Faculty Development in the AI Era

Siddhartha Paul Tiwari
https://orcid.org/0000-0003-1596-1501
Google Asia Pacific, Singapore

IGI Global
Scientific Publishing
Publishing Tomorrow's Research Today

Vice President of Editorial	Melissa Wagner
Director of Acquisitions	Mikaela Felty
Director of Book Development	Jocelynn Hessler
Production Manager	Mike Brehm
Cover Design	Jose Rosado

Published in the United States of America by
IGI Global Scientific Publishing
701 East Chocolate Avenue
Hershey, PA, 17033, USA
Tel: 717-533-8845 | Fax: 717-533-7115
Website: https://www.igi-global.com E-mail: cust@igi-global.com

Library of Congress Cataloging-in-Publication Data

Names: Tiwari, Siddhartha Paul, 1979- editor
Title: Faculty development in the AI era / edited by: Siddhartha Paul Tiwari.
Other titles: Faculty development in the artificial intelligence era
Description: Hershey, PA : IGI Global Scientific Publishing, [2026] | Includes bibliographical references and index. | Summary: "This book goes beyond surface-level training, focusing on how educators can adapt their practices, communicate complex ideas, and mentor students as they navigate a changing knowledge landscape"-- Provided by publisher.
Identifiers: LCCN 2025005851 (print) | LCCN 2025005852 (ebook) | ISBN 9798337312859 hardcover | ISBN 9798337312866 paperback | ISBN 9798337312873 ebook
Subjects: LCSH: Teachers--Training of--Technological innovations | Artificial intelligence--Educational applications
Classification: LCC LB1707 .F33 2026 (print) | LCC LB1707 (ebook) | DDC 370.71/1--dc23/eng/20250709
LC record available at https://lccn.loc.gov/2025005851
LC ebook record available at https://lccn.loc.gov/2025005852

British Cataloguing in Publication Data
A Cataloguing in Publication record for this book is available from the British Library.

Table of Contents

Detailed Table of Contents

By leveraging rapid advancements in AI technology, educators can meaningfully revolutionize the education. AI can also aid in attaining sustainable education. This chapter offers a wide-ranging guide for academicians navigating the fast-changing paradigm of Artificial Intelligence in education. It discusses the increasing presence of AI, outlining its brief history and discusses some of the main tools such as Intelligent Tutoring Systems, adaptive learning platforms, AI-powered assessment tools, and generative AI such as ChatGPT. Through practical case studies, the chapter illustrates the varied applications of AI in enhancing learning experiences, automating faculty tasks and investigate how faculty members perceive the AI tools. The chapter introduces key challenges and limitations. Ultimately, the chapter underscores the necessity for faculty to understand AI tools, best practices for faculty and adapt to their evolving roles in an AI-driven environment.

The integration of artificial intelligence (AI) technology occurs within both academic staff training programs and contemporary educational methods of teaching institutions. Educational facilities face implementation challenges with AI resources because faculty resists change and the costs for technology and infrastructure as well as privacy issues arise. Institutions need to establish financing methods and build ethical AI guidelines then educate their members about AI concepts. Existing universities implement AI systems for student education as well as faculty professional progress. Research teams work to develop sustainable ethical AI systems which will boost faculty preparing processes. Institutional deployment of ethical AI solutions gives teachers access to their advanced training systems. The resolution of operational obstacles will enable higher education to maximize the use of AI systems for faculty and professional development programs.

This chapter gives a detailed introduction to the principles of Artificial Intelligence (AI) particularly targeted at educators. With AI's rising presence in the educational sector, faculty members need to comprehend the underlying concepts of AI, its possible applications, and its ethical implications. The chapter begins with defining AI and addressing essential ideas and terminology that are crucial for educators. It then covers several AI tools and technologies that might boost teaching and learning, such as adaptive learning systems, AI-powered assessment tools, and intelligent tutoring systems. The chapter also discusses the ethical concerns surrounding AI, highlighting the significance of appropriate application in the classroom. Finally, the chapter examines the prospects and challenges of adopting AI in educational contexts and underlines its potential for faculty development, supporting continuous learning, and determining the future of education.

This chapter discusses strategic frameworks for integrating AI into higher education curricula in different domains. The examination begins with the conceptual and pedagogical changes needed to move from traditional educational frameworks to AI-augmented, learner-centric ones. The chapter discusses backward design, modular curricular architecture, and Bloom's Digital Taxonomy to explain AI integration design methods. Case-based applications in STEM, Humanities, Health, and Business demonstrate AI's importance in specialized education. Faculty preparation, resistance management, and ethical implications of co-creation and professional learning communities are also covered. The final section emphasizes assessment, scalability, and futurist perspectives to ensure institutional and curricular readiness. The chapter advocates for thoughtful, ethical, and humanistic AI in education.

This chapter examines the transformative impact of artificial intelligence (AI) on higher education, with a focus on enhancing faculty development and teaching methodologies. As AI reshapes curricular design, assessment, and research, educators must develop technological fluency alongside critical pedagogical skills to adapt to this evolving landscape. The chapter highlights strategies for integrating AI-driven tools to foster student engagement, personalized learning, and adaptive assessments while maintaining ethical standards, data privacy, and inclusivity. Practical frameworks and real-world case studies are provided to help faculty create student-centered and culturally sensitive learning environments that cater to diverse learners. Emphasis is placed on interdisciplinary collaboration among educators, researchers, and policymakers to promote innovation and knowledge exchange. The chapter underscores the importance of continuous professional development to ensure faculty remain adaptable to AI advancements while preserving the human values of education.

AI's quick growth is changing how we learn and work worldwide. This chapter looks at new AI tools, predicts tech advances, and explores their big impact on schools and workplaces. We'll list key tools like AI that create content, machine learning systems, and tech that understands human language. These are transforming how we learn, teach, and do business as AI spreads to most fields. Tech can do boring tasks, make learning better for each person, and give workers and students amazing new abilities. We'll point out the important tools driving new ideas now and likely to be big hits soon. Through a synthesis of current research, case studies, and expert insights, this chapter will provide a comprehensive perspective on how AI is redefining education and work, preparing readers for the opportunities and challenges of an AI-driven future.

Preface

The field of higher education is entering a defining period in which artificial intelligence is no longer a distant technological possibility, but a force reshaping teaching, learning, assessment, research, and institutional leadership. This transformation is especially significant for faculty members. Educators are challenged by the AI era not only to adopt new tools, but also to rethink the purposes, methods, ethics, and futures of educational practice. An intellectually grounded form of faculty development, pedagogically responsive, ethically conscious, and institutionally sustainable is required.

Faculty Development in the AI Era is intended to make a timely contribution to this evolving environment. The volume presents diverse perspectives on how educators, institutions, and academic leaders can understand, integrate, govern, and humanize artificial intelligence within higher education. The book addresses AI as a multidimensional phenomenon rather than as a purely technical intervention, which impacts curriculum design, classroom interaction, student support, teacher preparation, institutional strategy, digital wellbeing, interdisciplinary collaboration, employability, and educational equity.

A common theme throughout the chapters in this book is the recognition that faculty development in the AI age must begin with foundational literacy. To make informed pedagogical decisions, educators need a thorough understanding of AI concepts, tools, platforms, and applications. Several chapters introduce AI fundamentals for educators, examine chatbots and intelligent learning platforms, and discuss how applications such as ChatGPT are playing a growing role in personalised learning. Contributions such as these help de-mystify AI and position faculty as active interpreters and designers of technology-enhanced learning rather than passive users of externally imposed systems.

At the same time, the book emphasizes that effective AI integration cannot be reduced to the adoption of tools. Curriculum transformation, pedagogical redesign, and disciplinary relevance must all be addressed as part of faculty development. Chapters on AI-infused curriculum, agroforestry engineering education in Vietnam, and inclusive student-centered learning demonstrate that AI has a variety of meanings in different academic fields. In these chapters, it is demonstrated that meaningful integration must take into account context, discipline-specific learning outcomes, cultural realities, professional standards, and the lived needs of students and teachers.

The volume focuses on the ethical and human dimensions of AI-driven education. With the rapid expansion of artificial intelligence in higher education, there are difficult questions regarding academic integrity, bias, transparency, privacy, authorship, accountability, accessibility, and the changing role of human judgement. Faculty development must be anchored in values, as emphasized in the chapters on ethical considerations, digital wellbeing, responsible leadership, and learning agility. There is no need to compromise the relational, reflective, and emancipatory goals of education through the use of artificial intelligence. Instead, it should be geared towards strengthening inclusion, enhancing learner agency, increasing teacher capabilities, and enhancing access to quality education.

The book also focuses on leadership and institutional policy. The integration of artificial intelligence cannot be achieved solely through isolated experiments. Leadership, governance frameworks, institutional readiness, professional development systems, and sustained collaboration across departments and disciplines are essential. Chapters on strategic leadership and policy frameworks stress the need for institutions to move from fragmented adoption toward coherent, responsible, and future-oriented AI strategies. It emphasizes the importance of preparing academic leaders to manage risk, ensure quality, and balance innovation with educational objectives.

This volume also acknowledges that the future of faculty development is intertwined with the future of work. Emerging AI tools are already transforming the skills expected of graduates, the nature of professional practice, and the relationship between education and employability. The chapter on employment outcomes for psychology graduates, along with chapters on the future of education and work, situate AI in the broader context of transitions affecting labour markets, professional preparation, and graduate careers. The importance of preparing students for AI-mediated environments calls for faculty members to not only instruct students on how to use AI, but also teach them how to think critically, ethically, and creatively.

Among the collection's strengths is its breadth. It combines theoretical reflection, practical guidance, disciplinary case studies, educator and student perspectives, institutional policy discussions, and future-focused analyses. Chapters are divided into general higher education, teacher training, fine arts, engineering, psychology, leadership, curriculum design, and digital pedagogy. The fact that AI is interdisciplinary reflects the reality that it does not belong to any one field. The use of big data in academic settings is becoming a part of the shared infrastructure of academic life, while still requiring careful adaptation to local, institutional, and disciplinary contexts.

The book is intended for faculty members, academic developers, university leaders, policymakers, teacher educators, curriculum designers, researchers, and postgraduate students interested in the future of higher education. For educators seeking to understand artificial intelligence, for institutions designing faculty development programs, and for scholarly researchers examining the transformation of teaching and learning in the digital age, it may be useful as a guide.

The development of faculty today must cultivate technological fluency, ethical reasoning, pedagogical imagination, resilience, collaboration, and leadership. Educators must be able to navigate uncertainty while maintaining the human values at the core of education. Although artificial intelligence can generate content, recommend pathways, analyze data, and support personalised learning, it cannot replace the educator's role in shaping meaning, mentoring students, encouraging critical thinking, and furthering higher education's moral mission.

This volume is intended to contribute to a balanced and constructive dialogue. Chapters do not present AI as either a threat that should be rejected or as a miracle solution that should be embraced uncritically. They encourage readers to engage with AI as a powerful, contested, and evolving set of technologies that must be understood, governed, and aligned with educational values. This book thus asserts that the future of faculty development will not only be determined by what artificial intelligence can do, but also by what educators, institutions, and societies decide education should be.

Faculty Development in the AI Era is thus presented as both a scholarly resource and a practical invitation. It provides educators with the opportunity to learn, question, experiment, collaborate, lead, and reimagine their roles in the face of profound technological changes. In the AI era, it is more important than ever to make education thoughtful, inclusive, ethical, responsive, and humane, not simply to automate it.

CHAPTER OVERVIEW

Chapter 1 opens the volume with a pragmatic and timely guide for faculty navigating the expanding ecosystem of AI in education. From early developments to contemporary tools such as intelligent tutoring systems, adaptive platforms, and generative AI, the chapter situates technological innovation within day-to-day academic practice. Drawing on case-based insights, it demonstrates how AI can enhance learning, streamline instructional tasks, and reshape faculty roles, while also addressing persistent concerns around limitations and adoption. The discussion ultimately frames AI literacy and adaptability as essential competencies for educators in a rapidly evolving, technology-driven landscape.

Chapter 2 turns to the structural and ethical challenges that accompany AI-driven faculty development. It examines institutional barriers such as resistance to change, financial constraints, and privacy concerns, while advocating for comprehensive policy frameworks and ethical guidelines. By highlighting the need for awareness-building and sustainable implementation strategies, the chapter underscores how responsible integration can strengthen both teaching practices and professional development, provided that institutions proactively address operational and ethical complexities.

Chapter 3 provides a foundational orientation to AI tailored specifically for educators. It introduces key concepts, terminology, and applications, bridging technical understanding with pedagogical relevance. By exploring tools such as adaptive systems and AI-powered assessment alongside ethical considerations, the chapter equips faculty with the conceptual grounding necessary to engage critically and effectively with AI, positioning it as both an opportunity and a responsibility in shaping future educational practices.

Chapter 4 advances the discussion by focusing on curriculum design, offering strategic frameworks for embedding AI across disciplines. Through models such as backward design and digital taxonomies, it illustrates how curricula can transition toward learner-centered, AI-augmented structures. Case examples across diverse fields demonstrate the adaptability of AI integration, while attention to faculty readiness, resistance, and ethical co-creation highlights the institutional effort required to ensure scalable and meaningful transformation.

Chapter 5 examines the transformative role of AI in reshaping teaching practices and faculty development within higher education. Emphasizing the need for technological fluency alongside pedagogical sensitivity, the chapter presents practical frameworks and case studies that support personalized, inclusive, and student-centered learning environments. It also foregrounds collaboration and continuous professional development as critical drivers of innovation, ensuring that human values remain central amid technological change.

Chapter 6 looks ahead to the future, surveying emerging AI tools and forecasting their impact on education and the workforce. By synthesizing research, case studies, and expert perspectives, the chapter identifies key technological trends—such as generative systems and machine learning—and examines their capacity to transform learning, productivity, and innovation. It positions AI as a catalyst for both opportunity and disruption, urging readers to anticipate and prepare for its far-reaching implications.

Chapter 7 centers on teacher empowerment in the AI era, emphasizing the development of digital literacy and adaptive competencies. It explores how AI can enhance personalization, automate assessment, and reduce administrative burdens, while also acknowledging persistent challenges such as ethical concerns and inequities in access. The chapter advocates for sustained professional development and inclusive frameworks to ensure that educators can effectively and equitably integrate AI into their practice.

Chapter 8 shifts focus to interdisciplinary collaboration as a cornerstone of innovation in academia. It illustrates how cross-disciplinary partnerships can enrich teaching, research, and problem-solving, particularly in addressing complex global challenges. While acknowledging barriers such as institutional silos and resource constraints, the chapter offers strategies for cultivating collaborative cultures that drive creativity, knowledge exchange, and societal impact.

Chapter 9 explores the role of AI in fostering inclusive, student-centered learning environments. By leveraging data-driven insights, AI systems can tailor instruction to individual needs, enhancing accessibility and engagement. The chapter emphasizes the importance of collaboration among educators, policymakers, and technologists in establishing ethical and effective frameworks, positioning AI as a powerful tool for advancing equity and personalization in education.

Chapter 10 presents a focused case on the integration of AI within fine arts teacher training, highlighting both opportunities and tensions. It demonstrates how AI can support creative development, instructional design, and assessment, while also raising critical questions cultural authenticity and artistic integrity. The chapter advocates for a balanced, human-centered approach that preserves the essence of artistic practice while embracing technological innovation.

Chapter 11 examines the integration of AI into agroforestry engineering education, emphasizing the growing importance of digital competencies in environmental and agricultural fields. It outlines the role of technologies such as GIS and machine learning in modern curricula, while addressing practical considerations including infrastructure, faculty training, and industry collaboration. Ethical safeguards and alignment with global guidelines are presented as essential to responsible implementation.

Chapter 12 highlights the strategic role of leadership in guiding AI adoption within higher education. It explores emerging trends, ethical imperatives, and the necessity of transparency and inclusivity in AI systems. By emphasizing vision-setting, collaboration, and continuous professional development, the chapter provides a roadmap for institutional leaders to harness AI's potential while aligning it with academic and societal goals.

Chapter 13 delves into the evolving classroom, focusing on faculty resilience and transformative pedagogy in an AI-driven context. It examines how educators can adapt to challenges such as AI-generated content and shifting instructional roles, while leveraging innovative approaches like inquiry-based learning and adaptive assessment. The chapter reinforces the importance of critical thinking and ethical engagement, positioning faculty as facilitators of meaningful, technology-enhanced learning.

Chapter 14 offers an empirical perspective through a tracer study of psychology graduates, revealing gaps between educational preparation and employment outcomes. While noting engagement in further professional development, the chapter raises concerns employability and alignment with labor market demands. It underscores the need for continuous program evaluation and curricular refinement to better support graduate success.

Chapter 15 revisits the role of AI in faculty development, emphasizing its capacity to personalize learning experiences and enhance instructional effectiveness. By enabling adaptive, data-driven approaches, AI can reduce workload while supporting professional growth. The chapter reinforces the importance of understanding AI's evolving role in shaping teaching practices and lifelong learning for educators.

Chapter 16 concludes the volume by returning to leadership and policy frameworks, offering a comprehensive view of institutional strategies for AI integration. Drawing on established models of change management and technology adoption, it outlines pathways for effective implementation, supported by real-world case studies. The chapter emphasizes responsible innovation, governance, and strategic vision as essential components for embedding AI sustainably within higher education systems.

Chapter 1
Faculty Guide to AI Toolkit: Chatbots, Learning Platforms, and Beyond

Anand Jha
http://orcid.org/0000-0002-9570-1939
BSF Academy, Rustamji Institute of Technology, Tekanpur, India

Sanjay Patsariya
Rustamji Institute of Technology, Tekanpur, India

Saba Khan
http://orcid.org/0009-0008-1952-1881
Rustamji Institute of Technology, Tekanpur, India

Dharmendra Kumar Tripathi
Rustamji Institute of Technology, Tekanpur, India

ABSTRACT

By leveraging rapid advancements in AI technology, educators can meaningfully revolutionize the education. AI can also aid in attaining sustainable education. This chapter offers a wide-ranging guide for academicians navigating the fast-changing paradigm of Artificial Intelligence in education. It discusses the increasing presence of AI, outlining its brief history and discusses some of the main tools such as Intelligent Tutoring Systems, adaptive learning platforms, AI-powered assessment tools, and generative AI such as ChatGPT. Through practical case studies, the chapter illustrates the varied applications of AI in enhancing learning experiences, automating faculty tasks and investigate how faculty members perceive the AI tools. The chapter

DOI: 10.4018/979-8-3373-1285-9.ch001

introduces key challenges and limitations. Ultimately, the chapter underscores the necessity for faculty to understand AI tools, best practices for faculty and adapt to their evolving roles in an AI-driven environment.

1. INTRODUCTION

Overview of AI's Growing Role in Education

The rapid advancement of Artificial Intelligence (AI) has significantly transformed various sectors, and education is no exception (Vidalis & Subramanian, 2023). As AI technologies is evolving, Artificial Intelligence (AI) is playing a key role changing education and acting as a transformative force to influence educational landscapes (Pachaiyappan, 2024). AI is reshaping the way students learn, educators teach, and institutions operate through its transformative methods. AI tools such as WhatsApp chatbots, adaptive learning platforms and AI driven assessment tools etc. are enabling more education more personalized, efficient, and data-driven (Chetry, 2024; Šumak et al., 2024).

AI is helping student engagement, supports diverse and personalized learning styles, and lending a great help to a faculty in making their routine administrative tasks easier. This lets teachers spend more time on meaningful interactions tasks (Šumak et al., 2024). As classrooms are moving towards hybrid learning settings, AI is becoming more important in education institutions. It's crucial for educators to understand how AI can be used and its impact.

Effective AI integration in education necessitates strategic alignment with teaching goals, not just tool adoption. Faculty often struggle with the technology-pedagogy gap, overwhelmed by AI complexity. Understanding AI's potential allows for strategic use, enhancing, not replacing, human-centered teaching. Combining AI's data insights with pedagogical practices creates adaptive learning. Bridging this gap ensures technology complements faculty expertise, enriching education for both teachers and students (Kwid, Sarty, & Yang, 2024).

Importance of Faculty Understanding AI Tools

For faculty members, understanding these AI tools is no longer optional—it is essential. To realize AI's educational benefits, faculty require a deep understanding of its functionality and integration. Lacking this, misuse and missed opportunities are likely. Knowledge empowers educators to create engaging, personalized lessons with timely feedback. It also enables critical ethical assessment, ensuring responsible AI use. Informed educators confidently navigate AI, improving student outcomes and fostering dynamic classrooms. Continuous learning is essential, allowing faculty to leverage AI for enhanced pedagogy and a more effective learning experience. By understanding AI's capabilities and limitations, educators can maximize its positive impact on education.

Brief History of AI in Education

AI in education has progressed from basic automation to advanced personalized learning systems. Initially, AI handled tasks like automated grading and scheduling. Later, intelligent tutoring, adaptive platforms, and AI-driven assessments emerged, customizing education. Today, AI supports curriculum design and real-time feedback, changing knowledge delivery and measurement. Understanding this evolution helps educators grasp current AI applications and prepare for future technologies. Early AI focused on efficiency; now, it emphasizes personalization and deep analysis. This shift allows educators to enhance teaching and learning, providing a more tailored and effective educational experience for students.

Objectives of the Chapter

Objectives of the chapter are:

1. To equip faculty with a foundational understanding of key AI tools relevant to education, their applications, and their limitations.
2. To guide faculty in effectively and ethically integrating AI tools into their teaching practices, while navigating the evolving role of educators in an AI-driven environment.
3. To encourage proactive faculty development and a balanced approach to AI adoption, emphasizing its potential to enhance learning while acknowledging the importance of human interaction and sociocultural factors.

2. MAPPING THE AI TOOLKIT FOR LEARNING AND TEACHING

The integration of Artificial Intelligence (AI) is can be credited to the development of various AI-tools. These tools have transformed conventional teaching-learning methods by offering personalized educational, data-driven, and responsive & interactive experiences. This section explores key AI-powered academic tools such as Intelligent Tutoring Systems (ITS) (Akyuz, 2020; Kavita et al., 2025), Adaptive Learning Platforms, AI-Powered Assessment Tools, Virtual Assistants (Sharmila, Lakchudha, & Seervi, 2024), AI Agents (Istrate, 2024) & Chatbots, WhatsApp-based Chatbots and Generative AI tolls and their functionalities, roles and potential impact in the education.

Intelligent Tutoring Systems (ITS)

In 2015, the UN established 17 Sustainable Development Goals (SDGs) to address global challenges by 2030, with "quality education" as a crucial component (Wade, 2012) placed as SDG 4. SDG 4, "Quality Education," emphasizes inclusive and equitable lifelong learning for all.

Achieving sustainable education necessitates personalized, student-centred approaches, cultivating learners capable of driving sustainable development. By leveraging AI algorithms, sustainable education can be transformed through personalized learning. Analyzing student data allows for tailored experiences, leading to more effective and efficient learning outcomes for each student. Therefore, integrating modern information technologies like Intelligent Tutoring Systems (ITSs) is vital.

An Intelligent Tutoring System (ITS) in education is a computer-based teaching program that uses Artificial Intelligence (AI) to provide personalized, one-on-one instruction and immediate feedback to a student, much like an expert human tutor. It aims to replicate the benefits of personalized tutoring at a large scale by adapting the content, pace, and teaching methods based on the individual student's real-time performance, knowledge gaps, and learning style. Powered by AI, ITS act like an adaptive tutor for every student. They constantly analyse a learner's strengths and weaknesses to automatically tailor the pace, difficulty, and content focus. This customization not only supports diverse learning styles but also ensures instruction is precisely targeted to improve understanding and retention, helping each student master the material at their own, most effective speed.

A typical ITS consists of four core models that work together:

1. Domain Model: The content or expert knowledge to be taught (e.g., facts, concepts, problem-solving procedures).
2. Student Model: Tracks and assesses the student's current knowledge, mastery level, misconceptions, and learning progress. This is the "brain" that knows *what* the student knows.
3. Tutoring (or Pedagogical) Model: The teaching strategy that decides *how* to deliver instruction, *what* content to present next, and *when* and *how* to intervene with hints, explanations, or encouragement.
4. User Interface: The system's interactive environment through which the student and the system communicate (e.g., a chat interface, interactive problems, or gamified elements).

Diverging from traditional Computer-Assisted Instruction (CAI), which follows a fixed path, ITS dynamically adjusts based on real-time student assessment (Sharmila, Lakchudha, & Seervi, 2024; Istrate, 2024). The ITS strive to emulate personalized human tutoring, adapting learning to individual student needs, knowledge, and styles (Atun, 2020). This continuous adaptation ensures each student receives a unique learning experience, optimizing comprehension and progress.

From educators' perspectives, the ITS presents a valuable opportunity to enhance teaching and learning, rather than posing a threat or replacement. ITSs offer numerous advantages, notably facilitating individualized and differentiated instruction for diverse learners, a crucial element in transitioning from teacher-centered to student-centered methodologies (Ogunkunle & Qu, 2020; Silva et al., 2022). Furthermore, ITSs can alleviate teachers' workload by automating routine tasks such as grading, feedback delivery, allowing educators to dedicate more time to core teaching activities (Tobarra et al., 2021). Consequently, this fosters a culture of lifelong learning and professional development, benefiting both students and teachers.

An Intelligent Tutoring System (ITS) relies on a sophisticated architecture. The domain knowledge module stores subject expertise, enabling problem-solving and content creation. The crucial student model tracks individual understanding, skills, and preferences, shaping instructional choices. The tutoring module utilizes this data to select teaching strategies, provide feedback, and guide learning. Lastly, the interface module fosters student-system communication through diverse modalities, like text and graphics, ensuring an engaging and effective learning experience. These components work synergistically to deliver personalized, adaptive instruction, mimicking the benefits of one-on-one human tutoring.

ITS provides a significant leap forward from traditional methods by offering customized instruction that adapts to each student's learning style and speed. Through continuous assessment and immediate feedback, students can pinpoint and rectify errors, leading to enhanced comprehension (Atun, 2020).

Pros of ITS

ITS are designed to provide effective, individualized, and adaptive learning environments. The reason for the effectiveness of ITS is the use of on-screen agents and personalization within ITS which impacts student learning. They have the ability to modify their approaches based on the data obtained from both students and teachers (Atun, 2020). Some notable advantages of ITS are:

1. Personalized and Adaptive Learning:
   i. ITS can tailor instruction to individual student needs, learning styles, and paces, maximizing learning efficiency.

    ii. They provide customized feedback and content, ensuring students receive the right level of challenge and support.
2. Continuous Assessment and Feedback:
    i. ITS offer real-time assessment of student progress, allowing for immediate identification and correction of misconceptions.
    ii. This continuous feedback loop promotes deeper understanding and mastery of the subject matter.
3. 24/7 Availability and Accessibility:
    i. ITS can provide learning opportunities anytime and anywhere, offering flexibility for students with diverse schedules and needs.
    ii. This accessibility can be particularly beneficial for remote learners or those with disabilities.
4. Consistent and Objective Instruction:
    i. ITS provide consistent and unbiased instruction, eliminating the variability that can occur in human teaching.
    ii. They deliver standardized content and feedback, ensuring all students receive equitable learning experiences.
5. Data-Driven Insights for Educators:
    i. ITS can generate detailed data on student performance, providing valuable insights for educators to improve their teaching practices.
    ii. This data can inform curriculum development and identify areas where students need additional support.
6. Enhanced Student Engagement:
    i. Interactive and engaging interfaces, combined with personalized learning, can increase student motivation and engagement.
    ii. ITS can offer simulations, games, and other interactive elements to make learning more enjoyable.
7. Automation of Routine Tasks:
    i. ITS can automate tasks such as grading, and providing basic feedback, freeing up teacher time.
    ii. This allows teachers to focus on more complex tasks, such as individual student support.
8. Safe Learning Environment: ITS provide a safe place for students to practice, and make mistakes without fear of judgement.

Cons of ITS

Despite the benefits, there are potential challenges such as designing effective student models and tutoring strategies, curriculum integration requires expertise in both education and AI, which can be a complex and challenging task. Even with a well-designed ITS, ensuring effective instructor training remains a significant hurdle (Swanson, 2019). Ensuring that ITS are user-friendly and accessible to all students, regardless of their background or abilities, is essential but can be difficult to achieve (Atun, 2020). Some of the disadvantages of Intelligent Tutoring Systems (ITS) are:

1. High Development Cost and Complexity:
   i. Creating a robust ITS requires significant investment in terms of time, resources, and expertise.
   ii. Developing the domain knowledge module, student model, and tutoring module is complex and demands specialized skills in AI, education, and software development.
2. Limited Ability to Handle Complex or Ill-Defined Problems:
   i. ITS typically excel in well-structured domains with clearly defined rules and concepts.
   ii. They may struggle with complex, open-ended problems that require creativity, critical thinking, or nuanced judgment.
3. Potential for Over-Reliance and Reduced Human Interaction:
   i. Excessive reliance on ITS could diminish opportunities for students to engage in face-to-face interactions with teachers and peers.
   ii. This could impact the development of social skills, collaboration, and communication.
4. Difficulty in Modeling Affect and Motivation:
   i. While ITS can attempt to model student emotions, accurately capturing and responding to affective states like motivation, frustration, or boredom remains challenging.
   ii. This can limit the system's ability to provide truly personalized and engaging learning experiences.
5. Bias and Ethical Concerns:
   i. Like any AI system, ITS can inherit biases from the data used to train them, leading to unfair or discriminatory outcomes.
   ii. Data privacy and security concerns are also crucial considerations.
6. Lack of Teacher Familiarity and Integration Challenges:
   i. Teachers may have a lack of understanding of how ITS systems work, or how to properly integrate them into their teaching methods.
   ii. Integration into existing curriculums can also cause challenges.
7. Maintenance and Updates: ITS systems require consistent maintenance and updates to remain effective. Subject matter can change, and system bugs need to be fixed. This can cause additional expenses.

Adaptive Learning Platforms

Adaptive learning platforms employ AI algorithms to customize learning experiences, catering to individual student needs and learning paces (Sarnato et al., 2024). These platforms adjust content presentation based on a learner's skills, knowledge, and previous experiences, offering personalized learning paths (Sarnato et al., 2024). The integration of adaptive learning platforms enhances accessibility and flexibility while providing real-time analytics for personalized feedback, ultimately aiming to elevate student performance and engagement.

Since the pandemic and post-pandemic, technology has taken on a bigger role in how education is delivered because of rising digitization. These systems not only improve student outcomes but also assist educators by automating administrative tasks and streamlining resource allocation, enabling more efficient management of educational environments

Pros of Adaptive Learning Systems

1. Personalized Learning: Tailors the learning experience to each individual's needs, strengths, and weaknesses. Content and pace adjust based on performance, leading to more effective learning (Hakkal & Lahcen, 2021).
2. Increased Engagement and Motivation: Content that is appropriately challenging, customized and relevant keeps learners engaged and motivated. Features like gamification can further boost engagement (Austin-Gabriel et al., 2024).
3. Improved Learning Outcomes and Retention: Personalized learning paths and immediate feedback help learners master concepts more effectively, leading to better understanding and retention of information (Hakkal & Lahcen, 2021).
4. Real-time Feedback and Progress Tracking: Provides instant feedback on performance, allowing learners to identify and correct mistakes immediately. It also allows instructors and learners to track progress and identify areas needing improvement.
5. Efficient Use of Time: Learners can skip content they've already mastered and focus on areas where they need help and improvement, making learning more time-efficient by reducing time spent on concepts they already understand.
6. Accessibility and catering to Diverse Learning Styles: Adaptive systems can incorporate various content formats (videos, text, quizzes, interactive games) to suit different learning preferences (Yang, 2025).
7. Data-Driven Insights: Adaptive systems offer valuable data on student performance, enabling educators to refine teaching, identify struggling students, and personalize learning paths with real-time feedback. This allows students to learn

at their own pace and focus on areas needing improvement (Austin-Gabriel et al., 2024).

8. Scalability: Adaptive learning platforms can reach a large number of students with personalized learning experiences, making quality education more accessible.
9. Reduced Administrative Work: Automates tasks like grading and tracking progress, freeing up educators' time for more direct interaction with students.
10. Potential for Cost-Effectiveness: In the long run, adaptive learning can be more cost-effective than traditional methods by reducing the need for repetitive instruction and potentially replacing expensive textbooks.

Cons of Adaptive Learning Systems

Despite the benefits, the scaled adoption of AI-based adaptive learning platforms in schools is slow (Cukurova, Miao, & Brooker, 2023) due to various challenges ethical considerations. (Cukurova, Miao, & Brooker, 2023; Meylani, 2024). While teachers' knowledge, confidence, and product quality are important, factors such as minimizing additional workload, increasing teacher ownership and trust, generating support mechanisms, and ensuring ethical considerations are also essential for the adoption of AI in schools (Cukurova, Miao, & Brooker, 2023). Moreover, the existing AI mathematics learning platforms primarily focus on knowledge adaptivity, with less emphasis on emotional, motivational, or metacognitive adaptivity (Lee, Lee, & Kim, 2023). Some of the disadvantages of adaptive learning systems are:

1. Dependence on Technology: Requires reliable access to technology and internet which may not be available to all learners, creating a digital divide.
2. Reduced Human Interaction: The digital focus can limit face-to-face interaction with teachers and peers, which is crucial for some learners and for developing social skills.
3. High Initial Costs: Setting up and maintaining adaptive learning systems can be expensive, requiring investment in software, hardware, and training.
4. Not Suitable for All Subjects – Some topics require discussion, hands-on practice, or human interaction that AI cannot replicate effectively.
5. Resistance to Change – Educators and institutions may be hesitant to adopt new technology due to lack of training or skepticism.
6. Data Privacy Concerns: Collection and analysis of personal data raise concerns about privacy and security.
7. Potential for Over-reliance on Technology: Students may become overly dependent on technology, potentially hindering the development of critical thinking and problem-solving skills without technological aids.

8. Limited Scope of Assessment: Adaptive systems often focus on assessing specific knowledge and skills, potentially overlooking other important aspects of learning like creativity and collaboration.
9. Algorithmic Bias: If the algorithms are based on biased data, it can lead to unfair or inaccurate assessments and recommendations.
10. Implementation Challenges: Integrating adaptive learning systems into existing educational structures can be complex and may face resistance from educators and students accustomed to traditional methods.
11. Need for Teacher Training: Educators need training to effectively use and interpret the data from adaptive learning systems to support their students.
12. Content Quality Concerns: The effectiveness of adaptive learning depends on the quality of the educational content provided by the system. Poorly designed or inaccurate content can hinder learning.
13. Lack of Transparency: Some systems may lack transparency in how they make decisions about content delivery and assessments, making it difficult for learners to understand how their progress is evaluated.
14. Algorithm Bias – If not properly designed, adaptive systems may reinforce biases, leading to unfair learning experiences.
15. Ethical Concerns: Issues like data exploitation and the impact on student autonomy need careful consideration (Meylani, 2024).

AI-Powered Assessment Tools

AI-powered assessment tools are designed to improve grading accuracy, provide immediate feedback, and facilitate personalized adaptive testing. These tools can minimize bias and enhance fairness in grading, offering benefits such as mass Learning Management System (LMS) platforms. AI-driven evaluations also provide efficient and engaging environments for language learning and assessment, offering valuable feedback on fluency and pronunciation accuracy. The rapid advancement of AI has ushered in transformative opportunities across diverse sectors, with education emerging as a prominent focus

AI-powered assessment tools are used to improve grading accuracy, provide instant feedback, and personalize adaptive testing (Kavita et al., 2025). These tools can minimize bias, enhance fairness in grading, and offer benefits such as mass Learning Management System (LMS) platforms. AI-driven evaluations also offer efficient and engaging environments for language learning and assessment, providing valuable feedback on fluency and pronunciation accuracy (Ningsih, 2024).

AI-powered assessment tools are increasingly utilized in education to automate and enhance the evaluation of student work (Madhu et al., 2023). These tools leverage artificial intelligence and natural language processing to provide detailed feedback, detect plagiarism, and promote responsible research practices (Burkhard, 2023). While offering numerous benefits such as efficiency and personalized feedback, the adoption of AI-powered assessment tools also presents challenges including ethical concerns and the need for careful integration into teaching practices (Madhu et al., 2023; Burkhard, 2022).

The integration of AI in assessment not only streamlines the evaluation process but also offers opportunities for personalized learning and targeted interventions (Wang et al., 2024). As AI technologies rapidly advance, it is essential to understand their applications, benefits, and challenges in academic settings to ensure responsible and effective implementation (Raitskaya & Tikhonova, 2024).

Pros of AI-Powered Assessment Tools

1. Enhances writing quality: Offers text generation, proofreading, editing, annotation, paraphrasing, and translation.
2. Facilitates research and academic writing: Provides assistance in these areas and suggests strategies for hybrid AI-powered writing. offers strategies for hybrid AI-powered writing of various assignments and genres and improvements in writing quality (Raitskaya & Tikhonova, 2024).
3. Offers rapid text adaptation recommendations: Can provide detailed suggestions for text element adjustments within seconds.
4. Translation Capabilities: Assists in multilingual communication by offering accurate translations.
5. Improves English vocabulary learning: Positively impacts learning outcomes in EFL instruction and enhances learning efficiency when used for self-testing and in-class tests, effectively enhances vocabulary learning efficiency (Wang et al., 2024).
6. Streamlines communication and collaboration: Empowers committees and working groups to achieve goals effectively.
7. Aids in maintaining academic integrity: Can be used to detect plagiarism, prevent cheating, and promote responsible research practices (Madhu et al., 2023).

Cons of AI-Powered Assessment Tools

Some of the disadvantages of AI-powered assessment tools:

1. Potential for inconsistencies and errors: AI-powered writing tools can produce inconsistencies and errors, that students might not be aware of (Burkhard, 2022).
2. Lack of Human Judgment – AI tools may misinterpret context, tone, or intent, leading to inaccurate assessments.

3. Concerns about authorship and integrity: Raises questions about who the actual author is and the integrity of the submitted work (Raitskaya & Tikhonova, 2024).
4. Limited Creativity & Critical Thinking: AI-generated suggestions may lack originality and fail to encourage deeper analytical thinking.
5. Risk of overreliance: Students may become too dependent on these tools, hindering the development of their own writing skills (Raitskaya & Tikhonova, 2024).
6. Generation of misleading or false content: AI tools might produce inaccurate information.
7. Inaccurate referencing: AI-generated citations might be incorrect.
8. Inability to generate author's voice: The writing might lack the student's unique style and perspective.
9. Potential for unreflective and non-skeptical use: Students might accept AI-generated content without critical evaluation, leading to unintentional plagiarism (Burkhard, 2022).
10. Ethical concerns related to data privacy and mining: Storing and processing student data raises ethical issues and risks of data breaches.
11. Compliance with regulations like FERPA: Ensuring the tools adhere to privacy and data protection laws. It is important to use these tools in a responsible and ethical way and being aware of the limitations of these tools, and using them in conjunction with other measures to promote academic integrity (Madhu et al., 2023).
12. Cost & Accessibility Issues – Advanced AI assessment tools may be expensive and not accessible to all students or institutions.

AI Agents, Virtual Assistants and Chatbots

AI agents, virtual assistants, and chatbots are being used to streamline and augment learning processes by integrating pedagogical approaches with innovative technologies (Nze, 2024). These virtual assistants offer real-time, personalized support, making learning more interactive and tailored to individual student needs. Conversational AI in education is becoming increasingly prevalent, driven by advancements in AI and the growing demand for online learning (Ji & Yuan, 2022).

WhatsApp-based chatbots are explored for their potential in delivering education and support through a familiar and accessible platform (El Ayadi et al., 2023). These chatbots can address specific educational needs, such as providing health education to pregnant women or improving attitudes toward gender issues among adolescents. By offering interactive and readily available information, WhatsApp chatbots can enhance learning and engagement, particularly in underserved communities (Kaur et al., 2024; Lezama et al., 2023).

AI Agents, Virtual Assistants, and Chatbots are increasingly being integrated into education to offer personalized support, automate administrative tasks, and enhance learning experiences (Bekkar & Chtouki, 2024). These technologies, powered by artificial intelligence and natural language processing, provide opportunities to improve teaching and learning processes, but also pose challenges related to ethical considerations and the need for careful implementation (Istrate, 2024). Understanding their benefits and drawbacks is essential for educators and institutions to effectively leverage these tools in a responsible and ethical manner. Chatbots offer benefits such as teaching personalization, self-learning, and real-time feedback, making them emerging technologies with the potential to improve teaching and learning processes.

Pros

AI agents, virtual assistants, and chatbots offer numerous advantages in education including adaptive educational simulations, offering students personalized learning experiences, opportunities to practice skills (Mollick et al., 2024) and enhanced student support (Subiyantoro et al., 2023). AI agents can provide personalized learning experiences through adaptive educational simulations, offering students opportunities to practice skills in various scenarios (Gupta & Kaul, 2024). Virtual assistants can improve user acceptance and understanding, helping different users with their seeking tasks and improving the communication in education (Terzi, Akritidou, & Bibi, 2023). Chatbots can automate repetitive tasks, provide students with access to educational materials, and offer 24/7 support, which makes learning possible anytime and anywhere because of its ability to reply to chats automatically (Terzi, Akritidou, & Bibi, 2023). They can also enhance knowledge acquisition, research, and clinical decision-making. Furthermore, these technologies can streamline administrative tasks, allowing educators to focus more on teaching and student engagement (Terzi, Akritidou, & Bibi, 2023).

Cons

Despite the potential benefits, the integration of AI agents, virtual assistants, and chatbots in education also presents several challenges and limitations (Istrate, 2024). Ethical issues related to data privacy, algorithm bias, and the potential for misuse of data are significant concerns. Over-reliance on these tools may reduce human interaction and critical thinking skills, and can lead to a cold and impersonal interaction between teachers and students (Zou, 2024). There are also concerns that students might struggle with comprehending the chatbot's output, that the feedback provided by the AI writing assistant emerges as generic and lacking specificity, constraining its efficacy in guiding students' writing processes, and the unintentional risk of plagiarism when leveraging the tool (Negeri et al., 2024). Moreover, there is a need for clear guidelines and training for using AI chatbots to ensure that they are used effectively and ethically.

The Conversational AI for Content Creation

ChatGPT, a sophisticated chatbot developed by OpenAI, has rapidly gained attention in education and various other fields since its introduction in November 2022 (Gladstone, 2023). ChatGPT stands out from past AI because it can understand natural human language and create responses that make sense in context – something previously thought impossible. This groundbreaking achievement has garnered significant attention, revolutionizing how humans interact with computers. It rapidly gained over 100 million users in just two months, making it the fastest adopted technology on record.

It is designed to provide human-like text content by analyzing vast amounts of data and identifying statistical patterns from diverse sources such as textbooks, articles, and websites. While ChatGPT offers potential benefits for teaching, learning, and improving productivity, it also presents challenges related to accuracy, ethics, and the degradation of critical reasoning skills (Suhendi et al., 2024; Arista, Shuib, & Ismail, 2023).

The primary difference between ChatGPT and conventional LMS tools such as Canvas, Moodle, or Blackboard lies in their function. The LMS is a static content container and administrative system, while ChatGPT is a dynamic content generator and interactive dialogue partner. The following scenarios highlight how a faculty member might use each tool, demonstrating their distinct capabilities in the context of an AI integration into teaching-learning process.

Table 1. Creating and revising course content

Scenario	ChatGPT Use Case	Conventional LMS Tool Use Case	Comparison/Benefit
Lesson Plan Development	Faculty prompts ChatGPT to generate a complex case study on a specific ethical dilemma related to the course topic, including a scoring rubric.	Faculty uploads an existing case study document and a separate rubric file.	Generation vs. Storage: ChatGPT creates the content from scratch; the LMS simply organizes and delivers existing content.
Reading Accessibility	Faculty uses ChatGPT to simplify a dense academic abstract into a bulleted list for struggling students or to translate a key concept into a non-native language.	Faculty uses the LMS file repository to upload a separate, simplified PDF document or a pre-translated file.	Real-Time Adaptation: ChatGPT performs instant, on-demand modification of text; the LMS requires pre-made, static alternative resources.

Table 2. Student support and feedback

Scenario	ChatGPT Use Case	Conventional LMS Tool Use Case	Comparison/Benefit
24/7 Question Answering	A student may ask questions to ChatGPT which may be integrated as a *Virtual Teaching Assistant* at any time.	The student accesses static FAQ pages or course announcements posted by the faculty, or they post a question to a discussion board and must wait for a human response.	Conversational vs. Static: ChatGPT provides instant, conversational, and context-aware responses; the LMS provides delayed or predefined answers.
Draft Feedback	A student pastes an essay draft into ChatGPT and asks for feedback on their thesis statement's clarity and counter-arguments.	The student submits the essay file to the LMS Assignment Drop Box, where a human instructor or a simple plagiarism checker (a basic LMS tool) will later grade it.	Dialogue vs. Submission: ChatGPT offers iterative, formative, and detailed analytical feedback *before* submission; the LMS is primarily a one-way submission portal for summative assessment.

Table 3. Administrative tasks

Scenario	ChatGPT Use Case	Conventional LMS Tool Use Case	Comparison/Benefit
Analyzing Student Performance	Faculty uploads anonymized assignment data (e.g., a spreadsheet of grades and feedback comments) and asks ChatGPT to identify the top three common conceptual errors across the class.	Faculty uses the LMS Gradebook and Analytics Dashboard to view bar graphs of overall grade distributions and manually review individual submissions.	Insight Generation vs. Data Visualization: ChatGPT provides natural-language pattern recognition and qualitative synthesis; the LMS offers quantitative metrics and basic visualization.
Communication Drafting	Faculty prompts ChatGPT to draft an encouraging email to a group of students whose scores dipped below a certain threshold this week.	Faculty uses the LMS communication tool to select the students based on their grade and then manually types the email, or selects a basic, pre-set message template.	Automated Drafting: ChatGPT handles complex natural language composition; the LMS handles data filtering and sending the message.

Pros of ChatGPT in Education

ChatGPT can be a helpful tool for teaching and understanding fundamental concepts (Suhendi et al., 2024). It can boost student engagement by providing immersive, dynamic, and customized learning environments (Suhendi et al., 2024). In medical education, ChatGPT can improve personalized learning, clinical reasoning, and understanding of complex medical concepts (Sallam et al., 2023). It can also improve skills through step-by-step instructions and interactive content with instant feedback in dental education (Sallam et al., 2023). Additionally, ChatGPT can explain complex subjects and deploy interactive tools that aid in developing skills for patient counseling in pharmacy education (Sallam et al., 2023). In public health education, ChatGPT can provide explanations and case scenarios, and improve skills in data analysis and literature review. Moreover, ChatGPT can assist teachers by offering a comprehensive evaluation focused on accuracy, clarity, completeness, and technical terminology (Febrianti et al., 2024).

ChatGPT can be a helpful tool for students, offering assistance with studying and accelerating access to materials for research and assignments (Gladstone, 2023). It can increase student learning motivation by providing insight into various subjects. Students find that ChatGPT has features that are easy to use. ChatGPT can also improve overall literacy skills by helping students acquire new words, expressions, and information (Cha & Im, 2023). Furthermore, ChatGPT can broaden students' thinking by providing diverse points of view.

Cons of ChatGPT in Education

ChatGPT's innovative nature marks a significant step in learning technology, but its use in education warrants a cautious approach. On one hand, its ability to adapt and generate human-like responses offers a promising avenue for learning support (Arista, Shuib, & Ismail, 2023). On the other hand, a lack of appropriate design and stringent content management could result in substantial challenges regarding accuracy, ethical implications, and the upholding of values within Islamic religious education.

Excessive dependence on ChatGPT may weaken students' motivation and ability for autonomous learning and affect their personal growth and development (Liao, 2024). Students also face challenges in using ChatGPT-generated responses, such as the inability to express unique writing skills and difficulty revising those responses (Younes et al., 2024). Students also have concerns about the reliability and accuracy of the information provided by ChatGPT (Sun & Deng, 2024).

The most pronounced disadvantages of ChatGPT usage in education are:

1. Content Accuracy Concerns: A significant challenge lies in ensuring the accuracy of information from ChatGPT, especially within the education. ChatGPT's reliance on training data, rather than real-time verification, means it can sometimes provide incorrect or outdated information (Suhendi et al., 2024). This is a significant concern for subjects demanding precision and requires educators and students to verify its output. Many subjects including science, history necessitates the presentation of information that is both accurate and derived from

reliable, authentic sources. ChatGPT may inadvertently offer misinformation or misinterpretations. Therefore, relying on unverified AI content could result in confusion and erroneous interpretations of religious teachings (Suhendi et al., 2024).

2. Lack of Deep Understanding: While capable of summarizing, ChatGPT doesn't truly comprehend topics, hindering its ability to provide the nuanced insights needed for advanced learning and critical analysis (Suhendi et al., 2024).
3. Potential for Misuse: The ease with which ChatGPT can generate written work raises ethical concerns about academic integrity, requiring careful oversight in educational settings (Sun & Deng, 2024).
4. Impersonal Approach: ChatGPT's generalized responses fail to cater to individual learning styles, progress, or existing knowledge, limiting its effectiveness as a personalized learning aid.
5. Hindrance to Skill Development: Over-dependence on ChatGPT can prevent students from developing essential critical thinking and independent research abilities (Suhendi et al., 2024; Sun & Deng, 2024).
6. Text-Based Only: ChatGPT's inability to handle multimedia content limits its usefulness for subjects that benefit from visual, auditory, or interactive explanations, for example; science, art, and geography often rely heavily on visual aids. Education often benefits from diverse media formats to cater to different learning styles and make learning more engaging. ChatGPT's text-based nature can be limiting in this regard.

3. AI IN ACTION: ILLUSTRATIVE CASE STUDIES

AI tools offer a wide range of applications in education, transforming teaching and learning. Personalized learning platforms and intelligent tutoring systems adapt to individual student needs, providing tailored instruction and feedback. Assessment tools streamline assessment processes, while predictive analytics identify students needing support.

NLP tools aid in language learning and writing skill development. AI also enhances content creation, virtual assistance, and transcription/translation services. Learning management systems integrate AI for efficient course management. Furthermore, tools like VR/AR, gamification, and interactive whiteboards create engaging learning environments.

Below are some of the recent case studies of deployment of AI tools in educational context:

Case Study 1: An AI Assistant for Source Code Grading – TA Buddy

The study in (Nagakalyani et al., 2025) introduces *TA Buddy* – an AI-assisted tool designed to streamline the grading of source code in introductory programming courses. The tool uses *Code Llama*, a large language model fine-tuned on a dataset of graded programming assignments, to suggest grades for various criteria in a grading rubric. Human teaching assistants can then review, accept, or overrule these suggestions.

An evaluation of *TA Buddy* showed that it reduced grading time by 24% while maintaining a 90% agreement with purely manual grading (Nagakalyani et al., 2025). The tool also led to an increase in awarded marks, as it facilitated the awarding of partial credit for submissions with minor errors. The study concluded that *TA Buddy* effectively assists human TAs in grading source code, offering a more efficient and accurate alternative to traditional methods (Nagakalyani et al., 2025).

Case Study 2: AI-Powered Tools in Lithuanian General Education

The study in (Batuchina & Melnikova, 2024) examines the growing use of online learning platforms with integrated Learning Analytics (LA) and Artificial Intelligence (AI) tools in general education in Lithuania.

Learning Analytics (LA) in the context of AI tools and education is the process of collecting, measuring, analyzing, and reporting data about learners and their contexts to understand and optimize learning and the educational environment. LA is the engine that powers personalization. Key Functions of Learning Analytics within AI Tools include data collection, AI-driven modeling & analysis and decision making (prescriptive actions) for optimization.

Data Collection means AI tools continuously gather vast amounts of granular data on student interactions, including specific steps taken during problem-solving, types of errors or misconceptions, frequency of asking for hints or assistance, engagement levels and emotional states (in advanced systems.

In the step of AI-Driven Modeling & Analysis, the collected data is fed into sophisticated AI/Machine Learning algorithms to build the Student Model and Predict Outcomes. Building student model mean accurately assessing the student's current knowledge and skills, this step can be called Knowledge Tracing. Predicted outcomes are the output of predictive analytics means forecasting a student's future performance or identify those students who are at risk of failure.

The decision making (Tutoring Model) step utilizes the insights generated by the analytics directly inform the AI tutor's pedagogical decisions enabling it to:

- Adapt Instruction: Adjust the difficulty, pace, and content on-the-fly.
- Provide Targeted Feedback: Offer precise hints or explanations for specific mistakes.
- Recommend Resources: Suggest the next best activity or piece of content for that individual learner.

This study in Lithuanian general education schools monitored children's progress, engagement, and interest while using platforms like *LearnLab* and *Eduten Playground*, finding that students feel positive about using these platforms and become more engaged over time as they become familiar with the program's navigation and operation.

The study was conducted in schools participating in the DIMA project, focusing on platforms with AI and LA components like *LearnLab* and *Eduten Playground*. Data was collected using electronic questionnaires over three months (October-December 2020). The questionnaire, adapted from previous research, included questions on students' socio-demographic characteristics, device availability, usage conditions, and platform evaluation. 977 responses were received from students in grades 1-8 across 11 schools. Following observations were noted in the study (Batuchina & Melnikova, 2024):

1. Students generally showed a positive attitude towards online learning platforms.
2. There was an increase in student engagement as they became more familiar with the platforms' navigation and operation.
3. Most students initially used the platforms in school computer labs, but there was a shift towards more classroom use as schools acquired more devices.
4. Initially, students mainly worked individually on the platforms, but later there was an increase in collaborative use.
5. Students reported that it was easy to connect to the platforms and understand the tasks, with this ease increasing over time.
6. Students found learning with the platforms interesting and expressed a desire to continue using them.

The study indicates that student engagement in online learning platforms is influenced by both the platform's quality and the students' ability to navigate it. The findings suggest that as students become more comfortable with the platforms, their engagement and interest increase since these platforms enhance accessibility and flexibility in learning, providing real-time analytics for personalized feedback.

Case Study 3: Adaptive Learning Platforms

This study in (Isaeva et al., 2025) examines the integration of adaptive learning platforms and emerging computer technologies in education, assessing their impact on the learning process across diverse educational contexts. The study focuses on the role of AI tools in education, AI analytics, interactive elements, and gamification in enhancing learning outcomes. The research study uses a mixed-methods approach, combining qualitative analysis of educational platforms like Coursera, Khan Academy and edX with quantitative assessment of their features and effectiveness. Data is analyzed from educational institutions in Kyrgyzstan, Ukraine, and Azerbaijan.

The research study emphasizes that successful implementation depends on comprehensive planning, infrastructure readiness, and continuous professional development for educators. The study also acknowledges challenges like unequal access, insufficient teacher training, and technical limitations (Isaeva et al., 2025). The study indicates that the adaptive learning platforms enhance learning accessibility and flexibility with real-time analytics and virtual labs for remote practical training. Successful use requires planning, infrastructure, and teacher training (Isaeva et al., 2025).

Case Study 4: Intelligent Tutoring Systems

The study in (Rodrigues et al., 2013) talks about the case study presents EduTutor, an Intelligent Tutoring System (ITS) created for the Web-Based Aulanet Learning Management System (LMS), which focuses on subjects for the first cycle of studies of the Portuguese primary education system, between the first and the fourth year. Its purpose is to facilitate each student's understanding of the learning process in a virtual environment, acting as a personalized study guide. The system's architecture is designed to be easily integrated into higher levels of studies, different subjects, and several languages, and it is currently used in the Aulanet LMS platform (Rodrigues et al., 2013).

Case Study 5: ChatGPT Usage in Islamic Religious Education

The study in (Suhendi et al., 2024) presents a case study of using ChatGPT in the context of Islamic Religious Education, examining its potentials and the limitations. The study finds that ChatGPT has the ability to improve teaching-learning through facilitating lesson planning, offering plenty of information, and designing assessments. ChatGPT, for learners, can help with task accomplishment, provide learning and experimentation, and assist in product development and innovation.

But the research study also points out a number of challenges. It mentions that ChatGPT can give incorrect or outdated information, which is especially an issue in topics that need exact details (Suhendi et al., 2024). ChatGPT's inability to have deep knowledge can make it difficult for it to give well-rounded arguments and detailed explanations. There are ethical issues concerning ChatGPT usage, such as the possibility of academic dishonesty in the form of plagiarism and cheating. Also, ChatGPT's non-personalization and lack of context awareness constrain its capacity to address unique learning requirements. Relying too much on ChatGPT may also be detrimental to developing critical thinking skills and independent research capabilities (Suhendi et al., 2024). The research finds that although ChatGPT is full of promise for Islamic Religious Education, the teachers have to work actively in mitigating challenges involving accuracy, ethics, and maintaining Islamic values (Suhendi et al., 2024).

Case Study 6: ChatGPT to Enhance Learning Experience of College Students

This study in (Sun & Deng, 2024) examines college students' perceptions and experiences of using ChatGPT to enhance their experiential learning. The researchers designed a ChatGPT learning activity flow that corresponds to the four experiential learning steps: Experiencing - Reflecting - Thinking - Acting.

Data was collected from 39 students in a U.S. public university. The study revealed that students learned to use ChatGPT to explore questions of various knowledge types at different cognitive processes, under the guidance of their instructors. The findings suggest that the knowledge type of student-created prompts for ChatGPT and associated cognitive process depend on those of the first prompt provided by their instructors. While students were generally satisfied with the quality of the ChatGPT-generated information, some students expressed concerns about ChatGPT output. The study contributes to the literature on experiential learning and Bloom's Taxonomy. It also offers practical implications for educators and students on using generative artificial intelligence to achieve effective teaching and learning.

Case Study 7: ChatGPT Usage by Students for Written Communication Assignments

This study in (Younes et al., 2024) investigates the challenges and strategies employed by students in using ChatGPT for written communication assignments at a Malaysian university. ChatGPT is recognized as a powerful tool that can enhance teaching and learning across various educational contexts. The study involved 59 communication students who answered a self-developed questionnaire. The study suggests that while ChatGPT can be a valuable tool, it also presents challenges that both students and educators need to address. The findings indicate that students face challenges such as difficulty in expressing unique writing skills, dealing with inaccurate citation formats, and revising ChatGPT-generated responses. To address these challenges, students use strategies like adding ideas to ChatGPT-generated content, using ChatGPT for idea generation, paraphrasing, and replacing words with synonyms. The study also emphasizes the importance of developing institutional policies and guidelines to promote critical thinking and academic integrity in the use of AI-generated content.

4. AI'S IMPACT: IMPROVING EFFICIENCY FOR FACULTY AND OUTCOMES FOR STUDENTS

AI integration into the education offers several benefits to both faculty and students. AI capabilities extend beyond mere automation and can reform how education is delivered, assessed, and experienced. By leveraging AI tools thoughtfully and strategically, educators can foster more engaging learning environments, optimize their own time and resources.

Personalization and Engagement through AI

AI integration in education is creating personalized learning paths to boost student engagement. Conventional learning works in a one-size-fits-all manner, which tends to make some students feel disconnected or unable to cope, while others may not be challenged enough. AI solves this by studying the unique learning patterns of each student and corresponding them to strengths and weaknesses, performance metrics, dynamically adjusting the study materials, enabling the learning experience to be modified accordingly (Ogunkunle & Qu, 2020; Isaeva et al., 2025). Intelligent Tutoring Systems (ITS), for example, may give immediate feedback and modify exercise difficulty according to a student's performance. Adaptive learning platforms carry this further through curated content, resource recommendations, and even instructional pacing tailored to a student's learning style and preferences (Ji & Yuan, 2022).

Furthermore, AI-powered chatbots (Ningsih, 2024; Bekkar & Chtouki, 2024; Subiyantoro et al., 2023) and virtual assistants (Sharmila, Lakchudha, & Seervi, 2024; Terzi, Akritidou, & Bibi, 2023) can provide timely and relevant support to the students and answers to their questions, fostering a sense of autonomy in their learning. Beyond individualized learning, AI can also aid in to create more engaging learning environments experiences through interactive simulations, gamified learning modules powered by AI. By catering to diverse learning styles and providing personalized support and engaging content, AI has the potential to transform students from passive recipients of information into active participants.

Reclaiming Time: Streamlining Grading and Administration

AI integration saves faculty time by facilitating time-consuming tasks such as grading specially in objective assessments (Kavita et al., 2025), providing feedback, and managing administrative duties such as enrollment management, attendance tracking, and generating reports. AI-powered scheduling tools can assist in coordinating meetings and office hours, while chatbots can handle frequently asked questions from students, reducing the burden on faculty in responding to routine inquiries. Even for subjective assessments like essays and projects, AI tools can assist in identifying patterns, highlighting areas for improvement, and providing preliminary feedback on aspects like grammar and syntax.

Hence, faculty get more time to focus on more complex tasks that require human judgment and critical thinking and activities that directly impact student learning, such as developing innovative curriculum, preparing engaging lectures, conducting research. The time saved through AI integration can also contribute to a better work-life balance for faculty, reducing stress and burnout (Kavita et al., 2025).

Actionable Insights for Course Quality

AI provides data-driven insights to the faculty and educational institutions (Sarnato et al., 2024). By analyzing student performance data, engagement metrics, and feedback patterns, AI tools can identify areas where students are struggling, identify concepts that are particularly challenging, and highlight aspects of the curriculum or teaching methods that may need refinement (Boateng & Boateng, 2025). Learning analytics platforms, powered by AI, can visualize this data in meaningful ways, allowing faculty to gain a deeper understanding of student learning patterns and the effectiveness of their teaching strategies (Ogunkunle & Qu, 2020; Sarnato et al., 2024) For instance, if AI analysis reveals that a significant portion of students are consistently struggling with a particular concept, the faculty member can revisit their teaching methods for that topic. Similarly, if data indicates low student engagement with a specific type of assignment, the faculty member might consider redesigning the assignment to make it more relevant or engaging. Furthermore, at institutional level, aggregated data from AI-powered learning analytics can inform broader decisions about curriculum development, resource allocation, and the effectiveness of different educational programs. This data-driven approach not only benefits current students but also contributes to the continuous improvement of educational practices for future generations (Boateng & Boateng, 2025).

Fostering Equity: AI Tools for Inclusive Learning Environments

AI tools hold immense potential for supporting diverse learning needs and fostering a more inclusive educational environment (Gupta & Kaul, 2024). Recognizing that students learn at different paces and have varying learning styles and abilities, AI can be instrumental in creating personalized learning experiences that cater to these individual differences. Hence AI integration supports inclusive education i.e. ensuring support to underrepresented groups and everyone has fair access to a good education. Adaptive learning platforms can adjust the pace, content, and delivery method to suit each student's unique needs, ensuring that all learners have the opportunity to succeed (Yang, 2025). AI assistive technology can meet the different needs of disabled students (Yang, 2025). AI-powered text-to-speech and speech-to-text tools can facilitate access to course materials and communication for students with visual or auditory impairments. AI-driven translation tools can support students from diverse linguistic backgrounds, enabling them to engage with content in their native language.

Furthermore, by analyzing patterns in student performance and engagement, AI can flag students who may require additional assistance. AI can also contribute to creating more inclusive classroom environments by providing personalized feedback and support in a way that is non-judgmental and encouraging. Chatbots and virtual assistants can offer a safe space for students to ask questions and seek clarification without feeling self-conscious. The integration of AI in education has the potential to create a more equitable and inclusive learning environment where all students, regardless of their background, abilities, or learning styles, have the opportunity to thrive and reach their full potential (Yang, 2025).

5. CHALLENGES AND LIMITATIONS OF AI TOOLS

Potential Biases in AI Algorithms

AI algorithms can exhibit biases stemming from various sources, including the subjective factors and cognitive biases of algorithm designers, data bias, and algorithm biases (Li & Smith, n.d.). Generative AI models, such as ChatGPT, may inherit or amplify societal biases due to their training on extensive datasets (Li et al., 2023). In educational settings, the increasing integration of AI and algorithmic systems has raised critical concerns about their impact on educational equity. Algorithmic bias in education operates through multiple channels, from data collection and algorithm design to implementation practices and institutional policies (Boateng & Boateng, 2025). Studies indicate that relevant algorithms can lead to biased inferences about a number of factors, such as gender, race, ethnicity, socioeconomic status, and migration (Suna & Özer, 2025). Addressing algorithmic bias requires holding AI algorithm developers accountable, ensuring the accuracy of data mining, improving the transparency and interpretability of algorithms (Li & Smith, n.d.) and developing robust policies to mitigate ethical concerns and ensure equitable access to these technologies for all learners. Therefore, integrating AI responsibly and equitably is essential to optimize its benefits and address potential drawbacks.

Over-Reliance on Automation vs. Human Judgment

While AI has immense potential to transform learning experiences by providing personalized learning, immediate feedback, and access to enormous information. But there are concerns about overreliance on artificial intelligence will stifle the problem-solving and critical thinking capabilities of students by providing pre-programmed answers instead of encouraging independent thoughts (Shafei & Mahmood, 2025; Wang, 2024). The Digital Education Council Global AI Student Survey 2024, indicates that a majority of students express concerns about over-reliance on AI (Zaidy, 2024). Successful implementation requires a balanced approach, developing adaptable and culturally sensitive AI tools while investing in teacher training for effective human-AI collaboration (Vidalis & Subramanian, n.d.). The use of AI in educational assessment can lead to a lack of human interaction in the assessment process, which can be detrimental to students' learning experiences. Educators may miss important cues and nuances that can only be detected through human interaction. It is critical for transforming education by combining AI's data-driven insights with the human touch of educators. By integrating AI into traditional teaching methods and addressing issues such as ethics and equity, educational effectiveness can be improved and student engagement can be increased (Jantanukul, 2024)). Large language models (LLMs) deviate significantly from human judgments because they adhere strictly to policies, even when such adherence is impractical, suboptimal, or even counterproductive. Aligning LLMs with human judgment requires explicit training on how decisions are made, not just which decisions are made.

Data Privacy Concerns and Ethical Considerations

The use of AI in educational institutions raises ethical concerns, such as issues around data privacy, security and ownership of student data as well as concerns around using technology to replace human educators (Zou, 2024). AI advancements necessitate a critical review of data privacy policies in higher education to adapt to Big Data evolution. Preliminary findings indicate a growing interest in AI-based educational tools, along with a demand for rigorous training and ethical standards for their equitable application (Alawneh et al., 2024). It is essential to propose robust frameworks and strategies to safeguard the integrity and confidentiality of data in AI driven educational environments. AI raises challenges and concerns that require a thorough investigation of these ethical concerns and their potential societal implications.

Faculty Resistance and the Learning Curve in adopting New Technologies

Despite the growing number of AI-powered tools and application for supporting the teaching-learning process, there are still concerns and misunderstandings about acceptance in higher education, particularly among faculty members (Perez, 2024). A significant hurdle in adopting AI-powered tools stems from educators' limited understanding of the technology. Many lack the technical expertise to grasp the algorithms and their influence on assessment results. This lack of understanding is compounded by inadequate training on how to effectively utilize the AI tools.

Universities need to define AI's role on campus and establish guidelines on how faculty should use tools and recognize misuse (Yitages & Kasai, 2024). Increasing the literacy level and awareness of AI capabilities among students and teachers may help to mitigate the threats of AI implementation and ensuring the use of AI capabilities in the educational institutions (Perez, 2024). The study in (Iskandarova, Yusif-Zada, & Mukhtarova, 2024) finds that younger male faculty were most enthusiastic, however only a small percentage (6%) of educators have integrated AI tools like *ChatGPT* outside of STEM fields, with many (32%) expressing the need for further familiarity with such technologies. The study also observed positive changes in participants' knowledge and confidence levels post-training, emphasizing the significance of providing educators with robust training to enhance their AI literacy and teaching competencies (Iskandarova, Yusif-Zada, & Mukhtarova, 2024).

6. BEST PRACTICES FOR FACULTY USING AI TOOLS

Selecting Appropriate AI Tools for Different Teaching Contexts

Careful selection of AI tools is essential for diverse teaching contexts, requiring a focus on specific pedagogical goals and student needs. Faculty should prioritize

AI tools that demonstrably improve learning outcomes, learning objectives, and the diverse needs of their students. Identifying tools aligned with intended teaching outcomes is crucial, whether for enhancing writing skills using platforms like *Grammarly* and *Prowriting Aid*, or for research purposes with tools like Google Scholar (Rani, 2024). Adaptability and flexibility are key; faculty should select tools that accommodate various learning styles and educational settings, ensuring they enhance rather than complicate the learning process. This includes evaluating the AI tool's user-friendliness, its compatibility with existing educational platforms, understanding the capabilities and limitation and the availability of support and training for both faculty and students (Yitages & Kasai, 2024). A thorough evaluation process should inform the selection of AI tools, based on specific pedagogical goals and the learning context. Factors like the subject matter, learning objectives, student demographics, and available infrastructure are crucial considerations when choosing a tool. For example, an AI tool providing personalized feedback may be suitable for a large introductory course, while a tool that aids in generating creative content might be more appropriate for a writing-intensive seminar (Rani, 2024).

Cultivating AI Literacy: Essential Faculty Training

Comprehensive training and development programs are essential for faculty to effectively integrate AI tools into their teaching. These programs should aim to enhance educators' familiarity, confidence, and proficiency in using AI technologies (Perez, 2024). Furthermore, training should cover not only the technical aspects of AI tools but also pedagogical strategies for their effective implementation. Lack of training is identified as a significant barrier by 60% of teachers, to utilize AI tools effectively in their teaching practices (Roshan, Iqbal, & Qing, 2024). Training should address topics such as prompt engineering, understanding AI outputs, identifying potential biases, and adapting teaching methods to leverage AI effectively. Ongoing professional development is also essential to keep faculty updated on the rapidly evolving landscape of AI and its educational applications. Institutions should invest in workshops, online modules, and communities of practice to support faculty in developing their AI literacy and pedagogical skills (Roshan, Iqbal, & Qing, 2024). These initiatives should also focus on secure AI tools and technologies that evaluate students' reliance on such tools (Elalfy et al., n.d.).

AI literacy refers to the knowledge, skills, awareness and confidence that educators need to effectively understand, select, evaluate, and integrate AI-based tools in teaching and learning. It involves not only the technical understanding of how AI systems like chatbots, adaptive learning platforms, and analytics tools function, but also the ability to critically assess their benefits, limitations, and ethical implications. For faculty, AI literacy means being equipped to integrate these technologies responsibly into pedagogy, enhance student engagement. AI literacy encompasses the below mentioned skills:

1. Knowledge, Tool Familiarity & Selection: This involves grasping how AI systems function, their underlying concepts, and their applications in education. The practical ability to identify, understand the function of, and appropriately select different types of AI tools (e.g., Chatbots, Adaptive Learning Platforms). It also includes understanding the basics of AI, its history, and common applications
2. Pedagogical Integration: The skill to modify teaching approaches and create new pedagogies that are compatible with AI technologies, aligning them with learning outcomes.
3. Technical Confidence: The self-assurance and skill to implement, operate, and troubleshoot the AI applications in the classroom.
4. Ethical & Critical Awareness: Understanding the implications of using AI, including concerns about student data privacy, bias, and the appropriate boundaries of the technology.

Achieving the Hybrid Ideal: Balancing AI Tools with Human-Centric Teaching

Maintaining a balance between AI assistance and human interaction is crucial for effective teaching and learning, ensuring AI enhances rather than replaces the faculty role. This balance is vital for holistic student development and preventing over-reliance on AI (Yatani, Sramek, & Yang, 2024). While AI tools can automate tasks like generating initial drafts or providing instant feedback on basic concepts, human interaction remains essential for fostering critical thinking, emotional intelligence, and deeper understanding through discussions and mentorship. Faculty should strategically integrate AI to complement their role, designing activities that leverage AI for efficiency while preserving opportunities for meaningful human connection.

Strategies should focus on integrating AI to complement human teaching, particularly in early childhood education where AI lacks the ability to interpret social cues. Frameworks like "*Extraheric AI*" promote cognitive engagement by posing questions and offering alternative perspectives, encouraging critical thinking (Yatani, Sramek, & Yang, 2024). In corporate learning, hybrid models combining AI-driven processes with human interaction, feedback loops, and employee involvement can balance automation with empathy. Prioritizing learner needs and engagement allows educators to design human-centered AI systems that enhance learning without compromising essential human elements (Asemota & Owoeye, 2025).

Responsible AI: Addressing Bias, Fairness, and Ethical Governance

Faculty should proactively address the potential for bias and unfairness inherent in AI tools. Since AI models learn from data, pre-existing societal biases can be amplified in their outputs. Educators must critically assess AI tools for biases related to gender, race, socioeconomic status, and other factors. Understanding the algorithms and decision-making processes of AI tools is crucial for faculty to identify and mitigate bias. Furthermore, it's the responsibility of faculty to teach students how to critically evaluate AI outputs and understand the ethical implications of AI.

To responsibly integrate AI into education, it's crucial to address bias, ensure fairness, and uphold ethical considerations and transparency (Bing & Leong, 2025). Designing ethical AI systems involves mitigating bias with diverse and representative datasets, ensuring inclusivity for diverse learners, and safeguarding sensitive student data (Bing & Leong, 2025). Algorithmic bias often originates from unrepresentative historical data, while a lack of transparency can hide decision-making processes (Bing & Leong, 2025). Achieving fair, transparent, and trustworthy AI requires solutions like independent algorithm audits, explainable AI, and progressive regulations. Transparency in AI processes is vital for fostering trust among students, educators, and parents, demanding clear ethical guidelines and continuous professional development (Bing & Leong, 2025).

Faculty Responsibility in Ensuring Data Privacy and Security

AI in education demands faculty should take responsibility for ensuring privacy, security aspects of collected student data (Zou, 2024; Jose, 2024). Faculty must ensure that they and their students' data are protected when interacting with AI platforms. Protecting student data through access control, encryption, and updates is essential. Faculty perspectives should shape privacy policies, and incident analysis can improve them. E-learning platforms must prioritize data protection and follow privacy regulations. Balancing AI benefits with privacy is the key for the successful integration and use of AI and AI-powered tools in education (Jose, 2024).

Faculty responsibility involves understanding the data privacy policies of the AI tools being used, ensuring compliance with regulations like FERPA and GDPR, and educating students about responsible data sharing practices. Faculty should avoid inputting sensitive student information into AI tools that are not explicitly designed and secured for educational use. Institutions should provide clear guidelines and support to faculty on data privacy and security when using AI, and faculty should prioritize tools that offer robust data protection measures.

Some of best practices for faculty using AI tools in teaching-learning are:

1. Emphasize Critical Evaluation of AI Output: Faculty should train students to critically assess the information and content generated by AI tools. This includes verifying facts, identifying potential biases, and understanding the limitations of AI. Instead of blindly accepting AI output, encourage students to compare information from multiple sources, question the AI's reasoning (if possible), and consider the context in which the AI was trained. This practice fosters essential critical thinking skills in an age where AI-generated content is increasingly prevalent.
2. Design AI-Integrated Activities that Focus on Higher-Order Thinking: AI can automate some lower-level tasks, so faculty should leverage it to design activities that promote higher-order thinking skills like analysis, synthesis, and evaluation. For example, instead of asking students to use AI to summarize a text, ask them to use AI to generate different perspectives on a complex issue and then critically evaluate those perspectives, forming their own informed opinion. This shifts the focus from simple information retrieval to deeper engagement with the subject matter.
3. Promote Transparency and Ethical Use of AI: Faculty must explicitly discuss the ethical implications of using AI in academic work. This includes defining appropriate and inappropriate uses of AI, addressing issues of plagiarism and academic integrity in the context of AI-generated content, and discussing data privacy concerns related to AI tools. Setting clear guidelines and fostering open discussions about the responsible and ethical use of AI will help students navigate this evolving landscape with integrity.
4. Use AI as a Personalized Learning Assistant, Not a Replacement for Human Interaction: AI tools can be valuable for providing personalized feedback, identifying learning gaps, and offering tailored resources. Faculty should use AI to augment their teaching, not replace direct interaction with students. Human connection, mentorship, and the ability to address nuanced questions and emotional needs remain crucial aspects of effective teaching and learning. AI can free up faculty time for more meaningful student engagement.
5. Continuously Update Skills and Knowledge about AI Tools: The field of AI is rapidly evolving, and new tools and functionalities are constantly emerging. Faculty should commit to ongoing professional development to stay informed about the latest AI advancements and their potential applications in education. This includes exploring different AI tools, understanding their strengths and weaknesses, and learning effective strategies for integrating them into their teaching practices. Institutions should provide resources and support for such training.

7. CONCLUSION

This chapter has not only illuminated the transformative capabilities of AI but also highlighted the gravity of the balanced and thoughtful integration of these technologies within the academic landscape. The chapter has explored a range of AI tools, from intelligent tutoring systems, sophisticated learning platformsto generative AI like ChatGPT and chatbots, examining their practical applications and the challenges they present. The chapter discussion materialized three key parameters for faculty navigating this evolving educational environment.

1. Importance of understanding AI tools
2. Evolving role of educators in an AI-driven academic environment
3. Encouragement for proactive faculty development

Firstly, the *importance of understanding AI tools* cannot be overstated. The chapter has demonstrated that AI is no longer a futuristic concept but a present reality impacting teaching, learning, and assessment. Faculty who proactively engage with and understand the capabilities and limitations of the AI tools will be better equipped to leverage their strengths for pedagogical innovation, streamline administrative tasks, and ultimately, enhance student learning outcomes. Specialized training for faculty can ensure effective usage of AI tools.

Secondly, the *evolving role of educators in an AI-driven academic environment* is not simply a shift, but a recalibration. While AI tools can augment by automating certain aspects and tasks of teaching-learning process, they cannot replace the nuanced and critical role of faculty. The human element, encompassing sociocultural understanding, nuanced judgement, empathy ethical considerations, and the fostering of personal interaction, remains paramount. Hence, the educator's role shifts towards becoming a facilitator, curator, and critical thinker. Faculty must become instrumental and adept in integrating AI effectively, guiding students in critically evaluating AI-generated content, fostering human connection in a way that completes their expertise. The human element – empathy, nuanced judgment, and the ability to inspire – remains paramount, even as AI becomes a powerful pedagogical partner.

Finally, the chapter serves as an *encouragement for proactive faculty development*. The successful integration of AI tools requires a commitment to continuous learning and adaptation. The integration of the AI toolkit—from conversational chatbots like ChatGPT to enhanced LMS features—is not merely a technological upgrade; it is a fundamental shift in pedagogy that demands immediate institutional response. The implications extend beyond the classroom and into the institutional framework itself. For this transformation to be successful, universities must prioritize three interconnected areas: policy, training, and ethics. On the policy front, clear, actionable guidelines are required to differentiate between appropriate AI assistance and academic misconduct, safeguarding the integrity of assessment in an era of generative capabilities. Institutions must prioritize the need of comprehensive training to empower faculty to effectively utilize AI -tools and technologies. Simultaneously, comprehensive faculty training must evolve past simple tool introductions, focusing instead on prompt engineering, redesigning assignments for AI-proof critical thinking, and strategically leveraging AI to reduce administrative load.

The ethical and equity dimensions are paramount. The institutions should also focus on the development of robust frameworks to assess and mitigate the potential risks associated with AI, including data and algorithmic biases, transparency issues, demographic biases and impacts on student learning experience. Actively shaping the future of education in the age of AI calls for a collaborative effort among educators, technologists, and policymakers to ensure an inclusive, transparency. Ultimately, the successful deployment of the AI toolkit rests on the faculty's informed engagement, supported by responsive, ethical, and forward-looking institutional governance.

The AI toolkit presents both exciting opportunities and significant responsibilities for faculty. By embracing a cautious and proactive approach education institutions and faculty can navigate the evolving academic landscape and can harness the power of AI to enhance the learning experience which embraces equitable, supportive, and enriching learning environments which safeguards the core values of education and the vital role of human element in the teaching learning process. The future of education hinges on a hybrid approach that synergistically integrates technology and human factors to maximize learning outcomes for every student.

REFERENCES

Akyuz, Y. (2020). Effects of intelligent tutoring systems (ITS) on personalized learning (PL). *Creative Education, 11*(06), 953–978. DOI: 10.4236/ce.2020.116069

Alawneh, Y. J., Radwan, E. N. Z., Salman, F. N., Makhlouf, S. I. J., Makhamreh, K., & Alawneh, M. S. (2024). Ethical Considerations in the Use of AI in Primary Education: Privacy, Bias, and Inclusivity. In *2024 International Conference on Knowledge Engineering and Communication Systems (ICKECS)*. DOI: 10.1109/ICKECS61492.2024.10616986

Arista, L., Shuib, L., & Ismail, M. A. (2023). A Glimpse of chatGPT: An Introduction of Features, Challenges, and Threads in Higher Education. In *2023 International Conference on Informatics, Multimedia, Cyber and Informations System (ICIMCIS)*. DOI: 10.1109/ICIMCIS60089.2023.10349057

Asemota, M. O., & Owoeye, G. (2025). Integrating human-centric AI into corporate learning: Balancing automation with empathy. *Development and Learning in Organizations*.

Atmaja, S. A. (2025). Ethical Considerations in Algorithmic Decision-making: Towards Fair and Transparent AI Systems. *Riwayat: Educational Journal of History and Humanities*.

Atun, H. (2020). Intelligent tutoring systems (its) to improve reading comprehension: A systematic review. *Journal of Teacher Education and Lifelong Learning, 2*(2), 77–89.

Austin-Gabriel, B., Afolabi, A. I., Ike, C. C., & Hussain, N. Y. (2024). *AI and machine learning for adaptive elearning platforms in cybersecurity training for entrepreneurs*. Computer Science & IT Research Journal. DOI: 10.51594/csitrj.v5i12.1787

Batuchina, A., & Melnikova, J. (2024, May). Engagement of students in online learning platforms: follow-up study in lithuanian general education schools. In *society. Integration. Education. Proceedings of the International Scientific Conference* (Vol. 1, pp. 318-327). DOI: 10.17770/sie2024vol1.7866

Bekkar, H., & Chtouki, Y. (2024). Chatbots in Education: A Systematic Literature Review. In *2024 10th International Conference on Smart Computing and Communication (ICSCC)*. DOI: 10.1109/ICSCC62041.2024.10690334

Bing, Z. J., & Leong, W. Y. (2025). *Ethical Design of AI for Education and Learning Systems*. ASM Science Journal. DOI: 10.32802/asmscj.2025.1917

Boateng, O., & Boateng, B. (2025). *Algorithmic bias in educational systems: Examining the impact of AI-driven decision making in modern education*. World Journal of Advanced Research and Reviews.

Burkhard, M. (2022). Student perceptions of ai-powered writing tools: towards individualized teaching strategies. In *Proceeedings of the 19th International Conference on Cognition and Exploratory Learning in the Digital Age (CELDA 2022).*

Burkhard, M. (2023). How to deal with AI-powered writing tools in academic writing: a stakeholder analysis. In *Proceedings of the 20th International Conference on Cognition and Exploratory Learning in the Digital Age (CELDA 2023).*

Cha, M., & Im, H. (2023). A Study on the Case of Using ChatGPT in General English Classes. *Culture and Convergence, 45*(12), 175–184. DOI: 10.33645/cnc.2023.12.45.12.175

Chetry, K. K. (2024). Transforming education: How AI is revolutionizing the learning experience. *International Journal of Research Publication and Reviews, 5*(5), 6352–6356. DOI: 10.55248/gengpi.5.0524.1277

. Cukurova, M., Miao, X., & Brooker, R. (2023). Adoption of Adaptive Learning Platforms in Schools: Unveiling Factors Influencing Teachers' Engagement.

El Ayadi, E., Singh, P., Duggal, M., Kumar, V., Kaur, J., Sharma, P., Vosburg, K., & Diamond-Smith, N. (2023). Feasibility and acceptability of Saheli, a WhatsApp Chatbot, on COVID-19 vaccination among pregnant and breastfeeding women in rural North India. *BMJ Innovations, 9*(4), 195–206. DOI: 10.1136/bmjinnov-2022-001012

Elalfy, H., Mohmed, F., Elhay, B. A., & Elballat, A. (n.d.). The Attitudes of Faculty Staff Members and Their Assistants Towards Students' Use Of AI Tools In Scientific Research.

Febrianti, T. S., Fatimah, S., Fitriyah, Y., & Nurhayati, H. (2024). Leveraging ChatGPT for Scoring Students' Subjective Tests. *International Journal of Education in Mathematics, Science and Technology.*

Gladstone, R. (2023). *Using ChatGPT in the Classroom*. Spicer Adventist University Research Articles Journal. DOI: 10.56934/sauraj.v2i1.143

Gupta, M., & Kaul, S. (2024). *AI in Inclusive Education: A Systematic Review of Opportunities and Challenges in the Indian Context*. MIER Journal of Educational Studies Trends and Practices.

Hakkal, S., & Lahcen, A. A. (2021). An Overview of Adaptive Learning Fee-based Platforms. In *Proceedings of the 2nd International Conference on Big Data, Modelling and Machine Learning*. DOI: 10.5220/0010731400003101

Isaeva, R., Karasartova, N., Dznunusnalieva, K., Mirzoeva, K., & Mokliuk, M. (2025). Enhancing learning effectiveness through adaptive learning platforms and emerging computer technologies in education. *Jurnal Ilmiah Ilmu Terapan Universitas Jambi*, *9*(1), 144–160. DOI: 10.22437/jiituj.v9i1.37967

Iskandarova, S., Yusif-Zada, K., & Mukhtarova, S. (2024). *Integrating AI Into Higher Education Curriculum in Developing Countries. In 2024 IEEE Frontiers in Education Conference*. FIE.

Istrate, O. (2024). AI Agents in Education: An Early Systematic Review of Emerging Roles, Potential, and Limitations. *Revista de Pedagogie Digitală, 3*(1) 24-30. Bucure ti: Institutul pentru Educa ie. https://doi.org/.DOI: 10.61071/RPD.2496

Jantanukul, W. (2024). AI and Human Synergy: Utilizing AI to Enhance Teaching and Learning. *Journal of Education and Learning Reviews.*

Ji, S., & Yuan, T. (2022). Conversational Intelligent Tutoring Systems for Online Learning: What do Students and Tutors Say? In *2022 IEEE Global Engineering Education Conference (EDUCON)*. DOI: 10.1109/EDUCON52537.2022.9766567

Jose, D. (2024). Data Privacy and Security Concerns in AI-Integrated Educational Platforms. *Recent trends in Management and Commerce.*

Kaur, J., Sharma, P., Kumar, V., Duggal, M., Diamond-Smith, N., El Ayadi, A. E., Vosburg, K., & Singh, P. (2024). Exploring the Role of Chatbots in Tackling COVID-19 Vaccine Hesitancy among Pregnant and Breastfeeding Women in Rural Northern India. In *Proceedings of the ACM on Human-Computer Interaction*. DOI: 10.1145/3637332

Kavita, R. K., Samuel, & Ruby, J. (2025). Automated Grading and Feedback Systems for Programming in Higher Education Using Machine Learning. *Journal of Informatics Education and Research.*

Kwid, G., Sarty, N., & Yang, D. (2024). *A Review of AI Tools: Definitions, Functions, and Applications for K-12 Education.* AI, Computer Science and Robotics Technology.

Lee, G., Lee, Y. J., & Kim, H. (2023). *Analysis of adaptive learning in Korea's AI mathematics learning platforms*. Korean School Mathematics Society.

Lezama, E. E., Cabrera Echegaray, S. H., Rugel Medina, M. N., Carbajal Destre, P. E., & Ninaquispe Soto, M. E. (2023). Appropriation of Information Technologies during remote university education in Latin America. In *Proceedings of the 21th LACCEI International Multi-Conference for Engineering, Education and Technology (LACCEI 2023): "Leadership in Education and Innovation in Engineering in the Framework of Global Transformations: Integration and Alliances for Integral Development."* DOI: 10.18687/LACCEI2023.1.1.285

Li, M., Enkhtur, A., Yamamoto, B., & Cheng, F. (2023). *Potential Societal Biases of ChatGPT in Higher Education: A Scoping Review*. ArXiv.

Li, S., & Smith, T. M. (n.d.). Fairness and Inclusion in AI.

Liao, Z. (2024). *The Pros and Cons of Chatgpt Application in Higher Education - How to Be A "Middleman" Correctly.* Highlights in Business, Economics and Management. DOI: 10.54097/kdqm0k57

Madhu, M., Kumar, K. M., Pratyaksha, B., Sushmita, S., & Javed, G. S. (2023). Striking Ethical Balance in AI-TAI: Promoting Academic Integrity through AI-Powered Tools. In *2023 IEEE Technology & Engineering Management Conference - Asia Pacific (TEMSCON-ASPAC).*

Meylani, R. (2024). *A Critical Glance at Adaptive Learning Systems Using Artificial Intelligence: A Systematic Review and Qualitative Synthesis of Contemporary Research Literature.* Batı Anadolu Eğitim Bilimleri Dergisi.

Meylani, R. (2024). *A Critical Glance at Adaptive Learning Systems Using Artificial Intelligence: A Systematic Review and Qualitative Synthesis of Contemporary Research Literature.* Batı Anadolu Eğitim Bilimleri Dergisi.

Mollick, E. R., Mollick, L., Bach, N., Ciccarelli, L. J., Przystanski, B., & Ravipinto, D. (2024). *AI Agents and Education: Simulated Practice at Scale.* ArXiv.

Nagakalyani, G., Chaudhary, S., Apte, V., Ramakrishnan, G., & Tamilselvam, S. (2025, February). Design and Evaluation of an AI-Assisted Grading Tool for Introductory Programming Assignments: An Experience Report. In *Proceedings of the 56th ACM Technical Symposium on Computer Science Education* V. 1 (pp. 805-811). DOI: 10.1145/3641554.3701913

Negeri, U., Malik Ibrahim Malang, M., Yazid, S. R., & Dzulfikri, D. (2024). CHATGPT, SMART WRITING ASSISTANT CHATBOT FOR STUDENTS: AN ANALYSIS OF ITS DRAWBACKS. *Abjadia: International Journal of Education.*

Ningsih, F. (2024). *Analyzing students' English-speaking skills using Speechace: Insights from an AI-powered assessment tool*. Pedagogic Research-Applied Literacy Journal.

Nze, S. U. (2024). AI-Powered Chatbots. *Global Journal of Human Resource Management*.

Ogunkunle, O., & Qu, Y. (2020). A ādata mining based optimization of selecting learning material in an intelligent tutoring system for advancing STEM education. In *2020 International conference on computational science and computational intelligence (CSCI)*, Las Vegas, USA. DOI: 10.1109/CSCI51800.2020.00169

Pachaiyappan, P. (2024). Role of AI and ChatGPT in Promoting Holistic and Multidisciplinary Education: NEP-2020 Perspectives. *GRT Journal of Education. Science and Technology*, *2*(2), 35–40.

Perez, R. C. L. (2024). *AI in higher education: Faculty perspective towards artificial intelligence through UTAUT approach*. HO CHI MINH CITY OPEN UNIVERSITY JOURNAL OF SCIENCE - SOCIAL SCIENCES.

Raitskaya, L., & Tikhonova, E. (2024). Appliances of Generative AI-Powered Language Tools in Academic Writing: A Scoping Review. *Journal of Language and Education*.

Rani, B. T. (2024). *Artificial Intelligence tools in Learning English language and Teaching. How can be AI used for Language Learning*. Edumania-An International Multidisciplinary Journal. DOI: 10.59231/edumania/9085

Rodrigues, J. J. P. C., João, P. F. N., & Díez, I. D. L. T. (2013). Recent Advances in Intelligent Tutoring Systems: A Case Study.

Roshan, S., Iqbal, S. Z., & Qing, Z. (2024). Teacher Training and Professional Development for Implementing AI-Based Educational Tools. *Journal of Asian Development Studies*.

Sallam, M., Salim, N., Barakat, M., & Al-Tammemi, A. B. (2023). ChatGPT applications in medical, dental, pharmacy, and public health education: A descriptive study highlighting the advantages and limitations. *Narra J*, *3*(1), e103. DOI: 10.52225/narra.v3i1.103 PMID: 38450035

Sarnato, A. Z., Sari, W. D., Rahmawati, S. T., Hidayat, R., & Patry, H. (2024). The evolution of E-Learning platforms: From U-Learning to AI-Driven adaptive learning systems. *Journal of Social Science Utilizing Technology*, *2*(2), 289–300. DOI: 10.70177/jssut.v2i2.1131

Shafei, S., & Mahmood, S. (2025). Critical Analysis of the Impact of AI in Higher Education and Its Consequences on Students. *Journal of Information Systems Engineering & Management.*

Sharmila, V. C., Lakchudha, P. S., & Seervi, K. (2024, April). Conversational Chabot Builder-Smarter Virtuāal Assistants with Domain Specified AI. In *2024 Ninth International Conference on Science Technology Engineering and Mathematics (ICONSTEM)* (pp. 1-7). IEEE.

Silva, K., Induwara, R., Wimukthi, M., Poornika, S., Samaratunge Arachchillage, U. S. S., & Jayalath, T. (2022). E-tutor: Comprehensive student productivity management system for education. In *2022 4th International conference on advance ments in computing (ICAC)*, Colombo, Sri Lanka.

Subiyantoro, S., Degeng, I., Kuswandi, D., & Ulfa, S. (2023). *Exploring the Impact of AI-Powered Chatbots (Chat GPT) on Education: A Qualitative Study on Benefits and Drawbacks*. Jurnal Pekommas.

Suhendi, S., Yulianti, F., Isnaini, N. A., Jamal, J., Tamim, A., Wulandari, R., & Ruswandi, U. (2024). THE EMERGENCE OF CHATGPT: EXPLORING ITS POTENTIAL IN DESIGNING ISLAMIC RELIGIOUS EDUCATION LEARNING. *Edukasi Islami: Jurnal Pendidikan Islam.*

Šumak, B., López-de-Ipiña, D., Dziabenko, O., Correia, S. D., de Carvalho, L. M. S., Lopes, S., Pušnik, M. (2024, May). AI-Based Education Tools for Enabling Inclusive Education: Challenges and Benefits. In *2024 47th MIPRO ICT and Electronics Convention (MIPRO)* (pp. 472-477). IEEE.

Sun, R., & Deng, X. (2024). Using ChatGPT to Enhance Experiential Learning of College Students. In *Hawaii International Conference on System Sciences.* DOI: 10.24251/HICSS.2024.009

Suna, H., & Özer, M. (2025). The Human Complimentary Usage of AI and ML for Fair and Unbiased Educational Assessments. *Chinese/English Journal of Educational Measurement and Evaluation*, *6*(1). Advance online publication. DOI: 10.59863/YPKL4338

Swanson, T. (2019). The effectiveness of using intelligent tutoring systems to increase student achievement.

Terzi, A., Akritidou, E., & Bibi, M. (2023). Enhancing User Experience: Virtual Assistants in Greek University Helpdesk Service. In *Proceedings of the 27th Pan-Hellenic Conference on Progress in Computing and Informatics.* DOI: 10.1145/3635059.3635089

Tobarra, L., Utrilla, A., Robles-Gómez, A., Pastor-Vargas, R., & Hernández, R. (2021). A cloud game-based educative platform architecture: The cyberscratch project. *Applied Sciences, 11*(2), 1–22. *Article, 807.* Advance online publication. DOI: 10.3390/app11020807

Vidalis, S., & Subramanian, R. (n.d.). *Impact of AI Tools on Engineering Education. In 2023 Fall Mid Atlantic Conference: Meeting our students where they are and getting them where they need to be Proceedings.*

Vidalis, S. M., & Subramanian, R. (2023, October). *Impact of AI Tools on Engineering Education. In 2023 Fall Mid Atlantic Conference: Meeting our students where they are and getting them where they need to be.*

Wade, R. (2012). Pedagogy, places and people. *Journal of Teacher Education for Sustainability, 14*(2), 147–167. DOI: 10.2478/v10099-012-0014-8

Wang, Y. (2024). The Impact of AI Application in Education on Students. *Journal of Education, Humanities and Social Sciences.*

Wang, Y., Wu, J., Chen, F., Wang, Z., Li, J., & Wang, L. (2024). Empirical Assessment of AI-Powered Tools for Vocabulary Acquisition in EFL Instruction. *IEEE Access : Practical Innovations, Open Solutions, 12*, 131892–131905. DOI: 10.1109/ACCESS.2024.3446657

Yang, S. (2025). *The Role of AI in Achieving Inclusive Education.* Communications in Humanities Research. DOI: 10.54254/2753-7064/2024.19654

Yatani, K., Sramek, Z., & Yang, C. (2024). *AI as Extraherics: Fostering Higher-order Thinking Skills in Human-AI Interaction.* ArXiv.

Yitages, M., & Kasai, A. (2024). Faculty Opinions of AI Tools: Text Generators and Machine Translators. *American Journal of Undergraduate Research, 20*(4), 17–27. DOI: 10.33697/ajur.2024.102

Younes, Z. B. B., Hassan, I., Umar, M. M., Mustafa, N. H., Abdullah, A. T. H., & Azmi, M. N. L. (2024). *Challenges and Strategies for Using ChatGPT in Written Communication Assignments: A Study of University Students in Malaysia.* Arab World English Journal.

Zaidy, A. A. (2024). The Impact of Generative AI on Student Engagement and Ethics in Higher Education. *Journal of Information Technology, Cybersecurity, and Artificial Intelligence.*

Zou, Z. (2024). Exploring the Impact of Using Chatbots on Teacher-student Relationships in Today's Higher Education. *Journal of Education, Humanities and Social Sciences*.

Chapter 2
Addressing Challenges and Ethical Considerations in AI-Driven Faculty Development

Sandip Dey
http://orcid.org/0000-0002-1005-3304
Sukanta Mahavidyalaya, Dhupguri, India

ABSTRACT

The integration of artificial intelligence (AI) technology occurs within both academic staff training programs and contemporary educational methods of teaching institutions. Educational facilities face implementation challenges with AI resources because faculty resists change and the costs for technology and infrastructure as well as privacy issues arise. Institutions need to establish financing methods and build ethical AI guidelines then educate their members about AI concepts. Existing universities implement AI systems for student education as well as faculty professional progress. Research teams work to develop sustainable ethical AI systems which will boost faculty preparing processes. Institutional deployment of ethical AI solutions gives teachers access to their advanced training systems. The resolution of operational obstacles will enable higher education to maximize the use of AI systems for faculty and professional development programs.

DOI: 10.4018/979-8-3373-1285-9.ch002

1. INTRODUCTION

1.1 Overview of AI in Faculty Development

Through educational artificial intelligence (AI) transformations the effectiveness of both faculties training practices and learning activities has improved significantly. The practice of organizational progress assists instructors at all levels to refine their competency and pedagogical methodology. The analysis of extensive data by AI tools generates customized training recommendations (Zawacki-Richter et al., 2019). The systems evaluate exact knowledge gaps among instructors to provide suitable learning choices. Through AI the observation and evaluation of development have become more streamlined. AI-powered learning management systems use real-time feedback to supply information about faculty performance to educators (Wang et al., 2021). AI chatbots function as a helpful resource to deliver continuous support through guiding faculty members 24 hours per day. When we use AI we get more time in our hands. AI saves valuable faculty search time by automatically selecting appropriate academic resources (Popenici & Kerr, 2017). AI software helps create training application development systems that offer adaptable learning opportunities through which instructors can progress at customized speeds. Reliable artificial intelligence deployment in faculty development processes produces dilemmas about moral boundaries. Data privacy and fairness alongside other issues require attention because they determine responsible artificial intelligence usage.

Few recent works indicate that AI is increasingly an influential component in teaching and learning, yet faculty development is also posed with novel challenges due to its usage. Although AI tools may assist the teaching innovation, many teachers are not given clear guidelines and systematic training to utilize the technologies in an accountable manner (Holmes, 2023). The AI competency frameworks developed by UNESCO also explain that teachers must acquire more than technical skills, but also ethical awareness, as AI can influence equity, openness, and academic honesty (Mikeladze et al., 2024). A large part of the literature is that AI can personalize learning, automate routine activities, and assist in assessment, although little has been done to determine how faculty can be systematically trained to adopt AI into their instruction. Some studies have examined AI in curriculum design or grades assistance (De Cremer & Kasparov, 2021). There are fewer studies that focus on long-term faculty capacity building of institutions to determine problems like bias, data privacy, or accountability in AI.

These gaps are significant in that faculty are at the heart of the process of making sure that AI is employed ethically and productively in education. The purpose of this chapter is to bridge these gaps in the research with a practical faculty development strategy. It will not only examine the technical training requirements, but also highlight the ethical, cultural, and institutional factors that would determine how AI would be applied in classrooms. In such a way, the chapter attempts to advocate a moderate stance according to which AI could not discourage trust, equity, and professional values without causing harm to education.

1.2 Importance of Faculty Development in the Digital Era

Faculty development plays an essential role in the digital era because education experiences rapid transformations through technological changes. To stay current teachers, need to acquire both new teaching tools alongside new methods. Online platforms combined with virtual classrooms enable teachers to connect effectively with students through digital skills (Van Laar et al., 2017).

The analysis abilities of AI tools evaluate student performance while enabling teachers to create individualized educational approaches. Educational tools require proper training for faculty members to utilize them effectively (Alwaqdani, 2024). Untrained teachers frequently experience technology-related confusion together with a sense of being out of their depth. Through faculty development programs educators gain skills which enhance their teaching abilities. New educational strategies learned by teachers create lessons that grasp student attention. Mishra and Koehler (2006) suggested that trained faculty achieve better student educational results.

Education continues its transition toward global dimensions during the digital era. Educators must learn to teach students while considering multiple learning approaches and educational backgrounds as well as cultural diversity. Educational training makes it possible for educators to grasp these potential variations in a better way (Carey et al., 2018). School administrators who get professional training develop skills which support their career progress. New educational competencies lead teachers to both experience higher confidence and receive improved workplace motivation. Institutions gain from better trained faculty as their reputation improves (Anderson, 2008).

1.3 Objectives and Scope of the Paper

This paper aims to outline both the ethical dilemmas along with implementation obstacles when using AI to develop faculty competencies. Teaching and research together with leadership require faculty development to reach desired improvement levels (Darling-Hammond et al., 2017). AI technology applies more frequently to faculty development yet it introduces three major difficulties associated with fairness and privacy breaches combined with the challenge of adaptation (Gupta et al., 2023).

This document thoroughly explores these matters. Experts seek solutions to resolve artificial intelligence system bias and data protection vulnerabilities and education deficiency regarding AI technology (Qi et al., 2021). Research extends to discover guiding ethical standards for AI deployment with key principles of fairness accountability and transparency.

This work examines AI applications which enable personalized faculty training alongside data-driven testing and collaborative educational platforms (Orhani, 2023). Analysis of efficient professional growth AI tool implementations occurs through assessment of real-world examples at educational institutions (Wang et al., 2023). The study emphasizes both engineering components and societal and cultural barriers that emerge from implementing AI solutions in educational settings. AIT tools face barriers from both traditional beliefs about change as well as discriminatory platform usage patterns in developing nations (Miao et al., 2021).

2. THE ROLE OF AI IN FACULTY DEVELOPMENT

2.1 AI Tools and Technologies for Faculty Development

2.1.1 AI Tools for Teaching and Training Faculty

When educators use AI system examinations, they can discover more efficient instructional approaches. Through artificial intelligence systems Moodle and Blackboard create personalized educational recommendations for instructors (Capuano & Caballé, 2020). Intelligent educational systems linked student response data with performance records to develop fresh instructional blueprint proposals for educators. Intelligent tutoring systems in Carnegie Learning deliver customized educational instructions to teachers for their new teaching material as reported by (Mousavinasab et al., 2021). Process automation runs through these technological solutions to create workflow optimization that leaves teaching professionals with more time to focus on their development.

2.1.2 Virtual Assistance and Collaboration Technologies

The AI-enabled tools ChatGPT and IBM Watson Assistant supply instant responses about educational matters to teachers (Schön et al., 2023). Automated virtual assistants support faculty members to generate lesson plans while also sending emails and creating assessments. AI-powered collaboration tools Microsoft Teams and Slack break down communication hurdles between educators by enabling better team conversations while facilitating resource exchange. Students who use Oculus for Education benefit from teaching scenarios via virtual reality to help develop their educational strategies through virtual tests. Through diverse classroom management training faculty members learn practical skills that boost their effectiveness during student interaction (Marks & Thomas, 2022).

2.1.3 Analytics for Continuous Improvement

The setup enables teachers to use analytics tools which provide monitoring resources for checking performance levels and recognizing areas for self-improvement. AI technology functions as the support foundation for Tableau and Power BI platforms to analyze teaching data and create significant patterns (Lee et al., 2023). The analytic capabilities of dashboard systems enabled by artificial intelligence allow students' educational achievements and their engagement patterns to be accessible to educators. AI-powered predictive systems send alerts for instructors to provide additional support to students demanding additional help thus triggering immediate intervention (Umer et al., 2023). AI technology enables modern training programs to construct tailored feedback solutions that build continuous expert development capabilities for professionals. The technological breakthroughs allow continuous education development and flexible academic responses to transforming educational requirements.

2.2 Benefits of AI for Faculty Growth and Skill Enhancement

Through AI-enabled virtual instruction teachers access digital teaching standards together with essential educational content. Learning materials within these courses automatically adjust to match the instructional preferences of their individual instructors. When it comes to educational planning Coursera and edX together implement artificial intelligence systems to create personalized educational solutions for their teaching community (Xu, 2024). Online resources provide educators access to discover new teaching procedures and modern subject insights and classroom technology knowledge. Throughout its deployment AI analyzes the progression of educators through data evaluation to deliver systematic growth possibilities. Applications of these methods allow instructors to monitor educational to technological changes throughout the current era.

By bringing AI automation to the classroom teachers can handle their routine responsibilities like grading assignments while improving classroom time with students and pursuing professional development. The time teachers reserve out of their extended availability helps them work with students while moving forward professionally as instructors. It may require artificial intelligence systems for speeds deployment of precise grades (Alakoum et al., 2024). Through its features inside writing development Grammarly lets teachers transform their students' writing grammar abilities. Teacher users capitalize on ChatGPT to seek academic assistance in content generation while planning educational material and strategies. These modern teaching resources build contemporary educational frameworks that drive better teaching practices and inner efficiencies and more effective prospect results for teachers and pupils.

Artificial Intelligence provides teachers access to knowledge from worldwide experts who enable global collaboration. Relay conferences supported by AI translation software support international knowledge collaboration through borderless communication (AI-Youbi et al., 2020). The analytics through artificial intelligence enable educators to better comprehend how teaching emerges in various geographic regions. The combination of virtual reality (VR) and artificial intelligence simulations provides teachers with simulated teaching experiences across varying conditions. Their educational performance and self-assurance together with their abilities increase through this approach. Through AI-based systems teachers experience shorter development paths that lead to stronger professional outcomes.

2.3 Examples of Institutions Leveraging AI for Faculty Development

Research institutions employ artificial intelligence tools to both advance faculty development initiatives and enhance teaching methodologies. ECoach is an AI tool at the University of Michigan which delivers personalized pedagogical guidance to its faculty staff. Through this educational technology professors receive student assessments that provide directions for better engaging their students (Chatterjee et al., 2023). Georgia State University uses AI-based chatbots to support faculty through their educational workload and connection them to opportunities for improvement. Teachers experience shorter response times through these chatbots which allows them to dedicate more attention to their research and teaching activities (Nalyvaiko & Maliutina, 2021). AI tools enhance faculty member assessment of teaching approaches by providing suggestions from student performance data feedback. Through this analysis teachers can modify their instructional approaches for enhanced student success.

The Open Learning Initiative (OLI) at Carnegie Mellon University employs AI technology as part of its operations. Accessible data regarding student learning progression comes instantly through the platform which also empowers faculty to build better academic resources (Lakhavani et al., 2011). Stanford University boosts faculty growth by using adaptive learning platforms built with Artificial Intelligence. These educational platforms deliver modern teaching methods to educators who receive AI-directed developmental assessments (Southworth et al., 2023). Microsoft in partnership with IBM delivers AI-based workshops which unite universities worldwide for teaching professional development purposes after Microsoft declared its support in 2020 (Luckin et al., 2022) and IBM did so in 2021 (Pedro et al., 2019). The collaborative study demonstrates that artificial intelligence operates as both an educational tool which enhances teaching quality while keeping teachers proficient in modern educational methods.

New artificial intelligence applications, especially Large Language Models (LLMs), are changing the way faculty members develop by promoting adaptive learning, automatic content generation, and personal mentoring. Regional constraints however vary (through lack of infrastructural access or development in some countries, policy fragmentation in Europe or a lapse in cultural uptake in Asia) and lead to variable adoption rates. By bringing these solutions in line with the existing theory building models like AI Competency Standards by UNESCO, practices can be ensured to be ethically as well as inclusion and skill skill-based. This strategic orientation breeds context-specific solutions that are geographically sensitive at the same time practically applicable (Cukurova & Miao, 2024).

A set of AI tools for faculty development and their applications are presented in Table 1.

Table 1. AI tools for faculty development and their applications

Tool Type	Application in Faculty Development	Examples (Tools)
Automated Feedback Systems	Offers real-time feedback on teaching usefulness.	Perusall, Grammarly, Turnitin AI.
AI-Powered Learning Analytics	Tracks faculty and student engagement.	Coursera AI, Canvas Analytics.
Chatbots & Virtual Assistants	Supports faculty with administrative tasks. .	ChatGPT, IBM Watson.
AI-Based Recommendation Systems	Suggests personalized professional development resources.	LinkedIn Learning AI, Google Scholar AI.
AI-Driven Peer Review Systems	Enhances faculty research evaluation and collaboration.	Semantic Scholar

2.4 Faculty-led AI training programs

Few examples of programs that are led by faculty are addressed below.

1) University teach-the-teacher workshops where instructors are trained to create AI-conscious curricula and exams (e.g. campus Teaching with AI workshops and short courses) (Holmes & Tuomi, 2022).

2) Capacity-building summer schools / indaba in the region which combine actual ML practicums with faculty pedagogy (Deep Learning Indaba workshops serve as an example).
3) Multilateral professional development forced by multilateral agencies (UNESCO teacher/teacher-trainer guides, and AI competency frameworks to educators) (Cukurova & Miao, 2024).
4) Programs focused on providing the Southern institutions with the research-network led programs (AI4D/IDRC) to guide AI research and faculty training according to the needs of the Southern area (Wall et al., 2021).

Some real-world solutions that may address Global South resources inequality.

1) Train-the-trainer and modular OERs - scale effect. -- Prepare local faculty to cascade training with low-bandwidth open material.
2) Contextual learning programs and data sets - prioritize local issues and languages in such a way that faculty may train responsible AI (Holmes & Tuomi, 2022).
3) Blended & offline tooling - Integrate short face-to-face bootcamps with asynchronous micro-modules and lightweight toolchains to overcome connectivity constraints.
4) Sustainable financing and South-South partnership long-term grants, university networks, and mentorship to transfer leadership to local organizations (IDRC/AI4D models) (Wall et al., 2021).

2.5 Governance Models & Key Elements

1) Recommendation on the Ethics of Artificial Intelligence by UNESCO

The UNESCO focuses on the value-based model of governance that is based on human dignity and human rights, fairness, transparency, inclusivity, and sustainability and multi-stakeholder partnerships. Some of the most important principles are proportionality and do no harm, safety, and security, right to privacy and data protection, human oversight, awareness, and literacy, explainability, fairness and non-discrimination, and sustainability. They are expected to govern using mechanisms that are auditability, traceability, impact assessments, redress, and enforcement (Rios-Campos et al., 2023).

2) Hourglass Model of Organizational AI

This framework suggests that there should be layered governance at environmental, organizational and AI system levels. It traces governance throughout the entire lifecycle of AI systems, thereby providing ethical control over AI systems both in design and implementation to decommissioning. Applicable in the faculty development context where several phases (tool selection, implementation, review) are to be followed (Mäntymäki et al., 2022).

3) Model of AI Ethics Maturity (Whole organization approach)

The framework aimed to assist institutions in the transition of what ethical AI principles are to how to implement them. It defines maturity levels of the implementation of ethics in data science and AI practices, such as capacity building, governance policy, procedures, training, monitoring (Krijger et al., 2023).

4) Responsibility / Accountability & Stakeholder-Centric Framework

As an example, the "Privacy Ethics Alignment" framework, in which the roles of stakeholders are critical in the alignment of AI systems with privacy and ethics; or general Responsible AI Governance frameworks, in which accountability, clarity in oversight and multi-stakeholder input is prescribed. They are particularly applicable in ratings of faculty, students, and administration interests (Santos & Radanliev, 2024).

3. ETHICAL CONSIDERATIONS IN AI-DRIVEN FACULTY DEVELOPMENT

3.1 Privacy and Data Security Concerns

Training quality improves together with teaching standards through artificial intelligence systems which utilize data. Machine learning programs present dangers both to personal privacy and system security. Protected status extends to academic staff data consisting of personal information and records of performance together with feedback. Storage of faculty data remains at risk for theft or misuse when security measures are weak (Pechenkina, 2023).

3.1.1. Data Collection and Storage

Training quality improves together with teaching standards through artificial intelligence systems which utilize data. AI platforms process their massive data collection needs through their storage functionality. Information about faculty members alongside education methods and student performance data is collected by systems. Without the correct security measures hackers gain access to stored data. To guarantee protection of this information institutions should employ both encryption technologies alongside secure database management practices (Guliashki, 2023).

3.1.2. Data Sharing Risks

Data from faculty gets distributed to external companies through some AI technology choices. When universities hire AI service providers from outside their institutions there is risk. The sharing of data without permission leads to violations of privacy laws. All institutions need faculty approval before sharing academic data under current protocols (Lazăr et al., 2024).

3.1.3. Unauthorized Access

Airtight access restrictions must exist within AI systems. Any information system relies on proper access controls because unauthorized users can both view data and make unauthorized changes to it. Windward Professional Research notes that improper faculty information access could lead to inaccurate evaluations as well as wrongful faculty data usage. The combination between password security measures and multi-factor validation procedures and role-based permission systems should be implemented by faculty to avert unauthorized entrance (Yang & Beil, 2024).

3.1.4. AI Bias and Data Privacy

Databases used by artificial intelligence systems occasionally absorb various data biases that prove false or mistaken. AI systems utilizing unbalanced datasets develop faulty performance evaluation mechanisms for faculty members. All faculty members need the power to verify and correct their recorded information. Organizations must maintain transparency because only then conclusion of unfair treatment can be prevented (Memarian & Doleck, 2023).

3.1.5. Legal and Ethical Issues

The protection of faculty data in many nations comes through laws that include both the General Data Protection Regulation (GDPR) in Europe and matching legislation found across the United States. For safe operation universities need to maintain adherence to the applicable laws. All faculty members need detailed explanations of data collection processes and data usage purposes (Reidenberg & Schaub, 2018).

The ethical reasoning paradox and issues with global trends of artificial-intelligence represent one of the core issues in AI-based faculty development. Generative AI and LLMs also have a transformative potential in design regarding instructor training and curriculum structure, but also raise significant ethical issues. There is a potential threat of strengthening the stereotypes in the context of algorithmic bias, particularly when it comes to assessment and feedback. The collection of the faculty data is a privacy issue, which raises questions about informed consent and surveillance (Zuboff, 2023). In addition to ethical aspects, there are practical obstacles such as implementation cost and organizational policy to change which restrict implementation in settings where resource constraints exist (Brynjolfsson and McAfee, 2018). Although the global trends promote the scalability and personalization properties of AI, it is necessary to align these instruments with the ideas of equity, transparency, and affordability.

3.1.6. Best Practices for Privacy and Security

Encryption: Protects data from hackers.

Access Control: Data access and modification remain limited to select users.

Regular Audits: AI technology must stick to privacy requirements.

Transparency: Despite all regulations faculty must receive complete information regarding why their data gets handled.

Consent: Before any data sharing occurs, faculty members need to provide their explicit agreement.

The integration of AI into faculty development brings numerous advantages however privacy and security challenges remain as primary concerns. The protection of faculty data should include encryption approaches and stringent access protocols and clear data transparency measures. All organizations need to obey legal regulations to prevent privacy invasions. Ethical application of AI maintains both secure and fair procedures for faculty development (Saaida, 2023).

3.2 Bias in AI Algorithms and its Impacts

AI operates in faculty development alongside numerous other fields. However, AI can have bias. AI creates unfair treatment of people due to poor or insufficient data processing. The unjust treatment of faculty members and students develops from this situation.

3.2.1 Causes of AI Bias

AI models derive their biased nature from the data used for their training purpose. AI systems develop biased patterns when they are presented with an unbalanced training dataset. The research by Mehrabi et al. demonstrates that AI develops biases because data has sustained for centuries with unfair practices. The preferences demonstrated by past faculty recruitment processes toward male candidates may influence AI programs to also select candidates who identify as male for hiring positions (Mehrabi et al., 2021).

AI bias develops because of how AI models receive their design instructions. AI will deliver prejudicial outcomes to people when developers fail to conduct assessments for potential bias. Human decision-making factors throughout AI development processes lead to bias emergence. AI systems receive developers' biases without their awareness because these biases get incorporated into AI systems.

3.2.2 Impacts of AI Bias on Faculty Development

AI bias generates various impacts that affect the development of faculty members. The implementation of AI_Disruptive tools serves as an assistant for recruitment decisions and job advancements alongside employee assessment activities. AI systems showing bias could reduce the development opportunities of selected members of the faculty staff. The hiring tool analysis by Zou and Schiebinger, revealed that this system gives special treatment toward some demographic groups against others. This makes the system unfair (Zou & Schiebinger, 2018).

The application of AI systems leads to learning tools being detrimentally affected. The educational institutions deploy AI systems to evaluate faculty member teaching performance. Wrong evaluations would be sent to several faculty members when AI exposes biases in its system. Face recognition tools operated by AI systems produce higher error rates when used on darker skin pigmentation. The presence of identical prejudice within faculty evaluation devices endangers career development pathways.

3.2.3 Effects of AI on Teacher Student Relation

The implementation of AI in the learning process is turning the relationship between educators and learners into a two-sided process since it is offering chances and challenges. Tools powered by AI, such as adaptive learning systems and intelligent tutoring systems, along with individualized learning instruction and provision of timely feedback, automate tedious administrative processes for instructors. As a result, faculty can invest more time in mentorship and higher-level pedagogical responses that may result into an improvement in trust and exchange (Holmes & Porayska-Pomsta, 2023). Moreover, the AI-based analytics allow educators to more accurately identify the learning gaps and socio emotional needs and enhance the accommodations of more diverse learners

However, with a growing reliance on AI there is the danger of uncertainty on personalising the learning process. The most important human relationship on which also education is based can be undermined by the increased interaction of machines with students, leading to a lack of empathy and emotional attachment. Also, students can change their attitude regarding authority, perceiving AI systems as more objective or accurate as compared to human decision making, and the relational dimension of education is undermined. A bias favoring a large amount of data will run the risk of marginalizing the learners whose education patterns do not fit into the algorithmic forecasting (Luckin, 2018).

The main challenge in maintaining the authentic teacher-student relations involves establishing a reasonable balance between the efficiency of AI and the presence of the human touch and direction. Faculty development programs should, therefore, focus on not just technical integration of AI, but also ethics and relationship aspects associated with the use of AI.

3.2.4 Ethical Concerns

AI bias raises ethical concerns. The academic staff should have access to equal opportunities. AI creates discrimination because it chooses to prefer groups above others. The practice opposes both fairness standards and equal treatment. The designers of AI systems must focus on creating fair machines (Danks & London, 2017).

Another ethical issue is trust. The detection of AI bias by academic staff should create mistrust toward AI-based decision-making. AI bias generates weapons of math destruction which means AI generates significant damage when acting in crucial decisions. When AI shows bias in assessment processes it creates distrust between faculty members towards these assessment systems (O'neil, 2017).

3.2.5 Solutions to Reduce Bias

The implementation of AI bias reduction requires testing from both educational institutions and programming developers of their AI models. The training process for AI systems needs data from various backgrounds. The deployment of AI should include an assessment of fairness (Mitchell et al., 2019). When AI receives proper testing, it enables the reduction of bias.

Another solution is human oversight. AI systems should work under human supervision because they must not execute decisions independently. Humans should check AI's results. Human oversight of AI decisions enables detection and correction of bias (Raji et al., 2020).

Artificial Intelligence generates significant discriminatory challenges in the field of faculty development. Unfair results in the hiring process coupled with promotions and evaluations emerge from its biased operation. The situation is damaging both equality standards and trustworthy relationships between parties. To maintain fairness universities, need to conduct tests on their AI systems while employing human supervisors. AI bias reduction will create improved faculty development processes for all participants.

3.3 Balancing Automation with Human-Centered Development

Artificial Intelligence transforms how both faculty teaching methods and educational learning approaches operate. The automated system reduces the workload of repetitive tasks which faculty members need to perform. The system enables grading processes and generates feedback. Artificial intelligence lacks the ability to duplicate human attributes including empathy and creativity and critical thinking ability (Selwyn, 2019). Faculties must use AI automation to support human-led learning activities. The correct ratio between human involvement and artificial intelligence ensures AI supports teacher work instead of performing their tasks.

3.3.1 The Role of AI in Faculty Development

AI tools have multiple application areas that help academic faculty can leverage at their convenience. AI tools perform student performance assessment which generates customized learning recommendations. AI enables the deployment of virtual question-answering systems that serve students (Zawacki-Richter et al., 2019). Through automated processes organizations can conduct meeting scheduling while tracking student advancement and handling administrative responsibilities (Popenici & Kerr, 2017). The system provides features through which faculty members can allocate additional time to educational mentoring and teaching activities.

Putting too much faith in artificial intelligence systems has the potential to produce negative outcomes. Students lose their direct relationship with instructors because AI systems interact frequently. The decisions made by AI systems sometimes lack fair and unbiased judgments (Baker & Hawn, 2022). To learn AI systems, use data but any biases present in that data will automatically appear in the AI's output (O'Neil, 2017). AI-based faculty development requires human intervention because AI lacks full understanding of all educational requirements. Few examples of ethical considerations in AI-driven faculty development is presented in Table 2.

Table 2. Ethical considerations in AI-driven faculty development

Ethical Principle	Consideration	Examples
Fairness	The use of AI should not disadvantage for any group.	To ensure AI-based faculty estimations are bias-free.
Transparency	AI decision-making should be understandable.	To provide clear foundations for AI-generated endorsements.
Accountability	Institutions must be accountable for AI decisions.	To define who is liable for AI-based faculty assessments.
Consent & Privacy	Faculty should have control over their data.	To require clear consent for AI-driven performance trailing.
Sustainability	AI should line up with longstanding academic goals.	To ensure AI supports faculty development.

4. CHALLENGES IN IMPLEMENTING AI FOR FACULTY DEVELOPMENT

4.1 Technological Barriers and Infrastructure Limitations

AI provides teachers with opportunities to discover advanced learning subjects. AI implementation for faculty development requires careful implementation because of numerous obstacles. Multiple issues exist which obstruct the effective operation of AI systems. The primary difficulties surround poor technological installations along with inadequate infrastructure arrangements.

4.1.1 Limited Access to High-Quality Internet

AI needs fast internet. Many institutions which serve as educational facilities operate without providing adequate internet to their students. The functionality of AI tools suffers when there is not adequate internet connection availability (Hillier, 2020). The connectivity in many rural sections of the land is either sluggish or completely nonexistent. The lack of suitable AI tools makes teaching tasks difficult for educators. AI tools need online data. When internet speed weakens the tools cannot deliver proper outputs (Palvia et al., 2018).

4.1.2 Lack of Good Computers and Devices

AI tools need good computers. Many schools have old computers. The outdated nature of computers makes AI programs difficult to execute effectively. Online learning with AI tools requires both excellent camera and microphone capabilities

(Dogan et al., 2023). AI implementation by teachers proves challenging because faulty devices make their task impossible. Educational institutions use teacher-owned personal devices although these devices lack compatibility for running AI programs (Gonçalves, 2024).

4.1.3 High Cost of AI Technology

AI is expensive. The financial resources of numerous educational institutions are insufficient to acquire AI technology. Using AI tools and software and obtaining training for them implies steep financial costs. Due to restricted financing information technology solutions remain unattainable for educational institutions having limited financial resources. AI also needs updates. Updates cost money. The AI tools become extinct because schools lack sufficient funds to maintain them (Iftikhar et al., 2020).

4.1.4 Lack of Technical Support

AI technology expertise stands as a barrier for teachers because they lack proficiency in AI use. They need help. Most educational institutions lack employees who have expertise in AI technologies. Actual experts serve as the only solution for teachers who aim to solve AI-related problems. Most schools operate without internal groups that provide AI technical assistance. The use of AI technology by educators becomes jeopardized when they face issues with this technology (Chou et al., 2024).

4.1.5 Data Storage and Privacy Issues

AI needs a lot of data. Every educational institution requires protected facilities to maintain their data. The lack of effective data storage systems exists within multiple educational institutions. Data security risks allow hackers to obtain the information in their possession. Existence of personal information belonging to teachers and students becomes at risk. The operational requirements for AI tools require robust security measures. Security measures are needed to prevent AI from becoming hazardous (Watini et al., 2024).

4.1.6 Poor AI Integration with Existing Systems

Learning systems are currently being used within most educational institutions. The integration between AI and these existing systems must happen for success. Certain instances show that AI systems fail to produce suitable matches. Schools may need new systems. Establishing new technological infrastructures entails both monetary expenses and takes substantial periods of time. Old system incompatibility prevents AI from working properly thus making teachers reluctant to adopt the technology (Agre, 2014).

AI can help teachers grow. The poor performance of AI systems originates from inadequate internet connections along with outdated equipment and exorbitant fees along with limited availability of AI specialists and insecure data platforms and substandard system connectivity. Schools need better technology. Programs at both government and private levels need to guarantee schools achieve AI readiness status. AI will enhance faculty development when the identified issues find solutions.

4.2 Financial Constraints and Cost of AI Integration

Implementation of AI in the faculty development process is costly and may involve spending more than the resources available to the institutions which have limited budgets. The initial investment in AI in terms of software acquisition, high-performance computers, and specialized training courses pose a high barrier to smaller organizations and developing countries (Ananyi and Somieari-Pepple, 2023). The costs for installation, maintenance, savings on servers and processors, can enhance the expenses (Prasad et al., 2024).

Educating faculty on the use of AI is an added financial tension. Not only do workshops, support of the experts, and training of the skills require money, they also require faculty to spend time not teaching, which results in low productivity (Ziyautdinov, 2024). Also, teachers are unwilling to invest in professional development or learn more about new technologies, which slows their adoption (Knyazeva et al., 2022). AI is not a priority in the universities with limited budgets, as they usually allocate the necessary services instead (with delays or reduced adoption. Although automation and individualized learning have the potential to save money in the long term, institutions cannot calculate their investment payoff, which poses a question about sustainability (Prasad et al., 2024).

To address these obstacles, the institutions can turn to government support or collaboration with technology vendors. To save finances and make AI-based faculty development more realistic, it is important to think through financial planning, select specific tools, and have some external support. Few crucial challenges in AI-driven faculty growth are presented in Table 3.

Table 3. Key challenges in AI-driven faculty development

Challenges	Description	Examples
Bias in AI Systems	AI models may strengthen biases, that may lead to unfair treatment.	Gender bias in faculty assessment algorithms.
Data Privacy Issues	Ethical concerns about gathering and using faculty data.	AI tracking faculty performance without consent.
Lack of AI Literacy	Faculty may lack training to use AI tools in an effective manner.	Incapability to understand AI-generated feedback.
Resistance to AI Adoption	Faculty may fear job shift or loss of autonomy.	Uncertainty about AI grading or approval systems.
Transparency & Accountability	Trouble in understanding AI decision-making procedures.	Black-box AI models used for faculty valuation.

5. STRATEGIES FOR ADDRESSING CHALLENGES

5.1 Building Awareness and AI Literacy Among Faculty

AI is transforming the educational field, and it is important to know the principles of AI in faculty. However, most teachers are not well-informed, and they might be scared or intimidated when they must deal with the concepts of AI. At the institution level, it is thus important to have clear and accessible training strategies (Zawacki-Richter et al., 2019). Not only the understanding of definitions and applications, but also awareness of limitations and risks is AI literacy. By having knowledge of AI, teachers will be able to incorporate it in their teaching and research (Luckin et al., 2022).

Online training, workshops, and webinars are the major ways of training AI (Guilherme, 2019). Simple teachings and practical examples can assist teachers in visualizing how AI can be used to facilitate the work they do every day (Selwyn, 2019). Practical experiences are known to boost confidence, whereas learning groups enable teachers to share experiences and alleviate anxiety (Hashmi & Bal, 2024). Faculty are also guided through mentor-based support systems towards AI adoption. The problem with time is also present, since not all teachers have time to engage in self-directed learning. The organizations need to incorporate AI literacy in the professional development and staff meetings they have, to make sure learning is ongoing and systematic.

The next issue is the problem of job security. Educational leaders are afraid that faculty can be superseded, and AI needs to be positioned as an augmentative technology that facilitates teaching, not replaces human judgment (Selwyn, 2019).

Schools need to put in place fair use, data protection, and security policies to promote ethical usage (Jarke and Breiter, 2019).

Finally, the AI literacy will allow teachers to equip students with future requirements, reinforce pedagogy, and improve the quality of education (Zawacki-Richter et al., 2019).

5.2 Developing Transparent and Ethical AI Models

Faculty development has become an essential part of AI since its success is determined by transparency, fairness, accountability, and data privacy. Transparency means that users must be informed of the logic of AI decisions. Explainable AI (XAI) enhances the trust, as it explains how a recommendation is produced, i.e., why a specific teaching course is recommended (Gunning et al., 2019; Doshi-Velez and Kim, 2017). The level of AI acceptance among the faculty increases when systems can justify their decisions (Floridi and Cowls, 2022).

Prejudice minimization is also very important. As AI models can imitate discriminatory trends in training data, developers should consider numerous, representative datasets and accomplish regular bias testing. When biases are observed, they should be corrected immediately (Barocas et al., 2023). Accountability should be to the developers and the faculty. Faculty development should have guidelines on the use of AI in institutions, with the procedures in place to rectify errors and people as the ultimate decision-makers (Morley et al., 2021).

Another thing of priority is to protect data privacy. AI is based on sensitive data sets, and the institutions should impose clear policies regarding data collection, data storage, and application to protect the information of the faculty (Tsamados et al., 2021). Lastly, systematic auditing, constant upgrades, and ethics committees should be implemented as an approach to manage AI implementation in universities. The use of XAI and bias mitigation, accountability, and privacy protection guarantees that AI is a reliable and useful tool in the development of faculties (Jobin et al., 2019).

5.3 Securing Funding and Partnerships for AI Implementation

5.3.1 Importance of Funding and Partnerships

The implementation of artificial intelligence for faculty advancement requires financial backing and organizational support to succeed. Schools together with universities frequently lack necessary financial resources to implement AI systems (Jobin et al., 2019). The budget goes towards obtaining AI software alongside teacher training and system upkeep. Educational organizations gain access to easier AI deployment through strategic government-company alliances (Gabriel et al., 2022).

5.3.2 Government and Public Grants

Mastering AI in teaching receives financial backing through governmental grants. School grants from these institutions ensure institutions can use AI systems to enhance both teaching and learning practices Various nations operate funding initiatives which distribute financial aid to institutions that incorporate AI into their operations. The funding provided by public research organizations takes part in supporting AI project initiatives (Nikolinakos, 2023). The application process for these grants depends on submitting basic documentation which shows the value of AI technologies for trainer instruction.

5.3.3 Private Sector and Industry Collaborations

The education sector receives substantial investment of artificial intelligence technology from private businesses. Large technology companies minimize expenses by supplying financial support together with educational tools and institutional training to educational institutions (Esangbedo et al., 2023). Educational institutions may collaborate with these businesses to acquire complimentary AI software as well as price reductions. As part of their initiatives specific companies provide educational resources and guidance to professionals regarding AI-based teacher development.

5.3.4 Research and Development (R&D) Grants

University research groups obtain numerous grants which support AI experiments. The acquired funds are directed towards examining how AI contributes to faculty development (Miao et al., 2021). Several AI educational initiatives obtain financial support from worldwide organizations. The recipient funding supports AI development of educational tools suitable for teachers.

5.3.5 Crowdfunding and Community Support

A third funding approach for AI exists through crowdsourcing methods. Schools commonly conduct crowdfunding events where individuals donate minor monetary amounts for AI projects funding (Mao-Clark et al., 2024). The fundraising effort exists from both parents and alumni and education supporters. The support received from communities assists in spreading knowledge about the role of AI within faculty training.

5.3.6 Strategies for Addressing Funding Challenges

Acquiring AI funding remains hard but multiple methods exist for resolving this challenge. The process of obtaining multiple grants simultaneously stands as a strategy to obtain funding. Several academic institutions can unite in obtaining collective funding for AI research initiatives. Before seeking additional funds, one must establish successful pilot initiatives through which they can display impressive outcomes (Baker et al., 2023).

5.3.7 Ethical Partnerships in AI

Both parties involved in partnerships must establish relationships based on open communication. Schools need to select businesses operating with ethical AI practices. Any educational application of Artificial Intelligence requires protection of student privacy plus equal treatment opportunities. The implementation of ethical guidelines guarantees AI delivers equal advantages to every teacher and student.

5.4 Practical Strategies for Overcoming Resistance to AI in Faculty Development

Opposition towards the adoption of AI in higher education is often observed to be based on the concerns on the aspect of potential being replaced, loss of academic freedom, and lack of explicitly defined ethical issues. Streamlining these apprehensions would require a cocktail of real and sympathetic intercessions that are specifically crafted targeting both the faculty members and institutional controls.

5.4.1 Openness in Information and Creation of Awareness

The institutions are supposed to form organized discussion rooms whereby the faculty and administration are supposed to present their concerns openly. Honest and transparent communication that shows AI as more of an assistive tool than a replacement is effective in reducing the number of anxieties and was demonstrated in recent studies (Black, 2024).

5.4.2 Specific Training and Capacity Development.

Practical workshops and brief certification courses about AI literacy enable professors to play with AI technologies in a structured fashion. The practical experience has shown that these kinds of learning experience can help instill the understanding of AI as the facilitator of learners and pedagogy, and not a menace (Kim et al., 2022).

5.4.3 Showcasing Success Stories

The presentation of case studies of how AI has contributed to the efficiency of grading, curriculum design, and student engagement is a touch of reality when it comes to seeing the benefits. It is easy to see how peer-guided role models are more influential in contrast to top-down instructions and this argument is emphasized in modern research.. Here, models of Shared Governance and Policy Involvement are also available.

Engaging faculty and administration in AI policy writing would help in ensuring their views are not left out and thus they would have a sense of ownership and trust in AI initiatives.

5.4.4 Resolving the Ethical and Job Security issues.

Fears are mitigated through explicit promise as seen through clear policies which outlaw the substitution of faculty position to an AI based position. The institutions must promote AI as an assistant in the administration process and student analytics, possibly presenting the persistence of human pedagogy and mentoring as its priority.

5.4.5 Incentivizing Adoption

Faculty working with AI could be offered recognition, grants or workload re-alignment to encourage it gradually but under pressure-free conditions.

Resistance may be refitted through the lenses of empathy, collaboration, and value manifestation through prioritizing empathy, collaboration, and evidence of value. Whenever faculty and other administrators view AI as in line with academic values and professional development, its implementation becomes more of a joint opportunity than a contentious requisite.

5.4.6 Funding Partnerships

The formation of strategic funding partnering is an essential mechanism of making artificial intelligence tend to integrate faculty development programs. Joint agreements with government and non-governmental technological organizations, and educational funds can provide fiscal and technical resources (Starkey, 2020). These partnerships provide institutions with access to AI or training services and research grants, which lessens institutional reluctance, which is created by financial or resource constraints. In addition, collective efforts can spawn pilot studies which can empirically substantiate the usefulness of AI carrying out pedagogically and assessment settings.

5.4.7 AI Literacy Roadmaps

The conceptualization of design AI literacy roadmaps helps faculty members to build-up the competence and confidence incrementally (Holmes, 2020). The roadmaps should consider the traditional AI notions, ethical discussions, hands-on workshops, and continued mentorship. Heterogeneous levels of technological readiness are considered, and resistance to change abated through tiered learning trajectories (the first level beginning with awareness to the subsequent level being complete use of the technology). The significance of implementing AI literacy in faculty development programmes ensures the chances of success after introduction, and the enhancement of new pedagogic approaches.

6. CASE STUDIES: SUCCESSFUL IMPLEMENTATION OF AI IN FACULTY DEVELOPMENT

Case Study 1: AI-Powered Personalized Learning at Arizona State University

The faculty training programs at Arizona State University (ASU) utilize AI technology for enhancement. The university launched an AI system which supports teachers by enhancing their teaching abilities. The system provides immediate feed-back concerning teaching methods. The system evaluates educational recordings before delivering related recommendations. The AI system provides recommended online classes for faculty members to boost their professional capabilities.

The adaptive learning platform developed by ASU received collaborative creation help from CogBooks. Through this digital platform teachers gain the ability to develop improved learning programs. The system recognizes individual student requirements. Faculty members acquired skills to operate this technology through workshops which used artificial intelligence guidance. The workshops dedicated personal assistance to each instructor (Mishra & Smith, 2020).

The AI program at ASU enabled one of its professors to build better instructional methods for his classroom. Professor Master employed AI systems to obtain feedback which guided his lecture modifications. Students gained a better understanding of the taught material because of this approach. Student satisfaction levels at the institution increased based on data obtained by the university. Teacher growth within their profession becomes possible through AI implementation (Khine, 2024).

Case Study 2: AI-Based Teaching Assistants at Georgia Tech

Georgia Institution of Technology designed an AI system to improve teaching quality for their instructors. Jill Watson emerged as an AI system which served as a teaching assistant at Georgia Tech. Jill Watson operates as an automated assistant in online curriculum question response. Institutional employees gained proficiency in employing AI assistants within their educational activities.

Academic staff accessed their AI training sessions through online learning platforms. The programs demonstrated to teachers the entire process of AI assistant implementation and observation functions. Through its AI system the teachers obtained immediate responses for standard questions. Using AI assistants there was time conservation benefitting academic staff members. Professor staff members utilized their additional available time to enhance their educational programs (Sadera et al., 2024).

An instructor discovered valuable benefits from AI usage during classes with many students. Repetitive student inquiries were handled by the AI assistant. The instructor dedicated his instruction to advanced subject material. Students received a better learning experience because of the implementation. Research indicates that AI assistants received helpfulness feedback from 85% of student respondents. AI technology provided faculty members relief from stress by lowering their work demands (Hannan & Liu, 2023).

Case Study 3: AI-Powered Personalized Learning for Faculty

The University of California employed SmartLearn as their AI-based system to assist faculty members in their development process. The AI system processed information that involved faculty teaching approaches and student feedback together with academic research interests. The collected data served to generate individualized suggestions including training programs together with research partnership recommendations as well as educational enhancement suggestions (Holman et al., 2024).

Through its learning modules SmartLearn provided customized education to its faculty members. An AI system would propose digital pedagogy courses when a professor required better online teaching abilities. SmartLearn offered mentors to associate professors according to their preference of academic subjects. User interactivity alongside user input enabled this system to develop continuously (Bernacki et al., 2021).

Teaching effectiveness showed substantial improvement because SmartLearn was adopted as a new platform. The teaching and research abilities of faculty members improved according to their reports. Student satisfaction scores also increased. The university management team saw the platform's achievement so it began expanding its usage throughout various academic departments

The system faced ethical issues concerning the protection of data privacy during its operation. A few professors expressed doubts about the usage of their performance information. The university developed robust data protection rules while providing teaching personnel with the choice to decline artificial intelligence capabilities (Eden et al., 2024).

Case Study 4: IIT, Madras: AI, All: Scalable Faculty/Teacher Upskilling

The example of the AI for All program by IIT Madras, as well as the SWAYAM-Plus courses known as AI for Educators, represent a vast and low-barrier model of faculty training in which short, project-focused transit course modules, shared with free delivery. All teachers, including K-12 and college professors, are specifically aimed at by the programme matching abstract scholarly units (ethical AI, measurement of model outputs) with countries labs and small capacity capstone projects. The educational system mainly serves to reduce the barriers of entry and has the potential to demonstrate responsible AI. It is based on central planning curriculum and decentralized highlighting: basic material and data manipulation content was created by faculty at IIT and delivered via SWAYAM, and context-based laboratory sessions and mentoring by the partner units. The initiative has been successful based on two salient aspects: (1) the ability to operate at mass scale, based on the modularity of micro-courses, which does not require members of the faculty to go through any extensive sabbatical; (2) a thread of ethics and pedagogy that does not view AI as a technical ability but as a tool to re-evaluate the assessment practices and increase access. The metrics of early adoption and discussion coverage show that there are many cases of cross-disciplinary adoption of free, well-organized micro-credentials and integrated with institutionalized mentorship has the potential to jump start structure basic AI literacy among teachers. These factors make IIT Madras a copycat alternative to the resource-constrained systems in the Global South ('AI for All' 2.0, 2025).

Case Study 5: University of Cape Town: Contextualized AI Literacy, Decolonial Pedagogy

The University of Cape Town (UCT) introduces an opposing model that focuses on contextualization, critical literacy, and institutional reflexivity. The faculty work and dialogues of UCT anticipate authorship, accountability, and decolonization infrastructures enhanced in the curricular implementation of AI-based teaching and research. Instead of technical upskilling, UCT combined workshops about generating tools and getting new workflows reproduced with seminars that questioned power, bias, and local data governance so that the faculty could modify AI tools to local curricular objectives and local sensitivities around communities. Cross-departmental research units, AI research groups, teaching and learning centers provided institutional support, co-compressing material, and small grants were served to faculty to implement pedagogical pilot projects and reflective forums where faculty could share outcomes and revelation quandaries. Related institutional reports show that this bottom-up, iterative process has increased uptake in the humanities and social sciences areas where direct technical adoption has lagged by showing examples of use in the discipline and being clear and open about how to evaluate the results critically. Notably, the UCT model applies the focus on policy alignment (data ethics guidance and research oversight) and technical training, which will minimize downstream risks (misapplied models, data harms), and increase faculty confidence. Such a strategy exemplifies the ways of how ethical, situational pedagogy may become the basis of so-called successful implementation in institutions of higher learning that do not follow Western traditions (Muraina, 2022).

Other views of non-western institutions

1) National University of Singapore (NUS): Multidisciplinary research and executive and faculty upskilling programmes are merged in institutional centres including the NUS AI Institute which emphasizes the importance of bringing foundational AI research, pedagogy and industry collaboration to ensure faculty practice remains up to date and applied.
2) IITs / other Indian institutes (examples include: IIT Guwahati, IIT Kanpur, IIT Bhubaneswar): Frequent short-faultiness programmes (FDPs), or modular certificate proceeds reiterate pragmatic laboratories, laboratories-subsidized scale as well as prompt and fragmented moves across related colleges, with ill intent of featuring national-much-needed programs plan efforts as well-coordinated with neighborhood adviser work practical adoption and retaining control over ethics and pedagogy.

7. COMPARATIVE ANALYSIS BETWEEN AI TECHNOLOGIES IN THE DEVELOPMENT OF FACULTY

7.1 AI-powered papers writer applications

- Examples include ChatGPT, Grammarly and QuillBot.
- They offer support of writing, revising, and organizing of academic text.

- Ethical Considerations:
  -One problem is that this can result in excessive dependency on these tools and the disability to think critically.
  - Plagiarism can happen in case AI generated content is not referenced properly.
  - Educations continue to face problems with maintaining academic integrity.
- Effectiveness:
  - The tools increase the efficiency and clarity of writing.
  - They ease the learning of conventions of academic writing.

7.2 Intelligent Tutoring System (ITS)

- Such examples are Carnegie Learning and Squirrel AI.
- They provide individualized teaching and evaluation based on the speed of learning and understanding to a learner.
- Ethical Considerations:
  -Fair and reasonable daily supply of AI is necessary.
  -Before risking creating disparities among various groups of learners, algorithmic biases can irrespective of both groups.
- Effectiveness:
  - ITS intensify the student interests with personalized learning paths.
  - Instantaneous feedback consolidates instructional results.

7.3 AI-Driven Assessment Tools

- Such examples include Gradescope and Turnitin.
- They computerize grading processes and find cases of plagiarism.
- Ethical Considerations:
  - Openness in terms of grading standards is needed.
  - Equitable and precise evaluation should be strictly ensured.
- Effectiveness:
  - The instruments ease the grading workload on the instructors.
  - Summative assessment protects academic standards.

7.4 Artificial Intelligence-based Professional development software

- Examples include Illywees, Campus Coursera and LinkedIn Learning.
- They provide courses and materials, designed to increase faculty capabilities.

- Ethical Considerations:
  - There must be strong protective measures on privacy issues concerning user information.
  - Contextual relevance and content quality needs to be examined continuously.
- Effectiveness:
  - These mediums offer affordable opportunities of education.
  - They promote long-term career development.

7.5 Artificial intelligence: Ethics in nuclear faculty development

The implementation of AI in faculty development requires that they follow the ethics of responsible implementation.

Some of the major ethical principles are:

- **Transparency:** Openness as to the role of AI and constraints.
- **Accountability:** Creating responsibility of the results produced by AI.
- **Equity:** Providing just access and treatment of all members of the faculty.
- **Privacy:** The protection of the personal and institutional information.
- **Bias Reduction:** A carefully designed schedule of audits of AI systems to detect and remove bias.

These principles can reduce the risks and increase the positive effects of AI tools in the development of the faculty.

7.6 Suggestions on the way forward on the necessary integration of AI Tools in faculty development

- **Intensive Education:** Provide faculty training about effective, ethical use of AI.
- **Inclusion:** Ensure fair access to AI resources by faculty members.
- **Persistent Evaluation:** Analyze efficacy and ethical consequences of AI tools on regular basis.
- **Feedback Mechanisms:** Have in place organized avenues on which faculty offer feedback on AI application and experiences.
- **Ethical Audits:** Conduct regular audits in order to detect and remove any ethical issues in regards to the use of AI.

8. FUTURE DIRECTIONS

AI continues to expand its use for faculty advancement. AI technology introduces several new trends which enable teacher development. The educational tools of chatbots together with smart tutors provide teachers with assistance (Choudhary et al., 2024). AI systems provide training recommendations by evaluating what teachers need. AI analytics provide teachers access to their individual development progress data (Fuente & Fuente, 2022). The educational tools provided by technology create individualized and superior learning experiences for students.

AI utilization requires ethical as well as fair practices. AI exists to support teachers by preventing any form of harm as well as job retention. AI systems need to show teachers their operation dynamics. The protection of teacher information depends on proper regulations adopted by educational institutions. The focus of training will advise educators about proficient AI implementation (Bowen & Watson, 2024).

AI presents a significant role for the development of faculty skills. The artificial intelligence solution enables customized teacher training according to individual needs. AI enables faculty members to collaborate by exchanging educational concepts. The real-time capabilities of AI enable it to help teachers with their activities. Utilization of AI by educators leads to better teaching methods and enhancement in learning outcomes. The technique always requires safe and fair application (Morales-Forero et al., 2023).

9. CONCLUSION

AI brings extensive adaptations to the existing methods for faculty development. Through AI teachers obtain contemporary teaching practices alongside improving their instructional delivery methods. Businesses at present use AI technologies to create training platforms for their faculty staff members. AI technology develops customized education plans for students alongside providing support through feedback that helps them advance. The introduction of AI systems in faculty development faces various challenges that prevent users from adopting them.

The main concern pertains to both privacy matters and the protection of data. The protection of information stored during AI data collection activities needs to be established as a reliable system. Systematic bias creates problems for the implementation of AI algorithms throughout their operational framework. AI design standards decide which way the operation results in unfair conclusions. To achieve success in deployment it is essential to determine the perfect balance between robotic operations and human involvement. Organization leaders must provide staff members with assistance rather than replacing them with technological systems.

There are also practical challenges. Multiple establishments work without possessing appropriate technological hardware. Academic personnel show resistance against AI technology without understanding the principles of this technology. Several institutions face financial obstacles when purchasing AI tools because of their associated costs. For AI to function effectively institutions need financial resources as well as proper support systems for its correct application. Academic professionals need AI knowledge to solve the existing problems they encounter in their work. AI training needs to teach proper ethical models which will make its operations fair. Schools along with universities are required to establish partnerships with businesses and national authorities to obtain needed financial support. The implementation of AI yields positive outcomes when correctly deployed according to examples of successful projects.

Research indicates artificial intelligence has excellent promise to evolve faculty development approaches. AI technology implements responsible educational applications which maintain effective operational standards. AI-based systems properly implemented enhance faculty learning and combine this improvement with educational method transformations.

REFERENCES

Agre, P. E. (2014). Toward a critical technical practice: Lessons learned in trying to reform AI. In *Social science, technical systems, and cooperative work* (pp. 131-157). Psychology Press. 'AI for All' 2.0 (2025): https://www.iitm.ac.in/happenings/press-releases-and-coverages/ai-all-20-iit-madras-expands-swayam-plus-free-ai-courses [Accessed on 26th September, 2025]

Al-Youbi. A., Zahed, A. H., & Tierney, W. G. (2020). *Successful global collaborations in higher education institutions* (p. 93). Springer Nature.

Alakoum, A., Nica, E., & Abiad, M. (2024). Revolutionizing Faculty Performance Evaluation: The Future Role of Al in Higher Education. *Journal of Self-Governance & Management Economics, 12*(1).

Alwaqdani, M. (2024). Investigating teachers' perceptions of artificial intelligence tools in education: Potential and difficulties. *Education and Information Technologies*, •••, 1–19.

Ananyi, S. O., & Somieari-Pepple, E. (2023). Cost-benefit analysis of artificial intelligence integration in education management: Leadership perspectives. *International Journal of Economics Environmental Development and Society, 4*(3), 353–370.

Anderson, T. (2008). *The theory and practice of online learning*. Athabasca University. DOI: 10.15215/aupress/9781897425084.01

Baker, B., Mills, K. A., McDonald, P., & Wang, L. (2023). AI, concepts of intelligence, and chatbots: The "Figure of Man," the rise of emotion, and future visions of education. *Teachers College Record, 125*(6), 60–84. DOI: 10.1177/01614681231191291

Baker, R. S., & Hawn, A. (2022). Algorithmic bias in education. *International Journal of Artificial Intelligence in Education*, •••, 1–41.

Barocas, S., Hardt, M., & Narayanan, A. (2023). *Fairness and machine learning: Limitations and opportunities*. MIT press.

Bernacki, M. L., Greene, M. J., & Lobczowski, N. G. (2021). A systematic review of research on personalized learning: Personalized by whom, to what, how, and for what purpose (s)? *Educational Psychology Review, 33*(4), 1675–1715. DOI: 10.1007/s10648-021-09615-8

Black, E. S. (2024). *Working Smarter: A Quantitative Investigation Into Higher Education Faculty's Perceptions, Adoption, and Use of Generative Artificial Intelligence (AI) in Alignment With the Learning Sciences and Universal Design for Learning* (Doctoral dissertation, Drexel University).

Bowen, J. A., & Watson, C. E. (2024). *Teaching with AI: A practical guide to a new era of human learning*. JHU Press. DOI: 10.56021/9781421449227

Brynjolfsson, E., & McAfee, A. (2018). *Machine, Platform, Crowd: Wie wir das Beste aus unserer digitalen Zukunft machen*. Plassen Verlag.

Capuano, N., & Caballé, S. (2020). Adaptive learning technologies. *AI Magazine*, *41*(2), 96–98. DOI: 10.1609/aimag.v41i2.5317

Carey, R. L., Farinde-Wu, A., Milner, H. R., IV, & Delale-O'Connor, L. (2018). The culture and teaching gap: What is it, and how can teacher educators help to close it? *The Wiley handbook of teaching and learning*, 59-78.

Chatterjee, A., Pahari, N., Prinz, A., & Riegler, M. (2023). AI and semantic ontology for personalized activity eCoaching in healthy lifestyle recommendations: A meta-heuristic approach. *BMC Medical Informatics and Decision Making*, *23*(1), 278. DOI: 10.1186/s12911-023-02364-4 PMID: 38041041

Chou, C. M., Shen, T. C., Shen, T. C., & Shen, C. H. (2024). Teachers' adoption of AI-supported teaching behavior and its influencing factors: Using structural equation modeling. *Journal of Computers in Education*, •••, 1–44.

Choudhary, K., Ganguly, S., & Joseph, A. (2024). Revolutionizing Higher Education with AI: Opportunities, Challenges, and Future Trends. *Library of Progress-Library Science, Information Technology & Computer, 44*(3).

Cukurova, M., & Miao, F. (2024). *AI competency framework for teachers*. UNESCO Publishing.

Danks, D., & London, A. J. (2017, August). Algorithmic Bias in Autonomous Systems. In *Ijcai* (Vol. 17, No. 2017, pp. 4691-4697). DOI: 10.24963/ijcai.2017/654

Darling-Hammond, L. (2017). *Effective teacher professional development*. Learning Policy Institute. DOI: 10.54300/122.311

De Cremer, D., & Kasparov, G. (2021). AI should augment human intelligence, not replace it. *Harvard Business Review*, *18*(1), 1–8.

Dogan, M. E., Goru Dogan, T., & Bozkurt, A. (2023). The use of artificial intelligence (AI) in online learning and distance education processes: A systematic review of empirical studies. *Applied Sciences (Basel, Switzerland), 13*(5), 3056. DOI: 10.3390/app13053056

Doshi-Velez, F., & Kim, B. (2017). Towards a rigorous science of interpretable machine learning. *arXiv preprint arXiv:1702.08608.*

Eden, C. A., Chisom, O. N., & Adeniyi, I. S. (2024). Integrating AI in education: Opportunities, challenges, and ethical considerations. *Magna Scientia Advanced Research and Reviews, 10*(2), 006-013.

Esangbedo, C. O., Zhang, J., Esangbedo, M. O., Kone, S. D., & Xu, L. (2023). The role of industry-academia collaboration in enhancing educational opportunities and outcomes under the digital driven Industry 4.0. *Journal of Infrastructure. Policy and Development, 8*(1), 2569. DOI: 10.24294/jipd.v8i1.2569

Floridi, L., & Cowls, J. (2022). A unified framework of five principles for AI in society. *Machine learning and the city: Applications in architecture and urban design*, 535-545.

Fuente, R. O. D., & Fuente, R. O. D.Rodelio O Dela FuenteRomel O Dela Fuente. (2022). Faculty performance evaluation system with application of data analytics. *South Asian Journal of Engineering and Technology, 12*(1), 24–31. DOI: 10.26524/sajet.2022.12.05

Gabriel, F., Marrone, R., Van Sebille, Y., Kovanovic, V., & de Laat, M. (2022). Digital education strategies around the world: Practices and policies. *Irish Educational Studies, 41*(1), 85–106. DOI: 10.1080/03323315.2021.2022513

Gonçalves, B. F. (2024). Integration of artificial intelligence in teacher training: training to innovate in the digital age. In *Proceedings of the International Conferences on e-Learning and Digital Learning 2024, ELDL 2024; Sustainability, Technology and Education 2024, STE 2024*. IADIS.

Guilherme, A. (2019). AI and education: The importance of teacher and student relations. *AI & Society, 34*(1), 47–54. DOI: 10.1007/s00146-017-0693-8

Gunning, D., Stefik, M., Choi, J., Miller, T., Stumpf, S., & Yang, G. Z. (2019). XAI—Explainable artificial intelligence. *Science Robotics, 4*(37), eaay7120. DOI: 10.1126/scirobotics.aay7120 PMID: 33137719

Gupta, A., Dwivedi, D. N., & Shah, J. (2023). Ethical challenges for AI-based applications. In *Artificial Intelligence Applications in Banking and Financial Services: Anti Money Laundering and Compliance* (pp. 115–120). Springer Nature Singapore. DOI: 10.1007/978-981-99-2571-1_10

Hannan, E., & Liu, S. (2023). AI: New source of competitiveness in higher education. *Competitiveness Review*, *33*(2), 265–279. DOI: 10.1108/CR-03-2021-0045

Hashmi, N., & Bal, A. S. (2024). Generative AI in higher education and beyond. *Business Horizons*, *67*(5), 607–614. DOI: 10.1016/j.bushor.2024.05.005

Hillier, M. (2020). Bridging the digital divide with off-line e-learning. In *Expanding Horizons in Open and Distance Learning* (pp. 110–121). Routledge. DOI: 10.4324/9780429292941-8

Holman, K., Marino, M. T., Vasquez, T., Taub, M., Hunt, J. H., & Tazi, Y. (2024). Navigating AI-Powered Personalized Learning in Special Education: A Guide for Preservice Teacher Faculty. *Journal of Special Education Preparation*, *4*(2), 90–95. DOI: 10.33043/5b2xqcb3

Holmes, W. (2020). Artificial intelligence in education. In *Encyclopedia of education and information technologies* (pp. 88–103). Springer International Publishing. DOI: 10.1007/978-3-030-10576-1_107

Holmes, W. (2023). *The unintended consequences of artificial intelligence and education*. Education International Research.

Holmes, W., & Porayska-Pomsta, K. (2023). The ethics of artificial intelligence in education. *Lontoo: Routledge*, 621-653.

Holmes, W., & Tuomi, I. (2022). State of the art and practice in AI in education. *European Journal of Education*, *57*(4), 542–570. DOI: 10.1111/ejed.12533

Iftikhar, A., Musa, S., Alam, M., & Su'ud, M. M. (2020). Artificial intelligence based risk management in global software development: A proposed architecture to reduce risk by using time, budget and resources constraints. *Journal of Computational and Theoretical Nanoscience*, *17*(2-3), 878–885. DOI: 10.1166/jctn.2020.8735

Jarke, J., & Breiter, A. (2019). The datafication of education. *Learning, Media and Technology*, *44*(1), 1–6. DOI: 10.1080/17439884.2019.1573833

Jobin, A., Ienca, M., & Vayena, E. (2019). The global landscape of AI ethics guidelines. *Nature Machine Intelligence*, *1*(9), 389–399. DOI: 10.1038/s42256-019-0088-2

Khine, M. S. (2024). Using AI for Adaptive Learning and Adaptive Assessment. In *Artificial Intelligence in Education: A Machine-Generated Literature Overview* (pp. 341–466). Springer Nature Singapore. DOI: 10.1007/978-981-97-9350-1_3

Kim, I., Kang, K., Song, Y., & Kim, T. J. (2022). Application of artificial intelligence in pathology: Trends and challenges. *Diagnostics (Basel), 12*(11), 2794. DOI: 10.3390/diagnostics12112794 PMID: 36428854

Knyazeva, N., Mikhailova, I., Usmanova, N., & Shindina, T. (2022). Overcoming Barriers in Developing Digital Skills for Higher Education Teachers: Challenges and Solutions. *Review of Artificial Intelligence in Education, 3*(00), e024–e024. DOI: 10.37497/rev.artif.intell.educ.v3i00.24

Krijger, J., Thuis, T., de Ruiter, M., Ligthart, E., & Broekman, I. (2023). The AI ethics maturity model: A holistic approach to advancing ethical data science in organizations. *AI and Ethics, 3*(2), 355–367. DOI: 10.1007/s43681-022-00228-7

Lazăr, A. M., Repanovici, A., Popa, D., Ionas, D. G., & Dobrescu, A. I. (2024). Ethical Principles in AI Use for Assessment: Exploring Students' Perspectives on Ethical Principles in Academic Publishing. *Education Sciences, 14*(11), 1239. DOI: 10.3390/educsci14111239

Lee, A. V. Y., Koh, E., & Looi, C. K. (2023). AI in education and learning analytics in Singapore: An overview of key projects and initiatives. *Information and Technology in Education and Learning, 3*(1), Inv-p001.

Luckin, R. (2018). *Machine Learning and Human Intelligence. The future of education for the 21st century*. UCL institute of education press.

Luckin, R., Cukurova, M., Kent, C., & Du Boulay, B. (2022). Empowering educators to be AI-ready. *Computers and Education: Artificial Intelligence, 3*, 100076.

Mäntymäki, M., Minkkinen, M., Birkstedt, T., & Viljanen, M. (2022). Putting AI ethics into practice: The hourglass model of organizational AI governance. *arXiv preprint arXiv:2206.00335.*

Mao-Clark, X., Koh, Y., DeFranco, A., & Back, K. J. (2024). The Impact of Economic Policies on Creating Restaurant Startups. *Journal of Hospitality & Tourism Research (Washington, D.C.)*, •••, 10963480241292025.

Marks, B., & Thomas, J. (2022). Adoption of virtual reality technology in higher education: An evaluation of five teaching semesters in a purpose-designed laboratory. *Education and Information Technologies, 27*(1), 1287–1305. DOI: 10.1007/s10639-021-10653-6 PMID: 34257511

Mehrabi, N., Morstatter, F., Saxena, N., Lerman, K., & Galstyan, A. (2021). A survey on bias and fairness in machine learning. *ACM Computing Surveys*, *54*(6), 1–35. DOI: 10.1145/3457607

Memarian, B., & Doleck, T. (2023). Fairness, Accountability, Transparency, and Ethics (FATE) in Artificial Intelligence (AI), and higher education: A systematic review. *Computers and Education: Artificial Intelligence*, 100152.

Miao, F., Holmes, W., Huang, R., & Zhang, H. (2021). *AI and education: A guidance for policymakers*. Unesco Publishing.

Mikeladze, T., Meijer, P. C., & Verhoeff, R. P. (2024). A comprehensive exploration of artificial intelligence competence frameworks for educators: A critical review. *European Journal of Education*, *59*(3), e12663. DOI: 10.1111/ejed.12663

Mishra, P., & Koehler, M. J. (2006). Technological pedagogical content knowledge: A framework for teacher knowledge. *Teachers College Record*, *108*(6), 1017–1054. DOI: 10.1111/j.1467-9620.2006.00684.x

Mishra, P., & Smith, J. (2020). Known for whom we include: Designing models for lifelong education at Arizona State University. In *The 60-Year Curriculum* (pp. 87–103). Routledge. DOI: 10.4324/9781003013617-6

Mitchell, M., Wu, S., Zaldivar, A., Barnes, P., Vasserman, L., Hutchinson, B., Inioluwa, E. S., Raji, D., & Gebru, T. (2019, January). Model cards for model reporting. In *Proceedings of the conference on fairness, accountability, and transparency* (pp. 220-229). DOI: 10.1145/3287560.3287596

Morales-Forero, A., Bassetto, S., & Coatanea, E. (2023). Toward safe AI. *AI & Society*, *38*(2), 685–696. DOI: 10.1007/s00146-022-01591-z

Morley, J., Elhalal, A., Garcia, F., Kinsey, L., Mökander, J., & Floridi, L. (2021). Ethics as a service: A pragmatic operationalisation of AI ethics. *Minds and Machines*, *31*(2), 239–256. DOI: 10.1007/s11023-021-09563-w PMID: 34720418

Mousavinasab, E., Zarifsanaiey, N., & Niakan Kalhori, R., S., Rakhshan, M., Keikha, L., & Ghazi Saeedi, M. (. (2021). Intelligent tutoring systems: A systematic review of characteristics, applications, and evaluation methods. *Interactive Learning Environments*, *29*(1), 142–163. DOI: 10.1080/10494820.2018.1558257

Muraina, L. O. (2022). *Curriculum decolonization in the University of Cape Town: Research, policy and practice* (Master's minor dissertation, University of Cape Town). University of Cape Town.

Nalyvaiko, O., & Maliutina, A. (2021). Use of chat bots in the educational process of a higher education institution. Scientific notes of the pedagogical department, (48), 117-122.

Nikolinakos, N. T. (2023). *EU Policy and Legal Framework for Artificial Intelligence, Robotics and Related Technologies-The AI Act*. Springer International Publishing AG. DOI: 10.1007/978-3-031-27953-9

O'neil, C. (2017). *Weapons of math destruction: How big data increases inequality and threatens democracy*. Crown.

Orhani, S. (2023). Robots Assist or Replace Teachers in the Classroom. *Journal of Elementary and Secondary School*, *1*(1), 29–41. DOI: 10.31098/jess.v1i1.1418

Palvia, S., Aeron, P., Gupta, P., Mahapatra, D., Parida, R., Rosner, R., & Sindhi, S. (2018). Online education: Worldwide status, challenges, trends, and implications. *Journal of Global Information Technology Management*, *21*(4), 233–241. DOI: 10.1080/1097198X.2018.1542262

Pechenkina, K. (2023). *Artificial intelligence for good? Challenges and possibilities of AI in higher education from a data justice perspective. Higher Education for good: Teaching and learning futures (# HE4Good)*. Open Book Publishers.

Pedro, F., Subosa, M., Rivas, A., & Valverde, P. (2019). Artificial intelligence in education: Challenges and opportunities for sustainable development.

Popenici, S. A., & Kerr, S. (2017). Exploring the impact of artificial intelligence on teaching and learning in higher education. *Research and Practice in Technology Enhanced Learning*, *12*(1), 22. DOI: 10.1186/s41039-017-0062-8 PMID: 30595727

Prasad, K. R., Karanam, S. R., Ganesh, D., Liyakat, K. K. S., Talasila, V., & Purushotham, P. (2024). AI in public-private partnership for IT infrastructure development. *The Journal of High Technology Management Research*, *35*(1), 100496. DOI: 10.1016/j.hitech.2024.100496

Qi, P., Huang, J., Wu, Y., He, X., & Zhou, B. (2021). Conversational AI Systems for Social Good: Opportunities and Challenges. *arXiv preprint arXiv:2105.06457.*

Raji, I. D., Smart, A., White, R. N., Mitchell, M., Gebru, T., Hutchinson, B., Smith-Loud, J., Theron, D., & Barnes, P. (2020, January). Closing the AI accountability gap: Defining an end-to-end framework for internal algorithmic auditing. In *Proceedings of the 2020 conference on fairness, accountability, and transparency* (pp. 33-44). DOI: 10.1145/3351095.3372873

Reidenberg, J. R., & Schaub, F. (2018). Achieving big data privacy in education. *Theory and Research in Education, 16*(3), 263–279. DOI: 10.1177/1477878518805308

Rios-Campos, C., Vega, S. M. Z., Tejada-Castro, M. I., Viteri, J. D. C. L., Zambrano, E. O. G., Gamarra, J. M. B., & Vara, F. E. O. (2023). Ethics of artificial intelligence. *South Florida Journal of Development, 4*(4), 1715–1729. DOI: 10.46932/sfjdv4n4-022

Saaida, M. B. (2023). AI-Driven transformations in higher education: Opportunities and challenges. *International Journal of Educational Research and Studies, 5*(1), 29–36.

Sadera, E., Suonio, E. E., Chen, J. C. C., Herbert, R., Hsu, D., Bogdan, B., & Kool, B. (2024). Strategies and approaches for delivering sustainable training and professional development of graduate teaching assistants, teaching assistants, and tutors: A scoping review. *Journal of Applied Research in Higher Education, 16*(5), 2199–2215. DOI: 10.1108/JARHE-08-2023-0323

Santos, O., & Radanliev, P. (2024). *Beyond the algorithm: AI, security, privacy, and ethics*. Addison-Wesley Professional.

Schön, E. M., Neumann, M., Hofmann-Stölting, C., Baeza-Yates, R., & Rauschenberger, M. (2023). How are AI assistants changing higher education? *Frontiers of Computer Science, 5*, 1208550. DOI: 10.3389/fcomp.2023.1208550

Selwyn, N. (2019). *Should robots replace teachers?: AI and the future of education*. John Wiley & Sons.

Southworth, J., Migliaccio, K., Glover, J., Reed, D., McCarty, C., Brendemuhl, J., & Thomas, A. (2023). Developing a model for AI Across the curriculum: Transforming the higher education landscape via innovation in AI literacy. *Computers and Education: Artificial Intelligence, 4*, 100127. DOI: 10.1016/j.caeai.2023.100127

Starkey, L. (2020). A review of research exploring teacher preparation for the digital age. *Cambridge Journal of Education, 50*(1), 37–56. DOI: 10.1080/0305764X.2019.1625867

Tsamados, A., Aggarwal, N., Cowls, J., Morley, J., Roberts, H., Taddeo, M., & Floridi, L. (2021). The ethics of algorithms: key problems and solutions. *Ethics, governance, and policies in artificial intelligence*, 97-123.

Umer, R., Susnjak, T., Mathrani, A., & Suriadi, L. (2023). Current stance on predictive analytics in higher education: Opportunities, challenges and future directions. *Interactive Learning Environments, 31*(6), 3503–3528. DOI: 10.1080/10494820.2021.1933542

Van Laar, E., Van Deursen, A. J., Van Dijk, J. A., & De Haan, J. (2017). The relation between 21st-century skills and digital skills: A systematic literature review. *Computers in Human Behavior, 72*, 577–588. DOI: 10.1016/j.chb.2017.03.010

Wall, P. J., Saxena, D., & Brown, S. (2021). Artificial intelligence in the Global South (AI4D): Potential and risks. *arXiv preprint arXiv:2108.10093.*

Wang, X., Li, L., Tan, S. C., Yang, L., & Lei, J. (2023). Preparing for AI-enhanced education: Conceptualizing and empirically examining teachers' AI readiness. *Computers in Human Behavior, 146*, 107798. DOI: 10.1016/j.chb.2023.107798

Wang, Y., Liu, C., & Tu, Y. F. (2021). Factors affecting the adoption of AI-based applications in higher education. *Journal of Educational Technology & Society, 24*(3), 116–129.

Watini, S., Davies, G., & Andersen, N. (2024). Cybersecurity in Learning Systems: Data protection and privacy in educational information systems and digital learning environments. [ITEE]. *International Transactions on Education Technology, 3*(1), 26–35. DOI: 10.33050/itee.v3i1.665

Xu, Z. (2024). AI in education: Enhancing learning experiences and student outcomes. *Applied and Computational Engineering, 51*(1), 104–111. DOI: 10.54254/2755-2721/51/20241187

Yang, E., & Beil, C. (2024). Ensuring data privacy in AI/ML implementation. *New Directions for Higher Education, 2024*(207), 63–78. DOI: 10.1002/he.20509

Zawacki-Richter, O., Marín, V. I., Bond, M., & Gouverneur, F. (2019). Systematic review of research on artificial intelligence applications in higher education–where are the educators? *International Journal of Educational Technology in Higher Education, 16*(1), 1–27. DOI: 10.1186/s41239-019-0171-0

Ziyautdinov, J. (2024). TEACHER TRAINING FOR AI INTEGRATION: INTERNATIONAL BEST PRACTICES AND STRATEGIES. *Journal of Modern Educational Achievements, 5*(5), 186–191.

Zou, J., & Schiebinger, L. (2018). AI can be sexist and racist—It's time to make it fair. *Nature, 559*(7714), 324–326. DOI: 10.1038/d41586-018-05707-8 PMID: 30018439

Zuboff, S. (2023). The age of surveillance capitalism. In *Social theory re-wired* (pp. 203–213). Routledge. DOI: 10.4324/9781003320609-27

Chapter 3

AI Fundamentals for Educators: A Comprehensive Introduction

Mustafa Kayyali
http://orcid.org/0000-0003-3300-262X
Maaref University of Applied Sciences, Syria

ABSTRACT

This chapter gives a detailed introduction to the principles of Artificial Intelligence (AI) particularly targeted at educators. With AI's rising presence in the educational sector, faculty members need to comprehend the underlying concepts of AI, its possible applications, and its ethical implications. The chapter begins with defining AI and addressing essential ideas and terminology that are crucial for educators. It then covers several AI tools and technologies that might boost teaching and learning, such as adaptive learning systems, AI-powered assessment tools, and intelligent tutoring systems. The chapter also discusses the ethical concerns surrounding AI, highlighting the significance of appropriate application in the classroom. Finally, the chapter examines the prospects and challenges of adopting AI in educational contexts and underlines its potential for faculty development, supporting continuous learning, and determining the future of education.

INTRODUCTION

The landscape of education is experiencing a tremendous shift, driven primarily by the rapid expansion of technology. As educators, administrators, and politicians, we find ourselves at the crossroads of a new age in learning, when established techniques and practices are being challenged by the integration of artificial intelli-

DOI: 10.4018/979-8-3373-1285-9.ch003

gence (AI). This chapter discusses the underlying concepts of AI and its developing role in influencing the future of faculty development and lifelong learning, with specific emphasis on how it might boost instructional effectiveness, professional growth, and institutional success. The notion of AI—machines or systems capable of doing activities that traditionally require human intelligence—has been a source of intrigue and invention for decades (Lucci et al, 2022). Over time, AI has grown from a theoretical notion into a concrete and useful technology that pervades all areas of society. In the sphere of education, AI's potential to change teaching and learning processes has become increasingly clear. From tailored learning routes for students to AI-driven administrative operations, the prospects for AI to transform how humans connect with knowledge are huge and still mostly unexplored. Yet, the promise of AI in education extends well beyond student-centered applications; it offers equally revolutionary potential for the growth of teaching members.

Traditionally, faculty development has been anchored in the notion of ongoing professional learning, a fundamental component in the lifelong journey of educators who try to strengthen their teaching abilities, remain informed of new pedagogical trends, and expand their subject matter knowledge (Hill et al, 2021). These development programs have historically concentrated on face-to-face contact, with workshops, seminars, and conferences being the key vehicles for knowledge sharing. While these approaches have served their function, they are increasingly out of sync with the demands of modern educators. As the speed of technological change accelerates, faculty members must be equipped with new tools and chances for growth that reflect the changing demands of education in the digital age. Enter AI—a crucial technology that promises to transform the whole essence of faculty development. AI's unique capacity to analyze enormous quantities of data, discover trends, and tailor learning experiences presents a tremendous opportunity to revolutionize how faculty members develop and enhance their teaching abilities. By employing AI, faculty development programs can be personalized to the particular requirements of educators, ensuring that each educator receives the support and tools they require to succeed. AI-driven systems may provide tailored learning paths that reflect the specific skills, limitations, and ambitions of each faculty member, enabling them to interact with the most relevant materials at their speed and in a way that works best for them (ZONAID, 2024). AI can give real-time feedback and data, which is something that traditional faculty development methods have struggled to accomplish. With AI-powered technologies, educators may obtain immediate insights about their teaching performance, allowing them to make timely adjustments to increase student engagement, learning outcomes, and overall classroom effectiveness. This rapid access to data-driven insights makes the process of professional growth more dynamic, guaranteeing that faculty members are continually developing and adapting to the changing educational context.

However, the promise of AI does not end at faculty development; it also holds the key to boosting lifelong learning among educators. In a world where information and teaching tactics vary frequently, faculty members must consistently upgrade their skills and expertise. This is where AI can have a tremendous influence. Through AI-driven platforms, instructors may engage in continuing learning opportunities, accessing a wide range of materials suited to their unique needs and interests. Whether they want to learn about the newest pedagogical approaches, new technology, or trends in their subject, AI platforms may provide a personalized and adaptable learning environment that supports the continued growth of educators throughout their careers (Kayyali, 2024 B). As we investigate the future of AI in faculty development and lifelong learning, we must also analyze the wider environment in which these developments are taking place. The emergence of AI in education is not only about the tools themselves; it is also about the attitude and culture that we must build to truly embrace new technologies (Alam & Mohanty, 2023). Educators and institutions must transcend beyond the conventional limitations of teaching and learning, adopting an attitude of openness and adaptability to harness the full potential of AI. Faculty members, in particular, must be prepared to interact with AI not only as a tool but also as a partner in their continuous professional growth.

At the same time, there are problems and ethical issues that must be addressed as AI becomes increasingly incorporated into faculty development. As with any disruptive technology, AI presents problems regarding equality, privacy, access, and bias (Yu, 2020). How can we guarantee that AI technologies are available to all educators, regardless of their institution's resources? How can we preserve faculty members' privacy while deploying AI-powered tools that gather and analyze data on their teaching practices? How can we prevent prejudice in AI systems that may perpetuate current inequalities? These are crucial topics that must be examined as we move forward with AI in education. The objective of this chapter is to offer a comprehensive review of the role of AI in faculty development and lifelong learning. We will discuss the major ideas and terminologies related to AI, showing how these technologies may be exploited to enhance teaching methods, create ongoing professional growth, and support lifelong learning among educators. Additionally, we will examine the potential problems that come with the incorporation of AI into faculty development, presenting practical insights and suggestions for institutions, educators, and policymakers. As we dive into the future of AI in education, we must remember that the ultimate objective is not to replace human educators but to complement existing skills. AI can empower faculty members to be more effective professors, help them grow professionally, and enable them to remain lifelong learners in an ever-changing educational context. By adopting AI, we can unleash new possibilities for teaching and learning, opening the way for a future where education is more individualized, responsive, and impactful than ever before.

ARTIFICIAL INTELLIGENCE: A PRIMER FOR EDUCATORS

Artificial Intelligence (AI) is no longer a future perception. It is a dynamic and developing field that is increasingly transforming the world around us. From the way we interact and work to how we learn, AI has invaded practically every facet of daily life. For educators, this technology transformation brings both exciting potential and challenging obstacles. Understanding the principles of AI is vital for educators who wish to harness its potential in their classrooms and beyond.

In its simplest form, Artificial intellect refers to computers or systems that are meant to accomplish activities that traditionally require human intellect (Wang, 2019). These skills might range from detecting speech and analyzing visuals to making judgments and solving issues. At the heart of AI is the concept that robots may be designed to understand, learn, and adapt to new knowledge without human involvement. However, while the concept of robots "thinking" like humans may seem like science fiction, AI is founded on logical principles that are very much anchored in real-world technologies. AI is founded on numerous key principles, including machine learning, natural language processing, computer vision, and robotics (Soori et al, 2023). These domains, each with its own set of applications, present distinct possibilities for robots to duplicate or even surpass human talents in certain areas. Machine learning, for example, is a subset of AI that enables machines to learn from data (Sarker, 2021). This technique lets AI systems develop over time as they are exposed to additional knowledge, much like a student learning from experience. Natural language processing (NLP) allows machines to read, interpret, and synthesize human language, which is the backbone of many AI-powered technologies like chatbots and virtual assistants (Sridhar, 2024). Similarly, computer vision enables machines to detect and analyze pictures, making it feasible for AI systems to "see" and grasp the environment in a way that was previously reserved for humans. Robotics, another major field of AI, focuses on constructing devices that can execute physical tasks autonomously. For educators, understanding AI begins with identifying how technology might benefit teaching and learning. Over the past decade, we've watched the introduction of AI-driven solutions that have changed the educational environment (Shah, 2023). From personalized learning platforms that adapt to students' particular requirements to intelligent tutoring systems that give quick feedback, AI is being employed in creative ways to help both teaching and learning. These tools have the potential to make education more accessible, efficient, and entertaining. However, the integration of AI into education is not without its hurdles. It demands educators rethink old teaching techniques, adapt to new technology, and tackle ethical problems connected to data privacy and bias in algorithms.

One of the most important ways AI is transforming education is through the notion of individualized learning (Tapalova & Zhiyenbayeva, 2022). Traditionally, teaching approaches have followed a one-size-fits-all approach, where the speed and content of instruction are the same for every student in a class. This strategy can work effectively for some children but leaves others behind. AI offers the ability to develop individualized learning experiences that are tuned to the specific requirements, talents, and interests of each learner (Bhutoria, 2022). By assessing data on student performance and behavior, AI-powered systems may offer customized learning routes, tools, and activities that are best suited to each learner. This amount of flexibility may be a game-changer, particularly for children with unique learning requirements. For instance, students who are failing in specific areas might receive more practice or tailored instruction, while advanced learners can be challenged with more complicated content. Personalized learning helps create a more inclusive atmosphere where students may advance at their speed and attain their greatest potential. AI is also helping instructors improve their teaching techniques and promote student engagement (Almusaed, 2023). AI-driven solutions like chatbots, for example, allow students to ask questions and receive quick replies, offering 24/7 access to help (Martinez-Requejo et al, 2024). This not only relieves some of the load on instructors but also creates a sense of autonomy among students, as they may obtain aid outside of regular class hours. Additionally, AI may aid educators with grading and evaluation, saving critical time and allowing professors to focus more on interactive teaching and student interaction. AI may assess student responses to assignments and examinations, offer thorough comments, and even recommend areas for development. With AI, educators can make data-driven decisions about how to customize their teaching tactics, delivering tailored interventions when necessary and ensuring that every student is receiving the assistance they need.

Despite the tremendous potential of AI in education, there are various issues that educators must consider before using AI in their classrooms (Dimitriadou & Lanitis, 2023). One of the most serious problems is the ethical implications of AI. AI systems are only as good as the data they are trained on, and if the data is skewed, the system will reflect those biases. For example, AI systems used for student evaluation or admission choices may perpetuate existing disparities if they depend on biased data sets. In addition, there are worries regarding the privacy and security of student data. With the rising use of AI-powered systems that track student behavior and performance, educators must be diligent about securing students' personal information. Educators must guarantee that AI systems are transparent, responsible, and free from prejudice.

Another difficulty is the potential for AI to replace human instructors, a notion that has spurred significant debate in recent years (Aad & Hardey, 2025). While AI may automate certain duties, such as grading or providing feedback, it cannot replace the unique traits that human educators bring to the classroom, such as empathy, emotional intelligence, and the capacity to inspire and encourage students. AI should be considered as a tool that supports the work of instructors, not as a substitute. The role of educators will continue to be vital in leading students, promoting critical thinking, and establishing a supportive learning environment. AI can give great aid, but the human aspect of education remains irreplaceable. Educators must also examine the effects of AI on future employment (Fitria, 2023). As AI continues to evolve, there will be an increasing demand for professionals who are experienced in AI technologies and who understand how to utilize these tools effectively. For educators, this means educating students for a world where AI is a fundamental component of practically every business. In the classroom, this may entail teaching students about the foundations of AI, helping them develop critical thinking abilities, and encouraging them to engage with developing technology. Educators also need to be aware of the possible disruptions that AI may bring to various businesses and educate students about the changes that are likely to occur. By giving students a company foundation in AI and other new technologies, educators can ensure that they are equipped to flourish in a quickly changing employment market.

The future of AI in education is both exciting and uncertain (Pedro et al, 2019). While we have witnessed great improvements in AI technology, there is still much to learn about how best to integrate AI into education systems. However, one thing is clear: AI has the potential to disrupt education in ways that were formerly inconceivable. For educators, adopting AI entails being open to new possibilities, continually learning about developing technology, and finding ways to incorporate these tools into their teaching practice. It is not about replacing human educators but about increasing the learning experience for students, empowering instructors to focus on what they do best, and promoting an environment of continual development. As AI becomes increasingly incorporated into the educational ecosystem, educators must be knowledgeable about its possibilities and limits. By knowing the principles of AI, educators can make educated judgments about how to employ these technologies effectively, responsibly, and ethically (Nguyen et al, 2023). This will guarantee that AI becomes a powerful ally in the classroom, one that increases learning, encourages student achievement and prepares students for the future. AI provides immense promise for altering education, but it also demands educators to adapt, reflect, and continually interact with the technology. As we go ahead into the AI age, educators must take an active part in influencing how AI is utilized in their classrooms, ensuring that technology serves the best interests of students, creates a culture of equity, and contributes to the improvement of educational methods. Embracing AI in education is not only about staying ahead of the curve; it's about building a more dynamic, customized, and inclusive learning environment that can satisfy the different demands of today's learners. With the correct tools, techniques, and ethical concerns, AI may become a tremendous driver for good change in education.

THE ROLE OF AI IN MODERN EDUCATION

Artificial Intelligence (AI) has become a vital component of modern civilization, and its influence continues to spread in numerous fields (Sheikh, 2020). One of the areas where AI is having the most profound influence is education. The traditional classroom paradigm, with its emphasis on one-size-fits-all education, is gradually being altered by AI's capacity to personalize learning experiences to individual requirements. AI in education is not simply a passing trend; it is rapidly transforming the landscape of teaching and learning in ways that were formerly inconceivable. Educators, students, administrators, and politicians are all studying the numerous ways AI may improve education, making it more customized, accessible, and efficient. In many aspects, AI is becoming an educational companion, aiding both instructors and students in several capacities (Pokrivčáková, 2019). For instructors, AI offers technologies that help automate monotonous chores, such as grading and administrative work, freeing up time to focus on more meaningful interactions with students. For students, AI may function as a customized instructor, delivering rapid feedback and modifying learning materials to meet their requirements. It can assist in identifying areas of weakness and give focused solutions, enabling students to advance at their speed and eventually succeed. This capacity to respond to the particular requirements of each student is one of the primary ways AI is altering education.

Historically, the difficulty of addressing the different needs of children has been one of the most important challenges for educators. Each student learns in their way, at their speed, and with their own set of strengths and problems. Traditional teaching approaches, which typically rely on a predetermined curriculum provided consistently, cannot always account for these disparities (Oude Vrielink et al, 2019). Some students may struggle with the topic while others may find it too simple, leading to frustration and disengagement. AI, however, provides a solution. With its capacity to evaluate data and react in real-time, AI can create tailored learning experiences that meet students where they are. AI-powered systems, for example, may follow a student's progress, discover trends in their learning behavior, and change the material and difficulty level accordingly. If a learner is struggling with a specific idea, the system might suggest extra resources or tasks to reinforce that lesson. If a student is thriving, the system might give more demanding assignments to keep them interested and motivated. This dynamic, flexible approach to learning is what makes AI such a strong tool in education. By giving a personalized experience, AI ensures that each student has the support they need, which can eventually lead to higher education results. AI can help ease one of the major difficulties confronting education today: the scarcity of instructors. With classroom sizes continuing to expand and the demand for competent instructors sometimes surpassing supply, AI can play a vital role in filling the gaps. AI-driven systems may assist in grading, tracking progress, and delivering real-time feedback, all of which can significantly minimize the strain for instructors (Qazi et al, 2024). This offers instructors more time to focus on delivering high-quality education and interacting with students. Furthermore, AI-powered tutoring systems may give support to students outside of typical classroom hours, ensuring that aid is available whenever it is required. This is particularly beneficial in contexts where access to professors is limited, such as in distant or under-resourced locations.

Another major element of AI in education is its ability to democratize learning (Costa et al, 2022). Traditionally, access to great education has been constrained by geographic, economic, and social constraints. AI can tear down many of these obstacles. With online learning systems enabled by AI, students from all over the world may access high-quality instructional information at their leisure. These platforms may offer a wide range of learning tools, including video lectures, interactive quizzes, and individualized evaluations, all suited to the particular needs of each learner. As a result, students who may have previously had restricted access to educational opportunities may now take benefit of the same resources as their counterparts in more fortunate regions. AI also has the potential to increase accessibility for students with impairments (Abbasi et al, 2024). AI-powered solutions, such as speech recognition software, can aid students with visual or hearing impairments, enabling them to engage more completely with instructional content. For example, AI may transcribe lectures in real-time, making them accessible to students with hearing difficulties. Similarly, AI can read literature aloud for students with visual impairments, allowing them to access written resources that may otherwise be unavailable. This sort of support may considerably enhance the educational experience for students with impairments, providing they have the same opportunity to achieve as their classmates.

In addition to its capacity to customize learning and increase accessibility, AI is also playing an increasingly crucial role in evaluation. Traditional means of evaluation, such as tests and quizzes, typically fail to capture the entire spectrum of a student's talents (Rimm et al, 2021). They usually test knowledge at a specific moment in time and do not give a full picture of a student's development or learning style. AI-powered evaluations, on the other hand, may continually track a student's performance and present a more accurate and dynamic snapshot of their learning. These evaluations can be adaptive, altering the complexity of questions based on the student's replies, ensuring that students are continually pushed but not overwhelmed. Furthermore, AI can give fast feedback, allowing students to learn from their mistakes in real-time and make improvements to their strategy before it's too late (Chen et al, 2020). For instructors, AI can assist uncover trends and patterns in student performance that could otherwise be missed. By analyzing massive volumes of data, AI can find insights into how students are learning and where they may be suffering. For example, if a high percentage of students are performing poorly on a specific topic, it may suggest that the content is not being taught properly or that students need more time to learn the idea. Armed with this information, educators may change their teaching practices and give focused interventions to meet particular areas of need.

Despite the many benefits AI brings, some obstacles must be addressed (Ahmad et al, 2021). One of the key issues is the ethical implications of AI in education. AI systems rely on data to make judgments, and if that data is skewed, the system's suggestions will likewise be affected. This might have major consequences in education, particularly when it comes to topics like grading, admissions, and student assistance. For example, if an AI system is educated on biased data, it might accidentally favor certain groups of students over others, perpetuating existing disparities in the education system. To reduce this danger, it is necessary for educators, administrators, and regulators to carefully analyze the data used to train AI systems and ensure that it is as fair and representative as possible. Another fear is the possibility of AI to replace human professors. While AI can automate certain duties, like as grading and feedback, it cannot replace the crucial function that instructors perform in the classroom (Srinivasa et al, 2022). Professors are not only responsible for presenting material but also for developing connections, inspiring students, and giving emotional support. AI cannot duplicate the human touch that is so crucial in education. Instead of replacing professors, AI should be considered as a tool to enhance their jobs, allowing them to focus on more significant activities while automating monotonous or time-consuming operations. Professors will always be needed to lead students, stimulate creativity, and inspire the next generation of learners. The function of AI in modern education is diverse and continuously growing. It has the potential to alter teaching and learning in deep ways, from customizing education to enhancing accessibility and democratizing learning possibilities. AI may assist relieve the strain for instructors, giving real-time feedback to students, and ensuring that educational information is available to all. However, like with any new technology, some obstacles must be addressed, including ethical considerations and the necessity for human oversight. By adopting AI deliberately and responsibly, educators can unleash their full potential and create a more inclusive, efficient, and engaging educational experience for all learners. As we go deeper into the digital era, AI will surely continue to play a vital part in defining the future of education, and it is up to educators to ensure that it is employed in ways that benefit both students and society as a whole.

KEY CONCEPTS AND TERMINOLOGIES IN AI

In recent years, Artificial Intelligence (AI) has progressed from the world of science fiction to become a vital component of our daily life (Lee, 2020). From the way people interact with technology to how companies run, AI is reshaping the world in new ways. For educators, students, and professionals working in AI-related domains, grasping the essential ideas and terminology linked with AI is vital. It can be intimidating at first, as AI spans a wide range of technologies, techniques, and processes. However, breaking down these phrases and concepts into manageable chunks might assist in establishing a solid grasp of this difficult topic.

At its foundation, AI is the imitation of human intelligence in computers that are programmed to analyze, learn, and solve problems in a manner that replicates human cognitive processes (Dong et al, 2020). These computers are not merely executing pre-defined instructions; they can adapt, make judgments, and improve over time. While the scope of AI's possibilities is broad, grasping certain fundamental words and ideas will give a strong starting point for anybody wishing to study this topic. Machine Learning (ML) is possibly one of the most commonly recognized and essential ideas in AI (Kühl et al, 2022). It is the subset of AI that focuses on the development of algorithms and statistical models that allow computers to learn from and make predictions or judgments based on data. Unlike traditional programming, where explicit instructions are supplied to a computer, machine learning enables a system to improve its performance without being deliberately taught to do so (Fiebrink, 2019). By putting big datasets into a machine learning model, the system can find patterns, recognize trends, and make judgments without human intervention. A typical kind of machine learning is Supervised Learning, where the system is trained using labeled data. This implies that the input data is coupled with the proper output, and the system learns to map inputs to outputs by minimizing mistakes in its predictions. For example, a supervised learning system used to detect photographs of cats may be fed thousands of tagged images of cats and dogs. The algorithm would learn the distinctive aspects of a cat, such as the shape of its ears, eyes, and hair pattern, and use this information to categorize fresh photographs as either a cat or a dog.

Table 1. Core AI concepts for educators

Concept	Plain-English Definition	Typical Classroom Uses
Artificial Intelligence (AI)	Computational methods that perform tasks requiring human-like intelligence (perception, prediction, decision).	Personalized learning; smart search; automation
Machine Learning (ML)	Algorithms that learn patterns from data to make predictions or decisions without explicit rules.	Early-warning; adaptive content
Deep Learning (DL)	Neural networks with many layers that learn complex features from large datasets.	Vision (lab/AR), speech-to-text
Natural Language Processing (NLP)	Techniques for machines to understand and generate human language.	Chatbots; auto-feedback; translation
Reinforcement Learning (RL)	Agents learn actions by trial-and-error to maximize long-term reward.	Tutoring strategies; simulations
Learning Analytics	Collecting/analyzing learner data to inform teaching and support.	Dashboards; targeted interventions
	Fairness, transparency, privacy-by-design, and human oversight.	Consent; bias audits; appeals

On the other side, Unsupervised Learning incorporates algorithms that learn from data without labeled outputs (Neuer, 2024). The idea is to uncover patterns and correlations within the data without being specifically instructed on what to search for. A common example of unsupervised learning is clustering, where the algorithm puts similar data points together based on their intrinsic features. This strategy is widely used in data mining, customer segmentation, and anomaly detection, where the computer identifies hidden patterns in data that may not be immediately obvious.

Another major idea in AI is Deep Learning, a subclass of machine learning that employs neural networks with multiple layers to handle enormous quantities of data (Buduma et al, 2022). The term "deep" refers to the several layers in the neural network that allow the system to learn progressively complicated properties of the data. Deep learning has grown increasingly popular in domains such as picture and speech recognition, where the sheer complexity and amount of the data make typical machine learning approaches less successful. These deep networks can automatically extract high-level characteristics from raw input, making them incredibly successful at tasks like detecting objects in photos or transcribing spoken language. Within deep learning, Neural Networks play a crucial role (Bau, 2020). Neural networks are computer models inspired by the human brain, consisting of layers of linked nodes, or "neurons," that process input in parallel. Each neuron in a network is linked to other neurons, and the strength of these connections is modified during the learning process. The network learns to detect patterns by altering the weights of these connections based on the input data. This structure allows neural networks to learn complicated functions, making them useful tools for tasks such as image categorization, natural language processing, and even playing games.

When we talk about the Training of AI models, we are talking about the process by which a machine learning algorithm or neural network learns from data. During training, the system is provided with vast volumes of data and gradually improves its capacity to make predictions or choices by modifying the internal parameters of the model. The purpose of training is to decrease the discrepancy between the model's predictions and the actual results, a process known as optimization. Once a model has been trained, it may be assessed on new, unknown data to test its performance and generalizability. This is known as testing, and it is vital to demonstrate that the model does not only recall the training data but can generalize its knowledge to new, real-world scenarios.

In AI, it is also vital to comprehend the notion of Overfitting and Underfitting. Overfitting happens when a model learns the training data too well, capturing not just the underlying patterns but also the noise and random oscillations in the data (Montesinos López et al, 2022). This leads to a model that performs wonderfully on the training data but badly on fresh data since it has simply "memorized" the training instances rather than learning generalizable patterns. On the other side, underfitting happens when a model is too simplistic or not trained long enough to capture the underlying patterns in the data. In both circumstances, the model fails to generalize effectively to new data, which is why it is vital to establish the correct balance between overfitting and underfitting. A similar idea is Reinforcement Learning (RL), a sort of machine learning where an agent learns to make decisions by interacting with its environment. Unlike supervised or unsupervised learning, where the system learns from previous data, reinforcement learning includes learning by trial and error. The agent makes actions in the environment, receives feedback in the form of rewards or penalties, and modifies its behavior to optimize long-term benefits. This method has been effectively employed in domains like robotics, game-playing, and autonomous cars. Reinforcement learning methods enable robots to learn optimum behaviors and strategies via exploration and exploitation of their environments.

As AI grows increasingly ubiquitous, the relevance of Natural Language Processing (NLP) is likewise rising (Vinothkumar & Karunamurthy, 2023). NLP is the field of AI that focuses on allowing machines to perceive, interpret, and produce human language. Whether it's voice assistants like Siri or Alexa, chatbots, or language translation tools, NLP is the technology underpinning many of the services we use every day. NLP encompasses a range of tasks, from voice recognition (turning spoken language into text) to sentiment analysis (determining the emotional tone of a piece of text) and machine translation (translating text from one language to another) (Khurana et al, 2023). One of the key issues in NLP is dealing with the ambiguity and complexity of human language, which is continually developing and frequently context-dependent. AI systems in NLP must be able to handle subtleties, idioms, slang, and varied languages to comprehend and interact successfully with people. Computer Vision is another rapidly expanding topic within AI (Kakani et al, 2020). It focuses on helping robots to analyze and understand visual information from the world, such as photographs and movies. Through the application of deep learning, computer vision systems can distinguish objects, monitor motion, detect faces, and even evaluate medical pictures for symptoms of disease. Computer vision is utilized in a wide range of applications, from self-driving automobiles to facial recognition software and augmented reality systems. The area has achieved tremendous gains in recent years, mainly due to the development of more complex algorithms and the availability of enormous annotated datasets.

As AI systems grow more pervasive, the relevance of Ethics in AI cannot be emphasized (Hagendorff, 2020). One of the key problems is the Bias that may be built into AI systems. Because AI systems are commonly trained on enormous datasets, they may unwittingly learn and perpetuate the biases contained in the data. For example, if an AI system is educated on biased data, it may make judgments that favor one group over another, leading to discriminatory consequences. This can be particularly troublesome in sectors like hiring, financing, and law enforcement, where AI-driven judgments can have enormous consequences for humans. To address these concerns, it is necessary to guarantee that AI systems are open, responsible, and fair, with procedures in place to identify and reduce bias. Another key ethical concern is the possible Job Displacement induced by AI and automation (Khogali & Mekid, 2023). While AI can dramatically boost productivity and efficiency, it also raises questions about the future of labor. Many occupations, especially those involving repetitive activities, are at risk of being overtaken by AI systems (Todolí-Signes, 2021). This might lead to severe social and economic issues, particularly for people who are unable to adjust to new positions. Policymakers and educators must work together to ensure that workers are prepared with the skills essential to flourish in an AI-driven economy, including an emphasis on lifelong learning and the development of abilities that complement AI rather than compete with it. AI is a broad area that involves a range of technology and concepts. Understanding the fundamental words and principles underpinning AI is vital for anybody wanting to navigate this quickly expanding sector. From machine learning and deep learning to reinforcement learning and natural language processing, the topics taught here are simply the tip of the iceberg. As AI continues to evolve, it will likely present new ideas, challenges, and possibilities, and having a thorough knowledge of the underlying words and concepts will be vital for staying ahead of the curve. Whether you're an educator, a student, or a professional, knowing the vocabulary of AI is the first step toward unlocking its potential and contributing to the change of industry, education, and society as a whole.

AI TOOLS AND TECHNOLOGIES RELEVANT TO TEACHING AND LEARNING

The introduction of Artificial Intelligence (AI) has brought about major changes in the domain of education. Professors, students, and educational institutions alike are increasingly turning to AI tools and technology to enhance learning experiences, expedite administrative work, and encourage more individualized educational practices. The role of AI in teaching and learning is not only a question of automation; it entails revolutionizing how information is presented, tested, and applied, as well as how students engage with the subject (Makinde et al, 2024). AI technologies are not merely a trend—they are becoming crucial to the core fabric of modern education. In this part, we will analyze the most significant AI tools and technologies related to teaching and learning and discuss how they are transforming the educational environment. One of the key ways in which AI is being integrated into teaching is through customized learning (Pratama et al, 2023). Traditional classroom environments generally adopt a one-size-fits-all strategy, where a professor has to accommodate the demands of all students regardless of their specific learning speeds, styles, or needs. This can result in some students falling behind or getting disengaged. AI-powered customized learning platforms, however, overcome this difficulty by offering unique educational experiences for each learner (Ali et al, 2024). These platforms utilize algorithms that assess a student's performance, learning patterns, and preferences to offer information that is customized to their unique requirements. For instance, if a student succeeds in a certain area but fails in another, AI systems might adjust by giving more materials or practice tasks on the weaker topic. This tailored approach helps to optimize each student's potential, ensuring that they remain interested and motivated throughout their educational journey.

A significant AI technology that allows individualized learning is adaptive learning systems (Gligorea et al, 2023). These systems dynamically change the complexity of classes, assignments, and exams based on the learner's progress. For example, AI can determine how well a learner has grasped specific topics and adapt to the difficulty of following information appropriately. If the learner struggles with a specific issue, the system will present extra resources and support to help them comprehend the notion. Adaptive learning systems like DreamBox, Knewton, and Smart Sparrow are commonly utilized in K-12 education, as well as in higher education settings, to provide more individualized learning routes for students (Kabudi et al, 2021). By regularly monitoring student progress and intervening when required, these technologies offer a learning environment that promotes both remedial and advanced learning, providing each student with the best opportunity to succeed.

Another area where AI is making great gains is in automated grading and evaluation (Bulten et al, 2021). Grading may be a time-consuming and difficult activity for educators, frequently requiring substantial hours of labor to offer comments on assignments, essays, quizzes, and examinations. AI-powered grading systems are supposed to relieve this strain (Valavanidis, 2023). These systems employ natural language processing (NLP) and machine learning techniques to analyze student inputs. For example, AI can grade writings for grammar, spelling, consistency, and even the strength of arguments, offering prompt feedback to students. Some sophisticated systems are also capable of assessing more complicated characteristics of writing, such as tone, style, and the logical flow of ideas (Marzuki et al, 2023). Tools such as Turnitin and GradeScope employ AI to aid professors in grading textual content, while systems like Gradescope help automate the grading of multiple-choice questions and problem sets. The use of AI for automated grading not only saves time for professors but also strengthens the feedback loop for students. Rather than waiting for weeks to get feedback on their work, students may obtain quick insights into their strengths and flaws, helping them to grow consistently. Additionally, automated grading systems can assist minimize human bias in grading, assuring a fairer evaluation procedure. However, while AI-based grading systems are helpful, they still require close supervision by educators to guarantee accuracy and relevance, especially when assessing more subjective content like essays and research chapters. AI-powered solutions also offer a major increase in the area of intelligent tutoring (Rızvı, 2023). In a typical classroom context, it can be difficult for professors to deliver individualized attention to every student, especially in bigger classrooms. AI tutors address this gap by providing students with 24/7 assistance and instruction outside of classroom hours (Holstein et al, 2019). These intelligent tutoring systems employ AI to simulate the job of a human tutor, delivering rapid feedback, answering questions, and helping students comprehend tough ideas. One well-known example of this is Socratic, an AI-driven teaching software by Google that assists students with homework and gives explanations for numerous disciplines, including mathematics, physics, and literature (Clark, 2024). Another example is Duolingo, a language-learning website that employs AI to personalize courses to each learner's competency level and learning style (Sehlaoui, 2024). The AI inside Duolingo watches user progress and modifies the content, ensuring that learners are not swamped with tough material but are still challenged enough to make consistent progress. Intelligent tutoring systems have been proved to increase learning results by allowing students the ability to study at their own speed and receive real-time feedback on their performance. This enables students to feel more secure in their learning and more prepared for tests or other evaluations. Beyond tutoring, AI is also making its mark in the domain of virtual classrooms and online learning settings. The expansion of remote learning, particularly in the aftermath of the COVID-19 epidemic, has boosted the demand for AI solutions that may help promote efficient online teaching (Frenk et al, 2022). Virtual classrooms driven by

AI may imitate real-world classroom experiences, including features like automatic attendance monitoring, real-time feedback, and individualized learning experiences (Kayyali, 2020). Platforms like Zoom and Google Classroom use AI to enhance user experience and automate administrative chores, such as scheduling, alerts, and even tailored learning suggestions based on user activity and performance (Kayyali, 2025 A). AI tools are also helping to create more engaging and interactive learning experiences through immersive technology. Augmented Reality (AR) and Virtual Reality (VR), when paired with AI, are being utilized to build interactive learning environments that allow students to explore complicated subjects in ways that would be impossible in a regular classroom (Shirazi et al, 2024). For example, in medical education, students can employ AI-powered VR simulations to practice surgical skills or diagnose patients in a safe, virtual setting.

Similarly, AR technologies like Google Expeditions allow students to take virtual field excursions to historical locations or examine the human body in 3D, delivering an immersive, hands-on learning experience that traditional textbooks cannot mimic (Cowin, 2020). In research, AI-powered technologies are being used to imitate experiments and evaluate data. Labster, for example, is a virtual laboratory that employs AI to lead students through experiments, offering real-time feedback and allowing students to practice skills without the need for expensive laboratory equipment. These technologies not only promote engagement but also enable safe and cost-effective learning in areas that need substantial hands-on practice. AI's effect extends to collaborative learning as well. Through the use of AI-powered group work tools, students may participate in real-time collaboration, working together on projects and tasks in a virtual environment (Msambwa et al, 2025). These technologies can propose resources, offer feedback on group dynamics, and track each member's efforts, ensuring that cooperation is effective and equitable. For example, Slack and Microsoft Teams employ AI to improve communication, offer relevant resources, and even interact with other learning tools to support effective group work. AI may also assist in identifying learning patterns within a group, allowing educators to intervene when appropriate and give additional support when needed.

Another notable advancement in AI’s influence on teaching and learning is its capacity to boost accessibility for students with impairments (Garg & Sharma, 2020). AI technologies are breaking down barriers that have historically made education less accessible to students with visual, aural, or cognitive disabilities (Kayyali, 2024 A). Text-to-speech and speech-to-text technologies, for instance, allow students with visual impairments to access written information or aid students with hearing impairments by giving transcriptions of spoken lectures. Similarly, AI-driven solutions like Be My Eyes and Aira give real-time support to visually impaired students by linking them with sighted volunteers who can explain the scene or aid navigate educational situations. These methods guarantee that all students have equal opportunity to achieve, regardless of their specific problems. The potential for AI in education is immense, but it is not without obstacles. One of the key problems is the issue of data privacy. Many AI systems rely on enormous volumes of data to work properly, and the collecting and storage of student data pose issues about privacy and security. Educational institutions must guarantee that AI technologies comply with data protection standards and secure student information. Additionally, there is a need for openness in how AI technologies make judgments since instructors and students must have faith in the fairness and accuracy of these systems.

ETHICAL CONSIDERATIONS IN AI FOR EDUCATION

As Artificial Intelligence (AI) becomes more incorporated into education, its potential to improve teaching and learning is apparent (Pedro et al, 2019). The promise of tailored instruction, greater accessibility, and automated administrative activities presents tremendous opportunities for educators and students alike. However, with this transforming potential comes a plethora of ethical problems that must be properly explored. AI is not a neutral tool; it is influenced by the data it analyzes and the algorithms that drive it, and these factors can add prejudice, privacy problems, and other ethical challenges. As we accept AI's role in education, it is crucial to address these ethical challenges to guarantee that AI is employed responsibly and fairly in the educational environment. One of the most notable ethical challenges in AI for education is data protection (Nguyen et al, 2023). AI programs generally rely on enormous volumes of data to work properly, particularly when it comes to personalized learning algorithms. These technologies capture information on students' academic achievement, learning practices, preferences, and even personal qualities, such as their socio-economic status or language competence. This data, although beneficial for designing educational experiences, also raises substantial issues regarding student privacy. Educational institutions must ensure that any data collected is done so with the explicit consent of students and their families and that it is stored and used in compliance with data protection laws, such as the General Data Protection Regulation (GDPR) in Europe or the Family Educational Rights and Privacy Act (FERPA) in the United States.

The risk of AI undermining student privacy extends beyond the acquisition of personal data (Manheim & Kaplan, 2019). Many AI-powered applications are cloud-based, meaning that sensitive data is kept remotely on servers that might be subject to hacking or illegal access. A data breach might result in the exposing of sensitive student information, including academic records, health information, or even personal identifiers. The repercussions of such breaches are significant, not just in terms of possible identity theft but also in the destruction of trust between students, instructors, and institutions. To address these dangers, educational institutions must develop rigorous cybersecurity procedures to protect student data and guarantee that AI technologies are secure. The informed consent procedure becomes increasingly difficult as AI technologies progress (Kayyali, 2024 C). With AI systems capable of tracking students' interactions and activities across numerous platforms, it becomes difficult for students and parents to completely comprehend the amount of data being gathered and how it is being utilized. For instance, AI-powered learning systems may monitor students' engagement with specific lectures, their emotional reactions, or even their relationships with peers. While this information may help generate tailored learning experiences, students and their families must be made aware of what data is being gathered, how it will be used, and who will have access to it. Institutions must guarantee that AI-driven platforms are open in their data usage and provide clear, intelligible permission processes.

In addition to privacy problems, AI in education poses worries about prejudice and justice. AI algorithms are only as good as the data they are trained on, and if that data is skewed, the resultant conclusions or recommendations might likewise be prejudiced (Ferrara, 2023). For example, an AI-powered grading system could favor some demographic groups over others if it is educated on data that matches existing biases in traditional grading processes. Similarly, personalized learning systems that depend on data from prior students may perpetuate disparities if they predominantly reflect the experiences of students from wealthy backgrounds. This can lead to a situation where AI tools unintentionally amplify existing discrepancies in educational achievement. The problem of prejudice is particularly significant when it comes to AI's function in evaluation and grading. Traditional grading methods have always been criticized for their subjectivity and potential for prejudice, and AI-powered grading tools are no exception. For instance, algorithms that assess students' essays may be more inclined to prefer specific writing styles, language competence levels, or even cultural norms. This might result in biased judgments of students who do not fit within these parameters, particularly those from varied cultural or linguistic backgrounds. In such circumstances, AI might unintentionally hinder these students, thus entrenching educational inequities. To limit the danger of bias in AI systems, developers must guarantee that the data used to train these systems is varied, representative, and free from prejudice. This involves careful attention to the sources of data, as well as constant monitoring of AI technologies to discover and fix any biased outcomes. It is also crucial for educational institutions to have human oversight in the assessment process, ensuring that AI-generated findings are examined and understood by educators who understand the context of each student's performance.

Another ethical concern with AI for education is transparency (Memarian & Doleck, 2023). AI algorithms are generally considered "black boxes," meaning that it is difficult for people to grasp how the system makes judgments. This lack of transparency may be particularly worrisome in educational contexts, as students and instructors need to understand how grades are allocated, how learning suggestions are produced, and how AI technologies are influencing their educational experiences. For instance, if an AI-powered platform proposes specific learning materials for a student, the student and their instructor must understand why those resources were chosen and how they connect with the student's learning goals. Without transparency, students may believe that their educational experiences are being dictated by an opaque system, leading to a sense of disempowerment and mistrust. To enhance transparency, AI developers and educational institutions must guarantee that AI technologies are explainable and that users can comprehend the logic behind the system's judgments. This may entail providing explicit explanations of how algorithms function, how data is processed, and how decisions are made. It is also necessary for instructors to undergo training on how to analyze and explain AI-driven recommendations and assessments to students. In this approach, students and educators may engage with AI tools in a more informed and responsible manner.

While AI has the potential to expand accessibility in education, it also raises questions about equality (Bulathwela et al, 2024). AI-powered learning platforms and applications can help make education more accessible to students with disabilities by delivering text-to-speech, speech-to-text, and other assistive technologies. However, there is a concern that AI technology might worsen current inequities in access to education. For example, students from low-income families may not have access to the equipment or internet connectivity necessary to fully benefit from AI-powered learning tools. Similarly, remote colleges or colleges in underdeveloped countries may lack the infrastructure to allow the broad deployment of AI technology. In such circumstances, the digital divide might deepen, leaving poor students further behind. To overcome this issue, legislators, educators, and developers need to consider inclusive design while designing AI tools for education. This involves ensuring that AI-powered platforms are accessible to students with impairments, as well as ensuring that all students, regardless of their socio-economic level or geographic location, have access to the technology they need. Governments and educational institutions can also play a role by giving subsidies or funds to assist in the introduction of AI technology in underprivileged colleges.

The ethical issues of automation in education also demand study. AI-powered solutions may automate numerous administrative activities, like as grading, scheduling, and resource allocation, freeing up educators' time to focus on teaching and student engagement. However, this automation can also raise worries about the dehumanization of education. Education is not simply about the transfer of information; education is a highly human process that requires mentorship, emotional support, and social contact. As AI takes on more activities previously done by human educators, there is a risk that the human connection that is important to education might be weakened. The problem, then, is to establish a balance between embracing AI for its efficiency and ensuring that the fundamental human parts of education are retained (Rane et al, 2023). The ethical concerns surrounding AI in education are complicated and numerous. While AI has the potential to transform education by making learning more customized, accessible, and efficient, it also brings enormous ethical problems about privacy, prejudice, fairness, transparency, equity, and the humanization of education. To guarantee that AI is utilized ethically and responsibly in education, educators, technologists, and legislators must work together to address these challenges. By stressing openness, inclusion, and justice, and by ensuring that AI tools are aligned with the best interests of students, we can harness the power of AI to better education while maintaining core ethical values.

THE FUTURE OF AI IN FACULTY DEVELOPMENT AND LIFELONG LEARNING

Artificial intelligence (AI) has emerged as a disruptive force in many domains, and education is no exception. As technology continues to advance, its potential to enhance teaching and learning processes has become increasingly obvious. For faculty members, the future of AI promises a potential not simply for student learning advancement, but also for their professional progress (Celik et al, 2022). In this setting, AI is positioned to play a crucial role in professor development and lifelong learning. For educators, staying current with new trends, tools, and technology is no longer optional—it's vital. AI presents a unique potential to create personalized, adaptive, and data-driven learning experiences that may boost faculty abilities, improve teaching effectiveness, and promote ongoing improvement throughout their careers.

In the dynamic environment of higher education, faculty development programs are vital for ensuring that educators remain up-to-date with the newest pedagogical techniques and technical technologies (Kayyali, 2021). Traditionally, these programs have been face-to-face or cohort-based, delivering a one-size-fits-all approach. However, as the speed of technological innovation accelerates, there is a rising demand for more flexible and responsive faculty development approaches (Kayyali, 2022). AI can transform how these programs are planned and delivered by giving tailored and adaptable learning routes that respond to the specific requirements and aspirations of each instructor. The one-size-fits-all paradigm of traditional professional development is being replaced by tailored, AI-driven approaches that enable staff to learn at their speed, on their terms, and in ways that are most relevant to their teaching circumstances (Yang et al, 2019). One of the most interesting potentials for AI in faculty development resides in its capacity to create tailored learning experiences. Much like students, faculty members have various demands and areas of expertise. Some may be well-versed in conventional educational techniques but lack experience with new technological tools, while others may be technology experts but require help in increasing their subject matter expertise. AI-driven systems may assess individual faculty members' learning histories, teaching styles, and professional ambitions to design individualized development plans that correspond with their unique requirements. By integrating data from prior interactions, comments, and performance, AI may offer focused courses, tools, and activities that will help each educator improve in the areas most important to their current stage of growth (Ouyang et al, 2023). Through machine learning algorithms, AI systems may continually change the content and pace of learning based on the educator's development and performance. For example, if a faculty member is struggling with incorporating a certain technology into their classroom, AI may provide further resources, offer practice activities, and propose applicable best practices. On the other side, if an instructor is thriving in a specific area, AI can propose advanced content or push them to take on more challenging tasks. This dynamic, continuing feedback loop guarantees that faculty members are actively involved in the learning process, always updating and refining their teaching approaches in response to real-time data.

Figure 1. Weekly time reallocated by AI — Waterfall

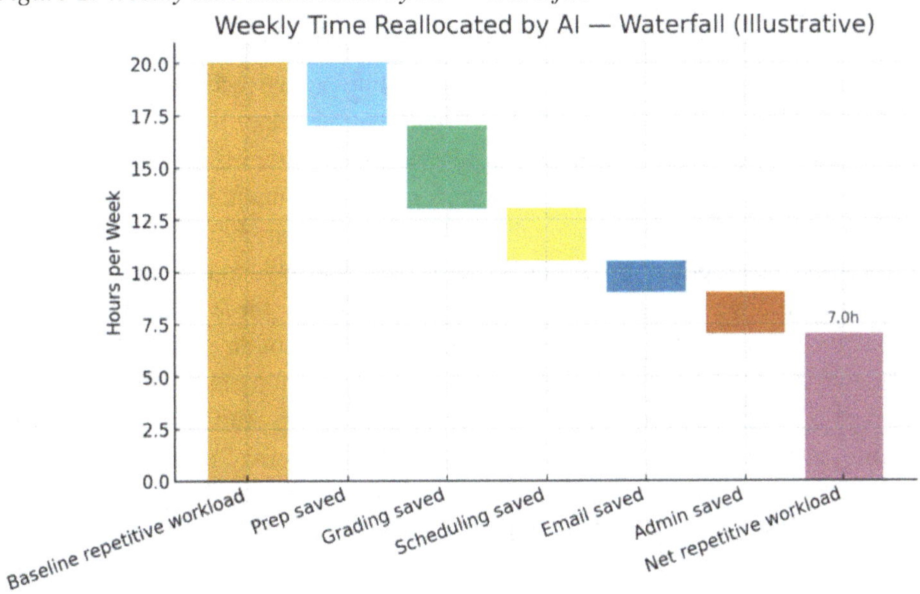

Beyond tailored learning experiences, AI may also assist faculty members better their teaching through the use of real-time feedback and statistics. In many faculty development programs, feedback is sometimes delayed, often coming weeks or even months after a teaching session has taken place. With AI, however, feedback may be immediate. For instance, AI-powered systems may evaluate classroom interactions, student engagement levels, and even mood to offer rapid feedback on teaching performance. This sort of data-driven feedback helps staff make rapid improvements to their teaching tactics, producing a more responsive and adaptable learning environment for their students. Real-time data may also help educators measure their professional growth over time, enabling them to create precise, quantifiable goals and assess their progress toward reaching them (Atlas, 2023). One area where AI is particularly well-positioned to have a substantial influence on professor development is in the arena of teaching assistants and mentorship programs. Faculty members typically find themselves managing a myriad of obligations, from preparing lectures to grading chapters, guiding students, and doing research. While many faculty members are devoted to mentoring junior colleagues, time restrictions and enormous workloads can make it tough to give individualized instruction to every mentee. AI may help bridge this gap by enabling virtual mentorship and assistance, providing advice, feedback, and support when faculty members need it the most. AI-powered teaching assistants may be integrated into faculty development programs to give rapid, on-demand help to educators who are seeking advice or direction on teaching tactics, technology use, or other professional development problems. By evaluating data about a faculty member's prior teaching experiences, AI may give targeted recommendations, resources, and solutions. Whether it's a question about adopting active learning practices, conducting online exams, or managing classroom dynamics, AI may serve as a trusted, non-judgmental helper that delivers helpful insights depending on the educator's requirements and circumstances.

Another area where AI can improve professor development is in the use of data analytics to inform instructional methods (Salas-Pilco et al, 2022). In conventional professional development programs, most of the feedback and direction are based on subjective observations or anecdotal evidence. While these techniques are essential, they may not always capture the complete picture of an educator's strengths and flaws. AI-driven systems, on the other hand, may acquire and analyze massive volumes of data regarding professor performance, from student assessments to teaching materials and classroom interactions. This data may be used to discover patterns, measure progress, and target areas for development.

For example, AI may evaluate a faculty member's lecture recordings to grade their speaking tempo, tone, and intelligibility (Saadia, 2023). It can then make ideas for improvement, such as slowing down during explanations or adjusting the tone to engage students more successfully. AI may also track how effectively students are interacting with the content, indicating which ideas may require extra explanation or which teaching strategies are most successful for particular learning types.

By integrating data analytics, faculty development programs may become more evidence-based, targeted, and outcomes-oriented. AI has the potential to facilitate lifelong learning among faculty members. In today's quickly changing educational scene, the need for continuing professional development is more critical than ever. Faculty members must continually adapt to new technology, teaching techniques, and research trends to remain relevant and successful. AI may play a significant part in this continuing process by allowing faculty members access to individualized learning materials and opportunities that meet their developing requirements.

AI-driven systems may provide faculty members access to on-demand learning resources, courses, and seminars that they can interact with at their leisure (Hamed & Ismael, 2024). For example, a faculty member who is interested in learning more about the newest breakthroughs in artificial intelligence may access a series of AI-focused courses, webinars, and publications customized expressly for their requirements. As their knowledge and experience improve, the platform may adapt, delivering more sophisticated content and challenges. In this approach, AI helps to guarantee that faculty members are regularly exposed to new ideas and advancements, encouraging a culture of lifelong learning. In addition to giving tailored learning possibilities, AI may also encourage cooperation and peer learning among faculty members. Traditional professional development programs frequently take place in isolation, with faculty members working separately or in small, cohort-based groups. However, with the aid of AI, educators may cooperate across institutions, disciplines, and geographic areas, sharing insights, resources, and best practices. AI-powered systems may link faculty members with colleagues who have similar interests or issues, allowing them to exchange ideas, engage in collaborative initiatives, and learn from each other's experiences. This sort of networked, peer-driven learning environment develops a feeling of community and encourages the sharing of information, skills, and resources.

Figure 2. Educator AI readiness: Baseline vs target (0–5)

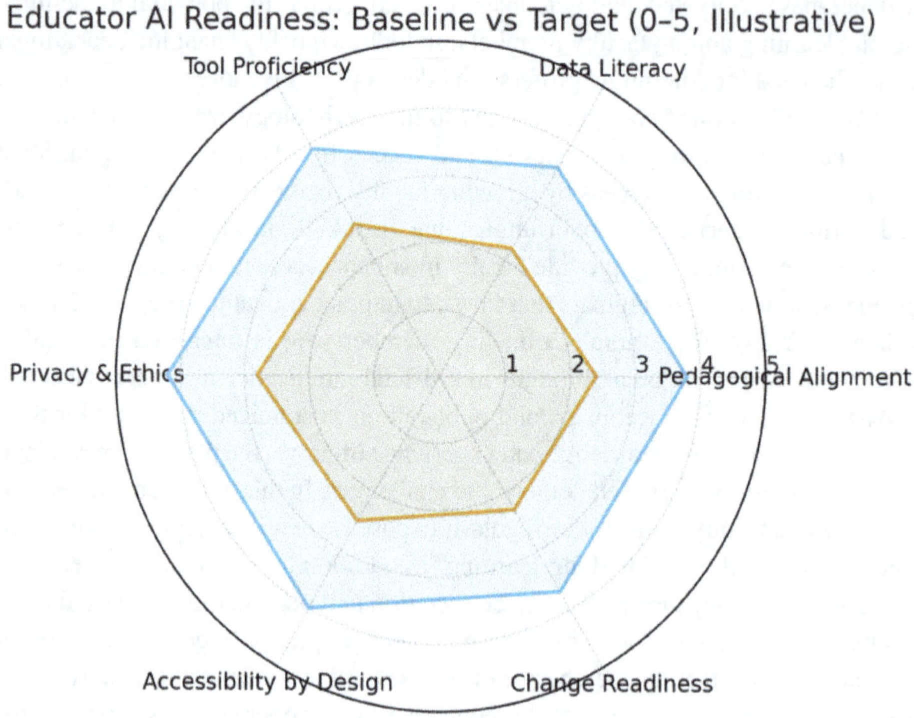

Despite the obvious benefits of AI in professor development and lifelong learning, there are also significant obstacles and ethical issues that must be addressed (Poquet & De Laat, 2021). One of the key challenges is the digital divide. While AI has the potential to boost professional development opportunities for many educators, access to AI-powered tools and resources is not ubiquitous. Faculty members in low-income or rural locations may have restricted access to essential technology or internet connectivity to properly benefit from AI-driven learning experiences. Addressing these equity challenges is vital to ensuring that AI's advantages are delivered equally and that all educators have the chance to grow their abilities. Another issue is the potential for over-reliance on AI. While AI may likely benefit faculty development programs, human judgment, and experience must remain at the heart of these projects (Ozmen Garibay et al, 2023). AI should be considered as a tool that supports, rather than replaces, human educators and mentors. Faculty development programs must continue to highlight the value of interpersonal communication, cooperation, and critical thinking—skills that AI, for all its accomplishments, cannot imitate. The future of AI in faculty development and lifelong learning is full of promise (Kayyali, 2025). As AI continues to improve, it provides educators the ability to engage in customized, adaptive, and data-driven professional development experiences that are suited to their particular needs and goals. AI-powered systems may provide real-time feedback, stimulate collaboration, and enable access to lifetime learning opportunities, ensuring that faculty members remain at the cutting edge of their disciplines. However, for AI to attain its full potential in faculty development, special attention must be paid to concerns of fairness, access, and ethical considerations. By finding the correct balance between AI and human knowledge, we may establish a future in which AI plays a vital role in helping educators and driving continual professional progress.

CONCLUSION

As we stand at the threshold of an educational revolution powered by artificial intelligence (AI), it is vital to focus on both the benefits and problems this transformational technology brings, particularly within the context of faculty development and lifelong learning. The integration of AI into education is not only a trend; it signifies a fundamental transformation in how teaching and learning are approached, understood, and experienced. While the full potential of AI in education has yet to be fully realized, its promise is undeniable, and its ability to enhance faculty development and support lifelong learning presents educators with a unique opportunity to redefine their professional growth, teaching practices, and ultimately, their impact on students. Throughout this chapter, we have covered the key ideas and terminologies that drive AI, examining the tools and technology that are already shaping the future of education. We have seen how AI can deliver specialized learning experiences, give real-time insights into teaching effectiveness, and create a dynamic and personalized approach to professional growth. Through these advancements, AI holds the potential to make faculty development more efficient, accessible, and impactful than ever before, allowing educators to stay at the forefront of teaching innovation and continually refine their expertise in response to the evolving demands of their discipline and the changing needs of their students.

Yet, like with any disruptive technology, the incorporation of AI into faculty development is not without its hurdles. Ethical problems, such as data privacy, bias in algorithms, and equal access to AI-driven resources, must be taken into account when educational institutions deploy these technologies. Ensuring that AI is utilized responsibly and ethically will need continual collaboration between educators, politicians, and engineers, with a common commitment to building systems that are transparent, inclusive, and free from prejudice. Moreover, the sheer nature of AI challenges traditional concepts of teaching and learning, pushing faculty members to adapt to new methods of engaging with technology, data, and students. This transformation will need a reassessment of how professional development is structured, with an emphasis on flexibility, accessibility, and the empowerment of professors to take charge of their learning journeys. For AI to fulfill its full potential in professor development and lifelong learning, institutions and educators must approach its adoption wisely and strategically. Institutions must invest in the infrastructure, training, and support necessary to guarantee that faculty members can easily integrate AI technologies into their teaching methods. Additionally, educators must be open to adopting AI as a partner in their professional progress, realizing that these technologies are not designed to replace human instructors but to enhance their skills and broaden their reach. Faculty members must become active participants in the process of technology adoption, engaging with AI tools, trying new teaching approaches, and regularly reporting on their experiences to maximize the benefits AI may bring. At the heart of AI's potential in education is its capacity to tailor learning and growth. The old one-size-fits-all strategy of faculty development no longer serves the demands of today's varied and dynamic teaching profession. AI gives the possibility to develop tailored learning experiences that correspond with individual objectives, interests, and areas of expertise. This customization allows faculty members to focus on the precise areas of their teaching that demand attention, whether that be topic knowledge, pedagogical tactics, or technological integration. As AI technologies grow, they will continue to offer increasingly sophisticated methods of personalizing development programs to match the particular requirements of each educator, offering continuing assistance that is both timely and relevant.

Another key benefit of AI in faculty development is the opportunity for real-time feedback. Traditional means of professional development, such as workshops and seminars, frequently lack the immediacy necessary to address difficulties that emerge in the classroom. In contrast, AI-driven technologies may deliver rapid, data-driven feedback that enables faculty to make modifications in real time. This rapid insight into teaching methods helps educators to take proactive efforts to improve their teaching efficacy, resulting in more engaged students and improved learning results. The capacity to evaluate classroom data and make actionable recommendations is one of the most effective components of AI since it allows instructors to constantly modify their approach and enhance their teaching tactics. In addition to increasing individual professor growth, AI also can promote a more collaborative and connected teaching community. AI technologies can allow the exchange of best practices, lesson plans, and resources, enabling faculty members to learn from one another and collaborate across academic boundaries. This collaborative atmosphere helps to break down silos inside institutions, enabling cross-departmental interaction and the sharing of ideas. AI-driven platforms may also assist peer mentorship and coaching, allowing faculty members the ability to get feedback from their peers and engage in meaningful professional interactions that stimulate growth and innovation.

REFERENCES

Aad, S., & Hardey, M. (2025). Generative AI: Hopes, controversies and the future of faculty roles in education. *Quality Assurance in Education, 33*(2), 267–282. DOI: 10.1108/QAE-02-2024-0043

Abbasi, M. U. R., Zulfiqar, A., Rasool, M. S., & Quadri, S. S. A. (2024). Impact of AI on the inclusion of Learners with Special needs: Public Policy Perspective in Contemporary Scenario. Arbor.

Ahmad, Z., Rahim, S., Zubair, M., & Abdul-Ghafar, J. (2021). Artificial intelligence (AI) in medicine, current applications and future role with special emphasis on its potential and promise in pathology: Present and future impact, obstacles including costs and acceptance among pathologists, practical and philosophical considerations. A comprehensive review. *Diagnostic Pathology, 16*(1), 1–16. DOI: 10.1186/s13000-021-01085-4

Alam, A., & Mohanty, A. (2023). Educational technology: Exploring the convergence of technology and pedagogy through mobility, interactivity, AI, and learning tools. *Cogent Engineering, 10*(2), 2283282. DOI: 10.1080/23311916.2023.2283282

Ali, M., Siddique, A., Aftab, A., Abid, M. K., & Fuzail, M. (2024). AI-Powered customized learning paths: Transforming data administration for students on digital platforms. *Journal of Computing & Biomedical Informatics, 6*(02), 195–204.

Atlas, S. (2023). ChatGPT for higher education and professional development: A guide to conversational AI.

Bhutoria, A. (2022). Personalized education and artificial intelligence in the United States, China, and India: A systematic review using a human-in-the-loop model. *Computers and Education: Artificial Intelligence, 3*, 100068. DOI: 10.1016/j.caeai.2022.100068

Buduma, N., Buduma, N., & Papa, J. (2022). *Fundamentals of deep learning: Designing next-generation machine intelligence algorithms.* O'Reilly Media, Inc.

Bulathwela, S., Pérez-Ortiz, M., Holloway, C., Cukurova, M., & Shawe-Taylor, J. (2024). Artificial intelligence alone will not democratise education: On educational inequality, techno-solutionism and inclusive tools. *Sustainability (Basel), 16*(2), 781. DOI: 10.3390/su16020781

Bulten, W., Balkenhol, M., Belinga, J. J. A., Brilhante, A., Çakır, A., Egevad, L., & Litjens, G. (2021). Artificial intelligence assistance significantly improves Gleason grading of prostate biopsies by pathologists. *Modern Pathology*, *34*(3), 660–671. DOI: 10.1038/s41379-020-0640-y

Celik, I., Dindar, M., Muukkonen, H., & Järvelä, S. (2022). The promises and challenges of artificial intelligence for teachers: A systematic review of research. *TechTrends*, *66*(4), 616–630. DOI: 10.1007/s11528-022-00715-y

Chen, L., Chen, P., & Lin, Z. (2020). Artificial intelligence in education: A review. *IEEE Access : Practical Innovations, Open Solutions*, *8*, 75264–75278. DOI: 10.1109/ACCESS.2020.2988510

Clark, D. (2024). *Artificial Intelligence for Learning: Using AI and Generative AI to Support Learner Development*. Kogan Page Publishers.

Cowin, J. B. (2020). Digital Worlds and Transformative Learning: Google Expeditions, Google Arts and Culture, and the Merge Cube. *International Research and Review*, *10*(1), 42–53.

Dimitriadou, E., & Lanitis, A. (2023). A critical evaluation, challenges, and future perspectives of using artificial intelligence and emerging technologies in smart classrooms. *Smart Learning Environments*, *10*(1), 12. DOI: 10.1186/s40561-023-00231-3

Dong, Y., Hou, J., Zhang, N., & Zhang, M. (2020). Research on how human intelligence, consciousness, and cognitive computing affect the development of artificial intelligence. *Complexity*, *2020*(1), 1680845. DOI: 10.1155/2020/1680845

Ferrara, E. (2023). Fairness and bias in artificial intelligence: A brief survey of sources, impacts, and mitigation strategies. *Sci*, *6*(1), 3. DOI: 10.3390/sci6010003

Fiebrink, R. (2019). Machine learning education for artists, musicians, and other creative practitioners. [TOCE]. *ACM Transactions on Computing Education*, *19*(4), 1–32. DOI: 10.1145/3294008

Fitria, T. N. (2023). The use of artificial intelligence in education (AIED): Can AI replace the teacher's role? *Epigram*, *20*(2), 165–187. DOI: 10.32722/epi.v20i2.5711

Frenk, J., Chen, L. C., Chandran, L., Groff, E. O., King, R., Meleis, A., & Fineberg, H. V. (2022). Challenges and opportunities for educating health professionals after the COVID-19 pandemic. *Lancet*, *400*(10362), 1539–1556. DOI: 10.1016/S0140-6736(22)02092-X

Gligorea, I., Cioca, M., Oancea, R., Gorski, A. T., Gorski, H., & Tudorache, P. (2023). Adaptive learning using artificial intelligence in e-learning: A literature review. *Education Sciences*, *13*(12), 1216. DOI: 10.3390/educsci13121216

Hagendorff, T. (2020). The ethics of AI ethics: An evaluation of guidelines. *Minds and Machines*, *30*(1), 99–120. DOI: 10.1007/s11023-020-09517-8

Hamed, A. E., & Ismael, B. B. (2024). AI-Driven Opportunistic Learning: Enhancing Personalized Educational Experiences for Arab Learners in the MENA Region. Journal of Scientific Development for Studies and Research (JSD), 5(20), 206_225-206_225.

Hill, H. C., Papay, J. P., Schwartz, N., Johnson, S., Freitag, E., Donohue, K., ... & Williamson-Zerwic, B. (2021). Improving teacher professional learning at scale.

Holstein, K., McLaren, B. M., & Aleven, V. (2019). Designing for complementarity: Teacher and student needs for orchestration support in AI-enhanced classrooms. In Artificial Intelligence in Education: 20th International Conference, AIED 2019, Chicago, IL, USA, June 25-29, 2019 [Springer International Publishing.]. *Proceedings*, *20*(Part I), 157–171.

Kabudi, T., Pappas, I., & Olsen, D. H. (2021). AI-enabled adaptive learning systems: A systematic mapping of the literature. Computers and education. *Artificial Intelligence*, *2*, 100017.

Kakani, V., Nguyen, V. H., Kumar, B. P., Kim, H., & Pasupuleti, V. R. (2020). A critical review on computer vision and artificial intelligence in food industry. *Journal of Agriculture and Food Research*, *2*, 100033. DOI: 10.1016/j.jafr.2020.100033

Kayyali, M. (2020). Post COVID-19: New era for higher education systems. *International Journal of Applied Science and Engineering*, *8*(2), 131–145. DOI: 10.30954/2322-0465.2.2020.6

Kayyali, M. (2021). Positive impact of high technology on higher education.

Kayyali, M. (2022). The Importance of Faculty Development in Higher Education. *International Journal of Higher Education Policies and Leadership*, *1*(1), 1–9.

Kayyali, M. (2024). A). Future possibilities and challenges of AI in education. In *Transforming education with generative AI: Prompt engineering and synthetic content creation* (pp. 118–137). IGI Global Scientific Publishing. DOI: 10.4018/979-8-3693-1351-0.ch006

Kayyali, M. (2024). B). Career development in higher education: Best practices and innovations. In *Advancing student employability through higher education* (pp. 1–19). IGI Global. DOI: 10.4018/979-8-3693-0517-1.ch001

Kayyali, M. (2024 C). Immersive Technologies: Virtual and Augmented Reality in Higher Education. In Reshaping learning with next generation educational technologies (pp. 99-114). IGI Global.

Kayyali, M. (2025 A). E-Learning Platforms and Their Influence on Lifelong Learning. In Impact of Digitalization on Education and Social Sustainability (pp. 155-176). IGI Global.

Kayyali, M. (2025). The Future of AI in Education: Predictions and Emerging Trends. Next-Generation AI Methodologies in Education, 367-406.

Khogali, H. O., & Mekid, S. (2023). The blended future of automation and AI: Examining some long-term societal and ethical impact features. *Technology in Society*, *73*, 102232. DOI: 10.1016/j.techsoc.2023.102232

Khurana, D., Koli, A., Khatter, K., & Singh, S. (2023). Natural language processing: State of the art, current trends and challenges. *Multimedia Tools and Applications*, *82*(3), 3713–3744. DOI: 10.1007/s11042-022-13428-4

Kühl, N., Schemmer, M., Goutier, M., & Satzger, G. (2022). Artificial intelligence and machine learning. *Electronic Markets*, *32*(4), 2235–2244. DOI: 10.1007/s12525-022-00598-0

Lee, R. S. (2020). Artificial intelligence in daily life.

Lucci, S., Musa, S. M., & Kopec, D. (2022). Artificial intelligence in the 21st century.

Makinde, A. I., Adeleye, S. A., Oronti, A. O., & Jimoh, I. T. (2024). Revolutionizing education. Artificial Intelligence for Wireless Communication Systems: Technology and Applications, 103.

Manheim, K., & Kaplan, L. (2019). Artificial intelligence: Risks to privacy and democracy. *Yale JL & Tech.*, *21*, 106.

Martinez-Requejo, S., García, E. J., Duarte, S. R., Lázaro, J. R., Sanz, E. P., & Vivas, G. M. (2024). AI-driven student assistance: chatbots redefining university support. In INTED2024 Proceedings (pp. 617-625). IATED.

Marzuki, W., Widiati, U., Rusdin, D., Darwin, , & Indrawati, I. (2023). The impact of AI writing tools on the content and organization of students' writing: EFL teachers' perspective. *Cogent Education*, *10*(2), 2236469. DOI: 10.1080/2331186X.2023.2236469

Memarian, B., & Doleck, T. (2023). Fairness, Accountability, Transparency, and Ethics (FATE) in Artificial Intelligence (AI) and higher education: A systematic review. *Computers and Education: Artificial Intelligence*, *5*, 100152. DOI: 10.1016/j.caeai.2023.100152

Montesinos López, O. A., Montesinos López, A., & Crossa, J. (2022). Overfitting, model tuning, and evaluation of prediction performance. In *Multivariate statistical machine learning methods for genomic prediction* (pp. 109–139). Springer International Publishing. DOI: 10.1007/978-3-030-89010-0_4

Msambwa, M. M., Wen, Z., & Daniel, K. (2025). The Impact of AI on the Personal and Collaborative Learning Environments in Higher Education. *European Journal of Education*, *60*(1), e12909. DOI: 10.1111/ejed.12909

Neuer, M. J. (2024). Unsupervised learning. In *Machine Learning for Engineers: Introduction to Physics-Informed, Explainable Learning Methods for AI in Engineering Applications* (pp. 141–172). Springer Berlin Heidelberg.

Nguyen, A., Ngo, H. N., Hong, Y., Dang, B., & Nguyen, B. P. T. (2023). Ethical principles for artificial intelligence in education. *Education and Information Technologies*, *28*(4), 4221–4241. DOI: 10.1007/s10639-022-11316-w

Oude Vrielink, R. A., Jansen, E. A., Hans, E. W., & van Hillegersberg, J. (2019). Practices in timetabling in higher education institutions: A systematic review. *Annals of Operations Research*, *275*(1), 145–160. DOI: 10.1007/s10479-017-2688-8

Ouyang, F., Wu, M., Zheng, L., Zhang, L., & Jiao, P. (2023). Integration of artificial intelligence performance prediction and learning analytics to improve student learning in online engineering course. *International Journal of Educational Technology in Higher Education*, *20*(1), 4. DOI: 10.1186/s41239-022-00372-4

Ozmen Garibay, O., Winslow, B., Andolina, S., Antona, M., Bodenschatz, A., Coursaris, C., Falco, G., Fiore, S. M., Garibay, I., Grieman, K., Havens, J. C., Jirotka, M., Kacorri, H., Karwowski, W., Kider, J., Konstan, J., Koon, S., Lopez-Gonzalez, M., Maifeld-Carucci, I., & Xu, W. (2023). Six human-centered artificial intelligence grand challenges. *International Journal of Human-Computer Interaction*, *39*(3), 391–437. DOI: 10.1080/10447318.2022.2153320

Pedro, F., Subosa, M., Rivas, A., & Valverde, P. (2019). Artificial intelligence in education: Challenges and opportunities for sustainable development.

Pokrivčáková, S. (2019). Preparing teachers for the application of AI-powered technologies in foreign language education. Journal of language and cultural education.

Poquet, O., & De Laat, M. (2021). Developing capabilities: Lifelong learning in the age of AI. *British Journal of Educational Technology, 52*(4), 1695–1708. DOI: 10.1111/bjet.13123

Pratama, M. P., Sampelolo, R., & Lura, H. (2023). Revolutionizing education: harnessing the power of artificial intelligence for personalized learning. Klasikal: Journal of education, language teaching and science, 5(2), 350-357.

Qazi, S., Kadri, M. B., Naveed, M., Khawaja, B. A., Khan, S. Z., Alam, M. M., & Su'ud, M. M. (2024). AI-Driven Learning Management Systems: Modern Developments, Challenges and Future Trends during the Age of ChatGPT. *Computers, Materials & Continua, 80*(2), 3289–3314. DOI: 10.32604/cmc.2024.048893

Rane, N., Choudhary, S., & Rane, J. (2023). Education 4.0 and 5.0: Integrating artificial intelligence (AI) for personalized and adaptive learning.

Rimm, S., Gilman, B., & Silverman, L. (2021). Nontraditional applications of traditional testing. In *Alternative assessments with gifted and talented students* (pp. 175–202). Routledge. DOI: 10.4324/9781003232988-10

Rɪzvɪ, M. (2023). Investigating AI-powered tutoring systems that adapt to individual student needs, providing personalized guidance and assessments. *The Eurasia Proceedings of Educational and Social Sciences, 31*, 67–73. DOI: 10.55549/epess.1381518

Saadia, K. H. (2023). Assessing the Effectiveness of Text-to-Speech and Automatic Speech Recognition in Improving EFL Learner's Pronunciation of Regular Past-ed.

Salas-Pilco, S. Z., Xiao, K., & Hu, X. (2022). Artificial intelligence and learning analytics in teacher education: A systematic review. *Education Sciences, 12*(8), 569. DOI: 10.3390/educsci12080569

Sarker, I. H. (2021). Machine learning: Algorithms, real-world applications and research directions. *SN Computer Science, 2*(3), 160. DOI: 10.1007/s42979-021-00592-x

Sehlaoui, F. Z. (2024). Integrating AI in Foreign Language Teaching and Learning: Learner Autonomy and Tool Utilization in an Algerian University. *Passerelle, 13*(2), 116–139.

Shah, P. (2023). *AI and the Future of Education: Teaching in the Age of Artificial Intelligence*. John Wiley & Sons.

Sheikh, S. (Ed.). (2020). *Understanding the role of artificial intelligence and its future social impact*. IGI Global.

Shirazi, B. N., Safavi, A. A., Aftabi, E., & Salimi, G. (2024, February). The Integration of Virtual Reality and Artificial Intelligence in Educational Paradigms. In 2024 11th International and the 17th National Conference on E-Learning and E-Teaching (ICeLeT) (pp. 1-6). IEEE. DOI: 10.1109/ICeLeT62507.2024.10493089

Soori, M., Arezoo, B., & Dastres, R. (2023). Artificial intelligence, machine learning and deep learning in advanced robotics, a review. *Cognitive Robotics*, *3*, 54–70. DOI: 10.1016/j.cogr.2023.04.001

Sridhar, V. (2024). *ChatGPT And Artificial Intelligence*. Academic Guru Publishing House.

Srinivasa, K. G., Kurni, M., & Saritha, K. (2022). Harnessing the Power of AI to Education. In *Learning, teaching, and assessment methods for contemporary learners: pedagogy for the digital generation* (pp. 311–342). Springer Nature Singapore. DOI: 10.1007/978-981-19-6734-4_13

Tapalova, O., & Zhiyenbayeva, N. (2022). Artificial intelligence in education: AIEd for personalised learning pathways. *Electronic Journal of e-Learning*, *20*(5), 639–653. DOI: 10.34190/ejel.20.5.2597

Todolí-Signes, A. (2021). Making algorithms safe for workers: Occupational risks associated with work managed by artificial intelligence. *Transfer: European Review of Labour and Research*, *27*(4), 433–452. DOI: 10.1177/10242589211035040

Valavanidis, A. (2023). Artificial intelligence (ai) applications. Department of Chemistry, National and Kapodistrian University of Athens, University Campus Zografou, 15784.

Vinothkumar, J., & Karunamurthy, A. (2023). Recent advancements in artificial intelligence technology: Trends and implications. Quing. *International Journal of Multidisciplinary Scientific Research and Development*, *2*(1), 1–11. DOI: 10.54368/qijmsrd.2.1.0003

Wang, P. (2019). On defining artificial intelligence. *Journal of Artificial General Intelligence*, *10*(2), 1–37. DOI: 10.2478/jagi-2019-0002

Yang, S., Tian, H., Sun, L., & Yu, X. (2019, June). From one-size-fits-all teaching to adaptive learning: The crisis and solution of education in the era of AI. []). IOP Publishing.]. *Journal of Physics: Conference Series*, *1237*(4), 042039. DOI: 10.1088/1742-6596/1237/4/042039

Yu, P. K. (2020). The algorithmic divide and equality in the age of artificial intelligence. *Florida Law Review*, *72*, 331.

ZONAID. M. (2024). SKILLSYNTH: AI DRIVEN PERSONALIZED EDUCATION PLATFORM (Doctoral dissertation, DAFFODIL INTERNATIONAL UNIVERSITY).

KEY TERMS AND DEFINTIONS

Adaptive Learning Systems: AI-driven educational platforms that adjust learning content, pace, and style based on a student's performance and needs, providing a more personalized learning experience.

AI-Powered Assessment: The use of AI in evaluating student performance through automated grading, real-time feedback, and data-driven insights to improve learning and teaching effectiveness.

Artificial Intelligence (AI): The simulation of human intelligence in machines that can perform tasks such as learning, problem-solving, and decision-making, often used in education for personalized learning and automation.

Ethical AI in Education: The principles and guidelines ensuring that AI applications in education are fair, unbiased, transparent, and respectful of data privacy while enhancing learning outcomes.

Faculty Development with AI: The use of AI-driven tools and analytics to support the continuous professional growth of educators by providing personalized training, feedback, and resource recommendations.

Intelligent Tutoring Systems (ITS): AI-based systems that provide personalized instruction and real-time feedback to students, mimicking the role of a human tutor in guiding learning.

Machine Learning (ML): A subset of AI that enables computers to learn patterns from data and improve performance on tasks without explicit programming, commonly used in adaptive learning systems.

Natural Language Processing (NLP): The AI capability that allows computers to understand, interpret, and generate human language, enabling applications like AI-powered tutoring and automated feedback tools.

Chapter 4
AI-Infused Curriculum: Strategies for Seamless Integration Across Disciplines

Andi Asrifan
http://orcid.org/0000-0002-9934-6129
Universitas Negeri Makassar, Indonesia

Rismawati Sudirman
http://orcid.org/0000-0001-8046-6764
Universitas Muhammadiyah Palopo, Indonesia

Vivit Rosmayanti
http://orcid.org/0000-0002-3648-9878
Universitas Negeri Makassar, Indonesia

La Sunra
http://orcid.org/0009-0003-7337-4126
Universitas Negeri Makassar, Indonesia

Jusrianto Jala
Universitas Muhammadiyah Sidenreng Rappang, Indonesia

Suci Amaliah
http://orcid.org/0009-0008-9315-1794
Universitas Negeri Makassar, Indonesia

ABSTRACT

This chapter discusses strategic frameworks for integrating AI into higher education curricula in different domains. The examination begins with the conceptual and pedagogical changes needed to move from traditional educational frameworks to AI-augmented, learner-centric ones. The chapter discusses backward design, modular curricular architecture, and Bloom's Digital Taxonomy to explain AI integration design methods. Case-based applications in STEM, Humanities, Health, and Business demonstrate AI's importance in specialized education. Faculty preparation, resistance management, and ethical implications of co-creation and professional learning communities are also covered. The final section emphasizes assessment, scalability, and futurist perspectives to ensure institutional and curricular readiness. The chapter advocates for thoughtful, ethical, and humanistic AI in education.

DOI: 10.4018/979-8-3373-1285-9.ch004

FOUNDATIONS OF AI INTEGRATION IN HIGHER EDUCATION CURRICULA

Beyond technology innovation, artificial intelligence is changing higher education teaching, governance, and culture. Universities must understand, place, and regulate AI in academic environments. Without a cohesive conceptual framework, AI discussions may become incoherent, tech-focused, or unrelated to education. A unifying conceptual framework for AI is essential for responsible integration, curriculum building, and connecting technological adoption with teaching, research, and public engagement goals. This section provides a conceptual framework for academic AI analysis, establishing the groundwork for future talks on implementation, equity, and ethics.

1.1 Conceptualizing AI in the Academic Context

Artificial Intelligence (AI) has become a revolutionary influence across various sectors, and its incorporation into academia is reshaping pedagogical, curricular, and institutional frameworks. In higher education, AI is increasingly regarded not just as a topic of study in computer science or engineering but as a cross-disciplinary catalyst that can transform the construction, delivery, and application of knowledge (Erduran & Levrini, 2024; Southworth et al., 2023; Tzirides et al., 2024). In the academic environment, conceptualizing AI necessitates a transition from perceiving it as an independent technology to recognizing it as a tool that augments cognitive, creative, and operational dimensions of teaching and learning.

Fundamentally, AI in education includes a wide range of intelligent systems, such as machine learning, natural language processing, robotics, computer vision, and generative algorithms. These systems provide real-time data analysis, adaptive feedback, automated content development, and tailored learning pathways (Badru et al., 2022; Bhutoria, 2022; García-Martínez et al., 2023). This requires faculty members and curriculum creators to reassess epistemological assumptions and pedagogical frameworks. Incorporating AI necessitates reimagining curricula that promote digital literacy, algorithmic reasoning, ethical consciousness, and interdisciplinary cooperation.

Furthermore, the integration of AI in academics is intricately linked to the fourth industrial revolution and the overarching digital transformation initiative. In response to the demand for future-ready graduates, schools can utilize AI-driven methodologies to cultivate more dynamic, inclusive, and learner-centered settings. This transition must be based on a critical comprehension of AI's implications, encompassing its advantages and hazards (Ng et al., 2023; Petridou & Lao, 2024). Concerns around prejudice, transparency, privacy, and the automation of cognitive labor necessitate curriculum design that prioritizes human-centered AI literacy.

Understanding AI within the academic framework necessitates an ecosystemic viewpoint that harmonizes technical advancement with educational integrity and institutional objectives. Faculty should be enabled to function as subject matter experts and as proficient facilitators in AI, capable of navigating intricate technologies, designing intelligent learning experiences, and critically assessing their consequences. This fundamental reconfiguration is essential for attaining seamless and sustained AI integration across disciplines, ensuring that higher education stays pertinent, adaptive, and robust in the era of intelligent systems.

1.2 Rationale for Cross-Disciplinary AI Integration

The justification for incorporating Artificial Intelligence (AI) across academic fields is its ubiquitous impact on all aspects of modern existence—economic, social, scientific, and cultural. Artificial intelligence is no longer only the province of computer scientists and engineers; it has emerged as a fundamental catalyst for innovation across various sectors, including healthcare, education, law, business, media, and the arts (Rashid & Kausik, 2024; Singh et al., 2023; Wang & Lester, 2023). This prevalence demands an educational approach that prepares learners with technical skills and critical, ethical, and creative qualities to interact effectively with AI in various circumstances.

As catalysts of social change, higher education institutions are distinctly equipped to address the requirements of a swiftly advancing knowledge economy. An interdisciplinary approach to AI integration guarantees that students from diverse academic backgrounds acquire vital literacies that go beyond conventional disciplinary limits (Petridou & Lao, 2024; Tzirides et al., 2024). These encompass data fluency, algorithmic reasoning, systems thinking, and ethical judgment. Integrating AI into the curriculum dismantles academic silos and promotes the multidisciplinary teamwork essential for addressing real-world challenges.

Moreover, AI's ability to customize learning, facilitate adaptive evaluation, and enhance instructional delivery is invaluable for improving educational fairness and efficacy. In fields such as education, psychology, sociology, and economics, AI enhances the examination of intricate behavioral and societal patterns. In the creative arts and humanities, AI facilitates innovative modes of expression and interpretive exploration (Nixon et al., 2024; Roshanaei et al., 2023). Integrating AI into various curriculum enables instructors to develop more pertinent, future-focused learning experiences that align with students' real-life experiences and professional ambitions.

The necessity to include AI across several disciplines is also strategic. As intelligent technologies more influence job markets, graduates must be equipped to interact with AI systems, evaluate their limitations, and devise inclusive digital futures. Institutions that actively integrate AI into their courses improve student employability and establish themselves as pioneers in educational innovation. An interdisciplinary AI curriculum promotes resilience, relevance, and responsibility—three fundamental pillars necessary for success in an AI-enhanced environment. The justification for cross-disciplinary AI integration is fundamentally based on the necessity to democratize AI knowledge, foster agile thinkers, and establish a higher education environment that is adaptable, inclusive, and socially sensitive.

1.3 Pedagogical Shifts in the Age of AI

The incorporation of Artificial Intelligence (AI) into educational frameworks is instigating substantial pedagogical changes, necessitating educators to reevaluate the principles, practices, and objectives of teaching and learning. Conventional instructional models focused on knowledge transfer are progressively being replaced by learner-centered, technology-enhanced teaching methods. These transformations are not simply incremental but fundamental, as AI reconfigures the roles of educators, the essence of content, and the learning process itself (Ng et al., 2023; Pahi et al., 2024).

A significant transformation is the shift from standardized education to individualized learning pathways. AI-driven systems can assess learner data instantaneously to customize material, tempo, and feedback according to individual student requirements. This adaptive feature improves engagement, facilitates individualized education, and accommodates various learning styles and capacities (Binhammad et al., 2024). Therefore, educators must transition from being mere content providers to being facilitators, learning architects, and curators of sophisticated content.

Furthermore, AI has implemented novel methods of evaluation and feedback. Automated grading, sentiment analysis, and intelligent tutoring systems facilitate ongoing, formative assessment that guides instructional decision-making. These tools alleviate administrative obligations, allowing educators to concentrate on advanced pedagogical objectives. Nonetheless, the dependence on algorithmic input necessitates that academics have a critical comprehension (Egunjobi & Adeyeye, 2024; Ma et al., 2024) of the biases, limitations, and transparency concerns intrinsic to AI systems.

Collaboration and creativity have become increasingly significant in AI-enhanced educational methodologies. With automation assuming ordinary cognitive functions, educators must cultivate skills that AI struggles to replicate—empathy, ethical reasoning, interdisciplinary synthesis, and critical reflection. Project-based, inquiry-driven, and experiential learning paradigms are crucial in cultivating these distinctively human abilities (At the Crossroads of Innovation: Embracing AI to Foster Deep

Learning in the College Classroom, 2024; Ng et al., 2023). In this setting, teaching serves as a collaborative arena for people and machines, wherein students participate in significant problem-solving, utilizing AI as both an instrument and a collaborator.

Furthermore, the advent of AI necessitates a reevaluation of curricular content. Educators must integrate digital ethics, algorithmic responsibility, and socio-technical analysis into learning objectives across several disciplines. Equipping students to thrive, operate, and govern in an AI-driven environment necessitates fostering both technical expertise and a profound understanding of AI's societal ramifications. Pedagogical transformations in the era of AI represent a reorganization of the educational experience—characterized by dynamism, personalization, ethical foundations, and alignment with the intricate realities of the digital age.

CURRICULUM DESIGN FRAMEWORKS FOR AI INTEGRATION

After studying AI theoretically, curriculum creation must incorporate AI-informed ideas. Conceptual clarity is insufficient without instructional frameworks that integrate learning objectives, assessment methods, and teaching activities quantitatively. Backward design and competency-based education allow for systematic integration of AI-enhanced learning into outcome-focused education. These strategies focus on explicitly defined competences and evidence-based evaluation to ensure academic rigor, accountability, and alignment with institutional learning objectives when integrating AI into curriculum planning.

2.1 Backward Design and Competency-Based Models

The incorporation of Artificial Intelligence (AI) in higher education necessitates a transformation in curriculum-building methodologies that prioritize clarity of intent, learner-focused outcomes, and interdisciplinary adaptability. Backward design and competency-based education (CBE) approaches provide effective frameworks for integrating AI-driven material with institutional objectives, curricular consistency, and individual student development. These methodologies allow educators to purposefully integrate AI literacy, digital ethics, and multidisciplinary skills into the core of academic curricula (Chiu et al., 2024; Nguyen, 2025; Tzirides et al., 2024).

Backward design commences with the end goal—establishing desired learning goals prior to selecting instructional techniques and assessment methodologies. This AI-integrated curriculum necessitates that faculty clearly define the knowledge and competencies students must acquire about AI technologies within their specific fields (Chiu et al., 2024; Pahi et al., 2024). Outcomes may encompass comprehending algorithmic logic, implementing machine learning principles, critically assessing

AI results, and addressing ethical considerations. Upon defining these outcomes, instructional content and learning activities are chosen to support students in achieving these objectives.

Competency-based methods enhance backward design by prioritizing the mastering of specific, quantifiable abilities over the mere fulfillment of seat-time or credit hours. AI-integrated competency-based education frameworks enable learners to advance at their own speed through content aligned with real-world difficulties. For example, health sciences students may exhibit proficiency in employing AI for diagnostic simulations, whereas business students may develop predictive models for market analysis (Carlgren, 2020; Gallagher & Savage, 2020; Vasquez et al., 2021). This model advocates for personalization, accountability, and equity, guaranteeing that learners achieve both conceptual comprehension and practical expertise.

Furthermore, both backward design and competency-based education prioritize assessment as a means of facilitating learning rather than solely for evaluation purposes. In AI-enhanced environments, evaluation activities can be supplemented with intelligent technologies that offer instantaneous feedback and performance analysis. These observations can guide student self-regulation and teacher interventions. Designers must guarantee that these assessments maintain transparency, fairness, and data privacy. The combined application of backward design and competency-based models provides a strategic framework for incorporating AI into curriculum development. They promote alignment among institutional goals, faculty development, and student achievement. Ultimately, these models facilitate the cultivation of graduates who are technologically proficient and ethically and socially accountable in their utilization of AI.

2.2 Modular Curriculum Architecture for AI Adaptability

As Artificial Intelligence (AI) technologies advance rapidly, higher education institutions must implement curricular frameworks that are intrinsically adaptable, scalable, and responsive to new advances. Modular curriculum architecture provides a strategic framework for assuring adaptation in AI-enhanced educational settings. By segmenting programs into distinct, autonomous learning modules, educators can create a curriculum that adapts to technology advancements while fostering multidisciplinary collaboration and learner independence (Hallenga-Brink et al., 2024; Perišić et al., 2023; Tong & Hu, 2024).

Modular curriculum architecture entails structuring content into units or micro-credentials that focus on certain competencies, concepts, or applications. This strategy enables institutions to incorporate fundamental, intermediate, and advanced AI topics across several disciplines. A modular design may encompass a basic education module on AI ethics, a discipline-specific module on AI tools in health informatics, and an advanced project-based module on AI implementation in business operations. This flexibility enables tailored learning trajectories while preserving curricular consistency (Kajiwara & Kawabata, 2024; Liang, 2024).

A primary advantage of modular design is its ability to provide iterative changes. The advancement of AI knowledge is swift, and conventional static curriculum sometimes fail to stay pertinent. Modular systems allow educators to modify, incorporate, or eliminate specific modules without affecting the entire curriculum. This guarantees that students interact with current information and tools that correspond with industry trends and technical standards. Furthermore, modular curriculum facilitate lifelong learning by enabling alumni and professionals to revisit certain modules as their skill requirements change.

Modularity further facilitates transdisciplinary integration. Institutions can create shared AI modules that are jointly implemented across departments, promoting collaborative instruction and the exchange of ideas. A module on natural language processing could benefit students in linguistics, computer science, and education. This enhances resource efficiency and fosters a multidisciplinary perspective crucial for addressing intricate real-world challenges (Bedewy & Lavicza, 2023; Perišić et al., 2023).

To properly utilize modular design, institutions must synchronize academic policies, learning management systems, and certification frameworks. Digital badges, stackable certificates, and competency transcripts offer transferable acknowledgment of accomplishment. Furthermore, it is essential to verify that modular content upholds academic rigor, effectively supports learning, and matches with broader program objectives. Modular curriculum architecture provides a flexible and robust framework for incorporating AI across several academic fields. It empowers learners, enhances institutional adaptability, and guarantees that higher education stays aligned with the changing landscape of intelligent technologies.

2.3 Aligning Bloom's Digital Taxonomy with AI-Driven Pedagogies

The incorporation of Artificial Intelligence (AI) into curriculum design requires a pedagogical framework to direct instructional tactics and learning outcomes. Bloom's Digital Taxonomy provides a comprehensive framework for aligning AI-enhanced learning activities within a systematic hierarchy of cognitive processes. By matching AI-driven tools and experiences with Bloom's revised taxonomy—from remembering to creating—curriculum designers can facilitate meaningful learning in ways that are both demanding and technologically pertinent (Abalkheel, 2022; Pahi et al., 2024).

Bloom's Digital Taxonomy enhances the original framework by integrating verbs and digital acts relevant to modern technology utilization. In the realm of AI-enhanced education, foundational cognitive skills like recall and comprehension can be supported by AI-driven information retrieval systems, intelligent teaching platforms, and natural language summarization tools. These technologies facilitate knowledge acquisition by offering learners immediate access to curated material, definitions, and contextual insights (Chen et al., 2023; Kerimbayev et al., 2025).

At the intermediate tier of the taxonomy—application and analysis—AI tools can facilitate enhanced engagement with content. Students may utilize machine learning algorithms on real-world datasets or examine AI-generated visualizations to derive conclusions and question assumptions. Artificial intelligence can facilitate inquiry-based learning by producing varied viewpoints, simulating problem scenarios, and providing adaptive simulations that promote analytical reasoning.

At advanced levels—evaluation and creation—AI-driven pedagogies empower learners to assess AI outputs, participate in ethical reasoning, and develop creative projects utilizing generative technologies. Engaging in activities such as evaluating chatbot responses, analyzing algorithmic fairness, or collaboratively creating works using AI systems illustrates this degree of cognitive involvement. These projects compel students to engage with AI while critically examining its logic, intent, and societal implications, thus cultivating metacognitive and ethical skills (Abdelwahab, 2024; Tzirides et al., 2024).

Crucially, synchronizing AI-driven teaching with Bloom's Digital Taxonomy guarantees purposefulness in curriculum development. Educators may align specialized tools, assignments, and evaluations with suitable cognitive levels, so maintaining academic rigor while utilizing the advantages of AI. This alignment facilitates individualized instruction by allowing tailored advancement through the taxonomy according to learner preparedness and performance ("Global Educational Studies Review," 2020; Pahi et al., 2024). Bloom's Digital Taxonomy offers a fundamental framework for creating AI-enhanced educational experiences that are developmentally suitable, intellectually stimulating, and pedagogically robust. When implemented judiciously, this concept converts AI from a mere technology accessory into a structured facilitator of advanced cognitive processes across several fields.

DISCIPLINE-SPECIFIC APPLICATIONS AND STRATEGIES

Discipline-level AI-enhanced learning is most visible with curriculum frameworks and competency-based models providing structure. Different academic disciplines use AI differently, affected by epistemology, educational aims, and evaluation techniques. STEM subjects are ideal for testing how generative AI may aid complex problem-solving, modeling, and experimenting. Investigating AI integration in STEM contexts shows how abstract design concepts are applied in the classroom and highlights discipline-specific possibilities and limitations that affect curricular innovation.

3.1 STEM Disciplines: Enhancing Problem Solving with Generative AI

The incorporation of generative Artificial Intelligence (AI) in Science, Technology, Engineering, and Mathematics (STEM) fields offers disruptive prospects for redefining problem-solving methodologies and altering conventional educational frameworks. STEM disciplines, being fundamentally analytical and solution-focused, benefit from the integration of AI technologies—especially generative AI models like large language models (LLMs), neural networks, and design-oriented AI systems—allowing students and educators to tackle intricate problems with enhanced creativity, accuracy, and computational capability (Black & Chaput, 2024; Liang, 2024; Moundridou et al., 2024).

Generative AI in STEM education can enhance key phases of the problem-solving process, from hypothesis formulation to model simulation. In engineering and design classes, students may utilize AI technologies to create prototypes, conduct simulations, and refine concepts based on immediate feedback. In mathematics and data science, generative AI facilitates learners in modeling patterns, detecting anomalies, and automating the creation of many issue variations for practice or evaluation (Moundridou et al., 2024; Tran & Murphy, 2023). These applications not only improve efficiency but also promote deeper engagement with knowledge through iterative, exploratory learning.

Furthermore, the utilization of generative AI facilitates transdisciplinary integration across STEM fields. Students may work on projects integrating AI with robotics, environmental modeling, or biomedical engineering, thereby enhancing computational thinking and systems analysis. AI techniques can elucidate intricate concepts—such as fluid dynamics or chemical structures—by visualizing and simplifying abstract data. This enables learners to interact more intuitively with scientific models and simulations, fostering confidence and conceptual mastery (AlShaikh et al., 2024; Black & Chaput, 2024; Saba et al., 2023).

Generative AI fosters inclusion and customisation in STEM education. AI can deliver personalized problem sets, provide clues or alternate explanations, and track student progress in real time using adaptive platforms. These skills are particularly advantageous in expansive or heterogeneous classes where differentiated education is required. Educators can concentrate on fostering inquiry, guiding collaboration, and evaluating higher-order reasoning (Du, 2022; Pahi et al., 2024; Swiecki et al., 2022).

The incorporation of generative AI in STEM education requires ethical and pedagogical deliberation. Students should be instructed not just in the utilization of these tools but also in the critical assessment of their outputs, comprehension of their limitations, and contemplation of the societal ramifications of AI-driven solutions. The responsible application of AI must be integrated into instructional design to guarantee that it enhances rather than supplants genuine problem-solving. Generative AI significantly enhances STEM education, allowing students to address challenges in more dynamic, data-intensive, and innovative manners.

3.2 Humanities and Social Sciences: AI in Discourse, Interpretation, and Content Creation

The integration of Artificial Intelligence (AI) into the Humanities and Social Sciences (HSS) in higher education presents new opportunities for enhancing conversation, improving interpretive approaches, and broadening creative expression. Despite the belief that HSS topics are ill-suited for technological integration, AI provides distinctive advantages that correspond with the analytical, reflexive, and narrative-oriented characteristics of these disciplines (Chapinal-Heras & Díaz-Sánchez, 2023; Christou, 2023; Zailuddin et al., 2024). Utilizing AI tools—such as natural language processing, sentiment analysis, and generative content platforms—students and academics can interact with texts, data, and cultural phenomena in a more critical and creative manner.

AI-driven discourse analysis advances the examination of language, politics, and society by facilitating extensive textual investigation. Natural language processing methods can examine political speeches, media narratives, historical documents, or literary corpora, uncovering trends, biases, and ideological frameworks. This computational perspective enhances conventional hermeneutic methods, promoting a hybrid approach of near and distant reading. In fields such as sociology and communication studies, these tools facilitate the extraction and visualization of themes from social media, policy documents, or interview transcripts (Cowhitt et al., 2024; Punziano et al., 2022; Vicari & Kirby, 2022).

AI-assisted annotation, translation, and semiotic analysis also enhance interpretive work in the Humanities. Machine learning algorithms can facilitate the detection of intertextuality, the classification of rhetorical tactics, or the comparison of story structures across diverse cultures and genres. This enables students to critically analyze meaning-making processes and cultural creation through multidisciplinary and technologically enhanced perspectives (Fyfe, 2022; Neumann & Waight, 2020). Furthermore, digital humanities initiatives utilizing AI tools frequently foster collaborative, inquiry-driven learning settings that integrate historical research, ethical analysis, and technological proficiency.

The generative capabilities of AI have revolutionized content creation in the arts and cultural studies. Students may engage with AI-generated poetry, art, music, or film scripts to investigate authorship, originality, and the aesthetics of automation. (Black & Chaput, 2024; Jen & Salam, 2024) These investigations offer a substantial basis for discourse concerning intellectual property, creativity, and the human role in a progressively mechanized world. In journalism and media studies, students may utilize AI to replicate newsroom operations, automate fundamental reporting tasks, or identify falsehoods. The implementation of AI in HSS necessitates a critical approach, focusing on concerns related to bias, agency, and representation. By integrating these considerations into curriculum design, educators may develop digital humanists and ethically aware social scientists capable of navigating and influencing AI-mediated environments.

3.3 Health and Business Fields: Simulation, Forecasting, and Decision Support

The incorporation of Artificial Intelligence (AI) into health and business education signifies a notable progression in applied learning, allowing students to participate in simulation-based environments, predictive modeling, and data-driven decision-making (Gibbons et al., 2021; Mohsen, 2023; Ortíz-Barrios et al., 2023). These domains, intrinsically intricate and context-dependent, gain from AI's ability to analyze extensive datasets, model dynamic systems, and facilitate real-time, evidence-informed decisions. As AI technologies become more integrated into professional practice, curriculum design must adapt to equip future healthcare providers and corporate leaders to critically and ethically employ these tools.

In health education, AI-driven simulations improve clinical training by mimicking patient interactions, diagnostic procedures, and emergency situations. Machine learning algorithms enable virtual patients to exhibit diverse symptoms according to user interactions, allowing trainees to enhance their diagnostic reasoning, communication abilities, and procedural knowledge in a risk-free setting. These simulations enhance adaptive learning by customizing feedback and scenarios according to the learner's performance, therefore augmenting retention and proficiency. AI-enhanced image recognition is likewise revolutionizing radiology and pathology education, providing immediate analysis of medical pictures and enhancing diagnostic precision.

In business sectors, AI facilitates predictive forecasting and decision-making assistance in finance, marketing, operations, and strategic management. Students can utilize AI-driven dashboards, scenario planning instruments, and algorithmic trading simulations to examine market patterns, evaluate risks, and enhance methods.

For instance, demand forecasting tools can model supply chain scenarios under diverse conditions, whereas consumer analytics platforms can facilitate segmentation, personalization, and campaign optimization. These applications connect theory and practice, fostering data literacy, strategic thinking, and agility (Badr & Ahmed, 2023; Rathipriya et al., 2022).

The incorporation of AI in both fields requires ethical and regulatory cognizance. Health-related concerns, including patient data confidentiality, algorithmic bias, and the limitations of machine-assisted diagnosis, require attention. In business, the issues of transparency, accountability, and labor automation necessitate rigorous examination. Educators must create learning experiences that integrate ethical reasoning and policy frameworks with technical skills. Integrating AI-driven simulation, forecasting, and decision-support technologies can transform health and business curriculum from static material delivery to immersive, systems-oriented learning. This corresponds with industry expectations and cultivates knowledgeable, flexible, and morally grounded people capable of navigating AI-enhanced situations.

3.4 Case Studies of AI Integration in Higher Education

Recent implementations of artificial intelligence in higher education illustrate both the revolutionary promise and the practical constraints of AI-enhanced curricula. At a prominent public institution, generative AI techniques were included into engineering and computer science curricula to facilitate design prototyping, code optimization, and simulation-driven problem solving. Students indicated heightened interest and efficiency in project development, while professors saw enhancements in iterative learning processes. Challenges arose concerning academic integrity and excessive dependence on automated outputs, leading the school to revise assessment techniques and prioritize rigorous review of AI-generated outcomes. This scenario demonstrates that the efficacy of AI relies on explicit pedagogical framing rather than unregulated access to tools.

A second scenario from a business school pertained to the application of AI-driven learning analytics to customize feedback and suggest learning pathways in introductory management courses. Although retention rates and formative assessment scores increased, the system initially did not support students with restricted digital access or irregular online engagement. This constraint underscored the peril of data-driven exclusion and prompted institutional investments in infrastructural support and equitable data governance standards. The event highlighted the necessity of synchronizing technology innovation with equity-focused execution.

A humanities-oriented institution implemented AI-assisted conversation analysis and writing support tools in its social science and literary departments. Faculty deliberately framed AI as a collaborative ally instead of an authoritative entity, necessitating that students evaluate algorithmic analyses and contemplate ethical ramifications. This method led to enhanced critical engagement, increased awareness of bias, and improved metacognitive abilities. Student feedback underscored the importance of supervised experimentation in preference to automatic ease.

These cases collectively demonstrate that effective AI integration in higher education is not just determined by technological capability. Successes arise when AI tools are integrated into deliberate educational frameworks, faculty facilitation, and ethical consciousness. Conversely, failures offer essential insights on assessment reform, equality protections, and the necessity for human-centered supervision. These observations indicate that scalable AI deployment necessitates ongoing reflection, contextual awareness, and institutional learning rather than a singular implementation.

FACULTY PREPAREDNESS AND CAPACITY BUILDING

4.1 Faculty Digital Readiness and Professional Learning Communities

The efficacy of AI-integrated courses depends not just on technology infrastructure but, importantly, on faculty preparedness and pedagogical competence. Faculty members are the principal agents of curriculum transformation, and their capacity to effectively incorporate artificial intelligence (AI) into instructional design necessitates a strong basis of digital preparedness and ongoing professional development. Establishing dynamic professional learning communities (PLCs) is crucial for developing collective capacity and promoting a culture of innovation in higher education institutions (Herron & Wolfe, 2021; Karim, 2024; Keese et al., 2023).

Faculty digital readiness includes technical competence, pedagogical expertise, and critical awareness regarding developing technologies. Although numerous educators have basic digital competencies, the use of AI presents additional layers of complexity. This encompasses comprehending machine learning principles, utilizing AI-driven tools for content creation and evaluation, and addressing ethical issues including data privacy, algorithmic bias, and automation (Must-Have Competencies and Skills in Our New AI World: A Synthesis for Educational Reform, 2024; Nguyen, 2025). Consequently, digital preparedness is dynamic and requires ongoing enhancement through iterative, practical interaction with AI tools in educational settings.

Professional learning communities provide a collaborative framework for fostering this preparedness. Professional Learning Communities (PLCs) are organized networks in which educators collectively develop knowledge, exchange effective practices, participate in peer mentoring, and jointly address instructional issues. In the realm of AI integration, PLCs can function as incubators for experimenting with AI-enhanced pedagogies, assessing emerging technologies, and collaboratively designing AI-infused learning modules across several disciplines (Ng et al., 2023; Pahi et al., 2024; Youn et al., 2024). This collaborative method not only democratizes knowledge but also alleviates emotions of isolation and reluctance among academics adapting to technological change.

Furthermore, PLCs facilitate reflective practice and multidisciplinary discourse, which are crucial for addressing the sociotechnical ramifications of AI. Faculty from various disciplines can investigate the alignment of AI with their academic frameworks, educational objectives, and student requirements. This cross-pollination enhances curriculum development and promotes collective accountability for ethical implementation (Kajiwara & Kawabata, 2024; Nguyen, 2025).

Institutional support is essential for the sustainability of these communities. Universities must allocate resources towards teacher development frameworks that encompass organized Professional Learning Communities, access to artificial intelligence technologies and instructional design assistance, and recognition mechanisms that promote creativity. Leadership endorsement, time allocation, and inclusive participation are essential elements for ensuring that Professional Learning Communities (PLCs) serve as catalysts for ongoing curricular innovation. Faculty digital preparedness and professional learning communities are essential for the effective and ethical integration of AI into higher education curricula. They enable educators to lead with assurance, instruct flexibly, and cooperate effectively in the era of intelligent technology.

In addition to informal professional learning communities, universities ought to implement structured faculty development programs centered on AI literacy and digital pedagogy. These may encompass tiered AI literacy programs, interdisciplinary teaching fellowships, and incentive-driven innovation awards that promote experimentation with AI-enhanced pedagogy. Structured programs enable professors to graduate from basic comprehension to sophisticated pedagogical implementation, while interdisciplinary fellowships promote collaboration across academic fields. Incentive methods, such as promotional recognition or awards for teaching innovation, further validate AI involvement as a scholarly pursuit rather than a mere technical talent.

4.2 Co-Creation of AI-Integrated Learning Experiences

The collaborative development of AI-integrated learning experiences signifies a revolutionary method in curriculum design, where faculty, instructional designers, and technology experts jointly create pedagogical solutions that utilize the capabilities of artificial intelligence (Moundridou et al., 2024). Transcending hierarchical methods of curricular innovation, co-creation acknowledges the collective expertise of academic communities and promotes shared ownership in the development of learning environments that are technologically sophisticated and pedagogically effective.

AI tools, albeit potent, necessitate contextualization within discipline-specific educational objectives and ethical frameworks. Co-creation enables professors to synchronize AI integration with their epistemological perspectives and pedagogical philosophies. For example, a language instructor might investigate the application of AI-generated text in narrative development, whereas a business faculty member could utilize AI tools for market modeling and forecasting (Giray et al., 2024; Mah & Gross, 2024; Nguyen, 2025). In all instances, collaborative design guarantees that the chosen tools and tasks are pertinent, rigorous, and attuned to learners' requirements.

Instructional designers are essential in this process by facilitating the alignment of learning outcomes, assessment methodologies, and digital pedagogies. They facilitate the conversion of educational objectives into scalable learning modules, integrating AI tools in ways that augment rather than detract from the learning experience (Madigan et al., 2023; Ng et al., 2023). Furthermore, technology experts provide technical insights about tool functionalities, integration standards, and data governance stipulations. This triadic collaboration among teachers, designers, and technologists establishes the basis for sustainable, cross-functional innovation ecosystems within universities.

Co-creation facilitates the integration of student perspectives into curriculum development. By involving learners in the design and assessment of AI-enhanced activities, instructors can gain a deeper insight into student expectations, preferences, and ethical considerations. This interactive strategy cultivates a sense of agency and belonging, while advancing digital citizenship and critical AI literacy.

Moreover, co-creation enhances institutional agility. As AI technologies advance, curriculum must remain flexible. Continuous collaboration among stakeholders guarantees that content is regularly updated and consistently aligned with evolving best practices. This method also enables the dissemination of scalable models (Pahi et al., 2024; Southworth et al., 2023) and toolkits among departments, fostering institutional consistency in AI implementation.

The co-creation of AI-integrated learning experiences is not simply a strategy for implementation; it is a pedagogical necessity. It cultivates a collaborative culture of inquiry, promotes interdisciplinary innovation, and guarantees that AI serves as a tool for empowerment rather than disruption in the academic experience.

Integrating student perspectives is crucial for substantive AI curriculum development. Surveys, reflective journals, and interactive design workshops enable learners in expressing their expectations, concerns, and ethical viewpoints concerning the utilization of AI. Collaborative design methodologies—where students jointly develop assignments, assess AI technologies, or suggest usage protocols—enhance agency and digital citizenship. These participatory techniques guarantee that AI integration aligns with learner realities and cultivates trust, relevance, and collective accountability in educational innovation.

4.3 Mitigating Resistance and Addressing Ethical Concerns

The incorporation of Artificial Intelligence (AI) into higher education curricula frequently encounters differing levels of opposition from faculty members. This reluctance may arise from perceived challenges to academic independence, apprehensions around technology displacement, or unease with unfamiliar instructional techniques. Faculty apprehension, compounded by genuine ethical concerns like as algorithmic bias, data privacy, spying, and the opacity of AI systems, must be recognized and aggressively addressed to guarantee responsible and inclusive adoption.

Addressing resistance necessitates a comprehensive strategy rooted in empathy, communication, and professional empowerment. Faculty development programs should extend beyond technical instruction to establish secure environments for critical inquiry and reflection. By fostering dialogues on AI's educational implications, disciplinary significance, and institutional effects, educators can examine AI's role not as a substitute, but as an enhancement of their teaching methodologies. Recognizing their knowledge and designating them as co-leaders in the AI integration process enhances agency and fosters trust (Giray et al., 2024; Moundridou et al., 2024; Pahi et al., 2024).

Ethical considerations must be tackled through deliberate curricular design and institutional policies. Faculty must be prepared to examine the ethical implications of AI tools utilized in instruction, especially concerning student data, predictive analytics, and automated decision-making. Incorporating digital ethics into training modules allows educators to identify potential harms and use mitigation techniques (Adams et al., 2023; Akgün & Greenhow, 2021; Dieterle et al., 2022). Transparent grading rubrics can enhance AI-generated feedback to promote fairness and accountability. Informed consent protocols can be implemented when AI systems monitor student behavior or participation.

Interdisciplinary collaboration is essential for addressing these difficulties. Involving specialists in computer science, law, philosophy, and educational technology can offer a comprehensive framework for comprehending and addressing the societal ramifications of AI. Ethical advisory boards or institutional review processes can govern the selection and implementation of AI tools in accordance with academic ideals and regulatory regulations (Tzirides et al., 2024). Institutions must have explicit ethical norms that embody concepts of openness, equity, inclusivity, and human oversight. Faculty must participate in the formulation of these policies to guarantee they embody varied perspectives and contextual realities.

Resolving opposition and ethical issues is not a secondary task; it is fundamental to the legitimacy and sustainability of AI in education. Equipping teachers with the necessary tools, voice, and ethical frameworks to critically engage with AI guarantees that technological progress is consistent with humanistic ideals and academic integrity. Ethical governance frameworks, including UNESCO's Recommendation on the Ethics of Artificial Intelligence and IEEE's Ethically Aligned Design, offer pragmatic principles for the ethical implementation of AI in education. Incorporating these concepts into curriculum design, faculty development, and institutional policy guarantees transparency, accountability, and human oversight. This alignment converts ethics from a theoretical issue into a practical application inside AI-augmented educational settings.

EVALUATION, SCALABILITY, AND FUTURE READINESS

5.1 Assessing the Impact of AI-Infused Curricula on Student Learning

As Artificial Intelligence (AI) becomes more integrated into higher education curricula, robust evaluation techniques are crucial to assess its true effect on student learning. The evaluation of AI-integrated curriculum should prioritize quantifiable learning results, cognitive involvement, and skill enhancement, rather than relying on anecdotal evidence or technological novelty. Effective assessment techniques validate the effectiveness of AI-enhanced instruction and inform ongoing curricular revision and instructional enhancement (Ma et al., 2024; Vasconcelos & Santos, 2023).

The initial round of evaluation entails defining explicit, AI-aligned learning objectives. These objectives may encompass students' capacity to critically interact with AI tools, use AI-assisted problem-solving techniques, or exhibit ethical reasoning in AI-mediated situations. These objectives must be specific to each subject while also corresponding with overarching competencies, including digital literacy, analytical reasoning, and data interpretation (Lo, 2025; Tzirides et al., 2024; Yang et al., 2025). Assessment procedures must be designed to evaluate both subject mastery and metacognitive development.

Artificial intelligence can function as an effective evaluative instrument. Intelligent tutoring systems and learning analytics platforms provide instantaneous data on learner behavior, advancement, and areas of difficulty. Data-driven insights facilitate formative assessment and prompt intervention. Nonetheless, dependence on algorithmic measures must be harmonized with human-centered methodologies that emphasize introspection, creativity, and critical thinking—elements of learning that AI cannot entirely measure. Qualitative assessments, including portfolios, reflective essays, and peer comments, are vital supplements to computerized evaluations (Grieve et al., 2021; Ma et al., 2024; Swiecki et al., 2022). Crucially, the assessment of AI-integrated courses must also take into account equity and accessibility. Data must be disaggregated to analyze how various student demographics—considering factors such as previous digital exposure, socioeconomic status, or language proficiency—interact with AI-enhanced learning environments. This research guarantees that AI does not unintentionally exacerbate educational disparities or establish new obstacles to participation.

Moreover, impact assessment must encompass not only academic success but also attitudinal and behavioral metrics, including student motivation, confidence in utilizing AI tools, and feelings of fairness and agency. Mixed-methods research strategies that integrate quantitative measurements with qualitative input offer a comprehensive knowledge of impact (Vieriu & Petrea, 2025).

Evaluating the efficacy of AI-integrated curriculum is a continuous process rather than a singular event. Institutions must cultivate a culture of evidence-based innovation where student learning outcomes dictate the selection, adoption, and refinement of AI technology. This dedication guarantees that educational transformation is rooted in pedagogical integrity and student-centered achievement.

To comprehensively assess the long-term effects of AI-integrated curriculum, institutions must implement longitudinal evaluation models that transcend immediate academic outcomes. Monitoring graduate employability, the evolution of critical thinking, ethical reasoning, and civic participation across time offers a more thorough evaluation of educational effectiveness. Mixed-method techniques that integrate learning analytics, alumni surveys, employer feedback, and reflective portfolios allow universities to analyze the impact of AI-enhanced learning on professional adaptability and social responsibility. This longitudinal evidence advocates for ongoing curriculum enhancement and guides policy decisions concerning the sustainable incorporation of AI in higher education.

5.2 Scaling AI Integration Across Institutions

Although pilot programs in Artificial Intelligence (AI)-integrated curriculum offer significant proof of concept, substantial transformation in higher education necessitates the expansion of these initiatives throughout institutional frameworks. Scaling AI integration requires more than just replication of technology tools; it necessitates a purposeful alignment of infrastructure, policy, education, and institutional culture. Effective scaling guarantees that AI evolves into a sustainable and equitable element of the educational framework, available to a variety of learners across disciplines, campuses, and modalities (Southworth et al., 2023; Tzirides et al., 2024).

The cornerstone of scalable AI integration is institutional vision and leadership dedication. Universities must define explicit objectives for AI integration that correspond with their academic purpose, workforce development initiatives, and digital transformation strategies. Strategic plans must delineate key domains for AI integration—such as fundamental curricula, multidisciplinary initiatives, or ongoing education—and establish frameworks for resource allocation, oversight, and continuous enhancement.

Infrastructure preparedness is an essential facilitator of scalability. Institutions must allocate resources to scalable learning management systems (LMS), cloud computing infrastructures, and secure data ecosystems that facilitate extensive AI tools and analytics. The enhancement of faculty ability through organized professional development programs that focus on both technical proficiency and pedagogical design is equally vital. Faculty champions and interdisciplinary teams can establish communities of practice, enabling peer-to-peer knowledge exchange and experimentation with scalable instructional methods (Eynon et al., 2024; Lee et al., 2023; Maimon & Schneider, 2023).

Scalability necessitates adaptation. AI integration must consider variations among disciplines, student demographics, and types of institutions. Modular curriculum design, open educational resources (OER), and configurable AI toolkits provide adaptable deployment while maintaining contextual significance (Pahi et al., 2024; Tzirides et al., 2024). Institutions may gain advantages by creating AI integration hubs or centers of excellence that aggregate resources, offer consultation, and assess developing technology.

Collaboration between institutions enhances scalability. Collaborations with other institutions, educational technology providers, and industry partners can establish common standards, minimize redundancy, and foster innovation. Programs like AI curriculum consortia or collaborative faculty development networks provide economies of scale and facilitate information exchange (Feuerriegel et al., 2023; Southworth et al., 2023).

Ethical scaling should serve as a fundamental concept. Institutions must guarantee that AI implementation adheres to principles of justice, transparency, and data stewardship. Consistent impact evaluations and participatory governance frameworks facilitate the protection of responsible development. Expanding AI integration within universities necessitates systemic thinking, coordinated efforts, and a sustained commitment to pedagogical innovation. When carefully executed, scalable AI efforts can cultivate robust, future-oriented learning environments that advantage both learners and society as a whole.

5.3 Foresight and Futures Thinking in AI Curriculum Development

The swift advancement of Artificial Intelligence (AI) technology necessitates a proactive and anticipatory strategy for curriculum creation. Instead of only responding to technology changes, institutions should integrate futures thinking and strategic foresight into their educational planning. This attitude allows educators to identify future trends, foresee skill requirements, and develop curricula that are adaptable, resilient, and morally sound in a swiftly changing global environment (Khadri, 2022; Kim et al., 2021; Pouru & Wilenius, 2021; Spanjol et al., 2022).

Futures thinking entails the methodical investigation of credible scenarios and the enduring implications of technological and societal transformations. In the realm of AI curriculum development, this entails transcending existing applications to explore how AI may transform knowledge domains, learning settings, and professional identities in the forthcoming decade (Petridou & Lao, 2024; Wang & Lester, 2023). Through horizon scanning, trend analysis, and scenario planning, educators can discern pivotal change agents—such as AI governance, quantum computing, neurotechnology, or digital labor—and integrate them into curricular dialogues and educational objectives.

Strategic foresight in AI education fosters innovation by promoting design for adaptation. Curricula must be modular, interdisciplinary, and frequently revised to incorporate developing tools, ethical discussions, and practical applications (Hazari, 2024; Tzirides et al., 2024; Xia et al., 2024). This necessitates institutions to implement flexible review processes, include stakeholder input, and foster ongoing collaboration among academic fields, industry specialists, and policymakers. This collaboration guarantees that AI-enhanced education stays pertinent, aligned with future demands, and attuned to both local and global requirements.

Incorporating futures literacy into curriculum development enhances students' capacity to act as agents of change. By engaging in critical inquiry, ethical reflection, and speculative design, learners can investigate future scenarios, contest deterministic narratives of AI, and envision inclusive, sustainable technology futures. Motivating students to collaboratively develop learning pathways and participate in anticipatory governance enhances their civic and digital competencies (Ng et al., 2023; Xia et al., 2024).

Futures thinking must be grounded on ethical foresight. Curriculum planners must examine not only the capabilities of AI but also its ethical implications and intended beneficiaries. This entails addressing issues of equity, power, environmental sustainability, and global justice. Prudent foresight guarantees that AI incorporation in education corresponds with overarching humanistic and global objectives. Including foresight and futures thinking into AI curriculum development transforms education from passive adaptation to proactive leadership. It provides institutions and learners with the resources to influence rather than be influenced by the forthcoming AI-driven futures.

5.4 Equity-Oriented Models for AI Access

Ensuring equitable access to artificial intelligence in higher education is a significant concern as institutions progressively incorporate AI into pedagogy, learning, and evaluation. In the absence of deliberate equity-focused frameworks, the implementation of AI may exacerbate pre-existing digital disparities associated with socioeconomic position, geographic location, and institutional capability. Mitigating these discrepancies necessitates strategic methods that emphasize accessibility, affordability, and inclusive infrastructure in conjunction with technological advancement.

A viable concept entails the utilization of open-source and cost-effective AI platforms that diminish reliance on proprietary technologies. Open-source tools enable schools to tailor applications to local requirements, enhance transparency, and encourage collaborative development among universities. When integrated with low-bandwidth design and offline capabilities, such platforms can enhance AI-assisted learning for students in resource-limited settings. Institutional licensing agreements that offer campus-wide access alleviate disparities by guaranteeing that AI technologies are accessible to everybody, rather being restricted to individuals who can afford separate subscriptions.

Government-led initiatives are essential in fostering fair access to AI. Public investment in digital infrastructure, national AI education frameworks, and shared cloud-based resources facilitates the scaling of AI integration in institutions while ensuring uniform quality standards. Inter-university consortia and public-private partnerships can enhance resource sharing, collaborative faculty training, and the establishment of unified ethical principles, while minimizing redundancy and disparities in capacity development across regions.

Equity-focused AI access at the institutional level necessitates intentional policy alignment. Universities must incorporate inclusion criteria into procurement decisions, data governance frameworks, and curriculum development. Support methods, such device lending programs, digital literacy training, and specialized academic assistance, guarantee that AI-enhanced learning settings are accessible to varied student demographics. Ultimately, equal access to AI is not merely a technical concern but a matter of governance and ethical obligation. Sustainable models prioritize human-centered design, shared accountability, and ongoing assessment to guarantee that AI functions as an instrument for enhancing participation instead of perpetuating exclusion.

CONCLUSION

The incorporation of Artificial Intelligence (AI) into higher education signifies a fundamental transformation in institutional methodologies for teaching, learning, and curriculum development. This chapter has illustrated that AI-enhanced education transcends technology fields; it is a transformative influence that encompasses all academic disciplines, redefining the learner experience, educational frameworks, and institutional functions.

By adopting design frameworks such as backward design, competency-based education, and modular curriculum structures, institutions may integrate AI effectively while adapting to the changing needs of industry and society. The integration of AI tools with Bloom's Digital Taxonomy guarantees that learning is both developmentally suitable and intellectually demanding, while specialized applications in STEM, Humanities, Health, and Business demonstrate the versatility and adaptability of AI technology.

Faculty are pivotal to this transformation. Enhancing their digital preparedness via professional learning communities and collaborative co-creation frameworks cultivates both capability and dedication. The ethical implications of AI must be perpetually addressed through institutional policies, multidisciplinary discourse, and critical pedagogy to guarantee that AI promotes rather than diminishes humanistic and democratic principles in education.

Furthermore, as AI tools and capacities advance swiftly, institutions must participate in foresight and futures thinking. This entails anticipating long-term consequences, developing adaptable curricula, and equipping students not only to navigate the future but to influence it responsibly. Strategic planning for scalability and effect evaluation is crucial to ensure coherence, inclusion, and sustainability within the academic ecosystem. In summary, an effective AI-integrated curriculum is characterized by technological innovation, instructional goal, ethical foundation, and global awareness. By fostering a culture of ongoing research, collaborative design, and adaptive leadership, higher education can fully harness AI to empower both learners and instructors in a deeply human-centered manner.

REFERENCES

Abalkheel, A. (2022). Amalgamating Bloom's Taxonomy and Artificial Intelligence to Face the Challenges of Online EFL Learning Amid Post-COVID-19 In Saudi Arabia. *International Journal of English Language and Literature Studies*, *11*(1), 16–30. DOI: 10.18488/5019.v11i1.4409

Abdelwahab, M. (2024). Artificial Intelligence Common Good in Research and Academics. *The Scholarship Without Borders Journal*, *3*(1). Advance online publication. DOI: 10.57229/2834-2267.1058

Adams, C., Pente, P., Lemermeyer, G., & Rockwell, G. (2023). Ethical principles for artificial intelligence in K-12 education. *Computers and Education Artificial Intelligence*, *4*, 100131. DOI: 10.1016/j.caeai.2023.100131

Akgün, S., & Greenhow, C. (2021). Artificial intelligence in education: Addressing ethical challenges in K-12 settings [Review of Artificial intelligence in education: Addressing ethical challenges in K-12 settings]. AI and Ethics, 2(3), 431. Springer Nature. https://doi.org/DOI: 10.1007/s43681-021-00096-7

AlShaikh, R., Al-Malki, N., & Almasre, M. (2024). The implementation of the cognitive theory of multimedia learning in the design and evaluation of an AI educational video assistant utilizing large language models. *Heliyon*, *10*(3), e25361. Advance online publication. DOI: 10.1016/j.heliyon.2024.e25361 PMID: 38352730

At the Crossroads of Innovation. Embracing AI to Foster Deep Learning in the College Classroom. (2024). https://er.educause.edu/articles/2024/7/at-the-crossroads-of-innovation-embracing-ai-to-foster-deep-learning-in-the-college-classroom

Badr, H., & Ahmed, W. (2023). A Comprehensive Analysis of Demand Prediction Models in Supply Chain Management. *American Journal of Industrial and Business Management*, *13*(12), 1353–1376. DOI: 10.4236/ajibm.2023.1312075

Badru, L. O., Vani, V., Lingam, G. I., & Khan, M. G. M. (2022). MERN Stack Web-Based Education Management Information Systems for Pacific Island Countries. *SN Computer Science*, *4*(1), 70. Advance online publication. DOI: 10.1007/s42979-022-01457-7 PMID: 36467856

Bedewy, S. E., & Lavicza, Z. (2023). STEAM + X - Extending the transdisciplinary of STEAM-based educational approaches: A theoretical contribution. *Thinking Skills and Creativity*, *48*, 101299. DOI: 10.1016/j.tsc.2023.101299

Bhutoria, A. (2022). Personalized education and Artificial Intelligence in the United States, China, and India: A systematic review using a Human-In-The-Loop model [Review of Personalized education and Artificial Intelligence in the United States, China, and India: A systematic review using a Human-In-The-Loop model]. Computers and Education Artificial Intelligence, 3, 100068. Elsevier BV. https://doi.org/DOI: 10.1016/j.caeai.2022.100068

Binhammad, M. H. Y., Othman, A., Abuljadayel, L., Mheiri, H. A., Alkaabi, M., & Almarri, M. (2024). Investigating How Generative AI Can Create Personalized Learning Materials Tailored to Individual Student Needs. *Creative Education, 15*(7), 1499–1523. DOI: 10.4236/ce.2024.157091

Black, J., & Chaput, T. (2024). A Discussion of Artificial Intelligence in Visual Art Education. *Journal of Computer and Communications, 12*(5), 71–85. DOI: 10.4236/jcc.2024.125005

Carlgren, D. (2020). Competency-based curriculum transition: A conceptual framework. *The Journal of Competency-Based Education, 6*(2), e1229. Advance online publication. DOI: 10.1002/cbe2.1229

Chapinal-Heras, D., & Díaz-Sánchez, C. (2023). A review of AI applications in Human Sciences research [Review of A review of AI applications in Human Sciences research]. Digital Applications in Archaeology and Cultural Heritage, 30. Elsevier BV. https://doi.org/DOI: 10.1016/j.daach.2023.e00288

Chen, B., Zhu, X., & Díaz del Castillo H, F. (2023). Integrating generative AI in knowledge building. *Computers and Education Artificial Intelligence, 5*, 100184. DOI: 10.1016/j.caeai.2023.100184

Chiu, T. K. F., Ahmad, Z., Ismailov, M., & Sanusi, I. T. (2024). What are artificial intelligence literacy and competency? A comprehensive framework to support them. *Computers and Education Open, 6*, 100171. DOI: 10.1016/j.caeo.2024.100171

Christou, P. (2023). The Use of Artificial Intelligence (AI) in Qualitative Research for Theory Development. *The Qualitative Report*. Advance online publication. DOI: 10.46743/2160-3715/2023.6536

Cowhitt, T., Brown, J. T., & Antonio, A. L. (2024). The emergence and evolution of ambiguous ideas: An innovative application of social network analysis to support systematic literature reviews. *Scientometrics, 129*(11), 7005–7033. Advance online publication. DOI: 10.1007/s11192-024-05144-7

Dieterle, E., Dede, C., & Walker, M. E. (2022). The cyclical ethical effects of using artificial intelligence in education. *AI & Society*, *39*(2), 633–643. DOI: 10.1007/s00146-022-01497-w PMID: 36185064

Du, Y. (2022). Application of the Data-Driven Educational Decision-Making System to Curriculum Optimization of Higher Education. *Wireless Communications and Mobile Computing*, *1*(1), 5823515. Advance online publication. DOI: 10.1155/2022/5823515

Egunjobi, D., & Adeyeye, O. (2024). Revolutionizing Learning: The Impact of Augmented Reality (AR) And Artificial Intelligence (AI on Education. *International Journal of Research Publication and Reviews*, *5*(10), 1157–1170. DOI: 10.55248/gengpi.5.1024.2734

Erduran, S., & Levrini, O. (2024). The impact of artificial intelligence on scientific practices: An emergent area of research for science education. *International Journal of Science Education*, *46*(18), 1982–1989. DOI: 10.1080/09500693.2024.2306604

Eynon, B., Iuzzini, J., Keith, H., Loepp, E., & Weber, N. (2024). Realizing the Promise of Professional Learning for Teaching, Equity, and Change. *Change*, *56*(1), 55–64. DOI: 10.1080/00091383.2024.2297637

Feuerriegel, S., Hartmann, J., Janiesch, C., & Zschech, P. (2023). Generative AI. *Business & Information Systems Engineering*, *66*(1), 111–126. DOI: 10.1007/s12599-023-00834-7

Fyfe, P. (2022). How to cheat on your final paper: Assigning AI for student writing. *AI & Society*, *38*(4), 1395–1405. DOI: 10.1007/s00146-022-01397-z

Gallagher, S. E., & Savage, T. (2020). Challenge-based learning in higher education: An exploratory literature review. *Teaching in Higher Education*, *28*(6), 1135–1157. DOI: 10.1080/13562517.2020.1863354

García-Martínez, I., Batanero, J. M. F., Cerero, J. F., & León, S. P. (2023). Analysing the Impact of Artificial Intelligence and Computational Sciences on Student Performance: Systematic Review and Meta-analysis. *Journal of New Approaches in Educational Research*, *12*(1), 171–197. DOI: 10.7821/naer.2023.1.1240

Gibbons, B., Fernando, M., & Spedding, T. A. (2021). Innovation Through Developing a Total Enterprise Computer Simulation: Teaching Responsible Decision Making. *Journal of Management Education*, *46*(1), 16–42. DOI: 10.1177/1052562920987591

Giray, L., Silos, P. Y. D., Adornado, A., Buelo, R. J. V., Galas, E. M., Reyes-Chua, E., Santiago, C. S., & Ulanday, M. (2024). Use and Impact of Artificial Intelligence in Philippine Higher Education: Reflections from Instructors and Administrators. *Internet Reference Services Quarterly*, *28*(3), 315–338. DOI: 10.1080/10875301.2024.2352746

Global Educational Studies Review. (2020). *Global Educational Studies Review.*, DOI: 10.31703/gesr

Grieve, R., Woodley, J., Hunt, S. E., & McKay, A. B. (2021). Student fears of oral presentations and public speaking in higher education: A qualitative survey. *Journal of Further and Higher Education*, *45*(9), 1281–1293. DOI: 10.1080/0309877X.2021.1948509

Hallenga-Brink, S. C., de Hei, M., Sjoer, E., Carlsson, C. J., Georgsson, F., Keller, E., McCartan, C., Enelund, M., Lyng, R., & Admiraal, W. (2024). Curriculum Agility principles for transformative innovation in engineering education. *European Journal of Engineering Education*, *1*. Advance online publication. DOI: 10.1080/03043797.2024.2398165

Hazari, S. (2024). Justification and Roadmap for Artificial Intelligence (AI) Literacy Courses in Higher Education. *Journal of Educational Research and Practice*, *14*(1). Advance online publication. DOI: 10.5590/JERAP.2024.14.1.07

Herron, J., & Wolfe, K. A. (2021). University Innovation Hubs & Technology-Enhanced Learning in K12 Environments. https://link.springer.com/article/10.1007/s11528-020-00575-4

Jen, S. L., & Salam, A. R. (2024). A Systematic Review on The Use of Artificial Intelligence in Writing [Review of A Systematic Review on The Use of Artificial Intelligence in Writing]. *International Journal of Academic Research in Progressive Education and Development*, *13*(1). Advance online publication. DOI: 10.6007/IJARPED/v13-i1/20584

Kajiwara, Y., & Kawabata, K. (2024). AI literacy for ethical use of chatbot: Will students accept AI ethics? *Computers and Education Artificial Intelligence*, *6*, 100251. DOI: 10.1016/j.caeai.2024.100251

Karim, A. M. (2024). Adapting to Change: A Qualitative Study on Continuous Professional Learning among Adult Learners. *International Journal of Academic Research in Business & Social Sciences*, *14*(11). Advance online publication. DOI: 10.6007/IJARBSS/v14-i11/23500

Keese, J., Ford, D. J., Luke, S. E., & Vaughn, S. M. (2023). An individualized Professional Development Approach for Training University Faculty in using a Technological Tool. *Education and Information Technologies, 28*(11), 14577–14594. DOI: 10.1007/s10639-023-11792-8 PMID: 37361749

Kerimbayev, N., Adamova, K., Shadiev, R., & Altınay, Z. (2025). Intelligent educational technologies in individual learning: A systematic literature review. *Smart Learning Environments, 12*(1), 1. Advance online publication. DOI: 10.1186/s40561-024-00360-3

Khadri, H. O. (2022). Becoming future-proof STEM teachers for enhancing sustainable development: A proposed general framework for capacity-building programs in future studies. *Prospects, 52*(3-4), 421–435. DOI: 10.1007/s11125-021-09588-0 PMID: 35368977

Kim, T., Yang, M., & Lim, S. (2021). Owning educational change in Korean schools: Three driving forces behind sustainable change. *Journal of Educational Change, 22*(4), 589–601. DOI: 10.1007/s10833-021-09442-2 PMID: 38624916

Lee, M., Horii, C. V., Austin, A. E., Avery, L., DeSanctis, M., Finkelstein, N. D., Miller, E., & Schaal, B. A. (2023). An Instructional-Workforce Framework for Coordinated Change in Undergraduate Education. *Change The Magazine of Higher Learning, 55*(1), 54. DOI: 10.1080/00091383.2023.2151809

Liang, J. (2024). Enhanced Art Design Education: Integrating Artificial Intelligence for Resource Optimization and Innovative Teaching. In Atlantis highlights in social sciences, education and humanities/Atlantis Highlights in Social Sciences, Education and Humanities (p. 239). Atlantis Press. https://doi.org/DOI: 10.2991/978-94-6463-560-7_29

Lo, L. S. (2025). AI Literacy: A Guide for Academic Libraries. *College & Research Libraries News, 86*(3). Advance online publication. DOI: 10.5860/crln.86.3.120

Ma, K., Zhang, Y., & Hui, B.-H. (2024). How Does AI Affect College? The Impact of AI Usage in College Teaching on Students' Innovative Behavior and Well-Being. *Behavioral Sciences (Basel, Switzerland), 14*(12), 1223. DOI: 10.3390/bs14121223 PMID: 39767364

Madigan, D. J., Kim, L. E., Glandorf, H. L., & Kavanagh, O. (2023). Teacher burnout and physical health: A systematic review [Review of Teacher burnout and physical health: A systematic review]. International Journal of Educational Research, 119, 102173. Elsevier BV. https://doi.org/DOI: 10.1016/j.ijer.2023.102173

Mah, D.-K., & Gross, N. (2024). Artificial intelligence in higher education: Exploring faculty use, self-efficacy, distinct profiles, and professional development needs. *International Journal of Educational Technology in Higher Education, 21*(1), 58. Advance online publication. DOI: 10.1186/s41239-024-00490-1

Maimon, E. P., & Schneider, C. G. (2023). Leading Academic Change. https://doi.org/DOI: 10.4324/9781003445593

Mohsen, B. M. (2023). Impact of Artificial Intelligence on Supply Chain Management Performance. *Journal of Service Science and Management, 16*(1), 44–58. DOI: 10.4236/jssm.2023.161004

Moundridou, M., Matzakos, N., & Doukakis, S. (2024). Generative AI tools as educators' assistants: Designing and implementing inquiry-based lesson plans. *Computers and Education Artificial Intelligence, 7*, 100277. DOI: 10.1016/j.caeai.2024.100277

Must-Have Competencies and Skills in Our New AI World. A Synthesis for Educational Reform. (2024). https://er.educause.edu/articles/2024/9/must-have-competencies-and-skills-in-our-new-ai-world-a-synthesis-for-educational-reform

Neumann, K., & Waight, N. (2020). The digitalization of science education: Déjà vu all over again? *Journal of Research in Science Teaching, 57*(9), 1519–1528. DOI: 10.1002/tea.21668

Ng, D. T. K., Leung, J. K. L., Su, J., Ng, C. W., & Chu, S. K. W. (2023). Teachers' AI digital competencies and twenty-first century skills in the post-pandemic world. *Educational Technology Research and Development, 71*(1), 137–161. DOI: 10.1007/s11423-023-10203-6 PMID: 36844361

Nguyen, V. (2025). The Use of Generative AI Tools in Higher Education: Ethical and Pedagogical Principles. *Journal of Academic Ethics, 23*(3), 1435–1455. Advance online publication. DOI: 10.1007/s10805-025-09607-1

Nixon, N., Lin, Y., & Snow, L. (2024). Catalyzing Equity in STEM Teams: Harnessing Generative AI for Inclusion and Diversity. *Policy Insights from the Behavioral and Brain Sciences, 11*(1), 85–92. DOI: 10.1177/23727322231220356 PMID: 38516055

Ortíz-Barrios, M., Arias-Fonseca, S., Ishizaka, A., Barbati, M., Avendaño-Collante, B., & Navarro-Jiménez, E. (2023). Artificial intelligence and discrete-event simulation for capacity management of intensive care units during the Covid-19 pandemic: A case study. *Journal of Business Research, 160*, 113806. DOI: 10.1016/j.jbusres.2023.113806 PMID: 36895308

Pahi, K., Hawlader, S., Hicks, E., Zaman, A., & Phan, V. (2024). Enhancing active learning through collaboration between human teachers and generative AI. *Computers and Education Open*, *6*, 100183. DOI: 10.1016/j.caeo.2024.100183

Perišić, A., Perisic, I., Lazić, M., & Perišić, B. (2023). The foundation for future education, teaching, training, learning, and performing infrastructure - The open interoperability conceptual framework approach. *Heliyon*, *9*(6), e16836. Advance online publication. DOI: 10.1016/j.heliyon.2023.e16836 PMID: 37484382

Petridou, E., & Lao, L. (2024). Identifying challenges and best practices for implementing AI additional qualifications in vocational and continuing education: A mixed methods analysis. *International Journal of Lifelong Education*, *43*(4), 385–400. DOI: 10.1080/02601370.2024.2351076

Pouru, L., & Wilenius, M. (2021). Building individual futures capacity through transformative futures learning. *Futures*, *132*, 102804. DOI: 10.1016/j.futures.2021.102804

Punziano, G., Falco, C. C. D., & Trezza, D. (2022). Digital Mixed Content Analysis for the Study of Digital Platform Social Data: An Illustration from the Analysis of COVID-19 Risk Perception in the Italian Twittersphere. *Journal of Mixed Methods Research*, *17*(2), 143–170. DOI: 10.1177/15586898211067647 PMID: 38603067

Rashid, A. B., & Kausik, M. A. K. (2024). AI Revolutionizing Industries Worldwide: A Comprehensive Overview of Its Diverse Applications. *Hybrid Advances*, *7*, 100277. DOI: 10.1016/j.hybadv.2024.100277

Rathipriya, R., Rahman, A. A. A., Dhamodharavadhani, S., Meero, A., & Yoganandan, G. (2022). Demand forecasting model for time-series pharmaceutical data using shallow and deep neural network model. *Neural Computing & Applications*, *35*(2), 1945–1957. DOI: 10.1007/s00521-022-07889-9 PMID: 36245796

Roshanaei, M., Olivares, H., & Lopez, R. R. (2023). Harnessing AI to Foster Equity in Education: Opportunities, Challenges, and Emerging Strategies. *Journal of Intelligent Learning Systems and Applications*, *15*(4), 123–143. DOI: 10.4236/jilsa.2023.154009

Saba, J., Hel-Or, H., & Levy, S. T. (2023). Promoting learning transfer in science through a complexity approach and computational modeling. *Instructional Science*, *51*(3), 475–507. DOI: 10.1007/s11251-023-09624-w PMID: 37192865

Singh, A., Kanaujia, A., Singh, V. K., & Vinuesa, R. (2023). Artificial intelligence for Sustainable Development Goals: Bibliometric patterns and concept evolution trajectories. *Sustainable Development (Bradford)*, *32*(1), 724–754. DOI: 10.1002/sd.2706

Southworth, J., Migliaccio, K. W., Glover, J., Glover, J., Reed, D. M., McCarty, C., Brendemuhl, J. H., & Thomas, A. (2023). Developing a model for AI Across the curriculum: Transforming the higher education landscape via innovation in AI literacy. *Computers and Education Artificial Intelligence*, *4*, 100127. DOI: 10.1016/j.caeai.2023.100127

Spanjol, J., Rosa, A., Schirrmeister, E., Dahl, P., Domnik, D., Lindner, M., de la Cruz, M., & Kuhlmann, J.-F. (2022). The potential of futures literacy for impact-oriented business schools. *Futures*, *146*, 103084. DOI: 10.1016/j.futures.2022.103084

Swiecki, Z., Khosravi, H., Chen, G., Martínez-Maldonado, R., Lodge, J. M., Milligan, S., Selwyn, N., & G sević, D. (2022). Assessment in the age of artificial intelligence. *Computers and Education Artificial Intelligence*, *3*, 100075. DOI: 10.1016/j.caeai.2022.100075

Tong, R. J., & Hu, X. (2024). Future of Education with Neuro-Symbolic AI Agents in Self-Improving Adaptive Instructional Systems. *Frontiers of Digital Education.*, *1*(2), 198–212. DOI: 10.1007/s44366-024-0008-9

Tran, H., & Murphy, P. J. (2023). Editorial: Generative artificial intelligence and entrepreneurial performance. *Journal of Small Business and Enterprise Development*, *30*(5), 853–856. DOI: 10.1108/JSBED-09-2023-508

Tzirides, A. O., Zapata, G. C., Kastania, N. P., Saini, A. K., Castro, V., Ismael, S. A., You, Y., dos Santos, T. A., Searsmith, D., O'Brien, C., Cope, B., & Kalantzis, M. (2024). Combining human and artificial intelligence for enhanced AI literacy in higher education. *Computers and Education Open*, *6*, 100184. DOI: 10.1016/j.caeo.2024.100184

Vasquez, J. A., Marcotte, K., & Gruppen, L. D. (2021). The parallel evolution of competency-based education in medical and higher education. *The Journal of Competency-Based Education*, *6*(2), e1234. Advance online publication. DOI: 10.1002/cbe2.1234

Vicari, S., & Kirby, D. P. (2022). Digital platforms as socio-cultural artifacts: Developing digital methods for cultural research. *Information Communication and Society*, *26*(9), 1733–1755. DOI: 10.1080/1369118X.2022.2027498

Vieriu, A. M., & Petrea, G. (2025). The Impact of Artificial Intelligence (AI) on Students' Academic Development. *Education Sciences*, *15*(3), 343. DOI: 10.3390/educsci15030343

Wang, N., & Lester, J. C. (2023). K-12 Education in the Age of AI: A Call to Action for K-12 AI Literacy. *International Journal of Artificial Intelligence in Education, 33*(2), 228–232. DOI: 10.1007/s40593-023-00358-x

Xia, Q., Weng, X., Ouyang, F., Lin, T., & Chiu, T. K. F. (2024). A scoping review on how generative artificial intelligence transforms assessment in higher education [Review of A scoping review on how generative artificial intelligence transforms assessment in higher education]. International Journal of Educational Technology in Higher Education, 21(1). Springer Nature. https://doi.org/DOI: 10.1186/s41239-024-00468-z

Yang, Y., Zhang, Y., Sun, D., He, W., & Wei, Y. (2025). Navigating the landscape of AI literacy education: Insights from a decade of research (2014–2024). *Humanities & Social Sciences Communications, 12*(1), 374. Advance online publication. DOI: 10.1057/s41599-025-04583-8

Youn, H., Park, N., & Murphy, R. M. (2024). Beyond writing a summary: Utilizing AI tools to enhance writing skills. *Communication Teacher, 1*. Advance online publication. DOI: 10.1080/17404622.2024.2396005

Zailuddin, M. F. N. O., Harun, N. A. N., Rahim, H. A. A., Kamaruzaman, A. F., Berahim, M. H., Harun, M. H., & Ibrahim, Y. (2024). Redefining creative education: A case study analysis of AI in design courses. *Journal of Research in Innovative Teaching & Learning, 17*(2), 282–296. DOI: 10.1108/JRIT-01-2024-0019

Chapter 5
Artificial Intelligence in Higher Education:
Transforming Faculty Development and Teaching Practices

Rashid Hashmi
http://orcid.org/0009-0006-3232-0705
Sharda University, India

ABSTRACT

This chapter examines the transformative impact of artificial intelligence (AI) on higher education, with a focus on enhancing faculty development and teaching methodologies. As AI reshapes curricular design, assessment, and research, educators must develop technological fluency alongside critical pedagogical skills to adapt to this evolving landscape. The chapter highlights strategies for integrating AI-driven tools to foster student engagement, personalized learning, and adaptive assessments while maintaining ethical standards, data privacy, and inclusivity. Practical frameworks and real-world case studies are provided to help faculty create student-centered and culturally sensitive learning environments that cater to diverse learners. Emphasis is placed on interdisciplinary collaboration among educators, researchers, and policymakers to promote innovation and knowledge exchange. The chapter underscores the importance of continuous professional development to ensure faculty remain adaptable to AI advancements while preserving the human values of education.

DOI: 10.4018/979-8-3373-1285-9.ch005

1. INTRODUCTION

When AI is applied in higher education, it marks an important change, impacting students and even how faculty approach their jobs. Recently, growing progress in generative AI, including large language models, computerized tutoring, machines that check assignments, and predictive analytics, has stirred both excitement and worry in schools. Even though certain stakeholders recommend using these tools to spark innovation in education, others are concerned about their potential impact on future teaching methods, ethics, and human involvement in schools. Hill (2023) found it appropriate to mention that it is unclear if AI will fade over time or permanently impact the academy. Because of the difference in opinions, it is vital to carefully study the use of AI in helping faculty and teaching in modern higher education.

AI has mostly been introduced in academics by assisting students with adaptive platforms for learning, intelligent tools for marking, virtual helpers, and data reports. Even so, the faculty's role in this technological change has not yet been fully explored. Bond (2023) explicitly questioned: "Who is guiding the education field in adopting AI?" This form of analysis points out that educators' views on AI are often overlooked by those who lead and supervise its adoption. Faculty play important roles beyond relying on new technology, as they organize education, share subject-based materials, and defend educational standards. Hence, the growth and progress of workers in AI should be a major issue that is given close attention now. Faculty development must now encompass not only traditional skills such as curriculum design and instructional delivery but also fluency in AI tools, ethical judgment in data use, and pedagogical adaptability in rapidly evolving digital ecosystems.

This transformation mainly focuses on a series of joining themes that show what today's faculty members must deal with and benefit from. Ethics plays a vital role since educators encounter problems associated with algorithm bias, keeping information secure, personal autonomy, and clear communication. If AI is used without considering ethics, it might inadvertently keep some students from accessing education or produce new barriers to learning using technology. As a result, AI-based teaching should always focus on making everyone feel included. Faculty should learn how to work with AI and ensure that all students benefit from its use. It requires educators to understand how students' social, economic, cultural, and language use impacts their interactions with AI in schools. Another significant aspect of this change is that now, more attention is being given to tailoring learning, and AI should make it work better for more individuals. Educational content, the pace of lessons, and feedback can be adjusted using machine learning to meet the needs of each person. Understanding the potential brings new duties for faculty members, who have to read the results of automated evaluations, observe class interaction, and steer students in the right direction when necessary. Personalized learning can't just be the work of machines; it also depends on the unique advice and perspective of a teacher. For this reason, training for educators should focus on empowering them to control algorithmic information while keeping the human side of teaching and mentoring solid.

Collaboration between different fields is seen as another crucial topic in discussing AI in higher education. Many AI tools for education are developed, applied, and evaluated together by teachers, computer experts, ethicists, and experts from the education and management fields. Therefore, faculty should develop the ability to work with others from different disciplines. This requires a shift in the traditional culture of academic silos toward more integrated and cooperative modes of knowledge production and problem-solving. Faculty development, in this regard, becomes not only a process of individual upskilling but also an opportunity to foster collaborative networks that support innovation grounded in shared values and mutual respect. AI could shape the future of education in positive and negative ways. Bali et al. urge people not to rely on technology alone to address tough issues in education. They, instead, support placing AI within the context of social, political, and educational issues. They further note that the role of AI in education will be shaped by decisions made by educators, schools, and policymakers today. These experts call for a future-focused mindset that relies on technology, considers ethics, and intends to impact education. As a result, how AI is applied in higher education is largely shaped by faculty, who ensure it supports the main principles within the field.

This chapter highlights the various effects of AI on faculty and how they teach in higher education. It aims to consider the benefits and challenges of using AI, develop guidelines for making it ethical and inclusive, and suggest ways in which faculty may benefit from AI. The chapter explains that, to enable educators to use AI properly, we need to focus on their learning, ethics, and ability to cooperate, especially by providing the right resources. No intake of AI in teaching and learning could be fair or beneficial for students if the teaching staff do not have adequate knowledge, skills, and values. The following sections explore the evolution of AI in education from initial computer-assisted learning experiments to its current use of generative AI and analytics. Following this, the core focus of the article will explore in greater detail the pedagogical, ethical, and organizational dimensions of AI use in faculty development. A set of practical solutions and recommendations will then be presented, grounded in real-world case studies and empirical research. Finally, the chapter will outline future research directions that can inform policy and practice, ensuring that AI's integration into higher education remains adaptive, accountable, and aligned with the public good. By covering AI in higher education, this chapter adds to the discussion on the future of teaching, updates the definition of academic work, and looks at the ethics involved in managing new technologies. The purpose is not only to examine or highlight AI, but to explore its effects on teachers and professors in higher education. Technology does not act by itself: they study, guide, and share its inventive process. Their improvement is necessary for higher education to remain ethical, welcoming to all, and successful in the future due to AI influence.

2. HISTORICAL TRAJECTORY OF AI AND TEACHING PRACTICES IN HIGHER EDUCATION

Before AI could enter higher education, there had to be many steps forward in technology, education, and understanding of fields of knowledge. To get a complete overview, it is important to see how AI-driven development in academia builds on the history of education and related technology changes in teaching. They have laid out the foundations for AI today, making clear how similar or different the new ideas are to older ones.

From the early days of lectures, education shifted into a focus on students and their abilities to work independently, ask questions, and participate in class activities. In the 1960s and 1970s, constructivist theories served as the primary reason why this shift gained the backing of many organizations. Those involved in faculty development during this phase mainly focused on designing lessons, communicating in the classroom, and learning about various subjects. In the late 1990s, the growing use of digital tools in education led educators to employ new teaching styles. They were the basis for developing advanced methods in digital education and prepared the way for the use of AI in educational software.

At the beginning of the 2000s, Learning Management Systems (LMS) appeared and began gathering information on student attendance, their test results, and their participation in online forums. The first use of analytics led to teachers relying on facts and numbers to influence their choices for teaching. It was a response to the increased focus on learning goals and responsibility across the globe in higher education. At times, the teachers' section experienced these changes as requirements set by others, which led to some accepting and some resisting them. The integration of AI into these environments added a new layer of complexity, transforming static analytics into dynamic, predictive models capable of forecasting student performance, recommending learning interventions, and automating assessment tasks.

2.1 Evolution of AI Integration in Higher Education

The chronological trajectory of AI in higher education can be framed around key milestones, each reflecting a shift in both technological capability and pedagogical ambition. From early rule-based systems that supported limited instructional automation to contemporary machine learning algorithms capable of generating content, the evolution has been rapid yet uneven across global contexts.

Table 1. Evolution of AI tools in higher education (2000–2025)

Year	Milestone	Description
2000–2005	Intelligent Tutoring Systems (ITS)	Rule-based systems offering limited, domain-specific feedback to learners
2006–2010	Early Learning Analytics	LMS data used for simple student performance dashboards
2011–2015	Natural Language Processing Tools	Basic AI chatbots and language assistance are integrated into online learning platforms
2016–2020	Predictive Analytics in Student Retention	Machine learning is used to forecast dropout risks and academic outcomes
2021–2023	AI-Enhanced Assessment & Content Generation	Automated essay grading, adaptive quizzes, and AI-generated readings were introduced
2024–2025	Generative AI and Faculty-AI Collaboration Platforms	Advanced AI tools co-create curricula and lesson plans; faculty development becomes AI-mediated

Caption: Milestones in the integration of AI in global higher education systems

This historical trajectory demonstrates that AI in higher education has shifted from peripheral experimental tools to core infrastructural elements. These developments are not merely technical but deeply pedagogical, necessitating an active faculty engagement to ensure alignment with educational values and practices.

2.2 Faculty Acceptance and Pedagogical Adaptation

Even though AI technologies are getting more advanced, acceptance by teachers has not caught up. Studies suggest that the integration of AI tools in teaching depends on how helpful educators find them, how easy they are to use, and how much their institution supports them (Ofosu-Ampong, 2024). In many situations, not having proper training, clear decisions about algorithms, and a clear goal for education discourages faculty from adopting education technology. Many times, faculty are presented with AI technology as a new policy rather than as a result of their involvement. Therefore, they tend to experiment with these technologies a little at a time, preferring not to use them widely in their teaching.

Additionally, Ofosu-Ampong (2024) suggests that acceptance on the faculty depends on the context of the subject area. Since STEM educators' methods often align with AI, they are more open to using it, whereas humanities and social sciences teachers usually doubt the way AI is based on certain ideas. Because there is a difference in disciplines, faculty development needs to suit the needs of each academic area. Teachers must also adopt technology and consider whether it supports the educational aims. It matters most when AI tools are made for purposes that do not fit with the values of academia. Therefore, faculty development should be looked at as helping educators understand how AI will influence their approaches to teaching, work, and self-image.

2.3 The Digital Turn and Engagement in Online Learning

With online learning being more popular, faculty have had to adjust many aspects of their teaching, including interacting with students. Activities in virtual classrooms often include webinars, taking part in forums, completing media-based tasks, and playing virtual games. He notes that teachers should not limit their use of digital tools to only advancing technology, as this could distract from the actual purpose of digital pedagogy. Dreamson sees digital engagement as best supported by design, reflection, and ongoing improvement, all facilitated by continuous faculty development.

As a result of the COVID-19 pandemic, online teaching became much more common, so being skilled at using technology became important for all faculty. Nevertheless, because of the quick move, teachers faced challenges in ensuring that their online classes were fair and well-designed. The use of AI for work has brought about excitement as well as concerns. Although AI can provide students with real-time feedback, suggestions, and advice, it can potentially lead to less interaction between the teacher and students.

According to Dreamson (2023), faculty members are expected to have the skills to reflect on their use of technology in teaching. As a result, faculty development must add content on critical digital pedagogy, media literacy, and reflective practices to help teachers work well with students using AI in online learning.

2.4 Regional Variations and Institutional Readiness

AI is adopted differently in higher education depending on the infrastructure, cultural attitudes, and the structure of each institution's governance, which vary region by region. The authors highlight that AI plans are an essential part of the educational systems in GCC countries. Usually, these approaches make AI a focal point in preparing schools and systems for the future. Even so, they suggest that schools and their faculty are not yet fully prepared for the changes the policies aim for.

In this region, the government is supporting AI through many projects, but facilities for faculty growth are not yet up to date. Some institutions find it difficult due to teacher resistance, lack of AI learning opportunities, and worries about inequalities in AI tools due to their Western development. In their study, Fadlelmula and Qadhi suggest adapting AI tools to support the region's specific traditions and language. They insist that it is important to include faculty at each stage of creating and using AI systems to show them why they matter.

It is clear from the regional analysis that special programs for faculty must address factors such as geopolitics, culture, and specific institutions. Trying to apply the same AI model in multiple contexts is unlikely to work well for the long term.

2.5 Transparency and Ethical Accountability

With AI used more in daily teaching activities, educators now pay more attention to transparency and accountability. Chaudhry et al. (2022) observe that several AI systems used within educational institutions hide what processes are involved in decision-making. Because of this mystery, faculty trust is harmed, and it raises issues about fair grading, keeping student data secure, and profiling. If an AI system marks a student's essay badly, the faculty member must be able to explain and verify that mark, especially if the student questions it. If the researchers do not share their algorithmic ideas, educators are put in a difficult situation. The authors propose that any AI system should be clear, allow users to control certain features, and undergo ethical review.

Such issues impact the way faculty is developed. Both the practical and the philosophical aspects of Artificial Intelligence must be taught to educators. Schools should ensure that students learn both how to use AI and how to handle ethical, thoughtful, and data management issues related to AI. AI has been introduced into higher education against a backdrop of innovation, educational progress, and social and cultural changes. The progress in teaching and using technology has prepared us for present-day AI-based teaching. Indeed, schools can use AI responsibly and effectively only with ready faculty, institutional assurance, factors from the region, and clear technology. Having this background information is necessary before developing faculty training that is inclusive, ethical, and focused on upcoming challenges.

3. FOCUS OF THE ARTICLE

Futuristic ideas about AI are gone; it has long been part of the main trends in teaching and learning, especially at university or high school. In this respect, the section below discusses how AI is changing how teaching and assessment are currently implemented. Such changes include adaptive surroundings for learning, using ethics when programming algorithms, teaching staff collaborating in classes, and developing skills in using technology at university. How AI shapes teaching and learning outcomes can be very challenging, yet it has significant upsides and challenges.

3.1 The Use of Adaptive Learning and Individualized Teaching

At the core of AI's potential in education is the ability to alter learning for each student individually. Personalization is mostly led by adaptive systems that use algorithms and keep re-examining results. Smart learning courses use analytics on students and well-planned sequencing to modify the level of tasks, how swiftly to present them, and the ways of teaching. They claim that adaptive technologies help guide students according to their learning needs, increasing their interest and success. They are not limited to how students think and learn; they also depend on a student's confidence and time spent on an activity, forming a more complete way of responding to students.

Lee and Cho (2015) explained that adaptive learning in the early stage relied on strict rules, which made it less practical for use in real school situations. As AI platforms have advanced, they can now use more advanced tools such as neural networks and probabilistic inferences. These models offer teachers suggestions on how to improve their teaching based on current students' performance. Nevertheless, introducing adaptive systems can be difficult because not all organizations are ready, their infrastructure may fall short, and teachers may not be properly trained in the required ways.

3.2 AI in Assessment: Innovations and Ethical Complexities

More use of AI in assessments leads to both positive and serious concerns. Automated systems to grade work, assess emotions in written student material, and measure potential outcomes are now used in testing. Bulut and colleagues (2024) review the role of AI in helping to streamline both formative and summative evaluation processes. According to them, intelligent tutoring systems review open-ended responses as they are being created and guide the learner in the same way teachers usually do.

On the other hand, Perkins et al. (2023) note that using algorithms to assess people can still result in biased conclusions due to the characteristics included in their training data. Using these tools might lead to the marginalization of students who do not speak, behave, or think the same way as most people. Consequently, creating an ethical framework is crucial for AI in the field of assessment. Regular audits of algorithms, being open about the use of data, and allowing human involvement should be part of the framework. Additionally, not being able to explain clearly how certain AI black-box systems make decisions makes it more difficult to ensure that student evaluation is fair and accountable.

3.3 Critical Digital Literacies and the Role of Faculty

With AI being used more in education, teachers should adjust the skills they have. Recently, faculty are required to manage digital tools and to help with the use of algorithms in the classroom. Raffaghelli (2024) defines critical digital literacies as including barely technical skills and also involving the ability to review digital resources, understand the behaviour of algorithms, and look ahead for the consequences of using technology in education. Changing the roles of faculty means universities should revisit their teacher training programs.

Across the world and between various subjects, digital literacy is not the same. Even though several instructors are highly skilled in using these technologies, others still have difficulty changing their approach from classic study methods to those backed by AI. Rather than letting teachers find and improve these literacies on their own, organizations ought to plan training sessions that address the needs of their specific disciplines and are pedagogically sound.

3.4 Co-Teaching and Faculty Upskilling

Faculty can now develop their skills in AI by using AI alongside other educators or by co-teaching with individuals with advanced technical knowledge. Lin and Cordie (2023) believe that co-teaching can help staff become more digitally proficient in settings where there are differences in digital literacy among teachers. Faculty can experience using AI tools in the classroom and gain guidance and help from both colleagues and the institution when co-teaching. Consequently, this model suggests that laws should be updated and pay needs to be reviewed. Co-teaching that supports growth in teaching requires coaches and teachers to spend time, be comfortable with each other, and revisit their work often. A lack of administrative help and good reasons for faculty may make them feel that co-teaching is just one more thing for them to do. Faculty members who work together in co-teaching must have related abilities and share the same teaching goals.

3.5 Navigating Legal and Ethical Frameworks

In higher education, AI raises various concerns about legal and ethical matters, including privacy of data, ownership of intellectual property, and possible harm from algorithms. According to Alasmari and Al-Zahrani (2025), few institutions have strong policies to direct the use of AI in classrooms and for assessment. In many cases, faculty and students deal with factors such as hidden data use, inadequate consent from participants, and vague responsibility measures.

Each nation has unique laws that make it harder for transnational educational activities to comply. Additionally, ethics involves questions about epistemic and pedagogical justice as well as following official rules. As an example, who is responsible for selecting the best learning methods in adaptive systems? How are unique or different student behaviors seen by the artificial intelligence used in education? Legal experts, ethicists, and educators have to play an active part over time in developing these governance styles.

Omari et al. argue that colleges and universities should involve faculty, students, IT specialists, and legal experts in the processes that guide their decisions. Using these methods allows AI to be used in ways that support a school's values and education system, not only for system efficiency. Since AI is used in schools in multiple ways, it is more important than ever for all parties to work closely together.

Table 2. Comparison of AI tools in teaching, assessment, and feedback

AI Tool	Function	Pedagogical Role	Key Ethical Consideration
Adaptive Learning Platforms	Adjust content in real-time	Personalize instruction	Data bias and transparency
Automated Essay Scorers	Grade open-ended responses	Expedite assessment	Fairness in linguistic diversity
Intelligent Tutoring Systems	Provide formative feedback	Support individualized learning paths	Human oversight and validity
Predictive Analytics Dashboards	Forecast academic performance	Inform pedagogical interventions	Consent and data protection
AI Chatbots	Respond to student queries	Enhance student engagement and support	Miscommunication risks

Caption: Comparative table of leading AI-driven educational technologies and their pedagogical roles.

Case Study Box: AI-Enabled Writing Assistant for Multilingual Learners

Lawrance et al. (2024) describe the application of an AI-powered writing assistance tool for multilingual learners in a public university in Asia. Instead of relying on multiple tools, the program offered instant fixes to grammar, recommended better words, and offered details helpful for users' native language. Although the initial response was positive and many saw improvements in their writing, some problems were marked in the study. Several times, the AI came up with culturally incorrect sentences and missed the specifics of writing in the field. The program needed adjustments made by faculty so that it supported, rather than replaced, the process of teaching. AI tools can help a lot in multilingual and multicultural contexts, though there are still some limits.

AI greatly impacts how teaching and assessment are carried out while posing a variety of problems. With adaptive technology, learners can choose a tailored approach to learning, while online assessment systems help in evaluating more students efficiently and quickly. At the same time, these advantages should be matched with careful attention to morals, proper faculty education, and models that ensure all are included. Future sections will study the role of universities in AI and analyse what lies ahead for AI in higher education.

4. SOLUTIONS AND RECOMMENDATIONS

Using AI in higher education involves upgrading technology as well as guiding teachers in adopting the changes. Now that AI is influencing the way universities teach, it is clear that faculty should have the skills needed to handle the new technology. Measures ought to cover areas such as ethics, equality in teaching, cross-field partnerships, and improvement over time. This section lists different solutions and models supported by evidence that help deal with the various difficulties of applying AI in colleges and universities.

4.1 Faculty Training through Inclusive Pedagogy

Ensuring that learning with AI is inclusive should be a priority, so no student is pushed to the side. McKnight and Morgan (2020) believe that models of "clinical teaching" should be promoted in higher education, as they help students understand their needs in different contexts and are adaptable to AI technology. Such models use constant formative feedback, flexible ways of teaching, and responsiveness to feelings, which AI can do with direction from trained teachers.

He further suggests considering computational inclusive pedagogy, a system that combines education with machine learning to fit every student's learning path. Faculty ought to be skilled in utilizing these tools and in reflecting on what they imply. Programs for training should add simulations to help instructors understand different types of students and detect biased algorithms. Business, AI, IT, and management can benefit from holding sessions together because they cover all aspects of AI.

4.2 Gamified and Transmedia Learning Approaches

They suggest that combining gamified and transmedia teaching with AI is useful for overcoming motivational issues and encouraging authentic engagement for students. This helps educators present lessons using storytelling, interactive activities, and instant feedback during virtual and augmented sessions.

One can organize workshops where instructors gain experience with designing gamified programs that align with AI analytics. In these talks, educators learn how data collected from students guides plot development, the way challenges increase, and other features. The ability to move across various media forms should be considered a necessary and important skill for teachers' training to use AI in education.

4.3 Ethical Content Delivery and AI Governance

Ensuring the ethical use of information is a main concern for AI in the classroom. Lee and Cho (2024) suggest using a method that guarantees tutors are aware of all the AI materials and how their presence in the classroom represents a respectful and clear approach toward students. According to the framework, instructors should regard ethical decision-making as an essential part of designing their courses.

Consequently, faculty development should add ethical reasoning training, so teachers can evaluate cases related to AI-based surveillance, methods of grading, and the use of data. Verma and Thelisson (2024) recommend that institutions should adopt the risk-based approach and focus on human involvement, as recalled in the European Union AI Act. Thus, learning by following guidelines can motivate faculty to act proactively in their roles and help them maintain moral class standards. Furthermore, educators should be aware of both the technical and moral aspects of AI. We should make sure that educators have opportunities to join forces with developers, legal advisors, and designers to address their main concerns and create needed solutions.

4.4 Institutional Models of Faculty Development for AI Integration

If AI integration is to succeed, faculty professional development should be expected and consistent. Organizations should follow models that support learning continuously, provide mentoring, and help everyone work together in unison. Table 3 shows different faculty development models and relates them to the important skills in the world of AI.

Table 3. Faculty development models integrating AI literacy

Faculty Development Model	AI Literacy Focus	Institutional Integration Strategy
Clinical Teaching Model	Contextual Data Use, Adaptive Feedback	Department-based mentoring
Gamified Pedagogical Workshops	Engagement Analytics, Behavioral Modeling	Cross-faculty digital labs
Computational Inclusive Pedagogy	Bias Recognition, Personalization Skills	Curriculum co-design units
Ethics Case-Based Learning	Governance, Transparency, Fairness	Policy-centered faculty learning circles
Transmedia Teaching Bootcamps	Cross-platform Design, AI Media Supervision	Media-education collaborative programs

Caption: Professional development models mapped against AI competencies

These models indicate that one-size-fits-all approaches to faculty development are insufficient. Universities should conduct needs assessments and personalize professional development pathways. In doing so, they address the varied digital literacies, pedagogical orientations, and disciplinary expectations of academic staff.

4.5 Faculty Collaboration and Interdisciplinary Pedagogy

Having faculty from various subjects work together is important when preparing for AI-enhanced teaching. As Lin and Cordie (2023) suggest, co-teaching models are effective methods for helping faculty improve their skills. With these models, teachers from computer science and education teams up to build AI-based lessons, share experience on teaching issues, and grow familiar with teaching methods.

Teaching institutions should allow co-teachers to adjust their schedules, praise their efforts in reviews, and provide them with teaching assistants who understand AI. Engaging in teamwork in classrooms encourages constant learning and opens up opportunities for all to share knowledge, which is necessary to match the pace of AI.

Forming labs that include collaborations among educators, AI developers, and policymakers encourages everyone to view the subject more comprehensively. These labs can enable faculty members to get involved with AI in teaching, develop pilot projects, write research papers, and use shared resources.

4.6 Policy Alignment and Compliance Training

Faculty needs to be involved in the process of making policies rather than just carrying out instructions from above. With regulations such as the EU AI Act becoming more widely known, teachers should learn about both legal and ethical requirements. The authors recommend creating helpful tools for staff that make it simpler to spot risks and decide on the best action or report the situation.

Faculty training for compliance should be included when new members join the faculty and be mentioned when the institution is being evaluated by an accrediting body. When this is done, the school's objectives and a person's methods of teaching are not conflicting, so everyone trusts AI technology more. Furthermore, the faculty should know about GDPR and other data protection and privacy laws that affect local areas. Teaching should center on the use, storage, and consent aspects of student data, as well as the role of AI, so professors are ready to challenge and improve their behaviour if needed.

Best Practices Checklist for Faculty Integrating AI Responsibly

- Understand the inclusive design principles of AI-enhanced learning tools
- Participate in ethics-based faculty training aligned with AI governance frameworks
- Engage in interdisciplinary co-teaching or collaborative lesson planning
- Use gamified and transmedia techniques to increase student engagement
- Regularly assess AI tools for bias, transparency, and effectiveness
- Align course design with data privacy and legal compliance requirements
- Actively contribute to institutional policy development on AI use in education
- Establish peer mentoring networks for continuous upskilling

4.7 Sustaining Change through Institutional Leadership

Changes in faculty development need to be supported by leaders. Those leading universities are responsible for teaching their faculty members about AI, including diverse groups in key decisions and acknowledging those who use AI in their pedagogy. McKnight (2023) points out that establishing inclusive and evidence-based practices for marginalized learners largely depends on leadership.

Making faculty development effective means changing the culture of the institution. Businesses should encourage new ideas, support mistakes as a learning opportunity, and focus on reflecting on their experiences. Leaders should be sure that teachers are recognized for using AI-based learning methods in their teaching.

Overall, supporting faculty in the use of responsible AI involves facing numerous challenges. Yet, it can be dealt with using ethical standards, inclusive lessons, joining expertise from different fields, and official support for development. Faculty members should be equipped to contribute to and design the changes brought about by AI in higher education.

5. FUTURE RESEARCH DIRECTIONS

While AI is becoming more popular in education, it has led to multiple issues that educators, researchers, and scholars must find answers for. While there have been significant initial studies, many aspects of introducing AI into education are still not fully understood, mainly those related to educators, ethics, and inclusivity in schools. Here, the main areas where research is lacking are highlighted, and directions for studies, including different fields and geographies, are offered, encouraging learning about both applications and concepts of AI in education.

5.1 Reframing Personalization: Between Utility and Surveillance

Giving students a personalized experience in education often means using AI, but this can result in greater surveillance. Falsk (2023) suggests that while AI promotes student-centered learning, no one has sufficiently asked whether this approach might be a new form of surveillance in the name of school efficiency. Adaptive learning systems are talked about more often than the problems that might arise from frequent data use.

Thus, it is important for future research to shift its view of personalization from a supposed positive to a questionable practice. Studies tracking the intellectual, emotional, and behavioral data of students in AI-personalized systems are required. Researchers should understand whether students respond differently to feedback and predictions offered by educational algorithms. Besides, additional qualitative studies should be conducted to understand how students' and faculty's views on surveillance in tech develop in diverse social situations. In addition, it is necessary to review how ready each institution is to deal with privacy when delivering personalized services. Reviewing different privacy laws in various countries can lead to effective guidelines that balance student protection and learning benefits.

5.2 Transparency and Explainability: Bridging Technical and Educational Discourses

Although algorithms are frequently discussed in the field of AI ethics, they are still not widely used in schools and universities. Chaudhry et al. (2022) argue that AI systems in education are often secrets to everyone except the creators, leaving teachers and others in the dark. Because the decisions are not clear enough to them, faculty cannot openly discuss AI grading or recommendations, and may face challenges when using data about student performance.

Moving forward, studies should produce and examine ideas that can help us explain AI in education. Users should be given helpful dashboards to show the basis of the decisions, which data is utilized, and the factors that impact the predictions. Researchers could see how applying visual tools could help teachers and trainers supervise the use of algorithms. It is also necessary for computer scientists, instructional designers, and educational researchers to collaborate so that the idea of explainability is included in AI systems from the beginning, not just tacked on later.

Researchers should also look into how transparency affects both student performance and views. Would AI feedback become more trustworthy for students if the reasons for the decision were explained? Can transparent practices help improve the acceptance of assessments made by machines? The topics in this list are rarely examined and still need to be studied in detail.

5.3 Positioning Educators in AI Research: From Implementers to Co-Creators

Despite the pedagogical implications of AI, educators remain underrepresented in research agendas shaping AI development and policy. Bond (2023) critiques the prevailing tendency in the literature to treat educators as passive implementers rather than active agents in AI integration. This epistemic marginalization risks producing tools and policies that are misaligned with instructional realities.

To counter this, future research must prioritize educator-centered studies that document the experiences, needs, and resistances of faculty navigating AI systems. This includes ethnographic accounts of classroom practices, action research projects led by faculty, and collaborative inquiries involving teachers as co-researchers. There is also a need for intersectional analysis that examines how faculty identity markers—such as gender, discipline, experience level, and cultural background—influence attitudes towards AI.

In addition to qualitative inquiries, large-scale mixed-methods studies can provide insights into faculty preparedness, trust levels, and training needs across different educational contexts. These data can inform institutional strategies for faculty development and curricular redesign. Research should also explore how faculty perceptions evolve, especially about exposure to AI training and participatory design initiatives.

5.4 Toward a Global Comparative Framework for AI Integration

The geographical and cultural concentration of AI education research in the Global North has resulted in a narrowed perspective that risks reproducing epistemic inequities. Regional studies—such as those from the Gulf Cooperation Council (Fadlelmula & Qadhi, 2023)—reveal that the socio-political context, technological infrastructure, and institutional mandates deeply shape how AI is adopted and perceived. Yet there is a lack of comparative frameworks that systematically analyze these variations.

Future research should prioritize cross-regional collaborations involving institutions from the Global South and underrepresented regions. These collaborations can uncover context-specific challenges and innovations that do not emerge in Western-centric research. For example, how does AI function in resource-constrained universities, or how do local data protection laws affect implementation in Sub-Saharan Africa or South Asia?

Additionally, there is scope for studies that examine the transferability of AI systems and pedagogical models across cultural and linguistic boundaries. Such research must go beyond technology adoption to critically assess cultural assumptions embedded in AI design and deployment. Participatory approaches involving local educators, students, and policymakers are essential to ensure relevance, equity, and sustainability.

5.5 Longitudinal and Multilevel Studies: Tracking the AI Trajectory in Education

Much of the existing research on AI in education remains short-term and exploratory. To truly understand the impact of AI, there is a need for longitudinal studies that track the evolution of teaching practices, learning outcomes, and institutional cultures over multiple academic cycles. These studies can reveal how AI integration matures, what unintended consequences emerge, and how institutional responses evolve.

Furthermore, multilevel studies that connect individual, institutional, and policy dimensions can offer a holistic picture of AI's educational ecosystem. For example, how do national AI policies influence institutional investment in AI tools, and how do these investments shape faculty development initiatives? Similarly, how do institutional values regarding innovation and inclusion influence the pedagogical choices made by individual instructors? Large-scale projects combining policy analysis, institutional ethnography, and classroom-level research are needed to map these complex interrelations. Such studies would require interdisciplinary teams and long-term funding, possibly through international research consortia or education ministries.

Figure 1. Future research trajectories in AI-driven education

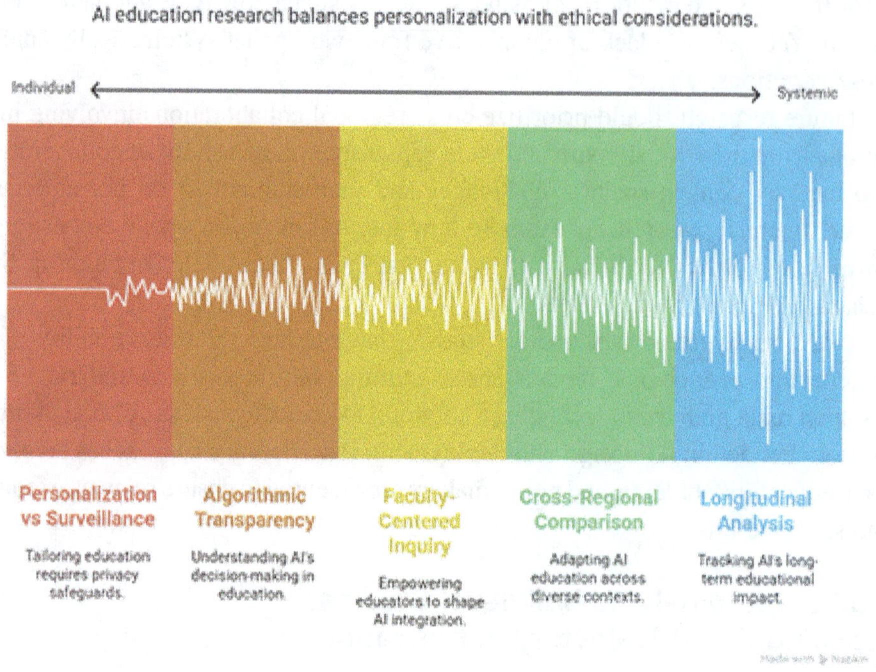

5.6 Building Interdisciplinary Research Ecosystems

A recurring theme across all proposed research directions is the necessity of interdisciplinary collaboration. The ethical, technical, and pedagogical challenges posed by AI in education cannot be adequately addressed within disciplinary silos. Future research must bridge the divide between educational theory, computer science, ethics, law, and public policy.

Creating interdisciplinary research centers focused on AI in education could facilitate sustained engagement across sectors. These centers should support joint appointments, collaborative grant applications, and public engagement initiatives. They could also serve as incubators for new methodological tools, such as ethical audits for AI systems or culturally responsive design protocols. By fostering such research ecosystems, higher education can not only respond to the challenges posed by AI but shape its future development in ways that prioritize human dignity, pedagogical justice, and global equity.

6. CONCLUSION

Artificial intelligence is bringing significant changes to higher education, and these are unlikely to fade or remain temporary. The chapter has explored how technology and educational goals are related in a quality education. The chapter repeatedly stresses that both innovations and future planning should be guided by ethics and long-term thinking.

What truly matters is that AI should be included in classrooms in a way that respects the role of humans and cares for every student. Although adaptive systems and other technologies are advancing, what truly matters is how teachers put them to use in education. Consequently, those involved in education are included in the central debates about AI.

Faculty should be developing their skills and understanding of ethics at the same time that technology is added to the university. For AI to be used ethically and effectively, professionals must continue their professional learning. Teaching staff must understand algorithms, as well as be trained to question technology that monitors people and apply fair approaches in teaching to avoid marginalizing students (Raffaghelli, 2024). Since artificial intelligence tools are currently being integrated, using and steering these tools is an important part of an educator's responsibility.

Additionally, the problems related to governance, following the rules, and ethics cannot be ignored. Alasmari and Al-Zahrani (2025) explain that the legal and ethical concerns involved in AI systems in universities are usually unprecedented. Institutions must therefore adopt transparent decision-making frameworks and compliance protocols that anticipate the socio-legal implications of deploying AI in classrooms. These frameworks should involve educators in their design and evaluation, recognizing the pedagogical expertise they bring to bear on matters of policy and implementation.

AI in universities must also encourage more multi-disciplinary strategies and active involvement in shaping new policies. People engaged in research, technology, and education should come together to set priorities for ethical design, applying new ideas to different cultures, and equal treatment of data. Stewart et al. (2023) maintain that AI for education relies on a vision that favors human wellbeing in the long term over simple improvements in results. All faculty development programs need to reflect the institution's goals about justice, inclusion, accessibility, and transformation.

To conclude, AI has played a major role in changing higher education, though its success will not rely only on technology. You can determine the level of success by looking at how institutions help teachers develop ethical approaches, continue their learning, and secure the main rights of students in mostly automated settings.

The chapter has explained how AI integration impacts the present and future of education, focusing especially on the faculty's leading role in this process.

We should continue to carefully watch and support the process, using creative ideas. Educational facilities ought to recognize that no AI tool provides immediate solutions. Therefore, they should focus on supporting faculty's decision-making, ethical thinking and inclusive planning. Only in these future situations will AI act as a positive influence instead of causing separation.

REFERENCES

Alasmari, T. M., & Al-Zahrani, A. M. (2025). Exploring the impact of artificial intelligence on higher education: The dynamics of ethical, social, and educational implications. *Education and Information Technologies.*

Bali, M., Stewart, B., Bozkurt, A., & Junhong, X. (2023). Speculative futures on ChatGPT and generative artificial intelligence (AI): A collective reflection from the educational landscape. *Teaching in Higher Education.*

Balzan, F. (2024). A computational model of inclusive pedagogy: From understanding to application. *International and Interdisciplinary Conference on Digital Environments.*

Bond, M. (2023). Systematic review of research on artificial intelligence applications in higher education – where are the educators? *International Journal of Educational Technology in Higher Education.*

Bulut, O., Beiting-Parrish, M., Casabianca, J. M., Slater, S. C., Jiao, H., Song, D., . . . Yildirim-Erbasli, S. N. (2024). The rise of artificial intelligence in educational measurement: Opportunities and ethical challenges. *arXiv preprint arXiv:2406.18900.*

Chaudhry, M. A., Cukurova, M., & Luckin, R. (2022). A transparency index framework for AI in education. *arXiv preprint arXiv:2206.03220.* DOI: 10.1007/978-3-031-11647-6_33

Deliyannis, I., Kaimara, P., Oikonomou, A., Fokides, E., & Miliotis, G. (2023). An innovative transmedia-based game development method for inclusive education. *Digital Culture & Education.*

Dreamson, N. (2023). Student interactivity and teacher participation: An application of legitimate peripheral participation in higher education online learning environments. *Journal of Educational Technology & Society.*

Fadlelmula, F. K., & Qadhi, S. M. (2023). A systematic review of research on artificial intelligence in higher education: Practice, gaps, and future directions in the GCC. *Education and Information Technologies.*

Falsk, R. (2023). *AI in education: Personalized learning and adaptive assessment.* ResearchGate.

Fowlin, J. M., Gallo, C., & Lilja, M. (2018). Gaining a global criminal justice perspective: A computer-supported collaboration between students in Sweden and the United States. *Journal of Criminal Justice Education, 29*(4), 531–550. DOI: 10.1080/10511253.2018.1426774

Hill, R. L. (2023). AI as fad or AI as lasting? Priorities for college faculty instructional development for generative artificial intelligence. *Irish Journal of Technology Enhanced Learning*.

Karimi, H., & Khawaja, S. (2023). The impact of artificial intelligence on higher education in England. *Creative Education, 14*(12), 2405–2415. DOI: 10.4236/ce.2023.1412154

Lawrance, J. C., Sambath, P., Shiny, C., Vazhangal, M., & Bala, B. K. (2024). Developing an AI-assisted multilingual adaptive learning system for personalized English language teaching. *10th International Conference on Communication and Signal Processing*. DOI: 10.1109/ICACCS60874.2024.10716887

Lee, Y., & Cho, J. (2015). Personalized item generation method for adaptive testing systems. *Multimedia Tools and Applications, 74*(19), 8571–8591. DOI: 10.1007/s11042-013-1421-0

Lee, Y., & Cho, J. (2024). Development of a content framework of artificial intelligence integrated education considering ethical factors. *International Journal on Advanced Science, Engineering and Information Technology, 14*(1), 205–213. DOI: 10.18517/ijaseit.14.1.19558

Lin, X., & Cordie, L. A. (2023). Co-teaching in higher education: Mentoring as faculty development. *International Journal on Teaching and Learning in Higher Education.*

McKnight, L. (2023). Teaching writing by formula: Empowerment or exclusion? *International Journal of Inclusive Education, 27*(5), 571–585. DOI: 10.1080/13603116.2020.1864790

McKnight, L., & Morgan, A. (2020). Why 'clinical teaching'? An interdisciplinary analysis of metaphor in initial teacher preparation. *Journal of Education for Teaching, 46*(1), 1–13. DOI: 10.1080/02607476.2019.1708629

Ofosu-Ampong, K. (2024). Beyond the hype: Exploring faculty perceptions and acceptability of AI in teaching practices. *Discover Education, 3*(1), 38. DOI: 10.1007/s44217-024-00128-4

Omari, A., Alyousef, A., & Fati, S. (2025). Governance and ethical frameworks for AI integration in higher education: Enhancing personalized learning and legal compliance. *Journal of Ecohumanism*, *4*(2), 80–86.

Perkins, M., Furze, L., Roe, J., & MacVaugh, J. (2023). The AI Assessment Scale (AIAS): A framework for ethical integration of generative AI in educational assessment. *arXiv preprint arXiv:2312.07086*.

Raffaghelli, J. E. (2024). Exploring teachers' perceptions of critical digital literacies and how these are manifested in their teaching practices. *International Journal of Educational Technology in Higher Education*.

Sajja, R., Sermet, Y., Cikmaz, M., Cwiertny, D., & Demir, I. (2023). Artificial intelligence-enabled intelligent assistant for personalized and adaptive learning in higher education. *arXiv preprint arXiv:2309.10892*.

Stewart, B., Bozkurt, A., Junhong, X., & Bali, M. (2023). Speculative futures on ChatGPT and generative artificial intelligence (AI): A collective reflection from the educational landscape. *Teaching in Higher Education*.

Verma, H., & Thelisson, E. (2024). Conformity assessment under the EU AI Act general approach. *AI and Ethics*.

KEY TERMS AND DEFINITIONS

Adaptive Assessment: A technology-driven evaluation method that adjusts the difficulty of questions in real time based on a learner's performance, offering a personalized and efficient assessment experience.

AI Transparency: The principle of making AI systems' processes, decision-making logic, and data use understandable and accessible to users, ensuring ethical accountability.

Digital Pedagogy: The application of digital tools and methodologies in teaching, learning, and curriculum design. It emphasizes learner engagement, interactivity, and the integration of technology in instructional practices.

Generative AI: A subset of artificial intelligence that creates new content, such as text, images, or audio, based on patterns learned from data. Tools like ChatGPT exemplify their use in educational content generation and assessment feedback.

Inclusive Education: An educational philosophy and practice that ensures all students, regardless of ability, background, or need, have equal access to learning opportunities and are supported through differentiated instruction.

Personalized Learning: A tailored educational approach where content, pace, and learning paths are customized to individual students' strengths, needs, and interests, often supported by AI analytics.

Chapter 6
Emerging AI Tools and the Future of Education and Work:
Identifying Emerging AI Tools, Forecasting Technological Advancements, and Anticipating the Changing

Samrat Kundu
http://orcid.org/0009-0004-9409-8041
Brainware University, India

ABSTRACT

AI's quick growth is changing how we learn and work worldwide. This chapter looks at new AI tools, predicts tech advances, and explores their big impact on schools and workplaces. We'll list key tools like AI that create content, machine learning systems, and tech that understands human language. These are transforming how we learn, teach, and do business as AI spreads to most fields. Tech can do boring tasks, make learning better for each person, and give workers and students amazing new abilities. We'll point out the important tools driving new ideas now and likely to be big hits soon. Through a synthesis of current research, case studies, and expert insights, this chapter will provide a comprehensive perspective on how AI is redefining education and work, preparing readers for the opportunities and challenges of an AI-driven future.

DOI: 10.4018/979-8-3373-1285-9.ch006

INTRODUCTION

Artificial intelligence has already begun to make some of the most visible changes to the field of education. Smart tutoring systems like MATHia, created by Carnegie Learning, can adjust to the needs of an individual learner and provide personalised instructions that enhance the learning process and outcomes (Luckin et al., 2016). Artificial intelligence-based services such as edX and Coursera suggest courses, monitor progress, and deliver quality education to students in distant regions, enabling the gaps in access to education to be eliminated (UNESCO, 2022). The labour force is changing simultaneously. AI helps in modular learning and micro-credentials that motivate individuals to continue acquiring skills in their work-life (McKinsey Global Institute, 2018). Engineering students can simulate prototypes with immersive technologies that integrate AI with virtual and augmented reality, and medical students can train for surgery in virtual reality to connect theory with practice (World Economic Forum, 2023). In most sectors, AI makes the company automate repetitive work, enhance human capabilities, and create new creative opportunities. AI is deployed by healthcare systems to diagnose and plan treatments more precisely using medical data, predictive algorithms to inform investment choices in the financial sector, and autonomous systems to revolutionise transportation by making it better with regard to mobility and logistics (Bengio et al., 2015). These developments are associated with obvious challenges. Robotisation poses a risk to certain conventional jobs and increases the level of demand in such skills as creativity, emotional intelligence and critical thinking (McKinsey Global Institute, 2018). Reskilling and tight collaboration of employers, teachers, and policy-makers are necessary to ensure that workers are flexible. The gig economy is also being pushed by AI, which pairs clients with freelance workers on sites like Upwork and Fiverr, making resilience and lifelong learning essential (Susskind and Susskind, 2015). Society needs to bridge the skill divide, facilitate adaptation and tackle ethical issues like bias, data privacy and equality in decision making to reap the full benefits of AI (OECD, 2021).

BACKGROUND

One of the most groundbreaking technologies of the twenty-first century and an already evolving way people learn and work is artificial intelligence (AI) (Brynjolfsson and McAfee, 2014).AI allows professionals, students, and educators to perform their tasks more creatively and efficiently by providing new tools and solutions. Due to the rapid development of technology, nowadays AI helps with tailored education, streamlined business operations, and the introduction of new occupational groups, but its implementation is also associated with issues that should be carefully considered to make education and employment inclusive and just (OECD, 2021). The old AI systems were only able to play games like chess or solve other simple problems, but today they apply complicated algorithms to comprehend language, analyse data and come up with correct decisions (Russell & Norvig, 2021). Generative AI models, including the GPT series, exhibit human-like writing, continue conversations and assist with creative work such as content generation (UNESCO, 2022). The tools DALL·E and MidJourney are visual tools that now enable professionals and students to transform ideas into images with minimum effort and make technology access more widespread than it used to be available to researchers.

These developments are a great advantage in education.

1. The AI tools like Khan Academy, Coursera, or Duolingo adapt the content according to personal pace and strengths of the learner (Luckin et al., 2016).
2. AI also enhances inclusiveness by assisting students with disabilities by signing using the help of AI-assisted sign-language interpreters, real-time text-to-speech services like Otter.ai and text-to-speech tools.
3. Automated grading, such as Gradescope, lessens the administrative work of teachers so that they can concentrate on mentoring.

Predictive analytics are used to identify students at risk of dropping out and provide timely intervention (McKinsey Global Institute, 2018).Recruitment applications like LinkedIn Recruiter and HireVue can filter applications within a few seconds, administer tests, and match talents with vacancies, which can save time and minimise discrimination (World Economic Forum, 2023). Repetitive and tedious tasks like data entry and invoice processing are done on automation platforms, such as UiPath and Blue Prism, which leave the rest of the staff to do the strategic work.AI can also enhance communication and collaboration by using writing assistants, such as Grammarly, planning software, such as Notion AI, and collaboration tools, such as Slack and Zoom. EdX and LinkedIn Learning are online learning platforms that apply AI in suggesting reskilling and upskilling paths to keep workers relevant in a rapidly evolving workforce. Artificial intelligence, combined with augmented and virtual reality in immersive technologies, can make learning engaging. They provide students with an opportunity to visit historical places, complete virtual experiments, or test engineering and medical practices in safe conditions (UNESCO, 2022). The education gap among well-endowed and underserved areas is also reduced by AI, which offers high-quality teachers and materials in virtual classrooms. AI can be used in the work environment to help turn routine into strategic decision-making. New job opportunities that are rising include data scientist, AI ethicist, and machine-learning engineer, and hybrid work models with the help of AI provide workers with more flexibility (World Economic Forum, 2023). Although these opportunities have been presented, there are still serious obstacles. The ethical standards must be high, and the algorithms should be supervised at all times because of concerns of privacy, the bias of algorithms, and accountability (OECD, 2021). Access to AI continues to be a problem of the digital divide in rural and low-income neighbourhoods. There is also the risk of automation replacing jobs, particularly those that are repetitive, but new jobs are introduced in the process. Businesses and authorities must invest in reskilling initiatives to ensure employees can adjust, and teachers should assist learners to retain the skills of critical thinking and problem-solving despite the use of AI (McKinsey Global Institute, 2018). There should always be a balance between technology and human interaction in the classrooms and the workplace.In the next few years, the education and employment systems will be more reliant on the fruitful collaboration between the artificial intelligence and humans. Instead of eliminating human effort, AI may be used as an instrument in the improvement of problem-solving, creativity, and decision-making in sectors. Nevertheless, this potential can be realised only in case the society manages to solve ethical, social, and economic issues which come with the advanced technologies. Policy makers must develop clear policies that emphasize on fairness, transparency and accountability in the design and implementation of AI. Ethics principles ought to be geared towards lessening the biases in power of algorithms, safeguarding the personal privacy, and guaranteeing that the advantages of automation are shared equally.The role of educators is an equally important one. Digital literacy and critical thinking should be included in the curriculum of schools and universities to provide students with knowledge on how to use AI tools and how to question and analyze them. Governmental and employer-driven lifelong learning programs will play a critical role in enabling employees who have to constantly change in response to changing technical demands. A change in this direction can be facilitated by business leaders through investing in employee training and creating work environments where machines and people can work together in harmony.With a culture of lifelong learning and responsible innovation, the society can utilize AI to produce new opportunities, enhance productivity, and increase knowledge access, and maintain human agency and creativity (Susskind and Susskind, 2015).

RELATED WORK

Artificial intelligence (AI) remains the development of the twenty-first century and still transforms the world of education and employment (Haenlein and Kaplan, 2019). Researchers have generated a rapidly expanding corpus of case studies and literature that AI technologies have an effect on society. Due to the quick advancements in automation, generative models, and machine-learning models, individuals who do not possess technical expertise are now able to generate content, process data, and develop products (Floridi and Chiriatti, 2020).ChatGPT and DALL·E are generative systems that enable users to create text and images in the near future, which reduces creative barriers and promotes novel learning and work methods (Bommasani et al., 2022). The intelligent tutoring systems offer real-time feedback and tailor content to the needs of an individual learner, which proves the prospects of feature-specific responses in online classes (Holmes et al., 2019). Online education organisations like edX and Coursera incorporate AI to suggest courses and monitor the progress of students, and provide students in underserved regions with access to quality education (Zawacki-Richter et al., 2019).

Simultaneously, the labour market demonstrates an increased interest in modular learning and micro-credentials that assist workers to keep their skills constantly updated in an AI-focused economy (Schroeder and Spann, 2020).

Technology and AI are transforming various sectors by improving efficiency, decision-making, and flexibility. Some key examples include:

- Gig-economy services (e.g., Upwork, Fiverr) use smart matching models to pair freelancers with customers, promoting flexible, task-based jobs (Manyika et al., 2017).
- Artificial intelligence (AI) in medicine enhances treatment planning and improves patient outcomes (Topol, 2019).
- Predictive algorithms in finance help improve risk management and guide investor strategies (Arner et al., 2016).

The field of transportation embraces connections to the autonomous sphere of logistics and self-driving cars that make the field safer and more mobile (Goodall, 2016).

In spite of these achievements, there are still significant challenges. Automation is causing certain traditional employment positions to be threatened, and reskilling and upskilling to become essential to enable employees to adjust to the new jobs (Frey and Osborne, 2017). Researchers note that AI will not replace human strengths, but creativity, emotional intelligence, and critical thinking will play a crucial role in the future (Bryson, 2019). There is also an interest in ethical concerns, such as algorithmic bias, transparency, and privacy threats based on personal data (Jobin et al., 2019). Researchers demand the implementation of tighter governance and cooperation among industry, academia, and governments to make sure that AI is beneficial and does not contribute to the further development of existing disparities (Whittlestone et al., 2019).VR and augmented reality (AR) allow virtual reality (VR) and artificial intelligence (AI) to offer deep, safe environments in which engineering and medical learners could practice and create the learning gap between theory and practice (Radianti et al., 2020).

This is evidenced by these examples that AI keeps enabling possibilities, and at the same time, needs to be monitored, and the human talent must be developed further to ensure an inclusive future.

PRELIMINARY THEORIES

Some early theories on the subject of artificial intelligence aimed to give the basics of the theory, technical principles, and social, ethical, and economic aspects of artificial intelligence. The understanding of these early views may serve to guide researchers and policymakers to make predictions about AI and preparations for the challenges that may arise when a growing number of people start depending on the technology in their day-to-day activities (Nilsson, 2010). The main topics are the philosophical foundations of AI, modes of learning, ethical paradigms, and the impacts of AI on education, labour, and society. Machine learning (ML) is a theory where algorithms can learn, identify patterns, and improve over time without explicit programming (Jordan & Mitchell, 2015). An even more developed subfield, deep learning, employs artificial neural networks that resemble the architecture of the human brain and drives breakthroughs in natural language processing, computer vision and speech recognition (LeCun et al., 2015). The techniques enable computers to comprehend human language, recognise objects in pictures and make complex decisions. These notions are extended by reinforcement learning (RL), which demonstrates how an artificial intelligence (AI) agent can learn by trial and error as it interacts with its environment. The system is rewarded or punished, and eventually, it will devise strategies that are the most successful in the long run (Sutton and Barto, 2018). Game-playing systems like AlphaGo and self-driving vehicles evidenced the use of RL in continuous improvement with feedback provided by a real or simulated environment (Silver et al., 2017). Explainable AI is another powerful concept and focuses more on transparency and interpretability to ensure that a user can understand the manner in which a model arrives at a decision (Doshi-Velez and Kim, 2017). Explainability can be of particular concern in the medical field, finance, and the criminal justice system, where the black box processes may cause unfair or unsafe results. Since most algorithms are trained on past data, which can be discriminatory in nature, they can perpetuate discrimination (Barocas and Selbst, 2016). Researchers suggest models, according to which fairness, accountability, and transparency will be in the first place to make sure that AI will benefit society as a whole (Floridi et al., 2018). The social good concept of AI suggests that technology must be used to assist all people and contribute to the elimination of such global challenges as poverty, health crises, and climate change (Vinuesa et al., 2020). The theories of the workforce emphasise that the automation of jobs requires reskilling of employees due to the shift in occupational character.

According to the so-called skills-gap hypothesis, the growing demand will be in the expertise of robotics, data science, and AI-related professional areas, which will need new education and training systems (Bessen, 2019). Contrary to it, the perspective of the so-called augmented intelligence argues that AI strengthens, but does not eliminate the human ability to operate, giving individuals the opportunity to concentrate on innovation, understanding, and sophisticated decision-making (Shneiderman, 2020). Education research evidences the assumption that AI may be applied to individualise the learning process by examining a group of student data and adjusting the instructions to the needs of individuals (Luckin and Holmes, 2017). The use of intelligent tutoring systems already demonstrates the potential of students to acquire knowledge at their own pace and to obtain precisely the respective support, which is necessary to democratise the process of obtaining high-quality education, irrespective of location or background.AGI is a system that is broadly cognitively endowed like humans and can carry out a variety of tasks without having to be programmed to accomplish any particular task (Goertzel and Pennachin, 2007).

Even though AGI remains a hypothetical project, its potential emergence creates serious governance, moral, and societal issues in the future (Bostrom, 2014).

FOCUS OF THE ARTICLE

The field of artificial intelligence (AI) is transforming education, work, and daily life at a pace that brings in the new opportunities of innovation and redefines the skills that will be demanded by the future workforce (Brynjolfsson and Mitchell, 2017). This paper sheds light on the new AI tools and discusses the future of technology and technology-related changes in higher education and the labour market. Other models, like the GPT family of OpenAI and DALL·E, can be used to produce text, imagery, music, or even computer code based on straightforward directives and assist writers, designers, and developers in their creative and technical work (Bommasani et al., 2022). Learning platforms that are AI-powered, such as Coursera, Udemy and Khan Academy, can suggest courses and even pace learning based on the progress of the specific learner (Zawacki-Richter et al., 2019).ITs offer personalised instructions and immediate feedback and do not necessarily involve numerous human educators (Holmes et al., 2019). Gradescope is an example of an assessment tool that is based on AI to grade essays and code assignments promptly and provide students with more detailed feedback to enable teachers to have more time to mentor. AI-based virtual assistants such as Google Assistant, Alexa, and

Siri facilitate office work, keep track of meetings, and provide responses, which enhance productivity at workplaces (Haenlein and Kaplan, 2019).

Diagnostic algorithms already exist in the field of healthcare that process medical images and genetic data to support physicians, reduce expenses, and enhance the quality of care (Topol, 2019).In the manufacturing, logistics, and agricultural industries, robotics and automation are further increasing, and as time goes on, various types of vehicles powered by robots and drone delivery are expected to be more advanced (Manyika et al., 2017).NLP allows the customer service bots to translate to a higher level and simulate conversation with people, which makes AI more approachable in everyday life (Jurafsky and Martin, 2023).In creative industries, it is employed in the areas of music composition, graphic design, and filmmaking, where AI tools like MuseNet are used to advance the ideas of the artists (Elgammal et al., 2017).

Universities use AI to propose courses that a student likes and can achieve success in, forming their own learning trajectory (Luckin and Holmes, 2017). The analytics are based on data, and they inform the design of the curriculum, allocation of resources, and the support provided to students (Ifenthaler and Yau, 2020).

Virtual classrooms and AI chatbots can be used to improve remote education because they provide real-time support and address large and heterogeneous groups of students (Chen et al., 2020).To equip graduates with AI-focused jobs, machine learning, robotics, and data science are progressively part of the curriculum (Gibson et al., 2021). The routine use of AI automation removes repetitive work, including data entry and customer services, but introduces new opportunities in developing AI systems, data analysis, and robotics (Frey and Osborne, 2017). The concept of reskilling and upskilling is necessary because employees are going to adjust to the changing job demands, and AI-based training systems assist individuals in learning at a comfortable pace (OECD, 2021). Predictive analytics and NLP are applied in recruitment to more effectively and objectively pair prospective employees with jobs (Bogen & Rieke, 2018). Other ways artificial intelligence tools can be used to promote collaboration include facilitating communication, project management, and decision-making in remote and hybrid work environments (Sarker et al., 2021).

In general, education and employment are becoming the target of automation, AI, and changing labour demand.AI will render the process of learning more democratic as it will enhance access to quality education across the globe and will allow teachers to learn more about their students and their needs. Simultaneously, it will change the existing occupations and introduce new fields of work. Employees with excellent knowledge of AI use will become extremely sought after, and the employees whose jobs are at risk of being automated will be forced to reskill and transfer to the new sectors to stay afloat (ILO, 2021).

PROPOSED METHOD

The presence of AI within education and the workforce has presented unique opportunities never before seen: creative opportunities, accessibility, and efficiencies. However, it requires a methodical strategy to promote effective change through well-conceived design, systematic implementation, and continual assessment of various avenues with the actual needs of teachers, students, employees, and employers (Bryson et al., 2023). The structure presented below is one of the many ways to actualise AI-induced change. It is conducted with stakeholder involvement and needs analysis.

In the educational contexts, schools will need to involve parents, administrators, instructors, and students to determine learning goals, resource gaps, and adoption barriers. This participatory approach ensures that AI adoption addresses real problems serving educational institutions. For instance, AI-driven platforms can sift through attendance, homework completion, and engagement with online learning tools to identify students who are at risk of falling behind. Involving parents or instructors in these processes allows institutions to locate interventions that are practical and culturally acceptable to all parties. Similarly, in the workplace, organisations, employees, human resources executives, and industry experts will map skills shortages, assess automation opportunities, and identify organisational issues. Such early-stage engagement prevents divergences from keeping AI relevant and applicable across both educational and employment settings (Jarke et al., 2022).

After the needs analysis, the next step is to select and customise the AI tools. Decision-makers should adopt criteria that place relevance first, then scalability and interoperability: relevance to local goals, scalability or possibility of expansion at a later stage. For example, an intelligent tutoring system could be developed by a university for regional languages and curricula to promote better student understanding and retention, whereas recruitment algorithms might be customised by a company to ensure fair and efficient assessment of candidates (Floridi et al., 2018). Appropriate customisation prevents incompatibilities with existing software systems, embraces cultural sensitivities, and meets legal requirements.

The support of capacity-building processes deserves to be mentioned along with the successful implementation of AI integration. This means developing the needed technical infrastructure, including good connectivity, sound hardware, and updated software, especially in contexts that are under-resourced or remote (OECD, 2021). A full range of workshops and hands-on training should then be provided to teachers, students, and employees to raise the level of efficiency in using AI tools. Structured change management approaches centred around transparent communication, the joint solving of problems, and early successes will diminish resistance and nurture a culture of change and continuous learning (West et al., 2019). Monitoring and evaluation mechanisms are likewise important. Performance indicators in education might encompass student engagement, learning outcomes, results in standardised tests, dropout rates, and teacher workload. Workplace metrics covering productivity, job performance, recruitment efficiency, and operational costs instruct in the practical use of AI. There is continual feedback through surveys, focus groups, and user analytics that update AI systems and training resources (Sarker et al., 2021). An accountability mechanism should rate AI algorithms through audits to eliminate instances of prejudice, discrimination, and unfair procedures (Jobin et al., 2019). Strict regulations on data protection, consistent with local and international standards, e.g., the General Data Protection Regulation (GDPR), must be employed to sustain trust and protect sensitive data. Another point worthy of attention is ensuring accessibility. AI must, therefore, be configured to serve, in the very least, users who have disabilities or less technical know-how to offer inclusion and equal opportunities (Whittlestone et al., 2019). Adaptive interfaces, voice-assisted commands, and multimodal feedback mechanisms, therefore, all stand as possible facilitators to bridge the digital divide. Furthermore, AI should be used to foster collaborative learning and team-based work both in educational setups and workplaces to develop interpersonal and problem-solving skills. Ultimately, a long-term perspective calls for consideration of sustainability and ethics. Schools and organisations should institute AI ethics committees responsible for implementation oversight, adjudication of ethical dilemmas, and guidance on responsible application practices. Combining stakeholder engagement, strategic customisation, solid infrastructure, constant monitoring, accessibility, and ethical oversight will make AI integration meaningful, equal, and measurable at educational and professional levels. This inclusive approach, which maximises AI potential while mitigating its associated hazards, will result in green pastures for entrepreneurship and adaptive learning ecosystems.

Lastly, AI implementation and maintenance require scalable and maintainable cloud-based systems that are more adaptable to context and cost. There should be collaboration between academia, industry, government, and non-profits so innovation may be pursued, and the outcome of education is dependent on the workforce demand (Manyika et al., 2017). Regular research and development, audits, and upgrading will keep these systems current, cost-efficient, and not obsolete (Brynjolfsson and McAfee, 2017). It is a voluntary approach to AI-education and the workforce based on participation, informed choice, non-discriminatory implementation, continuous assessment, and ethical control.

EXPERIMENTAL RESULTS

Being launched in a fast succession, AI-based transformations continue to impact education, labour, and daily life, with newer and newer efficiencies built to mitigate existing opportunities in creativity (Haenlein and Kaplan, 2019). Now, generative AI models such as GPT-4 and DALL·E generate text, images, and even code all from a short prompt. These systems are used to automate creativity, such as writing articles, writing marketing copy, or creating graphics, bringing down the cost and time previously spent on human labour (Bommasani et al., 2022). According to the researchers, GPT-4 produces multilingual scholarly drafts and customer-service messages, while DALL-E generates fast visual concepts for designers and advertisers. Applications like Duolingo or Khan Academy change the content on the move according to the level of advancement of each learner, thus enhancing engagement and retention (Zawacki-Richter et al., 2019). With autograding, plagiarism detection, and the provision of detailed, individualised feedback for students, Gradescope and Turnitin free up teachers for mentoring time (Chen et al., 2020). Research indicates such systems enhance accuracy in grading and minimise bias, besides providing better information on student performance. Pymetrics and HireVue are two platforms capable of analysing cognitive skills and behavioural information of the candidates to provide an efficient and quicker way to match the applicants with the vacancies and reduce bias (Bogen and Rieke, 2018). The AI-based career advice and tailored reskilling initiatives enable employees to take into account the future skill demands and shape workers for new jobs (OECD, 2021).

A combination of AI and quantum computing would allow a real-time study of complex systems, speeding up the discovery of new things in climatology, medicine, and cryptography (Arute et al., 2019). Robotics based on AI are already used in logistics, healthcare, and manufacturing, and schools have already implemented humanoid robots like NAO to assist in programming and interactive classes (Belpaeme et al., 2018).

IBM Watson Health and other medical systems are systems that process large volumes of data to enhance the detection and treatment of early diseases, beating conventional diagnosis systems in both speed and accuracy (Topol, 2019).

AI is increasingly finding applications in higher education to individualise the learning process, inform curriculum development, and forecast labour-market trends.DreamBox and Socratic have tools that adapt course content to individual student strengths, whereas predictive analytics can assist institutions in updating the programs in areas like data science, cybersecurity, and the creation of artificial intelligence (Ifenthaler and Yau, 2020). The hybrid and distance learning, which has been sped up due to the COVID-19 pandemic, is still a trend with AI chatbots and online classes that allow immediate feedback and smooth communication irrespective of the geographical location (Chen et al., 2020). These outcomes indicate quantifiable improvement in student achievement and career readiness.

In the future, scientists believe that AI will be united with robotics and quantum computing, introducing new functions and ethical dilemmas. Artificial general intelligence is a long-term goal that is theoretically feasible, although in some distant future, it may equip machines with abilities to carry out various cognitive functions presently in the domain of human beings (Bostrom, 2014). Such a scenario would give a chain reaction to reskilling and ethical monitoring. Altogether, experimental results of a few investigations state that either generative models or adaptive learning systems of AI are already performing the transformation in the classroom and workplace. Their evolution shall need adaptable educational courses, refresher training for workers, and good governance from which society ought to benefit while curbing the risks.

SOLUTIONS AND RECOMMENDATIONS

As an area of artificial intelligence (AI), higher education and the workforce, in general, are going through change, necessitating concerted efforts on the part of educators, industry leaders, governments, and learners themselves (Brynjolfsson and McAfee, 2017). AI-based customised learning interfaces, which include intelligent tutors and adaptive course platforms, enable students to study at their own pace and get instant feedback and progress evaluation (Zawacki-Richter et al., 2019). These systems enhance accessibility to students with disabilities because they accommodate individual needs, and they provide barrier-free learning environments.

AI and immersive technologies in the form of virtual and augmented reality (VR/AR) complement the training through a realistic experience: medical students may train in virtual surgeries, and engineering trainees may train on complicated equipment in a safe environment (Radianti et al., 2020). Such applications of AI as Google Socratic and Duolingo adaptive language platform can also be used to illustrate how AI can offer one-on-one assistance in subjects and ability level (Chen et al., 2020). At the workplace, AI automation is transforming the work environment by automating routine duties like data input and assisting in predictive analytics to make smarter decisions (Bughin et al., 2018). The innovations of natural language processing (NLP) allow conversational agents that speak almost perfectly fluently, translators, and literary writing tools that write speedily using AI assistance (Hirschberg and Manning, 2015). Generative AI can speed up product design, marketing, and prototyping, create more and encourage innovative thinking and collaboration worldwide (Bommasani et al., 2022). Robotic process automation (RPA) and AI-based recruitment systems simplify the process of hiring and workforce management and automatically match applicants with vacancies in a more effective way and with minimal bias, if properly supervised (Bogen & Rieke, 2018). The move toward education and work that is AI-integrated highlights the necessity of lifelong education and training of the faculty. To implement these technologies in curricula in a responsible manner, educators must be constantly trained to use AI tools, data analytics, and responsible practices (Luckin et al., 2016).

Micro-credentials, industry-academia relationships, and flexible online certifications can assist students and employees to remain up-to-date with the latest skills, such as machine learning, critical thinking and emotional intelligence (OECD, 2021). Although AI is used to automate routine tasks, it establishes new positions, like AI trainers, data ethicists, and machine-learning experts, highlighting the importance of soft skills, including innovation, problem-solving, and flexibility, as a complement to automation (Frey and Osborne, 2017).

Various stakeholders are recommended to implement:

1. Colleges must incorporate AI into their educational systems, make ethics more central to the curriculum, and train the faculty to use AI.
2. Governments should implement explicit AI application rules, invest in digital infrastructure, and invest in government-business projects to overcome the skills gap and enhance fair access to technology.
3. Industries are to devote their attention to the work where human creativity and empathy are needed, offer frequent AI upskilling, and use open-minded and bias-conscious AI systems.
4. Online courses, certifications, and AI-based career platforms should also help individuals (both students and job seekers) cultivate their lifelong learning habits to ensure that they stay competitive in the constantly evolving labour market.

To maximise the potential of AI to promote inclusion, efficiency and innovation in education systems and workplaces, these recommendations can be applied to promote ethical standards and social equity.

FUTURE DIRECTIONS FOR RESEARCH

Developed by AI, the new technology shapes human learning, teaching, and working, offering opportunities as well as posing challenges for human beings (Brynjolfsson & McAfee, 2017).In education, adaptive tutoring platforms, automated assessments, and real-time analytics deliver lessons based on student engagement between two levels of content, adjusting the pace at which they work for the learner on recognition and grasping concepts (Zawacki-Richter et al., 2019).

In the meantime, robotic process automation and machine-learning algorithms handle routine tasks, inferring data into decisions and supporting an enhanced level of productivity (Bughin et al., 2018). Considering these developments, it is clear that the need for human qualities such as creativity, critical thinking, and emotional intelligence will increase as AI systems focus on operational work (Frey & Osborne, 2017). Long-term considerations of how AI will transform labour markets and educational institutions should be considered as future research objectives.

While automation is likely to replace some occupations, it will also create new jobs that combine technical skills and creativity and require people to be constantly upskilled and reskilled (OECD, 2021). Scholars should examine lifelong learning strategies and consider how universities and employers could support continuous professional development as the technical landscape continues to evolve. On the other hand, increased usage of AI in classrooms raises questions about privacy, ethics, and the evolving roles of human instructors in highly automated environments (Williamson & Eynon, 2020). Ensuring that algorithmic bias is addressed, preserving private data, and insisting on transparent governance for AI will be the cornerstones for fair adoption (Binns, 2018). In fact, AI tools should really facilitate and augment human capabilities and not set themselves against these abilities.

The design of systems to facilitate human-machine interaction can consequently enhance creativity and collaboration in decision-making (Shneiderman, 2020). The focus is on human-AI collaborative teams and hybrid learning environments to discover opportunities in which AI tools may amplify human judgment and empathy instead of undermining them.

Given the dependence of AI on education and employment, any proactive research must project emerging technologies to social impacts so that policymakers can be guided toward deployment worthy of all members.

Key Terms and Definitions

Artificial Intelligence (AI): Computer systems designed to execute operations that generally require human intelligence, such as perception in natural language and pattern recognition (Russell & Norvig, 2021).

1. Machine Learning (ML): That subdivision of AI in which algorithms acquire experience from a data set, choosing to make predictions or decisions about new observations without being explicitly programmed (Goodfellow et al., 2016).

2. Natural Language Processing (NLP): Methods that enable machines to comprehend and generate human language under the auspices of AI to run chatbots or virtual assistants (Hirschberg & Manning, 2015).

3. Generative AI: AI models that create new text and new images or any sort of content from given training data, such as GPT-4 and DALL·E (Bommasani et al., 2022).

4. Personalised Learning: Teaching that is personalised for individuals based on their needs and preferences as determined by AI analytics (Holmes et al., 2019).

5. Ethical AI: Fairness, transparency, privacy, and accountability in the building and use of AI (Binns, 2018).

6. Robotic Process Automation (RPA): Software robots performing business-intensive processes repeatedly, thereby increasing the efficiency and accuracy of such processes (van der Aalst et al., 2018).

7. Augmented Intelligence: Designs that seek to ensure that AI systems somehow augment human decision-making rather than completely replacing it (Shneiderman, 2020).

By increasing the shared understanding and vocabulary around these terms, educators, industry leaders, and policymakers will be best equipped to realise the full potential of AI to create learning environments and workplaces that are creative, equitable, and sustainable.

CONCLUSION

The rapid ongoing development in technology is bringing transformations in education and jobs in various parts of the world. Today, Artificial Intelligence and Machine Learning aid teachers, students, and workers in carrying out their activities in a timely and precise manner. The learning that takes place in schools should be personalised, with lessons designed according to the needs of each student. Intelligent tutoring systems and adaptive platforms provide instant feedback both to students and teachers, fill the voids left in instruction, and generally provide quality education to all. They are capable of caring for menial tasks in offices, analysing complicated data, and making decisions that could further great acts in conjunction with human pluses. Therefore, it provides an opportunity to invest in creative potential and strategic thinking, thereby upgrading human potential in creativity, problem-solving, clear communication, and adaptability. Lends itself to fearless efforts; making an implementation comes with a few hang-ups. Great concerns about privacy protections, issues of fair use, and capitalism will cast the shadow of deepening the digital divide onto the technological front. Very clear policies, training, and indeed common good considerations must be placed into the business world and government sectors, as well as educational institutions.

The future lies in the ground relations between people and AI. By the mechanism of human assessment alongside the velocity and power of AI in society, the best education, new jobs, and solutions to problems shall be realised. The greatest achievements will be upon educators, businesses, and policymakers being partners in a shared commitment to equity, lifelong learning, and responsible use of technology.

REFERENCES

Arner, D. W., Barberis, J., & Buckley, R. P. (2016). The evolution of fintech: A new post-crisis paradigm? *Georgetown Journal of International Law*, *47*(4), 1271–1319.

Arute, F., Arya, K., Babbush, R., Bacon, D., Bardin, J. C., Barends, R., Biswas, R., Boixo, S., Brandao, F. G. S. L., Buell, D. A., Burkett, B., Chen, Y., Chen, Z., Chiaro, B., Collins, R., Courtney, W., Dunsworth, A., Farhi, E., Foxen, B., & Martinis, J. M. (2019). Quantum supremacy using a programmable superconducting processor. *Nature*, *574*(7779), 505–510. DOI: 10.1038/s41586-019-1666-5 PMID: 31645734

Barocas, S., & Selbst, A. D. (2016). Big data's disparate impact. *SSRN*, *104*(3), 671–732. DOI: 10.2139/ssrn.2477899

Belpaeme, T., Kennedy, J., Ramachandran, A., Scassellati, B., & Tanaka, F. (2018). Social robots for education: A review. *Science Robotics*, *3*(21), eaat5954. Advance online publication. DOI: 10.1126/scirobotics.aat5954 PMID: 33141719

Bengio, Y., LeCun, Y., & Hinton, G. (2015). Deep learning. *Nature*, *521*(7553), 436–444. DOI: 10.1038/nature14539 PMID: 26017442

Bessen, J. E. (2019). AI and jobs: The role of demand. *NBER Working Paper* No. 24235. https://doi.org/DOI: 10.3386/w24235

Binns, R. (2018). Fairness in machine learning: Lessons from political philosophy. *Proceedings of the 2018 Conference on Fairness, Accountability, and Transparency*, 149–159. https://doi.org/DOI: 10.1145/3287560.3287572

Bogen, M., & Rieke, A. (2018). Help wanted: An examination of hiring algorithms, equity, and bias. *Technology Science*. https://techscience.org

Bommasani, R., Hudson, D. A., Adeli, E., Altman, R., Arora, S., von Arx, S., & Liang, P. (2022). On the opportunities and risks of foundation models. *arXiv*. https://arxiv.org/abs/2108.07258

Bostrom, N. (2014). *Superintelligence: Paths, dangers, strategies*. Oxford University Press.

Brynjolfsson, E., & McAfee, A. (2014). *The second machine age: Work, progress, and prosperity in a time of brilliant technologies*. W. W. Norton & Company.

Brynjolfsson, E., & McAfee, A. (2017). *Machine, platform, crowd: Harnessing our digital future*. W. W. Norton & Company.

Brynjolfsson, E., & Mitchell, T. (2017). What can machine learning do? Workforce implications. *Science, 358*(6370), 1530–1534. DOI: 10.1126/science.aap8062 PMID: 29269459

Bryson, J. J. (2019). The past decade and the future of AI's impact on society. *Science, 366*(6468), 477–478. DOI: 10.1126/science.aay8424

Bryson, J. J., Diamantis, M. E., & Grant, T. D. (2023). Artificial intelligence: Governance and the new global order. *Annual Review of Political Science, 26*, 65–86. DOI: 10.1146/annurev-polisci-050722-041407

Bughin, J., Hazan, E., Ramaswamy, S., Chui, M., Allas, T., Dahlström, P., & Trench, M. (2018). *Skill shift: Automation and the future of the workforce*. McKinsey Global Institute.

Chen, L., Chen, P., & Lin, Z. (2020). Artificial intelligence in education: A review. *IEEE Access : Practical Innovations, Open Solutions, 8*, 75264–75278. DOI: 10.1109/ACCESS.2020.2988510

Doshi-Velez, F., & Kim, B. (2017). Towards a rigorous science of interpretable machine learning. *arXiv*. https://arxiv.org/abs/1702.08608

Elgammal, A., Liu, B., Elhoseiny, M., & Mazzone, M. (2017). CAN: Creative adversarial networks, generating "art" by learning about styles and deviating from style norms. *Proceedings of the 8th International Conference on Computational Creativity*, 96–103.

Floridi, L., & Chiriatti, M. (2020). GPT-3: Its nature, scope, limits, and consequences. *Minds and Machines, 30*(4), 681–694. DOI: 10.1007/s11023-020-09548-1

Floridi, L., Cowls, J., Beltrametti, M., Chatila, R., Chazerand, P., Dignum, V., Luetge, C., Madelin, R., Pagallo, U., Rossi, F., Schafer, B., Valcke, P., & Vayena, E. (2018). AI4People—An ethical framework for a good AI society. *Minds and Machines, 28*(4), 689–707. DOI: 10.1007/s11023-018-9482-5 PMID: 30930541

Frey, C. B., & Osborne, M. A. (2017). The future of employment: How susceptible are jobs to computerisation? *Technological Forecasting and Social Change, 114*, 254–280. DOI: 10.1016/j.techfore.2016.08.019

Gibson, D., Broadley, T., Downie, J., & Wallet, P. (2021). Artificial intelligence in education: Challenges and opportunities. *Educational Technology Research and Development, 69*(4), 201–216. DOI: 10.1007/s11423-020-09859-5

Goertzel, B., & Pennachin, C. (Eds.). (2007). *Artificial general intelligence*. Springer. DOI: 10.1007/978-3-540-68677-4

Goodall, N. J. (2016). Can you program ethics into a self-driving car? *IEEE Spectrum, 53*(6), 28–58. DOI: 10.1109/MSPEC.2016.7473149

Goodfellow, I., Bengio, Y., & Courville, A. (2016). *Deep learning*. MIT Press.

Haenlein, M., & Kaplan, A. (2019). A brief history of artificial intelligence: On the past, present, and future of artificial intelligence. *California Management Review, 61*(4), 5–14. DOI: 10.1177/0008125619864925

Hirschberg, J., & Manning, C. D. (2015). Advances in natural language processing. *Science, 349*(6245), 261–266. DOI: 10.1126/science.aaa8685 PMID: 26185244

Holmes, W., Bialik, M., & Fadel, C. (2019). *Artificial intelligence in education: Promises and implications for teaching and learning*. Centre for Curriculum Redesign.

Ifenthaler, D., & Yau, J. Y. K. (2020). Utilising learning analytics for study success: Reflections on current empirical findings. *International Journal of Learning Technology, 15*(1), 1–16. DOI: 10.1504/IJLT.2020.105995

International Labour Organisation. (2021). [*The role of digital labour platforms in transforming the world of work*. ILO.]. *World Employment and Social Outlook*, •••, 2021.

Jarke, J., Gerhard, U., & Busse, S. (2022). Co-creating AI: Stakeholder participation in the design of artificial intelligence. *AI & Society, 37*(1), 167–179. DOI: 10.1007/s00146-021-01172-4 PMID: 33867693

Jobin, A., Ienca, M., & Vayena, E. (2019). The global landscape of AI ethics guidelines. *Nature Machine Intelligence, 1*(9), 389–399. DOI: 10.1038/s42256-019-0088-2

Jordan, M. I., & Mitchell, T. M. (2015). Machine learning: Trends, perspectives, and prospects. *Science, 349*(6245), 255–260. DOI: 10.1126/science.aaa8415 PMID: 26185243

Jurafsky, D., & Martin, J. H. (2023). *Speech and language processing* (3rd ed.). Draft., https://web.stanford.edu/~jurafsky/slp3/

LeCun, Y., Bengio, Y., & Hinton, G. (2015). Deep learning. *Nature, 521*(7553), 436–444. DOI: 10.1038/nature14539 PMID: 26017442

Luckin, R., Holmes, W., Griffiths, M., & Forcier, L. B. (2016). *Intelligence unleashed: An argument for AI in education*. Pearson.

Manyika, J., Lund, S., Chui, M., Bughin, J., Woetzel, J., Batra, P., Ko, R., & Sanghvi, S. (2017). *Jobs lost, jobs gained: Workforce transitions in a time of automation*. McKinsey Global Institute.

McKinsey Global Institute. (2018). *Skill shift: Automation and the future of the workforce*. McKinsey & Company. https://www.mckinsey.com/business-functions/mckinsey-digital/our-insights

Nilsson, N. J. (2010). *The quest for artificial intelligence: A history of ideas and achievements*. Cambridge University Press.

OECD. (2021). *AI and the future of skills*. OECD Publishing., DOI: 10.1787/aa86e7b1-

OECD. (2021). *Skills outlook 2021: Learning for life*. OECD Publishing., DOI: 10.1787/0ae365b4-

Radianti, J., Majchrzak, T. A., Fromm, J., & Wohlgenannt, I. (2020). A systematic review of immersive virtual reality applications for higher education. *Computers & Education, 147*, 103778. DOI: 10.1016/j.compedu.2019.103778

Russell, S., & Norvig, P. (2021). *Artificial intelligence: A modern approach* (4th ed.). Pearson.

Sarker, I. H., Kayes, A. S. M., & Watters, P. (2021). Effectiveness analysis of machine learning classification models for predicting personalised context-aware smartphone usage. *Journal of Big Data, 8*, 1–28. DOI: 10.1186/s40537-021-00456-2

Schroeder, J., & Spann, M. (2020). Platform learning in multi-sided markets: The case of digital education platforms. *Electronic Markets, 30*(3), 531–546. DOI: 10.1007/s12525-019-00347-3

Shneiderman, B. (2020). Human-centred artificial intelligence: Reliable, safe & trustworthy. *International Journal of Human-Computer Interaction, 36*(6), 495–504. DOI: 10.1080/10447318.2020.1741118

Silver, D., Schrittwieser, J., Simonyan, K., Antonoglou, I., Huang, A., Guez, A., Hubert, T., Baker, L., Lai, M., Bolton, A., Chen, Y., Lillicrap, T., Hui, F., Sifre, L., van den Driessche, G., Graepel, T., & Hassabis, D. (2017). Mastering the game of Go without human knowledge. *Nature, 550*(7676), 354–359. DOI: 10.1038/nature24270 PMID: 29052630

Susskind, R., & Susskind, D. (2015). *The future of the professions: How technology will transform the work of human experts*. Oxford University Press. DOI: 10.1093/oso/9780198713395.001.0001

Susskind, R., & Susskind, D. (2015). *The future of the professions: How technology will transform the work of human experts*. Oxford University Press. DOI: 10.1093/oso/9780198713395.001.0001

Sutton, R. S., & Barto, A. G. (2018). *Reinforcement learning: An introduction* (2nd ed.). MIT Press.

Topol, E. J. (2019). High-performance medicine: The convergence of human and artificial intelligence. *Nature Medicine*, *25*(1), 44–56. DOI: 10.1038/s41591-018-0300-7 PMID: 30617339

UNESCO. (2022). *Artificial intelligence and education: Guidance for policy makers*. UNESCO Publishing. https://unesdoc.unesco.org

van der Aalst, W. M. P., Bichler, M., & Heinzl, A. (2018). Robotic process automation. *Business & Information Systems Engineering*, *60*(4), 269–272. DOI: 10.1007/s12599-018-0542-4

Vinuesa, R., Azizpour, H., Leite, I., Balaam, M., Dignum, V., Domisch, S., Felländer, A., Langhans, S. D., Tegmark, M., & Fuso Nerini, F. (2020). The role of artificial intelligence in achieving the Sustainable Development Goals. *Nature Communications*, *11*(1), 233. DOI: 10.1038/s41467-019-14108-y PMID: 31932590

West, D. M., Allen, J. R., & Grewal, R. S. (2019). *The future of work: Robots, AI, and automation*. Brookings Institution Press.

Whittlestone, J., Nyrup, R., Alexandrova, A., & Cave, S. (2019). The role and limits of principles in AI ethics. *Proceedings of the AAAI/ACM Conference on AI, Ethics, and Society*, 195–200. https://doi.org/DOI: 10.1145/3306618.3314289

Williamson, B., & Eynon, R. (2020). The global edtech industry and the pandemic: Digital education, AI and the new schooling normal. *Learning, Media and Technology*, *45*(4), 355–367. DOI: 10.1080/17439884.2020.1817766

World Economic Forum. (2023). *Future of Jobs Report 2023*. World Economic Forum. https://www.weforum.org/reports/future-of-jobs-report-2023

Zawacki-Richter, O., Marín, V. I., Bond, M., & Gouverneur, F. (2019). Systematic review of research on artificial intelligence applications in higher education. *International Journal of Educational Technology in Higher Education*, *16*(1), 39. DOI: 10.1186/s41239-019-0171-0

KEY TERMS AND DEFINITIONS

Artificial Intelligence (AI): Computer systems designed to execute operations that generally require human intelligence, such as perception in natural language and pattern recognition (Russell & Norvig, 2021).

Augmented Intelligence: Designs that seek to ensure that AI systems somehow augment human decision-making rather than completely replacing it (Shneiderman, 2020).

Ethical AI: Fairness, transparency, privacy, and accountability in the building and use of AI (Binns, 2018).

Generative AI: AI models that create new text and new images or any sort of content from given training data, such as GPT-4 and DALL·E (Bommasani et al., 2022).

Machine Learning (ML): That subdivision of AI in which algorithms acquire experience from a data set, choosing to make predictions or decisions about new observations without being explicitly programmed (Goodfellow et al., 2016).

Natural Language Processing (NLP): Methods that enable machines to comprehend and generate human language under the auspices of AI to run chatbots or virtual assistants (Hirschberg & Manning, 2015).

Personalised Learning: Teaching that is personalised for individuals based on their needs and preferences as determined by AI analytics (Holmes et al., 2019).

Robotic Process Automation (RPA): Software robots performing business-intensive processes repeatedly, thereby increasing the efficiency and accuracy of such processes (van der Aalst et al., 2018).

Chapter 7
Empowering Teachers for Adapting to AI-Driven Education Era

Y. Fathima
http://orcid.org/0000-0002-0045-1421
Jain (Deemed to be) University, India

Usha Prabhu
http://orcid.org/0000-0001-6219-5358
Jain (Deemed to be) University, India

N. Sathyanarayana
http://orcid.org/0000-0002-4185-7751
Jain (Deemed to be) University, India

Rachana Saxena
http://orcid.org/0000-0003-3514-2757
Jain (Deemed to be) University, India

Independent Researcher, India

ABSTRACT

This study examines the transformative impact of Artificial Intelligence (AI) on education, emphasising how AI technologies, such as machine learning, natural language processing, and predictive analytics, are reshaping teaching and learning. It highlights the necessity for teachers to develop digital literacy and adapt to AI-driven environments, ensuring effective integration into the classroom. The paper addresses AI's role in personalised learning, assessment automation, and reducing

DOI: 10.4018/979-8-3373-1285-9.ch007

administrative burdens. However, challenges such as resistance to change, ethical concerns, and digital divides persist. The research highlights the importance of ongoing teacher training, AI ethics, and inclusive practices in fostering an equitable learning environment. Recommendations focus on enhancing professional development, establishing AI ethics frameworks, and bridging the digital gap for AI-powered education.

1 INTRODUCTION TO AI IN EDUCATION

Learning and teaching approaches are being radically changed by artificial intelligence (AI) and are reshaping the learning process. Applications of artificial intelligence (AI) technologies, such as machine learning (ML), data analysis, and natural language processing (NLP), enhance teaching approaches, foster learner involvement, and enable personalisation of the experience (Luckin et al., 2018). Educators are empowered to analyse large sets of information and deliver personalised learning solutions by incorporating AI into learning. Artificial intelligence (AI) is revolutionising education through the applications of tools like predictive analysis, computerised tests, and intelligent tutoring systems (ITS) (Holmes et al., 2021).

1.1 AI in Education

The application of Artificial Intelligence (AI) to learning has generated an emerging literature that examines the transformative role and implications of AI for curriculum design, teacher training, and instructional strategies. Karataş et al. (2024) reflect upon how AI-supported curriculum adaptation revolutionises the learning practices through teachers' pattern mapping. This illustrates the interactive relationship between pedagogy and technology, where AI helps teachers adapt the curriculum more effectively to address the heterogeneity of learners. Similarly, Singh and Ram (2024) examine the extensive role of AI in teacher training, highlighting how AI tools are becoming increasingly vital to the professional development of teachers.

Parallel to this, Kadaruddin (2023) presents how AI can facilitate learning through innovative instructional designs that meet the evolving needs of learning. This is supported by Fatima (2024), who writes about learning to teach in the AI age, noting that despite AI's tremendous benefits, it challenges the boundaries of traditional instructional designs to the extent that a shift in instructional strategies is necessary. Ismail et al. (2024) further expound this notion by focusing on how teachers are trained to be future-ready, noting that AI literacy is essential to enable teachers to adapt to the new learning landscape.

Mayo (2024) further develops this concept by focusing specifically on integrating AI within the framework of artistic learning, asserting that AI presents new possibilities for artistic creation but also challenges the boundaries of learning content. Vu (2024) presents an overarching vision of the role of AI within the framework of the learning system, detailing both the challenges and the transformative potential that AI presents for redefining the operations of learning institutions and the delivery of learning. Another meta-theme throughout the literature pertains to teachers' attitudes toward AI-supported learning technologies. Nazaretsky et al. (2022) investigate how teachers' trust in AI technology can be established through professional learning programs, demonstrating that trust is a crucial factor in the successful integration of AI within the classroom. This informs the work of Meylani (2024), where the literature surrounding AI in teacher training is synthesised to generate qualitative findings about how AI is altering the training process for teachers and the instructional process.

The research provides an overarching perspective on the future role of AI in education and learning. It states that AI has the vast capability to transform the learning process, but also presents challenges to trust, flexibility, and future preparedness. The research highlights the importance of teachers developing AI literacy and being adaptable in implementing new instructional strategies that utilise AI effectively within the classroom.

1.2 Evolution of AI Technologies in Teaching and Learning

Over the last two decades, the use of AI in education has increased significantly due to improvements in information processing capacity, the availability of large datasets, and the emergence of sophisticated algorithms.

Table 1. Evolution of AI technologies in teaching and learning

Phase	Timeframe	Description	Tools	Citation(s)
Early Expert Systems	1960s–1980s	Rule-based expert systems provided simple tutorial support using pre-defined logic.	—	Carbonell, 1970
Intelligent Tutoring Systems (ITS)	1990s–2000s	Enabled adaptive learning by evaluating student progress and offering recommendations.	—	—
Overview: Growth in AI use in education	~2000s–present	Use has increased due to improved information processing capacity, the availability of large datasets, and the development of sophisticated algorithms.	—	—

continued on following page

Table 1. Continued

Phase	Timeframe	Description	Tools	Citation(s)
Machine Learning & Adaptive Learning	2010s to date	ML-based tools track learner activity and adapt content presentation.	Knewton; Coursera	Baker & Yacef, 2009
AI-Powered Chatbots & Virtual Tutors	2020s	Deep learning and NLP enable chatbots/ virtual tutors to aid students in real-time.	IBM Watson Tutor; Google Socratic	Bates, 2019
AI + AR/VR (Future Trend)	Future	Immersive, AI-based AR/VR will make learning more interactive and experiential.	—	Dede et al., 2017

Source: Authors' Composition

This progression highlights (Table 1) how AI technologies have continuously evolved to enhance educational experiences, making learning more efficient, engaging, and accessible. It traces an evident maturation from rule-based systems to data-driven adaptivity and then to NLP-enabled, real-time assistance, with an emerging horizon of immersive AR/VR. Early expert systems (1960s–80s) show AI as fixed logic supporting drills; ITS (1990s–2000s) marks the first real adaptivity by reacting to learner progress; the 2010s introduce machine-learning platforms that personalize at scale (e.g., Knewton, Coursera), shifting the teacher's role toward orchestration; the 2020s add chatbots/virtual tutors (e.g., IBM Watson Tutor, Socratic) that extend feedback and Q&A beyond class time; and the "future" row anticipates AI-infused AR/VR for experiential learning. Together, the phases imply (1) a steady increase in learner-model sophistication, (2) rising demands on teacher data literacy and pedagogy redesign, (3) a move from content delivery to continuous feedback and guidance, and (4) growing ethical and implementation considerations (privacy, bias, access) as systems become more autonomous and pervasive. Notably, the table also reveals gaps—some rows lack exemplars/citations—suggesting areas for strengthening the review. The "overview" row reminds us that the underlying drivers are computational, data availability, and algorithmic advances that continue to accelerate. For practice, the trajectory recommends a phased adoption approach: start with low-risk assistive tools (grading/feedback, chatbots), build teacher capacity for data-informed instruction, and then pilot immersive, high-engagement modalities where infrastructure allows—always with teacher agency, ethics, and equity at the centre.

1.3 Need for Teachers to Adapt in the AI Era

The integration of AI has significantly changed the teaching profession, requiring teachers to acquire new digital skills and pedagogical strategies (Pujeda, 2023).

AI supports personalised learning, automates routine tasks, and provides real-time analysis to help teachers maximise student engagement and performance (Mishra, 2024). Intelligent tutoring systems (ITS), adaptive learning systems, and AI-powered virtual assistants are examples of AI-powered tools used to develop student-centred learning environments (Kalyani, 2023). Research conducted by Sytnyk and Podlinyayeva (2024) revealed that insufficient AI training, ethical issues, and digital infrastructure shortcomings pose significant challenges that hinder the integration of AI into teaching. Furthermore, teachers voice concerns about algorithmic bias, the protection of students' data privacy, and the possibility that AI will replace human instructional functions (Vu, 2024). Specifically, AI-powered assessments and grading systems require careful monitoring to maintain fairness and precision in student performance evaluation (Adeniyi et al., 2024).

Teacher training programs specifically designed to tackle these issues have been proposed. Online certifications, workshops, and continuous professional development (CPD) courses on AI integration have been effective in equipping teachers with the requisite skills (Tarisayi, 2024). Furthermore, collaborations between educators, AI developers, and policymakers can help bridge the knowledge gap and ensure that AI tools are designed with teachers' needs in mind (Yadav, 2024). AI enables teachers to focus on mentorship, personalised learning, and fostering critical thinking (Amer-Yahia, 2022). The effective use of AI in blended learning, flipped classrooms, and hybrid models further supports a student-centred teaching approach (Jian, 2023); thereby, AI can be used as a collaborative teaching tool.

Individuals are driven by three innate psychological needs: autonomy (the need for self-direction and choice), competence (the need to feel capable and practical), and relatedness (the need to connect with others). When these needs are fulfilled, individuals exhibit higher motivation, engagement, and well-being. In education, student-centred learning, where AI-powered adaptive tools can enhance autonomy and competence, fosters self-driven learning experiences while maintaining meaningful teacher-student interactions to support relatedness.

The future of AI in education lies in the development of ethical AI policies, digital literacy initiatives, and equitable access to AI-powered learning environments (Ajuwon et al., 2024). Policymakers and institutions must invest in AI literacy for educators, ethical AI governance, and inclusive digital transformation strategies to ensure equitable integration of AI (Harry, 2023).

1.4 Research Gap & Research Design

- **Evidence gap:** Most guidance is tool-centric and generic; there is limited *local, teacher-centered* evidence about what actually works, for whom, and under what conditions.

- **Design gap:** Professional development often focuses on features, not pedagogy, ethics, or change management. This study will identify the design features of PD and coaching that genuinely build teacher agency.
- **Measurement gap:** Schools lack practical indicators to monitor teacher empowerment (beyond tool uptake). The study will propose locally meaningful measures (e.g., confidence in redesigning assessments, frequency of handling ethical decision-making scenarios, collaboration patterns).

This research is designed to *clearly surface and interpret the phenomena experienced by the local population and actual participants*—especially classroom teachers, school leaders, students, and families—such as:

1. **Capability–confidence dynamics:** The gap between teachers' technical skill, pedagogical judgment, and confidence to use AI responsibly with real students.
2. **Informal workarounds:** Unofficial practices (e.g., prompt-sharing, shadow lesson planning, use of personal accounts) that emerge when formal supports are missing.
3. **Equity frictions:** How bandwidth limits, device sharing, language/accent recognition, and accessibility tools affect different student groups—and how teachers compensate.
4. **Assessment and integrity shifts:** Classroom strategies to maintain authenticity of student work, redesign tasks, and provide feedback when AI writing and problem-solving are ubiquitous.
5. **Ethical dilemmas in the moment:** Decisions teachers make about data, consent, age-appropriateness, content filtering, and bias when AI outputs conflict with professional values.
6. **Professional identity and well-being:** Experiences of empowerment vs. deskilling, changes in teacher–student relationships, and emotional labour associated with rapid change.
7. **Participation in decision-making:** The degree to which teachers' voices shape procurement, policy, and curriculum alignment—and barriers to that participation.
8. **Community expectations and trust:** Local parents' and students' perceptions of AI in learning, and how teachers mediate these expectations.

2 THEORETICAL MODELS

A rigorous theoretical model must address the challenges of acclimating to new technology, empowering educators, and integrating AI into education. Employing various educational and psychological theories enhances pedagogical integrity and fosters students' engagement in education through the use of AI.

2.1 Technology Acceptance Model (TAM)

The Technology Acceptance Model (TAM) provides the appropriate instrument to analyse the motivations underlying educators' use and adoption of teaching tools infused with AI (Davis, 1989). According to the Technology Acceptance Model (TAM), the adoption decision relies on two major predictors:

- **Perceived Usefulness:** The degree to which teachers feel the quality of teaching is improved by AI
- **Perceived Ease of Use:** It captures educators' attitudes to the ease and usability of applying and acquiring AI in the classroom.

According to the Technology Acceptance Model, educators' acceptance of AI is influenced by their attitudes toward the technology's usability and feasibility. The emphasis on the perceivable advantages of using AI in education, along with the reduction in technical complexity, should be the primary focus of the course and exercise in professional development.

2.2 Substitution, Augmentation, Modification, Redefinition (SAMR) Model

Dr Ruben Puentedura developed the SAMR Model (Puentedura, 2013), which categorises technology integration into four increasingly higher levels that enable teaching and learning. Substitution supplants traditional tools with technology without altering their functional purpose (e.g., an e-textbook instead of a paper one). Augmentation makes tasks more efficient, such as the use of AI speech-to-text. Modification redesigns learning for extensive tasks, such as AI-adaptive tests. Redefinition makes new forms of learning possible that were previously impossible, such as AI-driven virtual simulations and global collaborative learning. The SAMR model supports teachers in effectively implementing AI to bring about meaningful pedagogical improvements and innovation in education.

2.3 Unified Theory of Acceptance and Use of Technology (UTAUT)

The Unified Theory of Acceptance and Use of Technology (UTAUT) by Venkatesh et al. (2003) builds upon the Technology Acceptance Model (TAM) by combining other determinants that influence the use of AI by teachers. Some of the key predictors that influence AI use and acceptance are:

1. Expectation of Performance: This refers to the teacher's anticipation that AI will enhance the effectiveness of instruction. Effort expectancy is also crucial because it measures the ease with which AI systems are used and interpreted.
2. Social Influence: Institutional support, policy frameworks, and peer networks are crucial for shaping teachers' interest in integrating AI into the classroom.
3. Supportive Factors: Effective AI integration relies on the administration's support, the availability of trained staff, and sufficient infrastructure. Leadership support, collaborative learning networks, and institutional preparedness are crucial for enabling teachers to implement AI-powered solutions effectively.

2.4 Technological Pedagogical Content Knowledge (TPACK)

The Technological Pedagogical Content Knowledge (TPACK) framework (Mishra & Koehler, 2006) integrates technology, pedagogy, and subject matter knowledge to inform practical digital instructional approaches. AI complements Technological Knowledge (TK) through automated grading, AI tutors, and personalised learning systems. AI facilitates personalised learning, real-time analysis, and differentiation within Pedagogical Knowledge (PK). At the same time, Content Knowledge (CK) is supported through AI-driven interactive simulations, smart recommendations for content, and virtual laboratories.

AI further develops Technological Pedagogical Knowledge (TPK) through gamification, AI-managed classroom management, and adaptive tests. Technological Content Knowledge (TCK) is further developed through automated content curation and AI-facilitated multilingual resources, enabling teachers to adapt the content and make it more accessible and interactive. AI transforms Pedagogical Content Knowledge (PCK) at the core by facilitating data-driven lesson planning, AI-facilitated formative tests, and student-centred feedback mechanisms.

By integrating AI into the TPACK model, teachers can enhance efficiency, reduce workload, and adopt innovative teaching methods. However, AI literacy, ethical AI use, and data privacy protection remain critical challenges. Professional development programs must ensure educators can effectively leverage AI while maintaining human-centred teaching approaches. AI-driven education holds great potential, but its success depends on strategic implementation and ongoing teacher empowerment.

2.5 Diffusion of Innovations Theory

Rogers' Diffusion of Innovations Theory (Rogers, 1995) explains how the adoption of AI spreads among teachers. This theory categorises educators based on their willingness to integrate AI:

1. **Innovators:** Early adopters who pilot and experiment with AI-based education tools.
2. **Early Adopters:** Teachers who recognise the potential in AI and use it strategically.
3. **Early Majority**: Teachers who adapt to AI only after optimal practices are established.
4. **Late Majority:** Educators who require extensive training and institutional support to use AI.
5. **Laggards:** Those who are resistant to the use of AI because they are reluctant or are technically incompetent. This model recognises the need to offer differential AI education to teachers at different levels of tech absorption.

2.6 Constructivist Learning Theory

The constructivist learning theory (DeVries, 2000) supports the idea that teachers should be facilitators rather than sole knowledge providers in AI-driven classrooms. AI enables:

1. **Student-Centred Learning:** Adaptive AI platforms personalise learning experiences.
2. **Collaborative Learning:** AI-driven discussion forums and interactive platforms encourage peer learning.
3. **Scaffolding Support:** AI-powered virtual assistants offer real-time feedback, enabling students to progress independently. Constructivist principles reinforce the idea that teachers should embrace AI as a co-teacher that enhances inquiry-based and active learning strategies.

2.7 Self-Efficacy Theory

Bandura's Self-Efficacy Theory (Bandura, 1977) emphasises the role of teacher confidence in the adoption of AI. Teachers with high self-efficacy are more likely to experiment with AI-driven methodologies. Key factors influencing teacher self-efficacy in AI integration include:

1. **Mastery Experiences:** Hands-on AI training workshops boost confidence.
2. **Vicarious Learning:** Observing successful AI implementation by peers.
3. **Social Persuasion:** Institutional encouragement and recognition of AI-driven teaching innovations.
4. **Emotional Arousal:** Reducing anxiety around AI through gradual exposure and professional support. This theory suggests that continuous professional development and peer collaboration can help teachers build confidence in using AI tools.

3 CONCEPTUAL FRAMEWORK ON EMPOWERING TEACHERS FOR ADAPTING TO AI-DRIVEN EDUCATION ERA

The heightened integration of artificial intelligence (AI) in education necessitates a paradigm shift in teaching practices, prompting educators to acquire new skills, reevaluate pedagogical strategies, and adopt technology-facilitated learning environments. This conceptual framework addresses teacher empowerment for AI-driven education, considering global trends and the Indian educational context.

Figure 1. Conceptual framework for empowering teachers in AI-driven education

The conceptual framework (Figure 1) for teacher empowerment in AI-based education focuses on the crucial factors that enable teachers to flourish in the AI-rich learning environment. AI literacy in teacher education is central to this, ensuring teachers possess a foundational knowledge to use AI tools in classrooms. When digital literacy and technological expertise are combined, teachers are better equipped to navigate the ever-changing nature of education.

A strong emphasis is placed on professional development and lifelong learning through CPD in AI skills and ethical AI training, promoting the responsible and inclusive use of AI. Teachers are incentivised to adopt student-centred and collaborative teaching methodologies and develop environments where they are facilitators and mentors. Pedagogic innovation and curriculum reform are also suggested to integrate AI meaningfully into classrooms, shifting away from traditional teacher-centred instruction to roles that better suit AI-augmented classrooms. Partnering with Ed-tech firms for reskilling is also a requirement, allowing teachers to stay updated on future AI trends.

4 CRITICAL DIMENSIONS OF TEACHER EMPOWERMENT IN AI-BASED EDUCATION

4.1 Digital Literacy and Technological Competence:

With the era of artificial intelligence (AI)-powered learning, digital competency and digital literacy are crucial for instructors. AI tools need an intrinsic understanding of digital environments, data analysis, and learning systems that are personalised to learners to enhance the efficacy of teaching and learning engagement (Zawacki-Richter et al., 2019). Teacher training programs must integrate AI literacy to help teachers effectively utilise AI-powered assessment tools, automated content curation, and personalised instructional techniques (OECD, 2021). This foundational understanding enables teachers to effectively utilise AI innovations to produce an interactive, evidence-informed learning environment.

4.2 Pedagogical Adaptation and Curriculum Innovation

AI has evolved traditional teaching methods into more interactive, student-centred methodologies. In contrast to traditional teaching, AI-driven education provides adaptive learning paths tailored to individual learners' needs and encourages self-paced learning (Luckin, 2018). To match the pace with these developments, the curriculum has to include AI-driven strategies like:

- Intelligent Tutoring Systems provide immediate feedback, monitor learners' progress, and modify instructional materials to enhance the learning experience.
- Computerised Assessment Tools: AI facilitates automated grading and assessment, relieving teachers' workload but providing consistent and accurate evaluation (Selwyn, 2019).
- Gamification and Simulation: Learning games and AI simulations enhance engagement through fun, interactive learning experiences.

By incorporating AI into the learning framework, education systems can facilitate an innovative, efficient, and personalised learning environment.

4.3 Ethical and Inclusive AI Practices in Education

While AI has numerous learning advantages, there are some ethical considerations to be taken into account to ensure its use is fair and appropriate. Teachers must be educated to manage data privacy, algorithmic bias, and the digital divide (Aiken & Epstein, 2020). Some of the key ethics are:

- Data Privacy and Protection: Schools must implement strong data governance principles to safeguard information about students from misuse.
- Bias within AI Algorithms: Educators must critically evaluate AI recommendations to prevent perpetuating biases that could disproportionately affect specific student groups.
- Closing the Digital Gap: AI learning must be inclusive to provide equal learning opportunities for students from diverse socio-economic backgrounds (UNESCO, 2022).

Educators can ensure a balanced, open, and inclusive online learning environment by utilising ethical AI.

4.4 Professional Development and Life-Long Learning

Continuous professional development (CPD) is essential for keeping teachers current with the rapid pace of technological innovation. CPD training must be used to upskill teachers to AI skills to allow them to integrate AI tools natively into teaching strategies (Hinojo-Lucena et al., 2019). Professional development can be made efficient through:

- Collaborations with Ed-Tech Companies and Universities: Such partnerships enable teachers to reskill and upskill through AI-powered learning management systems.
- AI Certification Programs and Workshops: Continuous AI training keeps teachers updated on AI advancements and teaching methodologies (Huang et al., 2020).

By fostering a lifelong learning culture, teachers can continually adapt their teaching methodologies to meet the evolving needs of AI-driven learning environments.

4.5 Teacher's Role in AI-Enhanced Classrooms

AI is a facilitative technology that enhances teachers' capability to deliver personalised and adaptive learning. AI enables:

- Personalised Learning Pathways: AI-driven analytics allows personalised learning, providing a customised learning experience (Schiff, 2021).
- Facilitation and Mentorship: Educators shift away from lecturing to mentorship, guiding learners through problem-solving, teamwork, and critical thinking, and utilising AI tools to aid in differentiation (Holmes et al., 2021).

By embracing AI-facilitated teaching, instructors can optimise class participation, enable independent learning, and deliver holistic intellectual development.

4.6 Global Perspectives on AI-Powered Teacher Empowerment

Globally, Nations have started to incorporate AI in education in various ways:

- In the United States, AI-powered adaptive learning systems, such as Knewton and Coursera, tailor student learning to their unique needs and provide targeted teacher interventions (Means et al., 2013).
- The European Union: AI competency models, such as DigCompEdu, provide structured teaching and educational guidelines (Redecker, 2017).
- In China, AI-powered student surveillance, including facial recognition and activity monitoring, is integrated into classrooms, where AI education studies receive robust investment (Zhai, 2021).
- Singapore: The Skills Future initiative promotes AI upskilling for teachers to provide technology-enabled lifelong learning (Goh & Tan, 2022).

4.7 Indian Perspective on AI and Teacher Empowerment

India is gradually embracing AI-enabled education, and leading examples include:

- National Education Policy (NEP) 2020: This policy recognises AI as an integral component of education in the future and mentions digital pedagogy for teachers (MHRD, 2020).
- The DIKSHA Platform provides digital teaching content and AI-powered assessment tools for teachers (NCERT, 2021).
- NITI Aayog's AI for All initiative focuses on upskilling teachers in AI to enhance technology-enabled learning opportunities (NITI Aayog, 2021).
- Ed-Tech Startups: Ed-tech start-ups, such as BYJU'S, Vedantu, and Embibe, utilise AI analytics to enhance teaching quality (Sinha, 2021).

5 CHALLENGES & THE ROAD AHEAD

Despite Progress, Several Challenges in AI's Adoption for Teachers' Empowerment

1. Digital Divide: In rural areas, a lack of access to AI tools and the internet constrains the scalability of AI-enabled education (UNESCO, 2022).
2. Resistance to Change: Teachers resist AI implementation due to inadequate awareness and concerns about job displacement (Schiff, 2021).
3. Policy and Regulation Loopholes: The adoption of AI in education requires strict policies to address ethical and data protection concerns (Aiken & Epstein, 2020).
4. To Overcome Barriers, Policymakers Must provide structured education and training in AI for teachers at different education levels. Develop AI-driven models to evaluate teachers and offer practical, adaptive teaching practices. Promote collaboration between industry, government, and academe for AI-powered innovations in education.

6 INTEGRATING THEORETICAL FRAMEWORK INTO PRACTICE

Applying such a theory may direct instructional strategies, AI implementation in policy, and teacher education. The following steps in practice align with theoretical models:

1. **Professional Development Initiatives:** Align AI education with TPACK so that technology supplements teaching for enhanced pedagogical impact.
2. **Institutional AI Support Structures:** Implement UTAUT principles to develop infrastructure, peer networks, and leadership-driven AI strategies.
3. **AI Adoption Plans:** Implement diffusion of Innovation strategies to identify and inspire initial adopters and stimulate greater teacher buy-in.
4. **Ethical AI Deployment:** Align Constructivist Learning and Self-Efficacy Theory to ensure AI augments, and does not replace, teaching by humans.
5. **Policy Recommendations:** Encourage governments and institutions to adopt AI education policies based on the foundations of TAM and UTAUT models and ensure access, quality, and continual learning for teachers.

7 FUNCTION OF AI IN MODERN CLASSROOMS

The incorporation of AI in today's classrooms greatly benefits teachers and students, redefining the education system completely. AI tools optimise evaluation and assessment practices, offer teachers digital teaching assistants, and track student progress through in-depth learning data. Observing AI's general educational capabilities, this study investigates how AI technologies enhance learning environments in terms of quality and student engagement.

7.1 AI-Powered Personalised Learning

AI-powered, personalised learning modifies course content to fit individual students' pace and learning style. Using student responses and the provision of personalised hints, smart teaching systems (ITS) improve understanding and retention of content (Chen et al., 2021). According to Popenici and Kerr (2017), AI-driven adaptive learning systems immediately modify the challenge level to fit both underachievers and high-achievers. Zawacki-Richter et al. (2019) state that in instances where learning obstruction exists, learners can access the immediate solution of AI-supported instructional software. This is an inclusive approach that accommodates various students and independent learning.

7.2 AI-Based Assessment and Feedback System

AI-based assessment tools enhance assessment processes with low teacher workload, ensuring fairness and accuracy. Automated grading systems use machine learning and natural language technologies to efficiently assess essays, multiple-choice questions, and quizzes (Burrows et al., 2015). AI-based systems provide students with real-time feedback to enhance their work before submission (Lu et al., 2018). Patterns in student mistakes are detected, and feedback is provided, thus helping teachers improve their instructional strategies. AI-based detecting tools for plagiarism uphold academic integrity through identifying plagiarised content (Foltz et al., 2019). Such technologies provide timely, data-driven feedback, enabling students to improve continuously.

7.3 Virtual Teaching Assistants and Chatbots

Virtual teaching assistants (VTAs) and AI-based chatbots enhance classroom engagement with on-demand student support. AI agents provide answers to standard questions, guide students through challenging material, and offer individualised learning plans (Gulson & Witzenberger, 2020). Chatbots supported by NLP interact with students in a conversational style, providing timely answers to questions and encouraging active learning (Winkler & Søllner, 2018). VTAs give instructors administrative relief in scheduling assignments and grading tests. AI frees instructors from low-level tasks, allowing them to focus on more engaging and high-level teaching activities.

7.4 AI-Driven Learning Analytics for Student Performance Monitoring

AI-powered learning analytics is crucial in tracking student performance and predicting scholastic success. Student data in large volumes is processed by machine learning models, analysing learning patterns and potential opportunities for scholastic failure (Siemens & Long, 2011). Predictive analytics guide teachers in implementing timely interventions for underachieving students, thereby improving student retention (Romero & Ventura, 2020). AI-powered dashboards offer a graphical representation of performance patterns, enabling individualised instructional modifications (Papamitsiou & Economides, 2014). In addition, learning analytics guides curricula design by pointing to efficiencies in teaching methodology. Educational institutions, through AI, can develop data-driven strategies to optimise student achievements.

8 CHALLENGES FACED BY TEACHERS IN THE AI ERA

8.1 Resistance to Technological Change

Teaching with artificial intelligence (AI) has radically reshaped teaching methods, yet numerous educators exhibit resistance to technological change. This resistance stems from a combination of factors, including unfamiliarity with the application of AI tools, fear of redundancy, and the inability to adapt to dynamically changing virtual environments (Selwyn, 2020). Resistance among veteran educators increases if they have not been sufficiently exposed to AI-informed teaching tools during teaching development (Tondeur et al., 2017). Institutional factors, including ineffective staff development programs, minimal technical support staff, and physical environment limitations, also enhance this resistance (Howard & Mozejko, 2015). Overcoming such challenges requires systematic training programs, change management initiatives, and a culture that encourages educators not to fear adapting to changing technologies and redundancy (Kirkwood & Price, 2014).

8.2 Ethical Challenges with AI-Enhanced Learning Environments

When educators utilise AI-enhanced teaching tools, various ethical issues arise. Williamson & Eynon (2020). Note issues of student data privacy, permission, and the security of student data concerning the use of student data in individualised teaching. Zawacki-Richter et al. (2019) state that educators struggle with the ethical dimension of AI-informed decision-making whenever the algorithm affects grading, student evaluation, and course recommendation. Bias in artificial intelligence (AI) also adds a further dimension of sophistication. Certain prediction tools may exacerbate existing educational disparities by giving an unfair preference to and perpetuating prejudice against specific student cohorts (Eubanks, 2018). Educators must be familiar with artificial intelligence (AI) to address such ethical challenges. This will protect students' rights and scholarly excellence, allowing them to review AI-informed teaching methods responsibly (Selwyn, 2019).

8.3 Lack of Proficiency and the Need for Reskilling

To keep pace with student learning, modern educators need to align competencies with the era of artificial intelligence and be subject to constant reskilling and upskilling. AI-assisted learning systems are transforming conventional teaching methods, equipping educators with digital competencies and technologies, and enabling the application of AI-assisted instructional design and data analysis (Luckin et al., 2016).

Most educators lack adequate education in AI competencies and digital literacy (Zhang & Aslan, 2021). Gudmundsdottir & Hatlevik (2018) note that the prospects for development differ per field, and educators struggle to apply AI effectively in the classroom. AI-assisted learning strategies must be emphasised during educator training programs so that educators will be competent enough to use technology instead of feeling it as a threat to their job security (Means et al., 2013).

8.4 Human and Artificial Intelligence Working Together in Educational Environments

One of the greatest challenges of AI-supported education is striking a balance between the roles of humans and AI in the classroom. AI's strengths include data-informed insights, automated administrative processes, and optimised individualised learning; however, humans perform better at providing adaptable teaching methods, mentoring, and social intelligence (Holmes et al., 2019). Compared with AI, teaching staff play a crucial role in children's social-emotional, imaginative, and critical skills (Selwyn, 2021). Over-reliance on AI by schools may be associated with de-personalised teaching, which can lower student participation and motivation (Schmid et al., 2021). To achieve the highest outcomes, education stakeholders should define the boundaries of AI application in the classroom and utilise the power of efficiency improvement while retaining educators at the centre of the teaching-learning experience (Knox et al., 2020).

9 AI-ENHANCED EDUCATION

9.1 Training in Artificial Intelligence and the Acquisition of Digital Skills

To enable educators to utilise AI-supported teaching effectively, a good understanding of AI and computer competencies is crucial. Teachers must understand how artificial intelligence works, its potential applications within teaching contexts, and the limitations of the technology (Zhang & Aslan, 2021). Teachers must be able to critically review the application of AI tools within teaching before such tools can be effectively applied within the teaching environment, and this involves an understanding of algorithmic decision-making processes, data protection, and the associated ethical issues (Selwyn, 2020). Digital competences training must incorporate AI-supported management of the teaching environment, AI-supported grading tools, and adaptation technologies (Holmes et al., 2019). Teachers must be actively taught about AI if they can take students through the technology change processes instead of reacting against it (Williamson & Eynon, 2020).

9.2 Curriculum Design and Training Programs in AI-Enriched Education

Pre-service training and regular professional development activities should be established to prepare educators for using AI in classrooms (Means et al., 2013). Artificial intelligence tools will significantly support class management and individualised teaching, and should be a major focus of CPD programs (Luckin et al., 2016). Educators can effectively fill the knowledge gap and utilise AI-supported teaching techniques through certification programs, seminar sessions, and educator training programs using AI (Gudmundsdottir & Hatlevik, 2018). The collaborative teaching techniques that enable educators to exchange suggestions on improving education through the use of artificial intelligence should also be incorporated into CPD programs (Schmid et al., 2021).

9.3 Educators and artificial intelligence inventors working together

Educators and AI technology experts should collaborate to develop an effective AI-informed system (Knox et al., 2020). Educators should be part of developing such tools and tools assessment and analysis to ensure that AI-informed instructional tools meet student demands and instructional objectives (Zawacki-Richter et al., 2019). By sharing knowledge of classroom dynamics, student engagement, curricula, instructional demands, and standards, educators can contribute to the design of instructional technology in collaboration with AI researchers (Williamson & Eynon, 2020). Discussions, focus groups, and educator-developer conversations should be initiated to ensure that AI technologies enhance educators rather than replace them (Eubanks, 2018).

9.4 Embracing a Growth Mindset in Integrating Technology

Teachers should not view technology as a threat, but rather as an opportunity to enhance teaching methods (Mangels et al., 2006). Allowing teachers to test AI tools, reflect on and assess their teaching methods, and accept technological innovations will enable schools to facilitate lifelong learning effectively (Selwyn, 2021). Mentor programs, school leadership encouragement, and appreciation for AI adoption programs will facilitate effective utilisation of AI-based teaching methods (Luckin et al., 2016). Teachers should develop a growth mindset to effectively use technological innovations and apply AI to facilitate inclusive education, differentiation, and student engagement (Schmid et al., 2021).

10 AI-BASED TEACHING TOOLS AND PLATFORMS

1. Learning Management System (LMS) with AI Enhancement: AI-assisted learning management systems provide students with individualised learning experiences by examining student performance metrics and customising the content accordingly (Holmes et al., 2019). Using Canvas, Blackboard, and Moodle tools, AI facilitates automatic grading, instant comments, and course suggestions based on individual needs (Zawacki-Richter et al., 2019). By applying such tools and technologies, educators can dedicate themselves to lesson planning and student engagement, while leaving administrative tasks behind (Williamson & Eynon, 2020).
2. AI-Enabled Content Generation and Curation Platforms: Educational tools based on artificial intelligence help educators prepare instructional materials easily. Quillionz and ScribeSense programs ease the preparation of customised tests and interactive and quiz materials, notes Selwyn (2021). AI-curated tools, such as Knewton and Smart Sparrow, track student participation, provide appropriate resources based on it, and offer a customised education experience (Zhang & Aslan, 2021).
3. Student Engagement and Class Management with AI-Powered Tools: AI-boosted engagement tools such as chatbots and virtual teaching aids keep learners active by giving real-time answers and interventions (Knox et al., 2020). Based on the results, Century Tech and the like leverage AI to gauge student engagement, identify knowledge deficits, and provide real-time interventions (Gudmundsdottir & Hatlevik, 2018). Classcraft is a good example of an AI-supported classroom management system that enables collaborative student participation and ease of behaviour monitoring (Selwyn, 2021).

11 ETHICAL & PEDAGOGICAL CONSIDERATIONS FOR AI INTEGRATION

1. Privacy and Information Security: AI instructional programs gather huge student data to deliver customised instruction. This raises concerns about privacy, ethical use, and data security (Williamson & Eynon, 2020). Schools and tertiary education institutions should honour provisions in regulations for data privacy, for example, the FERPA and General Data Protection Regulation (GDPR), to

safeguard private student data (Zawacki-Richter et al., 2019). Transparency in data gathering, guidelines for maintaining data security, and obtaining parental and student consent are necessary for AI use in teaching to be ethical (Holmes et al., 2019).

2. Concerns About AI Algorithms' Bias and Fairness: Educational AI systems are discriminatory and susceptible to unequal assessment results (Eubanks, 2018). Bias in training data, which can cause algorithmic bias, can penalise certain student groups (Zhang & Aslan, 2021). Cautious scrutiny of AI models in the contexts of equity and openness may help avoid such issues (Selwyn, 2020). The integration of educators, students, and policymakers in designing and testing AI services may help create more equitable learning environments (Knox et al., 2020).
3. Human and AI Cooperation in Decision-Making: AI can support educators' decision-making by analysing student performance and determining knowledge deficits. Human judgment will not be substituted with AI within the educational system; instead, it will be supplemented (Williamson & Eynon, 2020). Teachers will be solely responsible for making instructional decisions and will utilise AI insights to enhance student learning (Luckin et al., 2016). The greatest yield will be achieved if educators work alongside AI in a manner that allows them to review AI suggestions and ensure that automatic decisions are based on student needs and educational goals (Gudmundsdottir & Hatlevik, 2018).
4. Keeping Teachers in Their Roles of Mentor and Advisor: Teachers' teaching and mentoring roles continue to be crucial within classrooms due to the expanding power of AI (Holmes et al., 2019). Human skills, such as empathy, encouragement, and differentiated teaching, cannot be replaced by AI (Schmid et al., 2021). Teachers play a crucial role in developing children's social and emotional skills, fostering creativity within the classroom culture, and addressing the individual needs of each student (Selwyn, 2021). Through the use of AI, augmenting the efforts of human educators rather than replacing them, this balance can be established (Knox et al., 2020).

12 CASE STUDIES & BEST PRACTICES

Table 2. Summarised details of the real case studies and best practices

Theme	Context / Institution (Country)	AI tool/ approach	AI category	Level	What was implemented	Reported outcomes	Best-practice takeaway	Source
Key driver: efficient integration	Georgia Institute of Technology (USA)	"Jill Watson" is a teaching assistant who answers routine learner queries in online forums	NLP chatbot / AI teaching assistant	Higher ed	Deployed an AI TA to handle repetitive Q&A and triage student questions	Faster responses, lighter staff workload, high reported answer accuracy (~97%)	Start with well-scoped, low-risk tasks (routine Q&A), keep human oversight, track accuracy and satisfaction	Goel & Polepeddi, (2018)
Key driver: efficient integration	Squirrel AI (China)	Adaptive platform that sequences content to mastery	Intelligent Tutoring / Adaptive learning	K-12	Personalised practice paths based on ongoing performance	Reported gains in student achievement	Use mastery-based adaptivity; surface analytics that teachers can act on	Zawacki-Richter et al., (2019)
Importance of frameworks	Carnegie Learning (USA)	AI-informed math instruction that adapts problem-solving strategies	Intelligent Tutoring / Analytics-informed pedagogy	K-12 (Math)	The system tracks each learner and adjusts the method and problem sequence	Better retention and deeper understanding vs. regular classes	Align AI with pedagogy (not just content); embed formative checks	Holmes et al., (2019); Means et al., (2013)
Importance of frameworks	Finland (system level)	Policy and practice emphasise AI as a pedagogically aligned aid, not a replacement	System strategy / Pedagogical alignment	K-12 & beyond	Teachers remain central; AI is used for formative assessment and individualised feedback	Maintains educator agency while expanding feedback capacity	Position AI explicitly as augmentation; require formative uses and teacher control	Knox et al., (2020).
Real-life stories	Singapore high school	NLP tools for instant feedback on student writing	NLP-assisted writing feedback	Secondary	Automated, immediate comments on drafts	Stronger writing and higher engagement	Use rapid, rubric-guided feedback cycles; calibrate tool outputs with exemplars	Zhang & Aslan, (2021)
Real-life stories	India (inclusive classroom)	AI-adaptive tools to support mixed-ability learners	Adaptive learning / Assistive support	K-12	Differentiated content and pacing to include learners with diverse needs	Improved engagement, grades, and classroom climate	Leverage adaptivity for inclusion; monitor fairness, accessibility, and language support	Selwyn (2021)

Source: Author's Computation

Table 2 presents a summarised list of real-life case studies and best practices in implementing the application of artificial intelligence (AI) to the education system in various countries at different levels. The table identifies six key themes, spanning from the efficient integration of AI to real-life accounts of classroom implementation. Organisations, such as the Georgia Institute of Technology, Squirrel AI, and Carnegie Learning, have been among the first to develop new AI-based tools, including chatbots, adaptive platforms, and analytics-based pedagogy. These adoptions, whether in higher education or K-12 systems, have been shown to have practical advantages, including reduced staff workload, increased student access, improved retention, and higher teaching efficiency. The described results suggest that AI is more effective when implemented with caution in relation to pedagogy, rather than as an independent substitution. For example, whereas Finland focused on the policy-level positioning of AI as an augmentation tool, Singaporean schools utilised NLP tools to obtain instant feedback, demonstrating that context and usage determine effectiveness. The key takeaways from best practices have consistently emphasised the importance of human control, including formative check-ins and teacher oversight.

13 FUTURE TRENDS IN AI-POWERED EDUCATION & TEACHER READINESS

13.1 Educators and Policymakers

Educators' tasks will be adjusted with the addition of AI. The application of artificial intelligence will support educators in removing routine tasks, allowing them to focus on student engagement, critical thinking, and creativity (Holmes et al., 2019). The future will see educators acting as facilitators, supporting students with collaborative assignments that utilise AI tools to individualise their education (Selwyn, 2021). Future schools will adopt hybrid learning models based on the perspectives (Knox et al., 2020). The application of AI in curriculum delivery will enable educators to focus on students' social-emotional development and higher-order cognitive abilities.

13.2 Continuous Training for AI Integration

To thrive in an AI-enhanced world, educators should be equipped with programs that offer ongoing training and development (Means et al., 2013). Training should encompass the analysis of data, consideration of ethical issues, and the development of teaching strategies based on AI (Gudmundsdottir & Hatlevik, 2018). Training programs that incorporate AI into teaching strategies should be sponsored and supported by higher education institutions and the government (Zawacki-Richter et al., 2019). Additionally, facilitating collaborative work and exchanging knowledge on websites can enhance collaborative work and AI-supported teaching (Zhang & Aslan, 2021).

13.3 An Analysis of the Capacity of AI to Mitigate Achievement Differences within Academic Settings

Artificial intelligence can level the playing field regarding educational achievements by providing individualised learning experiences to students from diverse backgrounds and geographical locations worldwide (Eubanks, 2018). By analysing student performance metrics, artificial intelligence systems can personalise learning content and ensure disadvantaged populations have equitable access to education (Holmes et al., 2019). Last but not least, multilingual learners will be assisted using artificial intelligence speech recognition and language translation capabilities, thereby enhancing the accessibility and inclusion of education for all individuals (Williamson & Eynon, 2020). Equitable use of artificial intelligence will be ensured if the digital divide is bridged through the investment in physical and virtual infrastructure, as well as the enactment of specialised legislation (Knox et al., 2020).

13.4 Preparing Teachers for the Next Era of AI Innovation

Teachers will need to actively embrace emerging technology with the development of AI. AI-enhanced chatbots that support students, immersive AI-aided virtual environments, and natural language processing that aids in automatic assessments will be the future of education (Schmid et al., 2021). Teachers must stay up-to-date with technological innovations and receive regular training to keep pace with such transformations (Selwyn, 2021). Institutions need to cultivate an AI-ready culture by facilitating testing and experimentation with AI tools, developing cross-disciplinary collaborations, and constructing strategic models for integrating AI into the curriculum (Luckin et al., 2016).

14 CONCLUSION AND RECOMMENDATIONS

14.1 A Summary of Significant Factors

Using AI in classrooms has been a source of opportunity and hindrance for teaching staff members. The note factors include a shortage of training, ethical issues, resistance to change, and the equitable distribution of tasks between humans and AI (Selwyn, 2020). The judicious application of AI-supported interventions that boost individualised learning, simplify administrative tasks, and offer instant feedback must be done with consideration for ethical issues such as bias, data confidentiality, and overdependence on automation (Zawacki-Richter et al., 2019). Because educators have multiple responsibilities, including mentoring, facilitation, and leadership, they play a vital role in artificial intelligence (AI)- supported learning environments (Holmes et al., 2019).

14.2 Action Plan for Teachers Integrating AI into the Curriculum

To incorporate AI effectively into teaching activities, educators need to follow a systematic approach:

1. **Develop AI Literacy:** Teachers require training in the fundamentals of AI, data-informed decision-making, and algorithmic bias to make informed decisions about AI-enhanced instructional tools (Zhang & Aslan, 2021).
2. **Professional Growth:** Schools and institutions should offer workshops and training sessions to equip educators with the necessary skills (Gudmundsdottir & Hatlevik, 2018).
3. **Embracing AI as a Support Tool:** Instead of seeing AI as a replacement, educators should utilise AI as a supportive tool that complements teaching strategies, focusing on fostering critical thought and student engagement (Knox et al., 2020).
4. **Prevent Misuse of AI:** Teachers must be cautious regarding privacy issues and ensure that AI tools adhere to ethical standards and data safeguarding regulations **(Eubanks, 2018).**
5. **Engage in Peer Learning and Cooperation:** Constructing AI-informed teaching communities will facilitate the development of collaborative learning experiences, innovative teaching approaches, and best practices (Means et al., 2013).

14.3 Policy Recommendations for Training and Integration of AI

To maximise the potential of AI in education, schools and policymakers need to take the following steps:

1. **Unified AI Training Programs:** Institute compulsory AI literacy programs within educator training curricula in preparation of future educators for classrooms with AI integrated within them (Williamson & Eynon, 2020).
2. **AI Ethics Frameworks:** Establish ethical standards for using AI in education with openness, balance, and responsibility in AI-informed decision-making processes (Zawacki-Richter et al., 2019).

3. **Financing AI tools:** The government should allocate funding to provide schools with AI-enhanced teaching tools and staff development programs (Luckin et al., 2016).
4. **Monitoring and Evaluation:** Continuous assessment of AI integration effectiveness is crucial. Policymakers should establish evaluation mechanisms to measure AI's impact on learning outcomes and teacher engagement (Selwyn, 2021)
5. **Closing the Digital Divide:** Ensure inclusive access to AI technologies through investment in the digital infrastructure and support of disadvantaged schools and communities (Schmid et al., 2021).

15 SUMMARY

The study provides a comprehensive analysis of AI-informed education, offering an overview of how AI technologies, such as machine learning, natural language processing, and predictive analytics, enhance individualised teaching and learning techniques. AI has progressed from rule-based expert systems to modern adaptive systems that provide individualised student-centricity. The primary issues confronting educators in the AI era include resistance to change, ethical concerns, skills shortages, and the need to strike an optimal balance between human and AI-delivered teaching. Overcoming such issues involves empowering educators through AI training programs and workshops in staff development, as well as collaborative ventures with AI programmers. AI-informed teaching tools, such as LMS systems, tools that generate educational content, adaptive learning technology, and student engagement tools, ease administrative tasks, provide instant feedback, and construct an individualised teaching and learning experience. The ethical issues of data confidentiality, algorithmic bias, and the need for human oversight remain top concerns in AI applications. Case stories of using AI in schools and colleges demonstrate how educators have applied AI to make teaching and learning more effective and efficient. The study extends its focus to future directions, advocating for ongoing training of educators, the application of AI in addressing educational disparities, and preparing educators for future AI innovations. The study concludes with practical recommendations, including a call to policymakers to introduce standard training in AI, establish standards of AI ethics, allocate a budget for AI use, and bridge the digital gap in an effort toward an inclusive and beneficial system of AI-informed education.

REFERENCES

Aayog, N. I. T. I. (2021). *AI for All: India's AI strategy for inclusive education.* NITI Aayog, Government of India.

Adeniyi, I., Abimbola, C., & Adeleye, O. (2024). *A review of AI-driven pedagogical strategies for equitable access to science education.* Magna Scientia Advanced Research and Reviews., DOI: 10.30574/msarr.2024.10.2.0043

Aiken, M., & Epstein, B. (2020). *Artificial intelligence in education: The ethical considerations*. Springer.

Ajuwon, O., Animashaun, E., & Chiekezie, N. (2024). *Advancing human resources management practices in educational institutions: Enhancing teacher retention and student outcomes using AI.* International Journal of Management & Entrepreneurship Research., DOI: 10.51594/ijmer.v6i8.1367

Amer-Yahia, S. (2022). Towards AI-Powered Data-Driven Education. *Proc. VLDB Endow.*, 15, 3798-3806. https://doi.org/DOI: 10.14778/3554821.3554900

Baker, R. S., & Yacef, K. (2009). The state of educational data mining in 2009: A review and future visions. *Journal of Educational Data Mining*, *1*(1), 3–17.

Bandura, A. (1977). Self-efficacy: Toward a unifying theory of behavioral change. *Psychological Review*, *84*(2), 191–215. DOI: 10.1037/0033-295X.84.2.191 PMID: 847061

Bates, T. (2019). *Teaching in a digital age: Guidelines for designing teaching and learning*. Tony Bates Associates Ltd.

Burrows, S., Gurevych, I., & Stein, B. (2015). The Eras and Trends of Automatic Short Answer Grading. *International Journal of Artificial Intelligence in Education*, *25*(1), 60–117. DOI: 10.1007/s40593-014-0026-8

Carbonell, J. R. (1970). AI in CAI: An artificial-intelligence approach to computer-assisted instruction. *IEEE Transactions on Man-Machine Systems*, *11*(4), 190–202. DOI: 10.1109/TMMS.1970.299942

Chen, X., Xie, H., Zou, D., & Hwang, G. J. (2021). Application and Theory Trends in AI-Supported Personalized Learning: A Systematic Review. *Journal of Educational Technology & Society*, *24*(1), 24–43.

Davis, F. D. (1989). Perceived usefulness, perceived ease of use, and user acceptance of information technology. *Management Information Systems Quarterly*, *13*(3), 319–340. DOI: 10.2307/249008

Dede, C., Grotzer, T. A., Kamarainen, A., & Metcalf, S. (2017). Augmented reality in education. *Nature Human Behaviour, 1*(5), 219–220.

DeVries, R. (2000). Vygotsky, Piaget, and education: A reciprocal assimilation of theories and educational practices. *New Ideas in Psychology, 18*(2-3), 187–213. DOI: 10.1016/S0732-118X(00)00008-8

Eubanks, V. (2018). *Automating inequality: How high-tech tools profile, police, and punish the poor.* St. Martin's Press.

Fatima, S. (2024). *Teaching in The Age of Artificial Intelligence (AI).* International Journal For Multidisciplinary Research., DOI: 10.36948/ijfmr.2024.v06i03.22955

Foltz, P. W., Streeter, L. A., Lochbaum, K. E., & Landauer, T. K. (2019). Implementation and applications of the Intelligent Essay Assessor. *AI & Education, 7*(4), 295–310.

Goel, A. K., & Polepeddi, L. (2018). Jill Watson: A virtual teaching assistant for online education. In Learning engineering for online education (pp. 120-143). Routledge.

Goh, C., & Tan, D. (2022). AI-driven education policies in Singapore: Challenges and opportunities. *Educational Review, 74*(3), 215–230.

Gudmundsdottir, G. B., & Hatlevik, O. E. (2018). Newly qualified teachers' professional digital competence: Implications for teacher education. *European Journal of Teacher Education, 41*(2), 214–231. DOI: 10.1080/02619768.2017.1416085

Gulson, K. N., & Witzenberger, K. (2020). AI and the future of education: Beyond the human. *Educational Philosophy and Theory, 52*(8), 822–837.

Harry, A. (2023). *Role of AI in Education. Interdisciplinary Journal and Humanity.* INJURITY., DOI: 10.58631/injurity.v2i3.52

Hinojo-Lucena, F. J., Aznar-Díaz, I., Caceres-Reche, M. P., Trujillo-Torres, J. M., & Romero-Rodríguez, J. M. (2019). Artificial intelligence in higher education: An analysis of scientific production. *Journal of New Approaches in Educational Research, 8*(2), 9–17.

Holmes, W., Bialik, M., & Fadel, C. (2019). *Artificial intelligence in education: Promises and implications for teaching and learning*. Center for Curriculum Redesign.

Holmes, W., Bialik, M., & Fadel, C. (2021). *AI and education: The learning revolution.* Routledge.

Howard, S. K., & Mozejko, A. (2015). Teachers: Technology, change and resistance. In M. Henderson & G. Romeo (Eds.), Teaching and digital technologies: Big issues and critical questions (pp. 307-317). Cambridge University Press.

Huang, R., Spector, J. M., & Yang, J. (2020). *Emerging technologies for education: AI and digital learning transformation.* Springer.

. Ismail, A., Aliu, A., Ibrahim, M., & Sulaiman, A. (2024). Preparing Teachers of the Future in the Era of Artificial Intelligence. *Journal of Artificial Intelligence, Machine Learning and Neural Network.* .DOI: 10.55529/jaimlnn.44.31.41

Jian, M. J. K. O. (2023). Personalized learning through AI. *Advances in Engineering Innovation, 5*(1), 16–19. DOI: 10.54254/2977-3903/5/2023039

. Kadaruddin, K. (2023). Empowering Education through Generative AI: Innovative Instructional Strategies for Tomorrow's Learners. *International Journal of Business, Law, and Education.* .DOI: 10.56442/ijble.v4i2.215

Kalyani, L. (2023). *Revolutionizing Education: Artificial Intelligence's Pioneering Role in Shaping Tomorrow's Scholars.* International Journal of Multidisciplinary Research in Arts, Science and Technology., DOI: 10.61778/ijmrast.v1i2.6

Karataş, F., Eriçok, B., & Tanrikulu, L. (2024). Reshaping curriculum adaptation in the age of artificial intelligence: Mapping teachers' AI-driven curriculum adaptation patterns. *British Educational Research Journal.* Advance online publication. DOI: 10.1002/berj.4068

Kirkwood, A., & Price, L. (2014). Technology-enhanced learning and teaching in higher education: What is 'enhanced' and how do we know? A critical literature review. *Learning, Media and Technology, 39*(1), 6–36. DOI: 10.1080/17439884.2013.770404

Knox, J., Wang, Y., & Gallagher, M. (2020). Artificial intelligence and education in China. *Learning, Media and Technology, 45*(3), 279–293. DOI: 10.1080/17439884.2020.1754236

Lu, J., Bridges, S. M., Hmelo-Silver, C. E., & Chan, L. K. (2018). Learning analytics for assessment and feedback in higher education. *The Internet and Higher Education, 39*, 1–3. DOI: 10.1016/j.iheduc.2018.07.002

Luckin, R. (2018). *Machine learning and human intelligence: The future of education for the 21st century.* UCL Institute of Education Press.

Luckin, R., Holmes, W., Griffiths, M., & Forcier, L. B. (2016). *Intelligence unleashed: An argument for AI in education.* Pearson.

Mangels, J. A., Butterfield, B., Lamb, J., Good, C., & Dweck, C. S. (2006). Why do beliefs about intelligence influence learning success? A social cognitive neuroscience model. *Social Cognitive and Affective Neuroscience, 1*(2), 75–86. DOI: 10.1093/scan/nsl013 PMID: 17392928

Mayo, S. (2024). Co-creating with AI in Art Education: On the Precipice of the Next Terrain. *Education Journal, 13*(3), 124–132. Advance online publication. DOI: 10.11648/j.edu.20241303.15

Means, B., Toyama, Y., Murphy, R., Bakia, M., & Jones, K. (2013). The effectiveness of online and blended learning: A meta-analysis of the empirical literature. *Teachers College Record, 115*(3), 1–47. DOI: 10.1177/016146811311500307

Meylani, R. (2024). Artificial Intelligence in the Education of Teachers: A Qualitative Synthesis of the Cutting-Edge Research Literature. *Journal of Computer and Education Research, 12*(24), 600–637. Advance online publication. DOI: 10.18009/jcer.1477709

MHRD. (2020). National [Ministry of Human Resource Development, Government of India.]. *Educational Policy*, •••, 2020.

Mishra, P., & Koehler, M. J. (2006). Technological Pedagogical Content Knowledge: A framework for integrating technology in teacher knowledge. *Teachers College Record, 108*(6), 1017–1054. DOI: 10.1111/j.1467-9620.2006.00684.x

Mishra, S. (2024). Revolutionizing Education: The Impact of AI-Enhanced Teaching Strategies. *International Journal for Research in Applied Science and Engineering Technology, 12*(9), 9–32. Advance online publication. DOI: 10.22214/ijraset.2024.64127

Nazaretsky, T., Ariely, M., Cukurova, M., & Alexandron, G. (2022). Teachers' trust in AI-powered educational technology and a professional development program to improve it. *British Journal of Educational Technology, 53*(4), 914–931. DOI: 10.1111/bjet.13232

NCERT. (2021). *DIKSHA: A digital platform for teachers.* National Council of Educational Research and Training.

OECD. (2021). *AI and the future of skills in education.* Organisation for Economic Co-operation and Development.

Papamitsiou, Z., & Economides, A. A. (2014). Learning analytics and educational data mining in practice: A systematic literature review. *Computers & Education, 87*, 49–65.

Popenici, S. A., & Kerr, S. (2017). Exploring the impact of artificial intelligence on teaching and learning in higher education. *Research and Practice in Technology Enhanced Learning*, *12*(1), 1–13. DOI: 10.1186/s41039-017-0062-8 PMID: 30595727

Puentedura, R. R. (2013). SAMR: A contextualized introduction [PDF]. Hippasus. https://hippasus.com/rrpweblog/archives/2014/01/15/SAMRABriefContextualizedIntroduction.pdf

Pujeda, J. R. A. (2023). A systematic review of teachers' digital competencies and the adoption of artificial intelligence in enhancing learning experiences. *International Journal of Research and Innovation in Social Science*, *7*(12), 373–383. DOI: 10.47772/IJRISS.2023.7012031

Redecker, C. (2017). *European framework for the digital competence of educators: DigCompEdu*. European Commission.

Rogers, E. M. (1995). *Diffusion of innovations* (4th ed.). The Free Press., URL https://teddykw2.wordpress.com/wp-content/uploads/2012/07/everett-m-rogers-diffusion-of-innovations.pdf

Romero, C., & Ventura, S. (2020). Educational Data Mining and Learning Analytics: An Updated Survey. *Wiley Interdisciplinary Reviews. Data Mining and Knowledge Discovery*, *10*(3), e1355. DOI: 10.1002/widm.1355

Schiff, D. (2021). Education and AI ethics: Who teaches the machines? *AI & Society*, *36*(4), 977–989.

Schmid, M., Goertz, L., Behrens, J., & Fischer, F. (2021). The impact of artificial intelligence on learning, teaching, and education. *European Journal of Education*, *56*(3), 333–347.

Selwyn, N. (2019). *Should robots replace teachers? AI and the future of education*. Polity Press.

Selwyn, N. (2020). Re-imagining 'learning' and 'teaching' in the AI era: Looking beyond automation to 'AI' as an educational technology. *Digital Education Review*, *37*, 45–58.

Selwyn, N. (2021). The risks and opportunities of AI in education. *AI & Society*, *36*(4), 1099–1111.

Siemens, G., & Long, P. (2011). Penetrating the Fog: Analytics in Learning and Education. *EDUCAUSE Review*, *46*(5), 30–40.

Singh, V., & Ram, S. (2024). *Impact of Artificial Intelligence on Teacher Education*. Shodh Sari-An International Multidisciplinary Journal., DOI: 10.59231/SARI7669

Sinha, M. (2021). AI-driven learning analytics in *Indian ed-tech startups: A case study approach.* Educational Technology & Society, 24(1), 72–85.

Sytnyk, L., & Podlinyayeva, O. (2024). AI in education: Main possibilities and challenges. In Proceedings of the 8th International Scientific and Practical Conference" International Scientific Discussion: Problems, Tasks and Prospects (pp. 569-579).

Tarisayi, K. (2024). Preparing for AI's transformational potential: Rethinking teacher education in South Africa. *International Education Trend Issues*, *2*(1), 31–40. DOI: 10.56442/ieti.v2i1.364

Tondeur, J., van Braak, J., Ertmer, P. A., & Ottenbreit-Leftwich, A. (2017). Understanding the relationship between teachers' pedagogical beliefs and technology use in education: A systematic review of qualitative evidence. *Educational Technology Research and Development*, *65*(3), 555–575. DOI: 10.1007/s11423-016-9481-2

UNESCO. (2022). *AI in education: Global perspectives and best practices.* United Nations Educational, Scientific and Cultural Organization.

Venkatesh, V., Morris, M. G., Davis, G. B., & Davis, F. D. (2003). User acceptance of information technology: Toward a unified view. *Management Information Systems Quarterly*, *27*(3), 425–478. DOI: 10.2307/30036540

Vu, H. (2024). The Implications of Artificial Intelligence for Educational Systems: Challenges, Opportunities, and Transformative Potential. *The American Journal of Social Science and Education Innovations*. .DOI: 10.37547/tajssei/Volume06Issue03-17

Williamson, B., & Eynon, R. (2020). Historical trends and contemporary challenges in education and technology policy. *Oxford Review of Education*, *46*(3), 265–283.

Winkler, R., & Søllner, M. (2018). Unleashing the Potential of Chatbots in Education: A State-of-the-Art Analysis. *Proceedings of the International Conference on Information Systems*, 12(1), 45-59. DOI: 10.5465/AMBPP.2018.15903abstract

Yadav, B. (2024). Generative AI in the Era of Transformers: Revolutionizing Natural Language Processing with LLMs. *J. Image Process. Intell. Remote Sens*, *4*(2), 54–61. DOI: 10.55529/jipirs.42.54.61

Zawacki-Richter, O., Marín, V. I., Bond, M., & Gouverneur, F. (2019). Systematic review of research on artificial intelligence applications in higher education. *International Journal of Educational Technology in Higher Education*, *16*(1), 39. DOI: 10.1186/s41239-019-0171-0

Zhai, X. (2021). AI-powered education in China: Trends, challenges, and policies. *Educational Research Review*, *34*, 100419.

Zhang, Y., & Aslan, A. (2021). AI-driven educational innovations: Examining teachers' perspectives on AI applications in education. *Computers & Education*, *165*, 104–130.

Chapter 8

Faculty Interdisciplinary Collaboration:
Transforming Academia via Collaborative Partnerships

Wasswa Shafik
http://orcid.org/0000-0002-9320-3186
Dig Connectivity Research Laboratory (DCRLab), Uganda

ABSTRACT

Faculty interdisciplinary collaboration plays a pivotal role in fostering innovation, advancing research, and enhancing teaching in higher education. By bridging diverse disciplines, faculty members can address complex global challenges through integrative approaches that combine knowledge, methodologies, and perspectives from various fields. This collaboration promotes the development of innovative curricula, interdisciplinary research projects, and impactful solutions that transcend traditional academic boundaries. It also encourages knowledge sharing, creativity, and professional growth among educators and researchers. Despite its potential, interdisciplinary collaboration often faces challenges, including institutional barriers, differing terminologies, and resource constraints. This study explores strategies to overcome these obstacles, highlighting best practices for fostering collaborative environments that support interdisciplinary initiatives. This chapter offers insights into creating a culture of collaboration that drives academic excellence and societal impact.

DOI: 10.4018/979-8-3373-1285-9.ch008

1 INTRODUCTION

Interdisciplinary collaboration is an essential element in addressing the complex conundrums of education. Data from articles published in disciplinary associations' journals documents that interdisciplinary work is expanding. Between 1995 and 2024, estimates suggest that publications of interdisciplinary teams grew from around 2% or less of all published studies to more than 20%. Just over 60% of this interdisciplinary work is taking place within professional and clinical academic disciplines, with the remaining taking place in educational foundations and/or history (Gardner et al., 2024). This professional preparation has a long legacy in U.S. colleges and schools of education, aligning with the view that the work of educational professionals is complex and requires expertise from across a range of fields and disciplines. In higher education, interest and need for interdisciplinary work are growing at both undergraduate and graduate levels. The effect of worries and expectations about interdisciplinary work continues to persist, impeding the full potential of interdisciplinary work (Rodriguez et al., 2024). This is a time when no single field knows all that there is to know about its area of expertise, and the ever-growing availability of communication channels demands that specialists be able to convey new knowledge without the luxury of finding common language and agreements with every audience. Furthermore, the international nature of many fields, industries, and professions has increased the demand for professionals who can thrive in diverse and global environments, and colleges and universities must do more to graduate individuals who possess the knowledge, skills, and 'habits of mind' necessary to become principled and innovative contributors to our worldwide interconnected economy. This study seeks to unpack faculty interdisciplinary collaboration (van Schalkwyk & Blitz, 2024). Specifically, this analysis explores the benefits and challenges arising from faculty interdisciplinary collaboration in an era of increasing interest and expectation in the academic field.

Interdisciplinary collaboration within higher education has a long history. The earliest universities supported a broad-ranging education that prepared students to participate in societal governance as citizens rather than to work in specific avocations. Although the development of disciplines has long since replaced this comprehensive approach to support specialized training in careers, there has been a recent resurgence of interest in interdisciplinary or multidisciplinary approaches to college education (McNamee & Van Horn, 2024). Today's assorted silos were established relatively recently, especially in the natural sciences, through the functionalization of academic organizations in the economic boom of the 1950s. Between 1911 and 1958, nearly 40 percent of new natural science faculty members were appointed with institutional cross-appointments in areas such as agriculture, medicine, dentistry, engineering, or law. Currently, the increased competition for funding has required a "language of power" among colleagues with the resultant decline in understanding of other fields (Baker et al., 2024). But for college students to think and act intelligently in society, selective disregard of disciplinary perspectives in curricular programs further segregates knowledge.

Society's petrified knowledge structures are beyond the pale of the day's most pressing issues. Apprehension over the integration of knowledge has led some academic administrators to question the quality of interdisciplinary research as less rigorous or less organized than disciplines. However, an interdisciplinary approach often allows a more comprehensive examination of complex phenomena so that different research designs can triangulate on converging truths. Many contemporary college graduates will pursue careers and leadership positions solving problems that cut across traditional academic disciplines (Collazo et al., 2024). In other words, our society's demands oblige us to collaborate in preparing members of a new generation to do professional work that integrates different bodies of knowledge. In this manner, building support for interdisciplinary collaboration becomes an investment in the future of higher education. Given the societal relevance of this matter, there has already been a call for an interdisciplinary perspective on interdisciplinary programs of study. This calls for a preliminary analysis of faculty interdisciplinary collaboration in the contemporary university since faculty will be the leaders of such cross-disciplinary programs (Campbell et al., 2024). One of the solutions highlighted to help with some of the current challenges facing higher education is experiential learning, such as field-based education, service learning, project-based science, or conducting compelling interdisciplinary research programs. Prominent schools across the nation have faculty carrying out leading-edge research and who are furthermore taking time to transform undergraduate science and mathematics by making it more experientially oriented. Several studies argue that fostering such faculty interdisciplinary collaboration is important for needed reforms in the educational system (Green et al., 2024).

1.1 Definition and Scope

Faculty interdisciplinary collaboration is a joint or collective enterprise that differs from a multidisciplinary or combined approach, such as a project or curriculum that combines the work of separately functioning faculty members or a transdisciplinary or supradisciplinary approach that attempts to integrate or unify discrete knowledge and methods. Faculty interdisciplinary collaboration may have different forms. The most familiar form is a joint research project, where faculty from different disciplines contribute to formulating the research question, collecting and analyzing data, and interpreting and reporting the results. Another familiar form is collaborative teaching (Rokooei et al., 2024). Faculty interdisciplinary collaboration can also involve people from different departments working on curricular concerns, where all aspects of a program's operation are rich with teaching, learning, and integration topics. This may be from the research end, attempting to determine whether two or more groups of students learned as much as each other and the rest of the university's students, or from the practitioners or policy end, learning how promoting integrative knowledge enhances the economic leverage of the university graduates. Faculty work together on openly determined day-to-day issues or set broader visions, intentions, or strategies (Alizadeh et al., 2024). Whatever the source of interdisciplinary work, the partners must share their understanding in such a way that they can learn from each other's perspectives. In all cases, the faculty work together in order to generate a work product or process for others not concerned with, participating in, contributing to, or sanctioning the collaboration. An additional defining quality is the increasingly unique perspective that each partner contributes from a field that is distanced from the subject of the collaboration. Clearly, each field has its unique perspective, evidence, method, and intellectual virtues (Sharma, 2024). It is the special contribution of activity at the intersection that makes faculty interdisciplinary collaboration unique and potentially productive of new ideas or mechanisms.

1.2 Purpose of the Study

As the title of the study proposes, the principal goal of this research study was to explore ways in which faculty interdisciplinary work unfolds within a particular higher education context in the United States: a business and technology university. Through interviews and surveys with faculty members on campus, this study sought to understand, among other things, (A) the benefits of and motivations for interdisciplinary undertakings among higher education faculty members, (B) the challenges and barriers present in interdisciplinary efforts, and (C) potential strategies for creating an environment in which interdisciplinary efforts among faculty are supported. Particularly relevant to an exploration of interdisciplinary teaching, a subset of questions also asked about intersections between research and ways that interdepartmental work is encouraged or discouraged. A better understanding of interdisciplinary collaboration and its effects between and among non-science faculty provides unique and important contributions, yet evidence shows that too few faculty have the opportunity to engage in scholarly inquiry on approaches that have teaching and learning implications (Okpalauwaekwe et al., 2024). Specifically, the goal of this study was to uncover strategies for supporting faculty-inclusive practices in the service of students and faculty members in their development as teachers and scholars. As faculty work did not involve students engaged in scientific inquiry, we used inclusive rather than interdisciplinary. We anticipated that a better understanding of the challenges that faculty faced in incorporating disciplinary knowledge as part of their collaborative work would yield insight into the perceived dangers and attractions of engaging in integrative approaches (King et al., 2024). Such insights can help faculty coordinators become sensitive to barriers and challenges faced by faculty and suggest ways in which workshops and other training opportunities can be made more effective. Insights from the first study have already informed previous suggestive national conference presentations on ways to integrate faculty work campus-wide, advocating a systems approach. Just as support systems for "interdisciplinary work" need to be put in place before faculty members can be recruited, so will ongoing institution/activity support systems enhance the ability to engage faculty in inclusive rather than interdisciplinary programs (Bryant et al., 2024).

2 UNDERSTANDING INTERDISCIPLINARY ENVIRONMENT

Interdisciplinary work has garnered substantial attention within a myriad of disciplines and fields over the last few decades. Many definitions and nuances exist within the term interdisciplinary, but within higher educational settings, it is a term that describes the work among faculty to integrate, innovate, and collaborate across departments, divisions, and campuses. This has been done to amend a gap within higher education where the education of students has been approached with a reductionist intent, and they are not adequately prepared to address these complex and multidimensional problems that their professional careers will involve (Kunkel et al., 2024). Theoretical frameworks that inform interdisciplinary collaborative work are also vast, multitudinous, and dispersed. A handful of scholars have played a premier role in the field, and many influential studies have explored the benefits and challenges of interdisciplinary research and collaboration, which have influenced the research of this paper. Many different alternatives for classifying and categorizing interdisciplinary and transdisciplinary collaboration, creation, and research exist. This field is premised on the growing impacts and necessity of collaboration among faculty and thus has many studies on the benefits of collaborative experiences for students and faculty (Michael Nnaemeka Ajemba et al., 2024). Some scholars have classified the different types of collaborative work by disciplinary depth, levels of learner engagement and motivation, or the level of institutional integration. This literature review will show faculty, administrators, and educators working within a program's "beginning phase" the benefits and challenges of this fact in order for them to investigate and advocate for the needs necessary to encourage and maintain faculty interdisciplinary collaborative work. The previous literature also positions this research to expand and encourage consideration of the faculty perspective of their interdisciplinary work. The research offers a contributing and essential addition to the field, providing a new and thorough preliminary data analysis of faculty perception of their interdisciplinary work (Buckley et al., 2024).

Individual research on interdisciplinary collaboration in higher education has been criticized in the review for lacking extensive study or description of environmental and group context. This literature review responds to this challenge by articulating differences in grading rubrics, course types, and curricular levels of the faculty. Interdisciplinary education has also been paralleled with community-based learning in previous studies. Analysis of portfolios has emphasized the qualities of applications to organizations compared to the communities and individuals that portfolios identify (Martin, 2024). Analysis concerning educational benefits indicates the primary assessment link to self-regulated learning, altruistic values, academic and personal growth, and adult leadership. Improvement difficulties are responsible for analyzing the effects on faculty and students, and faculty interdisciplinary collaboration is also briefly investigated. The objectives include providing an overview of interdisciplinary (ID) language, theory, and knowledge that introduces the field of ID as a collaborative practice in higher education. Define the different classifications of interdisciplinary collaboration and give tangible examples for the classifications that identify the uniqueness and positives of the three introductory, entry-level college courses comprised of teacher participation (He, 2024). Analysis of the positives and negatives of faculty interdisciplinary collaboration will also be studied.

2.1 Concepts

Several definitions and concepts require clarification prior to delving into the study of faculty interdisciplinary collaboration. "Faculty collaboration" is a term commonly used in academic settings to describe a wide variety of cooperative activities among teachers or teachers and other agents. This term could include such varied activities as a supportive interchange of ideas or a division of labor in which small work groups engage in joint activity around a problem or issue. Similarly, "faculty" might refer not only to the appointed and tenured full-time instructors at higher education institutions but also to adjuncts, graduate teaching assistants, or learning professionals from nonacademic units (Rudd et al., 2024). Interdisciplinarity is a term with no agreed-upon definition or epistemology across academic literature. While in some cases, "scholarly" and "academic" are used interchangeably, in other instances, an absence of political ideology, class structure, or marketability distinguishes an academic scholar. Thus, "scholarly" work is characterized by "integrity, high ethical standards, due process, personal accountability, passion for professional excellence, and individual and corporate responsibility," while the scholarship is centered on faculty production of new knowledge and the sharing of this knowledge with the academic community. A further definition of "scholarship in teaching and learning" understands scholarship as "a rigorously intellectual endeavor aimed at the conduct and application of original research" at any educational level (Atkinson et al., 2024).

At the core of these diverse definitions is the understanding that faculty members do, or should, hold and apply responsibility for advancing student learning and understanding in their respective fields and should do so in a manner consistent with ethical and accurate research. Apply this understanding to preparing K-12 teachers and curriculum, and we might advance that such scholarship is expected to be "professionally relevant." The diverse and disaggregated understanding of the terms interdisciplinary appeal and interdisciplinarity serves not to create a singular, clear definition but rather to reveal the inextricable linkages between theoretical, practical, and technical aspects of prospective faculty work (Pierce et al., 2024). The significance of (or priority given to) pedagogy, technical instrumentality, community engagement, and service varies depending on the policy and management goals of the institution. Align faculty mission with broader university plans or objectives. The meaning of terms also varies by the details of institutional bylaws, requirements, and, indeed, cultural patterns such as how discipline-linked faculty tend to communicate. Institutionalization of interdisciplinary collaboration thus often serves as a complex mechanism for defining faculty work in accordance with institutional mandates (Peñaflor, 2024).

2.2 Theoretical Frameworks

The dynamic and relational nature of disciplines provides a foundation for understanding interdisciplinary collaboration in higher education. In theoretical terms, the different ways in which disciplines interact, integrate knowledge, and position themselves are the focus of various theoretical frameworks. These explain how disciplines are working and how they could be working differently. Here, we report two theoretical fields that provide the basis to guide the implementation of collaboration in university developments (Yeager-Okosi et al., 2024). Systems theory and social constructivism are two theoretical perspectives that can both appear in multidisciplinary or disciplinary contexts, highlighting either strategic or educational perspectives of institutional mission. From a strategic perspective, the dual perspectives of systems theory and social constructivism can mean that interdisciplinary collaboration is considered good practice or driving a good educational process. The understanding and acceptance of these frameworks by faculty leading and engaging in interdisciplinary collaborative activities are significant because they form the basis for considering and practicing involving another's expertise in learning and teaching (G. Katz et al., 2024). The first framework, systems theory, views interdisciplinary collaboration as a strategic process to guide practice. Systems theory provides a framework for gaining a functional understanding of interdisciplinary collaboration as an element of an institutional strategy to achieve a particular set of goals and to operate in a particular context. Systems theory also provides a practical guideline on how disciplines can effectively operationalize the development of an interdisciplinary collaborative practice that meets both institutional and operational needs, and that works with and moves beyond disciplinary learning and teaching (Ashilungu & Onyancha, 2024). The ability to do this is critical to gaining the buy-in of faculty required to turn the theory into reality.

3 TYPES OF INTERDISCIPLINARY COLLABORATION

Increasing interdisciplinary collaboration is an important goal in the challenges facing higher education, but little empirical research is available to assess the effectiveness of interdisciplinary approaches, describe mechanisms for establishing successful interdisciplinary projects, and explore tensions arising from collaborative activities. Research on both objectives and tensions will be of value to faculty in many institutions as they evaluate the opportunities and constraints related to developing interdisciplinary projects to advance a scholarly, research, or curricular agenda (Dexter et al., 2024). This presents findings from a three-year study at two public, comprehensive universities that bring perspectives on problem definition and project implementation. At these universities, collaborative work occurs among faculty members in multiple ways. Intra-faculty collaboration involves faculty members in the same department; at one institution, the department level is the most frequent site of collaboration. Department-level collaboration often includes contributions from all faculty in a department, while intra-faculty collaboration may involve only a portion of the department faculty. Inter-faculty collaboration involves faculty members from more than one department or college (Tippit et al., 2024). Despite the differences, neither approach dominates; most faculty are involved almost equally in all forms. Recent work asks some pertinent questions in an attempt to get at the mechanics of collaborative work. Given the richness of existing scholarship on collaboration, some specific challenges and benefits are addressed in more detail. Given that each circumstance of collaboration may require different protocols, a faculty centered on collaboration might consider the most relevant case and practical features for implications in its unique context (Riley et al., 2024).

3.1 Intra-Faculty Collaboration

The intra-faculty collaboration will have its distinct traits and benefits. The phrase 'intra-faculty' suggests faculty within the same department or discipline. So, a history faculty may have broadly aligned objectives for how they engage with interdisciplinary learning but will have research and teaching interests that overlap more with each other. Similar to the above, the alignment of departmental or disciplinary backgrounds among faculty gives an established community in which to launch into interdisciplinary research in pedagogy, as well as the existence of shared references to a common institutional culture (Falandry et al., 2024). Obviously, this may also depend on the size and remit of disciplines: a larger mathematics department is likely to have more inter-departmental links, adding more diverse approaches and practices to the table than a smaller Centre for American Literature. Despite the possibly narrow parameter for interlocutors, intra-faculty inquiry fosters a closer alignment of non-lesson learning and teaching about those areas we specialize (Padalulu & Malyo, 2024).

Our teaching may inform our research agenda in ways that proposals and presentations do not, and teaching in our domain foregrounds more concern in the 'what' and 'how' of learning and teaching. Committees in respective faculties can also support collaboration in respective areas. Collaborative links are forged and enacted through learning and teaching in the establishment of connections among faculty and interdisciplinary cultures (Bajwa et al., 2024). Again, examples of conference papers or successful bids for intra-faculty research projects will provide evidence of intra-faculty experience in directing curricula and engaging in research on learning and teaching. There is a first-hand account of an intra-faculty research project, the Embedded Values, situated in the Centre for Learning Excellence. Settings for teaching and learning increasingly recognize subject boundaries and pedagogies as increasingly diverse yet offer few opportunities for faculty to explore 'cutting-edge' research in pedagogical theories within a common framework (Gopal et al., 2024).

In terms of impact on students, by sharing common pedagogic and research objectives, a particular kind of teamwork is possible. Projects that draw on sub-disciplinary knowledge generate interdisciplinary knowledge. A group of staff researching and perhaps practicing teaching within the same area can give a more detailed understanding of a specialism that supports integration in our teaching. Collaboration among specialists who teach the same subjects allows reflexive, detailed comparison of the various teachings and philosophies around a subject. It goes beyond 'sharing practices' yet crucially draws on current themes in theory as they intersect with content (Turner et al., 2024). A good deal of practical work remains within the establishment of learning communities. Although easier to develop, one main current issue is the difficulty of maintaining focus and a robust will to sustain and grow an operational initiative beyond the identified and confined disciplinary threshold. There is a pressing need in higher education to address issues operating across disciplines that can be more costly to confront through a 'very narrow disciplinary door.' The excitement of the interdisciplinary focus often leads to stalling and absorption by those 'soloists' – i.e., the faculty who collaborate only within their sub-disciplines (Corte & Amrein-Beardsley, 2024). Note that this curricular and practical orientation does not sanction non-disciplinary or interdisciplinary work. It is a strategic approach, conscious of what is possible in the short to medium term, based on where the institution is currently in its development of faculties. It does not write off the interdisciplinary focus or non-disciplinary contexts but seeks to maximize our initial development of an interdisciplinary focus by occurring through a wide-ranging but limited array of disciplinary expertise. In future years, we would anticipate interim reports, a conference, and other similar research outputs to underscore this sub-disciplinary exploration and offer models, insights, and experiences gained (Gholamnia-Shirvani et al., 2024).

3.2 Inter-Faculty Collaboration

In inter-faculty collaborations, faculty who may come from different programs, departments, or divisions work together. The administration of administrative units from different faculties often seeks inter-faculty collaboration for two primary reasons: sharing resources and expertise and a focus on more than one potential solution to solve the suggestion. In this study, we will discuss the pedagogical or educational reasons to embark on inter-faculty collaboration, namely that the most innovative approaches may come from people who do not think alike (i.e., holistically inclusive of varying persons from diverse disciplines, including faculty, students, and other intended audiences) (Alkhateeb et al., 2024). Interdisciplinarity is an emerging concept in education, research, innovation, and intellectual life in recent years. Over the last couple of decades, interdisciplinarity as a buzzword has been flaunted across the globe, from research labs and faculty meetings to granting agencies and professional meetings. An interdisciplinary approach encourages interns to consider broad issues from diverse perspectives. It enables the exploration of some aspects of a given issue in terms of different identities and to discover the common qualities of the issue (Hamilton et al., 2024).

One of the earliest barriers to providing opportunities for inter-faculty initiatives is the structure of higher education curricula, which is divided into many disciplines, an inheritance from the Industrial Revolution. On the administrative level, departments are the basic units of approval for the staffing plan, teaching assignments, merit increases, and the development and implementation of policies and procedures. Deans and other senior administrators are organized in councils around these departmental lines. Inter-faculty initiatives organized for educational purposes may be perceived initially as barriers by administrators, who will point to the staff time required to invest in them (Tu et al., 2024). However, suppose the program has been marketed as offering transformative experiences, high utility per student cost, rewards for cross-institutional partnerships, recruitment of new students, scholarly publications, or presentations from faculty and students. In that case, financial disincentives will not have as negative an impact in terms of their decision to provide support. We would also suggest that once one or two inter-faculty initiatives have been institutionalized, the dean or other campus administrators will become stronger advocates given positive student evaluations. It might also facilitate administrative support and attract student participants if the program and related challenges can be tied to the institution's mission or a specific policy and the point of integration and implementation (Somerville et al., 2024).

4 PRACTICAL METHODOLOGY

The study employed a mixed-methods approach that included both qualitative and quantitative data collection and analysis. Qualitative data were obtained in the form of individual semi-structured interviews with a random, stratified sample of faculty, as well as with a sample of non-faculty stakeholders drawn from the aforementioned colleges in both Orlando and Miami. The quantitative data were obtained from a cross-sectional survey administered to faculty members in the same colleges. This data collection allows for triangulation across sources and methods, thereby enhancing validity (S. Katz & Deckman, 2024). For instance, qualitative data can offer an in-depth illustration of faculty perspectives, whereas quantitative data can permit an initial measurement of the representativeness of those qualitative data and a first cut at understanding their generalizability. We have continued to integrate and reanalyze both data types and will do so in discussing the results, though this paper's focus is on the qualitative data. One of the biggest benefits of a mixed-methods design is that it allows for capturing a diverse set of perspectives to validate the findings (Zhao et al., 2024). Indeed, diversity, in this case, can be conceived quite broadly: (i) such perspectives might be temporal – capturing snapshots of the way faculty collaboration was, is, and might be or should be; (ii) the perspectives also might be disciplinary, reflecting differences in the disciplines within the colleges; and (iii) the perspectives might be individual, representing unique answers from different individuals, or focused on interactions between faculty members, or among groups of people from the higher education communities, be they faculty members, students, administrators, or others (Eiswirth & Miller, 2024). When dealing with this text, readers need to remember that the influence of perspective permeates all aspects and findings, and as such, readers are encouraged to consider what underlies the apparent contradictions that arise herein, paying particularly close attention to both the methods of data collection and their results. The analysis herein, then, presents an almost kaleidoscopic view of the considerations that faculty members and stakeholders report on the issue of interdisciplinary faculty collaboration (Clipperton et al., 2024). This section further details the methodology, including the procedures for participant selection, ethical considerations, and the qualitative and quantitative data that were gathered.

4.1 Research Design

A research can follow a mixed-methods research design to explore how faculty who teach in interdisciplinary programs collaborate, and the benefits and challenges of such collaboration. Mixed-methods research is valuable in that the use of qualitatively and quantitatively driven results can enhance the depth of a study beyond what is possible with one method alone. In turn, qualitative results may be used to explain or build out from quantitative results, and vice versa. Interview narratives, survey responses, and statistical patterns can corroborate and otherwise strengthen a study's findings and also provide rich contexts that lack precedence in the literature (Chandra Shaw et al., 2024). We first conducted interviews that allowed key stakeholders to speak at length and share their personal experiences. The findings from the interviews were used to inform the design and focus of the online surveys. Data generated by the surveys were submitted for analysis using statistical and narrative methods. This design has many implications. First, using both of these approaches together can provide some corroboration of results and, therefore, offer a richness in data that neither method could provide alone (Corte & Amrein-Beardsley, 2024). Interviews create rich, descriptive data that might provide insights not previously identified in this field of research.

Additionally, qualitative data collected in interviews helps to build an understanding of complex and previously unidentified ideas. Integrating survey data collection with interviews ensures the surveys relate to the interviews qualitatively as well as psychometrically. To maximize retention and high response rates, an individualized email was written with surveys embedded from an approved list of potential interviewees and sent on our behalf by an administrative assistant or another trusted coordinator (S. Katz & Deckman, 2024). A reminder system was also put into place, whereby follow-up reminders were not done by us directly but by unique, trusted champions associated with a particular area or program that we were hoping to ensure participated in the survey. Finally, in the recruitment email and on the first page of the survey itself, the voluntary nature of the survey was emphasized, as well as the importance of the results, and data security and privacy information. Clearly worded informed consent statements were included on the first page of the survey. The study design addresses several potential threats to construct validity, and also attends to many of the threats to construct and internal validity of the survey (Alkhateeb et al., 2024). As well as external validity, the design of the study included consideration of selection and attrition biases that might occur as a result of the recruitment and follow-up procedures in this direction.

4.2 Data Collection Methods

For this study, we employed three methods to collect data. First, we created surveys to obtain quantitative data about the scale and scope of faculty collaborations at each of the six colleges. Second, we scheduled in-depth, face-to-face, semi-structured interviews with a subsample of faculty from each college to gain a deeper understanding of faculty perspectives and to verify the findings from the survey. Third, we conducted, at each college, a facilitated discussion that would (1) reflect the data that we had been collecting to confirm its accuracy and to add nuance to the findings and (2) assess the value of the various themes and subthemes that had been found. When taken together, we believe these instruments provided an appropriate level and quality of depth, detail, and breadth to capture the varieties of interdisciplinary collaboration and its nuances (Murakami et al., 2024). Our survey, interviews, and focus groups were designed iteratively, with input from members of the research team and an Advisory Committee composed of faculty and staff with expertise in interdisciplinary research and/or quantitative and qualitative research methods. The survey was designed to capture faculty demographics, identify the fields in which they primarily work, and begin inductive explorations into quantities and qualities of faculty collaborations (Pierce et al., 2024). It also captured faculty suggestions for additional key informants for the interview portion of the study. Focus group topics and interview questions were also subject to iterative input from the team and Advisory Committee and were constructed to help triangulate findings during the analysis of multiple data sets. Full consent was obtained prior to beginning the survey, interviews, or focus groups, and all data collection adhered to the principles of Full Board Review and the Preferred Reporting Items for Systematic Reviews and Meta-Analyses checklist (Riley et al., 2024).

5 BENEFITS OF INTERDISCIPLINARY COLLABORATION

Interdisciplinary collaboration in higher education represents an opportunity for colleagues across disciplines to generate new knowledge and develop complementary understanding, skills, and attitudes. From the instructors' perspectives, there are various potential benefits of collaboration that directly impact scholarship and teaching. Research teams often strive to incorporate individuals with diverse expertise in order to provide fresh perspectives and potentially refine project design and methods. Results from such research can prove beneficial to scholars, practitioners, and society based on the convergence of varied and ultimately mutually reinforcing ways of knowing (Rudd et al., 2024). Collaboration can also engender new abilities to engage students in deep learning and holistic understanding of knowledge, capitalizing on the differences in expertise between collaborators to make content relevant and to gain student buy-in. Evidence of interdisciplinary collaborations in academia can result in external funding to support future research efforts and programmatic activities. Collaborating with colleagues also represents an opportunity to create educational how-to manuals and workshops if research identifies evidence-based practices for application in educational contexts. Course development may represent a tangible outcome from interdisciplinary collaboration as new courses or learning experiences evolve from interactions with and between collaborators (Buckley et al., 2024; Michael Nnaemeka Ajemba et al., 2024). Students seek concrete examples of careers and professions, and collaboration can result in tangible opportunities for internships or perhaps co-authoring of journal articles or book chapters. Empirical evidence of the benefits of interdisciplinary collaboration may potentially lead to presentation and publication opportunities that will increase academic prestige and subject matter visibility. Data may also be used to support the development of interdisciplinary programs and degrees to attract and retain students (Green et al., 2024). By utilizing prescriptive educational development and evaluation methods and replicating and validating these potential benefits, faculty members and administrators will be able to demonstrate to various stakeholders the academic and professional utility that results from interdisciplinary collaboration.

5.1 Enhanced Research Opportunities

"There can often be a moment that is sort of like an aha moment where you really generate something new that you couldn't have otherwise." This quote comes from faculty participants in two different university-based faculty development programs that support interdisciplinary research collaborations. One initiative is an interdisciplinary research mentoring program designed to support teams of faculty who are embarking on interdisciplinary and team-based research projects. The other initiative is a faculty learning community that seeks to bring together faculty with shared interests. Both initiatives are run through large, research-intensive institutions (Rodriguez et al., 2024). Despite the differences in their objectives, iterations, and the faculty populations served, faculty in both initiatives echo the importance of combining knowledge from different fields and the ways in which doing so can lead to research and findings that are important and innovative. A growing number of articles in the literature are documenting high-impact interdisciplinary research projects at the higher education level. By combining disciplinary knowledge and expertise, these researchers share their results and suggest directions for the academy as a whole (Rokooei et al., 2024). Many of the interdisciplinary research project case examples embedded within these articles document how scholars are addressing complex problems, such as climate change, water quality, and food systems, by taking an interdisciplinary approach. The interdisciplinarity of these research projects has not only led to individual research productivity, such as publications but has also generated funding focused on solving "real world" problems. Scientists increasingly advocate for the integration of interdisciplinary research in undergraduate and graduate studies as well. Critics of this perspective argue that researchers and scientists should be well-versed in traditional methods and approaches that are specific to their disciplines. However, change is occurring—albeit slowly. In terms of changing the way that partnerships between undergraduate institutions and R1s function, one tool is to provide differential mentorship and support within existing programs to break down interdisciplinary research silos (Okpalauwaekwe et al., 2024).

5.2 Innovative Teaching Strategies

Innovative teaching strategies develop as a result of collaboration among colleagues from diverse disciplines, and especially as a result of interdisciplinary team teaching. Together, faculty can provide a context for adaptive and generative thinking, integrate multiple perspectives on a common theme into a course, help students understand the links between theory and practice across disciplines, and generally provide students with an insightful and holistic picture of their fields of study. Information about an institution's interdisciplinary teaching strategies has coalesced from interviews with educational leaders and scholars studying interdisciplinary efforts, and a study of the curricula at a number of schools (S. Katz & Deckman, 2024). Case studies of successful interdisciplinary programs consistently mention benefits to the students, such as increased and relevant knowledge. Results of interdisciplinary programs often include increased student understanding of another discipline, appreciation for another discipline's way of thinking, and a desire to spend more time in another field at the undergraduate level. The sharing of teaching practices is important to faculty. One case study of a faculty development program examines the assessment of teaching portfolios by faculty. Their data suggest that faculty appreciate the practical logistics of course content preparation and delivery (Tu et al., 2024). Faculty 'will pay attention to the manner in which they are disposed to think about the phenomenon in question, to talk about it, and to respond.' A study of interdepartmental faculty team teaching provides data on faculty benefits to academic improvement. There is a flow of knowledge of teaching practices and continuous improvement measures among faculty (Zhao et al., 2024). A study of faculty development programs shows data on faculty rewards in teaching improvement as a result of faculty collaboration, as presented in Table 1.

Table 1. Fostering faculty interdisciplinary collaboration approaches in this artificial intelligence era

Approach	Brief Description	Illustration	Impact	Reference
Sustainability	Long-term collaboration impact	Ongoing partnerships	Ensures continuity	(Gardner et al., 2024)
Leadership	Guiding collaborative efforts	Faculty coordinators	Ensures direction	(Rodriguez et al., 2024)
Integration	Merging ideas or methods	Unified frameworks	Reduces redundancies	(van Schalkwyk & Blitz, 2024)
Faculty	Academic staff in universities	Professors, Lecturers	Key stakeholders	(McNamee & Van Horn, 2024)
Teamwork	Group work dynamics	Joint projects	Strengthens outcomes	(Baker et al., 2024)
Collaboration	Working together	Research projects	Enhances productivity	(Collazo et al., 2024)
Synergy	Combined efforts	Collaborative programs	Greater impact	(Campbell et al., 2024)
Education	Teaching and learning	Interdisciplinary courses	Builds expertise	(Green et al., 2024)
Partnership	Formal collaboration	University partnerships	Shared resources	(Alizadeh et al., 2024)
Interdisciplinary	Involving multiple disciplines	STEM and Humanities	Promotes innovation	(Sharma, 2024)
Multidisciplinary	Combining varied fields	Engineering & Medicine	Broader perspectives	(Bryant et al., 2024)
Research	Systematic investigation	Published papers	Generates knowledge	(Okpalauwaekwe et al., 2024)
Innovation	Creative solutions	New technologies	Drives progress	(Buckley et al., 2024)

6 CHALLENGES OF INTERDISCIPLINARY COLLABORATION

The core idea of interdisciplinarity is that it requires engaging persons from multiple disciplines, given that a single discipline cannot achieve the development and understanding of knowledge and the complexity of problems. However, communication across disciplines can be difficult, as each discipline has its unique language, methodologies, and ways of thinking. Moreover, faculty face barriers in wanting to take part in interdisciplinary research and collaboration, many of these barriers stemming from faculty's lack of clarity about what is to be gained from interdisciplinary collaboration and research (Campbell et al., 2024). In some cases, disciplinary priorities get in the way of interdisciplinary collaboration. Disciplinary priorities are often the focus of faculty and with numerous internal and external forces on faculty, from research or departmental priorities to student advising, institutional service, and tenure and promotion. For faculty, time is a precious commodity, and to justify meaningful involvement in interdisciplinary programs, they must see the benefit of heavy time commitments. In addition to the individual and discipline challenges, many institutions support but do not fully integrate the work of existing shoulders across campus, and departments are funded differentially. While you may be given institutional support (IS) for your interdisciplinary work, few departments give tenure credit for participating in an interdisciplinary initiative (Alizadeh et al., 2024). Further, as our studies have shown, faculty opportunities for ongoing communication and collaboration can be quite limited because of scheduling and disciplinary differences. The assumptions, values, beliefs, and priorities that each discipline displays inevitably spill over and influence interdisciplinary collaboration. Differences in teaching loads leave some faculty with more time to develop an understanding of interdisciplinary work and to take part in planning and leading. Faculty are accustomed to working with people who share their discipline, adding another obstacle. Some faculty struggle with relinquishing financial and other resources for interdisciplinary coalitions or groups (Collazo et al., 2024).

6.1 Communication Barriers

Interdisciplinary collaboration presupposes the interaction between two or more people from different disciplines working jointly on a given project. An obvious challenge faced in interdisciplinarity, then, is associated with the necessity of understanding each other's jargon. Misinterpretation in interdisciplinary collaboration may occur due to differing styles of communication that result in misunderstanding and conflict (Riley et al., 2024). This can be seen in the following exchange:

- Xerox R&D project manager: Once we define the roles of the work and the process, we can then determine if the infrastructure is appropriate.
- Xerox PARC collaborator: Once the infrastructure is defined and the work and the process are fully parameterized, we can begin to migrate the parts of the process that are infrastructure-independent to new platforms or clients.

Both processes described above bear interesting implications for the development of a systematic approach that facilitates interdisciplinary collaboration. Outcomes from collaborative work between cognitive scientists and philosophers point to some possible positive impacts of the introduction of training in philosophical methodologies and concepts at the cognitive science undergraduate level, as well as the beneficial effects of recognizing where problems arise in interdisciplinary collaborations (Ashilungu & Onyancha, 2024). Developing a vocabulary that clarifies collaboration experiences in order to create a shared understanding of the variety of collaboration types is also likely to be very helpful. Facilitation or mediation that develops the necessary strategies to bridge communication gaps will, therefore, be the most direct method of facilitating collaboration (Falandry et al., 2024).

6.2 Resource Allocation Issues

Competition for limited resources across the institution can breed tensions in interdisciplinary work between faculty and their respective departments. Academic deans of interdisciplinary colleges or schools may struggle to distribute resource allocations in ways that adequately value and support diverse interdisciplinary activities because the dean's office is also highly resource-constrained. In larger institutions that generally fund departments rather than individual disciplines, department chairs who do not directly benefit from the initiative may resist reallocating shared resources to support the interdisciplinary, especially during budget shortages (S. Katz & Deckman, 2024). Finally, boundary-spanning units typically have their distinct administrative procedures that must somehow be made to work together. The growing field of centers, institutes, and initiatives presents a set of administrative challenges often related to resource allocation. For example, without shared fund accounting approaches and the ability to rent faculty time out to multiple entities, such centers often find it difficult to collaborate effectively because of the widespread perception of resource constraints. This is the resource allocation dimension of the sponsor's factor previously mentioned (Eiswirth & Miller, 2024; Shafik, 2023). Each of the challenges involves a resource allocation decision from senior administration, often the university president, provost, or at least a vice president. These challenges call for strategic attention, including possible organizational changes, if they are to be minimized. Clear vision, mission, goal statements, expectations, and built-in approaches for inter-departmental resource sharing and equity of access are just some of the necessary elements to create an environment that supports collaboration for interdisciplinary faculty research (Zhao et al., 2024). Transparent means also need to be available for interdisciplinary work resource distribution.

7 BEST PRACTICES (BP) FOR PROMOTING INTERDISCIPLINARY COLLABORATION

In some cases, administration and colleges or universities can implement or encourage BP that promote collaboration among faculty members from different disciplines and professional teams. Efforts to create a strong culture of collaborative work between disciplines require a strong commitment from the institution. To support this argument, BP from colleges and universities around the world are described. Policies have been created and incentives established to encourage faculty to work together on interdisciplinary research projects, courses, and programs (Padalulu & Malyo, 2024). In general, this includes one or more documents, such as plans, which state the value of collaborative efforts across disciplines. Leadership commitment is important to promote a connected institutional strategy of shared services. Faculty networks, collaboration, and interdisciplinary scholar groups can be used to promote connection. In some cases, a senior faculty leader was appointed to ensure the effectiveness of the large interdisciplinary conversion strategy. Working or consulting with an interdisciplinary education committee can also help promote the connection (Dexter et al., 2024). These include various practices and workspaces that encourage faculty from different fields to share and develop ideas. For example, some bold and cross-cultural spaces are equipped with students engaged in interdisciplinary conversation and subject education. Similarly, different professional teams have been brought together in open architecture spaces to work on interdisciplinary subjects. Other spaces include innovation studios and project spaces. In some large research institutions, directors have created efficient central spaces for large college and university activities (Yeager-Okosi et al., 2024). Therefore, some platforms can be specialized and equipped with appropriate technical equipment to promote the maritime journey.

7.1 Institutional Support

The long-term sustainability of interdisciplinary faculty projects rests on the development of a collaborative university structure, particularly fostered by IS. This support manifests itself in a number of ways. The most important institutional backing is the active support that department chairs, deans, and upper-level administrators can give to such interdisciplinary initiatives; having the administrative backing of these individuals in place makes it much easier for faculty to engage in such initiatives. The assignment of “faculty stewards” by top university administrators to shepherd an interdisciplinary initiative can also be helpful for faculty efforts (Rudd et al., 2024). Other tangible IS includes some of the following: providing a grant program via university-wide interdisciplinary centers or a cross-disciplinary body can be a useful way of steering some money to interdisciplinary work. Another way of providing tangible support is to either create or alter selection criteria for research proposals that require interdisciplinary collaboration. That is, ensure that the most highly scored proposals are those with an interdisciplinary component. This type of work can easily be done by a funder of your campus's research, but remember, funds to do so also need to be made available (Martin, 2024). Therefore, physical infrastructure and a clear interpretation of policies will also support and enable appropriate scholarly collaboration. Institutions need to ensure there are appropriate physical spaces available for faculty to meet and work together, a fact-finding cell for sharing equipment or financial and legal resources in interdisciplinary research enterprises. For such fundraising endeavors to gain traction, there must be policies in place that say the institution not only values faculty collaborative work but also rewards and promotes faculty for engaging in that work (Bryant et al., 2024). This requires a clear interpretation of faculty evaluation policies to explicitly reward faculty for their work in the areas of curriculum development and involvement in high-impact and engaged learning outside the classroom. We will show through a number of case study examples how faculty teams can accomplish enormous feats when provided the right support by both faculty colleagues and administrators. It is worth noting that in most of these case examples as well, a shared university vision and commitment to the collaborative process comes shining through. In other words, these are examples where the whole is greater than the sum of its parts (Rodriguez et al., 2024)!

7.2 Professional Development Opportunities

Workshops, seminars, or training that help faculty gain the necessary skills for interdisciplinary work are one way to provide professional development opportunities. At many institutions, workshops for faculty members cover a multitude of topics or activities, such as creative thinking, creativity, strategic planning, partnerships between academia and industry, strategic networking, and how to tackle grand challenges. Some programs also give a short-term publication, special academic recognition, or modest financial support for completing their programs or workshops (Ashilungu & Onyancha, 2024). The primary objective behind workshops is to provide individuals with the resources, skills, and support to initiate interdisciplinary initiatives that universities believe would be successful. Regular, ongoing professional development opportunities for faculty members would allow faculty members who wish to engage in interdisciplinary work to become skilled at the strategies necessary to succeed. Besides these regularly scheduled workshops, a mentorship plan could be established. Mentorship programs offer early success stories and insights from those who are new to interdisciplinary work, whether they are students or colleagues (Peñaflor, 2024). It has been suggested that experienced interdisciplinary scholars assess the novices with whom they partner. Establishing an interdisciplinary mentorship program could be an important tool for encouraging cooperation between individuals who work together and getting effective faculty collaboration off the ground. Institutions considering a faculty development plan should seek to help faculty members understand and participate in the processes and practices of interdisciplinary engagement. Offering convincing examples of what might be accomplished with properly supported interdisciplinary teamwork can be inspirational (King et al., 2024). Therefore, this chapter addresses IS related to the facilitation of interdisciplinary work.

8 SAMPLED CASE STUDIES OF SUCCESSFUL INTERDISCIPLINARY COLLABORATIONS

Communicating our changing world is just one of many initiatives that represent successful interdisciplinary collaborations in higher education. Faculty in four departments accounted for a range of points of view and productive tensions from natural and social sciences, communications, visual arts, and agriculture. These different vantage points, along with the jargon and methodologies that accompany them, ensure that interdisciplinary work can be difficult. "But the conversation you create also makes the outcomes more unique," according to a faculty member from Visual Arts. The group came together after responding to a call for proposals (Alizadeh et al., 2024). "Folders were full of ideas," notes a faculty member from LESC, "the hardest part was just getting it down to a manageable size... what is it we wanted to hone in on?" They chose to focus on the human costs of environmental change and specifically on the two Fijian communities of Yamata and Galoa that are currently in the midst of negotiating what to do as a country in the face of political and environmental compromise. Case study after case study discusses the demands interdisciplinary projects place on time, human and financial resources as well as on the outcomes (G. Katz et al., 2024; Yeager-Okosi et al., 2024). Outcomes, though, are rarely defined by researchers as academic articles, books, or peer-reviewed publications that might appear in discussions of research collaboration. Research outcomes are the literacies of successful interdisciplinary work: the ability to float between, accommodate, or juggle different perspectives, to draw out the best in a diversity of views, to apply approaches to different settings, and to work with constituencies who have other motives than yourself. Socially distributed within CE, it is these literacies that have made our team successful producers and trainers of interdisciplinary collaboration (Buckley et al., 2024; Michael Nnaemeka Ajemba et al., 2024). And, just as community engagement is valuable, advisor engagement is eminently valuable, bringing fresh, untold perspectives into academic space.

8.1 STEM and Humanities Integration

Integration efforts between science, technology, engineering, and mathematics (STEM) and the humanities often underscore the ways in which artists, humanists, or designers can contribute to STEM research, design, and teaching. While disciplinary boundaries around numbers and qualitative data remain important, recent case studies and position papers suggest that some of the most exciting collaborations might be between the quantitative methods of the social and natural sciences and qualitative humanities or arts (King et al., 2024). Notable projects that bridge STEM and the humanities include developing interdisciplinary research in scientific, ethical, philosophical, and policy matters related to the artificial intelligence revolution and projects that aim to integrate education in science, technology, engineering, and mathematics with the arts and humanities. While there are certainly challenges in bridging the two cultures of quantitative and qualitative, case studies such as these, suggest that there are also many fruitful ways to bring the two together (Riley et al., 2024). This kind of arts-science/humanities STEM integration can provide innovative and synergistic benefits that lead to enhanced engagement, teaching, and knowledge production in the humanistic and scientific realms. Many of the projects aim to engage students in active research or to craft addressing an interdisciplinary problem or issue. Importantly, these projects draw on the breadth and span of multiple schools and disciplines, which leads to the kind of diverse institutional investment needed to sustain interdisciplinary work within the university (Somerville et al., 2024). They also show the range and depth of cutting-edge humanistic STEM projects currently being pursued by faculty.

8.2 Community Engagement Projects

Community engagement projects are one of the most direct forms of interdisciplinary teaching and scholarship, providing a rich context within which participants can learn about new perspectives that complement or conflict with their own. On our campus, the last decade has seen a small explosion of initiatives whereby faculty and students have worked together with community organizations to address local challenges and opportunities. Modest IS has made possible more ambitious large-scale research projects, such as the two below, developed through collaboration with regionally based colleagues (Turner et al., 2024). In the interdisciplinary classroom, faculty report that their involvement with community-based engagement brought new energy and vitality to their classroom, offering both new ways of teaching their disciplines and new ways of interpreting disciplinary knowledge. But in community engagement, the reciprocal exchange between campus and community is unmistakably of the essence. New goals in the classroom must be negotiated between the faculty and their non-campus partners (Tippit et al., 2024). The pragmatics of addressing community-defined needs create a pedagogical environment markedly different from one that is driven by strictly academic goals. Though often the most appreciated, this kind of reciprocity is not about turning our campuses into nonprofits.

Rather, it seeks a kind of synergy, a form of educational enrichment that constitutes an essential educational aim: service learning. Thus we find that in the majority of our community-based courses, interdisciplinary or otherwise, our faculty have approached this model from an academic motivation that was then discovered to be beneficial to both the campus and the local community (Yeager-Okosi et al., 2024).

Interdisciplinary approaches to community improvement are certainly not new. For decades, traditional land-grant-based institutions have worked closely with local extension agencies toward practical outcomes in food and industry. More recently, increasingly innovative attempts at campus-community collaboration tend to fall under the broad rubric of an institution's "public service": witness, in higher education, the fledgling University Center and Program for Civic Engagement, the University of Vermont Helm's Scholars Program, and the many outreach projects and programs springing up on college campuses from coast to coast in response to recent calls for "engagement" by associations of colleges and universities (Atkinson et al., 2024). By emphasizing outreach and service, these models promote the development of effective pedagogy that goes beyond the confines of the disciplines. Few of them, however, promote a response to community need as a theoretical necessity for course design, and fewer still promote an interdisciplinary approach, one that delivers not only increased teaching and learning dividends but potentially greater stability and sustainability to the community (Tippit et al., 2024).

9 KEY FINDINGS AND IMPLICATIONS FOR PRACTICE

Based on the results of this study, we have identified a number of benefits and positive aspects of interdisciplinary collaboration among faculty in higher education. These can be organized into two main themes: improved research outcomes and more relevant and engaging learning and teaching. A number of challenges and concerns about faculty interdisciplinary collaboration were also identified. These can be categorized into three main themes: tensions in developing interdisciplinary work, the impact of non-disciplinary norms, and motivation (Rodriguez et al., 2024). However, for this report, the discussion focuses on the positive aspects and benefits of interdisciplinary collaboration. Based on the findings of this research, several areas of practice can be implemented in higher education institutions in order to support and enable faculty interdisciplinary collaboration: review mission groups funding schemes and processes, create supportive career pathways, provide training in soft skills, foster a culture of embracing experimentation and risk, and grow funds to support interdisciplinary projects (Bryant et al., 2024). Such a shift in institutional approach at a policy level will be vital since the findings of this research indicate that it is unlikely that any amount of collaboration at an operational level will enable interdisciplinary collaboration to truly flourish if this is not reflected at the level of institutional culture. The implication for all members of academic communities is clear, though: being proactive in building interdisciplinary collaboration, where required, will enable richer and more innovative academic work (Gopal et al., 2024). Moreover, fostering a supportive institutional environment, even by informal means, opens greater potential for academic practice.

9.1 Provide a longitudinal approach

As universities increasingly begin to implement interdisciplinary collaborative structures, it will be critical to examine how participants are being impacted over time. A key issue that longitudinal empirical studies would clarify is whether the benefits of faculty interdisciplinary collaboration are temporary. Another pressing research area is identifying the optimal timeframe for each form of interdisciplinary collaboration to deliver long-lasting effects (Tu et al., 2024). Ideally, this is probably the amount of time for faculty to complete a research project and achieve at least one major work product, or have lead members who are willing to invest several years in the collaboration. A longitudinal research perspective may answer a question such as: is a quantitatively small co-authorship network associated with one piece of faculty scholarship an early warning sign that the collaboration is doomed to only a limited number of written contributions despite the intentions to produce an interdisciplinary knowledge base encased in multiple works (Dexter et al., 2024)?

9.2 Apply multimethod research designs

Research designs that integrate both quantitative and qualitative methods can stimulate a broader and deeper understanding of faculty interdisciplinary collaborative processes and outcomes. Early empirical investigations pertaining to faculty interdisciplinary collaboration were conducted using cross-sectional research methods. The ridge of the corresponding method then moved toward team survey studies and formal modeling (Turner et al., 2024). The insight and depth of understanding into faculty interdisciplinary collaboration offered by these early empirical studies may have accordingly become increasingly diminished simply because the fields emphasized are those most easily addressed by large-sample surveys and computer programs. The combined empirical evidence, thereby largely confirmed by empirical research, likely stymies the research field of faculty interdisciplinary collaboration (Corte & Amrein-Beardsley, 2024; Zhao et al., 2024).

10 CONCLUSION

Based on the lived experiences of faculty across five institutions of higher education and a review of the interdisciplinary collaboration literature, the findings from this study discuss the multiple opportunities of engaging in interdisciplinary work as well as the challenges associated with these types of endeavors. Faculty members recognize both the potential benefits and frustrating obstacles faced when working collaboratively with others coming from a variety of disciplinary backgrounds. Based on our analysis, the benefits of interdisciplinarity for faculty and students alike include professional development and learning and transformed student programming, teaching, and learning. Yet, the challenges associated with interdisciplinary work can be substantial, including finding a shared language, managing conceptual differences, searching for time and funding, and confronting resistance from the newly developed bureaucracy. Faculty find participating in interdisciplinary work professionally and personally satisfying. Yet, most importantly, it has the potential to transform core professional practices, most notably the development of courses and the overall teaching and learning experience at the core of the undergraduate and graduate experience. In sum, interdisciplinary collaboration has the potential to improve the university experience. Interdisciplinary curriculum development will help develop the core competencies demanded by current and future employers. More importantly, however, is the manner in which a facilitated interdisciplinary approach to learning cultivates among students the superb capacity to skillfully and intelligently work with and across differences. Despite the numerous benefits associated with interdisciplinarity, interdisciplinary work in higher education is challenging. To be successful, therefore, institutions need to make participation in interdisciplinary work sufficiently inviting, feasible, and sustainable. Future research should further explore the challenges of interdisciplinary work, specifically from the faculty perspective. Given the many ways in which undergraduate and graduate students are experiencing interdisciplinary learning across the United States, we are learning that modern modes of interdisciplinarity are necessarily community-centered and engaged. Therefore, interdisciplinary becomes transdisciplinary as we are not just asking questions about social change but are actively and self-reflexively working for and catalyzing social change itself. If the previous century was the age of the expert, then the profile of the workforce in the next century will demand new competencies and knowledge.

REFERENCES

Ajemba, M. N., Iroanya, C. J., & Ironegbu, C. (2024). Assessment of faculty development programs in African Medical Schools: A systematic review. *World Journal of Advanced Research and Reviews*, *21*(1), 1723–1735. Advance online publication. DOI: 10.30574/wjarr.2024.21.1.0164

Alizadeh, M., Parmelee, D., & Nordquist, J. (2024). The Power of Metaphor: Learning Space and Faculty Development. *Medical Science Educator*, *34*(3), 543–550. Advance online publication. DOI: 10.1007/s40670-024-02024-w PMID: 38887419

Alkhateeb, N. E., Hormzyar, A. J., & Taha, H. I. (2024). Empowering Faculty Training Amidst COVID-19: Digital Badge as a Potential Pedagogical Tool. *Health Profession Education*, *10*(1). Advance online publication. DOI: 10.55890/2452-3011.1063

Ashilungu, M., & Onyancha, O. B. (2024). Faculty–librarian cooperation in collection development at the University of Namibia library, with special reference to electronic resources. *Collection and Curation*, *43*(1), 8–18. Advance online publication. DOI: 10.1108/CC-11-2022-0041

Atkinson, A. R., Abbott, C., Oswald, A., Boucher, A., Cavalcanti, R. B., Frank, J. R., & Snell, L. S. (2024). Strategies to Enable Transformation in Medical Education: Faculty and Trainee Development in Competence By Design. *Perspectives on Medical Education*, *13*(1), 85–94. Advance online publication. DOI: 10.5334/pme.960 PMID: 38343557

Bajwa, M., Ahmed, R., Lababidi, H., Morris, M., Morton, A., Mosher, C., Wawersik, D., Herx-Weaver, A., Gross, I. T., & Palaganas, J. C. (2024). Development of Distance Simulation Educator Guidelines in Healthcare A Delphi Method Application. *Simulation in Healthcare*, *19*(1), 1–10. Advance online publication. DOI: 10.1097/SIH.0000000000000707 PMID: 36598821

Baker, V. L., Christopher, A. N., & Noah, S. (2024). Expanding faculty development through capacity-building: An institutional case study. *Journal of University Teaching & Learning Practice*, *21*(2). Advance online publication. DOI: 10.53761/1.21.2.11

Bryant, B. H., Anderson, S. R., Brissette, M., Childs, J. M., Gratzinger, D., Johnson, K., Powell, D. E., Zein-Eldin Powell, S., Timmons, C. F., & McCloskey, C. B. (2024). Leveraging faculty development to support validation of entrustable professional activities assessment tools in anatomic and clinical pathology training. *Academic Pathology*, *11*(2), 100111. Advance online publication. DOI: 10.1016/j.acpath.2024.100111 PMID: 38560424

Buckley, E., Cooke, J., Whelton, H., & Barrett, A. (2024). 'Rules of engagement': Does competition drive engagement in faculty development. *The Clinical Teacher*, *21*(6), e13737. Advance online publication. DOI: 10.1111/tct.13737 PMID: 38291509

Campbell, J., Miehe, J., & Tice, M. (2024). Faculty Development on the Use of a Clinical Judgment Model in the Pre-licensure Nursing Curriculum. *Journal of Professional Nursing*, *51*, 9–15. Advance online publication. DOI: 10.1016/j.profnurs.2024.01.004 PMID: 38614679

Chandra Shaw, S., Datta, K., Lall, M., Jaipurkar, R., Shakya, A. K., & Kanitkar, M. (2024). Development of a hybrid undergraduate portfolio for the AETCOM module. *Medical Journal, Armed Forces India*, *80*(2), 192–198. Advance online publication. DOI: 10.1016/j.mjafi.2022.04.001 PMID: 38525458

Clipperton, S., McIntosh, L., Janssens, S., & Symon, B. (2024). Designing a faculty development programme for systems-focused translational simulation. *International Journal of Healthcare Simulation : Advances in Theory and Practice*, ptsg2886. Advance online publication. DOI: 10.54531/ptsg2886

Collazo, A., Walcher, C. M., & Campbell, K. M. (2024). Underrepresented in medicine (URiM) faculty development: Trends in biomedical database publication. *Journal of the National Medical Association*, *116*(2), 165–169. Advance online publication. DOI: 10.1016/j.jnma.2024.01.005 PMID: 38220585

Corte, C., & Amrein-Beardsley, A. (2024). Faculty/Staff Training to Examine Racial Implicit Bias: Findings and Implications for Creating Inclusive Educational Spaces. *Innovative Higher Education*, *49*(1), 133–151. Advance online publication. DOI: 10.1007/s10755-023-09673-6

Dexter, F., Epstein, R. H., & Hindman, B. J. (2024). Association between an anesthesia department development program for junior faculty and long-term production of publications: A longitudinal cohort study. *Journal of Clinical Anesthesia*, *92*, 111308. Advance online publication. DOI: 10.1016/j.jclinane.2023.111308 PMID: 38133566

Eiswirth, E., & Miller, A. (2024). Faculty-student authorship: Policy development. *Nurse Author & Editor*, *34*(1), e12058. Advance online publication. DOI: 10.1111/nae2.12058

Falandry, C., Bacchetta, J., Doret-Dion, M., Ferraro-Peyret, C., Confavreux, C. B., Douplat, M., Feugier, P., Friggeri, A., Bolze, P. A., Dargaud, Y., Messager, A., Wallon, M., Geffroy, L., Matillon, Y., & Bradwejn, J. (2024). Tailoring a specific medical leadership development program for faculty members: The Lyon-Ottawa experience. *Medical Education Online, 29*(1), 2308955. Advance online publication. DOI: 10.1080/10872981.2024.2308955 PMID: 38290044

Gardner, A. K., Rodgers, D. L., Steinert, Y., Davis, R., Condron, C., Peterson, D. T., Rohra, A., Viggers, S., Eppich, W. J., & Reedy, G. (2024). Mapping the Terrain of Faculty Development for Simulation: A Scoping Review. *Simulation in Healthcare, 19*(1), S75–S89. Advance online publication. DOI: 10.1097/SIH.0000000000000758 PMID: 38240621

Gholamnia-Shirvani, Z., Ahmady, S., & Habibi, A. (2024). Investigating effective factors in the development model of faculty members at Babol university of medical sciences. *Journal of Medical Education Development, 16*(52), 55–64. Advance online publication. DOI: 10.32592/jmed.2023.16.52.55

Gopal, B., Burlew, A. K., D'Souza, G., George, T. S., Varghese, K. J., & Raval, V. V. (2024). Facilitating Faculty Development for Training in Multicultural Competence in Health Service Psychology Graduate Programs Through an International Collaboration. *International Perspectives in Psychology : Research, Practice, Consultation, 13*(1), 24–39. Advance online publication. DOI: 10.1027/2157-3891/a000089

Green, T., Donovan, L., Gu, N., Ma, S., & Currry, D. J. (2024). Exploring Teaching and Research Practices During Cross-Cultural Collaboration: A Self-Study of Two Facilitator's Involvement in an International Faculty Development Program. *Studying Teacher Education, 20*(1), 65–86. Advance online publication. DOI: 10.1080/17425964.2023.2227649

Hamilton, S. R., Considine, C., Kunberger, T., Nilsson, T., Nolen, L., Saftner, D., & Saviz, C. M. (2024). Developing Faculty Leaders through the ASCE ExCEEd Teaching Workshop. *Journal of Civil Engineering Education, 150*(1), 05023006. Advance online publication. DOI: 10.1061/JCEECD.EIENG-1954

He, J. (2024). Professional Competence, Teaching Pedagogy, and Assessment Practices: Basis for Enhanced Faculty Development Plan. *Education Reform and Development, 6*(1), 65–77. Advance online publication. DOI: 10.26689/erd.v6i1.6218

Katz, G., Miloslavsky, E. M., Fernandes, A. D., & Bolster, M. B. (2024). Enhancing Faculty Development Through Compiled Verbal Feedback on Clinical Teaching From Trainees. *ACR Open Rheumatology, 6*(3), 139–144. Advance online publication. DOI: 10.1002/acr2.11638 PMID: 38155482

Katz, S., & Deckman, S. L. (2024). Adapting for Anti-Racism: Collaboratively Diversifying Faculty Open Professional Development. *New Review of Academic Librarianship, 30*(2–3), 273–282. Advance online publication. DOI: 10.1080/13614533.2024.2306356

King, N., Garrett, T., & Manjuck, A. (2024). Textbook Justice League: Creating a textbook affordability institute. *Journal of Academic Librarianship, 50*(1), 102836. Advance online publication. DOI: 10.1016/j.acalib.2023.102836

Kunkel, D. E., Tietze, M. F., Wilson, M., Fant, C. T., Rivard, M. J., Belchez, C. A., Forman, T. M., & Husson, N. M. (2024). Creating Case Studies for Digital Health and Technology Competency in Nursing. *Nurse Educator, 49*(1), 31–35. Advance online publication. DOI: 10.1097/NNE.0000000000001458 PMID: 37229722

Martin, M. M. (2024). Professional Standards for Teachers Landscape in the Standpoint of Teaching Profession: Insight from Higher Education Institution (HEI) Instructors. *International Journal of Learning. Teaching and Educational Research, 23*(1), 114–135. Advance online publication. DOI: 10.26803/ijlter.23.1.7

McNamee, T. C., & Van Horn, A. D. (2024). Faculty Development at Community Colleges in U.S. Rural Contexts. *Journal of Education Human Resources, 42*(1), 67–87. Advance online publication. DOI: 10.3138/jehr-2023-0051

Murakami, K., Ito, M., Nagata, C., Tsutsumi, M., Tanaka, A., Stone, T. E., & Conway, J. (2024). Japanese nurse academics' pedagogical development using collaborative action research. *Nurse Education Today, 132*, 106001. Advance online publication. DOI: 10.1016/j.nedt.2023.106001 PMID: 37890192

Okpalauwaekwe, U., Holinaty, C., Smith-Windsor, T., Barton, J. W., & MacLean, C. (2024). From field of dreams to back to the future? Exploring barriers to participating in continuing professional development (CPD) programs. *BMC Medical Education, 24*(1), 106. Advance online publication. DOI: 10.1186/s12909-024-05038-5 PMID: 38302979

Padalulu, L., & Malyo, T. (2024). Updates and Challenges in the Professional Development of Faculty Members: A Case Study at Okmin University. *Jurnal Ilmiah Mandala Education, 10*(1), 100. Advance online publication. DOI: 10.58258/jime.v10i1.6558

Peñaflor, M. (2024). Faculty Development Program (FDP) Of Selected Private Colleges In General Santos City: Its Impact On Organizational Commitment And Adaptive Performance, Basis For Enhanced Retention Program. [IJSRM]. *International Journal of Scientific Research and Management, 12*(03), 6089–6123. Advance online publication. DOI: 10.18535/ijsrm/v12i03.em13

Pierce, L., Stoecker, B., & Weber, M. (2024). Educating Educators With a Faculty Development Program for an Advanced Practice Fellowship. *Journal of Continuing Education in Nursing*, *55*(3), 105–107. Advance online publication. DOI: 10.3928/00220124-20240221-02 PMID: 38422990

Riley, T. D., Parascando, J. A., VanDyke, E., Stuckey, H. L., Dong, H., Pasha-Razzak, O., Kass, L. E., McCall-Hosenfeld, J., & Bronson, S. K. (2024). How Does a Junior Faculty Development Program Affect Burnout? A Mixed Methods Assessment. *Journal of Medical Education and Curricular Development*, *11*, 23821205231223294. Advance online publication. DOI: 10.1177/23821205231223294 PMID: 38322705

Rodriguez, M., Dooley, K. E., & Roberts, T. G. (2024). A Phenomenological Study of Intensive Experiential Learning for University Faculty Professional Development. *Journal of Experiential Education*, *47*(4), 685–703. Advance online publication. DOI: 10.1177/10538259241235915

Rokooei, S., Shojaei, A., & Ly, R. (2024). Faculty development program to enhance teaching quality in construction. *International Journal of Construction Management*. Advance online publication. DOI: 10.1080/15623599.2024.2304475

Rudd, M., Whicker, S., Mutcheson, R. B., Nagler, A., & Musick, D. (2024). Exploring Quality and Requirements in Faculty Development Related to Teaching. *The Journal of Continuing Education in the Health Professions*, *44*(4), 303–305. Advance online publication. DOI: 10.1097/CEH.0000000000000546 PMID: 38265363

Shafik, W. (2023). Introduction to ChatGPT. In *Advanced Applications of Generative AI and Natural Language Processing Models*. DOI: 10.4018/979-8-3693-0502-7.ch001

Sharma, P. (2024). Faculty competences development components: An integrated model for the development of educational leaders in technical education institutes. *International Journal of Educational Management*, *38*(2), 447–468. Advance online publication. DOI: 10.1108/IJEM-07-2023-0363

Somerville, S., Harrison, N., Lewis, S., & Colquhoun, N. (2024). Embracing a sustainable future: The development of a HYFLEX simulation faculty development module. *International Journal of Healthcare Simulation : Advances in Theory and Practice*, zsfd2733. Advance online publication. DOI: 10.54531/zsfd2733

Tippit, T. L., Chi, I., & Servey, J. T. (2024). A Model Curriculum For New Faculty Coaches in Undergraduate Medical Education. *Journal of Medical Education and Curricular Development*, *11*, 23821205231217896. Advance online publication. DOI: 10.1177/23821205231217896 PMID: 38204977

Tu, C. Y., Huang, K. M., Cheng, C. H., Lin, W. J., Liu, C. H., & Yang, C. W. (2024). Development, implementation, and evaluation of entrustable professional activities (EPAs) for medical radiation technologists in Taiwan: A nationwide experience. *BMC Medical Education*, *24*(1), 95. Advance online publication. DOI: 10.1186/s12909-024-05088-9 PMID: 38287396

Turner, A., Huth, K., Luff, D., Zendejas, B., Newman, L. R., & Leichtner, A. M. (2024). Lack of standardization and faculty development in pediatric colonoscopy: A qualitative study. *Journal of Pediatric Gastroenterology and Nutrition*, *78*(4), 948–956. Advance online publication. DOI: 10.1002/jpn3.12100 PMID: 38591669

van Schalkwyk, S., & Blitz, J. (2024). Curriculum renewal towards critically conscious graduates: Implications for faculty development. *Medical Education*, *58*(3), 299–307. Advance online publication. DOI: 10.1111/medu.15216 PMID: 37699795

Yeager-Okosi, S., Hall, A., & Quaicoe, N. (2024). Enhancing Effectiveness through Faculty Development Focused on Online Adjunct Faculty: A Comprehensive Investigation. *InSight: A Journal of Scholarly Teaching, 19*. DOI: 10.46504/19202402ye

Zhao, L., Dixon, R. A., Dousay, T. A., & Carr-Chellman, A. (2024). Exploring Faculty Perceptions of Outsourced Professional Development for Online Teaching and Learning. *TechTrends*, *68*(2), 268–280. Advance online publication. DOI: 10.1007/s11528-023-00923-0

Chapter 9
Fostering Student-Centered Learning Environments Using AI:
Creation of Inclusive and Accessible Guidance to Faculty

Anita Singh
Sharda University, India

Bhupinder Singh
http://orcid.org/0009-0006-4779-2553
Sharda University, India

Saurabh Chandra
http://orcid.org/0000-0003-4172-9968
Bennett University, Greater Noida, India

Liza Shoor
http://orcid.org/0009-0000-0085-3255
Punjab Agricultural University, Ludhiana, India

ABSTRACT

Students-centered learning environments need also to be inclusive, simultaneously personalizing and making accessible education. Using enormous data sets, AI systems can identify students' individual needs, learning patterns and problems to come up with what might be an effective instructional method for teachers. AI-powered adaptive learning platforms provide pupils with immediate feedback together with their learning process route in one place; advise troubleshooting solutions for those

DOI: 10.4018/979-8-3373-1285-9.ch009

directions when some turn useless on account of peculiar and inevitable reasons so students may always thrive. Collaboration between educators, policymakers and technologists is indispensable if a framework is to be established in which AI as an equalizer to equity, access and identity work collaboratively educators, administrators and technology developers need to collaborate on creating guidelines and standards for AI use in student-centered teaching. AI has the capacity to transform student-centered learning.

1. INTRODUCTION

AI-based tools like natural language processing (NLP) or sophisticated machine learning algorithms in our teaching resources make every effort to cover all manner of learning styles: they include facilities for students with disabilities such as text-to-speech (TTS) or customizable user interfaces that are speech-to-text. This enables educators to give themselves completely to activities like facilitating meaningful student interactions and cultivating critical minds in pupils. Predictive analytics can enable early identification of students who are at risk and offer timely intervention or academic support. In order to fully exploit AI's potential in the classroom, faculty must be trained in the use of AI tools and provided with guidance on how to incorporate them into their teaching while maintaining ethical standards and upholding students' privacy. Institutions should prioritize professional development training for teachers in subjects such as AI literacy, inclusive design, and student engagement strategies (Agbo et al., 2019).

Student-centered learning has come a long way since its early days, moving from the rigid and top-down pedagogies of an instructor-led classroom to adaptable and personalized Learning by Design. The education system was traditionally seen as a teacher-centric approach; where teachers determined the pace, content, and method of instruction. Although this model was useful for standardization of education, it often did not account for the different contexts, preferences and abilities of students. The push for student-centered learning arose from the understanding that students have different learning styles, and greater engagement, participation, and autonomy can result in better educational outcomes.

AI in education is changing how we teach by creating learning experiences that are tailored to each child's needs and make sure everyone can take part. This means moving away from the "stand and deliver" way of teaching and toward data-driven, student-centered learning that helps students do well and teachers make classrooms that are fair. Teachers can use AI tools to make learning environments that are perfect for each group of students, which gives each student a chance to do well. This overview shows how AI can help teachers make learning spaces that are open to everyone and easy to use.

AI will also be able to personalize learning by looking at students' data and changing the educational content based on their skills, limitations, and interests. For example, AI-powered platforms can check on a student's progress in real time, see where they are falling behind, and suggest activities or resources that are specific to them. It lets teachers go beyond just teaching in a way that works for everyone and gives each student the help they need based on how far they can go. AI does boring tasks for teachers, like grading and keeping track of students' progress, so they have more time to teach. This gives them the time they need to build important relationships with students, such as by mentoring and leading discussions.

1.1. Background and Significance: Evolution of Student-centered Learning

Having its foundations on constructivist theories, student-centered learning is a theory where the learner integrates knowledge through experiences, critical and problem-solving thinking. The role of experiential and social forms of learning in cognitive development. Their work was foundational to pedagogies that promote inquiry-based learning, project-based learning, and self-directed learning. Student-centered pedagogies have paved the way for more collaborative learning environments where technology could facilitate the exchange of ideas as early as the 21st century, offering progress toward a future where personalized learning could be enabled through digital platforms.

The major evolution of student-centered learning is the incorporation of digital technologies, enabling resources such as adaptive learning platforms, gamification, and multimedia content to accommodate a wide range of individual learning preferences. Access to knowledge has become increasingly democratized through the rise of online education, blended learning environments and open educational resources (OER), allowing learners to take ownership of their education outside the classroom. More and more institutions across the globe adopt flipped classrooms, competency-based learning and formative assessments that offer students ownership to engage with the courseware when they need (Apiola & Sutinen, 2021).

Yet, despite these developments, student-centered learning has a long way to go, especially in terms of inclusivity and accessibility. With not all students having the same access to digital tools and many educators shifting from traditional methods to more learner-centric styles, it does not come without a few drawbacks. Furthermore, student-centered learning can only be executed successfully when there are strong faculty support, institutional policies, and technical tools available to allow for personalized teaching. This is where Artificial Intelligence or AL is an increasingly critical piece offering insights and automation to help educators engage more deeply with students while they learn, meet them where they are, and on the right learning pathways.

The goal of AI-based education is to make sure that everyone can learn. AI tools can help students from different backgrounds or people who are very smart but have trouble reading. For instance, AI-powered tools like text-to-speech, real-time captioning, and language translation help students who have disabilities or who don't speak English as their first language fully understand the course material. You can use these tools to create content that everyone can access, like lecture transcripts or interactive workstream features for different kinds of learners. AI can also find bias in tests and teaching materials. This helps teachers make their lessons fairer by considering different points of view and making sure that everyone has the same chance in the classroom.

Access is important not just for the tech but also for AI's suggestions to teachers. AI-powered platforms help teachers make lesson plans that work for everyone by giving them evidence-based help. For example, AI can suggest ways to get students from different cultures involved or how to make projects easier for kids who learn in different ways. AI-based professional development tools can also help teachers teach in a way that works for all of their students. This will help them support all of their students. These ideas help teachers make their classrooms a place where every student feels valued and accepted.

1.2 Challenges in Traditional Faculty-driven Teaching Models

This approach has the teacher positioned as the main source of knowledge, and students are passive recipients of information through lectures, memorization and standardized testing. Though this manner of teaching maintains uniformity in curriculum delivery but does not even try to accommodate all individual needs, interests and learning types of students. Limitation of existing model all for cognitive capabilities and background of learners (Pollock et al. 2019) Students who struggle to keep the pace of the instruction may fall behind, while the ones able to easily grasp the concepts may think it is slow-paced or unchallenging for them. Such rigidity could lead to disconnection, a shrinking of motivation and in some cases, even greater dropout rates. In addition, traditional approaches utilize summative assessments which measure learning objectives after the fact, rather than formative assessments which enable instant feedback for improvement.

Faculty-directed teaching is, for the most part, a one- way concept with significant focus on content delivery but little or no security. We learn better by doing and students learn better when they engage in their own learning through discussions, hands-on projects and group problem solving, research shows. Yet traditional lecture-based teaching allows limited opportunities for this kind of interaction especially in large classroom environments. This model puts a great cognitive and administrative demand on faculties who have to prepare lectures, grade assignments, and organize the logistics of the course without being specifically enabled to give students individual attention (Lee et al., 2020).

The evolution to digital education has made social media based faculty an even more common occurrence, leaving all of us to ponder the true value of an instructor. Particularly, the COVID-19 pandemic required educational institutions across the globe to adopt remote forms of instruction, exposing faculty readiness gaps for online and hybrid instruction. Many professors had limited knowledge of digital literacy, strategies for engaging students in virtually mediated classrooms, and how technology can be utilized to support individualized forms of learning. This highlights the need for a more active model that incorporates technology to better assist both K-12 students as well as educators. The extendability of traditional faculty-centered socialization models often lack inclusivity. Rigid instructional structures tend to create barriers to quality education for students with disabilities, non-native language speakers, and students from marginalized backgrounds (Psycharis et al., 2018).

1.3 Role of AI in Transforming Education: Investigating AI-driven Tools for Student-centered Learning

While AI has become more normalized in our lives, like in the form of Google Assistant or Siri, an instance of a more exciting application is on its way to the education space. Utilizing new AI-powered tools and technologies, institutions are moving away from one-size-fits-all, instructor-led models toward dynamic, student-centered learning environments meant to meet a multitude of diverse needs, abilities and learning preferences. Instead, this influx of AI brings education a real (not an evolution of), and revolution of knowledge translation delivery, evaluation, and optimization, so leaners can be successful.

AI-based adaptive learning software has the ability to track such things as a student's strengths and weaknesses, his or her pace of learning, and how closely certain content matches those parameters, and present the right lesson, at the right level, at the right time. In contrast to many traditional systems that expect all students to progress through the same curriculum in lock-step fashion, AI-driven systems can allow learners to advance through the curriculum at their own pace, as demonstrated by individual understanding (Weintrop et al., 2016). AI-driven adaptive learning solutions like the AI Power tutor from Carnegie Learning provide immediate feedback and interactive experiences that guide students through complex concepts at a granular level with close support and step-by-step guidance. AI is also used to automate administrative tasks so that those teachers can spend their time with students. So, for example, automated grading allows teachers to measure assignments and tests more quickly which also helps in alleviating the stress of manual evaluation and ensuring uniformity in evaluation. The analytics all this data suggests on students' performance, patterns of engagement, what are they struggling to understand, where do they require intervention, are all delivered to the instructors through AI. This means that they will be able to give more personalized instruction and make sure that everyone is receiving help so that they do not fall behind.

AI is making education more accessible and equitable as well. Speech-to-text transcription and language translation assistants make it easier for both students with disabilities and those that are not native speakers to access learning material. Applications like Microsoft's Immersive Reader and Google's A.I.-driven live translation services are deconstructing language and accessibility barriers, creating more equitable classroom ecosystems. AI-powered chatbots and virtual assistants also assist students by responding to questions, providing learning recommendations, and guiding them through course content (Montiel et al., 2021). Again, I must stress, the advent of AI in education is not without the ethical implications that accompany the technologies that have become a ubiquitous part of our lives data privacy, algorithmic bias, over-reliance on automation. For students to remain at the center of their learning environments through the use of AI-driven education tools, it is critical that such tools be developed with transparency, fairness, and inclusiveness. AI is not just augmenting existing education systems, but changing them to be more inclusive, flexible and student-driven. With AI-derived insights and automation, faculty can design and personalize their own knowledge environment and curate effective learning rooms with increased student engagement and accessibility improving the quality of education for all learners (Qin, 2019).

2. STUDENT-CENTERED LEARNING IN THE AI ERA AND CORE PRINCIPLES OF STUDENT-CENTERED LEARNING

These systems can process huge amounts of data related to student performance, preferences, and progress to deliver real-time insights and recommendations. AI-powered learning management systems (LMS) and intelligent tutoring systems (ITS) can design personalized learning paths so that students receive resources and activities tailored to their learning needs, preferences, and pace Barcelos et al., 2022). AI brings a notable contribution to student-centered learning, namely, adaptive learning technology. Whereas traditional, static course materials provide the same content to all students regardless of their level of mastery, adaptive learning platforms dynamically tailor content to the individual student. This was a concept of the use of machine learning algorithms by these platforms to constantly evaluate the growth of students in real-time and adapt learning paths accordingly. Say if a student is having difficulty understanding a concept about the subject matter, the AI system will either provide extra clarifications, alternative learning materials, or even interact with a peer who can help the student make sense of the concept. On the other hand, learners who catch on quickly can be introduced to the next level of material, so that they're always appropriately engaged and challenged (Gross et al., 2024).

AI also promotes collaboration and active learning, both of which are important parts of student-centered learning. With the help of virtual teaching assistants and AI-powered discussion boards, students can talk to each other, share ideas, and take charge of their own learning. AI analytics can help teachers keep an eye on how well groups are working together and make sure that everyone is treated fairly. AI gives kids quick feedback on their work, which is very important because it gives them time to think about what they did and how they could do better, which helps them learn more.

AI could help students learn better by making the classroom a friendlier and easier place to be. AI helps the teachers create classrooms where all students can do well by removing obstacles, providing personalized learning, and giving teachers helpful tips. AI is getting better all the time, and so is its ability to make learning more fun and fair. It can also help students and teachers do their best in classrooms that are open to everyone.

2.1 AI-Powered Chatbots and Virtual Assistants

AI-powered Chatbots and virtual assistants help drive student-centered learning by offering support 24/7. These AI-driven systems can respond to questions, walk students through their course material, and even offer motivational feedback. This significantly cuts down on requirement for faculty availability and empowers students to manage their own schedules and learning process. Work with AI-powered analytics that help teachers to identify patterns in their students' behavior, including their level of engagement, learning gaps, etc., enabling timely intervention and personalized guidance. AI helps make education more accessible by providing accessibility features to students who have disabilities or are losing language. Actually instinct, speech-to-text and text-to-speech technologies assist students with hearing or visible impairments, and ai-based translation tools make availability to route fabric for those of a non-native language.

But incorporating AI into education is not without challenges and ethical concerns. Data privacy is a big one since AI systems depend on huge amounts of student data to work. The second dimension of trust in AI-driven education is maintaining trust through the ethical use of student data. There's also the danger of algorithmic bias, in which AI systems could unintentionally perpetuate existing inequalities if they are trained on biased data. It is crucial for both educators and institutions to strive towards using AI applications that seek equity, transparency, and inclusivity in education. AI opens a new interface for learning by enabling student-centered learning in a highly personalized, interactive and accessible manner (García-Peñalvo & Mendes, 2018). The AI pedagogy collaboration will greatly influence the future of education as technology continues to progress. This enables educators to shift to a more student agency and pedagogy, where the learning takes place in depth and is a lifelong activity by harnessing the power of AI. It's not about replacing educators, but giving them the tools to build more effective and meaningful educational experiences for students across the globe.

2.1.1 Fundamentals of Student-Centered Learning

The End is Student-Centered Learning In contrast to the traditional instructor-led approach, where students receive knowledge in a one-way manner, in student-centered learning, teachers need to give students more autonomy, more encouragement, and more personalized needs. While some aspects of education have transformed with technology, especially with the integration of artificial intelligence, we believe that some guiding principles must stay at the heart of student-centered learning. It is these tenets that work to create learning atmospheres centered on the needs, hopes and aspirations of the students.

2.1.2 Personalization and Differentiated Learning

Personalization is one of the key tenets of student-centered learning. Students differ from one another in terms of learning needs, cognitive capacity, and interests, hence designing educational experiences for individual variances are critical. AI and adaptive learning technologies enable this by reading the performance of students and changing the complexity and flow of delivery to the completion speed and knowledge level of the student. These groups are given differentiated instruction that allows them access to differentiated learning materials, support, and assessments tailored to their individual learning profiles. It enables a higher level of engagement, better retention rates, and a more profound grasp of concepts.

2.1.3 Active Learning and Engagement

Student-centered learning demands engagement rather than mere knowledge consumption. Strategies lie in active learning problem-solving, group discussions, hands-on projects, where students have the opportunity to experiment with knowledge outside of the classroom. To provide interactive learning environments, gamification and virtual simulations and even augmented reality experiences, this principle is enhanced through AI (Psycharis, 2018). These technologies authentically involve students, engendering experimentation, exploration, and immersive discovery. Active learning helps students own their learning process through building curiosity and creativity.

At the heart of student-centered education lies the belief that students should be empowered to take control of their own learning processe Unlike other forms of learning where it is more structured and guided, self-directed learning includes goal-setting, self-assessment and independent exploration of knowledge. AI-powered platform support autonomy by giving students personalized learning paths, recommending resources based on interest, and allowing flexible learning schedule. Students can monitor their progress, determine learning objectives, and get real-time feedback in AI-driven learning analytics. Learner autonomy fosters independence and self-directedness in students, guiding them to develop those necessary skills for lifelong learning through critical thinking and problem-solving abilities by promoting self-regulation and intrinsic motivation.

Learning is a social process, and student-centric education encourages peer to peer collaboration and interaction. Discussion boards, virtual classrooms, group project management tools and other AI-driven collaborative platforms allow students to communicate freely with one another. Similarly, AI language translation and speech recognition technologies remove communication barriers and facilitate global collaboration. The learning experience is further enriched by social aspects, minimizing isolation and encouraging teamwork, communication skills, and sharing of knowledge. AI allows educators to create a knowledge-inclusive community based on collaborative knowledge construction principles.

2.1.4 Practical and hands-on and Real-world Application

Student-centered learning moves from theory to application. Two very impactful curricular practices are experiential learning. AI enables experiential learning via VR (virtual reality) simulations, case studies relevant to industries, and AI-driven recommendation systems that are able to provide real-life projects relevant to a student's career goals (Bati et al., 2018). When educational institutions integrate attractive real-world applications into their curriculum, students learn skills that are occupationally relevant and, hence, help improve their employability and problem-solving abilities.

2.1.5 Using Formative Assessments for Timely Feedback

In traditional education frameworks, student performance is sometimes assessed through summative evaluations like standardized tests. But student-centered learning emphasizes formative assessment, giving ongoing feedback for improvement. Using AI-powered assessment tools, such have the ability to analyze student responses and identify misconceptions and provide individualized feedback in real-time. By employing automated grading systems, AI-powered writing assistants, and speech recognition-based evaluations, assessment processes become more efficient, enabling educators to concentrate on delivering valuable feedback. Assessment doesn't stop at the end of the study period but should be continual to ensure learning is not stagnant among the students.

2.1.6 Inclusivity and Accessibility

The main principle of student-centered learning is based on the idea that education is inclusive, meaning all students are able to fully participate regardless of their abilities, backgrounds, or learning preferences. Speech-to-text, text-to-speech, and AI-powered sign language interpretation are just a few examples of AI assistive technologies enabling students of all abilities to access learning resources effectively (Papadakis, 2020). Translation tools help multilingual learners which break the language barrier in education AI-based tools. AI-driven accessibility features ensure that all students have equal opportunity to succeed, and it therefore fosters equitable learning environments.

2.1.7 Teacher as Facilitator and Mentor

In learner-focused teaching, the teacher transitions from professor to guide and influencer. Rather than spoon feeding data, teachers facilitate personalized learning experiences, nurture academic progress, and promote critical thought. AI tools provide teachers assistance in the form of automation, analyzing students' performance, and offering data-driven insights. This enables educators to mentor, emotionally support and inspire a growth mindset in students. AI's integration facilitates individualized support and interaction, strengthening the bond between teachers and students. Following these key principles, student-centered learning with AI can be more engaging, equitable, and effective. Combining AI along with learner-driven pedagogies will guarantee that education is continually evolving, reactive and prepared for the future, furnishing students to prosper in a continually evolving global overview (Yadav et al., 2024).

3. AI-POWERED PERSONALIZATION IN LEARNING ENVIRONMENTS

The exponential growth of artificial intelligence (AI) and the implementation of it have created unprecedented changes in generations and occupations from healthcare to manufacturing, and now impacting the education system (Pollak & Ebner, 2019) (Saritepeci, 2020) (Buitrago-Florez, 2021). AI detects learning gaps at the earliest so that educators can step in with specific help before students start to lag behind. AI enables personalized learning recommendations by curating resources to suit individual learning goals and interests. These AI-based platforms such as Coursera, edX and Duolingo analyze user behavior to recommend courses, study materials and practice exercises according to the preferences of the student. By recommending a range of educational models, they offer options that include subject development, career paths, skills, and educational training programs that extend beyond pre-packaged courses. AI-based recommendation engines guide educators while customizing lesson plans and recommending additional learning materials adaptable to different learning requirements.

AI-powered personalization has proven vital to strengthening inclusivity and accessibility in education. Disabilities, language differences, and socio-economic constraints prevent the learning process for many students. AI-powered assistive tech helps fill these gaps by delivering personalized learning experiences for all students. Speech-to-text and text-to-speech tools support students with visual or hearing impairments, and AI-powered translation tools help non-native speakers access course materials in their language of choice (Gokçe & Yenmez, 2023). These AI chatbots and virtual assistants can allow for more one-on-one support of students with special needs, giving them the attention and guidance they require. Providing greater equity in education, these technologies ensure accessibility to engage in education for all students irrespective to their abilities.

The second critical aspect of AI-powered personalization relates to student motivation and engagement. Educational institutions and teachers are always looking for ways to improve passive learning and low retention rates in educational institutions. AI Overcomes These Difficulties Through Gamification, Interactive Simulations, And Immersive Experiences Within Personalized Learning Environments. Game-based learning strategies such as reward systems, leaderboards, or obstacles, are used by AI-based learning platforms to make learning more fun. VR/AR takes this engagement to the next level by immersing learners in their environments. For example, a medical student can practice surgeries on AI-generated patients in VR simulations while history students can go to virtual AR experiences of ancient civilizations. AI-powered personalization ecosystem supports collaborative and social learning experiences (Lodi & Martini, 2021). Whereas personalization focuses on how one individual is progressing, AI leverages social collaboration & baked-in peer interaction, ensuring students do not become islands in their own learning paths. AI-powered collaboration tools match students with peers, mentors, and instructors based on mutual interests, learning styles, and academic objectives. AI-driven discussion forums and peer-review systems promote knowledge-sharing and collective learning. AI-powered sentiment analysis tools gauge students' engagement levels in online discussions, highlighting those who might require more support or motivation to contribute.

While AI-driven personalization in educational environments can be extremely beneficial, there are ethical dilemmas and challenges associated with it. Data Privacy and Safety, First and Foremost AI systems depend on large amounts of data collection, which leads to concerns about the ways in which student information is stored, shared, and used. Educational institutions must also create strong data protection policies to ensure that the students' data is more secure and not misused. Another reason transparency around AI algorithms is critical so that bias doesn't inadvertently disadvantage some groups of students. This also means monitoring and evaluating AI-driven personalization continuously so as to ensure it is fair, unbiased, and inclusive. AI teacher may cause a decrease in the role of human educators. AI can certainly help refine knowledge and personalize learning, but it will never replace the human teachers who infuse creative thinking, mentorship and emotional intelligence into the learning experience. What all really want is a human-AI partnership educator using AI tools to inform their teaching while maintaining their human relationship with their students (Tsortanidou et al., 2019).

4. CREATING INCLUSIVE AND ACCESSIBLE LEARNING THROUGH AI

Artificial Intelligence (AI) has become an influential tool in transforming education, especially in promoting inclusivity and accessibility for a broader range of learners. Traditional education systems are struggling to cater to students of different abilities, learning styles and socio-economic backgrounds. Systemic barriers make it difficult for students even more so students with disabilities, students who are non-native language speakers, and students who come from marginalized communities to succeed in receiving a quality education. AI-based technologies provide solutions to fill these gaps and ensure that learning environments are tailored to every student's specific needs. The critical thing to understand about the wide use of AI in teaching/education is that we are bullish on the potential of educators to work with AI powered tools to turn education into individual equal opportunity sessions (Yilmaz Ince & Koc, 2021).

AI is the most beneficial tools for enhancing inclusivity in education. Classic classrooms are usually based on a set curriculum, which do not consider the different learning habits and speeds of the students. As a result, AI-driven learning platforms can create customized experiences based on the students' performance, preferences, and even engagement levels. Adaptive learning systems customize the level of material according to live progress, so that students are neither left behind nor bored. This customizability helps support students who might need more time to understand concepts, but also facilitates those who may need more challenging material to stay engaged (Sırakaya et al., 2020). AI-infused chat-partners like IBM Watson Tutor and AI-enabled virtual assistances in e-learning platforms serve as omnipresent mentors who respond to students' queries, provide explanation, and navigate them through the intricacies of difficult concepts. Adaptive assessments powered by artificial intelligence adapt the difficulty level and nature of the questions according to a student's capacity, providing a fair evaluation process (Valovičová et al., 2020). AI-powered grading systems apply machine learning algorithms to evaluate written assignments, coding projects, and even creative work, offering impartial and unbiased evaluations. By breaking away from one-size-fits-all assessment methods, AI creates a more inclusive academic environment that evaluates students based on their authentic capabilities, as opposed to their ability to meet conventional exam benchmarks.

AI bridges the digital divide also providing educational resources to students in underserved and remote areas. Some of these disparities stem from socio-economic disparities in access to quality teachers, textbooks, and structure (beyond the family) in which to learn. The advantage of AI-powered EdTech platforms like Khan Academy and Coursera is that they make educational content freely accessible to students all over the world (Lockwood & Mooney, 2017). AI powered mobile learning applications have made students accessible to lessons, practice exercises, and assessments through smartphones by lowering the need for investment in pricey infrastructure. AI-powered learning through satellite systems has also mushroomed in rural areas providing digital education to students who do not own a device with internet connectivity. AI also ensures equitable education facilities for students from various economic backgrounds.

Although AI can be used to create inclusive and accessible learning environments, the implementation of such technology is not without challenges. As AI systems depend on gathering, processing and analyzing large amounts of student data, data privacy and ethical issues are vital matters of concern. Educational establishments should have stringent data governance practices in place to mitigate abuse of sensitive, personal data. In addition of these endless-controls AI algorithms need to control to amend bias, discrimination, favoritism in personalized learning recommendation (Denning & Tedre, 2021). AI integration and teacher training are also critical in order to best leverage the benefits of AI-enabled inclusivity. Teachers need to be trained how to harness AI tools and design equitable education for all students.

While there are limitations AI is changing the game of education by allowing all types of learners to access knowledge free of barriers. From tailor-made learning pathways and assistive technologies to multilingual support and adaptable evaluations, AI-enabled advancements in Ed-Tech are dismantling age-old barriers to education. AI will allow educators to develop inclusive learning environments that will include students at all ability levels, ethnic backgrounds, learning needs and goals to ensure that no student is left behind. AI adoption towards inclusiveness will be successful only if data is secured, ethical values are maintained, and teaching staff is trained.

5. AI IN FACULTY DEVELOPMENT AND TEACHING STRATEGIES

AI is revolutionizing faculty development and how educators approach teaching since it provides educators with the tools required to ensure quality instruction, and by automating tedious administrative tasks and improving student engagement (Hsu & Liang, 2021). As a result, conventional faculty development programs need to be reformed to rely less on one-off workshops, manual grading, and generalised teaching styles which could fail to meet the needs of more modern and dynamic learners. But, with AI-powered innovations, educators can personalize instruction, automate clerical tasks, and track student performance in real-time while personalizing teaching strategies with data. Integrating AI into faculty development can help institutions ensure that educators mentor and capable of meeting the needs of contemporary education (Tedre & Denning, 2016).

The highest-impact areas that AI contributes to faculty development are through personalized professional learning. For instance, most training programmes for the educators typically goes with a straightjacket path not having customisation for their teaching patterns, level of expertise or areas of improvement. AI-powered learning platforms can analyze faculty strengths, weaknesses and instructional style and suggest personalized training modules. AI-enabled portals such as Coursera for Educators and LinkedIn Learning now recommend courses based on faculty requirements, helping them upskill at their own pace. AI-based feedback systems also analyze teaching effectiveness by assessing performance metrics from students, assisting educators to further refine their methodologies with exact interventions. Furthermore, being data driven ensures staff development is tailored to ensure ongoing professional development while keeping pace with emerging pedagogies.

AI also assists in curating and enhancing curriculum design and lesson planning. The approach is relatively new to academia; as teachers want to spend time working through course material, aligned with learning objectives and using varied course content (Agbo et al., 2021). Artificial Intelligence in Education domain with a focus on building intelligent, real-world, education focused recommender systems using advanced AI, such as machine learning and natural language processing (NLP) systems that eliminate the need for doing all of these tasks, by utilizing the wealth of educational data available and recommending the right course material, interactive content or optimizing the sequence of lessons based on intelligent algorithms. And platforms like Squirrel AI and Knewton use AI to optimize custom paths to suit both capabilities of students and necessities of institutions. This AI-powered help makes it possible for educators to create more actionable and engaging curricula in less time.

The major application of AI in faculty development can be in grading and assessment automation. Grading student assignments, quizzes and exams is usually a labour-intensive process prone to other human prejudices (Ulger, 2018). Examples of such grading systems include automating assessments through grading written responses, detecting plagiarism, and offering real-time feedback through AI-powered tools such as Gradescope and Turnitin. Machine learning-based rubrics allow AI algorithms to grade multiple-choice questions, coding assignments, and even essays. In addition to saving the faculty time, this automation helps streamline consistency and fairness. Additionally, AI-driven data analysis reveals common mistakes students make, so learning gaps can be filled.

AI also helps in data-driven decision-making regarding teaching strategies. Most traditional teaching methods, based on intuition and limited observational data, are used to assess student progress. With AI-enabled analytics, faculty gains the ability to access actionable insights that analyze student engagement, understanding levels, and performance trends. Using AI-enhanced learning management systems (LMS) like Blackboard, Moodle and Canvas, institutions track students' real-time interaction on different course materials and pinpoint where they struggle (Li et al., 2020).

AI-powered platforms, on the other hand, provide immediate feedback on student engagement and understanding, providing faculty with the ability to alter their teaching methodologies in real-time. AI-based emotion recognition systems, for instance, analyze students' expressions and engagement levels during lectures to gauge their understanding (Leonard et al., 2016). If students seem to be tuning out, the faculty can change up their teaching style, incorporate interactive elements, or present material in a different way. Their ability to adjust creates a more responsive, effective learning experience. AI is also improving faculty collaboration and peer learning. But how do you keep up with the latest pedagogical trends? Collaboration tools powered by AI, including Microsoft Teams, Google Scholar AI, and enhanced academic networks that integrate AI, help teachers share knowledge by providing insights on relevant research papers, summarizing academic conversations, and suggesting new teaching approaches. AI-powered platforms also help with collaborative lesson planning, enabling teachers to collaborate and iterate on course content in real-time.

Two important aspects of what AI has to offer to support faculty development is how it encourages more diverse and/or equitable teaching opportunities or outcomes. When many educators are still struggling to meet the needs of diverse learners be it disability, non-native language, or neurodiversity there is still a ways to go. AI Accessibility solutions help build tools to support different types of faculty, students, and staff by using machine learning technologies like real-time captioning, language translation, and adaptive content delivery. AI-based transcription services (Hava & Koyunlu Ünlü, 2021). The Real-time ai captioning generates captioning for any lecture concurrently which helps hearing impaired students. AI language translation tools also bridge the gap by making sure that students of different languages have access to educational material in their preferred language. Using these AI-driven approaches for accessible design, faculty can raise the learning experience for all students, regardless of ability or background.

While AI has many advantages, its use for faculty development raises challenges and ethical concerns. This over-reliance on AI in making instructional decisions opens the doors for algorithmic biases, misuse of data privacy, and the potential of over-automation stripping teaching of its human element. We need to train faculty to use AI responsibly, as the recommendations for AI-generated content should always vest on the betterment of classroom ethics. In addition, educational institutions should also develop policies that protect student data so that AI-driven decisions are transparent. Although AI is capable of enhancing the capabilities of faculty, it needs to be considered as an assistive instrument instead of a substitute for human teachers (Gonzalez-Perez & Ramírez-Montoya, 2022).

AI is changing how we approach faculty development and pedagogy by enabling personalized learning for faculty, optimizing class design, automating assessment processes, offering real-time analytics, and making classes more engaging. AI-powered tools for educators will embrace adaptive teaching practices, enhance collaboration and help create inclusive learning settings. But to successfully integrate AI into the classrooms, we need to approach it carefully, ethically, and aim for faculty training, moderation in using these tools, and, never forget, keep the human aspect of education. The extraordinary power of AI as it continues to develop as we know it will be a key driver of empowering educators and teaching strategy in the future.

6. CHALLENGES AND LIMITATIONS IN AI-DRIVEN STUDENT-CENTERED LEARNING

Although Artificial Intelligence (AI) has great potential in facilitating a student-centered learning environment, its incorporation is not without challenges and restrictions. The article also discusses the importance of addressing issues such as accessibility, data privacy, bias, limitations of technology, and human oversight in integrating AI into education (Iversen et al., 2018).

6.1. Technological Barriers and Digital Divide

They depend on internet connectivity; computing devices with advanced technology; and digital literacy Yet, around the world, especially in some of the most impoverished places, students do not have reliable high-speed internet connections, personal devices or even AI-fueled educational platforms. This creates an inequitable learning environment that ensures AI cannot serve all students equally. In industrialized nations, where such programs are starting to become more commonplace, there are also gaping holes in accessibility as many students at lower socio-economic levels cannot afford the latest apps or software programs. The solution to these problems lies not in technology, but in a commitment to fundamental rights, equality, and justice. Without adequate infrastructure and policies to boost equal access to AI as a form of data, there is a risk of AI reproducing pre-existing educational inequities rather than bridging the gap.

6.2 Data and Privacy

The second key limitation of AI-led student-centred learning is data privacy and security. AI systems need substantial amounts of student data to tailor pedagogical experiences, monitor academic development, and make suggestions (Miller et al., 2023).

6.3 Bias

AI systems learn from datasets that can be inherently biased, resulting in unjust recommendations for learning content and unfair evaluation results, resource distribution, and opportunities for learners. For instance, automated grading programs powered by AI have been criticized for privileging certain writing styles, dialects or socio-cultural perspectives, which leaves other students at a disadvantage (Bocconi et al., 2022). AI-enabled tutoring systems may survive unintentionally be biased by students each with learning processes which parallel the data in the AI is trained on, but they will concretely marginalise students with different cognitive or cultural modalities of learning.

6.4 Absence of Emotional Intelligence

The other major limitation of such AI-driven education is the absence of emotional intelligence and human touch. Student-centered learning focuses on personalized engagement, mentorship, and emotional support that AI is unable to effectively replicate. Yes, AI-powered chatbots and virtual assistants can answer questions asked or provide recommendations, but they are unable to truly understand how a student feels or their motivation level or personal setbacks. Teachers add empathy, push for what intellect development even means, and when to disguise any body language to reflect when a student is feeling overwhelmed. The overuse of AI in education may lead to these conditions that can bring up a depersonalized learning experience where students feel alone or unmotivated when they are not receiving the human element. AI is meant to supplement the teacher in classroom environments that are student-centered (Díaz, 2024).

6.5 Adaptability

The other challenge is whether AI recommendations are adaptive and accurate. Whereas AI-powered platforms offer personalized learning paths, they aren't always identical in diagnosing students' needs or predicting their pathways to learning. AI models use defined algorithms to work and may not consider unique student circumstances, such as temporary learning disabilities, stress, external pressures, or personal interests. An AI system could mistake a momentary slump for inability, and flatten diligence into academic helplessness, and worse: Speak tendencies out of a student's reach into their future by intervening or recommending things unsuitable for them (Norman & Zoncita, 2024). Monitoring and validation of AI outputs by educators is crucial to ensure that student-centered learning remains true to its goals.

6.6 Faculty Resistance

Faculty Resistance and the Need for AI Training It can be difficult to change how we think about education when we are so used to teaching in a certain way, which means many educators may be reluctant to use AI-powered tools simply because they are not familiar with them, fear that it will replace their jobs or be sceptical about how well it works. Moreover, incorporating AI into the teaching process requires specialized training that many faculty members don't have. Institutions need to be willing to invest in professional development programs that prepare educators to use AI effectively and ensure AI is complementary and not a replacement for their pedagogical expertise (Albuquerque et al., 2024). The way to help navigate these challenges is through collaboration, encouraging AI developers to work directly with educators to create a better understanding and implementation of intelligent systems that enhance teaching practices.

6.7 Ethical Considerations

Ethical considerations related to AI-driven decision making should be considered. AI-powered learning solutions and environments need to follow the pursuit of ethics, wherein, student well-being, academic integrity, and fairness are prioritized, which ultimately leads to a holistic learning/teaching culture. Automated Recommendation Systems that make decisions on grading, personalized Learning Pathways, and Student Evaluations should be implemented with transparency and have human oversight (Zahra et al., 2024). The employment of AI for observing student behaviors, engagement levels, and participation also presents ethical dilemmas regarding surveillance as well as potential abuse of AI within academic facilities. Nevertheless, the potential concerns due to the lack of regulation and data misuse remain.

AI-based student-centered learning represents a radical advancement in educational possibilities, complete with its own challenges and issues. To realize the potential promise of AI in student-centered learning, challenges related to digital accessibility, data privacy, algorithmic bias, emotional intelligence gaps, and faculty resistance will have to be resolved. Striking the right balance between AI's potential for improving productivity and the human need for empathy, ethical oversight, and equitable access will be critical to realizing that potential. Addressing these challenges proactively will allow AI-driven learning environments to be more inclusive, effective, and genuinely student-centered for all learners (Nicolaides et al., 2024).

7. CONCLUSION AND FUTURE SCOPE

AI-driven personalization in learning environments is transforming education by delivering customized and engaging learning experiences while ensuring inclusivity. AI creates personalized learning experiences that cater to the unique needs and pace of each student, ultimately helping them achieve their full potential. Although we have to address challenges like data privacy, algorithmic bias, human-AI balance, the advantages of AI-driven personalization overshadow the risks. But be it be the case exactly as depicted above, as AI progresses, the potential exists to make education more egalitarian, accessible, and efficient so that all learners across the globe can achieve their potential. Learning in the future will be personalized and AI-fueled, it will become the building block of every student, especially when they go to school.

With continuous advancements in machine learning, deep learning, and data-driven analytics, AI is making significant strides in enriching the educational experience and personalizing learning for students. More and more AI-driven personalized learning solutions will be developed, using real-time biometric feedback, affective computing and emotion recognition to adapt learning activities to students' emotional states. The AI led lifelong learning systems will be able to train individuals in continuously upskilling or reskilling as per the evolving demand of the job sector. AI-enabled personal learning assistant which will work like virtual tutors will guide students throughout their academic and professional career.

REFERENCES

Agbo, F. J., Oyelere, S. S., Suhonen, J., & Adewumi, S. (2019, November). A systematic review of computational thinking approach for programming education in higher education institutions. In *Proceedings of the 19th Koli Calling International Conference on Computing Education Research* (pp. 1-10). DOI: 10.1145/3364510.3364521

Agbo, F. J., Yigzaw, S. T., Sanusi, I. T., Oyelere, S. S., & Mare, A. H. (2021, October). Examining theoretical and pedagogical foundations of computational thinking in the context of higher education. In *2021 IEEE Frontiers in Education Conference (FIE)* (pp. 1-8). IEEE. DOI: 10.1109/FIE49875.2021.9637405

Albuquerque, U. P., Maroyi, A., Ladio, A. H., Pieroni, A., Abbasi, A. M., Toledo, B. A., Dahdouh-Guebas, F., Hallwass, G., Soldati, G. T., Odonne, G., Vandebroek, I., Vallès, J., Hurrell, J. A., Pardo de Santayana, M., La Torre-Cuadros, M. Á., Silva, M. T. P., Jacob, M. C. M., da Fonseca-Kruel, V. S., & Ferreira Júnior, W. S. (2024). Advancing ethnobiology for the ecological transition and a more inclusive and just world: A comprehensive framework for the next 20 years. *Journal of Ethnobiology and Ethnomedicine*, *20*(1), 18. DOI: 10.1186/s13002-024-00661-4 PMID: 38360640

Apiola, M., & Sutinen, E. (2021). Design science research for learning software engineering and computational thinking: Four cases. *Computer Applications in Engineering Education*, *29*(1), 83–101. DOI: 10.1002/cae.22291

Barcelos, T. S., & Silveira, I. F. (2022, October). Teaching computational thinking in initial series an analysis of the confluence among mathematics and computer sciences in elementary education and its implications for higher education. In *2012 XXXVIII Conferencia Latinoamericana En Informatica (CLEI)* (pp. 1-8). IEEE.

Bati, K., Yetişir, M. I., Çalişkan, I., Güneş, G., & Gül Saçan, E. (2018). Teaching the concept of time: A steam-based program on computational thinking in science education. *Cogent Education*, *5*(1), 1507306. DOI: 10.1080/2331186X.2018.1507306

. Bocconi, S., Chioccariello, A., Kampylis, P., Dagienė, V., Wastiau, P., Engelhardt, K., ... & Stupurienė, G. (2022). Reviewing computational thinking in compulsory education: State of play and practices from computing education.

Buitrago-Flórez, F., Danies, G., Restrepo, S., & Hernández, C. (2021). Fostering 21st Century Competences through Computational Thinking and Active Learning: A Mixed Method Study. *International Journal of Instruction*, *14*(3), 737–754. DOI: 10.29333/iji.2021.14343a

Denning, P. J., & Tedre, M. (2021). Computational thinking: A disciplinary perspective. *Informatics in Education*, *20*(3), 361.

Díaz, C. A. (2024). *From transdisciplinary concepts to undisciplined futures*. The Routledge International Handbook of Transdisciplinary Feminist Research and Methodological Praxis.

García-Peñalvo, F. J., & Mendes, A. J. (2018). Exploring the computational thinking effects in pre-university education. *Computers in Human Behavior*, *80*, 407–411. DOI: 10.1016/j.chb.2017.12.005

Gökçe, S., & Yenmez, A. A. (2023). Ingenuity of scratch programming on reflective thinking towards problem solving and computational thinking. *Education and Information Technologies*, *28*(5), 5493–5517. DOI: 10.1007/s10639-022-11385-x

González-Pérez, L. I., & Ramírez-Montoya, M. S. (2022). Components of Education 4.0 in 21st century skills frameworks: Systematic review. *Sustainability (Basel)*, *14*(3), 1493. DOI: 10.3390/su14031493

Gross, S., Kim, M., Schlosser, J., Mohtadi, C., Lluch, D., & Schneider, D. (2024, April). Fostering computational thinking in engineering education: Challenges, examples, and best practices. In *2014 IEEE Global Engineering Education Conference (EDUCON)* (pp. 450-459). IEEE.

Hava, K., & Koyunlu Ünlü, Z. (2021). Investigation of the relationship between middle school students' computational thinking skills and their STEM career interest and attitudes toward inquiry. *Journal of Science Education and Technology*, *30*(4), 484–495. DOI: 10.1007/s10956-020-09892-y

Hsu, T. C., & Liang, Y. S. (2021). Simultaneously improving computational thinking and foreign language learning: Interdisciplinary media with plugged and unplugged approaches. *Journal of Educational Computing Research*, *59*(6), 1184–1207. DOI: 10.1177/0735633121992480

Hutchins, N. M., Biswas, G., Maróti, M., Lédeczi, Á., Grover, S., Wolf, R., Blair, K. P., Chin, D., Conlin, L., Basu, S., & McElhaney, K. (2020). C2STEM: A system for synergistic learning of physics and computational thinking. *Journal of Science Education and Technology*, *29*(1), 83–100. DOI: 10.1007/s10956-019-09804-9

Iversen, O. S., Smith, R. C., & Dindler, C. (2018, August). From computational thinking to computational empowerment: a 21st century PD agenda. In *Proceedings of the 15th participatory design conference: Full papers-Volume 1* (pp. 1-11).

Lee, I., Grover, S., Martin, F., Pillai, S., & Malyn-Smith, J. (2020). Computational thinking from a disciplinary perspective: Integrating computational thinking in K-12 science, technology, engineering, and mathematics education. *Journal of Science Education and Technology*, *29*(1), 1–8. DOI: 10.1007/s10956-019-09803-w

Leonard, J., Buss, A., Gamboa, R., Mitchell, M., Fashola, O. S., Hubert, T., & Almughyirah, S. (2016). Using robotics and game design to enhance children's self-efficacy, STEM attitudes, and computational thinking skills. *Journal of Science Education and Technology, 25*(6), 860–876. DOI: 10.1007/s10956-016-9628-2

Li, Y., Schoenfeld, A. H., diSessa, A. A., Graesser, A. C., Benson, L. C., English, L. D., & Duschl, R. A. (2020). Computational thinking is more about thinking than computing. *Journal for STEM Education Research, 3*(1), 1–18. DOI: 10.1007/s41979-020-00030-2 PMID: 32838129

. Liu, H. P., Perera, S. M., & Klein, J. W. (2017). Using model-based learning to promote computational thinking education. *Emerging research, practice, and policy on computational thinking*, 153-172.

Lockwood, J., & Mooney, A. (2017). Computational Thinking in Education: Where does it fit? A systematic literary review. *arXiv preprint arXiv:1703.07659.*

Lodi, M., & Martini, S. (2021). Computational thinking, between Papert and Wing. *Science & Education, 30*(4), 883–908. DOI: 10.1007/s11191-021-00202-5

Miller, L. D., Soh, L. K., Chiriacescu, V., Ingraham, E., Shell, D. F., Ramsay, S., & Hazley, M. P. (2023, October). *Improving learning of computational thinking using creative thinking exercises in CS-1 computer science courses. In 2023 ieee frontiers in education conference (fie).* IEEE.

Montiel, H., & Gomez-Zermeño, M. G. (2021). Educational challenges for computational thinking in k–12 education: A systematic literature review of "scratch" as an innovative programming tool. *Computers, 10*(6), 69. DOI: 10.3390/computers10060069

Nicolaides, A., Lim, A., Herr, N., & Barefield, T. (Eds.). (2024). *Reimagining Adult Education as World Building: Creating Learning Ecologies for Transformation.* Taylor & Francis. DOI: 10.4324/9781003371359

Norman, P. D., & Zoncita, D. (2024). Elaborating the Efficacy of Outdoor Arts-based Cooperative Learning Experiences on the Latino Immigrant Students' Engagement, and Academic & Social Success in ESL-STEAM Education. *Available at SSRN* 4757518.

Papadakis, S. (2020). Evaluating a teaching intervention for teaching STEM and programming concepts through the creation of a weather-forecast app for smart mobile devices. In *Handbook of research on tools for teaching computational thinking in P-12 education* (pp. 31–53). IGI Global. DOI: 10.4018/978-1-7998-4576-8.ch002

Pollak, M., & Ebner, M. (2019). The missing link to computational thinking. *Future Internet, 11*(12), 263. DOI: 10.3390/fi11120263

Pollock, L., Mouza, C., Guidry, K. R., & Pusecker, K. (2019, February). Infusing computational thinking across disciplines: Reflections & lessons learned. In *Proceedings of the 50th ACM Technical Symposium on Computer Science Education* (pp. 435-441). DOI: 10.1145/3287324.3287469

Psycharis, S. (2018). STEAM in education: A literature review on the role of computational thinking, engineering epistemology and computational science. computational steam pedagogy (CSP). *Scientific Culture, 4*(2), 51–72.

Psycharis, S., Kalovrektis, K., Sakellaridi, E., Korres, K., & Mastorodimos, D. (2018). Unfolding the curriculum: physical computing, computational thinking and computational experiment in STEM's transdisciplinary approach. *European Journal of Engineering and Technology Research*, 19-24.

Pulimood, S. M., Pearson, K., & Bates, D. C. (2016, February). A study on the impact of multidisciplinary collaboration on computational thinking. In *Proceedings of the 47th ACM technical symposium on computing science education* (pp. 30-35). DOI: 10.1145/2839509.2844636

Qin, H. (2019, March). Teaching computational thinking through bioinformatics to biology students. In *Proceedings of the 40th ACM technical symposium on Computer science education* (pp. 188-191).

Saritepeci, M. (2020). Developing computational thinking skills of high school students: Design-based learning activities and programming tasks. *The Asia-Pacific Education Researcher, 29*(1), 35–54. DOI: 10.1007/s40299-019-00480-2

Sırakaya, M., Alsancak Sırakaya, D., & Korkmaz, Ö. (2020). The impact of STEM attitude and thinking style on computational thinking determined via structural equation modeling. *Journal of Science Education and Technology, 29*(4), 561–572. DOI: 10.1007/s10956-020-09836-6

Tedre, M., & Denning, P. J. (2016, November). The long quest for computational thinking. In *Proceedings of the 16th Koli Calling international conference on computing education research* (pp. 120-129).

Tsortanidou, X., Daradoumis, T., & Barberá, E. (2019). Connecting moments of creativity, computational thinking, collaboration and new media literacy skills. *Information and Learning Science, 120*(11/12), 704–722. DOI: 10.1108/ILS-05-2019-0042

Ulger, K. (2018). The effect of problem-based learning on the creative thinking and critical thinking disposition of students in visual arts education. *The Interdisciplinary Journal of Problem-Based Learning, 12*(1). Advance online publication. DOI: 10.7771/1541-5015.1649

Valovičová, Ľ., Ondruška, J., Zelenický, Ľ., Chytrý, V., & Medová, J. (2020). Enhancing computational thinking through interdisciplinary STEAM activities using tablets. *Mathematics, 8*(12), 2128. DOI: 10.3390/math8122128

Weintrop, D., Beheshti, E., Horn, M., Orton, K., Jona, K., Trouille, L., & Wilensky, U. (2016). Defining computational thinking for mathematics and science classrooms. *Journal of Science Education and Technology, 25*(1), 127–147. DOI: 10.1007/s10956-015-9581-5

Yadav, A., Mayfield, C., Zhou, N., Hambrusch, S., & Korb, J. T. (2024). Computational thinking in elementary and secondary teacher education. [TOCE]. *ACM Transactions on Computing Education, 14*(1), 1–16. DOI: 10.1145/2576872

Yilmaz Ince, E., & Koc, M. (2021). The consequences of robotics programming education on computational thinking skills: An intervention of the Young Engineer's Workshop (YEW). *Computer Applications in Engineering Education, 29*(1), 191–208. DOI: 10.1002/cae.22321

Zahra, A., Waheed, Z., Fatima, T., & Khong, K. W. (2024). Leveraging Technology for Environmental Awareness: Insights from Experimental Research with Middle School Students in Malaysia. *RMLE Online: Research in Middle Level Education, 47*(4), 1–17. DOI: 10.1080/19404476.2024.2322046

Chapter 10
Integrating AI to Enhance the Effectiveness of Fine Arts Teacher Training Programs in Vietnam

Hanh Cao Minh Hong
http://orcid.org/0009-0002-8828-736X
Saigon University, Vietnam

ABSTRACT

This chapter investigates the transformative potential of Artificial Intelligence (AI) in enhancing fine art teacher training programs in Vietnam. Grounded in an analysis of traditional program structures and contemporary educational demands, this study highlights how AI can support creative capacity building, and pedagogical training. Through literature synthesis and case studies from Vietnam and international contexts, this study identifies the role of AI in redefining instructional design, assessment feedback, and interdisciplinary integration in art education. At the same time, it critically examines concerns related to cultural authenticity, authorship, overdependence on automation, and the ethical boundaries of AI-generated art. The findings suggest that a phased, human-centered approach to AI integration can modernize Fine Arts education in Vietnam while preserving the core values of creativity, cultural identity, and pedagogical integrity.

DOI: 10.4018/979-8-3373-1285-9.ch010

INTRODUCTION

1.1. The evolution of AI applications in modern education

Modern education has undergone significant transformations under the influence of science and technology, particularly artificial intelligence (AI). Information technology (IT), together with AI, has facilitated a shift in the application and organization of learning models are applied and organized. Since the 2010s, the initial aim of integrating IT into higher education environments has been to comprehensively adjust the learning process. The impact of IT on educational programs has included a move toward personalized and distance learning, the support of virtual learning environments, and the promotion of flexible learner-centered approaches (Best & MacGregor, 2017; Tarnavska, 2013; UNESCO, 2014). Accordingly, IT has been proposed as a critical tool for transforming curricula and redesigning practical courses into online formats to meet the demands of a changing society. In parallel, the influence of IT on educators has been examined to enhance its educational effectiveness. Teachers are encouraged to integrate IT to support learners through mentoring, providing feedback, and facilitating learning (Baran, 2016; Belt & Lowenthal, 2020). Educators are expected to model technology integration and assist learners in developing technological competencies necessary for academic and professional success. This integration empowers learners by personalizing their learning experiences and fostering connected, meaningful engagement (Akwei et al., 2017; Baran, 2016; Tarnavska, 2013; UNESCO, 2014). Learners become more active in their educational journeys, selecting content that boosts motivation, enhances skills, and reshapes their perceptions of flexible and effective learning methods. Improvements have been noted in competencies such as teamwork, decision-making, and problem-solving. Moreover, some studies indicate that learners show greater interest in technology-integrated content, finding it more engaging than traditional linear teaching methods (Akwei et al., 2017; Best & MacGregor, 2017).

The 2020s marked a major transformation in educational technology, highlighted by the widespread emergence of AI. AI tools have begun to be recognized as instruments for enhancing productivity and fostering interdisciplinary learning (Jones, 2023). Generative AI (GenAI), in particular, has been embraced as a turning point in education, as it enables collaborative learning between humans and machines. Following the COVID-19 pandemic, the adoption of GenAI has accelerated owing to its capacity to assist educators in automating administrative tasks and providing rapid feedback to learners (Tahiru, 2021; Wang et al., 2024). Compared with earlier digital learning tools, the integration of AI in education offers unprecedented levels of personalized learning, automated instruction and feedback, system adaptability to individual learning pathways, and deep insights that contribute to more effective and tailored teaching and learning environments (Jones, 2023; Owoc et al., 2021; Shuliar et al., 2023; Tahiru, 2021; Wang et al., 2024). AI has shifted education from a reactive and generalized approach to one that is proactive and personalized, delivering clear benefits to both educators and learners. These include measurable improvements in learning performance and productivity (Table 1).

Table 1. Comparison of traditional educational technologies (EdTech) and AI in education with associated measurable benefits for educators and learners

Category	Traditional EdTech	AI in Education	Measurable Benefits	Beneficiary	Source
Personalized Learning	Limited implementation via preset modules; e-learning content lacks interactivity and real-time adaptability.	Real-time content adjustment based on learners' needs and outcomes.	Individual learning paths, higher engagement	Learners	Owoc et al., 2021; Shuliar et al., 2023; Wang et al., 2024
Assessment & Feedback	Manual grading; delayed feedback through Learning Management Systems (LMS); limited ongoing assessment support.	Immediate, intelligent, and personalized feedback through natural language processing (NLP) in education systems.	Faster comprehension, higher test scores	Learners	Owoc et al., 2021; Wang et al., 2024
Anxiety & Confidence	No emotional support; learners may feel anxious in self-directed or remote learning environments.	Adaptive AI tutors reduce learning anxiety by 20%	Higher motivation and self-efficacy	Learners	Wang et al., 2024
Administrative Automation	Basic LMS scheduling, manual grading and notifications; teacher/ instructor must perform all setup tasks.	Automated grading, emails, and tasks scheduling	Saves educator time and reduces workload	Educators	Owoc et al., 2021; Tahiru, 2021
Content Creation	Educators manually create all content; no automatic support for text or multimedia content generation.	AI supports test creation, lesson planning, and diverse assessment forms. AI-assisted generation of quizzes, syllabi, assessments	Reduced prep time, improved content quality	Educators	Jones, 2023; Owoc et al., 2021

continued on following page

Table 1. Continued

Category	Traditional EdTech	AI in Education	Measurable Benefits	Beneficiary	Source
Performance Prediction	Manual analysis using spreadsheets or dashboards; predictive models are limited.	Learner performance prediction based on learning data to identify at-risk students.	Early intervention, improved outcomes	Educators & Learners	Owoc et al., 2021; Wang et al., 2024
Creative Collaboration	Limited real-time tools (forums, wikis); lacks creative suggestion or co-creation features.	Tools like ChatGPT support brainstorming, interdisciplinary co-creation, and project suggestions.	Boosts engagement, critical thinking, creativity	Educators & Learners	Jones, 2023
Real-Time Adaptability	Manual content updates; minimal automation or system learning from past interactions.	Systems adapt and learn from each interaction based on recorded work history.	Continuous improvement of learning experience	Educators & Learners	Owoc et al., 2021; Wang et al., 2024

Thus, in the field of education, AI has emerged as an effective enabling technology for transforming teaching models and outperforming traditional technologies by creating more engaging, comprehensive, and distinctly personalized learning environments. Its ability to deliver measurable improvements, such as enhancing learning performance, increasing accessibility, and suggesting innovative teaching methods, highlights AI's potential to redefine the role of technology in modern educational models. By strategically leveraging the advantages of AI, higher education institutions can drive meaningful progress and better adapt to the rapidly evolving demands of contemporary education.

However, these developments are not without challenges. Issues of algorithmic bias, overdependence on automation, and the cultural mismatch between AI-generated content and local educational values are emerging as critical concerns, particularly in the creative and humanistic fields. As Vietnam moves toward modernizing its teacher training programs, particularly in Fine Arts education, the issue is how to integrate AI with responsibility, equity, and ethics.

1.2. Characteristics of Fine Arts Teacher training programs

The primary objective of Fine Arts Teacher training programs is to supply qualified visual arts educators for specific regions or roles related to art education. Throughout the 20th century, such programs were characterized by a set of core requirements concerning both artistic training and pedagogical competence.

First, the curriculum provided a solid foundation in various visual arts disciplines, including painting, design, sculpture, crafts, photography, and art history. Additionally, some programs advocated for interdisciplinary approaches, encouraging integration with general education subjects such as literature, science, mathematics, and foreign languages. This was aimed at meeting the diverse emotional and artistic intelligences of learners across different educational levels and backgrounds (Beymer, 1970; Engel, 1989; Kundis, 1954).

In addition, along with artistic expertise, these programs emphasized the development of pedagogical skills. Core competencies include child psychology, educational psychology, and methods of art instruction (Beymer, 1970; Kundis, 1954). Such training is essential for preservice Fine Arts teachers to understand the developmental stages and students' emotional needs, nurture creativity, and foster engagement in the classroom.

Finally, Fine Arts teacher training programs provide opportunities for extended teaching practicum, possibly lasting up to one year (Beymer, 1970). Preservice teachers were expected to gain experience across multiple grade levels and develop confidence, classroom management skills, and the ability to deliver effective instruction. Moreover, preservice Fine Arts teachers are often mentored by experienced senior teachers, ensuring that guidance is grounded in both artistic proficiency and practical teaching expertise (Engel, 1989; Kundis, 1954).

Overall, an effective Fine Arts Teacher Training program balanced artistic skill development with educational theory and pedagogical competence while focusing on nurturing students' personal qualities and capacities. In the 21st century, while these core elements remain, the focus has shifted toward interdisciplinary learning, technological proficiency, and equipping future teachers with the ability to navigate the challenges of a knowledge-based society. For example:

- Beyond artistic expertise, teachers now need interdisciplinary knowledge to guide instruction on real-world issues (Marshall, 2005; Smilan & Miraglia, 2009). Modern art education encourages students to use artistic practice to explore societal problems and promote collaborative inquiry-based learning that develops creativity, critical thinking, and social connections.
- In addition to psychology and pedagogy, programs must train students in digital and technological skills (Bequette & Brennan, 2008). Teachers are expected to help students create digital tools, such as photography, video editing, and animation, and use the media critically. Programs should include digital arts and media literacy to ensure that future teachers can effectively integrate technology.
- Furthermore, teachers must be prepared for rapidly changing social needs, diverse classrooms, increasing performance expectations from families and society, and technological advances in art (Kowalczuk-Walędziak et al., 2019; Lauwers, 2019). Students should receive short-term courses on 21st-century

skills and opportunities to integrate digital tools, contemporary art forms, and global issues into their teaching. Cultural competence and social collaboration must also be emphasized to equip future teachers in culturally and cognitively diverse learning environments (Blouin & Moss, 2015; Marshall, 2005; Smilan & Miraglia, 2009).

At its core, Fine Arts Teacher Training emphasizes foundational knowledge in visual arts and pedagogy. Programs traditionally focus on drawing, painting, sculpture, and crafts, alongside modules in psychology and instructional methods. Practical teaching experiences are central, with mentorship to build classroom confidence. In the 20th century, technology played a minimal role, and greater emphasis was placed on personal attributes like empathy and adaptability. However, modern programs are evolving to meet 21st-century demands by integrating interdisciplinary learning, digital literacy, and emerging tools in media arts and communication (Diagram 1). The role of art educators is expanding to include curriculum design, collaboration, and real-world application, highlighting the need for regular updates to training programs.

While Fine Arts Teacher Training programs around the world share common foundations, emphasizing artistic skill development, pedagogical knowledge, and practicum experience, they differ in how they respond to contemporary demands. In many Western institutions, there is a growing focus on interdisciplinary learning, digital media integration, and the use of AI to support both creative and instructional practices. By contrast, Vietnamese programs, though strong in traditional arts and pedagogy, have been slower to adopt emerging technologies and often lack systematic integration of digital or AI-based tools. However, recent curricular reforms in select Vietnamese universities signal a shift toward modernization, presenting both opportunities and challenges for aligning national fine arts education with global innovation trends.

1.3. Opportunities and cautions of applying AI in Fine Arts Teacher training programs

As Fine Arts Teacher Training programs evolve to meet the demands of a digital society, AI emerges as both a powerful enabler and a source of pedagogical tension. The creative and interdisciplinary nature of art education aligns well with AI's strengths, particularly its capacity to personalize learning, facilitate creative ideation, and deliver adaptive feedback. When used thoughtfully, AI can support preservice teachers in developing both artistic fluency and instructional competence.

AI-powered tools such as generative models, virtual tutors, and adaptive learning systems offer promising ways to enhance curriculum design and simulate diverse teaching scenarios. In particular, AI enables real-time customization of content, creative experimentation through image generation, and instant feedback tailored to individual learner needs (Kerimbayev et al., 2025; Wang et al., 2024). These capacities are well-suited to modern Fine Arts programs that emphasize differentiated instruction, cross-disciplinary learning, and digital media literacy.

Moreover, AI offers practical benefits for teacher development. Future educators can use AI to prototype visual materials, create multimedia content, and analyze classroom data to adjust teaching strategies. As the role of teachers expands to include instructional design and social facilitation, AI can help educators manage administrative tasks, anticipate learner needs, and promote reflective teaching practices (Ayanwale et al., 2024; Mustafa et al., 2024). Such tools hold particular promise for Vietnamese programs seeking to bridge traditional training methods with global educational innovation.

However, the integration of AI into Fine Arts education is not without risk. Overreliance on automation may compromise the development of foundational skills, such as hand drawing, visual analysis, and conceptual depth. Cultural originality and authorship may be diluted when students use AI-generated imagery without critical engagement. Ethical dilemmas, ranging from creative ownership to the opacity of algorithmic processes, raise concerns that are particularly relevant in artistic contexts, where authenticity and emotional expression are core values (Lockhart, 2024; Velasco et al., 2024).

Furthermore, disparities in digital infrastructure and training across countries, such as in Vietnam, may limit the equitable adoption of AI. Without proper support, students may struggle with prompt design, misinterpret AI feedback, or become passive users rather than critical creators. Therefore, while AI presents clear advantages, it must be integrated through a guided, reflective, and culturally responsive approach.

In summary, AI has the potential to enrich Fine Arts Teacher Training by expanding creative possibilities and enhancing pedagogical precision. Yet its success depends on how thoughtfully and ethically it is applied. For Vietnam, the challenge lies in balancing technological innovation with artistic integrity and educational equity, ensuring that AI complements, rather than compromises, the human-centered values of arts education.

LITERATURE REVIEW

2.1. Training and supporting creative capacity with AI integration

The integration of AI into fine arts education opens new opportunities to support creative thinking, motivate learners, and addresses the diverse needs of future teachers. Several recent studies highlight the potential of AI tools to assist in artistic exploration and idea development. For example, Zhou (2023) found that 86% of student teachers expressed excitement when first using AI-powered image generators, such as Midjourney and DALL-E. Many valued these tools for enhancing visual idea generation and helping students express concepts that were difficult to draw by hand. Similarly, Mayo (2024) emphasized that AI can act as a co-creator in the artistic process, not merely as a generator of content, encouraging students and educators to experiment collaboratively with machines.

However, these benefits are often dependent on users' digital fluency and conceptual clarity. Students who struggled to create accurate prompts or interpret AI-generated results reported lower engagement and creative frustration (Zhou, 2023). This points to the need for strong foundational training, not only in fine arts but also in prompt design and digital literacy. In Vietnam, this issue is also particularly relevant. While institutions in major cities, such as Ho Chi Minh City and Hanoi, have begun integrating multimedia arts and digital tools into their programs, others still focus primarily on traditional art forms, such as lacquer painting, folk printing, and sculpture. These forms require not only technical precision but also cultural understanding, which AI may not be able to replicate meaningfully.

A key theme across the literature is the tension between creative support and creative substitution. While AI tools such as Wombo Dream or Midjourney offer rapid visual ideation, they may encourage passive engagement if students rely too heavily on AI suggestions without developing their own visual thinking. Miralay (2024) noted that over-reliance on AI can reduce practice in hand drawing skills, which remain essential in many fine arts disciplines. In this regard, Velasco et al. (2024) proposed a useful model distinguishing between three levels of AI use in education: AI-controlled (passive), AI-assisted (collaborative), and AI-empowered (autonomous). They argued that truly creative use of AI requires learners to move beyond consuming outputs and engage critically with both the process and result.

These concerns are relatedly important in the Vietnamese context, where cultural heritage is a core part of the fine arts curriculum. Vietnamese artistic traditions often carry symbolic meanings, historical narratives, and community identities that AI systems trained on global image datasets may overlook or misrepresent. For instance, AI-generated "lacquer" textures may not reflect the material techniques or spiritual symbolism associated with traditional Vietnamese lacquer art. Educators must therefore play a guiding role in helping students interpret AI suggestions critically, encouraging adaptation rather than imitation.

Ethical concerns also arise around authorship and originality. As AI tools become more common in classrooms, questions about creative ownership and academic honesty become increasingly relevant. Some educators worry that AI-generated art may decrease the authenticity of students' work if they do not understand where the boundaries lie between assistance and creation (Miralay, 2024; Velasco et al., 2024). In Vietnam, where academic integrity and cultural values are emphasized, especially in fine arts teacher training, it is crucial that students are taught to reflect on their use of AI and be transparent about its role in their creative processes.

Moreover, digital literacy is not only about using tools effectively but also about developing a critical mindset. Mayo (2024) suggests that teachers should approach AI as a "virtual editor," interacting with it as part of a dialogical creative process. This includes writing thoughtful prompts, analyzing AI outputs, and revising work to align with personal and educational goals. For Vietnamese preservice teachers, this skill is essential, not only to support their future students in using digital tools but also to ensure that their teaching preserves artistic intention and cultural authenticity.

Overall, the use of AI in developing creative capacity shows strong potential when introduced as a supportive, reflective partner in the learning process. It can reduce technical barriers, inspire experimentation, and increase student motivation. However, these benefits are only realized when educators provide clear guidance, ethical boundaries, and training in both critical and creative thinking. As future Fine Arts teachers in Vietnam prepare to navigate an increasingly digital education environment as in worldwide, their ability to collaborate meaningfully with AI, without losing sight of traditional heritage, authorship, and intentionality, will be essential.

2.2. AI's impact on pedagogical training

Research on higher education and fine arts teacher training highlights the potential of AI to improve teaching and learning. Key contributions include real-time feedback, personalized instruction, adaptive platforms, and support for instructional design (Chen et al., 2022; Yusuf et al., 2025). Tools such as intelligent tutoring systems and conversational agents are increasingly applied to promote learner-centered practices and assist educators in curriculum development.

The literature suggests three main areas of impact. The first concerns pedagogical enhancement, where AI helps provide rapid feedback and personalized learning. Yusuf et al. (2025) describe how conversational agents adapt interactions to context, creating responsive learning environments. These systems not only support academic needs but also offer emotional encouragement, strengthening learner engagement.

The second area relates to barriers and preconditions. Bayaga (2025) argues that teacher attitudes and readiness strongly influence whether AI is adopted effectively. Even advanced systems may fail if educators approach them with skepticism or lack strategies for meaningful integration. Chen et al. (2022) also emphasize that robust infrastructure is essential for success, and without it, AI becomes an additional burden rather than support.

The third area addresses limitations in creative pedagogy. Habib et al. (2025) found that while AI can improve confidence and assist with idea development, it cannot substitute the reflective and process-oriented learning that is central to art education. Students value courses that foster exploration and experimentation, qualities that AI can supplement but not replace.

Applied to fine arts education, these findings show both promise and caution. Feedback in art training is not only technical but also interpretive and creative. AI can deliver instant suggestions, but if relied upon too heavily, there is a risk that lessons become standardized and student originality is reduced. This is especially significant in fine arts teacher preparation, where the aim is to cultivate both pedagogical skill and artistic sensitivity. Ethical concerns also arise, including authorship of AI-assisted lesson plans and the possibility of misrepresenting cultural traditions if datasets are biased toward various cultural visual forms.

In the Vietnamese context, these challenges are also amplified. Several teacher training programs still emphasize traditional pedagogy, with limited exposure to advanced digital tools. Although universities in central areas have integrated more multimedia courses, readiness for AI-enhanced pedagogy remains uneven. Infrastructure gaps and differences in digital literacy mean that AI adoption requires gradual, well-supported implementation.

Overall, AI has the potential to enrich pedagogical training in Fine Arts Teacher Education, but its success depends on both technical and human factors. It can personalize instruction and strengthen engagement, yet it must be integrated ethically and in alignment with local educational values. These insights provide a foundation for the structured integration model discussed in Section 3, which adapts international evidence to Vietnam's fine arts teacher training system.

2.3. Case studies: AI in creative higher education

To illustrate how AI is being implemented in the context of art education within specific higher education programs, this section presents selected case studies from Malaysia and the United States, representing two contrasting cultural and educational contexts: Eastern and Western. These real-world examples offer valuable insights for designing creativity-driven courses, fostering student engagement, and demonstrating the potential for enhancing pedagogical skills through AI integration in fine art teacher training programs.

Case Study 1: Innovation in Teaching Design Using AI Tools at University Malaysia Kelantan, Malaysia

At the Faculty of Creative Technology, Universiti Malaysia Kelantan (UMK), AI tools were integrated into three Fine Arts courses - "Production Design," "Mixed Media," and "Computer and Arts" - to explore their role in expanding students' creative capacity. The participants, ranging from the first to the third year, demonstrated adaptability, creative backgrounds, and technological fluency (Zailuddin et al., 2024).

In "Production Design," students often struggled to visualize abstract concepts like costume or scene design. The AI tool DALL·E was introduced as a visual partner to transform text prompts into image outputs. Students reported increased confidence and ideation. DALL·E offered diverse visual suggestions that students refined into hand-drawn or digital designs. Instructors stressed that AI should inspire, not dictate, creative decisions, preserving the focus on cultivating independent visual thinking.

The "Mixed Media" course introduced Wombo Dream to support ideation in 2D and 3D design. Students with limited artistic experience used Wombo to generate visual suggestions based on simple prompts. This tool encourages experimentation by breaking habitual visual thinking, reducing idea-generation time, and expanding exposure to new color schemes, forms, and textures.

In "Computer and Arts," first-year students explored digital technologies using beginner-friendly AI tools like Remove.bg and Prisma. Although technically simple, these tools have sparked creative thinking. For example, Prisma's stylized filters (e.g., Van Gogh-inspired) inspired students to develop posters, collages, or animations. AI is a visual catalyst that stimulates iterative creativity. By lowering technical barriers, AI empowers students to experiment and express ideas without fear of technical inadequacy, which is essential in early creative education.

Across all three courses, AI enriched creative learning by expanding visual choices and reducing barriers to expressions. Students who lack traditional drawing skills can still articulate ideas through image generation. One standout outcome was the democratization of creativity: students with diverse skill levels could meaningfully engage in visual storytelling. AI acted as a scaffold, not a shortcut, to support confidence and curiosity in creative practice.

Another pedagogical benefit emerged, namely prompt engineering as a learning tool. Students had to construct descriptive prompts that guided AI, encouraging reflection on visual elements, such as mood, setting, and composition. This prompted high-level thinking and deepened conceptual understanding. Particularly in "Production Design" and "Mixed Media," prompt writing fostered critical engagement with the creative process, transforming AI into a reflective collaborator.

Despite these benefits, challenges have surfaced. In all three courses, instructors and students raised concerns about overdependence on AI. While AI eased ideation, some students skipped the important steps in creative development. In "Production Design," the abundance of AI outputs led to "visual noise," making it hard for students to choose a clear direction. In "Mixed Media," repetition in AI styles raised concerns about formulaic or impersonal work. In "Computer and Arts," students sometimes chose visually appealing filters without deeper reflection on their narrative impact.

Another key issue is authorship. With AI-assisted creation, students and instructors questioned where creative ownership resides within the prompt, the selection and editing process, or the final output. This tension was particularly felt in "Mixed Media," in which some students perceived a loss of artistic control. These reflections underscore the need for educators to guide learners in asserting agency, reworking AI suggestions, and recognizing when to resist automated results.

Educators thus play a vital role not only in teaching tool usage, but also in preserving student intentionality. Students must be trained to interpret and reshape AI outputs in line with their vision. This fosters critical awareness and reinforces the ownership of their artistic voice. Without such guidance, there is the risk of superficial engagement or passivity in creative thinking.

In conclusion, the experimental use of AI in UMK's creative courses demonstrated a strong potential for expanding ideation, boosting engagement, and supporting expression, especially for students struggling with traditional techniques. AI's greatest contribution was its capacity to open new spaces for exploration, offering immediate and diverse input for artistic interpretation. However, it also brought challenges regarding depth, originality, and authorship. AI must not be seen as a creative solution but as a creative partner, effective only when paired with reflective pedagogy and intentional instructional design.

Ultimately, AI's role in art education is not to replace creativity, but to reframe how it develops. Educators must actively cultivate critical thinking, ensure ethical engagement with tools, and reaffirm students' creative agency. In doing so, AI becomes a medium for nurturing - not diminishing - the creative potential at the heart of fine art education.

Case Study 2: Teaching Art History Using Digital Technology and AI Integration at Lindenwood University, USA

At Lindenwood University, an innovative case study was launched to explore the educational potential of integrating AI tools into an online Ancient Art course, focusing on the historical period from Mesopotamia to the fall of Rome. Led by

James Hutson, this pilot initiative reimagined how students might engage with art history content, not through static lectures or textbook analysis, but through a dynamic exercise of using AI art generators to recreate iconic works from antiquity. The aim was not merely technical reproduction but to foster deeper visual literacy, formal analysis skills, and critical engagement with both historical forms and modern digital mediation.

Pedagogical design requires students to select a specific work from the course, analyze its visual elements through traditional formal analysis, and use that analysis to guide the creation of AI-generated replicas using platforms such as DALL-E 3, Craiyon, or Midjourney. Crucially, students were forbidden from including direct metadata, such as title, time period, or cultural origin, in their prompts. This ensured that the visual output relied on the descriptive precision and not on the AI's memory of the labeled datasets. What emerged from this exercise was not only a creative re-engagement with course material, but also a valuable exploration of how AI can augment, not replace, the student's interpretive agency in studying art.

The students' responses to the task revealed both enthusiasm and skepticism, capturing the ambivalent space that AI occupies in the educational process. AI has proved to be a valuable aid in visualizing complex architectural forms and compositional structures. For instance, students working on iconic structures such as the Parthenon or sculptural groups such as Laocoön leveraged iterative prompting to refine outputs that conveyed lighting, texture, and spatial dynamics with impressive nuances. These processes mirrored the iterative nature of sketching and conceptual design in traditional studio practice, and students reported that the trial-and-error format of prompt engineering deepened their understanding of the visual analysis.

One student, attempting to recreate the Nike of Samothrace, described the challenge of capturing a sense of dynamic movement and fabric flow. After multiple iterations, they found that refining phrases such as "forward thrust of the right leg" or "drapery clinging to torso in wind" improved the AI's output but also their own ability to describe what they saw. Thus, AI became both a mirror and a feedback loop for visual thinking.

However, not all experiences were smooth. Some students encountered frustration when the AI tools produced anatomically distorted figures or repeated stylistic clichés, especially with more accessible platforms such as Craiyon. One student expressed concern that the AI outputs, while visually intriguing, did not replicate the emotive force or cultural specificity of the original artwork. This tension raised essential pedagogical questions: Can AI capture the affective dimension of ancient sculpture or does it risk flattening it into an aesthetic style?

The reflective essays accompanying the image assignments added a critical layer to the process. Many students reported that while AI generators offered exciting possibilities for visualization, the act of translating observation into precise language - the prompt itself–solidified their analytical skills. Writing prompts such as "weathered Doric columns" or "broken pediment over empty interior" pushed students to go beyond surface-level descriptions and think in terms of form, structure, and context. Thus, prompt engineering was not just a technical skill but a cognitive and interpretive exercise aligned with the goals of formal analysis.

The ethical concerns were not considered. Several students expressed unease about the nature of AI training datasets, questioning whether the generated images constituted the original student work or derivative content. Others highlighted the risk of over-reliance on AI tools, warning that students might become passive in their engagement with art if the technology did too much of the "seeing" for them. These reflections signal a mature grappling with the philosophical implications of AI in art education and reaffirm the need for critical literacy as a core component of technology integration. Perhaps the most illuminating was the realization that AI could democratize certain aspects of creative engagement. Students without the strong drawing or modeling skills found in AI articulate visual ideas that would otherwise be locked behind technical barriers. Rather than diminishing their agency, AI amplified it in this context, provided that it was used reflectively and not uncritically. As one student wrote, "AI did not make my ideas; it helped me see them more clearly."

Ultimately, the case study at Lindenwood illustrates a balanced model for integrating AI into art history education - one that neither glorifies the tool nor rejects it but situates it within a structured, theory-informed framework. The project affirmed that AI can be a powerful ally in teaching visual analysis, provided it is used not as a crutch but as a collaborative lens through which students refine their observational and interpretive capacities. In the context of digital art history, such partnerships between human insight and machine capability may define the next chapter on how we teach and learn from the visual past.

FRAMEWORK FOR AI INTEGRATION IN VIETNAM

3.1. An overview of Fine Arts Teacher Training programs in Vietnam

Fine Arts Teacher Training programs in Vietnam currently emphasize both artistic practice and pedagogical competence, preparing graduates to teach in general education, as well as in specialized institutions. To examine the general structure of these programs, several representative curricula from reputable Vietnamese universities were selected, including

- Hanoi National University of Education (HNUE) and National University of Art Education (NUAE) in Northern Vietnam
- University of Arts, Hue University (HUFA) in Central Vietnam
- Ho Chi Minh City University of Fine Arts (HCMUFA) and Saigon University (SGU) in Southern Vietnam

(Sources: Hanoi National University of Education, 2025; Ho Chi Minh City University of Fine Arts, n.d.; National University of Art Education, n.d.; Saigon University, n.d.; University of Arts, Hue University, n.d.)

The institutions selected represent diverse regional educational contexts. The table below (Table 2) summarizes the training structures of the five Fine Arts Teacher Training programs from the aforementioned universities.

Table 2. Summary of the structure of five fine arts teacher training programs in Vietnam

Aspects	Similarities	Differences
General Knowledge	All programs include core courses in political education and physical education. Basic IT and foreign language training is commonly included.	- NUAE and HNUE place greater emphasis on political theory. - SGU places more focus on English language proficiency.
Art Knowledge & Skills	Programs include training in: - Artistic anatomy - Fundamentals of visual art - Art history - Composition & decorative arts - Electives in mixed media & digital creativity	- NUAE focuses more on traditional arts and media communication. - HNUE offers stronger components in 3D art exploration.
Pedagogical Knowledge & Skills	All programs include core pedagogy modules (e.g., educational psychology, art teaching methods). Internships are mandatory (8–12 weeks).	- NUAE emphasizes real-world teaching experience. - HNUE emphasizes school-based curriculum development. - HUFA emphasizes early fieldwork. - HCMUFA emphasizes creativity-focused teaching methods. - SGU frequently adopts practice-based approaches.
Technology and Digital Applications	All programs offer basic IT training and applied art tech modules.	- NUAE: ~7 credits in basic IT and applied media tech - HNUE: 8–10 credits in applied IT, multimedia, and optional 3D design - HUFA: 6–7 credits in basic IT and some multimedia exposure - HCMUFA: 15 credits in applied IT, graphic design, multimedia art - SGU: 12–15 credits in multimedia, photography, and applied graphics

In all Fine Arts Teacher Training programs, the general knowledge component is highly standardized across universities, reflecting consistent national requirements for foundational cognitive and skill development in higher education. Notably, the two institutions in Southern Vietnam demonstrate an emphasis on developing English proficiency, highlighting an increasing focus on foreign language competency among students.

Core artistic knowledge remains central to all programs, maintaining a strong foundation in traditional fine arts training. All universities rigorously incorporate figure drawing (via "Drawing" courses) and offer exposure to traditional art materials such as lacquer, silk painting, and woodblock printing. However, the degree of integration with modern practices varies. HUFA continues to prioritize classical training in figure drawing and art history, while HCMUFA has shifted toward contemporary practices such as 2D and 3D design. NUAE maintains a rich exploration of traditional media, while SGU balances traditional approaches with growing attention to applied graphics and photography. This uneven distribution reflects divergent readiness levels for adopting advanced technologies such as AI: institutions with stronger emphasis on digital and applied media (e.g., HCMUFA, SGU) are better positioned to integrate AI-based tools, whereas those anchored in traditional curricula may face greater transitional challenges.

Pedagogical training is strongly emphasized across all Fine Arts Teacher Training programs. Every institution includes subjects such as educational psychology, teaching methods, and practices or fieldwork experiences, though the duration and intensity differ. HUFA offers the longest field experience (14 weeks), providing deep immersion, while NUAE and HNUE spread practical training into multiple phases. Southern institutions such as SGU and HCMUFA adopt more practice-oriented approaches, reflecting a modern philosophy of gradually scaffolding pedagogical competencies. This alignment with practice-based training is significant for AI adoption, since teachers who already experiment with diverse instructional strategies may find it easier to incorporate AI-driven simulations, adaptive feedback tools, or digital lesson planning platforms into their practice.

The application of IT and multimedia is an emerging but uneven trend. HCMUFA and SGU stand out with substantial credits devoted to applied IT, multimedia art, and digital media, while NUAE and HUFA remain limited to basic IT literacy. HNUE takes a middle path, offering elective courses in multimedia and 3D design alongside traditional fine arts. This variety indicates that some universities are better prepared for AI integration, particularly those where digital literacy has already been incorporated into the curriculum. However, reliance on imported AI tools also raises concerns of cultural mismatch. For example, image-generation platforms often reflect Western artistic training datasets, which may distort or oversimplify Vietnam's unique traditions, such as lacquer painting or Đông H folk prints. Integrating AI into fine arts teacher education in Vietnam must therefore not only address technical readiness but also ensure cultural preservation and ethical use of digital tools.

In summary, Vietnamese Fine Arts Teacher Training programs are characterized by a strong base in traditional arts and pedagogy, with growing but uneven integration of digital and technological competencies. This unevenness underscores both the potential and the challenge of AI integration: while institutions with digital strengths are ready to explore AI-enhanced creativity and adaptive teaching, others must first build basic technological capacity. The path forward will require a balanced approach, leveraging AI to modernize curricula while guarding Vietnam's rich artistic heritage and culture.

3.2. AI adapts in training creativity in Fine Arts Teacher Training programs in Vietnam

Based on previous analyses and case studies, integrating AI into Fine Arts Teacher Training in Vietnam is both a significant opportunity and a necessary step. However, to be effective, it requires a structured and gradual strategy. This section proposes a three-phase approach that aligns international theoretical models, such as the AI Competency Framework by Velasco et al. (2024) and Bayaga's (2025) TOE and UTAUT models, with the specific conditions of Vietnam's teacher training programs.

In the Vietnamese context, readiness varies between institutions. Universities such as NUAE and HUFA, which remain focused on traditional fine arts and pedagogy, may start with basic AI integration. By contrast, HCMUFA and SGU, which already include multimedia and applied IT courses, are better positioned to experiment with more advanced phases of AI adoption. This uneven landscape highlights the need for a phased approach rather than a one-size-fits-all model.

Phase 1. Foundational (AI-Controlled)

In this first stage, AI is used under instructor guidance to build students' technical and pedagogical foundations. This includes structured feedback in courses such as anatomical drawing or composition, where instructors define benchmarks and AI provides rule-based evaluations. Students learn how to design prompts, interpret AI feedback, and compare it with traditional frameworks. In this way, they practice digital literacy while also strengthening their analytical skills. For institutions with limited digital resources, such as NUAE or HUFA, this controlled phase is a realistic entry point for AI use.

Phase 2. Experiential (AI-Assisted)

In the second stage, students use AI as a creative collaborator. This includes generating visual ideas through tools such as DALL-E or Wombo Dream, or practicing classroom simulations to prepare for real teaching. Here, AI supports ideation, experimentation, and adaptive lesson design, but students must still maintain conceptual direction and originality. Critical evaluation of AI outputs is emphasized to avoid superficial or repetitive results. For example, HCMUFA and SGU, with stronger multimedia foundations, can apply this stage in design-based courses and teaching practicums. According to the TOE and UTAUT frameworks (Bayaga, 2025), this phase also builds students' awareness of AI as a tool, not a replacement, encouraging responsible use in pedagogical contexts.

Phase 3. Innovation (AI-Empowered)

The final stage emphasizes independent creativity, curriculum design, and ethical responsibility. AI becomes fully integrated as a partner in lesson planning, interdisciplinary content creation, and adaptive teaching. Students apply AI to capstone projects, graduation portfolios, or independent research, while also learning how to address issues of authorship and authenticity. For example, just as students at Lindenwood University in the United States used AI to reinterpret ancient artworks (Hutson, 2024), Vietnamese students may use AI to develop teaching materials that blend traditional practices such as lacquer painting, Đông H woodcuts, or the Ly Dynasty's pattern with modern media. This phase requires not only technical fluency but also cultural awareness, ensuring that AI supports, rather than assimilating Vietnam's artistic heritage to Western artistic values.

Across all phases, there are challenges that remain. These include limited infrastructure in rural regions, uneven teacher readiness, and the danger of students relying too heavily on AI outputs. To address these risks, AI integration must be paired with faculty training, ethical guidelines, and continuous reflection. By doing so, AI can act as a scaffold for creativity and pedagogy, while preserving the authenticity of Vietnamese fine arts.

This three-phase model is summarized in Diagram 3. It ensures that AI is introduced gradually, allowing students to move from guided use to independent, responsible application. By aligning AI integration with both cognitive development and cultural values, the model balances innovation with tradition, helping future Vietnamese fine art teachers become creative, ethical, and adaptable educators.

3.3. Evaluation metrics for AI-enhanced training programs

To measure the effectiveness of AI integration in Fine Arts Teacher Training programs, it is essential to use a comprehensive evaluation framework that reflects both technological value and pedagogical outcomes. Building on the theoretical models of Sáez Velasco et al. (2024) and Bayaga (2025), this section proposes multidimensional criteria focused on creativity, pedagogy, ethics, and long-term application. In the Vietnamese context, these metrics must also reflect the diversity of institutions, from traditional programs to more digitally oriented ones.

Creative empowerment. The first criterion is the degree to which AI empowers students to explore ideas, experiment, and refine their artistic voice. In Vietnam, this means not only assessing AI-generated outputs but also examining how students adapt them to traditional practices. The key is whether students demonstrate independent agency in shaping AI-assisted work, rather than becoming passive consumers of automated suggestions.

Pedagogical adaptability. The second criterion is the ability to integrate AI into lesson planning and classroom practice. This includes designing learner-centered lessons, simulating teaching situations, and adapting to diverse student needs. For Vietnamese fine arts teacher training programs, this could involve assessing how preservice teachers use AI to create visual aids for school art classes, or how they adapt AI feedback into lesson revisions.

Ethical compliance. The third criterion addresses responsible AI use. This includes transparency about AI's role, respect for intellectual property, and sensitivity to cultural authenticity. In fine arts education, where originality is central, students must be guided to clearly differentiate between AI assistance and their own creative contributions. Vietnamese programs also need to guard against AI outputs that misrepresent cultural heritage or favor Western aesthetics over local traditions.

Attitudinal changes. The fourth criterion is the shift in students' and teachers' attitudes toward AI. In Vietnam, where digital resources are uneven and skepticism remains common, measuring confidence, motivation, and willingness to use AI is essential. Surveys and reflective journals can capture whether students feel empowered or alienated by AI tools.

Learning outcomes. The fifth criterion is improvement in both artistic and pedagogical results. This can be measured by comparing the quality of lesson plans, classroom activities, and creative projects between AI-assisted and non-AI student groups. However, evaluation should not only look at the final product but also at the creative process, such as whether AI encouraged experimentation, faster ideation, or more adaptive teaching strategies.

Sustainability and post-graduate use. The final criterion is whether graduates continue to use AI in their professional practice. Tracking the long term use of AI by alumni can indicate whether integration in training programs has lasting value. For Vietnam, this also reflects whether AI adoption is realistic given school resources, infrastructure, and cultural expectations.

To organize these criteria, the evaluation model is structured across three levels:

- Learner level: Focus on individual creativity, reflective journals, sketches, and AI tool usage.
- Teacher development level: Assess lesson design, classroom simulations, and ethical practices.
- System level: Evaluate curriculum integration, adoption rates, and stakeholder satisfaction.

In Vietnam, applying this three-phase model requires careful piloting. Institutions such as SGU or HCMUFA, with stronger digital foundations, can test the framework first, while traditional institutions may adapt gradually. Pilot programs should include both quantitative measures (rubrics, grades) and qualitative feedback (student reflections, faculty interviews).

In summary, evaluation should not focus only on how often AI is used, but on how it supports creativity, ethical practice, and long-term teaching capacity. By embedding these multidimensional criteria, Fine Arts Teacher Training programs in Vietnam can ensure that AI is used responsibly and meaningfully, enhancing both artistic education and professional readiness.

DRAWBACKS AND FUTURE DIRECTION

Despite the structured nature of the proposed AI integration framework in fine art teacher training programs, its practical application has several limitations that require further exploration and refinement. One significant challenge lies in the uneven readiness of institutions in terms of the digital infrastructure and pedagogical transformation. While universities such as HCMUFA and SGU have made strides in integrating digital media and applying IT skills into their curricula, others still rely heavily on traditional approaches with limited exposure to advanced digital or AI tools. This discrepancy may hinder the comprehensive implementation of the three-phase model in diverse educational settings.

Moreover, the shift from foundational to empowered AI usage requires sustained professional development and instructional innovation as outlined in the proposed model. Without adequate support in terms of training, time, and technical assistance, instructors may find it difficult to facilitate the transition from structured to student-led AI exploration. The integration of AI, especially at the "AI-Empowered" level, demands not only digital literacy, but also the ability to critically guide students through complex creative and pedagogical processes.

Another concern that has emerged through experimental case studies relates to ethical considerations, particularly regarding authorship and originality in AI-supported artistic production. Students and faculty members expressed uncertainty about the boundary between AI assistance and creative ownership. These concerns are particularly pronounced in art education, in which fostering personal expression and authenticity remains a core value. Therefore, future implementations must include explicit ethical guidelines and reflective training to help students navigate the nuanced relationship between human creativity and machine-generated content.

In addition, although the proposed multilevel evaluation model (learner–teacher–system) provides a comprehensive framework for assessing effectiveness, its empirical reliability and feasibility remain untested. To ensure its applicability, pilot implementation in selected institutions is necessary to refine the indicators, validate the assessment tools, and gather feedback from both faculty and students.

Without this practical testing, it would be difficult to measure the true impact of AI on learning outcomes and pedagogical development.

Future efforts should prioritize the development and evaluation of pilot programs based on the proposed framework. These experiments should focus on capturing not only quantitative improvements in learning outcomes but also qualitative shifts in student creativity, teaching practices, and institutional adaptability. Simultaneously, collaboration between art education institutions should be fostered to build shared resources, encourage innovation, and support consistent practices in AI-enhanced teaching.

Another direction involves the localization of AI tools to better reflect Vietnamese language, art forms, and educational values. Current tools, such as DALL-E or Wombo Dream, are largely developed in Western contexts, which may limit their cultural resonance and pedagogical relevance. Developing or adapting AI platforms to suit the Vietnamese fine arts education environment could significantly enhance its accessibility and impact.

Finally, ethical awareness and long-term professional applications should become integral parts of the training process. Students must be equipped with technical skills and the ability to critically reflect on their choices when using AI, ensuring that the use of technology does not diminish the role of human judgment and creativity. Institutional policy also plays a vital role in sustaining AI integration, which requires investment in infrastructure, curricular reform, and clear strategies for equitable access.

In summary, the integration of AI into Fine Arts Teacher Education presents significant and complex challenges. To move forward, a careful balance must be maintained between innovation and ethical responsibility and between technological empowerment and human agency. The proposed framework offers a foundation, but its success depends on ongoing adaptation, inclusive participation, and deep commitment to pedagogical integrity in the digital age.

CONCLUSION

The integration of AI into Fine Arts Teacher Training program represents a transformative opportunity to reimagine the structure, content, and delivery of pedagogical training in the digital age. Through a combination of literature analysis, case studies, and program evaluations across Vietnamese institutions, this chapter has demonstrated that AI is not merely a technical tool but also a catalyst for renewing creative education, enhancing teaching capacity, and shaping new models of learner engagement.

The proposed three-phase integration model, ranging from AI-Controlled to AI-Empowered learning, offers a developmentally appropriate pathway that aligns with the cognitive and pedagogical progression of fine art teacher trainees. The framework ensures that AI becomes a meaningful, ethical, and contextually relevant component of teacher education by embedding it into foundational, applied, and innovative learning stages. Moreover, this study emphasizes the importance of localized adaptation, ethical training, and interdisciplinary collaboration as key enablers for successful implementation.

At the program level, the findings highlight that, while the Vietnamese Fine Arts Teacher Training program already includes strong foundations in artistic skill development and pedagogical competence, further alignment with digital competencies and AI-assisted methodologies is both necessary and feasible. Practical examples from institutions such as UMK and Lindenwood underscore the global relevance of AI in art education and provide valuable insights into the challenges and success of implementation.

Ultimately, this chapter advocates for a shift in perspective from viewing AI as a supplementary tool to embracing it as a pedagogical partner in creative and teacher training processes. Future success will depend on the ability of educators, institutions, and policymakers to implement structured, ethical, and learner-centered strategies that ensure that AI integration enhances, rather than compromises, the core values of art and education. In doing so, Vietnam's Fine Arts Teacher Training program system can position itself at the forefront of educational innovation, preparing future teachers not only for today's classrooms, but also for the evolving landscapes of tomorrow.

REFERENCES

Akwei, C., Amoako, I., & Damoah, I. S. (2017). *The Role of Technology Innovation in Shaping Student Learning Experience in Higher Education.*

Ayanwale, M. A., Adelana, O. P., & Odufuwa, T. T. (2024). Exploring STEAM teachers' trust in AI-based educational technologies: A structural equation modelling approach. *Discover Education, 3*(1), 44. DOI: 10.1007/s44217-024-00092-z

Baran, E. (2016). Investigating faculty technology mentoring as a university-wide professional development model. *Journal of Computing in Higher Education, 28*(1), 45–71. DOI: 10.1007/s12528-015-9104-7

Bayaga, A. (2025). Leveraging AI-enhanced and emerging technologies for pedagogical innovations in higher education. *Education and Information Technologies, 30*(1), 1045–1072. DOI: 10.1007/s10639-024-13122-y

Belt, E., & Lowenthal, P. (2020). Developing Faculty to Teach with Technology: Themes from the Literature. *TechTrends, 64*(2), 248–259. DOI: 10.1007/s11528-019-00447-6

Bequette, J. W., & Brennan, C. (2008). Advancing "Media Arts" Education in "Visual Arts" Classrooms: Addressing Policy Ambiguities and Gaps in Art Teacher Preparation. *Studies in Art Education, 49*(4), 328–342. DOI: 10.1080/00393541.2008.11518745

Best, M., & MacGregor, D. (2017). Transitioning Design and Technology Education from physical classrooms to virtual spaces: Implications for pre-service teacher education. *International Journal of Technology and Design Education, 27*(2), 201–213. DOI: 10.1007/s10798-015-9350-z

Beymer, R. (1970). On Teacher Training. *Art Education, 23*(1), 36–37. DOI: 10.2307/3191402

Blouin, D. D., & Moss, A. R. (2015). Graduate Student Teacher Training: Still Relevant (and Missing?) 20 Years Later. *Teaching Sociology, 43*(2), 126–136. DOI: 10.1177/0092055X14565516

Chen, X., Zou, D., Xie, H., Cheng, G., & Liu, C. (2022). Two Decades of Artificial Intelligence in Education: Contributors, Collaborations, Research Topics, Challenges, and Future Directions. *Journal of Educational Technology & Society, 25*(1), 28–47.

Engel, J. B. (1989). Preserving Quality: Teacher Training from a Liberal Arts Perspective. *Phi Delta Kappan, 70*(6), 475–477.

Habib, S., Vogel, T., & Thorne, E. (2025). Student perspectives on creative pedagogy: Considerations for the Age of AI. *Thinking Skills and Creativity*, *56*, 101767. DOI: 10.1016/j.tsc.2025.101767

Hanoi National University of Education. (2025, April 26). *Fine Arts Teacher Training program*. https://hnue.edu.vn/tin-tuc/10600

Ho Chi Minh City University of Fine Arts. (n.d.). *Fine Arts Teacher Training program*. Retrieved April 26, 2025, from https://hcmufa.edu.vn/su-pham-my-thuat/

Hutson, J. (2024). *Integrating art and AI: Evaluating the educational impact of AI tools in digital art history learning*.

Jones, B. (2023). Breaking Boundaries with Generative AI: Good Practice of Unleashing the Power of ChatGPT for Inter- and Transdisciplinary Breakthroughs in the Age of Complexity. *Journal of the European Honors Council*, *6*(2). Advance online publication. DOI: 10.31378/jehc.177

Kerimbayev, N., Adamova, K., Shadiev, R., & Altinay, Z. (2025). Intelligent educational technologies in individual learning: A systematic literature review. *Smart Learning Environments*, *12*(1), 1. DOI: 10.1186/s40561-024-00360-3

Kundis, L. E. (1954). Teacher Training Programs in Art Education. *Art Education*, *7*(7), 5–19. DOI: 10.2307/3183906

Lauwers, G. (2019). Reshaping Teacher Training to Get the Right Education System for a Knowledge Society. In G. Lauwers, M. Kowalczuk-Walêdziak, A. Korzeniecka-Bondar, & W. Danilewicz (Eds.), *Rethinking Teacher Education for the 21st Century* (1st ed., pp. 43–53). Verlag Barbara Budrich. DOI: 10.2307/j.ctvpb3xhh.7

Lockhart, E. N. S. (2024). Creativity in the age of AI: The human condition and the limits of machine generation. *Journal of Cultural Cognitive Science*. Advance online publication. DOI: 10.1007/s41809-024-00158-2

Marshall, J. (2005). Connecting Art, Learning, and Creativity: A Case for Curriculum Integration. *Studies in Art Education*, *46*(3), 227–241. DOI: 10.1080/00393541.2005.11650076

Mayo, S. (2024). Co-creating with AI in Art Education: On the Precipice of the Next Terrain. *Education Journal*, *13*(3), 3. Advance online publication. DOI: 10.11648/j.edu.20241303.15

Miralay, F. (2024). Use of Artificial Intelligence and Augmented Reality Tools in Art Education Course. *Pegem Journal of Education and Instruction*, *14*(3), 44–50.

Mustafa, M. Y., Tlili, A., Lampropoulos, G., Huang, R., Jandrić, P., Zhao, J., Salha, S., Xu, L., Panda, S., Kinshuk, , López-Pernas, S., & Saqr, M. (2024). A systematic review of literature reviews on artificial intelligence in education (AIED): A roadmap to a future research agenda. *Smart Learning Environments, 11*(1), 59. DOI: 10.1186/s40561-024-00350-5

National University Of Art Education. (n.d.). *Fine Arts Teacher Training program.* Retrieved April 26, 2025, from https://spnttw.edu.vn/dao-tao/ke-hoach-dao-tao-toan-khoa-nam-hoc-2020-2021/

Owoc, M. L., Sawicka, A., & Weichbroth, P. (2021). Artificial Intelligence Technologies in Education: Benefits, Challenges and Strategies of Implementation. In Owoc, M. L., & Pondel, M. (Eds.), *Artificial Intelligence for Knowledge Management* (pp. 37–58). Springer International Publishing., DOI: 10.1007/978-3-030-85001-2_4

Sáez Velasco, S., Alaguero, M., Delgado-Benito, V., & Rodríguez-Cano, S. (2024). Analysing the Impact of Generative AI in Arts Education: A Cross-Disciplinary Perspective of Educators and Students in Higher Education. *Informatics (MDPI), 11*(2), 37. DOI: 10.3390/informatics11020037

Saigon University. (n.d.). *Fine Arts Teacher Training program.* Retrieved April 26, 2025, from https://daotao.sgu.edu.vn/index.php/van-ban/chuong-trinh-dao-tao

Shuliar, V., Shkurko, V., Polukhtovych, T., Semeniako, Y., Shanaieva-Tsymbal, L., & Koltok, L. (2023). Using Artificial Intelligence in Education. *BRAIN. Broad Research in Artificial Intelligence and Neuroscience, 14*(3), 3. DOI: 10.18662/brain/14.3/488

Smilan, C., & Miraglia, K. M. (2009). ART TEACHERS AS LEADERS OF Authentic Art Integration. *Art Education, 62*(6), 39–45. DOI: 10.1080/00043125.2009.11519044

Tahiru, F. (2021). AI in Education: A Systematic Literature Review. *Journal of Cases on Information Technology, 23*(1), 1–20. DOI: 10.4018/JCIT.2021010101

Tarnavska, T. (2013). The role and use of Information technology in higher education. *Edukacja - Technika - Informatyka, IV*(2), 98–103.

University of Arts. Hue University. (n.d.). *Fine Arts Teacher Training program.* Retrieved April 26, 2025, from https://tuyensinh.hueuni.edu.vn/Program/Detail/17

Wang, S., Wang, F., Zhu, Z., Wang, J., Tran, T., & Du, Z. (2024). Artificial intelligence in education: A systematic literature review. *Expert Systems with Applications, 252*, 124167. DOI: 10.1016/j.eswa.2024.124167

Yusuf, H., Money, A., & Daylamani-Zad, D. (2025). Pedagogical AI conversational agents in higher education: A conceptual framework and survey of the state of the art. *Educational Technology Research and Development, 73*(2), 815–874. Advance online publication. DOI: 10.1007/s11423-025-10447-4

Zailuddin, M. F. N. O., Harun, N. A. N., Rahim, H. A. A., Kamaruzaman, A. F., Berahim, M. H., Harun, M. H., & Ibrahim, Y. (2024). Redefining creative education: A case study analysis of AI in design courses. *Journal of Research in Innovative Teaching &amp. Learning, 17*(2), 282–296. DOI: 10.1108/JRIT-01-2024-0019

Zhou, C. (2023). Integration of modern technologies in higher education on the example of artificial intelligence use. *Education and Information Technologies, 28*(4), 3893–3910. DOI: 10.1007/s10639-022-11309-9 [illegible] and Technology, A. [illegible] (20[illegible]). [illegible] conversational agents in higher education: A conceptual framework and review of the state of the art. [illegible] Education Technology [illegible], [illegible]. [illegible] doi:10.1016/j.[illegible]

Zeng, [illegible] Reuben, M. H., [illegible] (20[illegible]). [illegible] education [illegible]. [illegible]

Zhao, [illegible] (2018). [illegible]

Chapter 11
Integration of Artificial Intelligence Tools Into the Agroforestry Engineering Curriculum

Fernando Aragon-Rodriguez
http://orcid.org/0000-0001-5417-4354
Universidad Miguel Hernández, Spain

Ivan Herranz-Matey
https://orcid.org/0000-0001-7959-0688
Universidad Politécnica de Madrid, Spain

Carmen Rocamora
http://orcid.org/0000-0002-0062-0598
Universidad Miguel Hernández, Spain

Andres Almeida-Nauñay
http://orcid.org/0000-0002-9742-9334
Universidad Politécnica de Madrid, Spain

Alicia Perdigones
http://orcid.org/0000-0001-8006-6437
Universidad Politécnica de Madrid, Spain

ABSTRACT

The present study explores how Artificial Intelligence (AI) technologies can be effectively embedded in agroforestry engineering education. It highlights the growing importance of digital competences and AI in agricultural, forestry, and environ-

DOI: 10.4018/979-8-3373-1285-9.ch011

mental sectors. The paper stresses that curricula must evolve to include tools like GIS, remote sensing, and machine learning, while also addressing faculty training, infrastructure needs, and licensing costs. University–industry collaboration is presented as crucial for aligning academic content with real-world demands. Ethical considerations—such as data privacy, algorithmic bias, and the role of human oversight—are emphasized, referencing UNESCO's guidelines. In conclusion, the study calls for comprehensive curricular reform, investment in infrastructure and educator training, and ethical safeguards to ensure graduates are well-prepared for a rapidly evolving, AI-driven job market.

THE UNIVERSITY–INDUSTRY RELATIONSHIP: A CORNERSTONE OF PROFESSIONAL TRAINING

The relationship between universities and industry has long been a central concern in higher education, one that has become increasingly critical in periods of rapid technological or economic change. It is widely acknowledged that a close and dynamic partnership between academic institutions and industry stakeholders is essential for ensuring that students receive up-to-date, high-quality training aligned with emerging technologies and market demands.

The primary objective of higher education institutions is to equip students with the competences necessary for a successful integration into the labor market. To achieve this, it is vital that academic staff remain abreast of technological advances while also ensuring that curricula remain sufficiently flexible to adapt to sectoral transformations. This calls for the active involvement of all stakeholders, including faculty members and university governance bodies.

In the field of agroforestry engineering, which encompasses agricultural, forestry, food, and environmental engineering, these transformations are primarily driven by technological developments. Over the past five years, the adoption of artificial intelligence (AI) has significantly accelerated change within the sector, necessitating corresponding updates in academic programs.

CURRICULAR STRUCTURE AND CORE COMPETENCES IN AGROFORESTRY ENGINEERING

The agroforestry engineering curriculum is inherently multidisciplinary, comprising instruction in biological sciences and agricultural, livestock, and forestry production, as well as rigorous training in mathematics, engineering, and economics. According to the American Society of Agricultural and Biological Engineers

(ABET, 2025), the curriculum must include mathematics through differential equations, and a foundation in both biological and engineering sciences that aligns with the program's educational objectives and practical applications in fields such as agriculture, aquaculture, forestry, and natural or human resources management.

Within this educational framework, both technical and transversal (or "soft") skills are emphasized. As noted by Indeed Mexico (2024), essential technical competences for agronomic engineers include a strong grasp of biological sciences, proficiency in the design and management of agricultural machinery, and the use of engineering software. Soft skills such as leadership, teamwork, and adaptability are also deemed critical.

The Official College of Agronomist Engineers of Central Spain and the Canary Islands (2024) highlights that the most in-demand technical skills in the field include crop and facility management techniques, knowledge of environmental and agri-food regulations, and familiarity with quality standards. Furthermore, it underscores the importance of digital proficiency, particularly in the use of tools such as GIS, AutoCAD, Excel, and specialized agricultural management and data analysis software.

In conclusion, the agroforestry engineering curriculum offers a comprehensive education that integrates biological, mathematical, and economic disciplines. This multidimensional approach fosters graduates' adaptability and holistic understanding of complex systems, with digital skills playing an increasingly prominent role in their professional preparation.

Agroforestry Engineering Labor Market

According to the U.S. Bureau of Labor Statistics (2024), employment in architecture and engineering occupations is projected to grow at a rate faster than the average for all occupations in the United States between 2023 and 2033. An estimated 200,000 new jobs per year are expected to arise, driven by both employment growth and the replacement of workers leaving the labor force. Within this broad field, agricultural, food, and environmental engineering disciplines are forecasted to experience particularly favorable employment trends. These positive prospects are largely attributed to the growing demand for sustainable and efficient solutions in food production and natural resource management. The only engineering discipline expected to face a downward trend is forestry engineering, a decline attributed to increased automation and technological advancements in the sector.

For agricultural engineers specifically, the Bureau projects an 8% increase in employment, driven by the necessity to develop sustainable and efficient agricultural systems. Similarly, environmental engineering roles are expected to grow by 7%, while occupations in agricultural and food science are anticipated to see an 8%

increase. This growth is closely linked to research in advanced agricultural production methods and the rising demand for healthy and sustainable food products.

Comparable projections have been published in Europe. The European Centre for the Development of Vocational Training (CEDEFOP, 2025) estimates a significant decline in employment among agricultural workers across Europe between 2022 and 2035. However, due to an ageing workforce and increasing retirements, approximately 1.8 million job vacancies are expected to emerge during this period. The report highlights that the integration of digital technologies—such as precision agriculture and automated machinery—is transforming the skill requirements of the sector, with a marked increase in demand for advanced digital and technical competences. While there will be fewer opportunities for low-skilled labor, the need for specialized professionals, particularly in environmental engineering, is expected to grow. These professionals will be essential in addressing pressing challenges related to energy efficiency, waste management, and environmental sustainability.

Furthermore, environmental policy developments and sustainability initiatives are reshaping occupational profiles, placing increasing emphasis on "green" skills and knowledge of the circular economy. While traditional agricultural roles may face employment challenges, the transition to more sustainable and technologically advanced practices is generating new opportunities for agricultural, agroforestry, and environmental engineers. Responding to these labor market trends will require sustained investment in education, training, and targeted skill development, particularly in digital and artificial intelligence (AI) competences.

Integrating Digital and AI Competences into Engineering Curricula

Engineering education has already begun incorporating digital skills into its curricula, with a particular focus on engineering software training. According to the Food and Agriculture Organization of the United Nations (FAO, 2025), agricultural engineers must be proficient in technologies such as Geographic Information Systems (GIS), remote sensing, big data analysis, and automation. These competences are considered essential for addressing challenges related to climate change, resource efficiency, and food security. Subsequent sections of this report will elaborate on the most relevant software tools for inclusion in agroforestry engineering programs.

A current priority for higher education institutions is to integrate AI training into engineering curricula with the same level of emphasis. Many of the benefits and challenges associated with software training are also applicable to AI education. Among the key benefits of incorporating specialized software and AI tools into the classroom are enhanced problem-solving skills, real-world application of knowledge, and improved employability. However, several challenges must be addressed:

- Faculty Training: Not all academic staff possess the required familiarity with emerging technologies and AI tools.
- Technical and Infrastructure Requirements: Adequate computing resources, reliable internet access, and properly equipped classrooms are essential for effective implementation.
- Licensing Costs: Commercial software can impose a significant financial burden on universities, particularly those with limited budgets.
- Continuous Updates: The rapid evolution of software and AI technologies necessitates frequent curriculum revisions to maintain relevance and effectiveness.

In conclusion, while the integration of AI and digital technologies into engineering education presents logistical and financial challenges, it is essential for preparing graduates to meet the demands of a rapidly changing and increasingly digital labor market.

Theoretical Frameworks for AI Integration in Engineering Education

The integration of artificial intelligence (AI) into engineering education can be better understood when anchored in established theoretical frameworks that explain how learning occurs, how competences are developed, and how educators adapt to pedagogical change.

From a constructivist learning perspective, knowledge is not passively transmitted but actively constructed by learners through interaction with their environment. In this regard, AI-based tools such as simulation platforms, intelligent tutoring systems, and generative AI applications can support learners in exploring complex engineering systems, testing hypotheses, and iteratively refining their understanding. Rather than replacing cognitive effort, AI can function as a mediating tool that enhances experiential engagement and supports deeper conceptual learning.

Closely related is experiential learning theory (Kolb), which emphasizes learning as a cyclical process involving concrete experience, reflective observation, abstract conceptualization, and active experimentation. AI-enabled environments—such as virtual laboratories, digital twins, and predictive modeling tools—facilitate this cycle by allowing students to engage in realistic problem-solving scenarios that mirror professional engineering practice. In agroforestry engineering, for example, AI-based crop simulation or environmental modeling systems enable students to experiment with variables that would otherwise be difficult or costly to manipulate in real-world contexts.

In parallel, faculty development frameworks, particularly communities of practice and continuous professional learning models, highlight that effective technology integration depends not only on individual skills but also on institutional culture, peer learning, and sustained professional support. Within this view, faculty adoption of AI is shaped by collaborative learning environments where educators share practices, co-develop materials, and collectively negotiate the pedagogical role of emerging technologies.

Together, these frameworks suggest that AI integration in engineering education is not merely a technological shift but a pedagogical transformation, requiring alignment between learner-centered approaches, experiential methodologies, and sustained faculty development structures.

Ethics in the Engineering Curriculum

Ethical education in engineering has gained increasing relevance over the past few decades, being recognized as a fundamental component in the development of socially responsible and professionally accountable engineers. Numerous scholarly studies have explored the incorporation of ethics into engineering programs, highlighting both notable progress and persistent challenges.

In the United States, the integration of ethics into engineering education has evolved considerably since the 1970s. Initially, ethical considerations were addressed only marginally within academic curricula. However, over time, a combination of factors—including changes to accreditation criteria by ABET, a heightened awareness of engineers' social responsibilities, and evolving market demands—has led to a more structured and comprehensive inclusion of ethics in engineering programs (Ocone, 2013). A similar trend has been observed in other countries.

A prominent approach in current educational practice is the model of ethics across the curriculum, which advocates for the integration of ethical considerations into technical subjects rather than relegating them to isolated modules. This pedagogical strategy fosters a more holistic understanding of ethics as embedded in professional practice. Nevertheless, ongoing challenges include the absence of consensus regarding ethical learning outcomes and a scarcity of empirical research to support evidence-based pedagogical practices (Kidd et al., 2020; Martin et al., 2021).

A particularly pressing contemporary issue is the ethical dimension of artificial intelligence (AI), which presents novel challenges for higher education and necessitates a strengthened focus on the ethical implications of AI technologies within university curricula. In this context, the UNESCO Recommendation on the Ethics of Artificial Intelligence (2021) provides a foundational international reference.

Adopted in November 2021, this UNESCO Recommendation offers a comprehensive global framework for guiding the ethical development and deployment of AI technologies. Recognized as one of the most significant policy texts in this domain, it acknowledges both the transformative potential and the associated risks of AI. It places a strong emphasis on human rights, environmental sustainability, and inclusive governance throughout the entire AI lifecycle.

The Recommendation articulates several core values:

- Human Rights and Dignity: AI systems must uphold and promote human rights, ensuring that their development and deployment do not compromise individual liberties or dignity.
- Environmental Flourishing: AI should contribute to environmental sustainability, reducing ecological footprints and fostering biodiversity.
- Diversity and Inclusion: AI technologies must respect cultural, linguistic, and gender diversity, ensuring equitable access and participation.
- Peace and Justice: The application of AI should support social cohesion, prevent conflict, and promote fairness and justice.

To operationalize these values, the Recommendation sets forth a series of ethical principles:

- Proportionality: AI applications should be appropriate to their intended purposes and must not cause harm to individuals or society.
- Safety: Systems must be robust, secure, and resilient to misuse or malicious interference.
- Fairness and Non-Discrimination: Measures should be taken to avoid bias in AI systems and to ensure fair treatment across demographic groups.
- Sustainability: AI must support the Sustainable Development Goals, balancing technological progress with environmental stewardship.
- Privacy and Data Protection: Individuals' rights to privacy must be safeguarded through transparent data governance frameworks.
- Human Oversight and Agency: Critical decisions, particularly those affecting human lives, must remain under human control, with AI serving as a support tool.
- Transparency and Explainability: AI systems must operate transparently and provide comprehensible explanations of their processes and decisions.
- Accountability and Responsibility: Clear mechanisms for accountability must be established, assigning responsibility for AI outcomes to appropriate stakeholders.

The UNESCO Recommendation thus serves as a comprehensive guide for the ethical governance of AI, underscoring the need to ensure that these technologies contribute to the common good and benefit all sectors of society. Its integration into engineering education is essential for preparing future professionals capable of navigating the ethical complexities of emerging digital technologies.

Applications of Artificial Intelligence in Agroforestry Engineering

The integration of artificial intelligence (AI) into agricultural engineering and the agri-food industry is advancing rapidly, particularly within the frameworks of precision agriculture and Industry 4.0. AI technologies are enhancing both the sustainability and operational efficiency of agro-industrial systems. Among its key applications, AI—particularly through deep learning—has been used for plant disease and pest detection via leaf image analysis, as well as for fruit yield estimation (Arakawa et al., 2024; Arogundade & Tochukwu, 2024; Zhang et al., 2023). Moreover, AI has contributed to the optimization of robotics in both agriculture and food industry contexts, enabling real-time field monitoring, soil condition analysis, and water usage management (J. Guo et al., 2025).

The development of Industry 4.0 has introduced transformative concepts such as big data analytics, the Internet of Things (IoT), and cloud computing, all of which are increasingly integrated with AI technologies (Hou et al., 2020). These innovations are contributing to more informed, data-driven decision-making processes across the agricultural value chain.

In addition to operational AI, generative AI tools, particularly those capable of producing textual content, are being applied in a range of administrative and technical activities. For instance, they are used to automate the drafting of environmental impact reports—embedding relevant local legislation—thereby reducing processing time and improving workflow efficiency. They are also useful in generating statistical analyses and conducting market research.

Given their growing relevance, these technologies should be systematically integrated into the curricula of engineering programs, ensuring that graduates possess the foundational knowledge and practical competences to engage with these tools effectively in professional settings (Southworth et al., 2023). This integration can be better understood through concrete examples of how AI is applied in agroforestry engineering teaching practice.

Case Examples of AI Integration in Agroforestry Engineering Education

The integration of artificial intelligence into agroforestry engineering education is increasingly reflected in practical, data-driven learning activities that connect theoretical knowledge with real-world applications.

Case Example: AI-Based Tractor Market Analysis for Agricultural Planning

A practical example of AI integration in agroforestry engineering education involves the use of machine learning models to analyze national tractor markets. In this approach, students work with datasets derived from agricultural ministry sources, including tractor registrations, farm census data, and farm income at the municipal level.

The analysis incorporates multiple variables such as tractor type (e.g., row crop, utility, specialty, compact), engine power, trim level (value, mid-spec, high-spec), and brand. Using AI-optimized models, students identify patterns in machinery adoption, regional demand, and correlations between farm income and equipment investment.

This type of project enables students to engage with real-world datasets, develop data analysis and modeling skills, and understand how AI can support decision-making in agricultural policy and agribusiness strategy.

Case Example: AI-Based Tractor Pricing Models in Engineering Education

Another applied example focuses on the development of predictive models for new and used tractor pricing. In this case, students analyze real market transaction data and explore how variables such as wheelbase, mass, engine power, transmission type, and user interface features influence pricing.

Students compare parametric and non-parametric machine learning models across datasets of varying sizes, examining how model performance changes depending on data availability. This approach highlights the advantages of AI-optimized parametric models in small-data contexts, which are common in specialized agricultural markets.

Through this exercise, students gain insight into model selection, data limitations, and the practical application of AI in equipment valuation and market forecasting, while strengthening their critical understanding of how different modeling approaches perform under real-world constraints.From a faculty perspective, implementing these types of activities presents several challenges. Instructors must design learning experiences that balance technical complexity with conceptual clarity, ensuring that students engage critically with model assumptions and limitations rather than relying unreflectively on computational outputs. Additionally, the use of real-world datasets requires careful curation and contextualization, reinforcing the evolving role of faculty as facilitators of data-informed and inquiry-based learning environments.

These illustrative examples highlight that the integration of artificial intelligence in engineering education extends beyond technological adoption to encompass pedagogical design, faculty preparedness, and institutional support. In this context, a series of critical questions emerge: Are universities prepared to address these technological shifts? Are faculty members adequately trained in AI and digital systems? Should teaching methods and assessment strategies be adapted to reflect these changes? Should the development of competences such as critical thinking be prioritized?.

Key Takeaways: AI Applications in Agroforestry Engineering

- AI is increasingly embedded in core agroforestry practices, including crop monitoring, yield prediction, and resource optimization.
- The educational value of AI lies not only in technical application, but in its ability to support problem-solving and data-driven decision-making.
- Generative AI expands possibilities for analysis, reporting, and creative problem exploration in engineering contexts.
- These developments require not only curriculum updates, but also significant adaptation in teaching practices and faculty competences.

Faculty Development: A Pressing Challenge

The integration of artificial intelligence (AI) into higher education has been widely recognized as a catalyst for pedagogical innovation, requiring continuous adaptation of teaching practices and faculty competences (Tan et al., 2025). In this context, faculty development is no longer a one-time activity but an ongoing process that must respond dynamically to rapid technological change (Ismail et al., 2024).

Despite this recognition, multiple studies indicate that a significant barrier to effective AI integration in education is the insufficient preparation of academic staff. The lack of targeted AI training, combined with varying levels of technological literacy across disciplines, limits educators' ability to meaningfully incorporate AI tools into their teaching practices (Kitcharoen et al., 2024; Tan et al., 2025). In some cases, limited motivation and institutional support further exacerbate this challenge (Aljemely, 2024). Additionally, structural constraints such as inadequate infrastructure and limited access to AI platforms restrict opportunities for experiential learning and experimentation.

These findings suggest that the challenge is not solely individual, but also institutional. Effective faculty development therefore requires systemic approaches that combine training opportunities, resource provision, and organizational incentives. Within this context, short-term targeted interventions have shown promising results. For example, the Artificial Intelligence of Things (AIoT) professional development model demonstrated that even brief, structured training programs can significantly improve faculty knowledge and confidence in using emerging technologies (Kitcharoen et al., 2024). However, such initiatives should be viewed as entry points rather than standalone solutions, as sustained competence development requires continuous engagement and institutional follow-up.

Closely linked to faculty development is the role of university–industry collaboration, which plays a crucial role in aligning academic training with evolving societal and labor market demands (Rossoni et al., 2023). These collaborations provide not only updated technical knowledge but also exposure to real-world applications of AI and digital technologies, thereby supporting both curriculum relevance and faculty upskilling.

Rather than viewing university–industry interaction as a set of isolated activities, it can be understood as a continuum of engagement. At one end are short-term exposure mechanisms, such as internships, technical visits, and guest lectures, which provide students and faculty with insights into current industrial practices. At a deeper level, collaborative formats such as joint research projects, industry-funded academic chairs, and co-designed curricula enable more structural integration of professional knowledge into academic programs. These long-term partnerships are particularly valuable for ensuring that educational content remains aligned with technological and labor market developments, although they require greater coordination and institutional commitment.

Importantly, in the context of AI and digital transformation, university–industry collaboration should not be limited to student employability. It also plays a critical role in faculty development by exposing educators to emerging tools, workflows, and problem-solving approaches used in professional environments. In this sense, industry engagement becomes a mechanism for continuous academic renewal, supporting educators in bridging the gap between theoretical instruction and applied technological practice.

Overall, the convergence of AI integration, faculty development, and university–industry collaboration highlights the need for a more interconnected model of higher education. Such a model positions educators not only as transmitters of knowledge, but as active participants in a continuously evolving ecosystem of technological and pedagogical innovation. The following sections further examine how these dynamics shape curriculum design and digital competence development in engineering education.

Key Takeaways: Faculty Development for AI Integration

- Faculty readiness is a central bottleneck in AI integration within higher education.
- Barriers include limited training, time constraints, lack of incentives, and uneven access to resources.

- Short, targeted training programs can significantly improve AI competences.
- Institutional support structures are essential to sustain long-term faculty engagement with AI.

EVOLUTION OF DIGITAL TOOLS IN ENGINEERING EDUCATION

Engineering education has undergone a profound transformation over recent decades, evolving from traditional lecture-based and paper-centered approaches toward digitally enriched and interactive learning environments. Early developments, such as the introduction of computers and programming tools in the mid-20th century, enabled engineers to perform complex calculations that were previously impractical. Subsequent advances, including the integration of Computer-Aided Design (CAD) in the 1980s, marked a shift toward visualization and simulation as core components of engineering training.

Today, this evolution has culminated in the widespread use of advanced digital tools—often grouped under Computer-Aided Engineering (CAE)—that allow students to model, simulate, and optimize systems across a wide range of engineering domains. These tools are now embedded in many engineering curricula, not merely as technical instruments, but as pedagogical resources that support experiential and problem-based learning.

From a teaching perspective, the value of digital tools lies less in their specific technical functionalities and more in their capacity to enhance learning processes. Simulation environments, for instance, enable students to explore complex, real-world scenarios in a safe and controlled setting, fostering experimentation, iterative thinking, and deeper conceptual understanding. Similarly, data-driven tools and digital platforms support the development of analytical skills and decision-making abilities that are increasingly essential in professional contexts.

In agroforestry engineering, the integration of digital tools is particularly significant due to the sector's reliance on spatial data, environmental monitoring, and resource optimization. Technologies such as Geographic Information Systems (GIS), remote sensing, and data analytics platforms enable students to engage with real-world challenges related to sustainability, land management, and agricultural productivity. These tools bridge the gap between theoretical knowledge and practical application, aligning academic training with industry needs.

However, the rapid expansion of digital technologies also raises important challenges for higher education institutions. One key issue concerns the selection and integration of appropriate tools within the curriculum. Given the vast and continuously evolving ecosystem of software, educators must prioritize pedagogical relevance over technical breadth, ensuring that tools are used to support learning objectives rather than introduced as ends in themselves.

Another critical consideration relates to accessibility and equity. While proprietary software often offers advanced capabilities, it may impose financial constraints on institutions and students. Open-source alternatives can mitigate these barriers, promoting wider access and fostering collaborative learning environments. Nonetheless, the choice between different types of tools should be guided by educational goals, institutional resources, and long-term sustainability.

For faculty, these developments imply a shift in roles and responsibilities. Educators are no longer solely transmitters of knowledge but facilitators of learning experiences in technology-rich environments. This transition requires not only technical familiarity with digital tools but also pedagogical strategies that effectively integrate them into teaching. Without adequate support and training, there is a risk that technology adoption remains superficial or fragmented.

In this context, the successful integration of digital tools in engineering education depends on a balanced approach that combines technological innovation with pedagogical reflection. Rather than focusing on the mastery of specific software packages, curricula should emphasize transferable skills such as critical thinking, problem-solving, and the ability to adapt to emerging technologies. This perspective is particularly relevant in the current context of artificial intelligence, where tools are rapidly evolving and reshaping both professional practice and educational environments.

Benefits of Using Software in University Engineering Education

The integration of computational programs in university-level engineering education is widely recognized as essential for adequately preparing students. The combination of traditional theoretical instruction with the practical application of mathematical and calculation software significantly enhances students' digital competences, problem-solving abilities, and readiness to face real-world engineering challenges.

Key benefits associated with the incorporation of software tools in engineering pedagogy include:

- Development of Advanced Digital and Analytical Skills: Through hands-on experience with tools such as Excel, MATLAB, and other mathematical software, students acquire crucial digital skills, including data analysis and modeling. These competences are regarded as valuable both for academic performance and future professional practice (Bogdanov et al., 2024; Sadikin et al., 2021). Additionally, the integration of such tools increases student engagement with computing and simulation, fostering a deeper understanding of mathematical concepts (Enelund et al., 2011).

- Enhanced Problem-Solving Capabilities: Software empowers students to address more complex and realistic problems that extend beyond the simplified examples commonly found in textbooks, thereby promoting deeper comprehension and learning (Whiteman & Nygren, 2000).
- Increased Engagement and Learning Efficiency: The use of educational software and simulation tools stimulates student activity, optimizes instructional time, and facilitates more effective and interactive learning experiences (Devin et al., 2020; Skafa et al., 2023).

To ensure meaningful learning outcomes through software use, a balanced integration of theoretical foundations and practical application is required. Students should first attain mastery of fundamental concepts prior to engaging with software tools.

Embedding software within cooperative learning and project-based courses or seminars fosters collaboration, critical thinking, and the application of digital tools to authentic engineering tasks. In cooperative learning environments, students of varying academic abilities collaborate in small groups toward shared objectives. Advocates of this approach assert that the active exchange of ideas within such groups not only enhances student interest but also cultivates critical thinking skills. Students assume responsibility for their tasks and manage their own learning, while instructors function as facilitators or guides. Interaction, mutual support, and the development of social skills—such as communication, negotiation, and respect for diverse perspectives—are strongly encouraged (Curtis & Lawson, 2019).

Online platforms, shared editing tools (e.g., Google Docs, Microsoft 365), discussion forums, and project management software enable synchronous or asynchronous collaboration regardless of physical location. These tools support task distribution, idea exchange, peer review, and collective knowledge construction, while also contributing to the acquisition of foundational digital skills. Collaborative presentation software (such as Google Slides or Prezi) allows groups to jointly create presentations that incorporate diverse viewpoints and competences.

Project-based learning is an educational methodology emphasizing problem-solving and meaningful learning, enabling students to autonomously organize knowledge, complete work products, and focus on scientific concepts and principles (Cole et al., 2002). Projects often have real-world applications, requiring students to apply knowledge and skills across multiple domains. The development of projects or products is vital for helping students integrate and reconstruct knowledge, enhance professional skills, increase discipline interest, and improve teamwork capabilities (P. Guo et al., 2020). Within this framework, the use of calculation and simulation software in instruction promotes the acquisition of tools essential for students' future professional careers.

For software integration in teaching to be successful, adequate coordination among faculty members is necessary to align software usage with course objectives and ensure that students do not circumvent fundamental learning. It is critical to guarantee comprehension of underlying principles to avoid inappropriate dependency on software for basic tasks. Consequently, assessment should not focus solely on the correct use of software but also evaluate conceptual mastery and the ability to apply engineering principles to interpret and validate results generated by digital tools. Educators must encourage critical and reflective software use, motivating students to understand the theoretical foundations supporting the calculations performed.

In conclusion, comprehensive engineering education requires a curriculum that combines a solid theoretical base with the practical application of software to facilitate meaningful learning. Guided introductions to software through seminars or hands-on classes aid familiarization with interfaces and applications, enabling a seamless transition from theory to practice. Opportunities for software use outside the classroom or scheduled hours motivate students to explore and deepen their understanding of topics of interest while seeking solutions to complex problems.

Recognizing the importance of integrating digital tools in education, many public institutions have established strategic plans to adapt education to the digital era. At the European level, the Digital Education Action Plan 2021-2027 (European Commission, 2020) was developed in response to the growing significance of digital technologies in education and training, catalyzed by the COVID-19 crisis. Its primary objective is to modernize educational and training systems for the digital age by enhancing the digital competences of all citizens and ensuring inclusive, high-quality education that prepares Europe for the dual ecological and digital transition. The plan is structured around two strategic priorities:

- Fostering a High-Performing Digital Education Ecosystem: Addressing technological gaps in infrastructure, devices, and organizational capacities is fundamental. This includes the ability to offer hybrid learning modes and ensure accessibility for all individuals regardless of socioeconomic status or location. Moreover, there is a need for high-quality digital educational content, user-friendly tools, value-added services, and secure platforms that respect privacy and ethical standards.
- Improving Digital Competences and Skills: It is critical to promote digital skills across all levels to drive growth, innovation, and build a more equitable and inclusive society. This encompasses not only technical skills but also digital literacy to manage information overload, distinguish facts from misinformation, and protect personal data.

Challenges of Artificial Intelligence

Artificial intelligence (AI) has become a transformative force in education, enabling new forms of personalized learning, intelligent tutoring, and data-driven decision-making. Key technological domains such as machine learning, natural language processing, computer vision, robotics, and expert systems contribute to these developments by supporting adaptive instruction, human–machine interaction, and automated educational support systems (Abioye et al., 2021). In particular, AI-powered tools can personalize learning pathways, enhance student engagement, and provide real-time feedback, thereby promoting autonomy and self-directed learning in engineering education (Baker & Inventado, 2014; Prather et al., 2023).

Beyond technical applications, AI is increasingly integrated into engineering education as a pedagogical enabler that supports problem-based learning and the development of analytical competences. In agroforestry engineering, these technologies contribute to more interactive and applied learning environments by simulating real-world systems and complex decision-making processes, thus aligning academic training with the demands of digitalized and automated industries.

In parallel, generative AI has introduced new opportunities for enhancing creativity, critical thinking, and iterative problem-solving. Through human–AI co-creation processes, students can explore multiple solution pathways, refine ideas, and engage in reflective learning activities. Evidence suggests that such interactions can enhance creative self-efficacy and innovation capacity when AI is used as a supportive rather than substitutive tool (Baltà-Salvador et al., 2025; Requejo et al., 2024). Similarly, prompt-based interaction with large language models encourages students to develop information literacy and critical reasoning skills, positioning them as active participants in the learning process (Cain, 2024).

However, despite these pedagogical opportunities, the integration of AI in education presents several significant challenges that must be critically addressed. A first challenge concerns conceptual and terminological ambiguity. The rapid evolution of AI technologies often leads to inconsistent definitions and misunderstandings among students and educators, complicating curriculum design and effective implementation (Levin et al., 2022).

A second challenge relates to the reliability and transparency of AI systems. AI tools may produce inaccurate, context-insensitive, or misleading outputs, particularly when applied to complex educational environments. This raises concerns regarding the validity of AI-supported decision-making in assessment, feedback, and student guidance (Kumar, 2021). Closely related to this issue is algorithmic bias, whereby AI systems may reproduce or amplify existing social inequalities embedded in training data, potentially affecting fairness in educational processes such as evaluation or admissions.

Ethical considerations also constitute a central challenge. Issues related to data privacy, accountability, and human oversight are particularly relevant in educational contexts where sensitive student data are processed. While AI can support personalization and automation, critical academic and pedagogical decisions must remain under human supervision to ensure ethical integrity and contextual judgment (Furman, 2024).

Institutional and pedagogical barriers further complicate AI adoption. Limited infrastructure, uneven access to digital tools, and resistance to technological change among faculty hinder effective implementation. These challenges reinforce the importance of sustained faculty development and institutional support, as previously discussed, to ensure meaningful integration of AI into teaching and learning practices (Mejía-Marín & Gómez-Rivero, 2024; Saura, 2022).

Another important concern is technological dependency. Excessive reliance on AI tools may reduce students' ability to engage in independent reasoning, problem-solving, and creative thinking. This dependency risks undermining the development of core professional competences required in complex and unpredictable real-world contexts (Morales-García et al., 2024; Zhang et al., 2024a).

Finally, the rapid pace of AI development introduces continuous challenges for curriculum design and instructional practice. Educators must constantly update content, methodologies, and assessment strategies to remain aligned with technological advancements, which places additional demands on institutional capacity and academic workload (Liu et al., 2025; Zhang et al., 2024b).

Key Takeaways: Challenges of AI in Engineering Education

- AI introduces significant ethical, pedagogical, and institutional challenges alongside its benefits.
- Risks include academic integrity issues, algorithmic bias, data privacy concerns, and overreliance by students.
- Faculty training and institutional readiness are critical to addressing these challenges effectively.
- The rapid evolution of AI requires continuous curriculum updates and adaptive teaching strategies.

Generative AI challenges

The extensive integration of generative artificial intelligence (GenAI) tools such as ChatGPT within higher education engenders profound and multifaceted challenges to conventional assessment methodologies (Steele, 2023). These challenges encompass concerns regarding academic integrity and potential detriments to student skill development (Bukar et al., 2024). Addressing these issues necessitates a critical re-evaluation of current assessment practices and the formulation of strategies to balance risk mitigation with the effective utilization of AI's benefits (McDonald et al., 2024).

A primary and widely acknowledged challenge is the considerable threat to academic integrity posed by GenAI tools (Bahroun et al., 2023). A scoping review indicated that 54% of examined articles identified this as a major concern. The capacity of GenAI, particularly ChatGPT, to produce coherent, human-like text with minimal input (Gimpel et al., 2023) complicates the differentiation between student-authored and AI-generated work. Empirical studies have demonstrated that neither students nor faculty can reliably distinguish essays written by humans from those generated by ChatGPT (Avila-Chauvet & Mejía, 2023; Kiryakova & Angelova, 2023). This capability fundamentally challenges the principle of originality that underpins scholarly work. Furthermore, AI-generated submissions have achieved high academic scores, including top grades across disciplines such as engineering, economics, medicine, and geography, casting doubt on the continued efficacy of traditional assessments like short-form essays.

Maintaining academic integrity remains imperative. The International Centre for Academic Integrity (ICAI) (Espinoza Vidaurre et al., 2024) emphasizes core values such as honesty, trust, justice, respect, responsibility, and courage—principles increasingly challenged by AI misuse. The rapid proliferation of AI in education has outpaced institutional policy development, precipitating conflicts among students, faculty, and administration over integrity issues (Artyukhov et al., 2024). Notably, some students report that AI use paradoxically disrupts their writing process by increasing their desire to retain control over their work, though concerns regarding dishonesty prevail.

Beyond academic integrity, AI integration raises a complex spectrum of ethical concerns (Von Garrel & Mayer, 2023). A systematic review identified thirty-eight distinct ethical issues associated with ChatGPT (Bukar et al., 2024), which were prioritized via the Analytic Hierarchy Process (AHP). The highest weighted concerns influencing policy decisions on AI use—restriction versus regulation—include copyright, legal, and compliance issues (17.31% weight). Large language models generate text by drawing on extensive external knowledge and sources (Qin & Zhang, 2024), prompting intellectual property considerations. Infodemics and misinformation are frequent concerns (12.96% frequency), reflecting AI's propensity to generate inaccurate or outdated content, thereby compromising educational quality (Sánchez-Prieto et al., 2025). Data privacy and confidentiality are also significant (12.86% weight), as AI systems process sensitive information, increasing risks of data breaches. Safety and security issues (10.50% weight) highlight potential cybersecurity threats. Finally, bias in AI outputs is a critical ethical problem (7.41%

frequency), as AI can perpetuate or amplify existing biases present in training data, resulting in unfair or discriminatory outcomes within educational contexts (Bukar et al., 2024; Cooper, 2023; Qin & Zhang, 2024).

Significant challenges arise regarding the influence of generative artificial intelligence (GenAI) on the development of student skills. A principal concern is the potential attenuation of students' self-assessment and critical thinking abilities (Samala et al., 2024; Steele, 2023). Excessive reliance on tools such as ChatGPT may impede the learning process by fostering passivity, diminishing students' autonomy, and undermining motivation for deep and sustained engagement with material. Such technologies threaten to devalue traditional academic competences, including the risk of atrophy in information retrieval skills if students become dependent on AI-generated aggregation (McDonald et al., 2024). Given the advanced capabilities of AI, it is imperative to emphasize the cultivation of future-oriented competences that are less susceptible to automation, such as critical thinking, creativity, and interpersonal communication (Bower et al., 2024; Shahzad et al., 2024). Consequently, assessment design should prioritize tasks that encourage the development and practice of higher-order cognitive skills, involving analysis, evaluation, and informed decision-making. While AI can support procedural tasks such as text generation, the essential cognitive labor of critically analyzing, synthesizing, and evaluating information from diverse sources remains inherently human (Fyfe, 2023). The critical challenge lies in ensuring that students employ AI as an augmentative tool rather than as a means to circumvent substantive learning.

In summary, the principal challenges posed by GenAI within university assessment contexts are substantial and interrelated. The risks to academic integrity—exemplified by plagiarism and the difficulty of differentiating AI-generated from student-produced content—necessitate a fundamental reexamination of assessment methodologies. Concurrently, the ethical implications encompassing copyright, privacy, bias, and misinformation warrant rigorous policy development and ethical scrutiny. Furthermore, the potential adverse effects on students' critical thinking, self-reliance, and intrinsic motivation underscore the need for pedagogical adaptations that foster skills complementary to, rather than competitive with, AI capabilities.

Strategies and Responses to Address Challenges

In response to the considerable challenges that GenAI presents in higher education assessment, institutions, educators, and students are implementing a range of strategic interventions. These responses reflect diverse philosophical approaches, ranging from cautious limitation to enthusiastic adoption, but share a consensus on the necessity of deliberate and adaptive strategies to navigate the evolving AI landscape effectively (Mao et al., 2024). At the institutional level, initiatives focus on policy formulation, ethical guidelines, and infrastructural adaptations. Universities are developing explicit frameworks governing GenAI use (Gimpel et al., 2023; McDonald et al., 2024), encompassing a spectrum from outright prohibition to unrestricted access, or delineating specific permissible and prohibited applications. Concurrently, awareness campaigns aimed at promoting the ethical and responsible use of GenAI are increasingly advocated (L. Xia et al., 2025). Moreover, there is growing acknowledgement of the need to establish novel validity standards for educational assessments in an AI-pervasive environment (Kaldaras et al., 2024), implying a systemic reconsideration of assessment design and validation.

At the pedagogical level, instructors are directly adapting teaching and assessment practices to transform GenAI challenges into opportunities for innovation (Gimpel et al., 2023). A commonly endorsed strategy involves fundamentally revising assessment formats to transcend tasks readily replicated by AI. This includes minimizing rote "busy work" and designing engaging assignments that require uniquely human capabilities beyond AI's current proficiency. Educators are shifting emphasis from recall-based or brief explanatory tasks toward assessments demanding higher-order cognitive skills such as critical analysis, complex reasoning, and integrative synthesis (Bower et al., 2024). Students are thus challenged to provide well-justified responses that demonstrate depth of understanding.

Alternative assessment modalities are increasingly adopted or explored, including authentic tasks that simulate real-world problem-solving, data interpretation, and case study analyses (Bower et al., 2024). Innovative formats such as podcast production or storyboard creation—where AI serves as a supplementary aid—are also being considered. Multi-stage assignments that assess iterative progress, such as requiring preliminary outlines prior to final submissions, enable evaluation of the learning process in addition to the product. Personalized assignments involving reflective writing or connections to personal experience resist facile AI replication. Grading rubrics are being refined to emphasize criteria aligned with higher-order thinking and knowledge integration.

Collaborative and peer-interactive tasks present further opportunities to reduce dependence on AI-generated work (Mao et al., 2024; Zastudil et al., 2023). Nonetheless, certain traditional methods, such as in-class writing, proctored examinations, and handwritten tests, retain value by limiting AI access during assessment. Oral examinations are increasingly considered for verifying comprehension and curtailing AI use, while some educators respond by increasing exam rigor.

Beyond modifications to assessment content and format, educators are focusing on incorporating AI literacy into curricula (Bower et al., 2024). A prevalent instructional approach emphasizes teaching students how to use AI responsibly and effectively—guiding its application to support tasks like information gathering, translation, or coding assistance. Importantly, instruction includes fostering understanding of AI's operational mechanisms, strengths, and limitations to promote critical engagement rather than passive acceptance of AI outputs. Ethical and responsible AI use is also foregrounded, with educators addressing dilemmas related to plagiarism, source citation, and academic integrity in an AI context (Wang, 2024). Some instructors utilize AI-generated content as pedagogical tools, encouraging students to critique, analyze, or scaffold their own work upon such examples, thus converting AI output into a learning opportunity.

Furthermore, AI tools are employed to generate teaching resources—examples, varied explanations, and formative assessments—and to facilitate instructional activities such as question generation and exam preparation (Mollick & Mollick, 2023; Qin & Zhang, 2024). Emerging pedagogical frameworks suggest that curricula may evolve to emphasize effective communication with AI, framing writing as a process of idea assembly and prompt engineering (Lau & Guo, 2023). The concept of "patchwriting", wherein students adapt source texts, might be reconceptualized as a constructive pedagogical strategy rather than solely as plagiarism, encouraging creativity and critical inquiry within a "remix culture".

At the student level, effective responses to the integration of AI necessitate the cultivation of essential competences and the adoption of responsible practices. Students must develop a comprehensive understanding of relevant legal frameworks and institutional regulations governing the use of AI in academic contexts. Furthermore, it is imperative that they cultivate self-regulation skills when interacting with AI technologies, including the refinement of prompt formulation strategies and reflective engagement with their own learning processes (Qin & Zhang, 2024; Samala et al., 2024; L. Xia et al., 2025). An important aspect of this development is the ability to exercise selective and deliberate engagement with AI, discerning when and how to utilize these tools to support learning effectively. Critical skills such as fact-checking, verification, and information literacy are indispensable for navigating the potential inaccuracies and biases inherent in AI-generated outputs. The aim of overarching is to leverage AI as an instrument for enhancing cognitive and metacognitive skills rather than allowing it to undermine critical thinking, self-assessment, and intrinsic motivation for deep learning. Students should be equipped to use AI as a complementary resource that augments human creativity and intellectual effort, rather than as a substitute.

Practical Recommendations for Educators and Institutions

- Integrate AI tools through project-based and applied learning activities rather than isolated technical instruction.
- Provide continuous, flexible training opportunities for faculty focused on pedagogical applications of AI.

- Redesign assessment methods to emphasize critical thinking, problem-solving, and process-based evaluation.
- Foster collaboration with industry partners to ensure curricular relevance and access to real-world applications.
- Establish clear institutional policies on ethical AI use, academic integrity, and data governance.

CONCLUSION: SUMMARY OF KEY POINTS AND FINAL PERSPECTIVES

The rapid advancement of artificial intelligence is fundamentally reshaping engineering education, particularly within agroforestry disciplines, by influencing its technological, pedagogical, ethical, and institutional dimensions. This study highlights that one of the central imperatives for higher education is the alignment of curricula with rapidly evolving technological developments and labor market demands. In this context, agroforestry engineering education must extend beyond traditional disciplinary foundations in biology, mathematics, and economics to include robust digital competences, particularly in artificial intelligence and data-driven technologies.

A key finding of this chapter is the strategic importance of university–industry collaboration in supporting this transformation. Partnerships with industry through internships, joint research initiatives, and co-designed curricula enable universities to maintain curricular relevance while ensuring that graduates acquire competences aligned with current professional practices. Such collaboration is particularly significant for the integration of AI-driven tools and digital technologies that are increasingly central to agricultural and environmental systems.

At the same time, the study identifies persistent structural challenges that may hinder effective implementation. Among the most critical is the limited preparedness of academic staff to integrate AI into teaching and learning processes. Existing gaps in faculty training, motivation, and access to appropriate technological resources represent significant barriers to the successful adoption of AI-enhanced pedagogies. These challenges underscore the necessity of sustained and systematic faculty development strategies as a core institutional priority.

Ethical considerations also emerge as a fundamental dimension of AI integration in education. Issues related to data privacy, algorithmic bias, transparency, academic integrity, and human oversight require careful governance to ensure that AI is deployed responsibly and equitably. In this regard, international frameworks such as the UNESCO Recommendation on the Ethics of Artificial Intelligence provide an essential reference for guiding institutional policies and educational practices.

Despite these challenges, artificial intelligence presents substantial opportunities to enhance the quality, creativity, and efficiency of engineering education. However, its effective integration requires a balanced and holistic approach that combines curricular reform, investment in infrastructure, faculty development, ethical governance, and strong engagement with industry stakeholders. Importantly, such transformation must also prioritize the development of critical thinking, creativity, and digital literacy among students, ensuring that AI is used as an augmentative tool rather than a substitute for human judgment and learning.

Research gaps and contribution of this chapter

Despite the growing body of literature on AI in education, several gaps remain. First, there is limited integration between technological perspectives and pedagogical frameworks, particularly in discipline-specific contexts such as agroforestry engineering. Second, existing studies often focus either on student learning or technological implementation, while insufficient attention is given to faculty development as a central enabler of AI integration. Third, there is a lack of comprehensive approaches that jointly address curriculum design, industry collaboration, and ethical governance within a unified framework.

Contribution of this Chapter

This chapter contributes to addressing these gaps by providing an integrated perspective that connects technological evolution, pedagogical transformation, faculty preparedness, and industry engagement within agroforestry engineering education. In doing so, it offers a structured understanding of how AI can be effectively incorporated into engineering curricula while maintaining alignment with ethical principles and labor market needs.

Practical Implications

From a practical standpoint, the findings underscore the need for coordinated action across multiple levels. Universities should prioritize curriculum redesign that incorporates AI competences in a structured and progressive manner. Faculty development programs must evolve beyond one-off training sessions to sustained professional learning ecosystems. Furthermore, institutional policies should explicitly support ethical AI use, infrastructure investment, and collaboration with industry partners to ensure relevance to real-world practice.

Final perspective

Ultimately, the future of engineering education lies in its ability to balance technological innovation with human-centered values. AI offers significant opportunities to enhance learning, creativity, and efficiency, but its success depends on thoughtful integration that prioritizes critical thinking, ethical awareness, and pedagogical intentionality. Engineering education must therefore evolve as a dynamic system—responsive to technological change while remaining grounded in its core educational mission of developing competent, reflective, and socially responsible professionals.

REFERENCES

Abioye, S. O., Oyedele, L. O., Akanbi, L., Ajayi, A., Delgado, J. M. D., Bilal, M., & Ahmed, A. (2021). Artificial intelligence in the construction industry: A review of present status, opportunities and future challenges. *Journal of Building Engineering*, *44*, 103299. DOI: 10.1016/j.jobe.2021.103299

Aljemely, Y. (2024). Challenges and best practices in training teachers to utilize artificial intelligence: A systematic review. *Frontiers in Education*, *9*, 1470853. Advance online publication. DOI: 10.3389/feduc.2024.1470853

American Society of Agricultural and Biological Engineers. ABET (2025). Criteria for accrediting engineering programs, 2025 - 2026. https://www.abet.org/wp-content/uploads/2024/11/2025-2026_EAC_Criteria.pdf

Arakawa, T., Tanaka, T. S. T., & Kamio, S. (2024). Detection of on-tree chestnut fruits using deep learning and RGB unmanned aerial vehicle imagery for estimation of yield and fruit load. *Agronomy Journal*, *116*(3), 973–981. DOI: 10.1002/agj2.21330

Arogundade, J., & Tochukwu, N. (2024). Maximizing crop yields through ai-driven precision agriculture and machine learning. *International Research Journal of Modernization in Engineering Technology and Science*, **•••**, 2582–5208. DOI: 10.56726/IRJMETS62193

Artyukhov, A., Wołowiec, T., Artyukhova, N., Bogacki, S., & Vasylieva, T. (2024). SDG 4, Academic Integrity and Artificial Intelligence: Clash or Win-Win Cooperation? *Sustainability (Basel)*, *16*(19), 8483. Advance online publication. DOI: 10.3390/su16198483

Avila-Chauvet, L., & Mejía, D. (2023). Can Professors and Students Detect ChatGPT Essays? SSRN *Electronic Journal, January*. DOI: 10.2139/ssrn.4373643

Bahroun, Z., Anane, C., Ahmed, V., & Zacca, A. (2023). Transforming Education: A Comprehensive Review of Generative Artificial Intelligence in Educational Settings through Bibliometric and Content Analysis. *Sustainability (Basel)*, *15*(17), 12983. Advance online publication. DOI: 10.3390/su151712983

Baker, R. S., & Inventado, P. S. (2014). Educational Data Mining and Learning Analytics. In Larusson, J., & White, B. (Eds.), *Learning Analytics*. Springer., DOI: 10.1007/978-1-4614-3305-7_4

Bogdanov, O., Butsenko, Y., Balina, O., & Bezklubenko, I. (2024). *Software Support for the Higher Mathematics Course at the Technical University*. Microsystems, Electronics and Acoustics., DOI: 10.20535/2523-4455.mea.314217

Bower, M., Torrington, J., Lai, J. W. M., Petocz, P., & Alfano, M. (2024). How should we change teaching and assessment in response to increasingly powerful generative Artificial Intelligence? Outcomes of the ChatGPT teacher survey. *Education and Information Technologies, 29(12).* Springer US. DOI: 10.1007/s10639-023-12405-0

Bukar, U. A., Sayeed, M. S., Fatimah Abdul Razak, S., Yogarayan, S., & Sneesl, R. (2024). Decision-Making Framework for the Utilization of Generative Artificial Intelligence in Education: A Case Study of ChatGPT. *IEEE Access : Practical Innovations, Open Solutions, 12*(June), 95368–95389. DOI: 10.1109/ACCESS.2024.3425172

Cain, W. (2024). Prompting change: Exploring prompt engineering in large language model AI and its potential to transform education. *TechTrends, 68*(1), 47–57. DOI: 10.1007/s11528-023-00896-0

Cole, K., Means, B., Simkins, M., & Tavali, F. (2002). *Increasing student learning through multimedia projects.* Association for Supervision and Curriculum Development., https://eric.ed.gov/?id=ED475526

Cooper, G. (2023). Examining Science Education in ChatGPT: An Exploratory Study of Generative Artificial Intelligence. *Journal of Science Education and Technology, 32*(3), 444–452. DOI: 10.1007/s10956-023-10039-y

Curtis, D., & Lawson, M. (2019). Exploring collaborative online learning. *Online Learning : the Official Journal of the Online Learning Consortium, 5*(1). Advance online publication. DOI: 10.24059/olj.v5i1.1885

Devin, V., Tkachuk, V., & Burdega, V. (2020). Usage of non-commercial educational software to calculate frame structures. *Electronic Scientific Professional Journal "Open educational e-environment of modern university", (8),* 8–16. DOI: 10.28925/2414-0325.2020.8.2

Enelund, M., Larsson, S., & Malmqvist, J. (2011, junio 20). Integration of a computational mathematics education in the mechanical engineering curriculum. *7th International CONCEIVE DESIGN IMPLEMENT OPERATE Conference (CDIO2011).* DOI: 10.4122/1.1000054473

Espinoza Vidaurre, S. M., Velásquez Rodríguez, N. C., Gambetta Quelopana, R. L., Martinez Valdivia, A. N., Leo Rossi, E. A., & Nolasco-Mamani, M. A. (2024). Perceptions of Artificial Intelligence and Its Impact on Academic Integrity Among University Students in Peru and Chile: An Approach to Sustainable Education. *Sustainability (Basel), 16*(20), 9005. Advance online publication. DOI: 10.3390/su16209005

European Commission. (2020). Digital Education Action Plan (2021-2027). Acceso disponible en: https://eur-lex.europa.eu/legal-content/EN/TXT/?uri=CELEX%3A52020DC0624

FAO. (2025). E-agriculture. https://www.fao.org/e-agriculture/

Furman, G. D. (2024). Enhancing Engineering Education: The Role of Artificial Intelligence in Personalizing Learning and Outcomes. In *2024 4th International Conference on Big Data Engineering and Education (BDEE)* (pp. 61-65). IEEE.

Fyfe, P. (2023). How to cheat on your final paper: Assigning AI for student writing. *AI & Society*, *38*(4), 1395–1405. DOI: 10.1007/s00146-022-01397-z

Gimpel, H., Ruiner, C., Schoch, M., Schoop, M., Hall, K., Eymann, T., Röglinger, M., Vandirk, S., Lämmermann, L., Urbach, N., Mädche, A., & Decker, S. (2023). Unlocking the power of generative AI models and systems such as GPT-4 and ChatGPT for higher education: A guide for students and lecturers (No. 02-2023). *Hohenheim Discussion Papers in Business, Economics and Social Sciences.* DOI: 10.13140/RG.2.2.20710.09287/2

Guo, J., Yang, Z., Karkee, M., Duan, J., & He, Y. (2025). Robotization of banana de-handing under multi-constraint scenarios: Challenges and future directions. *Artificial Intelligence in Agriculture*, *15*(1), 1–11. Advance online publication. DOI: 10.1016/j.aiia.2024.12.002

Guo, P., Saab, N., Post, L., & Admiraal, W. (2020). A review of project-based learning in higher education: Student outcomes and measures. *International Journal of Educational Research*, *102*, 101586. DOI: 10.1016/j.ijer.2020.101586

Hou, T., Cheng, B., Wang, R., Xue, W., & Chaudhry, P.E. (2020). Developing Industry 4.0 with systems perspectives. *Systems Research and Behavioral S e*, *37*, 741–748. DOI: 10.1002/sres.2715

Indeed Mexico. (2024). Cuáles son las habilidades de un ingeniero agrónomo. https://mx.indeed.com/orientacion-profesional/como-encontrar-empleo/habilidades-ingeniero-agronomo

Ismail, A., Aliu, A., Ibrahim, M., & Sulaiman, A. (2024). Preparing Teachers of the Future in the Era of Artificial Intelligence. *Journal of Artificial Intelligence. Machine Learning and Neural Network*, *4*(04), 31–41. DOI: 10.55529/jaimlnn.44.31.41

Kaldaras, L., Akaeze, H. O., & Reckase, M. D. (2024). Developing valid assessments in the era of generative artificial intelligence. *Frontiers in Education*, *9*, 1–10. DOI: 10.3389/feduc.2024.1399377

Kidd, D., Miner, J., Schein, M., Blauw, M., & Allen, D. (2020). Ethics across the curriculum: Detecting and describing emergent trends in ethics education. *Studies in Educational Evaluation*, *67*, 100914. DOI: 10.1016/j.stueduc.2020.100914

Kiryakova, G., & Angelova, N. (2023). ChatGPT—A Challenging Tool for the University Professors in Their Teaching Practice. *Education Sciences*, *13*(10), 1056. Advance online publication. DOI: 10.3390/educsci13101056

Kitcharoen, P., Howimanporn, S., & Chookaew, S. (2024). Mejora de las competencias de IA de Maestros a través de la Inteligencia Artificial de la Formación Profesional de Desarrollo Profesional de las Artes. *International Journal of Interactive Mobile Technologies (iJIM)*, *18*(02), pp. 4o15. DOI: 10.3991/ijim.v18i02.46613

Kumar, P. M. (2021). Special issue on Artificial Intelligence in Engineering Education. *Computer Applications in Engineering Education*, *29*(2), 311. Advance online publication. DOI: 10.1002/cae.22398

Lau, S., & Guo, P. (2023). From "Ban It Till We Understand It" to "Resistance is Futile": How University Programming Instructors Plan to Adapt as More Students Use AI Code Generation and Explanation Tools such as ChatGPT and GitHub Copilot. ICER 2023 - Proceedings of the 2023 ACM Conference on International Computing Education Research V.1, 106–121. DOI: 10.1145/3568813.3600138

Levin, B.A., Piskunov, A.A., Poliakov, V.Y., & Savin, A.V. (2022). Artificial intelligence in engineering education. *Vysshee obrazovanie v Rossii= Higher Education in Russia, 31*(7), 79-95. DOI: 10.31992/0869-3617-2022-31-7-79-95

Liu, Y., Jing, Y., Li, J., Dai, J., Hu, Z., & Wang, C. (2025). Application of AI in engineering education: A bibliometric study. *Review of Education*, *13*(1), e70044. DOI: 10.1002/rev3.70044

Mao, J., Chen, B., & Liu, J. C. (2024). Generative Artificial Intelligence in Education and Its Implications for Assessment. *TechTrends*, *68*(1), 58–66. DOI: 10.1007/s11528-023-00911-4

Martin, D. A., Conlon, E., & Bowe, B. (2021). A Multi-level Review of Engineering Ethics Education: Towards a Socio-technical Orientation of Engineering Education for Ethics. *Science and Engineering Ethics*, *27*(5), 60. DOI: 10.1007/s11948-021-00333-6 PMID: 34427811

McDonald, N., Johri, A., Ali, A., & Hingle, A. (2024). Generative Artificial Intelligence in Higher Education: Evidence from an Analysis of Institutional Policies and Guidelines. *Computers in Human Behavior: Artificial Humans*, *3*, 100121. DOI: 10.1016/j.chbah.2025.100121

Mejía-Marín, A. A., & Gómez-Rivero, J. O. (2024). Implementation of artificial intelligence in the educational processes of university teachers. DOI: 10.56294/dm2024.338

Mollick, E. R., & Mollick, L. (2023). Using AI to Implement Effective Teaching Strategies in Classrooms: Five Strategies, Including Prompts. SSRN *Electronic Journal*. DOI: 10.2139/ssrn.4391243

Morales-García, W., Sairitupa-Sanchez, L., Morales-García, S., & Morales-García, M. (2024). Development and validation of a scale for dependence on artificial intelligence in university students. *Frontiers in Education*, *9*, 1323898. Advance online publication. DOI: 10.3389/feduc.2024.1323898

Ocone, R. (2013). Engineering ethics and accreditation. *Education for Chemical Engineers*, *8*(3), e113–e118. DOI: 10.1016/j.ece.2013.07.002

Prather, J., Reeves, B., Denny, P., Becker, B., Leinonen, J., Luxton-Reilly, A., Powell, G., Finnie-Ansley, J., & Santos, E. (2023). "It's Weird That it Knows What I Want": Usability and Interactions with Copilot for Novice Programmers. *ACM Transactions on Computer-Human Interaction*, *31*(1), 1–31. DOI: 10.1145/3617367

Qin, Q., & Zhang, S. (2024). Visualizing the knowledge mapping of artificial intelligence in education: A systematic review. *Education and Information Technologies*, *30*(1). Springer US. https://doi.org/DOI: 10.1007/s10639-024-13076-

Requejo, W. S., Martínez, F. F., Vega, C. A., Martínez, R. Z., Cendrero, A. M., & Lantada, A. D. (2024). Fostering creativity in engineering design through constructive dialogues with generative artificial intelligence. *Cell Reports. Physical Science*, *5*(9), 102157. Advance online publication. DOI: 10.1016/j.xcrp.2024.102157

Rossoni, A. L., Vieira, E. P. G., & Rabelo, R. L. C. (2023). Barriers and facilitators of university–industry collaboration for research, development and innovation: A systematic review. *Journal of the Knowledge Economy*, *74*(3), 1841–1877. DOI: 10.1007/s11301-023-00349-1

Sadikin, A., Mustaffa, A., Hasbullah, H., Zakaria, Z., Hamid, M., Man, S., Hassim, M., Aziz, M., & Yusof, K. (2021). Qualitative Development of Students' Digital Skills by Integrating a Spreadsheet Software in First Year Introduction to Engineering and Seminar Course. *Int. J. Emerg. Technol. Learn.*, *16*. DOI: 10.3991/ijet.v16i18.24325

Samala, A. D., Rawas, S., Wang, T., Reed, J. M., Kim, J., Howard, N. J., & Ertz, M. (2024). Unveiling the landscape of generative artificial intelligence in education: a comprehensive taxonomy of applications, challenges, and future prospects. In *Education and Information Technologies* (Vol. 30, Issue 3). Springer US. DOI: 10.1007/s10639-024-12936-0

Sánchez-Prieto, J. C., Izquierdo-álvarez, V., Del Moral-Marcos, M. T., & Martínez-Abad, F. (2025). Generative artificial intelligence for self-learning in higher education: Design and validation of an example machine. *RIED-Revista Iberoamericana de Educacion a Distancia*, *28*(1), 59–81. DOI: 10.5944/ried.28.1.41548

Saura, J. (2022). A Teaching Guide for the Use of Artificial Intelligence Tools at Universities. *Advances in Electronic Government, Digital Divide, and Regional Development*, 309–321. Advance online publication. DOI: 10.4018/978-1-7998-9609-8.ch017

Shahzad, M. F., Xu, S., & Asif, M. (2024, May). Factors affecting generative artificial intelligence, such as ChatGPT, use in higher education: An application of technology acceptance model. *British Educational Research Journal*, *51*(2), 489–513. DOI: 10.1002/berj.4084

Skafa, E., Evseeva, E., & Korolev, M. (2023). DIGITAL APPROACH TO THE FORMATION METHODS OF ACTION ON MATHEMATICAL MODELING IN ENGINEERING EDUCATION. Izvestiya of the Samara Science Centre of the Russian Academy of Sciences. Social, Humanitarian, Medicobiological Sciences. .DOI: 10.37313/2413-9645-2023-25-92-55-62

Southworth, J., Migliaccio, K., Glover, J., Glover, J., Reed, D., McCarty, C., Brendemuhl, J., & Thomas, A. (2023). Developing a model for AI Across the curriculum: Transforming the higher education landscape via innovation in AI literacy. *Computers and Education: Artificial Intelligence*, *4*, 100127. Advance online publication. DOI: 10.1016/j.caeai.2023.100127

Steele, J. L. (2023). To GPT or not GPT? Empowering our students to learn with AI. *Computers and Education: Artificial Intelligence*, *5*, 100160. DOI: 10.1016/j.caeai.2023.100160

Tan, X., Cheng, G., & Ling, M. H. (2025). Artificial intelligence in teaching and teacher professional development: A systematic review. *Computers and Education: Artificial Intelligence*, *8*, 100355. DOI: 10.1016/j.caeai.2024.100355

The European Centre for the Development of Vocational Training. CEDEFOP. (2025). Skills forecast. https://www.cedefop.europa.eu/en/tools/skills-forecast

The Official College of Agronomist Engineers of Central Spain and the Canary Islands. (2024). Necesidades formativas más demandadas para los ingenieros agrónomos. https://agronomoscentro.org/articulos/competencias-profesionales-mas-demandadas-ingenieros-agronomos-espana

UNESCO. (2021). Recommendation on the ethics of artificial intelligence. https://www.unesco.org/en/articles/recommendation-ethics-artificial-intelligence

UNESCO. (2023). Oportunidades y desafíos de la era de la inteligencia artificial para la educación superior: una introducción para los actores de la educación superior. Acceso disponible en: https://unesdoc.unesco.org/ark:/48223/pf0000386670_spa

U.S. Bureau of Labor Statistics. (2024). Occupational outlook handbook. *Architecture and engineering occupations.* https://www.bls.gov/ooh/architecture-and-engineering/

Von Garrel, J., & Mayer, J. (2023). Artificial Intelligence in studies—Use of ChatGPT and AI-based tools among students in Germany. *Humanities & Social Sciences Communications, 10*(1), 799. Advance online publication. DOI: 10.1057/s41599-023-02304-7

Wang, C. (2024). Exploring Students' Generative AI-Assisted Writing Processes: Perceptions and Experiences from Native and Nonnative English Speakers. *Technology. Knowledge and Learning, 0123456789.* Advance online publication. DOI: 10.1007/s10758-024-09744-3

Whiteman, C., & Nygren, C. (2000). Achieving the Right Balance: Properly Integrating Mathematical Software Packages into Engineering Education. *Journal of Engineering Education, 89*(3), 331–336. Advance online publication. DOI: 10.1002/j.2168-9830.2000.tb00533.x

Xia, L., Shen, K., Sun, H., An, X., & Dong, Y. (2025). Developing and validating the student learning agency scale in generative artificial intelligence (AI)-supported contexts. *Education and Information Technologies, 0123456789*(10), 13999–14021. Advance online publication. DOI: 10.1007/s10639-024-13137-5

Zastudil, C., Rogalska, M., Kapp, C., Vaughn, J., & MacNeil, S. (2023). Generative AI in Computing Education: Perspectives of Students and Instructors. *Proceedings - Frontiers in Education Conference, FIE,* 1–9. DOI: 10.1109/FIE58773.2023.10343467

Zhang, N., Leong, W., Zhang, T., & Wei, C. (2024b). *Artificial Intelligence in Engineering Education: A Review of Pedagogical Innovations.* INTI Journal., DOI: 10.61453/INTIj.202446

Zhang, S., Zhang, C., Park, D. S., & Yoon, S. (2023, April 20). Editorial: Machine learning and artificial intelligence for smart agriculture, volume II. *Frontiers in Plant Science*, *14*, 1166209. DOI: 10.3389/fpls.2023.1166209 PMID: 37152126

Zhang, S., Zhao, X., & Kim, J. H. (2024a). *Do you have AI dependency? The roles of academic self-efficacy, academic stress, and performance expectations on problematic AI usage behavior. 21*, 1–14. https://doi.org/DOI: 10.1186/s41239-024-00467-0

KEY TERMS AND DEFINITIONS

Agroforestry Engineering: Agroforestry engineering is a discipline that integrates principles of agriculture and forestry to design, implement and manage production systems that combine crops, trees and often animals on the same area of land. Its main objective is to achieve sustainable production, while maximizing economic, social and environmental benefits. This is achieved by taking advantage of the interactions between agricultural and forestry components, which can lead to increased biodiversity, soil and water conservation, pest and disease reduction, and greater resilience to climate change.

Artificial Intelligence: Artificial Intelligence (AI) is the ability of machines to mimic and perform tasks that normally require human intelligence. This includes learning, reasoning, problem solving, perceiving and understanding language.

Competences: Competences or skills are the set of knowledge and attitudes that students acquire to perform effectively in their profession and in life. They include technical skills, critical thinking, communication, teamwork and problem solving.

Digital Tools: Digital tools are technological applications and platforms that support teaching and learning. They facilitate communication, access to resources, collaboration, content creation and academic management, optimizing the educational experience for teachers and students.

Grading rubrics: Are guidelines that establish clear criteria and performance levels for grading assignments or projects. They allow students and teachers to understand what is expected, ensuring a fair and transparent evaluation.

Hybrid learning: Learning methodology that combines face-to-face teaching with virtual activities. It allows students to participate in face-to-face classes while accessing resources and collaborating online, offering flexibility and optimizing the learning experience.

Online platforms: are virtual environments accessible via the Internet that centralize educational resources, facilitate interaction between students and teachers, and allow the management of courses, assignments and evaluations, making distance and blended learning possible.

Chapter 12

Leading the Way:
Strategic Leadership and Policy Frameworks for AI Integration in Higher Education

Md. Mazid-Ul-Haque
http://orcid.org/0000-0002-9091-7191
American International University-Bangladesh, Bangladesh

Md Mehedi Hasan Emon
http://orcid.org/0000-0002-6224-9552
American International University-Bangladesh, Bangladesh

ABSTRACT

This chapter explores the pivotal function of leadership in the implementation of AI inside higher education. It examines projected trends in AI integration, including the emergence of adaptive learning platforms, AI applications for student mental health assistance, and the growing need for explainable AI. The chapter examines ethical and social ramifications, highlighting the need of alleviating AI prejudice, safeguarding data privacy, and promoting openness in AI applications. Furthermore, it delineates tactics for influencing the future of AI-enhanced education, emphasizing the need of formulating a strategic vision, fostering multidisciplinary cooperation, and committing to continuous professional development for teachers and staff. By actively interacting with these components, institutional leaders may adeptly maneuver through the changing terrain of AI, guaranteeing that its incorporation is consistent with academic achievement and social advancement. The chapter finally promotes a progressive strategy to use the revolutionary capabilities of AI in higher education.

DOI: 10.4018/979-8-3373-1285-9.ch012

INTRODUCTION

The incorporation of Artificial Intelligence (AI) in higher education has become a revolutionary influence, altering pedagogical approaches, administrative procedures, and institutional management. AI-driven solutions provide unparalleled prospects for improving learning experiences, optimizing operations, and customizing instruction. Nonetheless, these developments also present intricate difficulties concerning ethics, data privacy, equality, and governance. As institutions traverse this changing environment, the significance of strategic leadership is crucial in guaranteeing that AI is implemented in accordance with academic integrity, institutional objectives, and social principles. Institutional leaders, such as administrators and politicians, are essential in guiding AI adoption by formulating comprehensive policies that reconcile innovation with ethical issues. Effective leadership in AI integration necessitates a proactive strategy that welcomes technological breakthroughs while addressing possible concerns, assuring inclusion and accessibility for various student groups. This requires the development of comprehensive policy frameworks, governance structures, and capacity-building efforts to empower teachers, staff, and students with the essential skills and knowledge to successfully engage with AI-enhanced education. This chapter explores the strategic leadership and policy frameworks necessary for the integration of AI in higher education. It offers pragmatic insights for synchronizing AI programs with institutional objectives, enhancing stakeholder engagement, and establishing governance frameworks that ensure transparency and accountability. The discussion aims to provide educational leaders with the knowledge to make educated choices on AI adoption by analyzing best practices, case studies, and emerging trends, therefore fostering a responsible and future-ready academic environment.

STRATEGIC PLANNING FOR AI INTEGRATION

The effective incorporation of Artificial Intelligence (AI) in higher education requires a thorough strategic vision that corresponds with an institution's purpose and long-term educational objectives. AI-powered technologies may improve educational experiences, optimize administrative functions, and enable data-informed decision-making. Nonetheless, its implementation must be directed by a well-articulated plan to guarantee ethical use, inclusion, and conformity with academic principles. In the absence of a systematic methodology, institutions may encounter issues like bias in AI models, data security vulnerabilities, and opposition to change from staff and students (Kunacheva et al., 2024). Consequently, institutional leaders must proactively develop frameworks that reconcile innovation with responsible execution.

ALIGNING AI ADOPTION WITH INSTITUTIONAL VISION

In order-to attain significant and enduring AI integration, institutions must synchronize AI activities with their fundamental purpose and strategic objectives. AI adoption must be integrated into institutional growth plans, regardless of whether the goal is to augment student engagement, boost operational efficiency, or promote research-excellence. An effective AI strategy should include fundamental principles like accessibility, inclusiveness, and academic integrity (Singh et al., 2024).

AI-driven adaptive learning systems provide tailored education, accommodating various learning styles and requirements. Research-focused universities may use AI for sophisticated data analytics, predictive modeling, and automated literature reviews. Moreover, institutions dedicated to expanding participation and inclusion must guarantee that AI solutions mitigate possible biases and improve accessibility for students with impairments (Mehta et al., 2023). By incorporating AI adoption into strategic planning, organizations may optimize advantages while minimizing risks linked to technology disruptions.

IDENTIFYING PRIORITY AREAS FOR AI-DRIVEN INNOVATION

The use of AI should focus on critical institutional sectors that provide the most benefit. Leaders must do a requirements assessment to identify areas where AI-driven solutions might improve productivity, engagement, and student achievements (George & Wooden, 2023). The priority areas encompass:

Teaching and Learning: AI has the potential to transform education via customized learning platforms, advanced tutoring systems, and automated assessment processes. AI-powered solutions such as chatbots and virtual assistants may aid students by offering immediate feedback and suggestions (Chen et al., 2023).

Administration: AI-driven solutions may improve enrollment management, resource distribution, and financial aid administration. Predictive analytics enables institutions to identify students at risk and execute early intervention initiatives (Zeineddine et al., 2021).

Student Support Services: AI-powered chatbots and virtual counselors may provide academic coaching, mental health assistance, and career help. These technologies may enhance human counselors, guaranteeing that students have prompt and individualized assistance (Alqahtani et al., 2023).

BUILDING CROSS-FUNCTIONAL TEAMS

To develop and execute a robust AI strategy, institutions must create interdisciplinary AI teams that integrate knowledge from several fields. These teams must include academic leaders, IT professionals, ethicists, faculty members, and student advocates to guarantee a balanced and ethical approach to AI implementation (Gurgu, 2022). Cross-functional teams are essential for managing AI installation, evaluating results, and assuring coherence with institutional objectives. They may also promote cooperation between educators and technologists, ensuring that AI technologies are pedagogically valid and morally accountable (Tariq & Sergio, 2024). Furthermore, these teams must establish explicit standards on data privacy, algorithmic transparency, and ethical AI use to cultivate trust and accountability in AI-driven efforts.

DEVELOPING ETHICAL AND INCLUSIVE AI POLICIES

The use of AI in higher education offers significant benefits while also posing essential ethical and inclusiveness challenges. Although AI may improve student learning, optimize administrative functions, and customize education, its use must be regulated by stringent laws that protect institutional integrity, data security, and student rights (Yadav, 2025). The lack of clearly defined AI policy may result in biased decision-making, violations of data privacy, and unforeseen repercussions that adversely affect certain student demographics. Institutions must proactively develop ethical rules that connect AI deployment with the ideals of openness, accountability, justice, and accessibility (Díaz-Rodríguez et al., 2023). By addressing these issues, colleges can guarantee that AI implementation stays inclusive, responsible, and advantageous to all stakeholders.

KEY PRINCIPLES FOR ETHICAL AI USE

In order-to encourage ethical AI adoption, organizations must include fundamental principles that guide the design, implementation, and regulation of AI systems. These principles should guarantee that AI serves as a means to improve education while mitigating concerns related to prejudice, privacy infringements, and unclear decision-making procedures (Manda et al., 2024). The fundamental concepts encompass:

Transparency: Institutions must explicitly convey the purpose of AI in decision-making processes, ensuring that students and faculty comprehend how AI-driven systems affect admissions, grading, and administrative operations (S. C. et al., 2024). Transparency entails offering justifications for AI-generated results, enabling users to contest or appeal choices as required.

Accountability: AI technologies must not function without human supervision. Institutions must designate accountability for AI-driven choices to certain stakeholders, including professors, IT professionals, and ethical (Franco D'Souza et al., 2024). A governance framework must be developed to oversee AI applications and address instances of algorithmic inaccuracies or ethical issues.

Bias Mitigation: AI algorithms are prone to bias, especially when trained on unrepresentative or historically biased datasets. Periodic audits must be performed to detect and rectify discriminatory trends in AI decision-making (Bansal et al., 2024). Moreover, AI developers must emphasize justice by ensuring that machine learning algorithms are constructed to be inclusive and equal across various demographic groups.

By integrating these concepts into AI governance frameworks, institutions may maintain ethical standards while using AI's potential to improve education.

ADDRESSING DATA PRIVACY AND ACCESSIBILITY

AI applications in education depend on vast amounts of student data, which raises considerable issues about privacy, security, and possible exploitation. Institutions are required to adhere to international and domestic data protection laws, including the General Data Protection Regulation (GDPR) in Europe and the Family Educational Rights and Privacy Act (FERPA) in the United States (Fazlioglu, 2021). These regulations delineate how educational institutions must manage personal data, guaranteeing that AI systems process information in a responsible and safe manner.

Data Privacy and Security Measures

Informed Consent: Students and professors must be informed about the collection, storage, and use of personal data by AI systems. Explicit opt-in and opt-out methods must be established to preserve user autonomy over personal information (Meszaros et al., 2020).

Data Encryption and Anonymization: Institutions must use robust encryption mechanisms to protect student data from cyber-attacks. Anonymization strategies enhance privacy by guaranteeing that AI models do not store personally identifying information (Villegas-Ch & García-Ortiz, 2023).

Third-Party Compliance: Numerous institutions engage with external AI providers for instructional technology. These suppliers are required to conform to institutional data security rules and uphold stringent ethical standards to avert data breaches (Dhirani et al., 2023).

Ensuring AI Accessibility for Diverse Students

In addition to privacy issues, AI must be engineered to provide accessibility for all students, including those with impairments and those from disadvantaged backgrounds. Institutions must guarantee that AI-driven technologies facilitate:

Students with Disabilities: AI-powered assistive technologies, such speech-to-text transcription services and adaptive learning platforms, may improve accessibility for students with visual, aural, or cognitive disabilities (Zdravkova, 2022).

Linguistic and Cultural Diversity: AI solutions must be designed to support multilingual students and various cultural viewpoints, guaranteeing that educational material is inclusive and representative (Başaran & Turan, 2024).

Internet and Technology Accessibility: Institutions must rectify digital disparities by guaranteeing that AI-enhanced educational resources are accessible to students with restricted internet connectivity or obsolete equipment (Yadav & Shrawankar, 2024).

By emphasizing both privacy and accessibility, institutions can provide a safe, inclusive, and equitable AI-driven learning environment for all students.

BALANCING INNOVATION WITH ACADEMIC INTEGRITY

As AI technologies progress, they present new obstacles to upholding academic integrity. As AI-assisted writing tools, automated research assistants, and plagiarism detection software proliferate, schools must formulate explicit norms for the ethical use of AI in coursework, research, and exams (Grassini, 2023).

Establishing Guidelines for AI-Assisted Learning

Permissible AI Use in Research and Writing: Institutions must delineate the permissible level of AI-generated material utilization in academic endeavors by pupils. For instance, while AI may aid in literature reviews and data analysis, it must not be used to produce whole research publications without appropriate credit (Lim et al., 2022).

Plagiarism Detection and AI-Generated Content: AI-driven plagiarism detection systems assist schools in recognizing academic misconduct. Nonetheless, rules must differentiate between genuine AI-assisted learning and unethical academic misbehavior (Zhang et al., 2025).

Examination Monitoring and AI's Role: AI-powered proctoring technologies are progressively used to oversee online examinations. Institutions must reconcile the need of deterring academic dishonesty with issues related to student privacy, algorithmic bias, and the psychological effects of AI monitoring (Fedele et al., 2024).

By formulating comprehensive academic integrity regulations, schools may adopt AI-driven innovation while maintaining the validity of academic output.

DEVELOPING ETHICAL AND INCLUSIVE AI POLICIES

The use of AI in higher education has significant prospects for augmenting learning experiences, optimizing operational efficiency, and facilitating data-informed decision-making. This implementation must be regulated by stringent ethical norms that mitigate associated dangers, including issues of fairness, openness, data privacy, and academic integrity. Institutional leaders are essential in creating regulatory frameworks that ensure institutional integrity, guarantee student rights, and foster ethical AI use.

KEY PRINCIPLES FOR ETHICAL AI USE

To establish an ethical framework for AI implementation in higher education, institutions must comply with fundamental principles that govern the responsible use of technology. ***Transparency*** is crucial for enabling stakeholders, such as students, teachers, and staff, to comprehend the function of AI in decision-making processes. Institutions must explicitly convey the use of AI technologies, the data they gather, and the manner-in which this data influences decision-making. This openness fosters trust and guarantees that stakeholders recognize the biases and limits inherent in AI systems (Felzmann et al., 2020).

Accountability is a fundamental tenet in the ethical use of AI. Institutions must designate accountability for AI results to certain stakeholders, establishing clarity on responsibility for the design, deployment, and oversight of AI systems. Implementing accountability structures, such as appointed oversight committees or positions, may assist organizations in managing the intricacies of AI deployment while fostering ethical norms (Ansarullah et al., 2024; Emon, 2025d).

Moreover, institutions have-to emphasize ***bias reduction*** via the frequent auditing of AI models to uncover and rectify any biases. AI systems often use historical data that may embody prevailing prejudices, thereby resulting in inequitable results for underrepresented populations (Stypinska, 2023). Through regular evaluations of AI technologies, institutions may use proactive strategies to mitigate bias and improve fairness in decision-making processes. This entails engaging many stakeholders in the design and assessment stages of AI applications to guarantee the consideration of varied views (Burr & Leslie, 2023).

ADDRESSING DATA PRIVACY AND ACCESSIBILITY

AI applications in education often aggregate extensive student data, prompting considerable worries about data security and possible exploitation. Institutions must adhere to international and national data protection laws, such the General Data Protection Regulation (GDPR) in Europe and the Family Educational Rights and Privacy Act (FERPA) in the United States, to secure student information (Alier et al., 2021). Formulating thorough data privacy regulations is crucial for guaranteeing the responsible use of AI technologies and safeguarding student data from unwanted access or misuse. Institutions must establish comprehensive cybersecurity protocols, perform routine data protection assessments, and provide training for academics and staff on optimal data privacy practices.

Moreover, AI-driven solutions must be developed to assist students with impairments and those from varied backgrounds. Accessibility should be a primary issue in the creation of AI technologies, guaranteeing that all students can use these tools (Mhlanga, 2023). Institutions have-to partner with accessibility specialists to develop AI applications that address diverse learning requirements, including assistive technologies that improve the educational experiences of students with impairments. By advancing accessibility in AI implementation, institutions may cultivate an inclusive educational climate that enables all students to thrive.

BALANCING INNOVATION WITH ACADEMIC INTEGRITY

Although AI technologies provide considerable opportunities for educational innovation, they also introduce issues about academic integrity. Institutions must establish explicit criteria for the acceptable use of AI in courses, research, and evaluations. Policies must delineate permissible methods for AI-assisted learning, including the utilization of AI technologies for research and writing assistance. It is crucial to distinguish between authentic AI applications that augment learning versus occurrences of academic misconduct, such plagiarism or contract cheating enabled by AI (Pudasaini et al., 2024). Institutions have- to provide training and tools for teachers and students to enhance comprehension of ethical AI utilization and the significance of academic integrity. This entails the creation of educational resources that delineate best practices for the responsible use of AI, highlighting the importance of original work and promoting critical thinking and creativity (Bahroun et al., 2023). Furthermore, rules must have stipulations for AI-based plagiarism detection systems to maintain academic integrity while acknowledging the valid applications of AI in education.

CONTINUOUS POLICY EVALUATION AND ADAPTATION

As AI technologies advance, the-regulations regulating their use in higher education must also develop. Institutions must establish mechanisms for the ongoing assessment and modification of AI policy to align with technical progress and evolving ethical concerns. This entails consistently obtaining input from stakeholders, including as students, professors, and industry experts, to evaluate the efficacy and pertinence of current policies (Mian et al., 2020). Moreover, institutions must participate in interdisciplinary research and cooperation to be abreast of the most recent advancements in AI ethics and education. This may include establishing collaborations with technology developers, legal specialists, and ethicists to guarantee that policies are based on contemporary best practices and encompass many viewpoints. By cultivating a culture of perpetual learning and adaptation, institutions may establish themselves as leaders in the ethical integration of AI while confronting the evolving difficulties posed by these technologies.

GOVERNANCE MODELS FOR AI IMPLEMENTATION

Establishing strong governance frameworks is essential for ensuring openness and accountability in the decision-making processes related to AI in higher education. As institutions progressively incorporate AI technology into their operations and educational structures, the need for explicit governance models becomes critical. These models are designed to guarantee that AI applications conform to institutional norms, uphold ethical standards, and safeguard the rights of all stakeholders. By establishing robust governance frameworks, higher education institutions may cultivate trust and cooperation while using AI's capabilities to improve learning and operational efficiency.

FRAMEWORKS FOR DECISION-MAKING AND ACCOUNTABILITY

Governance frameworks must define explicit roles and duties for AI supervision, enabling the integration of ethical and practical issues in all facets of AI deployment. A crucial element of these frameworks is the formation of AI Ethics Committees, responsible for verifying that AI applications comply with defined ethical norms and principles. These panels need to include a variety of stakeholders, including teachers, students, and specialists in ethics, technology, and law. Their main duty is to review proposed AI efforts and determine their conformity with institutional principles and ethical standards. AI Ethics Committees may mitigate possible ethical difficulties and promote a culture of responsible AI use via supervision and suggestions (Emon et al., 2025; Hagendorff, 2020). Besides ethical committees, organizations have-to designate Data Protection Officers (DPOs) tasked with overseeing compliance with data protection regulations pertaining to AI. Data Protection Officers (DPOs) are essential in ensuring that the collection, storage, and use of student data comply with applicable legal and regulatory standards, including the General Data Protection Regulation (GDPR) and the Family Educational Rights and Privacy Act (FERPA). DPOs decrease risks related to data breaches and illegal access by supervising data security procedures, so ensuring the privacy and rights of students (Bećirović, 2023). Furthermore, the establishment of AI Advisory Boards may provide strategic guidance on the implementation of AI technology inside the organization. These boards should include teachers, administrators, industry experts, and student representatives to ensure different viewpoints are incorporated into decision-making processes. AI Advisory Boards may uncover creative prospects for AI integration and solve possible obstacles and ethical issues by using the experience of diverse stakeholders (Hickman & Petrin, 2021).

CREATING ADVISORY COMMITTEES FOR AI GOVERNANCE

Establishing advisory groups focused on AI governance may augment an institution's capacity to manage the intricacies of AI adoption. These panels need should-have members from many groups, including professors, students, administrators, and external experts. Their main role is to provide insights on the- influence of AI on educational methodologies and to promote a culture of ongoing evaluation and ethical supervision. These groups may conduct frequent conversations to assess AI efforts, examine new technology, and provide best practices for AI adoption (Khan et al., 2025). Moreover, advisory committees may function as a forum for transparent discourse among stakeholders, facilitating the exchange of experiences and apprehensions about AI implementation in education. This collaborative method guarantees that the varied demands and viewpoints of all stakeholders are included in the formulation and execution of AI policies and projects. Moreover, advisory committees may connect technical and non-technical stakeholders, promoting a more thorough comprehension of AI technologies and its ramifications for higher education (Buckingham et al., 2024).

MONITORING AND EVALUATING AI INITIATIVES

Effective governance frameworks for AI deployment must have tools for the monitoring and evaluation of AI efforts. Institutions must establish assessment measures to analyze the efficacy of AI in several domains, including student learning results, operational efficiency improvements, and the ethical and societal ramifications of AI applications. A key component of this evaluation process is the assessment of AI's influence on student learning outcomes. Institutions need to collect data on academic achievement and engagement to assess the impact of AI-driven tools and technology on student success (Khan & Emon, 2025; Shoaib et al., 2024). Furthermore, quantifying operational efficiency improvements is crucial for assessing the return on investment for AI programs. Institutions may evaluate indicators such as cost savings, process enhancements, and resource allocation efficiency to determine the efficacy of AI applications in administrative operations. By showcasing concrete advantages, organizations may cultivate support for AI projects and justify further investments in technology (Khan et al., 2025; Wamba-Taguimdje et al., 2020).

FOSTERING A CULTURE OF CONTINUOUS IMPROVEMENT

For monitoring AI deployment efficiently, institutions must cultivate a culture of continual improvement. This entails the continual reassessment of governance frameworks and decision-making protocols to guarantee their relevance and responsiveness to new problems. Institutions must promote continuous professional development for teachers and staff to be informed about advancements in AI technology, ethics, and pedagogy. By investing in training and resources, institutions may enable stakeholders to make informed choices on AI use and contribute to the ethical governance of technology in education (Chan, 2023; Emon, 2025a). Furthermore, institutions must implement feedback systems that enable stakeholders to express their concerns and recommendations about AI programs. By proactively seeking feedback from academics, students, and other stakeholders, institutions may pinpoint areas for improvement and implement necessary modifications to their governance structures. This interactive method fosters accountability and transparency, hence augmenting confidence in the institution's AI endeavors.

CAPACITY BUILDING AND PROFESSIONAL DEVELOPMENT

Successful integration of AI in higher education necessitates that teachers and staff possess the requisite skills and expertise to properly use these technologies. The rapid advancement of AI necessitates a proactive strategy for capacity building and professional development, ensuring educators are adept in using AI technologies while being cognizant of its-ethical-ramifications and pedagogical uses. By investing in extensive training programs and promoting multidisciplinary cooperation, schools may enable their teachers and staff to fully use AI in their educational processes.

TRAINING PROGRAMS FOR FACULTY AND STAFF

Training programs designed for academics and staff should concentrate on three main areas: AI literacy, pedagogical applications, and ethical issues. AI literacy is essential for understanding the potential and limitations of AI systems. Faculty must be knowledgeable with the fundamental concepts of AI, including machine learning, natural language processing, and data analysis, to proficiently use these technologies into their pedagogical methods. Hermann (2022) underscore the significance of AI literacy, asserting that instructors with a robust comprehension of AI are more adept at directing students in their educational journeys and equipping them for a technology-oriented profession. Training programs should include the pedagogical uses of AI technologies, in addition to AI literacy. Educators must acquire the skills to integrate AI into their pedagogical approaches, therefore augmenting student engagement and boosting educational results. For example, intelligent tutoring systems and AI-driven analytics may provide customized learning experiences suited to the specific requirements of each learner. Almufarreh & Arshad (2023) assert that the incorporation of AI into educational methodologies not only enriches the learning experience but also enables educators to make data-informed choices that promote student achievement. Moreover, it is essential to examine the ethical implications associated with the use of AI in education. Faculty and staff must acknowledge the inherent biases in AI algorithms and comprehend the ethical ramifications of using these technologies in educational settings. Training programs must include debates on data protection, algorithmic transparency, and the obligation of educators to guarantee the ethical and equitable use of AI (Berendt et al., 2020). By embedding a robust ethical framework in training programs, institutions may equip educators to properly manage the intricacies of AI integration.

ENCOURAGING INTERDISCIPLINARY COLLABORATION

To provide a thorough and inclusive framework for AI education, universities must promote interdisciplinary cooperation across diverse academic disciplines, such as computer science, social sciences, and humanities. By cultivating collaborations across these disciplines, universities may get a more comprehensive grasp of AI and its ramifications across many professions. Interdisciplinary cooperation may foster creative research and pedagogical approaches that tackle the complex issues of AI integration. Integrating ideas from computer science with social science views may enhance educators' comprehension of the societal implications of AI technology. This methodology corresponds with the conclusions of a paper by the National Academy of Engineering, which promotes multidisciplinary cooperation to address the intricate social concerns presented by AI (Emon & Chowdhury, 2025). Furthermore, multidisciplinary cooperation may improve the formulation of AI curriculum that include multiple-viewpoints and promote inclusion in AI education. Incorporating academics from several disciplines in curriculum development enables institutions to create educational experiences that highlight the ethical, social, and cultural aspects of AI, equipping students to critically interact with these technologies in their future professions (Chiu & Chai, 2020).

PROMOTING LIFELONG LEARNING FOR LEADERSHIP AGILITY

Institutional leaders must foster lifelong learning and professional growth to adeptly manage the swiftly changing AI world. Leaders must be cognizant of developing AI trends, technology innovations, and changing rules via ongoing education, conferences, and knowledge-sharing platforms. Engaging in professional development opportunities enables leaders to acquire knowledge on optimal techniques for AI integration and deployment. Furthermore, participating in dialogues with colleagues and specialists in the domain cultivates a collaborative environment and facilitates the flow of information that may enhance decision-making at the institutional level. Emon (2025) assert that a dedication to lifelong learning among educational leaders improves their capacity to adapt to change and foster innovation within their institutions. Alongside participating in seminars and conferences, institutions may implement mentoring programs that link seasoned leaders with burgeoning experts in the discipline. Mentorship programs facilitate knowledge transfer and skill development, therefore nurturing the next generation of leaders prepared to tackle the problems and possibilities associated with AI integration in higher education.

COLLABORATING WITH INDUSTRY AND EXTERNAL EXPERTS

To improve the relevance and applicability of training programs, schools should interact with industry partners and external AI specialists. Interacting with technology industry specialists may provide professors and staff with insights into contemporary AI developments, applications, and workforce issues. Collaborations with business may enhance the creation of training programs that correspond with practical requirements, ensuring that instructors are adequately prepared to equip students for the job market's expectations. Moreover, corporate partnerships may provide chances for internships, guest lectures, and joint research, enhancing the educational experience for both teachers and students. Moreover, engaging external specialists in training sessions or seminars may augment the information imparted to academics and staff. These specialists may provide insightful viewpoints on innovative AI research, ethical implications, and effective implementation techniques, allowing institutions to remain at the vanguard of AI progress (Kanbach et al., 2024).

STAKEHOLDER COLLABORATION AND ENGAGEMENT

Involving many stakeholders is crucial for establishing a collective vision for the incorporation of AI in higher education. A collaborative strategy including teachers, students, industry partners, and other stakeholders may enhance the successful integration of AI technologies, ensuring they address the requirements of all participants. This chapter examines the significance of stakeholder cooperation, including techniques for engaging diverse groups, establishing partnerships for resource allocation, and maintaining transparent communication throughout the AI integration process.

INVOLVING FACULTY, STUDENTS, AND INDUSTRY PARTNERS

The participation of teachers and students is essential in determining the trajectory of AI integration inside educational environments. Institutions need to provide platforms for open discourse that let teachers and students to-express their concerns, expectations, and goals about AI's role in education. These forums may consist of seminars, focus groups, or town hall meetings, whereby stakeholders may articulate their experiences with AI technology and exchange thoughts on how these tools might improve teaching and learning outcomes. Chugh et al. (2023) emphasize the significance of faculty involvement in the decision-making process for the deployment of educational technology. Engaging educators in dialogues on AI integration enables institutions to comprehend the pedagogical ramifications of AI tools and guarantees alignment with their educational goals. Additionally, faculty contributions may pinpoint possible obstacles and opportunities for improvement, promoting a culture of ongoing evaluation and refinement of AI programs. Students, as the main beneficiaries of AI integration, must also be actively involved in the process. Their viewpoints may provide significant insights on the effects of AI technologies on their educational experiences and results. Institutions may engage students in joint research initiatives or focus groups designed to assess the efficacy of AI applications in educational settings. Alam & Mohanty (2023) underscore the importance of student participation in educational technology projects, indicating that students who perceive their opinions are valued are more inclined to adopt new technologies and participate actively in their learning. Alongside academic and student engagement, forging collaborations with industry partners is essential for comprehending AI developments and workforce demands. Partnering with technology firms and AI research institutes may provide organizations with knowledge about the most recent developments in AI technologies and their prospective uses in education. These collaborations may provide access to advanced AI technologies, resources, and knowledge, allowing universities to remain leaders in AI integration. Industry partners may contribute to curriculum development by supplying real-world case studies and examples that augment students' comprehension of AI applications across diverse industries.

BUILDING PARTNERSHIPS FOR RESOURCE SHARING

Collaboration with AI research institutions and technology firms may enhance knowledge transfer and provide access to state-of-the-art AI technologies. Forming alliances with research institutes may cultivate a culture of creativity and experimentation, motivating staff and students to investigate novel AI applications and approaches. These collaborations may facilitate cooperative research initiatives, conferences, and seminars that augment the institution's ability to incorporate AI proficiently. Institutions may partner with AI research institutes to create bespoke AI solutions designed to meet their unique educational requirements. Collaborative efforts between universities and research institutes can pinpoint domains where AI may have substantial influence, including customized education, predictive analytics, and administrative efficiency. Collaborative endeavors may result in the creation of novel technologies that improve teaching and learning results while tackling the specific issues encountered by each institution (Arinaitwe, 2021). Furthermore, partnerships with technology firms may provide universities-access to AI platforms, software, and tools that would otherwise be financially unfeasible. Numerous technology firms provide educational discounts or subsidies to facilitate AI integration in higher education. By using these resources, schools may augment their AI capabilities and provide staff and students with essential tools to investigate AI technologies in their educational practices. Establishing partnerships for resource sharing may also transcend AI-specific cooperation. Institutions may form cross-institutional collaborations to exchange best practices, research outcomes, and resources pertaining to AI integration. Establishing networks of institutions dedicated to investigating AI in education enables stakeholders to build a community of practice that promotes cooperation and information-exchange.

ENSURING TRANSPARENT COMMUNICATION

Clear communication is vital for cultivating trust and inclusion among stakeholders throughout the AI integration process. Institutions must articulate AI policies and choices transparently across several channels, such as institutional webpages, policy briefings, and stakeholder meetings. This openness may elucidate AI technology and guarantee that all stakeholders comprehend their roles and duties in the integration process. Effective communication of AI policy must address several facets, including data protection, ethical implications, and the anticipated results of AI implementation. Institutions must notify stakeholders on the use of AI technology in educational environments, the data to be gathered, and the safeguards implemented to protect student privacy. A research by Rezaei et al. (2024) emphasizes the significance of openness in fostering trust among stakeholders, indicating that explicit communication might mitigate apprehensions related to data security and ethical considerations surrounding AI technology. Besides policy communication, institutions must participate in continuous discussion with stakeholders to get input and resolve emerging problems. Consistent stakeholder meetings, surveys, and feedback systems may provide significant information into the efficacy of AI projects and identify areas for improvement. By actively seeking advice from professors, students, and industry partners, universities may show their dedication to collaborative decision-making and responsiveness to stakeholder requirements. Furthermore, institutions must contemplate the establishment of a centralized communication platform that aggregates information pertinent to AI integration. This website may function as a central repository for stakeholders to get materials, updates, and best practices about

AI technology. Establishing a designated area for AI-related discourse enables organizations to cultivate a feeling of community and cooperation among stakeholders, hence improving the efficacy of AI integration initiatives.

CASE STUDIES AND BEST PRACTICES

The use of AI in higher education has shown transformational capabilities, raising student performance, increasing operational efficiency, and promoting novel pedagogical approaches. This chapter examines many successful case studies of AI implementation in higher education, together with insights from institutional leaders and essential takeaways for reproducible success.

SUCCESSFUL AI ADOPTION IN HIGHER EDUCATION

Case Study 1: AI-Powered Predictive Analytics for Student Retention at a U.S. University

A prominent instance of effective AI implementation is the use of predictive analytics at Georgia State University (GSU) in the United States. GSU adopted an AI-powered predictive analytics approach to detect students at risk of attrition. The method evaluates many data sources, such as academic achievement, attendance records, and demographic information, to forecast which students may have difficulties in maintaining their studies. The institution used this prediction model to develop targeted interventions, including individualized advising and academic support services. For example, when the system recognized a student as being in danger, an adviser would contact them to provide support, urging the student to use relevant options. This effort led GSU to claim a notable rise in student retention rates, escalating from 72% to 82% over five years. This instance underscores the efficacy of AI in tackling student retention issues and illustrates the significance of data-informed decision-making in higher education.

Case Study 2: AI-Driven Automated Grading Systems Improving Assessment Efficiency in European Institutions

In Europe, institutions such as the University of Amsterdam and the University of Edinburgh have effectively used AI-driven automated grading systems to improve assessment efficiency. These systems use machine learning algorithms to assess student inputs, delivering prompt response while ensuring consistency and equity in grading. At the University of Amsterdam, the automated grading system was originally evaluated in large-scale courses with thousands of students. The AI system evaluated multiple-choice questions and short-answer essays, providing prompt feedback to students. This not only alleviated the grading burden for professors but also enabled students to get prompt feedback on their performance, hence enhancing learning outcomes. The efficacy of these automated grading systems highlights the capacity of AI to optimize assessment procedures, allowing educators to devote more time to interactive instruction and individualized student assistance. Furthermore, these methods have shown significant use in big lecture courses, where providing personalized feedback is often difficult.

Case Study 3: Intelligent Tutoring Systems Enhancing Personalized Learning at an Australian University

An intelligent teaching system (ITS) has been created at the University of Sydney in Australia to improve tailored learning experiences for students in computer science courses. This AI-driven platform customizes- to each student's learning style, speed, and preferences, delivering personalized exercises and feedback according to individual advancement. The ITS evaluates student interactions and performance metrics to pinpoint areas of difficulty and modifies the learning trajectory appropriately. The method promotes enhanced student engagement with course content by providing tailored suggestions and resources. A pilot research revealed that students using the ITS exhibited significant improvement in their comprehension of intricate programming topics, resulting in superior overall course grades relative to their counterparts not employing the system (Wang et al., 2024). This scenario underscores the significance of AI in promoting individualized learning experiences, allowing students to advance at their own speed while obtaining tailored assistance. As AI technologies advance, Intelligent Tutoring Systems are expected to significantly influence the future of education by addressing varied student requirements.

Case Study 4: AI-Powered Career Counseling and Job Matching at a Canadian University

The University of Toronto has built an AI-driven platform for career counseling and job matching to aid students in career planning and job searching. The system evaluates student profiles, including abilities, interests, and academic achievement, to align them with relevant career prospects and internships in real time. The platform utilizes natural language processing to evaluate job descriptions and discern the skills and competences necessary for diverse positions. It subsequently offers students tailored suggestions for employment vacancies, internships, and networking prospects that correspond with their profiles. The system also provides materials for résumé development and interview preparation. The deployment of an AI-driven career counseling platform has led to increased job placement rates among students, with several individuals obtaining internships and employment that closely correspond to their abilities and interests (Wong, 2024). This instance illustrates the capacity of AI to improve career services in higher education, therefore equipping students more effectively for the job market.

LESSONS LEARNED BY INSTITUTIONAL LEADERS

The effective use of AI in higher education has yielded significant insights from institutional leaders. Best practices recognized by leading institutions underscore the significance of governance, faculty development, and open communication. A crucial lesson is the need of instituting strong governance frameworks to supervise AI ventures. Institutions have-to establish AI ethics committees to guarantee compliance with ethical norms in AI applications and adherence to data protection rules. Governance frameworks must explicitly define duties for decision-making, accountability, and risk management concerning AI integration (Díaz-Rodríguez et al., 2023). A crucial observation is the need for extensive faculty training programs centered on AI literacy and pedagogical applications. Faculty members must possess the knowledge and abilities to properly integrate AI technologies into their pedagogical methods. Continuous professional development opportunities enable educators to remain updated on the latest breakthroughs in AI technology and their educational consequences (Alam, 2021). Finally, clear communication with stakeholders is crucial for establishing confidence and promoting a culture of cooperation. Institutions must provide explicit information about AI projects, encompassing their objectives, execution procedures, and any effects on students and staff. Involving stakeholders in dialogues on AI policies and practices may alleviate worries and foster a mutual understanding of the advantages and difficulties associated with AI integration.

KEY TAKEAWAYS FOR REPLICABLE SUCCESS

In order-to replicate the results shown in the case studies and best practices examined, institutions should concentrate on the following essential insights:

Establishing a Clear AI Strategy Aligned with Institutional Goals: Institutions must establish a holistic AI strategy that corresponds with their purpose, vision, and objectives. This plan must delineate the anticipated results of AI integration, the particular uses-of AI technology, and the resources necessary for its execution.

Prioritizing Ethical AI Implementation and Stakeholder Engagement: Ethical issues must be paramount in the deployment of AI. Institutions must emphasize openness, accountability, and equity in their AI activities. Involving stakeholders throughout the decision-making process guarantees the consideration of many viewpoints and a comprehensive evaluation of AI's possible effects on students and professors.

Investing in Continuous AI Education and Training: In order-to utilize AI's capabilities, schools must engage in continuous education and training for teachers, staff, and students. Professional development programs must prioritize the enhancement of AI literacy, comprehension of the ethical ramifications of AI technology, and the formulation of pedagogical methods for the integration of AI tools in education.

Monitoring and Evaluating AI Initiatives: Institutions must implement stringent evaluation criteria to consistently measure the effectiveness of AI projects. By evaluating student performance, operational efficiency, and ethical issues, institutions may make data-driven decisions to improve their AI programs and ensure they meet their objectives.

Fostering a Culture of Innovation and Collaboration: Institutions must cultivate an environment that encourages innovation and collaboration among scholars, students, and industry participants. Creating platforms for open dialogue, information exchange, and interdisciplinary collaboration may foster the development of innovative AI applications and enhance the entire educational experience.

FUTURE DIRECTIONS FOR LEADERSHIP IN AI ADOPTION

As AI technology advances swiftly, leaders in higher education must foresee forthcoming trends and problems to guarantee the successful and ethical incorporation of AI in academic settings. Leadership is crucial in navigating this changing environment, necessitating a proactive strategy to use the advantages of AI while confronting ethical and social concerns. This part examines projected trends in AI integration, the necessary preparations to tackle ethical issues, and the vision for creating the future of AI-enhanced education.

ANTICIPATING TRENDS IN AI INTEGRATION

Increased Reliance on AI-Driven Adaptive Learning Platforms

A prominent trend in AI integration is the increasing dependence on adaptive learning systems that use AI algorithms to customize educational experiences for individual students. These systems evaluate student data to discern learning patterns, strengths, and areas needing improvement, enabling tailored training. Studies indicate that adaptive learning may result in increased student engagement and superior learning results (Vanbecelaere et al., 2020). Purdue University, among other schools, has effectively integrated adaptive learning technology into its curriculum, leading to increased retention rates and enhanced academic performance among students (Arockia et al., 2024; Emon, 2025b). As AI-driven adaptive learning platforms advance, institutional leaders must provide resources for infrastructure, training, and support to enable professors and students to successfully engage with new technologies.

Expansion of AI Applications in Student Mental Health Support

A notable trend is the proliferation of AI apps aimed at enhancing student mental health. As universities acknowledge the significance of mental health in academic achievement, AI-powered solutions like chatbots and virtual counseling platforms are being included into student services. These technologies may provide round-the-clock assistance, give coping mechanisms, and enable access to mental health services.

The University of Michigan has implemented an AI-driven mental health chatbot that assists students in managing their emotions and offers customized resources according to their feedback (Patel & Indurkhya, 2024). This trend indicates a transition towards comprehensive strategies for student support, necessitating that institutional leaders prioritize the adoption of AI solutions that improve mental health services while safeguarding student privacy and confidentiality.

Growing Emphasis on Explainable AI in Decision-Making

As AI systems increasingly influence decision-making, the focus on explainable AI (XAI) is anticipated to intensify. XAI seeks to make the decision-making processes of AI systems comprehensible to users, enabling stakeholders to grasp the rationale behind AI-generated suggestions. This openness is essential in higher education, where choices about admissions, grading, and resource distribution may profoundly affect students and teachers. Leaders in higher education must promote the creation and incorporation of XAI frameworks inside their institutions. This entails educating professors and staff on the interpretation of AI outputs and facilitating informed decision-making based on these insights. Institutions that emphasize XAI will cultivate confidence in AI systems while also improving accountability and ethical concerns in its deployment (Agrawal, 2024).

PREPARING FOR ETHICAL AND SOCIETAL IMPLICATIONS

As AI technologies infiltrate higher education, leaders must proactively confront the ethical and social ramifications linked to AI implementation. This encompasses issues pertaining to AI bias, digital spying, and the safeguarding of student data.

Addressing AI Bias

AI systems possess bias commensurate with the data used for their training. If the foundational data exhibits historical biases, the AI may sustain these biases in its decision-making processes. Research indicates that AI algorithms used in admissions procedures may unintentionally favor certain demographic groups, leading to inequitable results (Emon, 2025c; Roshanaei, 2024). Institutional leaders must implement measures to guarantee that the data used in AI systems is representative, varied, and subject to frequent audits to mitigate bias.

Navigating Digital Surveillance

The rapid growth of AI in higher education engenders apprehensions around digital monitoring and privacy. Institutions may use AI-driven monitoring systems to assess student involvement and performance; nevertheless, these systems may infringe upon students' privacy and foster a culture of surveillance. Leaders must balance the use of AI to improve educational experiences with the preservation of student autonomy and privacy rights (Berendt et al., 2020). Institutions must formulate explicit regulations about the utilization of AI monitoring systems, guaranteeing that students are apprised-of data collecting methods and that their permission is secured. Furthermore, leaders must cultivate an ethical culture that emphasizes openness and responsibility in AI deployment.

Protecting Student Data

The safeguarding of student data is essential as educational institutions increasingly depend on AI systems that handle sensitive information. Institutional leaders must guarantee adherence to data protection standards, including the Family Educational Rights and Privacy Act (FERPA) in the United States and the General Data Protection Regulation (GDPR) in Europe. To protect student data, colleges must establish stringent cybersecurity protocols, do regular audits of AI systems, and provide training for teachers and staff on data privacy standards. By emphasizing data security, leaders may cultivate trust with students and stakeholders while promoting a safe educational environment.

SHAPING THE FUTURE OF AI-ENHANCED LEARNING

Effective AI leadership in higher education must be progressive and linked with the concepts of academic achievement, institutional integrity, and social advancement. Institutional leaders need to contemplate the following ways to influence the future of AI-enhanced education:

Developing a Strategic AI Vision

Institutional leaders must formulate a definitive strategic vision that corresponds with the institution's objectives to facilitate the successful integration of AI in education. This vision must include the prospective advantages of AI, including enhanced student performance, operational efficiency, and creative pedagogical approaches. By formulating a comprehensive plan, leaders may mobilize resources and get support from academics, staff, and stakeholders.

Fostering a Culture of Continuous Improvement

Leaders need to foster a culture of perpetual enhancement that promotes experimentation and innovation using AI technology. This entails establishing venues for teachers and staff to exchange their experiences, problems, and achievements in the implementation of AI solutions. By cultivating a collaborative atmosphere, schools may use collective knowledge to improve AI applications and augment their efficacy in facilitating student learning.

Engaging in Interdisciplinary Collaboration

The implementation of AI in higher education requires interdisciplinary cooperation. Leaders need to promote multidisciplinary collaborations among computer science, education, psychology, and other pertinent disciplines to create comprehensive AI solutions that tackle intricate educational issues. By promoting cooperation, universities may develop holistic AI systems that improve teaching and learning while accommodating many viewpoints.

Promoting Lifelong Learning for Faculty and Staff

As AI technologies advance, institutional leaders must emphasize continuous learning opportunities for academics and staff. Professional development programs need to emphasize the augmentation of AI literacy, ethical issues, and the pedagogical uses of AI technologies. By investing in ongoing education, institutions can guarantee that educators stay abreast of the newest developments in AI and are prepared to use these technologies successfully in their pedagogical methods.

Building Partnerships with Industry

Leaders need to pursue collaborations with industry pioneers and AI research institutions to promote knowledge transfer and access to advanced technology. Partnering with technology firms may provide universities with information about nascent AI trends, labor demands, and novel uses of AI in education. These collaborations may provide students with significant chances for internships, networking, and practical experiences.

CONCLUSION

The use of AI in higher education offers a revolutionary potential for institutions to improve teaching, learning, and administrative functions. This chapter has shown that the successful implementation of AI requires a comprehensive strategy including governance, capacity development, stakeholder engagement, and ethical issues. Primarily, developing strong governance frameworks is essential for ensuring openness and accountability in AI decision-making. By defining supervision responsibilities and establishing advisory committees, institutions may guarantee that AI applications comply with ethical norms and adequately meet the varied demands of students and teachers. Assessing and appraising AI efforts via explicitly defined measures will augment the efficacy and influence of these technologies on academic achievement and operational productivity. Moreover, the enhancement of skills and professional growth for teachers and staff is crucial for the effective incorporation of AI. Training programs centered on AI literacy, pedagogical applications, and ethical issues will enable educators to use AI technologies proficiently in their instructional methodologies. Promoting multidisciplinary cooperation will enhance AI education, enabling institutions to provide a holistic and inclusive learning environment. Involving many stakeholders, such as academics, students, and industry partners, is essential for establishing a collective vision for AI integration. By promoting open conversation and guaranteeing clear communication, organizations may cultivate trust and encourage a collaborative culture. Collaborations with industry and AI research institutions will improve resource allocation and provide access to advanced technology, therefore augmenting the educational experience. An analysis of case studies and exemplary practices from leading institutions highlights the significance of strategic planning, ethical execution, and stakeholder involvement in attaining reproducible success in AI deployment. By analyzing these experiences, institutions may formulate explicit AI strategies that correspond with their objectives, emphasize ethical issues, and provide resources for ongoing education and training for their professors and staff. Institutional leaders must stay alert in forecasting future trends in AI integration. This encompasses the adoption of AI-driven adaptive learning platforms, the enhancement of apps for student mental health assistance, and the prioritization of explainable AI in decision-making processes. Leaders must proactively confront the ethical and social ramifications of AI adoption, including AI bias, digital spying, and the safeguarding of student data. The future of AI in higher education depends on visionary leadership dedicated to creating an innovative, ethical, and inclusive learning environment. By using AI to improve academic achievement and institutional integrity, leaders may foster societal advancement and equip students for the challenges of a more digital landscape. The integration of AI is not just a technical pursuit but a significant chance to transform the educational environment for future generations.

REFERENCES

Agrawal, G. (2024). Accountability, Trust, and Transparency in AI Systems From the Perspective of Public Policy: Elevating Ethical Standards. In *AI Healthcare Applications and Security, Ethical, and Legal Considerations* (pp. 148–162). IGI Global Scientific Publishing. DOI: 10.4018/979-8-3693-7452-8.ch009

Alam, A. (2021). Possibilities and Apprehensions in the Landscape of Artificial Intelligence in Education. *2021 International Conference on Computational Intelligence and Computing Applications (ICCICA)*, 1–8. DOI: 10.1109/ICCICA52458.2021.9697272

Alam, A., & Mohanty, A. (2023). Educational technology: Exploring the convergence of technology and pedagogy through mobility, interactivity, AI, and learning tools. *Cogent Engineering*, *10*(2), 2283282. Advance online publication. DOI: 10.1080/23311916.2023.2283282

Alier, M., Casañ Guerrero, M. J., Amo, D., Severance, C., & Fonseca, D. (2021). Privacy and E-Learning: A Pending Task. *Sustainability (Basel)*, *13*(16), 9206. DOI: 10.3390/su13169206

Almufarreh, A., & Arshad, M. (2023). Promising Emerging Technologies for Teaching and Learning: Recent Developments and Future Challenges. *Sustainability (Basel)*, *15*(8), 6917. DOI: 10.3390/su15086917

Alqahtani, T., Badreldin, H. A., Alrashed, M., Alshaya, A. I., Alghamdi, S. S., bin Saleh, K., Alowais, S. A., Alshaya, O. A., Rahman, I., Al Yami, M. S., & Albekairy, A. M. (2023). The emergent role of artificial intelligence, natural learning processing, and large language models in higher education and research. *Research in Social & Administrative Pharmacy*, *19*(8), 1236–1242. DOI: 10.1016/j.sapharm.2023.05.016 PMID: 37321925

Ansarullah, S. I., Kirmani, M. M., Alshmrany, S., & Firdous, A. (2024). Ethical issues around artificial intelligence. In *A Biologist's Guide to Artificial Intelligence* (pp. 301–314). Elsevier., DOI: 10.1016/B978-0-443-24001-0.00018-X

Arinaitwe, D. (2021). Practices and strategies for enhancing learning through collaboration between vocational teacher training institutions and workplaces. *Empirical Research in Vocational Education and Training*, *13*(1), 13. DOI: 10.1186/s40461-021-00117-z

Bahroun, Z., Anane, C., Ahmed, V., & Zacca, A. (2023). Transforming Education: A Comprehensive Review of Generative Artificial Intelligence in Educational Settings through Bibliometric and Content Analysis. *Sustainability (Basel), 15*(17), 12983. DOI: 10.3390/su151712983

Bansal, U., Bharatwal, S., Bagiyam, D. S., & Kismawadi, E. R. (2024). Fraud Detection in the Era of AI: Harnessing Technology for a Safer Digital Economy. In *AI-Driven Decentralized Finance and the Future of Finance* (pp. 143–164). IGI Global Scientific Publishing. DOI: 10.4018/979-8-3693-6321-8.ch006

Başaran, O., & Turan, S. (2024). Reimagining Local Solutions to Global Challenges in Education: A Cross-Cultural Examination. In *Cultural Awareness and Diversity Management in Contemporary Education* (pp. 99–192). IGI Global Scientific Publishing. DOI: 10.4018/979-8-3373-0402-1.ch004

Bećirović, S. (2023). Privacy and Personal Data Protection in Digital Pedagogy. In *Digital Pedagogy* (pp. 83–96). Springer., DOI: 10.1007/978-981-99-0444-0_7

Berendt, B., Littlejohn, A., & Blakemore, M. (2020). AI in education: Learner choice and fundamental rights. *Learning, Media and Technology, 45*(3), 312–324. DOI: 10.1080/17439884.2020.1786399

Burr, C., & Leslie, D. (2023). Ethical assurance: A practical approach to the responsible design, development, and deployment of data-driven technologies. *AI and Ethics, 3*(1), 73–98. DOI: 10.1007/s43681-022-00178-0

Chan, C. K. Y. (2023). A comprehensive AI policy education framework for university teaching and learning. *International Journal of Educational Technology in Higher Education, 20*(1), 38. DOI: 10.1186/s41239-023-00408-3

Chen, Y., Jensen, S., Albert, L. J., Gupta, S., & Lee, T. (2023). Artificial Intelligence (AI) Student Assistants in the Classroom: Designing Chatbots to Support Student Success. *Information Systems Frontiers, 25*(1), 161–182. DOI: 10.1007/s10796-022-10291-4

Chiu, T. K. F., & Chai, C. (2020). Sustainable Curriculum Planning for Artificial Intelligence Education: A Self-Determination Theory Perspective. *Sustainability (Basel), 12*(14), 5568. DOI: 10.3390/su12145568

Chugh, R., Turnbull, D., Cowling, M. A., Vanderburg, R., & Vanderburg, M. A. (2023). Implementing educational technology in Higher Education Institutions: A review of technologies, stakeholder perceptions, frameworks and metrics. *Education and Information Technologies, 28*(12), 16403–16429. DOI: 10.1007/s10639-023-11846-x

Dhirani, L. L., Mukhtiar, N., Chowdhry, B. S., & Newe, T. (2023). Ethical Dilemmas and Privacy Issues in Emerging Technologies: A Review. *Sensors (Basel)*, *23*(3), 1151. DOI: 10.3390/s23031151 PMID: 36772190

Díaz-Rodríguez, N., Del Ser, J., Coeckelbergh, M., López de Prado, M., Herrera-Viedma, E., & Herrera, F. (2023). Connecting the dots in trustworthy Artificial Intelligence: From AI principles, ethics, and key requirements to responsible AI systems and regulation. *Information Fusion*, *99*, 101896. DOI: 10.1016/j.inffus.2023.101896

Emon, M. M. H. (2025a). Leveraging AI on Social Media & Digital Platforms to Enhance English Language Teaching and Learning. In *AI-Powered English Teaching* (pp. 211–238). IGI Global Scientific Publishing., DOI: 10.4018/979-8-3373-1952-0.ch007

Emon, M. M. H. (2025b). Circularity Meets AI: Revolutionizing Consumer Engagement Through Green Marketing. In *Transforming Business Practices With AI-Powered Green Marketing* (pp. 169–208). IGI Global Scientific Publishing. DOI: 10.4018/979-8-3373-3017-4.ch007

Emon, M. M. H. (2025c). Purpose-Driven Intelligence in Green Marketing: Leveraging AI for CSR-Centric and Sustainable Brand Positioning. In *Transforming Business Practices With AI-Powered Green Marketing* (pp. 89–122). IGI Global Scientific Publishing. DOI: 10.4018/979-8-3373-3017-4.ch004

Emon, M. M. H. (2025d). Navigating the Digital Labyrinth: Personal Data Privacy and Security at Individual and Organizational Levels. In *User-Centric Cybersecurity Implications for Sustainable Digital Transformation* (pp. 257–288). IGI Global Scientific Publishing. DOI: 10.4018/979-8-3373-3171-3.ch008

Emon, M. M. H., & Chowdhury, M. S. A. (2025). Safeguarding Student Data: Privacy and Security Challenges in AI-Powered Education Tools. In *Enhancing Student Support and Learning Through Conversational AI* (pp. 191–228). IGI Global Scientific Publishing. DOI: 10.4018/979-8-3373-3316-8.ch008

Emon, M. M. H., Nath, A., & Nipa, M. N. (2025). *AI for a Greener Tomorrow: Harnessing Artificial Intelligence for Environmental Sustainability*. IGI Global Scientific Publishing., DOI: 10.4018/979-8-3373-2387-9.ch010

Fazlioglu, M. (2021). *The United States and the EU's General Data Protection Regulation.*, DOI: 10.1007/978-94-6265-407-5_10

Fedele, A., Punzi, C., & Tramacere, S. (2024). The ALTAI checklist as a tool to assess ethical and legal implications for a trustworthy AI development in education. *Computer Law & Security Review*, *53*, 105986. DOI: 10.1016/j.clsr.2024.105986

Felzmann, H., Fosch-Villaronga, E., Lutz, C., & Tamò-Larrieux, A. (2020). Towards Transparency by Design for Artificial Intelligence. *Science and Engineering Ethics*, *26*(6), 3333–3361. DOI: 10.1007/s11948-020-00276-4 PMID: 33196975

Franco D'Souza, R., Mathew, M., Mishra, V., & Surapaneni, K. M. (2024). Twelve tips for addressing ethical concerns in the implementation of artificial intelligence in medical education. *Medical Education Online*, *29*(1), 2330250. Advance online publication. DOI: 10.1080/10872981.2024.2330250 PMID: 38566608

George, B., & Wooden, O. (2023). Managing the Strategic Transformation of Higher Education through Artificial Intelligence. *Administrative Sciences*, *13*(9), 196. DOI: 10.3390/admsci13090196

Grassini, S. (2023). Shaping the Future of Education: Exploring the Potential and Consequences of AI and ChatGPT in Educational Settings. *Education Sciences*, *13*(7), 692. DOI: 10.3390/educsci13070692

Gurgu, E. (2022). *Leadership on Ethical Bases in the University Environment to Improve Standards in Higher Education.*, DOI: 10.4018/978-1-6684-5195-3.ch003

Hagendorff, T. (2020). The Ethics of AI Ethics: An Evaluation of Guidelines. *Minds and Machines*, *30*(1), 99–120. DOI: 10.1007/s11023-020-09517-8

Hermann, E. (2022). Artificial intelligence and mass personalization of communication content—An ethical and literacy perspective. *New Media & Society*, *24*(5), 1258–1277. DOI: 10.1177/14614448211022702

Hickman, E., & Petrin, M. (2021). Trustworthy AI and Corporate Governance: The EU's Ethics Guidelines for Trustworthy Artificial Intelligence from a Company Law Perspective. *European Business Organization Law Review*, *22*(4), 593–625. DOI: 10.1007/s40804-021-00224-0

Kanbach, D. K., Heiduk, L., Blueher, G., Schreiter, M., & Lahmann, A. (2024). The GenAI is out of the bottle: Generative artificial intelligence from a business model innovation perspective. *Review of Managerial Science*, *18*(4), 1189–1220. DOI: 10.1007/s11846-023-00696-z

Khan, T., & Emon, M. M. H. (2025). The role of digital supply chain practices in enhancing firm performance: Insights from the manufacturing sector of Bangladesh. *Brazilian Journal of Operations & Production Management*, *22*(2), 2493. DOI: 10.14488/BJOPM.2493.2025

Khan, T., Emon, M. M. H., Rahman, K. M., Nipa, M. N., & Fuad, M. N. (2025). The Role of AI in Driving Customer Engagement Through Technological, Organizational and Environmental Enablers in E-Commerce. *2025 International Conference on Quantum Photonics, Artificial Intelligence, and Networking (QPAIN)*, 1–6. DOI: 10.1109/QPAIN66474.2025.11171949

Khan, T., Emon, M. M. H., Rahman, M. A., Hamid, A. B. A., & Yaakub, N. I. (2025). Bridging the Gap: Realizing GreenTech Potential. In *AI and Green Technology Applications in Society* (pp. 91–122). IGI Global Scientific Publishing. DOI: 10.4018/979-8-3693-9879-1.ch004

Kunacheva, N., Niyomves, B., & Kenaphoom, S. (2024). Innovative Strategies and Future Trends: The Next Paradigm of Education Management. In *Modern Management Science Practices in the Age of AI* (pp. 181–210). IGI Global Scientific Publishing. DOI: 10.4018/979-8-3693-6720-9.ch007

Lim, W. M., Kumar, S., & Ali, F. (2022). Advancing knowledge through literature reviews: 'what', 'why', and 'how to contribute.'. *Service Industries Journal*, *42*(7–8), 481–513. DOI: 10.1080/02642069.2022.2047941

Manda, V. K., Christy, V., & Jitta, M. R. (2024). Ethical AI and Decision-Making in Management Leadership. In *Ethical Dimensions of AI Development* (pp. 197–226). IGI Global Scientific Publishing., DOI: 10.4018/979-8-3693-4147-6.ch009

Mehta, P., Chillarge, G. R., Sapkal, S. D., Shinde, G. R., & Kshirsagar, P. S. (2023). Inclusion of Children With Special Needs in the Educational System, Artificial Intelligence (AI). In *AI-Assisted Special Education for Students With Exceptional Needs* (pp. 156–185). IGI Global Scientific Publishing. DOI: 10.4018/979-8-3693-0378-8.ch007

Meszaros, J., Ho, C., & Corrales Compagnucci, M. (2020). Nudging Consent and the New Opt-Out System to the Processing of Health Data in England. In *Legal Tech and the New Sharing Economy* (pp. 93–113). Springer., DOI: 10.1007/978-981-15-1350-3_5

Mhlanga, D. (2023). Open AI in Education, the Responsible and Ethical Use of ChatGPT Towards Lifelong Learning. In *FinTech and Artificial Intelligence for Sustainable Development. Sustainable Development Goals Series* (pp. 387–409). Palgrave Macmillan, Cham. DOI: 10.1007/978-3-031-37776-1_17

Mian, S. H., Salah, B., Ameen, W., Moiduddin, K., & Alkhalefah, H. (2020). Adapting Universities for Sustainability Education in Industry 4.0: Channel of Challenges and Opportunities. *Sustainability (Basel)*, *12*(15), 6100. DOI: 10.3390/su12156100

Patel, N. S., & Indurkhya, N. (2024). *The Rise of Intelligent Machines* (1st Editio). Chapman and Hall/CRC. DOI: 10.1201/9781003469551

Pudasaini, S., Miralles-Pechuán, L., Lillis, D., & Llorens Salvador, M. (2024). Survey on AI-Generated Plagiarism Detection: The Impact of Large Language Models on Academic Integrity. *Journal of Academic Ethics*. Advance online publication. DOI: 10.1007/s10805-024-09576-x

Rezaei, M., Pironti, M., & Quaglia, R. (2024). AI in knowledge sharing, which ethical challenges are raised in decision-making processes for organisations? *Management Decision*. Advance online publication. DOI: 10.1108/MD-10-2023-2023

Roshanaei, M. (2024). Towards best practices for mitigating artificial intelligence implicit bias in shaping diversity, inclusion and equity in higher education. *Education and Information Technologies*, *29*(14), 18959–18984. DOI: 10.1007/s10639-024-12605-2

S. C. V., Vidhyapriya, P., & V. P., A. (2024). The Role of AI in Transforming Assessment Practices in Education. In *AI Applications and Strategies in Teacher Education* (K. Keeley, pp. 43–70). IGI Global Scientific Publishing. DOI: 10.4018/979-8-3693-5443-8.ch003

Shoaib, M., Sayed, N., Singh, J., Shafi, J., Khan, S., & Ali, F. (2024). AI student success predictor: Enhancing personalized learning in campus management systems. *Computers in Human Behavior*, *158*, 108301. DOI: 10.1016/j.chb.2024.108301

Singh, J. P., Mishra, N., & Mishra, K. K. (2024). Promoting Academic Integrity: Strategies and Challenges in Higher Education. In *Higher Education and Quality Assurance Practices* (pp. 191–224). IGI Global Scientific Publishing. DOI: 10.4018/979-8-3693-6765-0.ch007

Stypinska, J. (2023). AI ageism: A critical roadmap for studying age discrimination and exclusion in digitalized societies. *AI & Society*, *38*(2), 665–677. DOI: 10.1007/s00146-022-01553-5 PMID: 36212226

Tariq, M. U., & Sergio, R. P. (2024). *Nurturing Digital Citizenship in Society 5.0 Through AI and Computational Intelligence Education* (pp. 59–84). DOI: 10.4018/979-8-3693-4326-5.ch003

Vanbecelaere, S., Van den Berghe, K., Cornillie, F., Sasanguie, D., Reynvoet, B., & Depaepe, F. (2020). The effectiveness of adaptive versus non-adaptive learning with digital educational games. *Journal of Computer Assisted Learning*, *36*(4), 502–513. DOI: 10.1111/jcal.12416

Villegas-Ch, W., & García-Ortiz, J. (2023). Toward a Comprehensive Framework for Ensuring Security and Privacy in Artificial Intelligence. *Electronics (Basel), 12*(18), 3786. DOI: 10.3390/electronics12183786

Wamba-Taguimdje, S.-L., Fosso Wamba, S., Kala Kamdjoug, J. R., & Tchatchouang Wanko, C. E. (2020). Influence of artificial intelligence (AI) on firm performance: The business value of AI-based transformation projects. *Business Process Management Journal, 26*(7), 1893–1924. DOI: 10.1108/BPMJ-10-2019-0411

Wang, R., Zulkifli, N. N., & Mohd Ayub, A. F. (2024). Investigating the Impact of the Stratified Cognitive Apprenticeship Model on High School Students' Math Performance. *Education Sciences, 14*(8), 898. DOI: 10.3390/educsci14080898

Wong, L. P. W. (2024). Artificial Intelligence and Job Automation: Challenges for Secondary Students' Career Development and Life Planning. *Merits, 4*(4), 370–399. DOI: 10.3390/merits4040027

Yadav, S. (2025). Leveraging AI to Enhance Teaching and Learning in Education. In *Optimizing Research Techniques and Learning Strategies With Digital Technologies* (pp. 211–238). IGI Global., DOI: 10.4018/979-8-3693-7863-2.ch008

Yadav, U., & Shrawankar, U. (2024). *Artificial Intelligence Across Industries.*, DOI: 10.4018/979-8-3693-5443-8.ch010

Zdravkova, K. (2022). *The Potential of Artificial Intelligence for Assistive Technology in Education.*, DOI: 10.1007/978-3-031-04662-9_4

Zeineddine, H., Braendle, U., & Farah, A. (2021). Enhancing prediction of student success: Automated machine learning approach. *Computers & Electrical Engineering, 89*, 106903. DOI: 10.1016/j.compeleceng.2020.106903

Zhang, L., Amos, C., & Pentina, I. (2025). Interplay of rationality and morality in using ChatGPT for academic misconduct. *Behaviour & Information Technology, 44*(3), 491–507. DOI: 10.1080/0144929X.2024.2325023

KEY TERMS AND DEFINITIONS

Adaptive Learning: An educational approach using AI algorithms to tailor the learning experience according to individual student requirements, preferences, and performance, hence facilitating customized teaching and enhancing learning results.

AI Ethics Committees: Entities formed inside enterprises to monitor the ethical ramifications of AI technology, guaranteeing that AI applications comply with ethical norms and do not reinforce prejudices or injustices.

AI-Driven Mental Health Support: The use of AI technology, including chatbots and virtual counseling platforms, to provide students with mental health resources and assistance, therefore addressing their emotional and psychological well-being.

Data Protection Officer (DPO): An appointed professional tasked for ensuring adherence to data privacy standards inside an organization, specifically with the acquisition, storage, and processing of personal data.

Explainable AI (XAI): A collection of procedures and methodologies in AI development designed to elucidate the decision-making mechanisms of AI systems, hence fostering transparency and accountability in the formulation of AI-generated recommendations.

Interdisciplinary Collaboration: The integration of information, processes, and viewpoints from several academic fields to formulate complete solutions, especially in tackling the intricate issues posed by AI in education.

Lifelong Learning: The perpetual quest for knowledge and skills throughout an individual's life, highlighting the need for continuing professional development for educators and staff to remain abreast of advancing AI trends and applications.

Stakeholder Engagement: The continuous pursuit of knowledge and skills throughout an individual's life, highlighting the need of continuing professional development for educators and staff to remain abreast of advancing AI trends and applications.

Chapter 13

Navigating the AI-Driven Classroom: Building Faculty Resilience and Transformative Pedagogy

Muhammad Usman Tariq
http://orcid.org/0000-0002-7605-3040
Abu Dhabi University, UAE & University College Cork, Ireland

ABSTRACT

The rapid integration of artificial intelligence (AI) in education is reshaping traditional teaching methodologies, necessitating a shift in faculty roles, pedagogical strategies, and institutional frameworks. Navigating the AI-Driven Classroom: Building Faculty Resilience and Transformative Pedagogy explores how educators can adapt to this evolving landscape by developing resilience, fostering digital literacy, and implementing innovative teaching approaches. This chapter examines the challenges faculty face, including AI-driven content generation, ethical considerations, and the need for continuous professional development. By analyzing transformative pedagogical models, such as inquiry-based learning and adaptive assessment strategies, the chapter highlights how AI can enhance student engagement and personalization in learning. The role of faculty as facilitators of critical thinking and ethical AI use is emphasized, ensuring that technology serves as a tool for empowerment rather than replacement.

INTRODUCTION

Educational practices have experienced fundamental transformations through the fast adoption of artificial intelligence (AI), which creates new potential doors

DOI: 10.4018/979-8-3373-1285-9.ch013

and substantial obstacles for educational staff. People utilize AI-based tools and platforms throughout their education experience to substantially modify how students learn, how learners interact with their educators, what constitutes student evaluation methods, and how university administrators work. AI delivers efficiency through personalized content delivery systems and automated grading technologies, which restructure typical instructor responsibilities in education. The traditional role of senior educators who managed classroom discussions has evolved into an adaptive teaching requirement in digital learning systems, which demands their dual insights into technology platforms and educational development. This study investigates the educational resilience techniques that professors need to implement for success in AI-enabled educational spaces (Adeoye & Otemuyiwa, 2024). Teachers must adapt because AI automates repetitive tasks, including assignment evaluation, plagiarism detection, and recommendation system operation for student materials. New technological systems help reduce administrative work, but at the same time, they disrupt the institutional roles of instructors. The use of AI-grade programs provides a precise evaluation of multiple-choice exams and short-answer questions to decrease faculty grading work, which frees time for personalized education. The adoption of these systems raises doubts regarding clear evaluation methods when applied to subjective assignments, as human judgment plays an important role in evaluating essays (Mustafa, 2023). Teaching faculty must merge AI systems with their educational methodology to preserve academic quality, because automated systems should not diminish deep student comprehension. Student performance analytics through AI systems create individualized learning tracks that detect specific learning obstacles to guide learners toward appropriate resources that help fill educational gaps (Tariq, 2025a). Carnegie Learning's MATHia platform automatically adjusts learning difficulty based on student advancement to provide personalized lessons. Personalized instruction benefits student learning, but it causes faculty members to question what features should guide student learning experiences. Educators need to restructure their curriculum delivery methods to support critical thinking instruction rather than content transmission once AI assumes dominant control over student learning decisions. Higher resilience levels emerge when educators accept AI as their performance assistant instead of their competition and exploit its capabilities to boost human teaching quality (Mustafa, 2023).

Implementing AI into educational systems sparks difficulties in its acceptance because faculties resist changing their approach. Educational faculty members worry about diminished independence, depreciation of their professional knowledge base, and moral questions regarding AI in teaching practices. There is a fear that AI-generated educational content, along with automated teaching systems, could replace educational personnel to the extent that faculty involvement becomes unnecessary. However, valid issues do not recognize how AI can enhance teaching practices. The use of artificial intelligence allows teachers to direct their efforts toward advanced educational functions, such as mentorship and research-based teaching, together with intellectual dialogue, instead of managing repetitive administrative work. Higher-level strategic adaptation enables faculty members to transform AI into improved professional capabilities instead of facing feelings of imminent threat (Adeoye & Otemuyiwa, 2024). Additionally, faculty resilience in AI-driven classrooms necessitates a strong foundation in digital literacy and ongoing professional development. Educational staff who have not received proper instruction on AI technology face large gaps in their understanding, which prevents them from integrating AI properly. Educational institutions need to establish professional development opportunities for instructors that will teach them concrete skills along with the faith to handle AI resources competently. Educational institutions adopting AI-enhanced learning systems need to establish carefully designed workshops, together with hands-on instruction and peer mentoring programs, which aid users through their transition process. The evaluation demonstrates that technology changes more rapidly than academic professional development initiatives, making both institutions and educators implement new technological systems at different rates. This gap requires continuous learning from institutions to ensure that faculty members become part of AI's educational framework development beyond being simple adopters (Yadav, 2025; Tariq, 2025b). The practice of faculty resilience extends to the evaluation of both moral ethical conduct and instructional practices in higher education. The perfect nature of AI remains elusive because algorithms contain biases that lead to educational inequities, which negatively affect groups of students. Automated scoring of student essays, together with facial recognition systems, tends to demonstrate discriminatory biases toward race, gender, and socioeconomic background, resulting in inconsistent student treatment. Institutes of higher learning should perform consistent assessments of their AI system tools, as these technologies should uphold academic integrity and the principles of fairness and inclusiveness. The active investigation of AI applications by faculty members helps institutions achieve ethical and responsible AI implementation (Mustafa, 2023). The success of AI-driven education depends heavily on faculty members who display a willingness to adapt, evaluate AI implications, and design contemporary educational practices. The main objective of this chapter is to equip teachers with essential tools, strategic approaches, and meaningful insights that enable them to approach the transformation with assurance. Education faculties can positively use AI capabilities to establish revolutionary learning areas that serve students while strengthening their creative skills, critical thinking, and collaborative abilities. Through this effort, educators can enhance their roles in the future and help form a learning system that integrates AI technology into a human-centered educational standard (Adeoye & Otemuyiwa, 2024).

BACKGROUND

The ability of teaching staff to handle both technological progress and educational uncertainties through the ongoing development of digital learning methods defines their resilience in AI-driven educational systems. Modern resilience in AI-enhanced education differs from traditional resilience in that it requires faculty members to actively approach new technologies and test their boundaries through continuous educational development. Academic staff must develop a positive attitude toward adjustment instead of letting resistance deter them because AI represents an advantage that strengthens their instructional practices in educational settings (Swargiary, 2024). AI-equipped education depends heavily on adaptability for its resilience to succeed. The rapid entry of AI tools into universities has led to the demand for teachers to adopt adaptable instruction methods that include intelligent tutoring systems, automated grading software, and AI-produced content. Instead of using AI grading assistance to reduce their evaluation power, teachers can maximize administrative efficiency, which in turn gives them time for student-specific educational approaches. Gradescope has proven its worth by utilizing AI for grading assistance, thus reducing instructor workloads to enable better application of higher educational methods. Complete technological adoption in education goes beyond equipment distribution because organizations need motivated staff to test traditional procedures and implement modern teaching strategies (Singh, 2024). Building resilience through faculty learning communities (FLCs) enables peers to share knowledge while receiving mutual support to develop it. AI integration succeeds through combined efforts that require different educational backgrounds to work together. Academic institutions can achieve greater faculty dedication toward AI systems and improved tool-handling abilities by conducting organized AI training, including discussion-based activities and team-based tasks. Arizona State University serves as an example of an institution that has developed AI-focused professional development programs to help faculty members discover AI applications for their disciplines (Swargiary, 2024). Figure 1 provides overview of important elements that support faculty resilience.

Figure 1. Framework for faculty resilience in AI-enhanced education

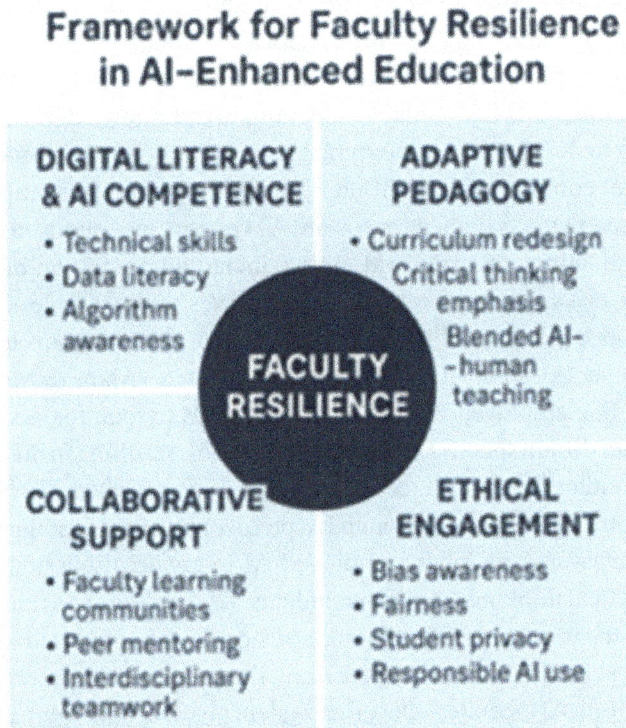

The ability of faculty members to transform their instructional methods through technological progress while handling the unknown aspects of the digital learning environment qualifies as resilience in AI-driven education. Modern resilience in AI-enhanced education differs from traditional resilience in that it requires faculty members to actively approach new technologies and test their boundaries through continuous educational development. Academic staff must develop a positive attitude toward adjustment instead of letting resistance deter them because AI represents an advantage that strengthens their instructional practices in educational settings (Alam & Mohanty, 2024). Adaptability is a fundamental element that supports resilience functions in AI-enhanced educational settings. The rapid entry of AI tools into universities has led to the demand for teachers to adopt adaptable instruction methods that include intelligent tutoring systems, automated grading software, and AI-produced content. Instead of using AI grading assistance to reduce their evaluation power, teachers can maximize administrative efficiency, which in turn gives them time for student-specific educational approaches. Gradescope has proven its worth by utilizing AI for grading assistance, thus reducing instructor workloads to enable better application of higher educational methods. Therefore, technology access alone is insufficient for successful adaptation, as successful adaptation requires both experimental character and careful assessment of outdated methods and innovative teaching principles (Swargiary, 2024). Building resilience through faculty learning communities (FLCs) enables peers to share knowledge while receiving mutual support to develop it. AI integration succeeds through combined efforts that require different educational backgrounds to work together. Academic institutions can achieve greater faculty dedication toward AI systems and improved tool-handling abilities by conducting organized AI training, including discussion-based activities and team-based tasks. Arizona State University serves as an example of an institution that has developed AI-focused professional development programs to help faculty members discover AI applications for their disciplines (Alam & Mohanty, 2024; Tariq, 2025c). She employed AI tracking dashboards to monitor student progress, which helped her design specific intervention methods, resulting in improved student retention. The judicial use of AI technology proves that student-teacher bonds will improve rather than fade away. Through his philosophy courses at the University of Edinburgh, Professor Alex Taylor employed AI to create discussion prompts that enhanced analytical thinking among his students. AI functions as a thinking catalyst, demonstrating the necessity of faculty supervision for AI-supported learning activities (Strielkowski et al., 2024). The preceding illustrations demonstrate that faculty resilience within an AI-operated education system involves active engagement rather than simple technological acceptance. The educational process necessitates that faculty members actively participate with AI systems while assessing their effects on teaching practices and developing instructional approaches that maximize their benefits. Teachers who achieve the highest success within AI-enhanced educational environments understand that AI operates as an enhancement of their mentoring and inspirational abilities. The combination of adaptability training and educational progress alongside moral AI advocacy enables faculty members to direct educational evolution toward a beneficial transformation (Alam & Mohanty, 2024).

Educational processes have experienced profound transformations because of artificial intelligence (AI) integration into the education industry, which affects both classroom methods, teacher responsibilities, and student evaluation standards. AI-powered tools present multiple benefits for enhancing efficiency and personalizing education, but educators face growing difficulties due to the rapid advancement of AI technologies in the educational field. Traditional instructional practices of faculty members must transition into enhanced teaching with AI tools while also coping with automatic assessment and data-driven educational decision systems. The growing use of AI-powered educational tools in educational institutions makes faculty members' adaptability and creative thinking imperative factors for producing successful learning results and institutional achievement (Eslit, 2023). The educational field uses a wide range of technological tools to develop AI-based education through adaptive learning systems, AI-driven chatbots, virtual instructional aides, and computerized grading systems. These innovations prove their ability to improve learner participation while providing instant response capabilities. Through Carnegie Learning's MATHia software, AI engines analyze students' solving methods to create customized help, enabling individualized instruction. The academic integrity monitoring process has changed significantly because of AI-powered writing assistants, including Grammarly and Turnitin's AI-driven plagiarism detection tools. These educational tools have established new capabilities for instructors; however, they force both faculty and traditional teaching methods to reshape their educational practices (Singh, 2024). AI-driven classrooms present a pivotal obstacle because of their ability to replace the typical responsibilities of educational staff. AI systems that perform basic functions, such as grading tasks and content delivery, make some educators anticipate that their role might function as a supporting player to technology. AI technology improves teacher capabilities rather than removing their roles, as it allows educators to spend more time on tasks that require critical thinking and individual student assistance. Faculty who actively use AI should relocate their work toward creative development and ethical judgment, together with human-centered problem-solving, which remains outside AI capabilities (Eslit, 2023; Tariq, 2025d). Automated tools for student essay analysis can only provide grammar and structure checks, while trained faculty instructors maintain unique skills for understanding rhetoric, cultural context, and argumentation. Educational institutions need to invest in sustained programs for faculty development that will teach both digital literacy and new teaching methods utilizing AI. Professionals teaching at educational institutions often resist the new implementation of AI because they have not received sufficient AI technology training. Essentially, structured AI training programs result in educators who demonstrate more willingness and competence when attempting new tools for educational development. The Massachusetts Institute of Technology (MIT) has formed AI-focused professional development programs to build practical usage strategies for AI in classroom settings for its faculty. Training programs focus on both teaching technical AI operations and promoting ethical thinking to enable educators to review AI in educational applications (Awadallah Alkouk & Khlaif, 2024).

The main challenge in AI-driven education extends beyond technical implementation to maintaining responsible and fair usage of AI tools. When AI systems are improperly designed and lack assessment, they maintain and spread educational inequalities through biased operations. Standardized testing and admissions decisions that utilize AI systems have documented issues with biased algorithms that affect fairness and transparency in the system. The main stakeholders in AI implementation – faculty members – need to fully participate in sustaining ethical practices in

AI integration for education. The implementation of AI-based assessment practices requires faculty members to verify data sources, develop unbiased algorithms, and continuously supervise AI-assisted evaluation processes. The essential training requirement for faculty members needs to include labeling AI's ethical practice so that they can make educated choices when incorporating AI technology (Eslit, 2023). The psychological and emotional aspects of technological change affect faculty members in AI-driven educational settings. Academic staff must undergo complete cognitive and emotional adjustments when they shift from standard instructional practices to AI-reinforced instructional techniques. Academicians with traditional classroom habits find it difficult to handle digital learning platforms that heavily depend on AI communication systems.

Organizations that focus on staff health and develop resilience programs can help create solutions to these difficulties. The Center for Teaching and Learning at Stanford University helps faculty members manage digital exhaustion and implement technological tools effectively through mentorship initiatives (Awadallah Alkouk & Khlaif, 2024). The educational achievements of faculty members who understand and adapt to AI demonstrate how their resilience, combined with their willingness to transform, results in better teaching outcomes. Academic members of the College of Education at the University of Florida use AI discussion systems to create interactive learning environments supported by students. AI-driven analytics integrated into teaching programs help educational staff detect student difficulties early and deliver focused intervention activities, thus boosting student success. The University of Melbourne uses artificial intelligence to create simulations that help strengthen hands-on educational experiences within medical and engineering training curricula. AI enriches faculty-student connections if academia uses it strategically during educational processes (Qudrat-Ullah, 2024). AI technologies should be led by faculty's active collaboration to determine their integration procedures rather than being implemented as passive recipients by academics. Academic institutions need to establish spiritual settings for teachers to voice their opinions on AI integration to ensure that it supports pedagogical objectives before administrative effectiveness. An open dialogue between faculty members is necessary when making AI policies to prevent technologically driven choices that minimize costs instead of enhancing education standards (Awadallah Alkouk & Khlaif, 2024). Employees in faculty roles face both promising opportunities and demanding challenges because of AI-powered classroom environments. The educational revolution made possible by AI will succeed to the extent that faculty members successfully incorporate and mold its implementation into teaching and learning. To ensure that AI-driven education continues to be a tool for empowerment rather than disruption, it is crucial to build faculty resilience through ongoing learning, ethical AI engagement, and institutional support. In addition to navigating the intricacies of AI, educators can spearhead meaningful and student-centered changes in 21st-century education by cultivating a culture of flexibility and pedagogical creativity (Kayal, 2024; Tariq, 2025e).

Transforming Pedagogy with AI

The implementation of artificial intelligence (AI) systems in educational institutions creates an excellent opportunity to modernize standard teaching practices. The historical education system focused on established curricula, lectures, and broad assessment methods. Recent technological developments based on AI have created dynamic educational methods that deliver personalized content using data-driven approaches to suit individual students. Educational evolution requires more than just new tools, as it means completely redesigning how instructors create lesson plans, evaluate student advancement, and determine which decisions require technological assistance versus human expertise (Barrera Castro et al., 2024). The educational world is being transformed by AI because it perfects conventional classroom practices. Large information transmission through lectures retains effectiveness, but it fails to provide tailored instruction and perform immediate student understanding adjustments. Carnegie Learning's AI-enabled tutoring systems offer teachers the opportunity to change standard educational practices because they provide distinct learning assistance to students based on their individual educational requirements. Student-centered learning methods have emerged through AI-powered learning systems as they replace previous memorization methods (Barrera Castro et al., 2024). AI tools can significantly improve the design process of educational curricula. Teachers who develop curricula have always relied on standardized learning objectives combined with past student data and institutional regulations to develop curricula. AI analytical tools allow instructors to update curriculum organization by processing current student interaction, understanding, and performance metrics. Knewton applies AI-driven machine learning to adjust course materials through its curriculum management tools, which then support each learner's unique progression speed. Educators gain the power to create flexible programs by utilizing these technologies, which improve student participation and prevent sudden losses of enrollment data and achievement improvements (George, 2023). AI has changed assessment procedures through the implementation of adaptive testing methods and personalized evaluation systems. The current exam system, together with standardized tests, loses valuable student-learning information because it fails to measure diverse educational experiences and aptitudes. AI assessment tools create detailed evaluation outcomes that analyze both correct and incorrect answers, along with students' approach to solving problems. Students benefit from AI evaluation on Gradescope, which evaluates their handwritten answers while offering feedback about their solution techniques instead of focusing solely on their end responses. Educators can gain better knowledge of student problem-solving processes through these tools to improve their lesson content. The evaluation protocols generated by AI assessment systems minimize grading bias because they establish uniform metrics to prevent subjective grading decisions from human evaluators (Barrera Castro et al., 2024).

Almost every aspect of education receives improved direction through AI technology, which specializes in individualized feedback delivery. The traditional practice of delivering personal feedback to students took up substantial amounts of educator time because faculty members hit limits in their workload capacities. AI-powered feedback platforms, such as Turnitin Feedback Studio and Grammarly's writing evaluations, provide instant feedback to students to develop their writing, critical thinking, and grammar skills. Automated assessment tools show strength in handling linguistic and structural problems but cannot handle the profound level of human-grade feedback, especially regarding complex arguments and creative and original work. The optimal implementation of AI for feedback systems requires AI to manage standard procedural feedback, while human experts should concentrate on providing detailed evaluative assessments (Karam, 2023). The benefits of AI in education require careful evaluation to address the problems that arise from its implementation. The main issue arises from leaning too heavily on AI systems while diminishing the importance of human contact. Education requires more than transferring information through the integration of mentorship, emotional intelligence, and social learning activities. The processing capabilities of AI systems remain high, but they lack the human ability to express empathy, understand contextual situations, and demonstrate moral behavior (George, 2023).

When evaluating student discussion participation, an AI system lacks an understanding of the social elements and emotional factors that impact student learning. Educational personnel must ensure that AI functions support the essential human skills needed for instruction. Schools face difficulties due to ethical concerns arising from the use of AI in education. AI platforms access student data to enhance educational outcomes; however, this practice raises questions about protecting information along with obtaining proper authorizations and compensation for underlying system issues. The occurrence of historical educational biases in training datasets can cause AI models to strengthen educational inequalities during operation. An important case of AI-related dispute involves university admissions systems that use algorithms because certain models discriminate against less privileged students because their training data contain built-in biases. Faculty members should participate in thorough debates that discuss responsible AI implementation in classrooms to establish unobstructed and fair AI regulatory frameworks (Karam, 2023). To create successful instructional choices, both human intuition and AI analysis must work together. AI provides instructors with data-based suggestions; however, faculty members must use their expertise to evaluate these system recommendations. A trained educator would recognize the student's anxiety when AI recommends more algorithmically generated exercises for struggling math students. The significant role of human intuition emerges in designing suitable interventions because experts understand the source of the learning problems. This integration demonstrates the potential of AI for educational improvement through proper implementation. The adoption of predictive analytics based on artificial intelligence at Georgia State University allows faculty members to identify students who face academic risk so that they can provide the required interventions that boost student retention numbers (Ozer et al., 2024). An AI chatbot named "Alex" operates at Arizona State University to support students by assisting their algebra learning, which results in better problem-solving capabilities through interactive educational exercises. The use of artificial intelligence creates more inclusive and effective learning environments when implemented through strategic measures. The purpose of AI technology in educational transformation is to deliver advanced educational tools that help instructors enhance their instructional methods while retaining the human elements of teaching. Teaching professionals who apply AI developments in their practice design unique educational experiences that use student analytics for educational improvements while keeping human connections at the forefront of learning. Future educational applications of AI will succeed only when teachers maintain control over AI tools to combine automated infrastructure with human interaction standards and innovative creations in their classrooms. Proper balance management enables educators to access the full potential of artificial intelligence to develop a transformative learning experience that places students at its center (Karam, 2023).

AI AND STUDENT ENGAGEMENT

The integration of artificial intelligence (AI) in education has transformed student connectivity through personalized lesson experiences that utilize both interactive and immersive teaching methods. Standard educational spaces deliver effective structured teaching; however, they fail to keep students engaged because they apply identical teaching methods to every student. AI tools create individualized learning experiences that help students achieve better understanding, motivation, and success outcomes. Educators can create engaging learning environments that adapt to individual student requirements by deploying interactive AI tools alongside adaptive learning platforms and AI-driven feedback systems (Bohara & Rana, 2024). AI technology leads to significant improvements in student engagement through the creation of interactive learning environments. Students benefit from AI-powered chatbots and virtual tutors coupled with game-based platforms because these tools deliver immediate feedback, which enhances learning accessibility while making it more interesting for students (Husain, 2023). Duolingo represents an AI-driven language learning app that implements three gamification methods such as personal progress tracking and individual quizzes in combination with rewarding students to perpetuate their educational journey. The system analyzes user behaviors to modify difficulty rates and content distribution while finding the perfect challenge threshold that leads users to maintain continuous involvement. Through its chatbot named "Jill Watson" Georgia Tech helps students receive quick responses to course inquiries, which promotes better course content interaction. The implemented educational tools enhance both student learning speed and build environments that encourage students to actively engage with their coursework (Hutson & Rains, 2024). Student engagement receives further development through dynamic learning solutions that adjust instruction by processing immediate student performance information. Traditional education represents its curricula as static documents that lack accommodations for personal student understanding variations and mastery of the subject material. Knewton, Squirrel AI, and Smart Sparrow leverage AI algorithms to evaluate student work and follow student development while modifying instructional content. These programs pinpoint the subjects in which students falter and offer pertinent materials to boost comprehension. For instance, Squirrel AI, which is popular in China, uses machine learning algorithms to identify students' areas of weakness and suggest tailored courses, greatly enhancing student performance and retention. AI ensures that students stay interested in the course rather than being irritated by too-easy or too-hard content by adjusting to their own speed (Bohara & Rana, 2024).

Beyond customization, AI-powered advances have greatly increased student success and motivation. AI-powered solutions for augmented reality (AR) and virtual reality (VR) provide immersive learning environments that humanize abstract concepts. AI-driven simulations are used in STEM education by platforms such as Labster, which allows students to perform virtual biology and chemistry experiments in authentic laboratory environments. By giving abstract ideas a more tangible form, these simulations encourage curiosity and active learning. In a similar vein, medical students may view and work with 3D models of human organs in interactive anatomy classes made possible by Microsoft's AI-powered HoloLens, which enhances their comprehension via practical investigation. Educators can use AI and immersive technology to produce captivating learning experiences that improve motivation and understanding (Husain, 2023). Notwithstanding these developments, using AI to engage students raises several issues that require careful consideration. AI tools run the risk of decreasing human connection in the classroom, even while they may customize learning.

Learning is more than just taking in facts; it also involves teamwork, communication, and critical thinking skills that are best cultivated through interpersonal interactions. An overreliance on AI-powered tools, including chatbots and automated tutors, might reduce the possibilities for mentoring and peer interaction and result in a more solitary learning environment. To solve this, educators need to integrate AI tools in a manner that balances social learning, group discussions, and instructor-led assistance (Bohara & Rana, 2024). The possibility that AI may strengthen prejudices in schooling is another concern. Numerous AI-powered systems depend on algorithms trained on historical data, which might unintentionally maintain disparities in access to learning materials. An AI-driven platform might not adequately serve students from underrepresented or underprivileged backgrounds, for example, if it is largely trained on data from high-achieving students. Furthermore, if AI-driven interfaces are not created with accessibility in mind, students with impairments may encounter difficulties using them. Careful planning, open algorithms, and ongoing monitoring are necessary to ensure that AI technologies foster diversity and avoid biased learning results (Husain, 2023). Despite these obstacles, AI can undoubtedly transform student engagement. As evidenced by successful case studies, AI may greatly improve learning outcomes when used carefully. Higher course completion rates have resulted from the deployment of AI-driven tutoring systems at the Arizona State University to help students who struggle with algebra understand arithmetic concepts. Similarly, teachers at the Open University in the UK can offer early interventions and assistance because AI-powered analytics analyze student participation and forecast academic success. These illustrations show how AI can be deliberately included to produce a more effective, individualized, and interesting learning environment (Hutson & Rains, 2024). AI's contribution to student engagement is centered on its capacity to enhance learning through motivation, interaction, and adaptability of the learning process. The secret to its success, however, is not to replace human instructors but rather to enhance their knowledge with insights from artificial intelligence. The responsible use of AI by educators can help them develop engaging and inclusive learning environments that meet the demands of a wide range of students while maintaining the fundamentally human aspects of instruction. AI's role in education will be determined by its capacity to supplement, not replace, the social, cognitive, and emotional components of learning, keeping students interested in ways that are both pedagogically sound and technologically sophisticated (Bohara & Rana, 2024).

Ethical Considerations in AI Integration

Educational institutions now use AI innovations to generate substantial progress, which optimizes both educational results and individual teaching approaches, in addition to enhancing student engagement. Educational innovations create substantial ethical problems regarding privacy issues, while causing problems with equitable treatment and biases, alongside academic integrity matters. Educational institutions face risks when AI systems operate without ethical guidance, as this could strengthen social gaps, break student privacy, and challenge academic standards. Educational institutions need to provide safeguards to protect the responsible and ethical use of AI-driven tools because they continue to adopt such tools (Oyedotun, 2024). AI-enhanced classrooms have a major ethical concern in protecting student privacy through data security standards. The educational technology infrastructure that integrates artificial intelligence gathers significant student data from metrics on performance, habit patterns, and behavioral patterns. Valuable educational data pose privacy issues regarding storage locations, circulation methods, and deployment practices. Student data remain at risk of compromise when its management falls short because it becomes susceptible to breaches from unauthorized parties who might also use it commercially (Long et al., 2024). A 2020 ProctorU data breach unveiled sensitive student information to the public, exposing vulnerabilities of artificial intelligence technologies in the educational sphere. Such risks require proper mitigation through institutions by adopting strict data governance policies, encryption techniques, anonymization methods, and defined data retention policies. AI-driven education requires students and educators to receive complete information about data collection procedures, as well as knowing who handles their data and how it will be utilized to establish transparency and consent protocols (Oyedotun, 2024).

Equity represents another important challenge after privacy in AI adoption. AI possesses educational accessibility opportunities; however, its improper design and execution might worsen existing educational inequalities. Many AI-driven learning resources demand reliable Internet connectivity, recent technology appliances, and digital competency skills that some students lack, particularly those from poor areas or remote regions. The digital divide creates unequal access to AI-enhanced learning experiences, which strengthens educational inequalities among students (Mishra, 2024). AI learning recommendations and assessments produce inaccurate results because AI algorithms identify groups that belong to privileged demographics when trained on such datasets. Facial recognition AI methods used in educational settings are ineffective for students of color because they receive poor recognition outcomes from discriminatory training information. Educational institutions must develop AI tools for inclusive purposes, offer substitute learning materials to students who lack access to advanced technology, and validate AI frameworks for unbiased operation. An additional major ethical concern about AI relates to its biased behavior, which requires thorough examination. Ideological biases present within stored educational records tend to persist and possibly intensify during the training of AI algorithms. The improper use of AI-driven grading systems based on biased student performance datasets from the past can lead to unfairly negative outcomes for some students (Mishra, 2024). The application of algorithm-driven assessment for A-level exams in 2020 revealed bias when it negatively affected students from disadvantaged areas, causing major backlash that forced policy changes in the UK. The lack of female candidates in historical evaluation samples used by university hiring tools makes these AI systems unintentionally bias selections towards male applicants over female peers. The elimination of biases in AI tools is possible through continuous monitoring alongside dataset refinement to ensure fairness, which also depends on diverse representation (Singh, 2024). The core issue is the implementation of proper ethical guidelines to guide AI decision-making processes. The integration of AI systems requires institutions to implement policies that guarantee fairness, full accountability, and complete transparency. The requirements of AI-driven learning tools include stable internet access, up-to-date devices, and digital literacy skills, which some students do not have access to, such as students who come from low-income areas and rural locations. Educational inequalities worsen because numerous students lack equal access to AI-enhanced learning possibilities due to the digital divide (Strielkowski et al., 2024).

The use of AI algorithms trained with data from privileged groups creates underrepresenting population assessments that produce both inaccurate evaluation results and biased learning suggestions. Researchers have proven that educational facial recognition Artificial Intelligence provides inferior results for students of color because it relies on training data containing racial biases. Educational institutions should follow three steps to address these inequities: develop inclusive AI tools, establish various learning materials for students with limited technological access, and work to eliminate bias from AI creation (Singh, 2024). The ethical issues associated with AI bias require thorough evaluation for resolution. Ideological biases present within stored educational records tend to persist and possibly intensify during the training of AI algorithms. AI-driven grading systems could produce unwanted outcomes when using performance data from students, which contain existing systemic biases to assess future students. The application of algorithm-driven assessment for A-level exams in 2020 revealed bias when it negatively affected students from disadvantaged areas, causing major backlash that forced policy changes in the UK (Strielkowski et al., 2024). The lack of female candidates in historical evaluation samples used by university hiring tools makes these AI systems unintentionally bias selections towards male applicants over female peers. AI tools require permanent surveillance to identify and improve biases, and their decision-making processes should depend on diverse datasets containing representative data to achieve fairness. Ethical frameworks must be established to guide AI decision-making systems to avoid these challenges. The integration of AI systems requires institutions to implement policies that guarantee fairness, full accountability, and complete transparency (Strielkowski et al., 2024).

Faculty Professional Development for AI Competency

The rapid advancement of artificial intelligence (AI) in education necessitates a significant shift in faculty's professional development. The technological transformation of education through AI requires educators to learn specific competencies that help them to implement these tools properly and morally. The inability to receive proper training and ongoing skill development creates challenges for faculty members when they try to extract maximum value from AI platforms, which produces both performance problems and opposition, together with ethical concerns. Educational institutions need to develop complete professional development plans that enhance instructors' knowledge about AI, along with digital skill development, so that they can use AI responsibly. When designing AI-focused professional development educational programs, teachers need to receive initial training that builds their understanding of Artificial Intelligence principles. Teachers with extensive discipline experience might struggle to understand AI concepts because of their minimal engagement with AI; thus, they often develop incorrect ideas and show reluctance toward AI use in education. AI training for educators should begin with essential AI education focusing on machine learning, natural language processing, and predictive analytics, which must be presented through methods that relate to educational instruction. Workshops should demonstrate how AI operates behind Carnegie Learning's MATHia personalized learning solution and the role of ChatGPT chatbots in lesson planning support. Faculty members can gain a better practical understanding of AI through practical exposure to real classroom examples. Educational enhancements in professional development require the development of specific AI skills, whereby educators become proficient users who can evaluate and apply relevant AI tools for instructional needs. The requirement of AI fluency covers both technical expertise and competence in evaluating AI recommendations, recognizing algorithmic biases, and identifying ethical risks. Educators need training to check AI grading systems that prevent selected student groups from receiving unfairly negative results. Training programs must include this case study to allow faculty members to learn how to adopt AI in a critical manner.

Education professionals must develop digital literacy competence to function effectively when AI tools become dominant in instructional environments. Digital content creation and data analytics knowledge and abilities, together with online instructional design abilities, are required to work with AI-driven platforms. Educational staff should receive training in operating AI-based learning management systems, such as Canvas or Blackboard, that contain built-in tracking features for student achievement progress. Educators who use the strength of these tools succeed in developing better teaching approaches while learning to help students in need quickly and deliver tailored learning solutions to them. Learning programs must teach responsible data practices that allow education professionals to comply with GDPR, FERPA privacy regulations, and other related laws. Faculty members must be trained to assess student data security to avoid accidental violations that could result from insufficient understanding (Chisom & Osawaru, 2023). Data interpretation is an essential yet often neglected aspect of proficiency in artificial intelligence systems. AI insights gain their real value when faculty members effectively interpret and respond accordingly. AI produces predictive models for student engagement and retention combined with performance; however, these data outputs require faculty members to conduct an analytical review before adopting them in practice. Students might receive failing risk predictions from AI algorithms based on data patterns, but faculty need to check whether extra factors, such as personal issues, are responsible rather than actual learning deficiencies. Statistical understanding must be the central focus of training because it helps professors recognize the difference between associated patterns and actual cause-effect relationships when evaluating AI analytical data.

The training of faculty to use AI practices should have three key components which include practical workshops with AI tools and opportunities for interdisciplinary education and ongoing learning support. The development of AI competency demands beyond traditional lecture-based learning because faculty members need interactive sessions that allow them to experiment with AI tools while discussing practical applications. The institutions of MIT and Stanford created AI laboratories to allow their educators to evaluate AI applications within virtual classroom environments that promote practical educational experiences. The collaboration of educators with data scientists at Arizona State University allows faculty members to work together with AI specialists to develop AI enhancements in academic programs (Chisom & Osawaru, 2023). Profession-wide development programs for teachers of AI systems need to operate continuously instead of delivering sporadic singular training sessions. Educational institutions need to create micro-credentialing systems that enable teachers to obtain digital badges based on their proficiency in AI skills, such as adaptive learning, ethical AI applications, and data-based choices. AI training courses delivered through Coursera and edX enable faculty to acquire informative modules while working online at their convenience. Colleges should set up AI mentorship schemes that pair experienced technology faculty members with colleagues to teach them and establish AI integration practices that involve mutual educational assistance. Professional development centers focusing on Artificial Intelligence must address the existing barriers preventing faculty from joining training programs. Resistance to adopting AI in teaching tends to arise because faculty members worry that technology might substitute educators, yet they face skepticism about how AI may improve educational practice. Training programs need to teach that AI serves as an assistant tool for instruction, instead of replacing human teachers, to address faculty concerns. AI tools such as Grammarly and Turnitin enhance the teacher feedback process by taking care of standard assessments to enable instructors to devote their attention to advanced evaluative activities. The implementation of AI as an assisting technology helps educational institutions gain faculty cooperation and actively participate in sustaining educational excellence. Faculty training regarding AI competencies is important for educational development beyond the present day. When faculty lack sufficient training, they become less effective at using AI in their practice to improve student learning outcomes. By creating organized, practical, and continuous AI professional development programs, educational institutions may enable teachers to use AI in a responsible, moral, and creative way. Faculty members can confidently negotiate the difficulties of integrating AI by having the necessary digital literacy, data interpretation skills, and AI fluency. This will guarantee that AI transforms education rather than disrupts it (Chisom & Osawaru, 2023).

Fostering Collaboration in an AI-Enhanced Academy

Higher education innovation depends on collaborative efforts that are becoming increasingly essential in educational institutions that use AI technology. AI tools transform teaching and research, along with administration processes and faculty; therefore, they need to break away from academic silos to establish collective knowledge development practices. Academia will benefit maximally from AI by building platforms for collaborative exchange, establishing diversity-based education networks, and establishing institutional AI implementation initiatives. When the transformative capabilities of AI lack effective implementation and deployment, they result in minimized functionality, which reduces their useful impact on research activities alongside teaching excellence. Interdisciplinary teamwork enables schools to maximize the use of artificial intelligence through various teaching perspectives. The impact of AI extends across the entire academic landscape because it serves purposes in both computer science and dozens of other subjects, including humanities, social sciences, business, and healthcare. Members from various academic areas contribute distinct understandings of how AI technology improves educational methods and research methodology development. To enhance the quality of natural language processing models, an English professor working on AI-generated essay feedback teams up with a data scientist who ensures that AI responses match pedagogical purposes. Medical educators must collaborate with AI specialists to develop virtual patient simulations that enhance medical education through realistic data-based learning scenarios. These partnerships assist faculty members in constructing AI solutions that fulfill their discipline requirements while maintaining ethical and educational principles (Capinding & Dumayas, 2024).

The advantages of teaming up experts across disciplines are hindered by some academic departments that maintain distinct boundaries or fail to show backing or discredit the importance of AI technology within their subject areas. To address these obstacles, faculty need to implement deliberate methods, including university-designed academic program exchanges and shared collaborative research projects. Through their AI research hubs, Stanford and MIT combine different academic departments to conduct joint projects to enhance AI initiatives in research and education. Higher education institutions use these programs to facilitate interdisciplinary discussions and provide research tools that allow faculty to experiment with artificial intelligence in their domains. Building structured cooperation mechanisms enables educational institutions to dismantle departmental barriers, which subsequently establishes collective AI research practices. The establishment of communities of practice represents an important approach to support faculty members who need to exchange AI-related knowledge and practical guidance to overcome obstacles. A community of practice unites educators who focus on AI-enhanced teaching through interactions that enable members to co-create strategies and exchange ideas while mutually supporting one another during AI implementation. AI teaching cohorts must become part of the university framework, enabling faculty to gather regularly for AI tool implementation discussions with their courses. The group discussed both automated grading via AI and the use of AI-generated content for creating lesson plans, as well as ways to minimize bias from algorithmic assessment tools. AI-resistant faculty members find support through such communities, which also help them continuously advance their skills. Advanced technology institutions have created successful community-based programs that use artificial intelligence for education (Capinding & Dumayas, 2024). Figure 2 reinforces the AI argument for balanced AI-human integration in education.

Figure 2. Balanced model of AI–human integration in education

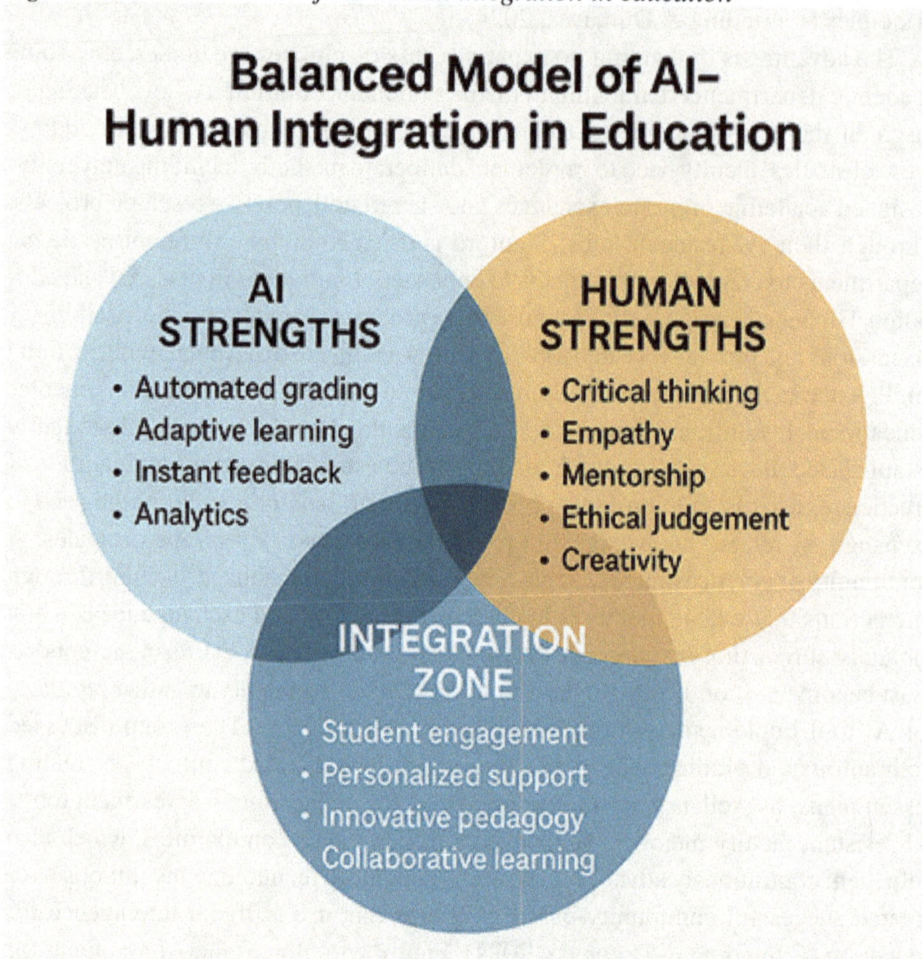

The "Learning Futures Collaboratory" at Arizona State University serves as an interdisciplinary faculty organization whose mission focuses on researching the effects of AI on educational processes. The faculty achieves AI-driven learning solution design through workshops, hackathons, and team-based projects. Through its "Teaching and Learning Lab" service, Harvard University offers faculty members the chance to evaluate AI teaching methods by reviewing practical AI educational examples and case studies. University-wide efforts have proven that faculty collaborative networks drive the growth of supportive AI adoption programs based on evolving mutual accomplishments in their work. Institutional leadership and established policies are essential elements for building a learning environment enhanced through AI applications. An AI experimentation platform requires universities to develop policies that allow testing while placing ethical concerns at the core. The adoption of AI across disciplines will increase when educational facilities receive funding to support research through grants, launch AI literacy programs, and implement training for faculty development. The University of Helsinki delivers its free "Elements of AI" curriculum to faculty members and students who learn the basic knowledge of AI that applies universally across educational areas. The AI teaching infrastructure at Carnegie Mellon University supports faculty members through facilities that combine AI tools with specialists who teach ongoing education on AI educational methods (Capinding & Dumayas, 2024). The implementation of institutional AI initiatives requires proper planning to prevent the amplification of social discrepancies between university staff and the increase in digital separation between teachers. The limited reach of AI adoption in technology departments creates feelings of exclusion and professional inadequacy among faculty from other disciplines. Colleges need to create comprehensive programs for training faculty in AI, regardless of their natural skill level in technology. University policies must handle three main ethical AI matters: safeguarding data privacy, enhancing algorithm visibility, and minimizing bias. Educational institutions must create AI ethics bodies that provide direction regarding safe AI implementation, thus supporting instructors in resolving moral issues after installing AI teaching tools. The development of a collaborative learning environment with AI support requires institutions to build an integrated strategy for disciplinary teamwork with instructor-run professional exchange activities supported by robust administrative backing. The combined efforts of faculty members collaborating across disciplines and participating in structured knowledge-sharing communities and institutional-level support systems give them the capacity to extract AI's transformative value while simultaneously reducing possible dangers. University institutions that focus on collaborative initiatives will position AI to support innovation without generating division, thus establishing an academic climate that benefits faculty members and their students (Capinding & Dumayas, 2024).

CASE STUDIES: REAL-WORLD APPLICATIONS OF AI IN TEACHING AND RESEARCH

The adoption of AI tools in educational research and instruction has brought revolutionary transformation to colleges, as teachers use AI resources for student learning improvements, operational management optimization, and scientific exploration advancement. These beneficial AI advancements have introduced certain obstacles that require proper university navigation. Real-life examples of faculty members who effectively use AI in their university work demonstrate the key benefits and implementation challenges of AI-driven education technologies (Bura & Myakala, 2024). The computer science department at the University of California, Berkeley, uses AI-powered personalized learning systems to enhance introductory programming education. These systems monitor student performance as it happens and identify specific topics where students need help before creating individualized exercises to solidify understanding. Student involvement alongside academic success improved significantly after implementing the Codio AI tool, as their failure rates decreased by 25% over two years (Long et al., 2024). Students initially doubted the AI evaluations because they believed that AI would provide insufficient depth or subtlety of human feedback. The teaching staff adopted a combination strategy that used AI to deliver fast responses about coding assignments, but they added human input from professors to enrich AI assessments by providing qualitative feedback. This case study shows how AI system improvements help learning, yet require human involvement to preserve educational quality in teaching methods. Harvard Business School succeeded in harnessing AI technology by implementing AI-based simulations, which helped faculty teach business strategy and decision-making to students (Long et al., 2024). Students use StratX and similar AI platforms, which model market realities, to perform experiments on business plans through interactive virtual market environments. Machine learning algorithms incorporated into these simulations reveal quantifiable decision results to students, who use this information to enhance their risk assessment and analytical abilities. The introduction of AI-based simulations improved student engagement by 40% according to faculty reports, as students preferred active learning through simulations over traditional case study discussions. The main difficulty for faculty members was maintaining the development of critical thinking in students, as students seemed to depend heavily on AI recommendations. Student use of AI gained approval through a combination of written reflections and peer discussions to validate their decisions, but also showed human involvement with AI insights (Bura & Myakala, 2024; Nisar et al., 2023).

The research division at Stanford University, led by faculty members, developed AI applications for medical education improvement, especially within radiology training programs. Students and clinical staff achieve better medical imaging interpretations through AI recognition systems, which lead to precise diagnoses and enhanced patient welfare. Students at Stanford Medical School learned radiology diagnosis using AI assistance, which led to a 15% better evaluation performance than their traditional peers. The medical training enhancement capacity of AI was confirmed through these results, but the faculty members expressed concerns about AI diagnostic dependence. The curriculum taught AI as an addition to clinical expertise instead of AI being used to replace clinical capabilities to help students acquire a balanced set of capabilities that unite AI support with medical experience (Liando & Tatipang, 2024). The University of Michigan introduced AI-based grading methods to automate assessment tasks in large introductory classes when faculty employed artificial intelligence for assignment and examination grading. The AI grading software Gradescope reduces the teacher's workload by performing automated evaluations for large student populations with instant grading results. The reduced grading period experienced by faculty members enabled them to allocate 60 percent more hours between student mentoring and course material assessment and improvement. The decision to use AI algorithms faced issues mainly due to potential grading bias in subject classes with undefined assessment standards. Regular evaluations of AI grading were combined with human oversight activities to guarantee fairness and accuracy in the grading process (Bura & Myakala, 2024). This example demonstrates that although AI improves assessment efficiency, the faculty must continue to monitor assessment processes to prevent bias and ensure transparency. Teaching and research adoption of AI by faculty members leads to established accomplishments, but they also encounter institutional and ethical barriers that emerge in their pathway. The University of Toronto experienced implementation challenges because faculty members leading AI educational initiatives discovered that the varied AI understanding levels between students and instructors became barriers to implementation. Certain students, mainly from underrepresented groups, confronted difficulties in obtaining access to AI-related educational materials, resulting in diminished digital proficiency. The institution structured specific training sessions and workshops to ensure equal access to AI equipment and knowledge bases for all members. This situation demonstrates why institutions should focus on resolving digital inequalities before introducing AI technology into educational environments (Liando & Tatipang, 2024).

AI in education reaches its maximum effectiveness when used as an additional instrument that supports conventional educational approaches instead of completely replacing traditional teaching practices. Faculty members achieve AI-based tool adoption success through careful combinations of technological efficiency and human supervision, which makes AI beneficial to learning rather than harmful. Continuous monitoring and faculty training, together with ethical considerations and student acceptance, will solve the problems that emerge during AI implementation (Bura & Myakala, 2024). The adoption of AI technology within these institutions produces tangible benefits, leading to better student involvement and increased student continuation, together with faster grading processes and better research precision. These achievements bring an essential task to address the negative side effects, which include algorithmic discrimination, a decrease in critical thinking capability, and unbalanced digital technology access. To ensure that AI is a tool that enhances learning and research outcomes rather than a crutch that compromises academic rigor, faculty members must critically approach AI integration. These case studies illustrate the larger reality of AI in education: it is a revolutionary tool, but its application requires careful planning, teacher readiness, and institutional backing. Teachers may traverse the AI-driven academic landscape more effectively, utilizing its advantages while reducing its hazards, by taking lessons from both achievements and setbacks (Liando & Tatipang, 2024).

FUTURE TRENDS AND OPPORTUNITIES

Artificial intelligence will progressively advance its impact on education, transforming educational approaches for instructors while transforming student learning methods. The development of three key AI technologies, including generative AI combined with adaptive learning systems and intelligent tutors, will enable teachers to deliver customized educational interactions that will also improve instructional efficiency. The progress of AI technology creates barriers that trigger faculty to transform their teaching approaches while building student competency in AI-powered industrial requirements. The future development of AI integration requires educators to learn about its trends, as this knowledge will determine their effectiveness in maintaining educational relevance (Koseda et al., 2024). Generative AI is the most powerful advancement in AI because it generates human-like text, images, and code. Educators currently employ ChatGPT, along with Claude and the Gemini system from Google, to support students during their writing projects and brainstorming activities and solve problems in their assignments. These educational support tools will progress to develop better capabilities, allowing students to experience complex simulations alongside scenario-based learning. Students majoring in medicine can conduct surgical exercises in lifelike AI-managed virtual reality facilities without endangering actual patients. Using AI, students studying law can take part in courtroom simulations that automatically adjust their challenges according to their presented arguments. Educational staff must acquire mastery of these new tools to apply them properly because their main purpose should be to advance learning instead of substituting crucial thinking abilities (Kumbo & Hayuma, 2023).

Adaptive learning technologies serving students through artificial intelligence are now expanding across educational institutions to deliver tailored instruction based on individual needs. The educational platforms of Carnegie Learning and Knewton already provide personalized educational experiences, and developers aim to enhance the technology by utilizing AI for early predictions of learning gaps. The implemented systems allow faculty to deliver specialized assistance; however, privacy issues and algorithmic prejudice emerge due to their use (Khine, 2024). Educational inequalities will strengthen unless AI systems receive proper management because high-tech students will succeed through AI-based systems, while other students will fall behind. Institutions must ensure that AI tools use open methods combined with balanced distribution and inclusion strategies during their development to reduce this risk. The integration of AI technology in higher education calls for faculty members to teach students about new workforce requirements. The technical operations performed by AI systems now prompt organizations to focus on human capabilities, which encompass analytical reasoning and creative thinking abilities paired with ethical problem-solving capacities. Curriculum development by educators needs to include these capabilities to teach students how to use AI tools effectively while acquiring the capability to evaluate and understand AI outcomes. The integration of AI market analysis tools into business case studies at educational institutions requires students to understand the advantages and restrictions of AI-generated information (Mishra, 2024). Faculty members must assume leadership roles as mentors because their responsibilities will expand to ultimately surpass those of existing industrial practices. AI control over knowledge delivery requires educators to instruct students on ethical AI use, multidisciplinary problem-solving, and human-dedicated innovation. Funding from institutions should support teacher development initiatives that teach AI knowledge competency and motivate joint investigations of AI's effects on education. AI in education will create new prospects but also introduce complex issues in the upcoming years. The integration of artificial intelligence technology with human expertise and core ethical values will allow faculty to develop a learning environment in which AI assists education processes without eliminating the primary responsibility of educators (Khine, 2024; Mittal & Gaballa, 2025).

CONCLUSION

Artificial intelligence is being incorporated into education to enhance teachers' talents and change the educational process, not to replace them. Faculty members are essential to keep AI adoption human-centered, moral, and intentional. Instead of seeing AI as a disruptive force, educators need to embrace technology as a collaborator that can improve student engagement, expedite administrative processes, and provide more individualized learning pathways. Nonetheless, this shift necessitates that educators cultivate resilience, flexibility, and a thorough comprehension of AI's possibilities and constraints of AI. To apply AI in ways that are consistent with pedagogical best practices, educators, researchers, and policymakers must collaborate. This entails investing in multidisciplinary cooperation, professional development, and ongoing assessment of how AI technologies affect student results. For instance, learning gaps have decreased and student retention rates have increased in colleges that have used AI-driven adaptive learning platforms. However, these advantages are only achievable if educators possess the information and abilities necessary to employ AI sensibly, minimizing biases and retaining students as active learners rather than passive consumers of AI-generated content. Institutions must establish an academic climate that strikes a balance between technical innovation, ethical issues, and human oversight to truly embrace AI as a partner in education. To realize this vision, faculty members must not only embrace AI technologies but also critically interact with them to ensure that they promote accessibility, inclusion, and student empowerment. Teachers may turn AI from a simple technological development into a driving force for a more dynamic, egalitarian, and progressive academic environment by cultivating ongoing learning and cooperation.

REFERENCES

Adeoye, M. A., & Otemuyiwa, B. I. (2024). Navigating the future: Strategies of EdTech companies in driving educational transformation. *JERIT: Journal of Educational Research and Innovation Technology*, *1*(1), 43–50. DOI: 10.34125/jerit.v1i1.10

Alam, A., & Mohanty, A. (2024). Integrated constructive robotics in education (ICRE) model: A paradigmatic framework for transformative learning in the educational ecosystem. *Cogent Education*, *11*(1), 2324487. DOI: 10.1080/2331186X.2024.2324487

Awadallah Alkouk, W., & Khlaif, Z. N. (2024, December). AI-resistant assessments in higher education: Practical insights from faculty training workshops. []. Frontiers Media SA.]. *Frontiers in Education*, *9*, 1499495. DOI: 10.3389/feduc.2024.1499495

Barrera Castro, G. P., Chiappe, A., Becerra Rodríguez, D. F., & Gonzalo Sepulveda, F. (2024). Harnessing AI for Education 4.0: Drivers of personalized learning. *Electronic Journal of e-Learning*, *22*(5), 01–14. DOI: 10.34190/ejel.22.5.3467

Bohara, D. K., & Rana, K. (2024). Unmasking teachers' proficiency in harnessing artificial intelligence (AI) for transformative education. *SN Social Sciences*, *4*(11), 203. DOI: 10.1007/s43545-024-01003-7

Bura, C., & Myakala, P. K. (2024). Advancing transformative education: Generative AI as a catalyst for equity and innovation. *arXiv preprint arXiv:2411.15971.*

Capinding, A. T., & Dumayas, F. T. (2024). Transformative pedagogy in the digital age: Unraveling the impact of artificial intelligence on higher education students. *Problems of Education in the 21st Century, 82*(5), 630-657.

Eslit, E. (2023). Thriving beyond the crisis: Teachers' reflections on literature and language education in the era of artificial intelligence (AI) and globalization.

George, A. S. (2023). Preparing students for an AI-driven world: Rethinking curriculum and pedagogy in the age of artificial intelligence. *Partners Universal Innovative Research Publication*, *1*(2), 112–136.

Husain, N. (2023). Educational renaissance: Unleashing the potential of interdisciplinary AI integration. *Journal of Environmental Science and Technology*, *2*(1), 159–166.

Hutson, J., & Rains, T. J. (2024). *Charting the AI transition in education and business environments: Navigating the generative inflection point for Industry 4.0 success.* Taylor & Francis. DOI: 10.4324/9781003512813

Karam, J. (2023). Reforming higher education through AI. In *Governance in Higher Education: Global Reform and Trends in the MENA Region* (pp. 275–306). Springer Nature Switzerland. DOI: 10.1007/978-3-031-40586-0_12

Kayal, A. (2024). Transformative pedagogy: A comprehensive framework for AI integration in education. In *Explainable AI for Education: Recent Trends and Challenges* (pp. 247–270). Springer Nature Switzerland. DOI: 10.1007/978-3-031-72410-7_14

Khine, M. S. (2024). Ethics, and the future of education in an AI-driven world. In *Artificial Intelligence in Education: A Machine-Generated Literature Overview* (pp. 629–735). Springer Nature Singapore. DOI: 10.1007/978-981-97-9350-1_6

Koseda, E., Reeve, C., Fascia, M., McIntosh, B., & Cohen, I. (2024). Globalization, education, policy, and curricula issues: Education 4.0: Digital disruption and innovative solutions as pedagogical drivers in higher education. In *Fourth International Handbook of Globalisation, Education and Policy Research* (pp. 541–584). Springer. DOI: 10.1007/978-3-031-67667-3_30

Liando, N. V. F., & Tatipang, D. P. (2024). *Enlightened minds: Navigating the nexus of artificial intelligence and educational modernization*. Penerbit Tahta Media.

Long, K. C., Gunder, A., Robinson, B., Davis, V. L., Barth, D., & Fairfax, M. E. (2024). *Leading the AI revolution: The crucial role of HBCUs in steering AI leadership*. Online Learning Consortium.

Mishra, R. (2024). Embracing a paradigm shift: Transitioning from traditional teaching methods to AI-based NLP education. *Research and Reviews in Literature. Social Sciences*, •••, 75.

Mustafa, D. (2023). Smart classrooms, bright minds: The intersection of education and artificial intelligence. *Journal of Environmental Science and Technology*, *2*(1), 150–158.

Nisar, A., Bashir, I., & Ahmad, A. (2023). Experience of academia with artificial intelligence as adaptive pedagogy. *Pakistan Social Sciences Review*, *7*(3), 657–669.

Oyedotun, T. D. (2024). Digital pedagogy: The role of e-learning tools in facilitating 21st-century skills. *International Journal of Innovation in Education*, *9*(1), 32–46. DOI: 10.1504/IJIIE.2024.144155

Ozer, M., Kose, Y., Kucukkaya, G., Mukasheva, A., & Ciris, K. (2024). Adapting to the AI disruption: Reshaping the IT landscape and educational paradigms. *arXiv preprint arXiv:2409.10541*.

Qudrat-Ullah, H. (Ed.). (2024). *Empowering educational leaders using analytics, AI, and systems thinking*. IGI Global. DOI: 10.4018/979-8-3693-7190-9

Singh, R. (2024). Navigating through education 5.0 era: Imperative competencies for success. In *Preconceptions of Policies, Strategies, and Challenges in Education 5.0* (pp. 33-50). IGI Global.

Strielkowski, W., Grebennikova, V., Lisovskiy, A., Rakhimova, G., & Vasileva, T. (2024). AI-driven adaptive learning for sustainable educational transformation. *Sustainable Development*.

SWARGIARY, K. (2024). Embracing AI in education: A guide for teachers. *LAP.*

Tariq, M. U. (2025a). Gamification and Virtual Reality: Transforming Early Childhood Language Learning. In Manditereza, B. (Ed.), *Digital Pedagogy in Early Childhood Language Development* (pp. 25–52). IGI Global Scientific Publishing., DOI: 10.4018/979-8-3693-7437-5.ch002

Tariq, M. U. (2025b). Empowering Learning Through Networked and Connected Education: Case Studies in Digital Engagement. In Gierhart, A. (Ed.), *Cases on Enhancing P-16 Student Engagement With Digital Technologies* (pp. 169–198). IGI Global Scientific Publishing., DOI: 10.4018/979-8-3693-5633-3.ch007

Tariq, M. U. (2025c). Beyond the Classroom: The Sustained Influence of Educators on Student Success. In West, E. (Ed.), *Former Educators' Roles in Supporting Student Growth and Learning* (pp. 321–346). IGI Global Scientific Publishing., DOI: 10.4018/979-8-3693-6427-7.ch013

Tariq, M. U. (2025d). Sustainability of Quality Processes in Higher Education: Strategies for Continuous Improvement. In Saeed, S., Rana, O., & Dhanaraj, R. (Eds.), *Higher Education and Quality Assurance Practices* (pp. 305–334). IGI Global Scientific Publishing., DOI: 10.4018/979-8-3693-6765-0.ch011

Tariq, M. U. (2025e). The Belmont Report: Guiding Ethical Principles in Human Research. In Throne, R. (Ed.), *IRB, Human Research Protections, and Data Ethics for Researchers* (pp. 245–268). IGI Global Scientific Publishing., DOI: 10.4018/979-8-3693-3848-3.ch010

Yadav, S. (2025). Advancing education with AI-driven education for diverse learners: Integrating AI into pedagogical practices. In *Integrating AI Into Pedagogical Education* (pp. 49–80). IGI Global Scientific Publishing.

KEY TERMS AND DEFINITIONS

Adaptive Learning: AI-powered educational systems that modify content delivery based on individual student progress and needs.

AI Ethics in Education: The study of ethical issues such as bias, privacy, and academic integrity in AI-supported learning environments.

Digital Literacy: The ability of faculty to effectively navigate, evaluate, and implement AI-driven tools in educational settings.

Faculty Resilience: The ability of educators to adapt, innovate, and thrive in AI-enhanced learning environments.

Transformative Pedagogy: Teaching approaches that integrate AI to enhance critical thinking, personalization, and student engagement.

Chapter 14

Pioneering Pathway as a Tracer Study on Employment Outcomes of the BS Psychology Class of 2022:

The Inaugural Graduates From the K-12 Program

Eugene Mark B. Lopez
Laguna State Polytechnic University, Philippines

Jherwin Pagkaliwagan Hermosa
http://orcid.org/0000-0001-8562-3028
Laguna State Polytechnic University, Philippines

ABSTRACT

The study also highlighted a small number of graduates pursuing further education, with eight enrolled in a Career Transition Program (CTP) and one in a Master's program, indicating a commitment to professional development. Despite the strong foundation provided by their education, the high unemployment rate suggests challenges in finding relevant employment opportunities in psychology. This research underscores the importance of evaluating and refining the BS Psychology program to better prepare graduates for the job market.

DOI: 10.4018/979-8-3373-1285-9.ch014

CHAPTER I

Background of the Study

Understanding the career paths of BS Psychology graduates is crucial for evaluating the effectiveness of the program and ensuring that it meets industry demands. This study examined the employment status of these graduates, revealing that a significant number are engaged in roles that align with their field of study. To further enhance their professional preparedness, the curriculum must evolve to address the specific requirements of clinical, educational, and industrial settings.

In clinical work, it's vital to enhance the curriculum with more clinical psychology courses and practical training opportunities. This will better equip students for clinical roles, where specialized skills are essential. Additionally, encouraging graduates to pursue further certifications or advanced studies can significantly boost their employability in clinical settings, where advanced qualifications are often a prerequisite for career progression.

For those pursuing careers in the educational field, strengthening partnerships with schools and universities can create more internship opportunities and job placements. Expanding courses in educational psychology and counseling will provide graduates with the knowledge and skills needed to excel in educational roles. Similarly, for graduates entering the industrial sector, integrating more industrial-organizational psychology content and offering targeted workshops on human resources, employee training, and organizational development will ensure that they are well-prepared to meet the demands of this dynamic field.

Theoretical Framework

Schomburg's (2010) study, "Concept and Methodology of Tracer Studies–International Experiences," highlights the critical role tracer studies play in aligning educational programs with job market demands. These studies offer valuable insights into the effectiveness of academic training, yet they are not without challenges. One significant hurdle is the difficulty in locating and engaging graduates to complete surveys. Additionally, as Schomburg (2010) points out, graduates may struggle to see the connection between their academic knowledge and their professional lives, which can affect the depth and accuracy of the feedback collected. However, when effectively utilized, the findings from tracer studies can drive meaningful educational reforms, aiding planners in shaping more relevant and effective curricula.

Addressing unemployment, particularly in developing countries with rapidly growing populations, requires coordinated efforts from both governments and private organizations. Job creation and the establishment of new industries not only help balance high population growth but also contribute to national stability and economic health. By providing employment opportunities, these initiatives can enhance resource efficiency and reduce the social issues, such as crime, that are often associated with high unemployment rates. The positive ripple effects of such efforts underscore the importance of a responsive and dynamic approach to education and job market alignment.

While these broader economic challenges are significant, this paper focuses specifically on examining the employment outcomes of graduates. It aims to determine the percentage of graduates who secure their first job shortly after completing their studies. By analyzing key aspects of graduates' employment profiles, the research seeks to assess how well their academic preparation aligns with job market expectations. The insights gained from this study are intended to guide curriculum development and institutional improvements, providing data-driven recommendations to enhance the relevance and effectiveness of educational programs.

Significance of the Study

1. The primary goal for the College is to conduct a comprehensive tracer study of the work profiles of BS Psychology graduates from the class of 2022. This initiative is designed to assess and evaluate the effectiveness of the program's curriculum. By identifying the skills and training programs that are most relevant to the job market, the College aims to enhance its educational offerings, particularly in key areas such as clinical psychology, educational psychology, and industrial-organizational psychology. This alignment with current industry demands is essential for preparing students for successful careers.
2. For other Higher Learning Institutions, this study underscores the importance of aligning program offerings with the evolving needs of the job market. By identifying high-demand subjects within the BS Psychology program, such as clinical and industrial-organizational psychology, institutions can tailor their curricula to ensure graduates possess the skills and knowledge most sought after by employers. This focus not only enhances the employability of graduates but also strengthens the institution's reputation for producing job-ready professionals.
3. The involvement of the Commission on Higher Education (CHED) is crucial in advancing curricular and program development across the country. By engaging with the findings from this tracer study, CHED's Curricular & Program Committee can strategically design or redesign academic programs to better align with industry trends. This collaboration ensures that educational institutions are offering programs that meet the latest demands of the job market, particularly in clinical, educational, and industrial settings, thereby contributing to the ongoing growth and relevance of higher education in the Philippines.

Scope & Limitation of the Study

This tracer study focuses exclusively on graduates of the Bachelor of Science in Psychology program from the academic year 2022 at the College of Arts & Sciences, Laguna State Polytechnic University, San Pablo City Campus. The decision to target this specific program arises from its availability at the selected campus, enabling a concentrated and in-depth exploration of graduate outcomes.

Conducted in the second quarter of 2023, the study examines the graduates' personal profiles, work experiences, and perceptions through a comprehensive survey. This survey evaluates the relevance of their education, the development of their skills, and gathers their recommendations for program enhancement. The study is deliberately limited to graduates of the BS Psychology program at the San Pablo City Campus to maintain focus and specificity.

The primary objective of this research is to trace the employment trajectories of these graduates, analyzing whether the skills and competencies they acquired during their college years are significant and applicable in their professional roles. Additionally, the study assesses how these skills have evolved since entering the workforce. The insights gained will inform recommendations for refining the BS Psychology program, including suggestions for new training initiatives to further enhance graduate preparedness and success.

Objectives of the Study General Objective

To provide comprehensive data on the employment and professional trajectories of the 2022 graduates from the College of Arts & Sciences, with a focus on BS Psychology graduates who completed the K-12 Program prior to college.

Specific Objectives:

1. To determine the Alumni Profile of BS Psychology graduates from the College of Arts & Sciences who underwent the K-12 Program.
2. To present data of Alumni Work Profiles of BS Psychology graduates, highlighting their employment status, work related in course and nature of work related to Psychology.
3. To analyze the extent to which these graduates are employed in roles related to their field of study, specifically within Clinical Work, the Educational Field, or the Industrial Setting.
4. To identify and assess the relevance of the work these graduates are engaged in, in relation to their psychology education and training.

LITERATURE REVIEW

1. Factors that Affect Graduates' Employment Competencies

Advancing Tracer Studies for Curriculum Enhancement: Insights from Lange (2001). In Lange's (2001) work on manual tracer studies, the study underscores the pivotal questions that should guide such inquiries. Primarily, the focus revolves around evaluating the impact of courses offered, with a keen interest in understanding if graduates secure employment post-graduation and whether they attain a satisfactory income in the labor market. Equally significant is the exploration of how graduates apply the skills and knowledge acquired, identify areas where additional training is required, and cultivate the necessary competencies.

The study advocates for a holistic approach to post-graduate support, emphasizing the necessity of further training initiatives, including skill courses and additional mechanisms to bolster employment opportunities for graduates. It critically examines the efficacy of support services currently in place.

Key findings from the study illuminate the pressing need to update curricula and refine training delivery methods. Tracer studies emerge as instrumental tools for ongoing monitoring and self- evaluation, providing valuable insights into the alignment of training programs with market needs and employer expectations. The study identifies the dynamic labor market trends, delineates areas of potential growth within courses, and underscores the measurable and positive social and economic impact attributed to the training offered.

In essence, this research not only validates the relevance of tracer studies but also positions them as indispensable tools for institutions seeking continuous improvement. The study advocates for an adaptive and responsive approach to training, ensuring that educational offerings align with market demands, thereby fostering the success of graduates and contributing meaningfully to social and economic development.

2. The Role of Higher Education Institutions for Graduate's Work Competitiveness

Advancing Graduate Employability: Insights from Noteworthy Studies Nordin's (2009) exploration in "Enhancing Graduate Employability: Issues, Concerns, and the Way Forward" sheds light on the evolving landscape where merely possessing academic knowledge is insufficient for recent graduates. The contemporary job market demands a fusion of academic prowess with practical skills to bolster employment prospects. Higher Education Institutions (HEIs) are urged to adapt, transitioning from traditional centers of moral and intellectual development to dynamic hubs for professional training. The imperative is to align education and training with market demands, ensuring responsiveness to the dynamic needs of various economic sectors.

Echoing this sentiment, Mercado (2009) highlights the Commission on Higher Education's (CHED) initiative in the Philippines, spearheading Graduate Tracer Studies (GTS) among selected HEIs. The purpose is twofold: to gauge if courses meet the needs of industry and society and to enable HEIs to align their efforts with industry manpower requirements (CHED CMO #s 38, s. 2006, 11, s. 1999).

Lalican's (2007) study underscores the symbiotic relationship between the acquisition of knowledge, skills, and competencies during undergraduate specialization and the subsequent enhancement of productivity, efficiency, and expertise in graduates' current roles.

Examining employment status, Miranda (2000) outlines criteria for deeming employment as regular, offering a legal perspective on the nature of employment agreements. This serves as a backdrop for understanding employment dynamics in subsequent studies.

Yangco's (2007) study reveals that Electrical and Computer Engineering graduates are predominantly employed, with a focus on permanent positions. Unemployed respondents express a desire for overseas employment, emphasizing the importance of enhancing skills related to information technology and improving facilities for hands-on training to augment curriculum effectiveness.

In Diestro's (2013) exploration, the majority of graduates are employed in their respective fields, with those unemployed citing reasons such as pursuing higher studies or engaging in domestic responsibilities. This dual perspective provides a comprehensive understanding of post-graduation trajectories.

Together, these studies paint a comprehensive picture of the challenges and opportunities in the dynamic landscape of graduate employability, offering valuable insights for institutions aiming to enhance their curricula and foster greater alignment with industry needs.

RESEARCH PARADIGM

STATEMENT OF THE PROBLEM

This study aimed to trace the career paths of graduates from the Bachelor of Science in Psychology program at Laguna State Polytechnic University's San Pablo City Campus, College of Arts & Sciences. Specifically, the research sought to answer the following questions:

1. What are the personal profiles of the graduates in terms of:
    1.1 Gender
    1.2 Year of Graduation
    1.3 Educational Attainment (BS, CTP, Master's, Doctorate, or Currently Pursuing Another Course)
2. What is the employment status of the graduates?
    2.1. Employed
    2.2 Unemployed
3. How closely is their current work related to their psychology degree?
    3.1. Related to the Course
    3.2 Not Related to the Course
4. What is the nature of their work within the field of psychology?
    4.1 Clinical Work
    4.2 Educational Field
    4.3 Industrial Setting

HYPOTHESIS

1. There is a **significant trace** of the **personal profiles** of the graduates Profile of BS Psychology graduates from the College of Arts & Sciences who underwent the K-12 Program in terms of gender, year of graduation, and educational attainment.
2. A **majority of BS Psychology graduates are employed** within two years of graduation.
3. BS Psychology graduates who are employed are more likely to be working in **jobs closely related to their course of study.**
4. The nature of work among employed BS Psychology graduates is **significantly distributed across clinical work, educational fields, and industrial settings.**

CHAPTER II

Research Design

The researchers utilize a Descriptive Research Design to carefully track the professional paths of graduates. This involves a comprehensive survey assessing graduates' current employment status, examining the relevance of the skills and competencies they acquired during their studies, and evaluating their development based on these skills.

Connecting this research to clinical work, educational fields, and industrial settings highlights the importance of relevant training in ensuring graduates are equipped to meet real-world challenges. In clinical contexts, understanding how academic skills translate into patient care and therapeutic practices is vital for effective practice. In educational fields, this research can inform teacher training programs, ensuring educators possess the necessary competencies to foster student success. In industrial settings, aligning training with industry standards enhances graduates' readiness to contribute to organizational goals, ultimately benefiting both the individuals and the sectors they enter. This holistic approach not only supports individual career development but also strengthens the overall workforce by producing graduates who are well-prepared to excel in their chosen fields.

Research Methodology

The researchers used a Descriptive Research Design to gather clear information about the career paths of graduates, focusing on their employment or self-employment after college. They collected data from the BS Psychology alumni records at Laguna State Polytechnic University, specifically using the LSPU SPCC Alumni Profile & Work Profile Worksheet. This tracing project for the 2022 graduates started in 2023 and continued into early 2024.

To gather detailed information, the researchers used various methods to distribute the survey. They employed modern communication tools like messaging apps, group polls, and Google Mail to send out the questionnaires. They also relied on the help of graduates' former advisers, friends, and family to assist in the data collection. This diverse approach ensured a thorough and reliable dataset, enabling an in-depth examination of the post-graduation experiences of BS Psychology alumni.

Population and Sample

In 2022, a total of 157 graduates completed the Bachelor of Science in Psychology program at Laguna State Polytechnic University San Pablo Campus. The graduates were identified using the official list from the LSPU SPCC Alumni Affairs Office. This list includes important information such as the graduates' names, gender, area of specialization, current jobs, and average monthly salaries, providing a clear overview of their activities after graduation.

Data Gathering Procedures

To thoroughly track the graduates' profiles and career paths, the researchers used reliable employment data from the Laguna State Polytechnic University Alumni Placement Office. This trustworthy information formed the basis for creating each graduate's personal and work profiles.

Statistical Tool/s

In the analysis of the personal and work profiles of BS Psychology graduates, the researchers employed descriptive statistics as a cornerstone of their methodology. Specifically, they harnessed the power of Frequency Count (f) and Percentage (%) to discern patterns within the identified graduates based on various criteria. This analytical approach, presented succinctly in tables, sheds light on the most prevalent characteristics among the surveyed graduates. Additionally, the study employs percentages to ascertain the proportion of graduates whose current work aligns with their major in college, providing a nuanced perspective on career relevance.

CHAPTER 3

Results and Discussion

Table 1. Alumni profile of the BS psychology graduates from 2022

Year Graduated	*No. of Graduates*
2022	*157*
Total	*157*
Gender	
Male	*26*
Female	*131*
Educational Attainment	
Bachelor's Degree	*159*
CTP/ Ongoing	*8 Ongoing*
Master's Degree/ Ongoing	*1 Ongoing*
Doctorate Degree/ Ongoing	*0*
Taking- Up another Course	*0*

Table 1 provides a the profile of BS Psychology graduates from 2022. It includes information on the number of graduates, gender distribution, educational attainment, and further academic or professional pursuits. A total of 157 students graduated with a BS Psychology degree during the three- year period. The majority of graduates were female (131), while a smaller number were male (26). This indicates a significant gender disparity in the field. A large majority (157) of graduates achieved a Bachelor's Degree. Additionally, eight graduates were currently enrolled in a CTP (Career Transition Program), while one was pursuing a Master's degree, and none were enrolled in a Doctorate program. No graduates were reported to be taking up another course, such as a BS Law degree.

The predominance of female graduates suggests that there might be underlying societal or cultural factors influencing career choices in psychology. The high number of graduates with a Bachelor's Degree indicates that many are likely seeking immediate employment or further education in related fields. The presence of graduates enrolled in CTP or pursuing higher degrees suggests a desire for professional development and specialization. Information on the employment rates and career paths of the graduates would provide a more complete picture of their post-graduation experiences.

In conclusion, the data presented in Table 1 provides valuable insights into the profile of BS Psychology graduates from 2022. However, further analysis and research are needed to understand the factors influencing their career choices and outcomes.

Table 2. Alumni work profile of BS psychology graduates from 2022

Employment Status of BS Psychology Graduates 2022	*75 (47.77%) of 157 graduates*
1. Employed	*75 (47.73%)*
2. Unemployed	*82(52.23%)*
Work Related Status	
1. Work Related to Field	*65 (86.67%)*
2. Work Unrelated to Field	*10 (13.33%)*

Table 2 provides information on the work profile of BS Psychology graduates from 2022, specifically their employment status and the relevance of their jobs to their field of study. A majority of graduates (75, or 47.73%) were employed, while 82 (52.23%) were unemployed. Among those employed, a significant portion (65, or 86.67%) were working in jobs related to their field of study (psychology), while 10 (13.33%) were in unrelated fields.

The relatively high unemployment rate among psychology graduates suggests that finding relevant employment in the field can be challenging. The majority of employed graduates were working in psychology-related fields, indicating that many are able to leverage their education to secure relevant jobs. The 13.33% of graduates working in unrelated fields may be exploring alternative career paths or facing difficulties in finding psychology-specific opportunities.

The data only represents a single year (2022). Trends and changes in employment rates and job relevance may have occurred in subsequent years. Understanding the factors influencing employment outcomes, such as geographic location, specific areas of specialization within psychology, and economic conditions, would provide a more comprehensive analysis.

The data presented in Table 2 provides insights into the post-graduation employment experiences of BS Psychology graduates from 2022. While a majority of graduates were employed, finding relevant work in the field can be challenging for some. Further research is needed to explore the factors affecting employment outcomes and identify strategies to improve career prospects for psychology graduates.

Table 3. Nature of work related to BS psychology graduates from 2022

Employment Status of BS Psychology Graduates 2022	
Employment Status of BS Psychology Graduates 2022	*75 (47.77%) of 157 graduates*
Nature of Work Related to Psychology	
a. Clinical Work	***30 (40%) of 157 BS Psychology Graduates of 2022***
b. Educational Field	***22 (30%) of 157 BS Psychology Graduates of 2022***
c. Industrial Setting	***23 (30%) of 157 BS Psychology Graduates of 2022***

Table 3 provides information on the nature of work for employed BS Psychology graduates from 2022, focusing on the specific areas within the field where they are employed. The most common area of employment was clinical work, with 30 graduates (40%) engaged in this field. This suggests a strong demand for psychologists in clinical settings. A significant number of graduates (22, or 30%) were working in the educational field, indicating a growing demand for psychologists in educational institutions. Another 23 graduates (30%) were employed in industrial settings, suggesting that psychology is increasingly being applied in corporate environments.

The data highlights the diverse career paths available to BS Psychology graduates, with opportunities in clinical settings, education, and industry. The high percentage of graduates in clinical work and the growing presence in educational and industrial settings suggest a strong demand for psychologists in various sectors. The results may indicate a trend towards specialization within the field, with graduates seeking jobs that align with their specific interests and skills. The data only represents a single year (2022).

Trends and changes in the nature of work may have occurred in subsequent years. The distribution of graduates across different work areas may vary depending on geographic location and regional demand for psychologists. The data presented in Table 3 provides insights into the nature of work for employed BS Psychology graduates from 2022. The results indicate a strong demand for psychologists in various sectors, including clinical settings, education, and industry. This suggests that graduates have diverse career opportunities available to them, depending on their interests and skills.

Table 4. Percentage of Graduates' personal profiles—including gender, year of graduation, educational attainment and employment area of BS psychology graduates from 2022

Gender and Employment Status:	*(1) The majority of graduates were female (131 out of 157).*
Year of Graduation:	*47.73% are employed within the first year.*
Educational Attainment and Employment Status:	***(1) Most graduates (157) attained a Bachelor's degree, and employment appears to be positively correlated with psychology-related fields*** ***(2) (8) eight are enrolled in a Career Transition Program (CTP)*** ***(3) One (1) is pursuing a Master's degree*** ***(4) The high percentage of employed graduates (65 out of 75) working in psychology-related fields (86.67%)***
Employment Areas:	***(1) 40% of graduates working in clinical roles*** ***(2) 30% in education*** ***(3) 30% in industrial settings***

Table 4 provides information about the majority of graduates were female (131 out of 159). This could indicate a gender bias in the field of psychology, which may affect the overall employment status, though the gender breakdown is not provided specifically for employed versus unemployed graduates. However, it's important to note that the higher female population may correlate with employment, given the large number working in psychology-related fields.

At the same rate, Since all 159 graduates completed their degree in 2022, they are part of the same cohort, which limits variations related to graduation year. However, the data can still reflect trends about how recent graduates transition into the workforce, such as the fact that 47.73% are employed within the first year.

Moreover, most graduates (159) attained a Bachelor's degree, and employment appears to be positively correlated with psychology-related fields for those with this level of education. Interestingly, a small number (eight) are enrolled in a Career Transition Program (CTP), and one is pursuing a Master's degree, suggesting that while most graduates begin their careers with a Bachelor's, some continue their education for specialization or career shift. The high percentage of employed graduates (65 out of 75) working in psychology-related fields (86.67%) indicates that a Bachelor's in Psychology is highly valued in certain fields like clinical, education, and industrial work.

Lastly, Employment is strongly aligned with the field of study. The data shows 40% of graduates working in clinical roles, 30% in education, and 30% in industrial settings, highlighting that most graduates find jobs in areas directly connected to their degree. This is a positive outcome for those seeking employment in psychology-related fields.

In summary, the percentage of graduates' personal profiles and their current employment status suggests that while gender and educational attainment (Bachelor's degree) are factors, the most significant correlation is between the graduates' chosen field of study and their employment in psychology-related jobs. The relatively high employment rate (47.73%) suggests that psychology graduates are in demand in relevant sectors, though a larger proportion (52.23%) remain unemployed, possibly indicating gaps in the job market or the need for further specialization (such as a Master's degree).

CHAPTER 4

Summary of Findings

The profile of BS Psychology graduates from 2022 reveals that a total of 157 students completed their degree, with a significant gender disparity evident as 131 were female and only 26 were male. Most graduates (157) achieved a Bachelor's Degree, indicating a strong focus on undergraduate education. A small number of graduates are pursuing further studies, with eight enrolled in a Certificate of Teaching Proficiency (CTP) and one pursuing a Master's degree. This suggests that while many graduates are ready to enter the workforce, there remains an interest in professional development and specialization within the field.

Employment outcomes for the graduates show that 75 (47.73%) were employed, while 82 (52.23%) were unemployed. Among those employed, a significant majority (65 or 86.67%) found jobs relevant to their field of study, indicating that many were able to leverage their education effectively. However, the 13.33% working in unrelated fields highlights the challenges some graduates face in securing psychology-specific roles. This relatively high unemployment rate suggests that finding relevant employment in psychology can be challenging for graduates.

The nature of work among employed BS Psychology graduates indicates strong demand across various sectors. Clinical work was the most common area of employment, with 30 graduates (40%) engaged in this field. Additionally, 22 graduates (30%) were working in educational settings, and another 23 (30%) were employed in industrial environments. This diversity in career paths suggests that psychology graduates have ample opportunities depending on their interests and skills. However, further research is needed to understand the factors influencing employment outcomes and to identify strategies for improving career prospects for psychology graduates.

Findings of the Study

Based in the results of the study, the following findings are made:

1. A total of 157 students graduated with a BS Psychology degree in 2022.
2. The majority of graduates were female (131), while males accounted for a smaller number (26),
   indicating a significant gender disparity in the field.
3. Most graduates (159) achieved a Bachelor's Degree, reflecting a focus on undergraduate education.
4. Eight graduates were enrolled in a Career Transition Program (CTP), one was pursuing a Master's degree, and none were enrolled in a Doctorate program.
5. The presence of graduates in CTP and pursuing higher degrees suggests a desire for professional development and specialization in psychology.
6. Among the graduates, 75 (47.73%) were employed, while 82 (52.23%) were unemployed.
7. Of those employed, a significant portion (65 or 86.67%) were working in psychology-related fields, while 10 (13.33%) were in unrelated jobs.
8. The most common area of employment for graduates was clinical work (30 graduates or 40%), followed by education (22 graduates or 30%) and industrial settings (23 graduates or 30%).
9. The data indicates a strong demand for psychologists in various sectors, particularly clinical, educational, and industrial fields.
10. There is a need for further analysis of employment outcomes, geographic influences, and factors affecting career choices to better understand the post-graduation experiences of BS Psychology graduates.

CONCLUSIONS

On the source of the findings, the following conclusions are made:

1. A significant correlation exists between graduates' personal profiles—including gender, year of graduation, and educational attainment—and their current employment status.
2. The majority of BS Psychology graduates secure employment within two years of completing their degree.
3. Employed BS Psychology graduates are predominantly engaged in positions closely aligned with their field of study, reflecting the applicability of their education.
4. The work undertaken by employed BS Psychology graduates is significantly spread across various sectors, including clinical practice, educational institutions, and industrial environments.

RECOMMENDATIONS

Based on the findings and conclusions made, the following are recommended:

1. The school should establish robust career services that provide comprehensive support for psychology graduates. This could include workshops on job search strategies, resume writing, interview preparation, and networking opportunities with professionals in the field. Additionally, partnerships with local organizations and businesses could facilitate internships and job placements, helping students gain relevant experience and secure employment in psychology-related fields.
2. The college should consider developing specialized tracks within the psychology program that align with current job market demands, such as clinical psychology, educational psychology, and industrial-organizational psychology. By offering elective courses or concentrations in these areas, the college can better prepare students for specific career paths, making them more competitive in the job market and increasing their employability upon graduation.
3. Higher education institutions should invest in ongoing research to track the career trajectories of psychology graduates. By collecting data on employment rates, job relevance, and alumni experiences, schools can gain insights into the factors affecting graduate success. This information can inform program improvements, curriculum adjustments, and targeted support services, ultimately enhancing the overall educational experience and outcomes for future students.

REFERENCES

Commission on Higher Education. (1999). *CHED CMO No. 11, s. 1999: Revised policies and standards for teacher education*. Manila, Philippines: Author.

Commission on Higher Education. (2006). *GTS manual and lectures: CHED CMO No. 38, s. 2006, policies, standards, and guidelines for BSBA*. Manila, Philippines: Author.

Diestro, R. F. (2013). *An inventory of the perceptions and employment data of the graduates of Bachelor of Science in Office Administration at Rizal Technological University*. Rizal Technological University.

Lalican, N. M. (2007). *Tracer study of agriculture students*. University of the Philippines Los Baños.

Lange, R. (2001, May). *Manual tracer studies*. FAKT GmbH (sponsored by AG KED).

Mercado, F. M. (2009). *A tracer study of MSEUF graduates*. Enverga University.

Miranda, G. S. (2000). *Labor-management Relations*. National Book Store.

Nordin, M. K. (2009). Enhancing graduate employability: Issues, concerns and the way forward. Minister of Higher Education Malaysia.

Rizal Technological University. (2012). *Academic journal: Research papers* (Vol. II). Author.

SAS Institute Inc. (1999). *Computing chi-square test for one-way frequency table*. Author.

Schomburg, H. (2010). Concept and Methodology of Tracer Studies œ International Experiences

Yangco, O. B. (2007). Assessment of RTU ECE Graduates' Employability. Rizal Technological University, Mandaluyong City.

Chapter 15
Role of AI in Faculty Development in Current Scenario

Deepa Sharma
http://orcid.org/0000-0003-4374-917X
Maharishi Markandeshwar (Deemed to be) University, India

ABSTRACT

AI in education helps teachers customize instructional content to meet their needs. This allows teachers to work at their own pace, participate in activities that suit their learning preferences, and take charge of their own education. Using AI assistants to differentiate assignments and provide a data-driven, adaptive exercise improves the learning process overall, reducing the burden on the teacher. In today's era, it becomes important to know the role of artificial intelligence (AI) on the teaching development of faculty members.

BACKGROUND

The scientific field of artificial intelligence creates and studies devices that are intended to enhance human intelligence. AI's primary goal is to speed up and increase the efficiency of normal processes that is, if it has been properly installed and supported. As a result, more businesses around the world are implementing AI. The majority of AI tools adhere to three fundamental principles:

The majority of AI tools adhere to three fundamental principles:

Learning: Getting the new experience, analyzing it, and developing new behavioral models.

Self-correction: Improving algorithms to guarantee the most precise outcomes.

DOI: 10.4018/979-8-3373-1285-9.ch015

Reasoning: Selecting particular algorithms to accomplish a given task.

History of AI: With roots in the early days of contemporary computing, the idea of artificial intelligence (AI) has been around for a number of decades (Maity et al, 2019). The history of artificial intelligence covers the various ways term has been used in movies and television shows as a crude catch-all for the anxiety that technology is taking over our life. Naturally, this is a false portrayal, particularly in the films Blade Runner and 2001: A Space Odyssey, where human-like robots rebel against their creators.

WHO CREATED ARTIFICIAL INTELLIGENCE?

Although the renowned test was named after Alan Turing, John McCarthy is typically credited with creating artificial intelligence. The word was credited to him at a meeting for a 1956 summer artificial intelligence research project at Dartmouth (Zhang et al, 2018). A large portion of the early basic research of AI theory was based on this gathering. From there, institutions like the Defense Advanced Research Projects Agency (DARPA) in the United States carried on with the creation of AI. Street mapping, which enabled users to examine immersive interactive maps of cities, was one of DARPA's experiments in the 1970s. Numerous developments that we currently utilize in our daily lives have been made possible by the research and development of other AI programs over time (Hazaimeh et al, 2024).

HISTORY OF AI IN FACULTY DEVELOPMENT PROGRAM

Though there were early discussions about AI in education in the 1980s, it wasn't until the 2010s that widespread implementation in faculty training started to take hold, with a focus on using AI tools for personalized learning, assessment, and instructional design. The integration of AI into faculty development programs is a relatively recent development, with significant growth occurring in the last decade as advancements in AI technology have made it more accessible and relevant for educators, particularly with the rise of machine learning and deep learning techniques. Important moments in the history of faculty development using

1. **AI Initial exploration in the 1980s and 1990s:** Early studies on artificial intelligence (AI) in education concentrated on fundamental ideas like intelligent tutoring systems and expert systems. Some faculty development programs included introductory workshops on these subjects, but adoption was constrained by technological limitations. The 2010s saw a resurgence of interest in AI-based

educational tools due to developments in machine learning algorithms such as neural networks and cloud computing platforms. This sparked a wave of faculty development programs that introduced educators to tools like intelligent chat bots, adaptive learning platforms, and automated grading (Lourenço et al, 2018).

3. **Concentrate on particular uses (from 2015 onward):** These days, faculty development programs focus more and more on particular AI applications that are pertinent to their field, such creating tailored learning modules, integrating AI-powered feedback mechanisms in evaluations, and employing AI for data analysis in research (Rasheed et al, 2016). Giving faculty members a basic understanding of AI principles such as data analysis, machine learning, and natural language processing would help them appreciate the capabilities and constraints of AI tools (Lohman et al, 2006). Key elements of AI in programs for teacher development:
    a. **Practical instruction:** Providing hands-on seminars where instructors can test out various AI tools and platforms to gain expertise in integrating them into their instruction.
    b. **Moral considerations:** Discussing the moral ramifications of AI in education, such as concerns about algorithmic prejudice, data privacy, and accessibility.

Significance of AI in faculty development program: Explore the untapped potential of generative artificial intelligence for faculty development. This session is intended to serve as a useful and concise guide. In this workshop you will be presented with five easy-to-implement strategies when producing faculty professional development materials (Dubey et al, 2015). Each suggestion is carefully crafted to build on the one before it, providing a thorough and systematic understanding of how generative AI can revolutionize your situation Because AI is so good at providing individualized learning experiences; it is completely changing the job of teachers. These cutting-edge AI systems can quickly and precisely identify a student's strengths and weaknesses in each topic, enabling lessons to be tailored to each student's individual abilities without passing judgment (Nafukho et al, 2017). We will discuss everything from the fundamentals of AI in education to its specific, useful uses in your day-to-day dealings with teachers. Below some goals we described:

- Learn about the fundamentals of generative artificial intelligence and how it can be used in educational and faculty development environments.
- Determine and evaluate potential applications of AI in the production and improvement of faculty professional development materials.
- Learn how to successfully integrate AI techniques and tools into programs for faculty development.

- Examine how AI can be used to provide effective, efficient, and interesting professional development opportunities for faculty members.
- Think about the practical difficulties, data privacy issues, and ethical implications of implementing AI in faculty development.

Introduction: Education is at a turning point in the digital age. The field of faculty development is constantly changing along with technology. The way educators teach, interact, and develop is being revolutionized by artificial intelligence (AI), which is more than just a supporting tool (Brandt et al., 2019). AI applications in education can help professors and students create and curate information more easily and promote interactive collaboration. These resources assist educators in creating curriculum-aligned content, guaranteeing that learning resources successfully address the various needs of students. Commonplace situations like retail purchase forecasting, online customer care interactions and financial services fraud detection are examples of AI use cases. Teacher performance data, including grades, feedback, and student evaluations, can be analyzed by AI to pinpoint areas in which teachers need to grow and to offer tailored professional development feedback (Baruch et al, 2022). AI's primary objective is to replicate human intelligence and carry out difficult human activities faster and more effectively. AI has the potential to significantly speed up the teaching-learning process in the educational industry. By giving teachers the ability to customize their learning experiences, analyze teaching performance data to pinpoint areas for improvement, automate administrative tasks, create personalized learning materials, and provide real-time feedback, artificial intelligence (AI) plays a significant role in faculty development in the current educational landscape. This allows teachers to stay abreast of emerging trends in their field and continuously improve their teaching practices. In the field of education AI to provide interesting and educational instructional materials or additional content can be advantageous for both teachers and students. In a lot less time than it would typically take to construct a new curriculum unit, teachers can produce complete lesson or unit plans. Artificial intelligence (AI) systems more especially, AI-powered systems are excellent at helping students understand difficult ideas. AI instructors can provide explanations that align with individual learning patterns through interactive simulations and individualized feedback, promoting a deeper comprehension of difficult subjects. AI uses adaptive learning platforms and gamified content to make learning more dynamic and interesting. AI is used by apps like Kahoot! and Minecraft: Education edition to produce dynamic tests and simulations that react to user input, retaining students interest and motivation (McCallum et al, 2024)Teacher performance data, including grades, feedback, and student evaluations, can be analyzed by AI to pinpoint areas in which teachers need to grow and to offer tailored professional development feedback. By automatically producing code fragments or complete functionalities, AI-powered solutions can help engineers and drastically cut down on development time. Instead of generating code, finding bugs, and testing, this automation frees up developers to concentrate on higher-level tasks like problem-solving and architectural design (Ayeleke et al, 2019). Principal effects of AI on teacher development include:

1. **Tailored Educational Routes:** AI algorithms can identify a faculty member's teaching style, areas of strength, and areas for improvement to create customized learning modules and professional development courses that will ensure targeted improvement.
2. **Data-Driven Feedback:** AI can analyze performance metrics, classroom observations, and student feedback to provide detailed insights into teaching effectiveness, highlighting areas where a faculty member can improve.
3. **Automated Content Creation:** AI can create lesson plans, presentations, and practice quizzes based on specific learning objectives, saving faculty time and allowing them to focus on more creative aspects of teaching.
4. **Real-time Assessment:** AI-powered tools can provide immediate feedback on student performance during assessments, enabling faculty to modify their teaching strategies in real-time.
5. **Adaptive Learning Platforms:** AI-driven platforms can adjust the pace and complexity of instruction to meet each faculty member's unique learning needs.
6. **Research Support:** By helping professors with data analysis, literature reviews, and research proposal formulation, artificial intelligence (AI) can make research projects more effective and significant.
7. **Micro-learning Modules:** AI may produce brief, focused learning modules that fill in particular skill shortages, giving faculty members on-demand access to pertinent professional development.
8. **Virtual Coaching and Mentorship:** Faculty members can receive individualized coaching and feedback from AI-powered virtual assistants that mimic in-person conversations with peers or mentors. AI can help researchers by providing strong instruments to improve productivity, precision, and creativity. By using AI to manage massive datasets, automate literature reviews, find hidden patterns, and produce new ideas, researchers can free up more time to concentrate on other aspects of their work, such as formulating research questions and analyzing findings. Additionally, by streamlining administrative duties like grant writing and peer review management, AI gives scholars more time to concentrate on scholarly work and further their areas understanding. During a faculty development program, AI can assist teachers in interacting directly with various technologies: Get Real-World Experience: Gaining practical experience aids

in your comprehension of the capabilities, constraints, and possible uses of AI in both educational and professional settings.

9. **Improve your instructional strategies:** You can find new methods to improve student engagement, expedite administrative duties, and customize learning experiences by experimenting with AI tools.
10. **Keep up with technological advancements:** Consistent engagement with AI platforms guarantees that you stay abreast of the most recent advancements in AI, equipping you to successfully integrate these innovations into your curriculum.

WHY AI USED IN EDUCATION SECTOR?

Further, the landscape of postsecondary education is changing due to technological advancements such as gamification, AI and machine learning, and virtual and augmented reality. To date, much of the conversation around these technologies has centered on how they impact students, institutional norms, or ethical conduct, with little attention paid to helping staff develop the adaptive skills needed to succeed in these unpredictable times. How, then, can faculty development be reconsidered to accommodate the rapidly evolving field of artificial intelligence in higher education? Faculty development has generally been more ad hoc or opportunistic, with a few notable exceptions. As a result, faculty development curriculum often evolves on its own rather than being purposefully aligned with recognized competencies. Despite its flaws in concept and execution, competency-based medical education has benefited from a comprehensive, integrated, and systematic approach based on good educational principles and integrated curricula that all assist in the development of competencies to meet societal demands. Similar systems approaches that support and maximize faculty development will be beneficial in the AI era, including some below points:

1. **Determine the needs of the faculty in relation to AI:** Coming up with suggestions about what faculty members need to know in order to employ AI effectively would be the first step. This process should ideally involve a whole community with a variety of skill sets to think holistically and intelligently about these needs rather than happening in a vacuum. Among their many responsibilities are those of administrators, mentors, leaders, researchers, and teachers. As such, the necessity for fluency should be adjustable to everyone. Furthermore, in a sector that is changing so quickly, faculty members should be prepared to assess and adapt to new advancements. What are the necessary abilities from an AI perspective?

2. **Match skills to needs that have been recognized:** The competencies needed to address those needs are taken into consideration in the second stage. For instance, knowledgeable instructors must understand how AI functions, its inherent benefits and drawbacks, and how to optimize its strengths and minimize its drawbacks if one of the course's objectives is to teach students about the ethical application of AI. How to effectively use AI to precisely narrow down a literature review may be another faculty need related to a research function. Understanding how AI searches are conducted is necessary for this.
3. **Create the curriculum for faculty development in AI:** The curriculum would then consciously map those needs and competences, taking into account the following: which skills and information must be taught in a sequential manner, and which are stand-alone? What are the benefits of having a trusted coach and an AI community of practice? These inquiries must take into account the fact that faculty members will have diverse backgrounds, specializations, and passions, which means that there must be a mechanism for students to enroll in the course at different stages. They must also take into account the way the curriculum is being taught, including the possibility of in-situ faculty development for AI.
4. **Continuous evaluation:** Although it has a great deal of promise to support and encourage learning, assessment has not traditionally been a part of faculty development. Because assessment and evaluation have traditionally been high-stakes, value-laden, without clear benchmarks for their various functions, and not supported or motivated, many faculty members avoid this. Learning is known to be greatly improved when performance feedback is used for introspection and learning rather than for passing judgment. Faculty could compare their knowledge to their defined desired competency for the role being created in this self-directed, scaffold reflection, or a mentor or coach could facilitate it. A competency-based faculty development system's facilitators would intentionally foster professional development. Ideally, an assessment of the efficacy would also be included.

LITERATURE REVIEW

According to Kulal (2024) the goal of the current study was to investigate how FDP can improve teachers' abilities by utilizing cutting-edge teaching strategies and contemporary technology. Additionally, to assess how FDPs affect teachers' attitudes and drive to incorporate cutting-edge teaching innovations into their lesson plans. The investigation was carried out in two stages using a pre-post study design: Phase I took place one week prior to FDP (August 14–20, 2023), and Phase II took place one week following FDP (15–21, 2023). Participants in the FDP were asked to complete standardized questionnaires, and a statistical tool for social sciences was used to process and evaluate the data. According to the report, instructors who participate in FDP have a major impact on their adoption of cutting-edge pedagogical strategies and technological integration in the classroom. This supports the UNSDG-4 and indirectly advances high-quality education generally. The study also showed that an effective FDP improves teachers' attitudes and philosophies on students overall learning and growth in addition to advancing teaching techniques. According to Zekaj (2023) focused on how the use of AI in academic settings can impact teaching strategies, personalized learning experiences, and administrative processes, the purpose of the study was to examine the potential benefits and drawbacks of such implementation. The quality of each article's content and relevance to the study questions were evaluated to perform a full analysis of the integration of AI in instructional faculty support. The results suggest that AI-driven technologies such as ChatGPT and intelligent tutoring systems can greatly enhance training and promote adaptive learning, leading to better learning outcomes. AI can also improve administrative processes and encourage student-centered learning. This study enhances our understanding of the role of AI in supporting academic staff by addressing both its benefits and limitations. This study lays the foundation for future research and the creation of best practices for integrating AI in academic settings by pointing out critical gaps and challenges. According to Hannan and Liu (2023) this study examined the evaluation of artificial intelligence (AI) applications in higher education institutions (HEIs). The findings of this study in HEIs demonstrate the effective use of AI technology in three key college operations domains: enrollment management, student support, and learning environment. The results revealed important implications for HEIs that adopt AI early, giving them a competitive edge. According to Al-Mughairi and Bhaskar (2024) this paper examined what motivates and what hinders teachers from adopting ChatGPT for teaching and the study advances the knowledge of teachers perspectives on the use of ChatGPT in the classroom. The results showed that policymakers can create appropriate regulations and service providers can adapt their products to teachers' needs by taking teachers perspectives into account. Higher education institutions (HEIs) will find the study findings useful in developing regulations that guarantee the proper and efficient use of ChatGPT. According to Bhaskar and Gupta (2024) the purpose of this study is to examine how educators view the inclusion of ChatGPT, an AI language model, within management education. Educators were requested to discuss perceived benefits, drawbacks, and ways to scale up ChatGPT for management education as widely as possible as part of the current study. Additionally, to provide information about factors that encourages or hinders the use of ChatGPT in Indian management education. In the current study, educators spoke about the many benefits of ChatGPT when it comes to management education. Nine distinct sub-themes relating to the benefits of ChatGPT in management education were identified from the comments of the interviewed instructors. Similarly, educators' responses to a survey about the drawbacks of ChatGPT in management education were categorized into six sub-themes that emerged during the interviews. Additionally, when teachers were interviewed about possible ways to improve ChatGPT for management education, their answers were categorized into seven sub-themes that represented the various ways suggested by teachers. According to Kashiramka and Sushil (2021) using India as a case study, the aim of this research was to establish a hierarchy of critical success criteria that impact higher technical education institutions. The study attempts to determine the relationships between 10 critical success elements to improve the performance of these institutions using total explanatory structural modeling (TISM). Using the answers of 18 subject-matter experts, the study uses total explanatory structural modeling (TISM) to understand the hierarchy and interactions of the components. The results suggest that the success of institutions is primarily driven by autonomy, accountability, and availability of sustainable funding. Establishing centers of expertise and providing infrastructure act as amplification factors. Academic performance and student placement process are driven by factors, such as the introduction of new programs and their accreditation, improving faculty quality, research output, and performance of academically weak students. According to Pillai and Kaushik (2024) this study defined the technology adoption model (TAM) and context-specific variables to examine students' adoption intention (ADI) and actual usage (ATU) of artificial intelligence (AI)-based teacher bots (T-bots) for learning. The adoption of T-bots for learning was investigated using a mixed-method strategy that used quantitative and qualitative techniques. NVivo 8.0 was utilized to analyze the interview data from 45 principals, directors, deans, and professors. A total of 1,380 college students were polled, and the Partial Least Squares Structural Equation Modeling (PLS-SEM) method was used to analyze the data. Perceived intelligence, anthropomorphism, perceived utility, customization, interaction, perceived trust, and perceived ease of use were the precursors of the T-bot's ADI. Stickiness to learn from human teachers in the classroom negatively moderates the link between the ADI and T-bots' ATU. It understands senior officials' perspectives on the use of T-bots in Indian higher education institutions. According to Hazaime (2024) the study discussed that artificial intelligence (AI) is a rapidly developing field that has the potential to transform almost every industry and aspect of civilization. It is anticipated that when AI develops further, it will create a more dynamic, effective, and personalized educational system that supports lifelong learning and adjusts to the needs and pace of each student. In this study, we investigate the AI acceptance model in higher education (HE) using human interaction-based criteria, such as openness to experience, attitudes, and capabilities. We hypothesized that perceived benefits would increase the acceptance of AI in higher education.

The findings show that perceived benefits and adoption of AI in higher education in the Arab world are positively and significantly correlated with adopted attitudes. The findings also show how digital elements indirectly influence AI adoption when benefits are recognized, which was important for model validation. According to Jafri (2024) the purpose of this study was to determine the opportunities and difficulties associated with artificial intelligence (AI) in higher education at Tehran University. AI PhD students from Tehran University in 2022-2023 participated in this study. The participants were chosen through the technique of purposive sampling; interviews were done with 15 AI PhD students who were subject matter experts. The study's findings also add to the body of information about how AI will affect higher education in the future, as academics need to learn more about how AI will affect higher education in the future. According to Spenneman (2024), the use of generative artificial intelligence (GenAI) language models to write assignment content is well established. The aim of this article was to evaluate the feasibility of the suggested solutions and to explore the extent to which GenAI can be used to avoid detection when commissioning and submitting contract-written assignments. However, while most of the recommended tips were low-probability of being caught, tips on hiding plagiarism and content mixing, as well as tips on avoiding distractions, are more likely to remain undetected. The authors came to the conclusion that ChatGPT can be successfully used as a brainstorming tool to advise cheating, but its effectiveness depends on how attentive assignment markers are and how well the cheating student can distinguish between the two. According to Aad and Hardey (2024) the purpose of this paper was to investigate the revolutionary effects of GAI on higher education, with an emphasis on the changing roles of professors in the classroom. The results show that GAI now challenges the traditional educational model by creating biased and commercially driven learning environments. Even though GAI has the potential to improve education, its independent nature often puts commercial interests ahead of educational objectives. The ability of generative artificial intelligence (GAI) to produce unique content through natural language processing and comprehensive language models has led to its explosive rise in recent years. According to Burger et al. (2023) the paper explored how artificial intelligence (AI) is currently useful in research and how it enhances different research techniques. The practical case study of systematic literature reviews (SLRs) is the main emphasis of this paper, which aims to offer guidelines for using AI in the process. The results show that although the guidelines were created for the literature review case, they can be applied to a wide range of research areas, such as quantitative research, data qualification, research on unstructured data, qualitative data, and even numerous support functions and repetitive tasks, *etc.*

CHALLENGES ARISE AI IN FACULTY DEVELOPMENT PROGRAM

Large volumes of data are used by AI systems, which may eventually be essential for preserving data security and privacy since they may reveal private information (Felix et al, 2020). To prevent leaks, breaches, and misuse, data security, availability, and integrity must be guaranteed. Fear that teachers would become overly dependent on these AI-powered technologies is another major issue with AI in education (Ayeleke et al, 2019). Additionally, student's run the danger of cyber security issues when they use this technology. Faculty members concur that the ethical issues surrounding AI's use are the main source of difficulty, especially when it comes to unfair AI use in research, misleading information, and the diminished role of teachers in the learning process. Important details regarding these difficulties:

1. **Quick evolution of the field:** Because AI is always evolving; academics must stay up to date on new tools, algorithms, and applications.
2. **Curriculum development:** Since there isn't a single, approved curriculum for teaching AI, instructors must create their own syllabi and course materials, which can take a lot of time and vary in quality.
3. **Gap in technical expertise:** Some professors might not have the requisite technical training in mathematics or computer science to completely understand intricate AI ideas.
4. **Financial constraints:** A lot of universities might not have enough money to set up AI labs with the required technology and software, which would limit the availability of hands-on training chances.
5. **Multidisciplinary nature:** It can be difficult to coordinate the cooperation of specialists from different fields when integrating AI into multiple disciplines.
6. **Ethics:** Teachers must get instruction on the moral ramifications of artificial intelligence, such as bias, data privacy, and responsible AI development.
7. **Inclusivity and accessibility:** It might be challenging to guarantee that all faculty members, irrespective of their backgrounds, have equal access to high-quality AI training.

CHALLENGES FACED FACULTY TOWARDS FACULTY DEVELOPMENT PROGRAM

In addition to juggling the demands of a busy academic schedule, faculty development programs frequently face obstacles such as a lack of time for faculty participation, limited resources, low motivation, poor collaboration, difficulty measuring program effectiveness, resistance to change, diverse faculty needs, and ensuring the transfer of learned skills back to the classroom (Turunen et al, 2016). Principal obstacles in programs for faculty development describe below:

1. **Time restrictions:** Attending development events can be challenging for faculty members who frequently have a lot of administrative and instructional duties.
2. **Lack of funds and resources:** The breadth and caliber of development activities may be constrained by a lack of funds to cover program expenses such as travel, outside speakers, and technological requirements.
3. **Individualized needs:** It might be difficult to create programs that meet the needs of all faculty members because they come from a variety of areas and backgrounds.
4. **Evaluation and impact measurement:** It might be challenging to show how faculty development programs directly affect the caliber of instruction and the learning outcomes of students.
5. **Opposition to change:** Because they are accustomed to their current practices, some faculty members may be reluctant to embrace new teaching strategies or tactics they have learnt in development programs.
6. **Absence of follow-up and support:** Development programs may not be as successful if there is insufficient post-program assistance and little opportunity to put newly acquired skills to use.
7. **Bad program design:** Learning outcomes may be hampered by inadequate curriculum creation, a dearth of pertinent content, or inefficient teaching strategies.
8. **Limited cooperation:** The execution and efficacy of faculty development initiatives may be hampered by a lack of cooperation between administrators and faculty.
9. **Institutional culture:** Implementing programs successfully may be hampered by a culture that does not prioritize faculty development or professional development.

FACTORS SUPPORTING TO CONDUCT OF AI SUCCESS IN EVERY FIELD

Artificial intelligence (AI) has transformed many industries with the development of Generative AI (GenAI). However, careful preparation and execution, supported by a clearly defined program charter, are necessary for the effective deployment of AI. A crucial component or requirement necessary to accomplish the intended results of a project or endeavor is known as a vital success factor. These crucial success characteristics should be outlined in the AI program charter, which will direct the project from start to finish and guarantee alignment with corporate goals and efficient use of resources. Below we discussed the success factors for AI in FDP success concentrating on key areas that can make or destroy AI projects.

1. **Executive Support and Leadership:** The effectiveness of AI depends heavily on the backing of senior leadership. Executives are crucial in obtaining the required funding, setting priorities for AI initiatives, and cultivating an innovative culture. Their dedication fosters organizational support, guaranteeing that AI projects get the time and funding they require to be successful.
2. **Create an AI Steering Committee:** Since several AI projects frequently operate simultaneously, an AI Steering Committee can offer the required supervision and coordination. Representatives from a range of departments, including the technical, security, and data and analytics teams, should be on this committee. The committee guarantees resource optimization, consistency, and alignment with strategic goals by coordinating these efforts.
3. **Form Partnerships:** Internal teams might not have access to the specialized knowledge, cutting-edge tools, and strategic insights that partnerships with technology suppliers and consulting firms offer. These collaborations lower the possibility of expensive errors by giving businesses access to state-of-the-art technology, accelerating time-to-market, and implementing best practices. Consulting partners also offer insightful information sharing and strategic direction, guaranteeing that AI projects are in line with corporate objectives and have the potential to yield substantial benefits.
4. **Effective business strategy:** A business strategy that is in line with the intended business outcomes Organizations must coordinate their AI activities with their overarching business strategy in order to optimize the impact of AI. This entails drafting a value story that explains in detail how AI helps achieve company goals and incorporating the intended business outcomes into the charter of your AI program. AI may be fully utilized by rethinking and recalibrating business processes around it, which will lead to notable gains in productivity, creativity, and customer happiness. Any AI initiative must start with the definition of precise, quantifiable business outcomes. These goals direct the creation and application of AI technologies, guaranteeing that they produce observable advantages.
5. **Quality Data:** AI relies heavily on high-quality data. Clean, varied, and representative datasets are essential for the successful application of AI. It is essential to invest in data collecting, cleaning, and governance procedures. To create and work with AI models, organizations should make sure that data is impartial and pertinent to the issue domain.
6. **Building a skilled team:** It is impossible to overestimate the significance of having a team of data scientists, machine learning engineers, domain experts, and AI specialists. The technical and business facets of AI initiatives should

be thoroughly understood by this team. Programs for ongoing training and development can support the preservation and expansion of this knowledge.

7. **Run-time considerations:** The long-term viability of the solution set depends on an economical and efficient run-time environment. For AI systems to operate successfully in production, an effective run-time infrastructure that satisfies requirements for cost, performance, security, monitoring, logging, and management must be designed. Constant observation guarantees that AI models function as intended, quickly identifying and resolving problems. Thorough logging helps with performance optimization by facilitating debugging and offering insights into model behavior. To ensure long-term dependability and performance, effective management entails regular changes to accommodate shifting conditions and requirements as well as continuous cost and security monitoring.
8. **Scalability and Flexibility:** These two factors should be considered when designing AI systems. AI systems must be able to develop and adapt as business requirements change.
9. **Iterative Development Process:** AI development can be improved continuously by using an iterative technique. Teams are able to gradually improve models and algorithms through rapid prototyping and frequent feedback loops. This method guarantees that the AI solutions closely match user expectations and business requirements while also speeding up the development process.
10. **Integration Strategy and Architecture:** Smooth integration with current systems, business procedures, and data is essential to maximizing AI's capabilities. By utilizing the advantages of existing infrastructure, this strategic integration reduces disruption and guarantees the seamless integration of AI improvements into day-to-day operations (Lourenço et al, 2018). Driving efficiency and effectiveness and allowing enterprises to take advantage of AI capabilities while preserving operational continuity and optimizing value require a strong integration strategy and architecture (Dubey et al, 2015). In the last we say that Successful AI implementation calls for more than just cutting-edge technology; it also calls for strong leadership, competent staff, high-quality data, strategic alignment, efficient run-time management, and solid integration. Organizations may successfully negotiate the intricacies of artificial intelligence (AI) and fully utilize its potential to generate business transformation and competitive advantage by concentrating on four crucial success elements and creating a thorough program charter (Dubey et al, 2015).

CHANGING FACULTY DEVELOPMENT PROGRAM THROUGH AI

AI integration in faculty development is a revolution, not only a fad. Teachers may improve their abilities, interact with students more successfully, and provide a vibrant, progressive learning environment by adopting AI. The future of faculty development appears to be more promising than ever, with AI at the forefront. Below we described the some points:

1. **Creating the future:** In a world where user experience is paramount, traditional design concepts are no longer adequate. AI-powered UX/UI design classes are becoming the new standard, allowing teachers to design interfaces that are not only useful but also user-friendly and captivating. These courses enable faculty members remain ahead of the curve by utilizing AI to provide real-time feedback, individualized learning paths, and predictive analytics.
2. **AI's creative method:** AI's generative AI platform distinguishes itself by offering customized UX/UI design courses that are adapted to different learning preferences. Imagine a course that provides resources and assignments that are precisely in line with your development, all while adjusting in real-time based on your interactions.
3. **Redefining professional identity with ai personal branding tools**: AI personal branding technologies are enabling educators to precisely create and maintain their professional identities in a time when having a digital presence is crucial. To create a unified and powerful online identity, these tools examine publications, social media activity, and even teaching methods.
4. **A New Paradigm for AI in education strategy**: In the field of education, strategic planning has frequently been a reactive procedure (Turunen et al, 2016). AI is changing the game by making proactive, data-driven tactics possible. AI is making educational strategy more dynamic and flexible, from forecasting enrollment trends to customizing courses based on student performance data.
5. **AI-Powered language teaching resources or dismantling barriers**: Teaching languages has always been a challenging task. These days, AI solutions are making this process easier by providing virtual language coaches, individualized learning modules, and real-time translation. By removing obstacles that previously appeared insurmountable, these tools improve language learning's effectiveness and accessibility.
6. **AI in higher education:** The effects of AI on higher education go well beyond conventional instruction. AI is changing what it means to be an academic institution in the twenty-first century, from improving research capacities to automating administrative jobs.

7. **AI Mentorship Programs:** Leading the next generation a key element of faculty development is mentoring. AI-powered mentorship programs provide individualized coaching by linking mentors with educators according to their individual needs and professional objectives. These initiatives make use of data to offer practical insights, guaranteeing that mentoring is successful and significant.
8. **AI in employee performance evaluations:** Conventional performance evaluations are frequently biased and subjective. AI is transforming this by providing data-driven performance evaluations that offer unbiased analysis and useful suggestions. By assisting educators in identifying their areas of strength and progress, these evaluations promote ongoing professional development.
9. **AI as the new normal in online education:** Online instruction is now a standard feature of education rather than a temporary repair. By providing real-time feedback, individualized learning experiences, and interactive technologies that increase the effectiveness and engagement of virtual classrooms, artificial intelligence is improving online education.
10. **Developing the future with AI software engineering:** Lastly, the core of all these advancements is AI software engineering. Software engineers are building the instruments that will influence faculty development in the future by constructing AI algorithms and systems that are suited to educational requirements.

RELATIONSHIP OF AI AND FACULTY DEVELOPMENT PROGRAM

The goal of an artificial intelligence (AI) faculty development program is to give teachers the know-how to successfully incorporate AI tools and methodologies into their research, teaching practices, and curriculum development. This will enable them to take advantage of AI's potential to improve student learning and further academic research in a variety of fields.

1. **Knowing the fundamentals of AI:** Giving educators a basic understanding of AI topics, such as data analysis, machine learning, and natural language processing, would enable them to better understand how AI can be used in the classroom.
2. **Finding possible uses:** Investigating different AI-powered resources and platforms that can be employed in the classroom, including intelligent content production tools, virtual tutors, adaptive learning software, and automated grading systems.
3. **Personalized learning strategies:** Discovering ways to use AI to modify lessons according to each student's unique needs, learning preferences, and strengths

in order to create a more individualized educational experience. Faculty development programs that teach educators how to use AI for personalized learning can entail the creation of tailored learning pathways for students based on their unique requirements and learning styles.

4. **Data analysis and interpretation:** Gaining the ability to examine student data produced by AI systems in order to spot trends, monitor development, and make wise judgments about education.
5. **Ethical considerations:** Talking about the moral ramifications of implementing AI in the classroom, such as issues with algorithmic bias, data privacy, and accessibility.
6. **Curriculum integration:** Instruction on how to smoothly integrate AI tools into the current curriculum and create classes that use AI features to improve student learning.
7. **Practical experience:** Giving educators the chance to test out AI tools in a real-world environment will help them gain confidence when implementing AI in the classroom.
8. **Increased efficacy in the classroom:** Teachers can better meet the needs of each individual student by using AI tools, which improves engagement and learning outcomes.
9. **Improved professional development:** Teachers can stay current and flexible in the ever-changing educational scene by keeping up with cutting-edge technology like artificial intelligence.
10. **Enhanced student motivation:** AI-enabled personalized learning can increase students' motivation and interest.
11. **Streamlined administrative tasks:** AI can automate monotonous procedures, giving teachers more time to concentrate on educational activities that have a greater impact.
12. **Empowering Teachers:** AI faculty development programs give teachers the knowledge of AI principles, applications, and ethical issues they need to apply AI tools in the classroom with assurance.
13. **Assessment and Feedback:** Faculty development programs can concentrate on helping instructors enhance their assessment techniques by using AI-powered systems that can evaluate student replies and offer real-time feedback.
14. **Enhancement of Research:** Teachers can learn how to use AI to analyze data, identify patterns, and formulate new research questions as part of their research projects.
15. **Curriculum Design:** By helping teachers integrate AI-based learning projects and activities into their classes, faculty development programs can help them adjust their curricula to the rapidly changing technology environment. All things considered, an AI FDP enables teachers to take use of artificial intelligence's

promise to give their pupils a more engaging, customized, and productive learning environment.

Here are some examples of how faculty development programs might incorporate AI:

a. **Practical workshops:** arranging for faculty members to try out various AI tools and platforms in order to have firsthand experience.
b. **Case studies:** Talking about actual instances of AI being applied in education to identify best practices and possible difficulties.
c. **Expert lectures:** Asking AI experts to discuss the most recent developments in the field and how they affect education.
d. **Peer review and cooperation:** Encouraging faculty members to exchange experiences and work together on projects pertaining to the use of AI in the classroom. All things considered, the interaction between AI and faculty development programs is essential to guaranteeing that teachers are prepared to use AI technology to improve student learning outcomes and adjust to the changing nature of education.

ROLE OF A1 CONTRIBUTION IN FDP ORGANIZED

AI in education helps customize learning content to meet the needs of students and teachers. AI is being used more and more in education to customize lessons for both teachers and students. It provides personalized learning content according to their aptitude, passion, and learning preferences (Bilal et. al 2019). AI determines patterns of learning challenges or understanding gaps by analyzing teacher and student performance data. The way we teach and learn is changing as a result of the widespread use of technology in education. One of the innovative ways to tailor the experiences of various learning groups, instructors, and tutors is artificial intelligence. Artificial intelligence techniques can be used in the following ways to enhance study procedures:

1. Customize Instruction: By determining a student's strengths and weaknesses, artificial intelligence creates a customized study plan for each student that takes their knowledge gaps into account. AI increases students' efficiency by customizing their lessons to meet their unique demands. Using the Knowledge Space Theory as a guide, many businesses train their AIs to identify and depict knowledge gaps while accounting for the intricacy of scientific concepts and their relationships that is, how one might inform another or serve as a foundation for bridging a gap. By accommodating each learner's specific needs and preferences, artificial intelligence

(AI) in e-learning makes personalized learning experiences possible. Learner data, including performance, learning style, and progress, can be analyzed by intelligent algorithms to customize activities and content to meet each learner's specific needs. By addressing their areas of strength and weakness and maximizing their learning outcomes, this personalization guarantees that students receive training that is tailored specifically to them. Learners with different backgrounds and levels of prior knowledge benefit the most from personalized learning. AI algorithms are used in personalized learning to evaluate student data and adjust training. For example, an AI-powered e-learning platform can modify a course's pace, content, and degree of difficulty in response to a learner's performance and preferences.

2. **Create Smart Content**

- AI can be used to create digital learning interfaces with customizable options, digital textbooks, study guides, bite-sized lessons, and much more.
- AI can also be used to create and update learning content, which keeps the information current and adapts it to various learning curves.
- Information visualization AI can power new ways of perceiving information, including simulation, visualization, and web-based study environments.

The process of creating content for eLearning can be automated with AI. Algorithms for natural language production may convert unstructured data into accessible, coherent writing, which enables teachers to produce excellent instructional materials more quickly. AI-powered content production systems may also evaluate vast volumes of data, including research papers, articles, and textbooks, to select current and pertinent content for students. This saves teachers time and gives students access to a wide range of resources. The development of interesting and dynamic learning resources is encouraged by intelligent content creation, which also improves instructional design. AI algorithms are used in intelligent content creation to automate the production of superior educational resources. An AI-powered tool, for example, may evaluate enormous volumes of data and select pertinent materials, including articles, videos, and interactive components.

3. Participate in the Automation of Tasks

Teachers might use AI to streamline time-consuming procedures like grading, assessing, and responding to students. Do you recall the tips that Gmail gives you when you compose messages based on the summary of your previous and present messages as well as the fundamentals of business vocabulary? Having this feature on any learning platform or learning management system that anticipates feedback. By giving AI a set of repetitive jobs, teachers may focus on more important things, like self-education, improving the quality of the classes, and judging assignments that are impossible for AI to handle.

4. Provide tutoring

Personal study programs that are always changing consider the gaps that students need to fill in their own sessions. Students who receive one-on-one tutoring and support outside of the classroom are better able to stay up with their studies and avoid their parents having to struggle to explain algebra to their children. Teachers save a ton of time by using AI tutors because they don't have to spend as much time explaining difficult subjects to students. Students can avoid embarrassment by asking for more guidance in front of their peers by using chatbots or AI virtual personal assistants.

5. Make sure students with special needs have access to education

Students with learning difficulties can now connect in new ways thanks to the deployment of cutting-edge AI technologies. Students with special needs, such as those who are deaf and hard of hearing, visually challenged, or have Autism Spectrum Disorder (ASD) can now access education thanks to artificial intelligence. Any group of students with unique needs can benefit from the successful training of artificial intelligence technologies.

6. Systems for Intelligent Tutoring

Intelligent tutoring systems driven by AI are meant to mimic one-on-one tutoring by offering students individualized help and direction. These systems evaluate student performance, pinpoint problem areas, and provide tailored feedback and remediation using machine learning algorithms. In order to encourage mastery, intelligent tutoring systems can modify their lessons in real time by adding new materials or changing the level of difficulty in response to student success. This individualized teaching method boosts students' self-esteem and enhances their comprehension of challenging ideas.

7. Processing Natural Languages

A subfield of artificial intelligence called natural language processing (NLP) makes it possible for computers to comprehend and communicate in human language. NLP technology enables chat bots, automatic language tests, and feedback in eLearning. NLP-powered language assessment programs may examine student work and offer immediate feedback, assisting students in developing their writing abilities. On the other hand, chat bots can improve learner support and engagement by helping students by responding to their inquiries, offering clarifications, and assisting them with the course contents. NLP makes eLearning more inclusive and learner-centric by improving accessibility and communication. Automated language evaluations and feedback in eLearning are made possible by natural language processing. An NLP-powered application, for example, can examine a student's written response to an essay question, assess its grammar and coherence, and offer immediate feedback on areas that need work.

8. Acquiring Knowledge about Analytics

Strong learning analytics are made possible by AI, giving teachers important knowledge on the behavior, performance, and engagement of their students. Artificial intelligence (AI) algorithms can spot trends, patterns, and opportunities for development by examining data gathered from students interactions with digital platforms. In order to improve the learning experience, educators can use learning analytics to monitor student progress, evaluate the efficacy of instructional tactics, and make data-driven decisions. Improved learning outcomes can be achieved, for instance, when teachers use analytics to identify challenging students and offer tailored interventions or modify their teaching strategies. AI is used in learning analytics to evaluate student data and give teachers insightful information. AI systems, for instance, can assist teachers in tracking student's progress, identifying problem areas, and making data-driven decisions by examining learner interactions and performance trends.

9. Astute Evaluation and Input

AI can expedite the eLearning assessment procedure. AI-powered automated assessment solutions can effectively analyze student performance and offer real-time feedback on tests, assignments, and quizzes. These tools help learners' ongoing development by analyzing replies, identifying trends, and providing tailored feedback. AI can also facilitate adaptive testing, which ensures the right amount of challenge and engagement by modifying the questions' difficulty according to student responses. Both students and teachers gain from the evaluation process' increased efficacy and efficiency due to intelligent assessment and feedback.

10. Early Intervention and Predictive Analytics

Predictive analytics driven by AI can identify students who may be struggling or at risk of falling behind. By evaluating learner data, including behavior, performance, and engagement, AI algorithms can produce early warning signals that enable teachers to step in and offer focused assistance. Predictive analytics-based early intervention techniques can increase retention rates and avoid learner disengagement. To make sure that struggling students get the help they need and advance in their educational path, educators can provide tailored interventions, such as more resources, one-on-one support, or targeted interventions.

FUTURE IMPACT OF AI ON FACULTY DEVELOPMENT PROGRAMS

Faculty development programs could be one of the many facets of higher education that artificial intelligence (AI) has the potential to transform. These programs are intended to improve university faculty members' research capacities, technological know-how, and pedagogical abilities. Faculty development programs can be changed to better suit the changing demands of educators in the digital era by incorporating AI technologies. This paper investigates the significant effects of AI on university faculty development programs, looking at the advantages, difficulties, and potential ramifications.

1. Enhanced personalization and customization: The capacity to tailor learning experiences for individual educators is one of the main benefits of integrating AI into faculty development programs. Customized professional development plans can be created by using AI-driven systems that evaluate data on faculty members' teaching preferences, styles, and areas for growth. Based on the unique requirements and objectives of every faculty member, these platforms can suggest pertinent materials, workshops, and training courses by utilizing machine learning algorithms. By improving efficacy, motivation, and engagement, this individualized strategy eventually equips teachers to flourish in their positions.

2. Lifelong learning facilitation: Faculty development programs could become dynamic, ongoing learning environments thanks to AI technologies. Faculty members can access a wide range of resources, such as online courses, virtual simulations, and interactive tutorials, at any time and from any location with AI-powered learning platforms. These platforms enable self-directed learning and exploration by accommodating different learning styles and speeds. AI-enabled faculty development programs help teachers to stay up to date with new discipline ideas, technological breakthroughs, and pedagogical trends by encouraging a culture of lifelong learning.

3. Enhancement of teaching and research capabilities: Faculty members' effectiveness and productivity can be increased by utilizing AI technologies and applications to enhance their teaching and research capabilities. AI-powered virtual assistants, for instance, can automate repetitive administrative duties like maintaining course materials, setting up appointments, and grading assignments, giving teachers more time to devote to more important pursuits. Furthermore, big datasets can be analyzed by AI-driven analytics tools to find trends, patterns, and insights that are pertinent to study and education. Faculty members can more accurately and efficiently discover research possibilities, refine instructional tactics, and make data-informed decisions by utilizing predictive analytics.

4. Promotion of inclusive and accessible practices: AI technologies have the potential to advance inclusive and accessible practices in programs for faculty development, guaranteeing that all educators have fair access to opportunities for professional growth. Faculty members with a range of requirements and preferences, including those who are disabled or have language problems, can receive individualized accommodations and support services via AI-driven systems. Additionally, text-to-speech apps and voice recognition software are examples of AI-enabled content delivery systems that can improve usability and accessibility for teachers with different learning preferences and styles. AI-enhanced faculty development programs can create a more varied and encouraging learning environment for teachers by emphasizing accessibility and inclusivity.

5. Problems and things to think About: Although AI has the potential to revolutionize education, there are a number of problems and things to think about when incorporating it into faculty development programs. To protect sensitive data and preserve faculty members' trust, issues with data privacy, security, and the moral application of AI algorithms must be resolved. Furthermore, to guarantee that educators have the information and abilities to use AI technology in an ethical and successful manner, continuous professional development and training are required. The risk of algorithmic bias and prejudice in AI-driven decision-making processes should also be reduced, especially in areas like performance reviews, hiring, and promotion.

RECOMMENDATIONS

We hear from a lot of academic institutions that are seeking to create local legislation because they are having trouble managing artificial intelligence. The main issue with artificial intelligence regulation is that technology is always changing. As a result, regulations need to be revised frequently, and employees need to be informed of any new developments. As a result, it would make more sense to have an understanding document that can discuss the new capability more broadly, something that all organizational components should take into account. We outline our thoughts and provide a specific example of what such an understanding document might include in the following sections. After that, any institution can take the recommendations and create their own version. Personalized learning experiences, thorough teacher training on AI use, ethical considerations, and equitable access to AI tools, and curriculum development that integrates AI literacy to prepare students for the future of technology are all important factors to consider when advocating for AI integration in the education sector. Always put the welfare of students and responsible use of AI first to prevent potential biases and privacy issues. Below some important suggestions for using AI in education:

1. Make use of AI-powered tools to adjust the pace and substance of instruction to the needs and learning preferences of each unique learner. Put in place adaptive learning systems that change according to the performance and growth of the students and teachers. Use AI-driven analytics to develop focused solutions for kids who are having difficulty.
2. Give teachers plenty of chances for professional growth so they can successfully use AI tools into their lesson plans. Pay attention to potential biases in AI algorithms, data privacy issues, and ethical AI use.
3. Use AI to grade assignments automatically and provide students feedback right away. Use AI-powered solutions to ensure the integrity of assessments and detect plagiarism. Create more thorough evaluation techniques that go beyond conventional testing and use AI to examine student achievement in various areas.
4. Address possible digital gaps by guaranteeing that every student has equitable access to AI-powered resources. Use AI-powered assistive technology to help students with disabilities.
5. Teach students about the potential and moral implications of artificial intelligence by integrating AI literacy into the curriculum. Create educational materials that equip students to use and create AI technology critically.
6. Make use of AI to automate administrative duties such as creating reports, scheduling, and monitoring attendance and provide precise rules for the ethical application of AI in education, including safeguarding student privacy. To guarantee fair results for every student, keep an eye out for and correct any potential biases in AI algorithms.

LIMITATIONS OF THE STUDY AND IMPLICATIONS OF FUTURE RESEARCH

This research examined the role of AI in faculty development program in the current scenario in the education sector which was included in the systematic review.

In future, apart from the education sector, the entire profit and non-profit organization, startup schemes to make the public aware, women empowerment, banking sector and other sectors can be investigated and accurately analyzed. Future research will specifically investigate how the role of AI is affecting which sector the most.

CONCLUSION

In conclusion, there is a great deal of potential for changing the face of higher education through the incorporation of AI into faculty development programs. AI technology can help educators succeed in the digital era by improving personalization, supporting inclusive practices, boosting teaching and research capacities, and enabling lifelong learning. But in order to fully utilize AI in faculty development, issues with algorithmic bias, data privacy, security, and ethical use must be resolved. Prioritizing cooperation, openness, and fairness is crucial as academic institutions continue to adopt AI-driven innovations in order to maintain faculty development programs efficacy, inclusivity, and responsiveness to the changing requirements of both teachers and students. AI has enormous potential for faculty development program, but its application necessitates rigorous evaluation of social, ethical, technological, and cultural aspects. AI poses questions around data privacy, bias, and cultural acceptability even if it has the potential to improve teacher education, improve instructors' abilities, and enable individualized learning. The creation of a thorough framework that guarantees AI's appropriate use is crucial to ensuring that it is utilized to its maximum potential in teacher education. Education is not an exception to the growing usage of artificial intelligence (AI) in many domains to increase efficacy and efficiency. The efficacy and beneficial effects of FDPs in the education sector are strongly supported by this systematic review and meta-analysis. It has been demonstrated that FDPs help faculty members in the education sector develop their teaching, assessment, research, leadership, and administrative capabilities. Although there is no single, uniform framework for teacher education, programs can be designed and modified to meet students' needs and desired objectives. These initiatives require funding, space, administrative support, resources, and dedication. Despite the fact that institutions implement such programs, there is no well-established theoretical framework that can be applied to other institutions. These findings encourage educators to create a framework for instruction that accurately takes into account faculty's knowledge and demands. Essential components of faculty development that give teachers the means to instruct and reinforce their fundamental knowledge should be incorporated into institutional support initiatives. Because each discipline has different dynamics, a conveniently customized environment is provided to meet the goals established through the FDP process.

REFERENCES

Aad, S., & Hardey, M. (2024). Generative AI: Hopes, controversies and the future of faculty roles in education. *Quality Assurance in Education*. Advance online publication. DOI: 10.1108/QAE-02-2024-0043

Al-Mughairi, H., & Bhaskar, P. (2024). Exploring the factors affecting the adoption of AI techniques in higher education: Insights from teachers' perspectives on ChatGPT. *Journal of Research in Innovative Teaching & Learning*. Advance online publication. https://doi.org/DOI: 10.1108/JRIT-09-2023-0129

Bhaskar, P., & Gupta, P. K. K. (2024). Delving into educators' perspectives on ChatGPT in management education: A qualitative exploration. *Interactive Technology and Smart Education*, *21*(4), 645–671. DOI: 10.1108/ITSE-08-2023-0169

Bilal, B., Guraya, S. Y., & Chen, S. (2019). The impact and effectiveness of faculty development programs in fostering faculty knowledge, skills, and professional competence: A systematic review and meta-analysis. *Saudi Journal of Biological Sciences*, *26*(4), 688–697. DOI: 10.1016/j.sjbs.2017.10.024 PMID: 31048993

Brandt, J. O., Bürgener, L., Barth, M., & Redman, A. (2019). Becoming a competent teacher in education for sustainable development: Learning outcomes and processes in teacher education. *International Journal of Sustainability in Higher Education*, *20*(4), 630–653. DOI: 10.1108/IJSHE-10-2018-0183

Burger, B., Kanbach, D. K., & Corvello, V. (2023). On the use of AI-based tools like ChatGPT to support management research. *European Journal of Innovation Management*, *26*(7), 233–241. DOI: 10.1108/EJIM-02-2023-0156

Felix, C. V. (2020). The role of the teacher and AI in education. In *International perspectives on the role of technology in humanizing higher education* (Vol. 33, pp. 33–48). https://doi.org/DOI: 10.1108/S2055-364120200000033003

Hannan, E., & Liu, S. (2023). AI: New source of competitiveness in higher education. *Competitiveness Review*, *33*(2), 265–279. DOI: 10.1108/CR-03-2021-0045

Kashiramka, S., & Sushil, S. (2021). Critical success factors for next generation technical education institutions. *Benchmarking*, *28*(5), 1605–1621. DOI: 10.1108/BIJ-06-2018-0176

Lohman, M. C. (2006). Factors influencing teachers' engagement in informal learning activities. *Journal of Workplace Learning*, *18*(3), 141–156. DOI: 10.1108/13665620610654577

Lourenço, M. (2018). Internationalizing teacher education curricula: Opportunities for academic staff development. *On the Horizon*, *26*(2), 157–169. DOI: 10.1108/OTH-07-2017-0053

Maity, S. (2019). Identifying opportunities for artificial intelligence in the evolution of training and development practices. *Journal of Management Development*, *38*(8), 651–663. DOI: 10.1108/JMD-03-2019-0069

McCallum, L. (2024). New takes on developing intercultural communicative competence: Using AI tools in telecollaboration task design and completion. *Journal for Multicultural Education*, *18*(1–2), 153–172. DOI: 10.1108/JME-06-2023-0043

Pillai, R., & Kaushik, N. (2024). Students' adoption of AI-based teacher-bots for learning in higher education. *Information Technology & People*, *37*(1), 328–355. DOI: 10.1108/ITP-02-2021-0152

Turunen, T. (2016). Professional development through reflection in teacher education. *Teaching and Teacher Education*, *55*, 198–206. DOI: 10.1016/j.tate.2016.01.014

Zekaj, R. (2023). AI language models as educational allies: Enhancing instructional support in higher education. *International Journal of Learning. Teaching and Educational Research*, *22*(8), 120–134. Advance online publication. DOI: 10.26803/ijlter.22.8.7

Zhang, J., Yuen, M., & Chen, G. (2018). Teacher support for career development: An integrative review and research agenda. *Career Development International*, *23*(2), 122–144. DOI: 10.1108/CDI-09-2016-0155 [illegible] M. (2016). [illegible] transformational [illegible] teacher education: [illegible] Opportunities for academic staff development. [illegible] DOI: [illegible]

Mass, K. (2020). [illegible] for [illegible] learning and development [illegible] DOI: [illegible]

McCallum, [illegible] (2021). [illegible] development [illegible] practice. Using [illegible] and [illegible] DOI: [illegible]

[illegible] (2020). [illegible] learning in higher education. *Information Technologies in Education*. DOI: [illegible]

[illegible] (2016). Professional development [illegible] DOI: [illegible]

[illegible] (2019). [illegible] support [illegible] DOI: [illegible]

[illegible] higher education [illegible] research [illegible] DOI: [illegible]

Chapter 16
Strategic Leadership and Policy Frameworks for AI Integration in Institutions

Satya Subrahmanyam
http://orcid.org/0000-0003-0441-2742
Holy Spirit University of Kaslik, Lebanon

Danielle Khalife
Holy Spirit University of Kaslik, Lebanon

ABSTRACT

The integration of Artificial Intelligence (AI) in higher education requires strategic leadership and effective policy frameworks to ensure its successful adoption. This chapter explores the pivotal role of leadership in navigating AI's influence on teaching, research, and administration. It emphasizes the importance of transformational leadership, governance models, and ethical considerations in guiding AI deployment. The chapter examines theoretical frameworks such as the Technology Acceptance Model (TAM) and Kotter's 8-Step Change Model to support AI adoption. It also discusses faculty development strategies, policy guidelines, and real-world case studies from institutions like MIT, University of Helsinki, and Arizona State University. The chapter concludes with recommendations for fostering responsible AI innovation in academic environments.

DOI: 10.4018/979-8-3373-1285-9.ch016

1. INTRODUCTION

1.1 AI's Transformative Role in Higher Education

The field of artificial intelligence (AI) has become one of the most radical technologies of the 21st century, which has significantly changed the landscape of industries, societies, and institutions on the global scale. Industries in higher education are experiencing undergone fundamental changes through AI in teaching, learning, research and administration. Adaptive learning, intelligent tutoring, and predictive analytics are some of the AI-enabled tools that are being embraced by universities to tailor the learning of students, boost retention, and enhance institutional efficiency (Dwivedi et al., 2020). In addition to pedagogy, AI facilitates research innovation by using big data analysis, natural language processing, and automated repetitive tasks, so that scholars can commit higher-level intellectual input. In the administrative context, AI-based solutions streamline enrollment management, resource allocation, and academic advising, which enhances institutional performance. Hence, AI does not merely transform academic experience, but it also changes the strategic mission of the institutions of higher learning.

1.2 The Importance of Strategic Leadership in AI Adoption

Although the potential of AI in technology is generally underestimated, it is clear that the successful implementation in higher education needs visionary and strategic leadership. Strategic leadership offers focus, vision, and flexibility to address uncertainties involved in the integration of disruptive technologies (Subrahmanyam, 2025). University leaders have the role of balancing between the opportunities presented by technology and the maintenance of the traditional academic values like equity, inclusivity, and academic freedom. Leaders who promote the culture of innovation also make sure that faculty, staff, and students accept AI as an addition to, but not the substitution of the human expertise. In the absence of good leadership, there are the risks of fragmentation in implementation, change resistance and ethical issues in institutions. Hence, leadership is significant in the operationalization of AI as a strategic resource in line with the strategic plans of the institution, whilst reducing the risks of algorithm prejudice, data confidentiality, and expanding digital divides.

1.3 The Rationale for Establishing Policy Frameworks

Strategic leadership alone is insufficient without robust policy frameworks that institutionalize AI integration. Policy frameworks provide structured guidelines for decision-making, implementation, and evaluation of AI initiatives. They help address challenges related to governance, accountability, and compliance with ethical and legal standards (Zawacki-Richter et al., 2019). Policies on data management and privacy ensure that the deployment of AI systems respects student rights, while frameworks for transparency and accountability promote trust among stakeholders. In addition, policy frameworks establish mechanisms for capacity building, ensuring faculty and staff are adequately trained to utilize AI effectively. A well-defined policy environment also helps institutions avoid ad hoc adoption of AI technologies, fostering long-term sustainability and alignment with national higher education priorities. In this sense, policy frameworks serve as both a protective and enabling mechanism, balancing innovation with regulation.

1.4 Objectives and Scope of the Chapter

The chapter, titled *Strategic Leadership and Policy Frameworks for AI Integration in Institutions*, seeks to explore the dual roles of leadership and policy in shaping the sustainable integration of AI within higher education. Its primary objective is to highlight how strategic leadership guides institutions in aligning AI adoption with their mission, vision, and values, while policy frameworks provide the structural foundation to support these efforts. The scope of the chapter extends to examining case examples, identifying best practices, and analyzing challenges that institutions encounter in AI integration. Specifically, it addresses how leaders can cultivate organizational readiness, how policies can mitigate ethical and operational risks, and how both leadership and policy can together foster a culture of innovation and inclusivity. Eventually, the chapter aims to provide a holistic understanding of how higher education institutions can leverage AI responsibly, ensuring that technological advancements contribute meaningfully to educational quality, equity, and sustainability.

By situating AI integration at the intersection of leadership vision and policy frameworks, the chapter underscores the necessity of coordinated and forward-looking strategies. AI has immense potential to enrich higher education, but realizing its benefits require more than technical adoption - it demands thoughtful leadership and resilient policies that guide institutions through the complexities of digital transformation.

2. STRATEGIC LEADERSHIP IN THE AI ERA

The subject of artificial intelligence (AI) implementation in higher education goes beyond technological preparedness and it demands visionary leadership to help institutions make complicated transitions. The strategic leadership here considers foresight, dynamism, and making ethical decisions to streamline AI implementation with academic missions. Leaders can make a central role in creating sustainable, inclusive, and future-ready academic ecosystems in the age of AI by building innovation, training faculty, and responsible execution of the same.

2.1 Defining Strategic Leadership in the Context of AI

The integration of artificial intelligence (AI) into higher education requires leaders who can envision, adapt, and strategically guide institutions through profound technological change. Strategic leadership in the AI era refers to the capacity to align institutional goals with emerging technological opportunities while anticipating challenges and fostering resilience. Unlike traditional leadership, which often emphasizes stability and operational efficiency, strategic leadership is inherently future-oriented and adaptive (Subrahmanyam, 2025).

A defining element of strategic leadership in this context is visionary thinking. Leaders must articulate a clear, compelling vision of how AI can enhance teaching, research, and administration while preserving the academic values of equity and inclusivity. This vision is not static; it requires constant adaptation as AI technologies evolve rapidly. Adaptive leadership enables institutions to respond to uncertainty by experimenting with new approaches, learning from outcomes, and scaling effective practices (García-Morales et al., 2021).

Strategic foresight also plays a critical role, enabling leaders to anticipate long-term implications of AI adoption. Through foresight, leaders can identify potential disruptions, assess institutional readiness, and prepare faculty and students for future demands. Innovation management becomes essential, as leaders must encourage a culture where experimentation with AI tools is welcomed, evaluated, and refined. This process ensures that AI adoption is not merely reactive but strategically embedded in institutional missions and pedagogical practices (Dwivedi et al., 2020).

2.2 Roles of Leaders in AI Integration

Strategic leaders play multiple roles in enabling successful AI integration within higher education. One of the most critical responsibilities is institutional vision-setting. Leaders must establish a coherent narrative for AI adoption, linking it to the institution's broader mission. By framing AI as a tool to enrich learning outcomes, promote research excellence, and enhance inclusivity, leaders provide a sense of direction and legitimacy to AI initiatives (Zawacki-Richter et al., 2019).

Equally important is building AI-readiness among faculty and staff. Readiness entails not only technical competence but also cultural acceptance of AI as a driver of transformation. Leaders facilitate readiness by offering professional development, creating collaborative spaces for faculty experimentation, and encouraging cross-disciplinary learning communities. By empowering educators with digital skills and pedagogical strategies, leaders mitigate resistance and foster a climate of innovation (Subrahmanyam, 2024).

Another essential leadership role involves facilitating resource allocation and capacity building. AI integration demands significant investments in infrastructure, software, and human capital. Leaders must ensure that resources are equitably distributed to prevent digital divides within the institution. Beyond financial investment, capacity building includes strengthening institutional support structures, such as IT services, research centers, and innovation hubs, that can sustain AI initiatives. This role emphasizes the leader's responsibility to mobilize resources strategically and ensure that technological integration aligns with long-term sustainability (García-Morales et al., 2021).

2.3 Leadership Competencies for AI Transformation

For AI integration to succeed, leaders must possess specific competencies that go beyond traditional leadership skills. One critical competency is digital literacy and data-driven decision-making. Leaders must understand the fundamentals of AI technologies, including their capabilities, limitations, and implications for pedagogy and governance. Digital literacy enables informed decision-making, while data-driven leadership ensures that policies and strategies are grounded in evidence, such as learning analytics and performance metrics (Priyanka et al., 2025).

Ethical inclusive leadership is another important competency. Use of AI presents serious ethical issues that include bias in algorithms, privacy of data, and equal access. The leaders who are strategic should be committed to ethics, so that AI systems will be clear and responsible and correspond with the institutional values. Inclusive leadership implies the promotion of fair access to the use of AI tools, the absence of the exclusion of vulnerable groups, and the establishment of a culture of trust and shared accountability (Zawacki-Richter et al., 2019).

Effective AI transformation requires change management and collaborative leadership. AI adoption often disrupts established practices and provokes resistance. Leaders must act as change agents, guiding institutions through transitions by communicating openly, addressing concerns, and involving stakeholders in decision-making. Collaborative leadership emphasizes the importance of collective action, where faculty, staff, students, and external partners work together to co-create AI strategies. This participatory approach not only enhances buy-in but also strengthens institutional resilience in the face of technological disruption (Subrahmanyam, 2025).

Figure 1. Strategic leadership in the AI era (Author, 2025)

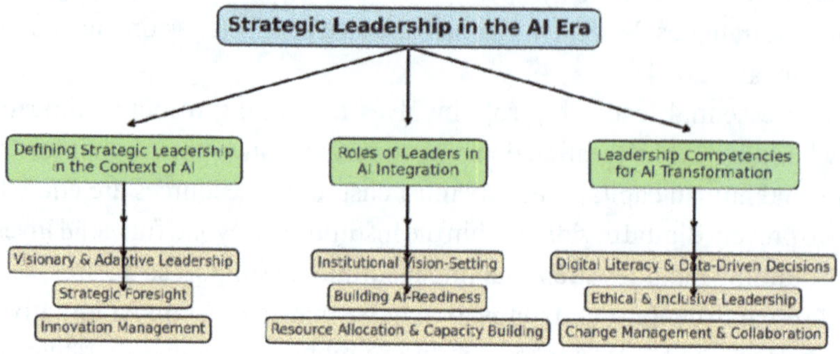

Strategic leadership in the AI era represents a convergence of vision, adaptability, and competence. Leaders must anticipate technological change, set a clear institutional direction, and build readiness among faculty and staff. They must also secure resources, champion ethical practices, and foster collaborative cultures that embrace innovation. By embodying digital literacy, ethical responsibility, and changing management skills, strategic leaders ensure that AI integration strengthens rather than undermines the core mission of higher education. In the end, leadership in this era is not about adopting technology for its own sake but about strategically harnessing AI to enhance learning, research, and equity in sustainable ways.

3. POLICY FRAMEWORKS FOR AI INTEGRATION

The fast integration of artificial intelligence (AI) in higher education is an indicator of why serious policy frameworks are needed to direct the responsible application of AI. Good policies provide guidance on governance, ethics, data security, and academic integrity, and AI should and should not be used to sabotage institutional missions. Policy frameworks promote global in line with local realities to protect equity, transparency and accountability and facilitate sustainable innovation in teaching, research and administration in different educational ecosystems.

3.1 Need for Policy Frameworks in Institutions

The integration of artificial intelligence (AI) into higher education is not solely a technological challenge; it is a governance and ethical imperative. Policy frameworks serve as the foundation for ensuring that AI adoption is ethical, equitable, and sustainable. Without clear policies, institutions risk deploying AI tools in ways that may exacerbate inequalities, compromise academic values, or create legal liabilities (Subrahmanyam, 2024).

One of the most critical needs for policy frameworks lies in ensuring ethical, equitable, and responsible AI use. Universities must safeguard fairness in the application of AI tools, particularly in areas such as admissions, grading, and predictive analytics, where biased algorithms could disadvantage vulnerable groups. Ethical policies ensure that AI functions as an enabler of access and inclusion, not a source of discrimination.

Protection of academic integrity, privacy, and data security is another urgent question. AI systems have a tendency to operate on extensive student and faculty data, such as performance history, student identifiers, and web history. Strict guidelines in relation to data collection, storage and sharing should therefore be developed by policies. Without these measures, the institutions will threaten the level of trust among the stakeholders and break the laws in the European region like the General Data Protection Regulation (GDPR) (Dwivedi et al., 2020). Initiating the fight against academic dishonesty also requires the regulation of AI application in the academic evaluation of students, so that automation facilitates and does not threaten the integrity of the learning outcomes.

Table 1. The need for policy frameworks in AI integration

Policy Need	Purpose	Institutional Implication
Ethical, equitable, and responsible use	Ensure fairness and prevent bias in AI-driven decisions	Protects students and staff from discrimination and ensures inclusivity
Academic integrity, privacy, and security	Safeguard personal data and preserve authenticity of academic practices	Builds trust, ensures compliance with legal frameworks (e.g., GDPR), and maintains integrity

3.2 Core Dimensions of AI Policy in Institutions

Policy frameworks for AI integration should be multidimensional, addressing governance, ethics, data management, teaching, and research.

Governance Policies. Effective governance requires institutions to establish formal structures such as AI committees, task forces, or advisory boards. These bodies ensure accountability by monitoring AI adoption, setting standards, and reviewing outcomes. Governance frameworks also delineate responsibilities across administrative, academic, and technical domains, enabling coordinated and transparent decision-making (Subrahmanyam, 2024).

Ethical Guidelines. Policies must embed principles of fairness, transparency, and bias mitigation into all AI applications. Guidelines should mandate regular algorithm audits to detect discriminatory patterns and require explainability mechanisms that allow users to understand how AI-generated decisions are made. Transparency in AI deployment builds trust among faculty and students, while fairness ensures that technology contributes to inclusive learning environments (Zawacki-Richter et al., 2019).

Data Governance. Since AI relies heavily on data, policies must prioritize privacy, security, and informed consent. Universities should implement encryption, anonymization, and secure storage practices to safeguard sensitive information. Consent protocols are particularly important, ensuring that students and staff are aware of and agree with how their data is being used. Clear policies on data sharing with third-party vendors are also necessary to prevent misuse or unauthorized access (Dwivedi et al., 2020).

Academic Policies. Academic policies are critical as AI has an increased role in the areas of teaching, learning and assessment. Schools need to establish reasonable applications of AI in classrooms, including adaptive learning systems, plagiarism detectors, and AI-assisted grading. It must be made clear in policies that faculty members should play a role in monitoring these tools where AI should only supplement human judgment and not displace it. Students ought to have academic policies that regulate the ethical application of AI like prohibiting generative AI in assignments to achieve integrity (Garcia-Morales et al., 2020).

Research Policies. As AI increasingly shapes academic research, institutions must adopt policies that govern AI-driven research practices. Standards for data ethics, reproducibility, and collaboration with industry partners must be established. These policies ensure that AI-supported research adheres to academic values of transparency, integrity, and societal contribution. Policies should encourage interdisciplinary collaboration, recognizing that responsible AI research often spans computer science, education, ethics, and social sciences (Subrahmanyam, 2025).

Table 2. Core dimensions of institutional AI policies

Policy Dimension	Focus Area	Examples of Policy Actions
Governance Policies	Establishing accountability structures and oversight	Creation of AI committees; clear reporting and monitoring mechanisms
Ethical Guidelines	Embedding fairness, transparency, and bias mitigation	Algorithm audits; explainability requirements; stakeholder engagement
Data Governance	Managing privacy, security, and consent protocols	Data anonymization, encryption, and clear consent frameworks

continued on following page

Table 2. Continued

Policy Dimension	Focus Area	Examples of Policy Actions
Academic Policies	Regulating AI in teaching, learning, and assessment	AI-assisted grading oversight; plagiarism detection guidelines; rules for student use of AI
Research Policies	Standards for AI-driven research and collaborations	Data ethics standards; guidelines for industry partnerships; reproducibility requirements

3.3 Global and National Policy Influences

Institutional policies cannot exist in isolation; they must align with broader global and national frameworks. Benchmarking against international AI education policies provide valuable guidance. Organizations such as UNESCO and the Organisation for Economic Co-operation and Development (OECD) have developed frameworks emphasizing human-centered and ethical AI use in education. UNESCO's 2020 recommendations stress inclusivity, fairness, and cultural sensitivity, while the OECD highlights transparency and accountability in AI governance (UNESCO, 2021; OECD, 2019). Aligning with such benchmarks ensures that institutional policies are consistent with global best practices and support international collaboration.

At the same time, institutions must localize frameworks to cultural and institutional contexts. Higher education systems differ significantly across regions in terms of governance models, resource availability, and societal expectations. A university in a developing country may prioritize policies for digital equity and infrastructure access, while institutions in advanced economies may focus more on sophisticated data governance and advanced AI research collaborations. Localizing frameworks ensures that policies are both relevant and actionable, avoiding the pitfalls of one-size-fits-all models (Subrahmanyam & Kaspard, 2025).

Table 3. Global and national policy influences on institutions

Policy Source	Key Principles/Recommendations	Implications for Institutions
UNESCO (2021)	Human-centered AI, inclusivity, cultural sensitivity, ethical deployment	Institutions should prioritize equity and tailor AI policies to diverse learner populations
OECD (2019)	Transparency, accountability, trust, and responsible innovation	Benchmarking institutional policies against international AI governance standards
National Frameworks	Context-specific education, legal compliance, and cultural adaptation	Localized policies reflecting institutional capacities, national priorities, and societal needs

Policy frameworks are indispensable to the sustainable integration of AI in higher education. They safeguard ethics, ensure data privacy, and preserve academic integrity while providing governance structures that foster accountability and innovation. By addressing dimensions such as governance, ethics, data management, academic practices, and research standards, institutions create comprehensive environments for responsible AI use. Benchmarking against global frameworks like those of UNESCO and OECD while localizing policies to institutional contexts ensures relevance and inclusivity. Ultimately, robust policy frameworks empower institutions to harness AI's transformative potential while upholding responsibility to students, faculty, and society.

4. INSTITUTIONAL STRATEGIES FOR FACULTY DEVELOPMENT IN THE AI ERA

Artificial intelligence (AI) is rapidly transforming higher education, presenting both challenges and opportunities for faculty members. As universities adopt AI for teaching, research, and administration, faculty development becomes a cornerstone for institutional success. Equipping educators with the right skills, pedagogical approaches, and support systems ensures that AI strengthens rather than disrupts the academic mission. Institutional strategies for faculty development in the AI era can be conceptualized across three dimensions: capacity building, curriculum and pedagogy, and support systems.

4.1 Capacity Building

Capacity building involves equipping faculty with the knowledge and confidence to effectively use AI tools in their professional practice. Training programs tailored to faculty needs are essential, covering not only technical skills but also pedagogical integration. Structured workshops on AI-powered learning management systems, adaptive teaching platforms, and automated grading tools enable educators to harness AI to improve efficiency and personalization (Chen et al., 2020).

In addition to technical training, AI literacy initiatives promote a broader understanding of how AI functions, its societal implications, and its ethical challenges. Long and Magerko (2020) emphasize that AI literacy goes beyond tool proficiency, fostering the ability to critically evaluate algorithmic decision-making and its influence on education. Such literacy empowers faculty to make informed choices about when and how AI should be used in the classroom or research environment.

Interdisciplinary learning opportunities are also crucial. AI impacts all academic fields, from healthcare to the arts. Faculty development programs that bring together educators from diverse disciplines create shared spaces to explore AI applications in their respective domains. As Rienties and others (2023) argue, collaborative and interdisciplinary professional learning strengthen institutional resilience by encouraging cross-pollination of ideas and teaching practices.

4.2 Curriculum and Pedagogy

AI not only transforms how faculty teach but also reshapes what they teach. One strategy for faculty development involves integrating AI-related content across disciplines. Universities should encourage faculty to embed AI themes into existing curricula, ensuring students in all programs develop essential competencies. Law faculty may address AI in legal reasoning, while economics departments may integrate machine learning applications in data analysis. Subrahmanyam (2025) highlights that embedding AI into mainstream curricula equips students with critical digital skills needed in an AI-driven labor market.

Another institutional priority is developing policies for AI-assisted teaching and assessment. Faculty must understand not only the technical aspects of using AI grading tools or intelligent tutoring systems but also the ethical implications of fairness, transparency, and student privacy. According to Knox (2020), AI in assessment raises important questions about accountability, necessitating clear policies that guide faculty in balancing efficiency with equity.

Pedagogical innovation through AI requires support for new teaching methods. AI tools can personalize learning experiences by adapting to student needs, but faculty must be trained to interpret system outputs and intervene when necessary. Alfredo et al. (2024) argue that effective pedagogy in the AI era blends human judgment with algorithmic insights, ensuring that technology complements rather than replaces the educator's role.

4.3 Support Systems for Faculty

Beyond training and curricular adaptation, institutions must create supportive ecosystems that sustain faculty engagement with AI. One approach is providing incentives for AI-driven innovation, such as research grants, fellowships, or recognition programs for faculty who pioneer innovative AI applications. These incentives encourage experimentation and signal institutional commitment to advancing AI integration (Popenici & Kerr, 2017).

Another critical element is collaborative research and knowledge-sharing platforms. Establishing AI-focused centers, cross-departmental working groups, and online faculty communities allows educators to share resources, co-develop teaching materials, and collaborate on interdisciplinary projects. Subrahmanyam (2025) notes that such platforms enhance knowledge transfer and prevent fragmentation in institutional AI adoption.

Finally, continuous professional development pathways are essential given the rapid pace of AI evolution. Unlike one-off workshops, ongoing opportunities - such as micro-credentialing, online certification programs, and regular refresher courses - enable faculty to stay current with emerging AI technologies. Ahn (2024) argues that continuous development not only sustains technical competence but also cultivates a growth mindset among faculty, positioning them as lifelong learners alongside their students.

Figure 2. Faculty development strategies (Author, 2025)

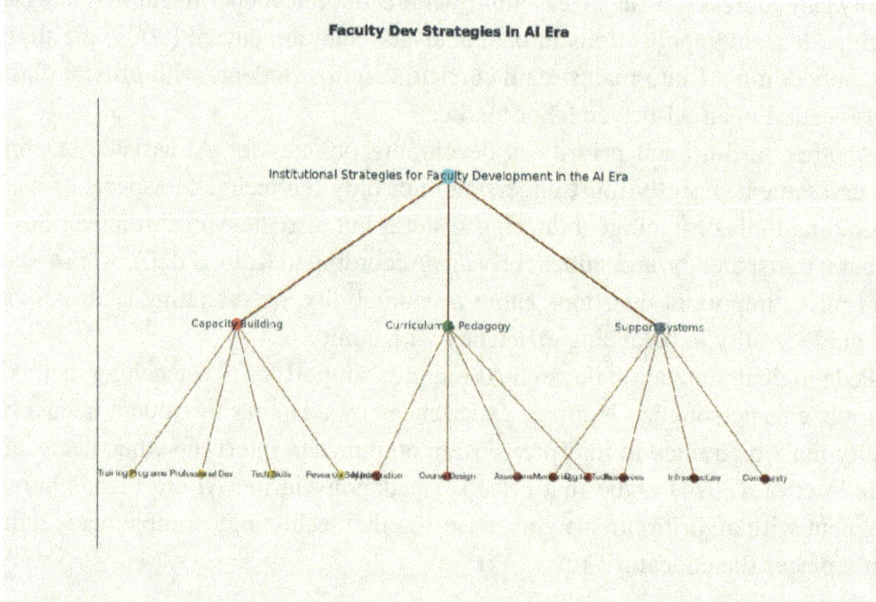

Institutional strategies for faculty development in the AI era must extend beyond simple technical training. Capacity building equips faculty with the skills and literacy to critically and effectively use AI. Curriculum and pedagogy strategies ensure AI is meaningfully integrated into teaching and assessment, while clear policies safeguard equity and integrity. Support systems provide incentives, collaborative platforms, and continuous pathways for professional development.

Together, these strategies foster an institutional culture in which faculty are not passive adopters of AI but active leaders shaping its responsible use. As higher education continues to adapt to the AI revolution, comprehensive faculty development is indispensable for aligning technological innovation with academic values and preparing both educators and students for the future.

5. CHALLENGES AND CONSIDERATIONS IN AI INTEGRATION

The introduction of artificial intelligence (AI) to universities and colleges has a huge potential but involves a serious number of challenges that should be introduced with caution. As institutions shift to integrating AI into the teaching, research, and administration processes, they are faced with numerous challenges such as cultural resistance and ethical dilemmas as well as infrastructural differences. These issues should be known to create responsible approaches to ensure that innovation and academic values are balanced.

5.1 Resistance to Change and Digital Divides

Faculty, staff, and student resistance to change is one of the most endemic issues in AI implementation. As most teachers worry, AI can take their jobs, or undermine their work, which causes most teachers to doubt and resist the use of AI tools (Mhlanga, 2023). Natural anxiety arising due to the steep learning curve of AI technologies may be faced by faculty members who were previously not exposed to online tools. This opposition might slack down the speed of implementation and restrict the transformational influence of AI.

Closely linked to resistance is the issue of digital divides. While some faculty and students have access to advanced digital resources, others face barriers due to limited access to devices, reliable internet, or training opportunities. According to Ribeiro and Subrahmanyam (2021), the digital divide in higher education became particularly visible during the COVID-19 pandemic, where inequities in access to technology hindered equitable learning outcomes. Without deliberate efforts to bridge these divides, AI adoption risks exacerbating inequalities rather than alleviating them.

5.2 Ethical Dilemmas and Academic Integrity Concerns

AI raises complex ethical questions that affect both teaching and research. Algorithms used in adaptive learning platforms, admissions systems, or plagiarism detection software can unintentionally reproduce biases embedded in the data they are trained on. As Floridi (2021) argues, the opacity of AI systems makes it difficult to ensure fairness, accountability, and transparency, especially when decisions significantly affect academic progression.

Another key concern is academic integrity. Tools such as AI-based writing assistants and generative platforms raise questions about authorship, originality, and the role of human intellectual effort. Faculty must grapple with distinguishing between legitimate learning support and potential academic dishonesty. Bittle and El-Gayar (2025) highlights that AI-generated content challenges traditional definitions of plagiarism, requiring institutions to revise their academic policies to address this new reality. Ensuring ethical use of AI thus demands both robust policy frameworks and heightened faculty awareness.

5.3 Policy Gaps and Regulatory Uncertainties

Despite the growing momentum of AI adoption, there remain significant policy gaps and regulatory uncertainties. At the institutional level, many universities have not yet established comprehensive guidelines on AI use in classrooms, assessment, or research collaboration. Globally, governments and international organizations are still debating frameworks for AI governance, leading to uncertainty about compliance requirements.

UNESCO (2021) has called for global standards that emphasize human-centered and ethical AI in education, but implementation at the national and institutional levels remains uneven. OECD (2019) emphasizes responsible innovation, but regulatory clarity on issues such as data ownership, accountability, and liability is still evolving. As a result, institutions are left navigating a fragmented policy environment, often relying on ad hoc rules rather than cohesive frameworks (Hwang & Tu, 2021). This uncertainty complicates long-term planning and discourages faculty from experimenting with AI-driven practices.

5.4 Balancing Innovation with Tradition in Academic Practices

Higher education institutions face the delicate task of balancing innovation with tradition. On one hand, AI promises efficiency and personalization in teaching and research; on the other, academia is deeply rooted in traditions of human intellectual engagement, mentorship, and critical discourse. Overemphasis on AI-driven automation risks reducing learning to transactional processes and undermining the values of critical thinking and creativity (Knox, 2020).

While AI-assisted grading can streamline assessment, it may overlook the nuanced judgments that educators provide. Over-reliance on AI in teaching could shift focus away from the relational aspects of education, such as mentoring and collaborative learning. As Selwyn et al. (2021) argue, universities must ensure that the use of

AI complements, rather than substitutes, the human dimensions of academic life. Maintaining this balance requires careful pedagogical design and thoughtful institutional leadership.

5.5 Resource and Infrastructure Disparities Between Institutions

Finally, the successful integration of AI is often hindered by resource and infrastructure disparities across institutions. Leading universities with strong financial capacity can invest in state-of-the-art AI systems, advanced data centers, and faculty training programs. In contrast, smaller or underfunded institutions struggle to secure even basic technological infrastructure. This disparity risks creating a two-tiered system of higher education, where resource-rich universities advance rapidly with AI while others lag behind.

According to Al-Shaer and Hattab (2025), disparities in infrastructure and funding amplify existing inequalities in higher education, particularly in developing regions. Without equitable access to AI tools and training, many institutions risk being excluded from global advancements in digital education. This imbalance not only affects institutional competitiveness but also undermines the goal of inclusive education. Addressing this challenge requires coordinated efforts from governments, policymakers, and international organizations to provide support and resources for under-resourced institutions.

Table 4. Challenges and considerations in AI integration in higher education

Challenge	Description	Implications for Institutions
Resistance to Change & Digital Divides	Faculty and students may resist AI adoption due to lack of digital skills or fear of technology; disparities in access to digital tools exacerbate inequity.	Slows down adoption; creates unequal learning opportunities across diverse student groups.
Ethical Dilemmas & Academic Integrity	Concerns over plagiarism, bias in algorithms, and misuse of AI in assessments challenge academic values.	Risk of compromised academic standards; potential erosion of trust in institutional practices.
Policy Gaps & Regulatory Uncertainties	Lack of clear guidelines on AI governance, data usage, and accountability creates ambiguity.	Limits institutional ability to standardize AI practices; increases vulnerability to legal and reputational risks.
Balancing Innovation with Tradition	Integrating AI while preserving core pedagogical values remains a tension in higher education.	Challenges in maintaining human-centered teaching practices while embracing technological efficiency.
Resource & Infrastructure Disparities	Unequal distribution of funding, expertise, and infrastructure across institutions.	Creates a widening gap between technologically advanced institutions and under-resourced ones.

The integration of AI into higher education is a complex endeavor fraught with challenges that go beyond technology. Resistance to change and digital divides hinder widespread adoption, while ethical dilemmas and academic integrity concerns raise questions about fairness and accountability. Policy gaps and regulatory uncertainties complicate governance, while the need to balance innovation with academic traditions highlights the cultural dimensions of AI adoption. Resource disparities across institutions risk entrenching inequalities in access to AI-driven opportunities.

These challenges demand a complex solution, and they include effective leadership in the institutions, policies, ethical protection, and the fair distribution of resources. Only in the light of addressing and addressing those considerations, higher education may leverage the transformative power of AI without betraying its mission of promoting knowledge, equity, and human development.

6. CASE STUDIES AND BEST PRACTICES

The analysis of artificial intelligence (AI) implementation in higher education case studies offers important details about the successful implementation strategies and lessons. The best organizations in the world like MIT, Stanford, and the University of Helsinki show how innovative thinking and powerful policies are propelled by leadership. The developing world universities emphasize the necessity of contextual adaptation. Collectively, these cases demonstrate the best practices in terms of balancing the use of technology and ethics, inclusivity, and institutional sustainability.

6.1 Global Examples: Institutions Leading in AI Integration

Globally, several higher education institutions are at the forefront of integrating artificial intelligence (AI) into teaching, research, and administrative processes. The Massachusetts Institute of Technology (MIT) has been recognized for embedding AI into both its research agenda and pedagogical practices. Through its Schwarzman College of Computing, MIT has created interdisciplinary opportunities where AI intersects with fields such as biology, social sciences, and ethics, ensuring that AI is not confined to technical disciplines alone (Massachusetts Institute of Technology, 2020). Stanford University's Human-Centered AI Institute emphasizes the development of AI that is socially responsible, supporting both technological innovation and ethical frameworks for its application (Stanford Institute for Human-Centered Artificial Intelligence, 2022).

In Europe, the University of Helsinki launched the "Elements of AI" course in collaboration with Reaktor, which has become one of the most widely accessed online AI education programs globally (University of Helsinki, 2020). By offering the course free of charge and in multiple languages, the institution has democratized access to AI knowledge and inspired similar initiatives across Europe and Asia. Asian universities have also been pioneers in AI integration. Tsinghua University in China established the Institute for AI Industry Research, aligning educational strategies with national AI policies to advance research and innovation (Tsinghua University, 2021). These global leaders demonstrate that successful AI adoption is not limited to a single geography but emerges through institutional vision, investment, and alignment with broader societal needs.

6.2 Regional Perspectives: AI Adoption in Developing Contexts

While advanced economies have resources to lead large-scale AI projects, developing regions also exhibit promising initiatives. In India, the Indian Institute of Technology (IIT) Hyderabad launched a B.Tech program in AI in 2020, marking the country's first undergraduate program solely dedicated to the field (IIT Hyderabad, 2019). This program represents a proactive step in building AI-ready human capital for the nation's growing digital economy. In Africa, the University of Pretoria has been instrumental in advancing AI research through its Centre for Artificial Intelligence Research, which collaborates with governments and industries to address pressing regional challenges such as healthcare and agriculture (University of Pretoria, 2022).

In Latin America, AI adoption in higher education has been slower but significant. The Monterrey Institute of Technology in Mexico has integrated AI into blended learning environments, providing predictive analytics to improve student performance and retention (García-Peñalvo et al., 2020). These examples highlight that despite financial and infrastructural constraints, institutions in developing contexts are leveraging AI strategically, often tailoring applications to local challenges such as expanding access, addressing skill gaps, and improving governance.

6.3 Insights Gained: Effective Leadership Models and Policy Implementation

From these global and regional cases, several insights emerge regarding best practices in AI integration. First, effective leadership is central to AI adoption. MIT and Stanford demonstrate that visionary leadership, with a strong commitment to interdisciplinary collaboration, creates a fertile ground for sustainable AI integration (Luckin, 2017). Leaders in these institutions not only set an ambitious vision but also foster inclusive cultures that encourage faculty and students from diverse disciplines to participate in AI-related initiatives.

Second, the importance of policy frameworks cannot be overstated. The University of Helsinki's global outreach with "Elements of AI" reflects the value of aligning institutional policies with wider societal goals of inclusivity and democratization of knowledge (University of Helsinki, 2020). In developing contexts, localized policy frameworks that account for infrastructural realities are crucial. The University of Pretoria's work demonstrates how policies designed with regional priorities in mind can ensure AI serves as a tool for development rather than deepening inequality (University of Pretoria, 2022).

Third, best practices show that resource allocation and strategic partnerships are critical. Institutions such as Tsinghua University and Monterrey Institute of Technology have effectively leveraged collaborations with government and industry to enhance institutional capacity, ensuring sustainable AI adoption (Subrahmanyam, 2025). Partnerships provide not only financial and technological resources but also create pathways for students and faculty to engage with real-world AI applications.

Finally, an overarching lesson is the need to balance innovation with ethics and tradition. Stanford's Human-Centered AI model underscores the necessity of ethical guardrails, ensuring AI complements rather than replaces human judgment in education (Stanford Institute for Human-Centered Artificial Intelligence, 2022). Institutions that integrate ethical considerations into their AI strategies are more likely to earn trust from faculty, students, and the broader public.

The case studies from global leaders like MIT, Stanford, and the University of Helsinki, along with regional perspectives from India, Africa, and Latin America, illustrate the diverse ways AI is being integrated into higher education. The insights derived from these examples emphasize that successful AI adoption requires visionary leadership, robust policy frameworks, strategic partnerships, and an unwavering commitment to ethical and inclusive practices. Collectively, these best practices offer a blueprint for other institutions seeking to navigate the complex yet rewarding journey of AI integration in the academic sphere.

7. FUTURE DIRECTIONS

As artificial intelligence (AI) continues to evolve, higher education must anticipate future opportunities and challenges through proactive leadership and policy innovation. The next phase of AI integration will extend beyond current applications to emerging technologies such as generative AI and quantum computing. Institutions must prioritize inclusive, ethical, and human-centered approaches, ensuring innovation complements academic values. Exploring future directions offers guidance for leaders, policymakers, and faculty in building resilient, forward-looking educational ecosystems.

7.1 The Evolving Role of Strategic Leadership in an AI-Driven Academic Ecosystem

As artificial intelligence (AI) continues to reshape higher education, strategic leadership will become increasingly pivotal in navigating complex institutional landscapes. Leaders will need to act not only as administrators but as visionaries who anticipate technological disruptions and guide their institutions toward adaptive responses. Emerging studies highlight that leadership in the AI era requires balancing technological innovation with humanistic values to maintain institutional trust and relevance (Cheung et al., 2021). Strategic leaders are expected to cultivate institutional agility, ensuring that universities can pivot quickly in response to advances such as generative AI and adaptive learning systems. This involves fostering a culture of continuous innovation, cross-disciplinary collaboration, and future-focused decision-making (Luckin, 2017).

Leadership will also evolve into a more participatory model, where stakeholders across faculty, students, and industry partners co-create the AI ecosystem of an institution. Such shared leadership not only builds resilience but also reduces resistance to technological change, making integration smoother and more sustainable (García-Peñalvo et al., 2020). Eventually, leaders who align AI strategies with institutional missions and societal needs will position their universities at the forefront of global academic transformation.

7.2 Policy Frameworks for Emerging Technologies

The rapid rise of generative AI tools such as ChatGPT, DALL·E, and other large language models highlights the urgency for robust policy frameworks that extend beyond traditional AI use. Policies must address issues of authorship, intellectual property, and academic integrity as generative AI blurs boundaries between human and machine-generated work (Dwivedi et al., 2022). Likewise, the potential of quantum computing in research and data analysis underscores the necessity of forward-looking regulations that anticipate disruptive innovations. Institutions that proactively craft policies for these emerging technologies will reduce risks of misuse while enabling innovative applications.

The policy frameworks must be focused on accountability, transparency and fairness. The 2021 Recommendation on the Ethics of Artificial Intelligence by UNESCO proposes that the world should engage in collaboration in order to protect human rights and academic freedoms when using AI (UNESCO, 2022). Universities are able to localize such international guides and therefore enable them to be relevant to the local culture and yet they are able to maintain international standards. The policies of data governance will have to grow in order to cover the issues of algorithmic bias, cybersecurity risks, and equality of access to the high-tech solutions (Floridi, 2019). In this respect, policymakers, industry and civil society are necessitated that the leaders get involved in co-developing responsive, ethical and adaptive regulatory mechanisms.

7.3 Towards Inclusive, Responsible, and Human-Centered AI Integration

Efficiency or innovation alone should not be used to define the future of AI in the field of higher education since the potential of technology lies in its ability to encourage inclusive and human-oriented practices. Researchers emphasize that the need to establish equal access to AI-driven tools and electronic sources should take precedence in order to close the expanding digital divide between resource-endowed and underfunded schools (University of Pretoria, 2022). The integration of AI on human factors entails the development of systems that complement the efforts of human beings, but not to supersede them so that the educational process can be a process of relationships and transformation.

There is also a need to deal with ethical dilemmas within institutions by providing extensive AI literacy programs that should equip faculty and students with the ability to engage critically with AI applications. The idea of responsible integration involves the incorporation of concepts of fairness, transparency, and inclusiveness into all areas of AI use (Whittlestone et al., 2019). Intelligent adaptive learning systems could be tailored to individualize learning and actively track biases, which could discriminate against some population groups. Through inclusiveness, higher education will have the ability to make AI empowerment and not an exclusion tool.

7.4 Recommendations for Institutional Leaders, Policymakers, and Faculty Developers

Looking ahead, a multi-stakeholder approach is essential for maximizing the benefits of AI while mitigating its risks. For institutional leaders, the priority should be to develop AI strategies that align with long-term academic missions and societal goals. Leaders should invest in faculty development programs that enhance digital literacy, encourage interdisciplinary research, and reward innovation in AI-driven pedagogy (Ratten, 2020). Establishing institutional AI ethics boards can help monitor implementation and ensure accountability.

For policymakers, there is a need to create adaptive regulations that evolve with technological advancements. Governments can facilitate collaborations between universities, industries, and international bodies to harmonize policies and share best practices (Dwivedi et al., 2022). Investment in digital infrastructure and equitable funding models will also be crucial to prevent disparities in AI adoption across regions and institutions.

Faculty developers play a central role in bridging policy and practice. They should design professional development pathways that integrate AI training with pedagogical strategies, enabling faculty to confidently use AI tools while maintaining academic integrity (García-Peñalvo et al., 2020). Knowledge-sharing platforms can facilitate collaboration across disciplines, allowing best practices in AI integration to be scaled effectively.

Figure 3. Future directions (Author, 2025)

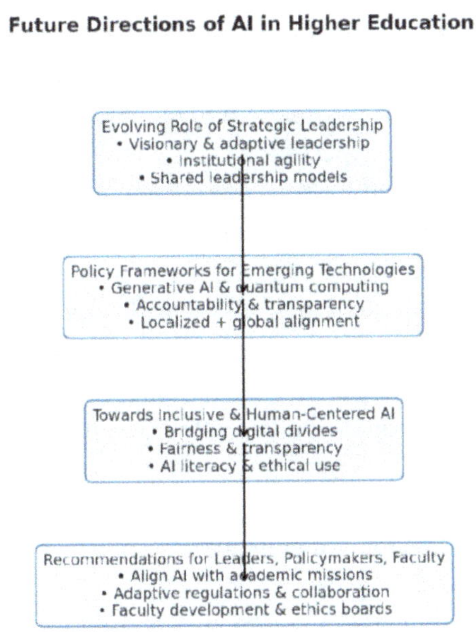

The future of AI within the sphere of higher education is positive and complicated at the same time as it requires leadership that is visionary, solid policies, and inclusive strategies. With the development of AI into generative and even quantum-enhanced AI, the institutions will need to become nimble, moral and focused on humans. With the focus on inclusivity, the creation of future-oriented policies, and the preparation of educators with the skills to work with AI, higher learning has the potential to use the power of AI to transform learning, research, and societal impact by focusing on inclusivity, creating forward-looking policies, and providing faculty with the skills to operate with AI. The responsibility of developing this future is shared by strategic leaders, policymakers, and faculty developers alike and is the one in which technological advances are welcomed without undermining those values which constitute education.

8. CONCLUSION

Strategic leadership and well-designed policy frameworks play a crucial role in successfully integrating AI into educational institutions. Effective leadership sets the vision and tone for innovation, while policies provide the necessary structure to guide ethical, equitable, and impactful AI adoption. Together, they create an environment where faculty can confidently develop the skills needed to embrace new technologies, enhancing teaching and learning outcomes.

The relationship between leadership, policy, and faculty development is deeply interconnected. Leadership inspires commitment and allocates resources, policies establish clear standards and expectations, and faculty development ensures educators have the knowledge and tools to implement AI effectively. This symbiosis fosters a culture of continuous improvement and adaptability, which is essential in the rapidly evolving AI landscape.

Institutions must actively align their vision with strategic leadership and robust policy frameworks to ensure sustainable AI adoption. This alignment not only drives innovation but also protects stakeholders and promotes inclusivity. By prioritizing these elements, education providers can create forward-looking environments that empower both teachers and students, ultimately preparing them for the challenges and opportunities of the future. The time for action is now - embracing this integrated approach will define the next era of education.

REFERENCES

Ahn, H. Y. (2024). AI-Powered e-Learning for lifelong learners: Impact on performance and knowledge application. *Sustainability (Basel), 16*(20), 9066. DOI: 10.3390/su16209066

Alfredo, R., Echeverria, V., Jin, Y., Yan, L., Swiecki, Z., Gašević, D., & Martinez-Maldonado, R. (2024). Human-centred learning analytics and AI in education: A systematic literature review. *Computers & Education: Artificial Intelligence, 6*, 100215. DOI: 10.1016/j.caeai.2024.100215

Bittle, K., & El-Gayar, O. (2025). Generative AI and academic integrity in higher education: A systematic review and research agenda. *Information (Basel), 16*(4), 296. DOI: 10.3390/info16040296

Chen, X., Xie, H., Zou, D., & Hwang, G.-J. (2020). Application and theory gaps during the rise of artificial intelligence in education. *Computers and Education: Artificial Intelligence, 1*, 100002. DOI: 10.1016/j.caeai.2020.100002

Cheung, S. K. S., Kwok, L. F., Phusavat, K., & Yang, H. H. (2021). Shaping the future learning environments with smart elements: Challenges and opportunities. *International Journal of Educational Technology in Higher Education, 18*(1), 16. Advance online publication. DOI: 10.1186/s41239-021-00254-1 PMID: 34778521

Dwivedi, Y. K., Hughes, D. L., Coombs, C., Constantiou, I., Duan, Y., Edwards, J. S., Gupta, B., Lal, B., Misra, S., Prashant, P., Raman, R., Rana, N. P., Sharma, S. K., & Upadhyay, N. (2020). Impact of COVID-19 pandemic on information management research and practice: Transforming education, work, and life. *International Journal of Information Management, 55*, 102211. Advance online publication. DOI: 10.1016/j.ijinfomgt.2020.102211

Dwivedi, Y. K., Hughes, L., Baabdullah, A. M., Ribeiro-Navarrete, S., Giannakis, M., Al-Debei, M. M., Dennehy, D., Metri, B., Buhalis, D., Cheung, C. M. K., Conboy, K., Doyle, R., Dubey, R., Dutot, V., Felix, R., Goyal, D. P., Gustafsson, A., Hinsch, C., Jebabli, I., & Wamba, S. F. (2022). Metaverse beyond the hype: Multidisciplinary perspectives on emerging challenges, opportunities, and agenda for research, practice and policy. *International Journal of Information Management, 66*, 102542. DOI: 10.1016/j.ijinfomgt.2022.102542

Floridi, L. (2019). Translating principles into practices of digital ethics: Five risks of being unethical. *Philosophy & Technology, 32*(2), 185–193. DOI: 10.1007/s13347-019-00354-x

Floridi, L. (2021). Introduction – The importance of an ethics-first approach to the development of AI. In Floridi, L. (Ed.), *Ethics, governance, and policies in artificial intelligence* (pp. 1–4). Springer., DOI: 10.1007/978-3-030-81907-1_1

García-Morales, V. J., Garrido-Moreno, A., & Martín-Rojas, R. (2021). The transformation of higher education after the COVID disruption: Emerging challenges in an online learning scenario. *Frontiers in Psychology, 12*, 616059. Advance online publication. DOI: 10.3389/fpsyg.2021.616059 PMID: 33643144

García-Peñalvo, F. J., Corell, A., Abella-García, V., & Grande, M. (2020). Online assessment in higher education in the time of COVID-19. *Education in the Knowledge Society, 21*, 12. Advance online publication. DOI: 10.14201/eks.23086

Hwang, G.-J., & Tu, Y.-F. (2021). Roles and research trends of artificial intelligence in mathematics education: A bibliometric mapping analysis and systematic review. *Mathematics, 9*(6), 584. Advance online publication. DOI: 10.3390/math9060584

Hyderabad, I. I. T. (2019). *IIT Hyderabad launches B.Tech in Artificial Intelligence* [Press release]. Indian Institute of Technology Hyderabad. https://iith.ac.in

Knox, J. (2020). Artificial intelligence and education in China. *Learning, Media and Technology, 45*(3), 298–311. DOI: 10.1080/17439884.2020.1754236

Long, D., & Magerko, B. (2020). What is AI literacy? Competencies and design considerations. In *Proceedings of the 2020 CHI Conference on Human Factors in Computing Systems* (pp. 1–16). Association for Computing Machinery. https://doi.org/DOI: 10.1145/3313831.3376727

Luckin, R. (2017). Towards artificial intelligence-based assessment systems. *Nature Human Behaviour, 1*(3), 0028. Advance online publication. DOI: 10.1038/s41562-016-0028

Massachusetts Institute of Technology. (2020). *MIT Stephen A. Schwarzman College of Computing: Impact Report 2019-2020.* MIT Schwarzman College of Computing. https://computing.mit.edu/wp-content/uploads/2020/11/SCC-Impact-Report-2020.pdf

Mhlanga, D. (2023). Digital transformation in education: Opportunities, challenges and future directions of AI in higher education. *Education Research International, 2023*, 7605075. Advance online publication. DOI: 10.1155/2023/7605075

OECD. (2019). Recommendation of the Council on Artificial Intelligence. OECD., OECD/LEGAL/0449.

Popenici, S. A. D., & Kerr, S. (2017). Exploring the impact of artificial intelligence on teaching and learning in higher education. *Research and Practice in Technology Enhanced Learning*, *12*(1), 22. Advance online publication. DOI: 10.1186/s41039-017-0062-8 PMID: 30595727

Priyanka, T., Singh, A. K., Kaushik, V., Sripriya, G., Suthar, M. B., & Subrahmanyam, S. (2025). AI in leadership decision-making and strategy formulation. *Journal of Informatics Education and Research*, *5*(2), 1967–1975. DOI: 10.52783/jier.v5i2.2654

Ratten, V. (2020). Coronavirus and international business: An entrepreneurial ecosystem perspective. *Thunderbird International Business Review*, *62*(5), 629–634. DOI: 10.1002/tie.22161

Ribeiro, N., & Subrahmanyam, S. (2021). Emotional challenges of teaching online during the pandemic. In Uddin, M., Sony, K. K., & Verma, N. (Eds.), *Psychosocial issues in COVID-19 pandemic* (pp. 244–255). SHINE Publication. RED.

Rienties, B., Divjak, B., Eichhorn, M., Iniesto, F., Saunders-Smits, G., Svetec, B., Tillmann, A., & Zizak, M. (2023). Online professional development across institutions and borders. *International Journal of Educational Technology in Higher Education*, *20*(1), 30. Advance online publication. DOI: 10.1186/s41239-023-00399-1 PMID: 37251087

Selwyn, N., Pangrazio, L., & Cumbo, B. (2021). Attending to data: Exploring the use of attendance data within the datafied school. *Research in Education*, *109*(1), 72–89. DOI: 10.1177/0034523720984200

Stanford Institute for Human-Centered Artificial Intelligence. (2022). *2020–2021 Annual Report*. Stanford University.

Subrahmanyam, S. (2024). Implementing agile talent management practices to adapt to changing higher education landscapes. In Kayyali, M. (Ed.), *Cultivating creativity and navigating talent management in academia* (pp. 187–210). IGI Global Scientific Publishing., DOI: 10.4018/979-8-3693-6880-0.ch009

Subrahmanyam, S. (2024). The role of leadership in nurturing innovation and creativity among faculty and staff. In Kayyali, M. (Ed.), *Cultivating creativity and navigating talent management in academia* (pp. 449–468). IGI Global Scientific Publishing., DOI: 10.4018/979-8-3693-6880-0.ch021

Subrahmanyam, S. (2025). Corporate Sustainability Leadership in a Technology-Driven Educational Environment. In Dall'Acqua, L., & Gironacci, I. (Eds.), *Navigating Complexity, AI, and Legal Challenges in Organizations* (pp. 177–208). IGI Global Scientific Publishing., DOI: 10.4018/979-8-3373-2419-7.ch008

Subrahmanyam, S. (2025). Developing Mindful Leaders for Global Change: Cultivating Awareness and Resilience to Navigate a Complex World. In Baez, M. D. (Ed.), *Strategic Approaches to Mindful Leadership and Change Management* (pp. 1–34). IGI Global Scientific Publishing., DOI: 10.4018/979-8-3693-7066-7.ch001

Subrahmanyam, S. (2025). Integrating AI and AR Into Teaching and Scholarly Communication. In Vrba, J., & Huynh, T. (Eds.), *Revolutionizing Academic Research With AI and Augmented Reality* (pp. 179–212). IGI Global Scientific Publishing., DOI: 10.4018/979-8-3373-1414-3.ch006

Subrahmanyam, S. (2025). Preparing Doctoral Students for Future Global Research Landscapes. In Tariq, M. (Ed.), *Improving Doctoral Education and Research Development for Sustainability* (pp. 239–270). IGI Global Scientific Publishing., DOI: 10.4018/979-8-3373-0225-6.ch008

Subrahmanyam, S. (2025). Qualitative Research Designs in Higher Education. In Mdikana, A. (Ed.), *Social Implications of Research in Higher Education* (pp. 263–296). IGI Global Scientific Publishing., DOI: 10.4018/979-8-3373-0654-4.ch010

Subrahmanyam, S. (2025). Strategic Collaboration and Partnerships in R&D for Innovation. In Martínez-Falcó, J., Sánchez-García, E., & Marco-Lajara, B. (Eds.), *Research and Development Practices in Innovation* (pp. 283–314). IGI Global Scientific Publishing., DOI: 10.4018/979-8-3373-0812-8.ch010

Subrahmanyam, S., & Kaspard, J. A. (2025). Strategic Management of Higher Education Institutions' Internationalization Efforts. In Berberich, B., & Berberich, R. (Eds.), *Higher Education Institution Strategies for Internationalization* (pp. 125–156). IGI Global Scientific Publishing., DOI: 10.4018/979-8-3373-1092-3.ch005

UNESCO. (2021). *AI and education: Guidance for policy-makers*. UNESCO. https://unesdoc.unesco.org/ark:/48223/pf0000376709

UNESCO. (2022). *Recommendation on the Ethics of Artificial Intelligence*. UNESCO. https://unesdoc.unesco.org/ark:/48223/pf0000379920

University of Helsinki. (2020). *Elements of AI [Online course]*. University of Helsinki. https://www.elementsofai.com

University of Pretoria. (2022). *Reimagining universities: Research Report*. University of Pretoria. https://www.up.ac.za/media/shared/520/2022/university_of_pretoria_publication-online.zp224510.pdf

Whittlestone, J., Nyrup, R., Alexandrova, A., & Cave, S. (2019). The role and limits of principles in AI ethics: Towards a focus on tensions. In Conitzer, V., Hadfield, G. K., & Vallor, S. (Eds.), *Proceedings of the 2019 AAAI/ACM Conference on AI, Ethics, and Society (AIES '19)* (pp. 195-200). ACM. https://doi.org/DOI: 10.1145/3306618.3314289

Zawacki-Richter, O., Marín, V. I., Bond, M., & Gouverneur, F. (2019). Systematic review of research on artificial intelligence applications in higher education – Where are the educators? *International Journal of Educational Technology in Higher Education, 16*(1), 39. Advance online publication. DOI: 10.1186/s41239-019-0171-0

KEY TERMS AND DEFINITIONS

AI Literacy: AI literacy encompasses the knowledge and skills required by educators, students, and staff to understand, evaluate, and effectively use AI tools in teaching, learning, and research contexts.

Artificial Intelligence (AI): AI refers to computer systems or algorithms designed to perform tasks that typically require human intelligence, such as problem-solving, learning, reasoning, and decision-making.

Change Management: Change management is the structured approach leaders use to transition institutions from traditional practices to AI-enhanced processes, ensuring minimal resistance and greater adoption.

Data Governance: Data governance refers to the policies and practices that ensure responsible management of data, including privacy, security, and consent, particularly in AI-driven academic systems.

Digital Divide: The digital divide describes the unequal access to digital technologies and AI resources between well-resourced and underfunded institutions, creating disparities in opportunities for faculty and students.

Ethical AI: Ethical AI refers to the development and application of AI systems that are transparent, unbiased, accountable, and aligned with human rights and academic integrity.

Generative AI: Generative AI is a subset of artificial intelligence that creates new content, such as text, images, or code, by learning patterns from existing data. Tools like ChatGPT and DALL·E exemplify this innovation.

Human-Centered AI: Human-centered AI emphasizes the design and implementation of AI systems that augment human capacities, uphold ethical values, and prioritize inclusivity, fairness, and transparency.

Policy Frameworks: Policy frameworks are structured sets of principles, guidelines, and regulations that provide governance, accountability, and direction for the ethical and effective integration of AI in institutions.

Strategic Leadership: Strategic leadership is the practice of guiding an institution through complex challenges by setting a long-term vision, fostering adaptability, and enabling innovation, particularly in the context of technological transformation.

About the Contributors

Siddhartha Paul Tiwari, PhD, FRAS, FRAI is an award-winning academic, technologist, and researcher known for his significant contributions to educational innovation, mobile technology, digital strategies, and ICT. He earned his doctorate from The Southeast Asia Interdisciplinary Development Institute (SAIDI), Philippines.

***

Andrés Almeida-Ñauñay holds a PhD in Agricultural Engineering from the Polytechnic University of Madrid. His research activity is focused on the application of remote sensing for agro-environmental purposes and the application of artificial intelligence for agroforestry data analysis. He began his scientific career studying bird populations in rural environments, with a particular focus on the cleaning and management of spatial databases. Subsequently, he has actively participated in numerous research projects, both national and international, mainly oriented to the download and analysis of high and low spatial resolution images, including products from the MODIS collection and data obtained by unmanned aerial vehicles (UAV). Thanks to this experience, he has developed an interdisciplinary profile that complements several lines of research. Currently, he is an assistant professor at the Polytechnic University of Madrid, in the Department of Agroforestry Engineering, within the Electrical Engineering Unit.

Suci Amaliah is an enthusiastic educator and emerging researcher whose work centers on innovative English language teaching and creative pedagogy. She is committed to the idea that language learning should empower students to explore the world, express themselves confidently, and develop skills essential for the 21st century. Her teaching philosophy emphasizes communication, collaboration, critical thinking, and creativity, ensuring that learners engage meaningfully with both content and context. Her research explores the intersection of technology, culture, and language learning, with studies covering topics such as project-based learning, culturally responsive writing instruction, polysemy awareness through podcast-based activities, and evolving perspectives of Gen Z learners. She has contributed to several international publications discussing language learning challenges, classroom innovation, and culturally grounded pedagogical practices. Beyond the classroom, she actively participates in community development initiatives, offering training for teachers and students on digital learning, creative writing, and academic skill-building. Her work reflects a passion for nurturing learner autonomy and supporting educational transformation through practical, accessible, and culturally sensitive approaches. Suci is widely recognized for her engaging teaching style, strong rapport with students, and dedication to continuous improvement. She strives to inspire young learners to grow with confidence, curiosity, and a deep appreciation for meaningful learning experiences.

Fernando Aragon-Rodriguez holds a PhD in Agricultural Engineering from the University of Cordoba and is an assistant professor in the area of Agroforestry Engineering, within the Department of Engineering at the Miguel Hernández University. He holds a Master's degree in Projects and Management of Agroindustrial Plants from the University of Cordoba and another Master's degree in Big Data and Business Analytics from the European University Miguel de Cervantes. His main research area is agricultural mechanisation, focusing on fruit harvesting machinery, automation of agricultural processes and pre-harvest and post-harvest quality assessment, for which he uses various enabling technologies (IoT, AI, cloud computing, etc.) and sensors (vibration, image, NIR, GNSS, etc.). He teaches the subjects 'Agricultural Mechanisation', 'Agricultural Farm Engineering' and 'Works and Facilities Engineering' within the Degree in Agri-Food and Agri-Environmental Engineering and the subject 'Management of Agri-Food Equipment and Facilities' within the Master's Degree in Agronomic Engineering. He has participated in several projects related to the development of prototypes for the mechanised harvesting of table olives and oranges for juice, mechanised collection and application of pollen, implementation of the internet of things for the regulation and action on environmental conditions and development of telecommunications architectures.

Andi Asrifan is an accomplished educator and academic leader with a Doctorate in Education, specializing in English Language Education from Universitas Negeri Makassar. With a strong academic foundation, he holds a Master's degree in the same field and a Bachelor's degree in Secondary Education. His dissertation focused on developing bilingual educational materials, reflecting his commitment to enhancing language education. Dr. Asrifan has extensive experience in various educational roles, including serving as the Head of the International Affairs Office at Politeknik Negeri Nunukan and as the Head of the Institute for Student Development and Alumni at Universitas Muhammadiyah Sidenreng Rappang. He is also an active member of several professional organizations, including the Linguistics Society of Indonesia and TEFLIN. In addition to his administrative roles, Dr. Asrifan is a passionate advocate for educational innovation and has participated in numerous international conferences and webinars, sharing his insights on language teaching and curriculum development. His dedication to professional development is evident through his participation in various training programs.

Guruprasad B.G, M.Com, Ph.D. (MBA), is an author, innovative thinker, devoted educator, and strategic leader in education management. He is a professor and principal at Surana Evening College in Bangalore. He has been recognized as a Commerce research guide at the University of Mysore. He was the Syndicate and Academic Council Member of Bangalore University, Jnana Bharathi Campus in Bengaluru. He has almost a decade and a half of teaching and industrial experience. 20 research papers published in ABDC-indexed journals, Scopus-indexed publications, and UGC care-listed journals. He has written over 22 textbooks.

Hanh Cao Minh Hong, since joining Saigon University, Hanh has focused on teaching and studying Fine Arts practice and education. She has been a lecturer in the Faculty of Arts since 2015, working to incorporate modern methods and technologies into Fine Arts education while maintaining a connection to local socio-cultural traditions. From 2020 to 2024, she has been involved in projects exploring contemporary approaches to Fine Arts education, aiming to balance traditional values with modern developments in the field. Looking ahead, Hanh plans to expand her research on innovative teaching methodologies, particularly focusing on the integration of digital tools and interactive platforms to enhance creativity and engagement in Fine Arts education, while continuing to uphold the importance of cultural heritage in artistic practice.

Saurabh Chandra is an accomplished legal scholar and currently serves as an Associate Professor & Assistant Dean at the School of Law, Bennett University, India. With a robust academic foundation, he earned his Bachelor of Arts and Bachelor of Laws (B.A. LL.B.) from the prestigious Aligarh Muslim University (A.M.U.). He further specialized in Business Laws, completing his Master of Laws (LL.M.) at the renowned National Law School of India University (NLSIU), Bangalore. Dr. Chandra's academic journey culminated in a Doctorate in Law (Ph.D.) from the esteemed National Law University (NLU) Delhi. In addition to his impressive legal education from some of India's most prestigious institutions, Dr. Chandra also holds a master's degree in Management with specialization in Human Resources in Management and another in Journalism and Mass Communication. With more than sixteen years of teaching experience, he has numerous publications to his credit. His expertise is complemented by a robust portfolio of scholarly publications. By bridging the gap between theoretical insights and real-world applications, Dr. Chandra's work serves as a valuable resource for academics, legal practitioners, and industry professionals alike. Dr. Chandra brings a wealth of experience in Academic Administration, having successfully held various key administrative positions. His diverse qualifications and extensive experience make him a distinguished figure in the academic and legal communities.

Sandip Dey was an Associate Professor and the HOD with the Department of Computer Science and Engineering, Global Institute of Management and Technology, India. He worked as an Assistant Professor in OmDayal Group of Institution and Camellia Institute of Technology for several years. Before that he worked as a Lecturer in Narula Institute of Technology. He is currently an Assistant Professor in the Department of Computer Science, Sukanta Mahavidyalaya, Jalpaiguri. He has coauthored one book titled "Quantum-Inspired Metaheuristics for Image Analysis"; Publisher: John Wiley & Sons, UK, coedited three books, and authored or coauthored about 60 research publications in international journals, book chapters, and conference proceedings. His research interests include soft computing, hybrid intelligence, quantum computing, and image analysis. Dey reviewed several international peer-reviewed journals like Applied Soft Computing, Swarm and Evolutionary Computation, Information Sciences, Journal of Computational Science, Engineering Applications of Artificial Intelligence, Expert Systems With Applications, Advanced Engineering Informatics, IEEE Transactions on Signal Processing and so on.

Md Mehedi Hasan Emon is an SDG-focused research practitioner with expertise in Artificial Intelligence (AI), digital transformation, supply chain management, sustainability, marketing analytics, and Educational Technology (EduTech). With an interdisciplinary foundation bridging Management Information Systems, Marketing, and Operations & Supply Chain Management, he contributes to AI-driven Industry 4.0 and 5.0, digital innovation, and sustainable business ecosystems in emerging economies. His research aligns with the United Nations Sustainable Development Goals (SDGs), reflecting a commitment to sustainable industrial transformation and green innovation. He has been involved in multiple UGC-funded research projects through the Centre for Higher Studies and Research (CHSR) and the BUP Research Centre (BRC) at Bangladesh University of Professionals, contributing to project coordination, research design, data analysis, and reporting on AI adoption, digital supply chains, sustainability practices, and consumer behavior. He has also contributed to European Union-funded collaborative research initiatives. His scholarly contributions include journal articles, conference papers, book chapters, and edited books such as Sustainable Operations in the Age of AI and Big Data and Enhancing Sustainability in Global Supply Chains With Big Data Analytics. He focuses on AI adoption, digital supply chain integration, sustainability performance, green innovation, cybersecurity behavior, and AI-enabled marketing systems, and serves as a peer reviewer for international journals and publishers. His research interests span AI, sustainable supply chains, digital transformation, green marketing, consumer trust, cybersecurity adoption, and technology acceptance, with a focus on how AI reshapes organizational capabilities, enhances sustainability outcomes, influences consumer behavior, and transforms strategic decision-making. Through academic excellence, grant-funded research, industry analytics expertise, and international collaboration, he advances evidence-based, technology-enabled, and innovation-driven development in Bangladesh and beyond.

İlkim Ecem Emre is research assistant at Marmara University, Business Informatics Department. She earned a BA in Business Informatics from Marmara University in 2015. In 2017, she received her MSc from İstanbul University, Informatics Department. Currently she is studying on data mining techniques for her thesis. Her research areas are data mining, machine learning, knowledge society, and knowledge management.

Y. Fathima, BBA.,MFC.,MBA.,M.Phil.,DGT.,Ph.D.,is an Professor in the Department of Commerce, School of Commerce at Jain (Deemed-to-be University) Bangalore. An accomplished educator with demonstrated ability to teach, motivate, and direct students while maintaining high interest and achievement. Articulate communicator able to effectively interact with diverse population of students at a variety of academic levels. She has 18 years of Teaching Experience and 10 years of Research experience. She has published papers in reputed journal and authored 4 books.

Rashid Hashmi is a senior journalist having a vast experience of over 22 years in Broadcast, Digital and Print Media. He has worked as an EXECUTIVE EDITOR and SENIOR ANCHOR in leading national news channel India News. During his TV NEWS career of almost two decades he worked in various roles in Dainik Jagran Newspaper, ETV, Total TV, FM News and India News. Prof. Rashid Hashmi anchored, debated and did ground zero reporting of various parliamentary and assembly election. He Interviewed prominent political, sports and bollywood personalities such as all of the ministers of Yogi Cabinet, various Union Ministers,

Gen VK Singh, Amar Singh, Azam Khan, Shivpal Yadav, Raja Bhaiya, Sakshi Maharaj, Pravin Togadia, Vinay Katiyar, Indresh Ji, Malini Awasthi, Ravi Kishan, Hans Raj Hans, Digvijay Singh during parliamentary elections 2019, cricketer Yuvraj Singh, Kangana Ranaut, Sunny Leone, Shahid Kapoor, Alia Bhatt, John Abraham etc.

Jherwin P. Hermosa is an Associate Professor 3 at the Laguna State Polytechnic University in San Pablo City Campus. Dr. Hermosa earned his Doctor of Education in Educational Management in 2023 from the same university. He also holds degrees in Philosophy and Theology from Rome, Italy. Dr. Hermosa currently teaches Social Sciences and Philosophical Subjects at both the Undergraduate and Graduate Program levels. Additionally, he serves as an editorial board member for the International Review of Social Sciences Research and member of the Philosophical Association of the Philippines (PAP). Dr. Hermosa has authored books such as Foundations of Education (2022) Philosophy of Education (2023) and Advanced Social Philosophy (2024), and Ethics: A Guide to a Moral Living (2025) along with numerous scientific articles and literary works that have been published internationally. Currently, he is pursuing a Juris Doctor degree at San Pablo Colleges, College of Law. Dr. Hermosa's research interests primarily focus on the social sciences, philosophy, educational management, and law.

Iván Herranz-Matey, with over 24 years of experience in the agricultural engineering sector, Ivan Herranz-Matey has enjoyed roles at a world-leading provider of agricultural machinery and services. With a career that has spanned multiple engineering disciplines—including product definition, design, manufacturing, after-sales support, customer experience, asset optimization, and go-to-market strategy—across various European market. Significant involvement in the advancement of precision agriculture technologies and service-based solutions. Currently expanding focus from the corporate sector to academia, with an emphasis on sharing practical knowledge, fostering collaboration with students and faculty to exchange ideas, collaborate, and continue learning and growing within an academic environment.

Jusrianto Jala, S.Pd., M.Pd. completed his undergraduate studies in Indonesian Language and Literature Education at STKIP Muhammadiyah Sidenreng Rappang in 2010. He later earned a Master's degree in Indonesian Language Education from the Graduate School of Universitas Muhammadiyah Sidenreng Rappang in 2021. His educational journey reflects a strong commitment to lifelong learning, shaped by diverse academic and social experiences across different regions in Indonesia. In 2024, he was appointed as a permanent foundation-based lecturer at Universitas Muhammadiyah Sidenreng Rappang, a position he currently holds. His academic interests focus on Indonesian language education, literature pedagogy, and instructional development, with particular attention to contextual and community-based learning. Through teaching and academic engagement, he is committed to contributing to the advancement of Indonesian language education in higher education settings.

Mustafa Kayyali is an ardent advocate for excellence in higher education, driven by a relentless pursuit of quality, recognition, and innovation. My journey in academia started with a Master's in Quality Management and Evaluation in Higher Education from Universitat Oberta de Catalunya, followed by a Ph.D. in Quality Management from Azteca University. These academic pursuits have laid a strong foundation for my expertise in Accreditation, Quality Assurance, and Higher Education Rankings. As an entrepreneur, researcher, translator, and publisher, I am deeply involved in various facets of the academic world. My diverse interests encompass Management, Translation, Interpretation, and Academic consulting, contributing to a well-rounded understanding of the industry. Throughout my career, I have made significant contributions to academic literature, with more than 40 published papers and 30 book chapters to my name. Additionally, I take pride in having translated 6 books, bridging language gaps, and promoting knowledge exchange on a global scale. I am committed to fostering positive change in higher education and contributing to its continuous improvement.

Eugene Mark B. Lopez is a dedicated educator and researcher with a strong passion for literature, language, and educational innovation. He authored the study "Designing Comics-Based Worktext for World Literature: Input to Enhanced Reading Comprehension and Vocabulary Skills of College Students," which was published in international journals and highlights effective interventions in teaching literature. Currently, he is pursuing a research project that aligns with academic standards, focusing on innovative teaching approaches. With a deep interest in creative learning tools, Eugene is also developing a cellphone-based game designed to teach literature and fiction, integrating elements from both classic and contemporary works. Beyond research, he is the creator of the Literary Legends Trading Card Game (TCG), a project that merges literary analysis, gamification, and educational technology to make literary studies more engaging and accessible for learners. Eugene's passion for storytelling extends to his creative writing endeavors; he is currently working on a novel in English, which he plans to translate into Filipino, reflecting his commitment to promoting literary appreciation in diverse contexts.

Anita Maharani is an expert in Human Resources. She published more than 20 international journal articles.

Md. Mazid-Ul-Haque is working as an Assistant Professor in the Department of Computer Science at American International University- Bangladesh. He has completed both his Master of Science in Computer Science degree and Bachelor of Science in Computer Science and Engineering degree from American International University- Bangladesh. He did his HSC at Notre Dame College, Dhaka. Previously, he worked as a Lecturer and as an Instructor in the Department of Computer Science at American International University- Bangladesh. His research interests include ML, Wireless Communication, WSN, etc. He was born in Kushtia. He has a strong passion and dedication for teaching and research work. He believes in hard work and sincerity for achieving life goals. Apart from teaching, his hobbies include playing football, traveling, watching movies, and reading newspapers.

Alicia Perdigones holds a PhD in Agricultural Engineering and is a professor at the Universidad Politécnica de Madrid. She develops her teaching work in the area of agroforestry engineering, combining this activity with her professional activity through the design of electrical installation projects in public parks and gardens. She is also involved in research on the improvement of energy efficiency in agro-industrial facilities. Alicia is the coordinator of the educational innovation group in Engineering Projects. In addition to co-authoring a book chapter on the difficulties in implementing artificial intelligence in teaching for sustainable engineering, she has written articles on teaching improvement for the journals "Assessment and Evaluation in Higher Education" and "European Journal of Engineering Education."

Usha Prabhu, is a senior academician having 23+ years of teaching experience – at UG & PG levels, aware of new changes in the education sector like the implementation of the National Education Policy, a member of the Syllabus Revision Committee -PG Level MBA at Bangalore University. She holds three Master degrees - MA, M. Phil, MBA, UGC- NET qualified and holds Ph.D from Bangalore University, presently working at Jain(Deemed-to-be University.· She has authored 2 books - Organization Behaviour for MBA and Entrepreneurship Skill for III semester B. Com published by Sapna Book House. She has published 12 research papers in International Journals, presented 9 research papers at International Conferences and 3 research Book Chapters(Scopus indexed).

Rismawati Sudirman is a distinguished academic and consultant with a robust focus on sustainability reporting. She currently holds the position of lecturer and Head of the Quality Assurance Institute at Universitas Muhammadiyah Palopo, where she has been pivotal in ensuring the quality of university processes and outputs since February 2020. Additionally, she serves as an Assurer for Sustainability Reporting at the National Center for Sustainability Reporting in

Jakarta, specializing in the evaluation of sustainability reports for mining companies across Indonesia. Her academic qualifications are extensive, comprising a Bachelor's degree in Economics and Accounting, a Master's degree in Accounting Science, and a Doctorate in Accounting from Universitas Brawijaya, Malang. Rismawati is also a certified specialist in sustainability reporting, risk management, and tax planning, holding several prestigious certifications including Certified Sustainability Reporting Specialist (CSRS) and Certified Risk Management Practitioner (CRMP). In her professional capacity, she has provided consultancy services in financial management and tax compliance for companies such as PT. Reski Barito Timur and PT. Helay Raya. Furthermore, she has authored multiple publications on taxation and management, contributing significantly to the academic community. Her interests in reading, writing, and travel reflect her commitment to lifelong learning and professional growth in her field.

Carmen Rocamora Osorio is PhD in Agricultural Engineering from the Polytechnic University of Valencia and Professor at the Miguel Hernández University (UMH) of Elche. She is also a member of the Institute for Agri-food and Agri-environmental Research and Innovation (CIAGRO). She develops her work in the area of agroforestry engineering, within the Department of Engineering of the University Miguel Hernández. She is part of the Research Group "Water and Energy for Sustainable Agriculture". Her research interests focus on energy efficiency in irrigation systems, the implementation of precision agriculture technologies (especially in smart greenhouses), and the application of artificial intelligence in agriculture to improve productivity and sustainability.

Vivit Rosmayanti, S.Pd.I., M.Pd was born in Botta on June 26, 1987. She has over 10 years of experience teaching at the University. She obtained a bachelor's degree in English Education from Alauddin State Islamic University. She completed her master's and doctoral degrees in English Education from Makassar State University. She is currently a lecturer in the Post Graduate Program, Department of English Education at Makassar State University, South Sulawesi, Indonesia. She is also actively writing research articles to be published in nationally and internationally accredited journals. She has written in some chapter books, monographs, and reference books. She is interested in teaching methods for teaching English. Her research interests include language teaching methodology, ICT instruction, and ESP teaching. She can be contacted at email: rosmayantivivit@gmail.com

Sam Rany is the Vice-Rector of the National University of Battambang (NUBB), a public university in northwest Cambodia, which he joined in 2008. He has served as the Cambodian Director of the Confucius Institute at the National

University of Battambang since 2019. He received his Ph.D. in Education from the School of Educational Studies at the University of Science Malaysia (USM) in 2016. In 2017 and 2022, he graduated from the Royal School of Administration in Cambodia with diplomas in public administration, leadership, and innovation programs. He graduated with Bachelor's and Master's Degrees in Law (LL.B & LL.M) at the Royal University of Law and Economics (RULE), Cambodia, in 2004 and 2007, respectively. He is also actively involved in some projects, including Erasmus+, KOICA, JICA, USAID, and WB. He is currently a NUBB project coordinator for the World Bank-funded Higher Education Improvement Project (HEIP, 2018–2024). Legal Studies, Public Policy and Administration, Educational History and Cooperation, Educational Leadership and Management, and other types of social research were all things he was interested in. His email address is samrany82@gmail.com

N Sathyanarayana has over 15 years of teaching experience at both undergraduate and postgraduate levels. He holds a Master of Business Administration degree from Visvesvaraya Technological University (VTU) and a Master of Commerce degree from Periyar University. He has completed his Ph.D. in Banking and Finance from Dayananda Sagar University. Currently, he serves as an Assistant Professor in the School of Commerce at Jain (Deemed-to-be University), Bangalore. He has published 24 research papers in international journals, including three indexed in Scopus, and seven papers in national journals. Additionally, he has presented 14 research papers at international conferences and 11 at national conferences. He has co-authored two books at the national level and contributed nine Scopus-indexed book chapters.

Rachana Saxena is presently working as Professor at School of Commerce, Jain (deemed-to-be) University, Bengaluru. She has experience of more than 20 years in Research and Teaching. She is a curriculum and content development expert in accounting and taxation courses. She has authored many books in the area of accounting, management and banking. She has many international and national research paper publications to her credit. She is an invited keynote speaker in various international conferences. She holds PhD in Commerce with dual specialization of finance and tourism.

Wasswa Shafik (Member, IEEE) received a Bachelor of Science degree in information technology from Ndejje University, Uganda, a Master of Engineering degree in Information Technology (Computer and Communication Networks) from Yazd University, Iran, and a PhD in Computer Science with the School of Digital Science, Universiti Brunei Darussalam, Brunei Darussalam. He is also the Founder and Research Director of the Dig Connectivity Research Laboratory (DCRLab) after serving as a Research Associate at the Network Interconnectivity Research Laboratory at Yazd University. Prior to this, he worked as a Community Data Analyst at Population Services International (PSI-Uganda), a Community Data Officer at the Programme for Accessible Health Communication (PACE-Uganda), a Research Assistant at the Socio-Economic Data Centre (SEDC-Uganda), Uganda, an Assistant Data Officer at TechnoServe, Kampala, Uganda, and Asmaah Charity Organization as Cheif Executive Officer. He has hundreds of publications with renowned publishers. His research interests include Artificial Intelligence, Neural Networks, Computer Vision, Smart Agriculture, Digital Health, and Green Computing.

Deepa Sharma has done Ph.D., MBA in Human Resource Management, currently working as Assistant Professor at MMIM, Maharishi Markandeshwar (Deemed to be University), NAAC Accredited Grade 'A++' University, Mullana, Ambala (Haryana). She has more than 9 years of experience in academics. She has written 61+ research papers for various Scopus and UGC listed referred National & International Journals and 13 papers appear on SCOPUS Preview.

Liza Shoor is a distinguished scholar who earned her Ph.D. from Punjab Agricultural University (PAU), Ludhiana, India, with her research affiliated to the School of Business Studies at PAU. Her academic pursuits are centered on the evolving landscape of consumer behavior, with a particular focus on impulse buying in the digital era.

Bhupinder Singh working as Professor at Sharda University, India. Also, Honorary Professor in University of South Wales UK and Santo Tomas University Tunja, Colombia. His areas of publications as Smart Healthcare, Medicines, fuzzy logics, artificial intelligence, robotics, machine learning, deep learning, federated learning, IoT, PV Glasses, metaverse and many more. He has 3 books, 139 paper publications, 163 paper presentations in international/national conferences and seminars, participated in more than 40 workshops/FDP's/QIP's, 25 courses from international universities of repute, organized more than 59 events with international and national academicians and industry people's, editor-in-chief and co-editor in journals, developed new courses. He has given talks at international universities, resource person in international conferences such as in Nanyang Technological University Singapore, Tashkent State University of Law Uzbekistan; KIMEP University Kazakhstan, All'ah meh Tabatabi University Iran, the Iranian Association of International Criminal law, Iran and Hague Center for International Law and Investment, The Netherlands, Northumbria University Newcastle UK,

Satya Subrahmanyam is a double PhD Postdoctoral scholar with expertise in Leadership, HR Practices, Business Analytics, Startups, and Soft Skills, contributing to academic and industry innovation. Currently, I serve as Professor and Dean (Research) at the Holy Spirit University of Kaslik (USEK), Lebanon, where I lead research and innovation activities to enhance academic quality and standards. I began my academic career at Ambedkar Open University, India. During my tenure as Principal with the Ministry of Education, Republic of Maldives, I was associated with Cambridge University and the University of London. As an academic entrepreneur, I am the Managing Partner and Trust Member at Vignan Institute of Technology and Management, Odisha, fostering its growth into a leading institution. At the Catholic University in Erbil, I advanced education and employment as Professor, Research Centre Director, and Lifelong Learning Centre Director, launching impactful programs. My academic journey includes two master's degrees, an M.Phil., two doctorates, and a postdoctoral qualification from Polytechnic Institute of Leiria, Portugal.

La Sunra, M.Hum, is a senior lecturer in the English Education Department at Universitas Negeri Makassar, Indonesia. He earned his doctoral degree in English Education from the Graduate School of Universitas Negeri Makassar. His research interests include reflective teaching, classroom interaction, formative assessment, EFL speaking pedagogy, and digital literacy in teacher education. Dr. La Sunra has published extensively in both national and international journals. His notable publications include studies on reflective practice, questioning strategies in microteaching, politeness strategies in online classrooms, critical thinking through reflective journals, and the impact of formative assessment on student motivation. His recent works explore project-based learning, differentiated instruction, and scaffolding in EFL settings, with articles appearing in journals such as Asian EFL Journal, International Journal of Language Education, ELT Worldwide, EduLine, Klasikal, and ELS Journal on Interdisciplinary Studies in Humanities. Beyond publishing, he actively serves as a facilitator and resource person in workshops on teaching strategies, classroom management, and educational innovation. With his dedication to advancing language education, Dr. La Sunra continues to contribute significantly to the professional development of pre-service and in-service English teachers in Indonesia.

Muhammad Usman Tariq has more than 16+ year's experience in industry and academia. He has authored more than 200+ research articles, 110+ case studies, 120+ book chapters and several books other than 4 patents. He is founder and CEO of The Case HQ, a unique repository for courses, narrative and video case studies. He has been working as a consultant and trainer for industries representing six sigma, quality, health and safety, environmental systems, project management, and information security standards. His work has encompassed sectors in aviation, manufacturing, food, hospitality, education, finance, research, software and transportation. He has diverse and significant experience working with accreditation agencies of ABET, ACBSP, AACSB, WASC, CAA, EFQM and NCEAC. Additionally, Dr. Tariq has operational experience in incubators, research labs, government research projects, private sector startups, program creation and management at various industrial and academic levels. He is Certified Higher Education Teacher from Harvard University, USA, Certified Online Educator from HMBSU, Certified Six Sigma Master Black Belt and has been awarded PFHEA, SFSEDA, SMIEEE, and CMBE.

Index

A

C

D

E

F

G

H

I

K

L

M

P

R

S

T

W

www.ingramcontent.com/pod-product-compliance
Lightning Source LLC
LaVergne TN
LVHW062336300926
849161LV00007B/1713